Breogán's Lighthouse
An Anthology of Galician Literature

Breogán's Lighthouse
An Anthology of Galician Literature

Edited by
Antonio Raúl de Toro Santos

Francis
Boutle
Publishers

First published by Francis Boutle Publishers
272 Alexandra Park Road
London N22 7BG
Tel/Fax: 020 8889 7744
info@francisboutle.co.uk
www.francisboutle.co.uk

Writings included in this anthology were translated as follows:
Poetry – John Rutherford: all poetry (except V. Araguas' poems, translated by
Mike Warren-Piper).
With the Translation Workshop of the Centre for Galician Studies at the
Queen's College, Oxford: R. Dieste's *Fearful Blandina* and *New York is Ours*,
Marilar Alexandre, Xurxo Borrazás, Marina Mayoral, Xavier Queipo, and
Xelís de Toro.
Medieval prose – John Rutherford.
Prose – David Clark: M. Valladares, Rosalía de Castro, López Ferreiro, Lamas
Carvajal, Lugrís Freire, Lesta Meis, V. Risco, A. D. Rodríguez Castelao, R.
Otero Pedrayo, Suso de Toro (*The Hunting Shadow*, with A. R. de Toro).
Anne MacCarthy and Juan Casas: Rafael Dieste, R. de Valenzuela, E. Blanco
Amor, A. Fole, A. Cunqueiro, Celso E. Ferreiro, X. Neira Vilas, C. Gonsar, M.
X. Queizán, X. L. Méndez Ferrín, C. Casares, X. M. Martínez Oca, Alfredo
Conde, Xavier Alcalá, Carlos Reigosa, Víctor Freixanes, Margarita Ledo, A.
Rei Ballesteros.
Alan Floyd and Ana Gabín: X. Rábade Paredes, Darío X. Cabana, X. M.
Álvarez Cáccamo, Xosé Miranda, Suso de Toro, Manuel Rivas, Antón Reixa,
Gonzalo Navaza, X. Cid Cabido, Xosé C. Caneiro, Miguelanxo Murado.

Lesser used Languages of Europe series editor: Alan M. Kent

ISBN 978 1 903427 51 4

Acknowledgments

Our heartfelt appreciation to the following persons and institutions that collaborated in the publication: the translators for their arduous yet challenging task; Ramón Gutiérrez, Gonzalo Navaza, Luciano Rodríguez, Manuel Bragado and Editorial Xerais de Galicia for giving permission to reproduce most of the texts included in the anthology; Editorial Galaxia, Sotelo Blanco, Edicións do Castro, Espiral Maior, Deputación Provincial de A Coruña; Ediciónes Positivas, La Voz de Galicia, Pero, Meogo, Akal, Bahía Edicións, Nós, Ediciones B, Vía Láctea, Edicións, do Cerne, Castrelos, Sons Galiza Libros, Noitarenga, Edicións Celta (a full list of publishers and texts appears at the back of the book); Dirección Xeral de Creación e Difusión Cultural (Xunta de Galicia) and Centro Ramón Piñeiro para a Investigación en Humanidades for their valuable sponsorship, without which this anthology could not have been completed; Manuel González for believing in this project; the staff of the Amergin University Institute for Irish Studies of the University of Coruña; John Rutherford, Director of the Centre for Galician Studies at the Queen's College, University of Oxford, for giving his rights to some of the texts, and María Liñeira, David Longrigg, Bella Whittington, Ben Cahill, Laura Sáez Fernández, Francisco Dubert, Ramón Mariño Paz, Emilio Ínsua González for their collaboration, and Pablo Cancelo for his technical assistance and guidance. We would also like to thank those who, in one way or another, helped to finish this anthology of Galician literature.

The following internet tools have also been of great help: *TILGA, BVG, TMILG, Dicionario de dicionarios*, and *Dicionario de dicionarios do galego medieval*.

Contents

Medieval Literature
Secular Poetry
Songs of Women in Love (Cantigas de amigo)

The Nineteenth Century
Early Writings

The Pre-Revivalists

The Revival

The Twentieth Century

The First Thirty Years

The Recovery
Eduardo Blanco Amor (1897–1979)

Ánxel Fole (1903–1986)
From Á lus do candil (By the Light of a Candle)

María Mariño Carou (1907–1967)
From Verba que comenenza (Words that Begin)

Aquilino Iglesia Alvariño (1909–1961)
From Corazón ao vento (Heart in the Wind)

From Cómaros verdes (Green Field-Ridges)
From Nenias
From Lanza de soledá (Lance of Solitude)

Ricardo Carballo Calero (1910–1990)
From Salterio de Fingoi (The Fingoi Psaltery)

From Futuro condicional (Future Conditional)

Álvaro Cunqueiro (1911–1981)
From Merlín e familia e outras historias (Merlín and Family and Other Stories)

From Escola de menciñeiros (School of Bonesetters)
From Xente de aquí e de acolá (People from Here and There)
From Cantiga nova que se chama ribeira (New Lay Called Waterside)
From Dona do corpo delgado (Lady with the Slender Body)

Foreword

An anthology of Galician literature, such as this, has been a notable absence both in Galicia and in English-speaking countries for a long time. The literary history of Galicia over the last eight hundred years, especially after the revivalist movements in the nineteenth century and the consolidation of writing in the native language in the twentieth, made it absolutely necessary to publish an anthology in English. Like all collections of translations, this makes the Galician literary heritage available to a wider reading public, other than the Galicians or the Spanish. Thus, readers in English have access to a culture and literature which, otherwise, would have been closed to them by the barriers of language. We hope that this effort to bring part of our cultural tradition into English will contribute to an appreciation of a unique way of perceiving the world which has been practically hidden until recently.

Some individual works have been translated into English and issued by small independent publishers mostly, during the last twenty years. A few anthologies, of contemporary poetry mainly, and short stories, have also been published, such as *Contemporánea* (1995), *Galician Generation of the Eighties: Three Poets* (1999), *To Visit Me the Sea: Galician Poetry 1930–1996* (2000); *A tribo das baleas: An Anthology of the Latest Galician Poetry* (2001), *Poetry Is the World's Great Miracle: Poets of Galician PEN Club* (2001), *Rosalía de Castro: Selected Poems*, (2007); *Manuel Rivas: From Unknown to Unknown* (2009), *Xosé Luís Méndez Ferrín: Them and Other Stories* (1996), *By the Paths of Literature: Galician Writers of PEN* (1993) and *From the Beginning of the Sea: Anthology of Contemporary Galician Short Stories* (2008). Special mention should be made of Jonathan Dunne's interesting and fresh *Anthology of Galician Literature 1196-1981* (Edicións Xerais and Galaxia, 2010), which covers a selection of Galician literature up to 1981, but leaves out the rich flowering of the last thirty years.

Important though these publications may be in helping one to become familiar with Galician writing in English, there was a widely-felt need for a new comprehensive anthology which would contain highlights from Galician literature from its beginnings to the present time. Our aim here was to provide an all-embracing view of it, in English, for those readers who want to learn more about the literary and cultural heritage of Galicia, a country situated on the northwestern part of the Iberian Peninsula. It goes without saying, of course, that we do not aim at exhaustiveness (something which is true of all anthologies). In our view, however, the excerpts and poems selected give a short yet comprehensive account of Galician literature to the present day.

In this anthology there is a striking presence of poetry that tells of the hardships that Galicians suffered until recently. In the past it was always fairly easy to publish individual poems in periodicals. Excerpts from novels are most prominent in the 20th century, as might be expected. As for drama, the first playwrights worth considering were first published only at the end of the nineteenth century. All the poems, as well as the prose and drama excerpts, however, shed light on the struggles, mentality and character of a people living for centuries in this corner of the Iberian peninsula, with a unique culture, language and literature almost unknown in the anglophone world.

We have mostly used *Literatura galega*, by Ramón Gutiérrez, Gonzalo Navaza, and Luciano Rodríguez (2000), as a starting point to which more material was added. The selected texts have been preserved as they were first published wherever it was possible so that the reader can appreciate the development of Galician. We are deeply indebted to Luciano Rodríguez for his able assistance and comments.

Breogán's Lighthouse suggests a transcendental viewpoint on Galician literature: it is a symbol of a cultural tradition that passes through geographical and linguistic boundaries. Breogán's tower and lighthouse witnessed the expeditions of the Milesians, that crossed the sea to land in Ireland, (if we are to believe *The Book of Invasions*). This was the first contact between people from this region and other European countries. We do hope that the lighthouse in the title illuminates and guides those who approach Galicia in spirit so that they can appreciate the concealed heritage of an ancient people and widen their knowledge of other cultures – which, after all, is one of the chief objectives of any translator.

A Short Introduction to Galician Literature

In the Medieval period, between the twelfth and fourteenth centuries, there flourished a poetic movement in the Galician language throughout the West of the Iberian Peninsula, in the area which today is Galicia and Northern Portugal. This corpus has been handed down to us in the form of the *Cancioneiros*.

Galician Medieval poetry was written in a highly elaborated Galician in the kingdoms of Galicia (before and after the independence of Portugal), León and Castile. The actual birthplace of the author was never taken into consideration. On the other hand, Galician Medieval prose, which was very scarce, consisted mainly of translations of works written in other languages. From the fifteenth century onwards, sociolinguistic circumstances of the age favoured the independence of Portuguese with respect to Galician and the division of the Galician and Portuguese literature, bringing with it a blossoming of language and literature in the independent kingdom of Portugal, and a period of decadence in Galician language and literature, known now as the Dark Centuries.

The twelfth century was a splendid period in the history of Galicia. The substantial rise in population allowed for the extension of agriculture and fishing and a subsequent increase in mercantile activity based on the agricultural products, which were taken to the towns to be exchanged for manufactured goods.

This saw as a consequence an urban renaissance, with the birth of a bourgeoisie grouped into guilds, which were established in districts and streets depending on the trade. The towns, as opposed to the rural areas, were the dominion of kings and feudal lords.

It was also in the twelfth century when the age known as the Compostelan Era began, thanks to the Archbishop Diego Xelmírez, who brought splendour to Santiago de Compostela, both in terms of economic wealth and of culture. The secular verses of the troubadors, the arrival of Romanesque art through the French Order of Cluny, St James' Way, and the composition of the *Codex Calistinus* all bore witness to this cultural boom.

From the thirteenth century onwards, the bourgeoisie started to show an interest in political power, and this led to struggles between this emerging class and the lay and religious aristocracy. At the end of the thirteenth century, however, Europe started to undergo a great crisis which would worsen in the fourteenth century.

Despite the crisis in the fourteenth century a slow recovery took place which gave way to the economic growth of the fifteenth century and in the pursuit of new exotic markets, especially by the Crowns of Castile and Portugal. For a long time Galician society advanced hand in hand with the rest of Europe. In the mid fifteenth century, however, great social and political conflict arrived in the shape of the *revoltas irmandiñas* which consisted of a series of anti-feudal uprisings. All the sectors involved (the peasants, the bourgeoisie and low level landholders) saw their economy being strangled by feudalism, and through these uprisings aimed at the overthrow of the feudal system. The Crown and the Church, however, despite their initial support for or tolerance of the revolt, allied with the Great Lords and thus maintained the stagnation of Galician socio-political life.

From 1482, Isabella I of Castile (after her victories in the internal wars) with her consort Ferdinand II of Aragón, started what was called by Padre Zurita the "process of taming and castration of the Kingdom of Galicia", placing Galicia under harsh political, linguistic and cultural bondage, whose consequence would be the centuries of silence, the Dark Centuries.

In literature, secular Galician verse grew out of Provençal poetry. This poetry, unlike Galician verse from the sixteenth, seventeenth and eighteenth centuries, has survived up to the present. It was claimed for a long time that Galician troubadour poetry was a simple imitation of Provençal verse. The reader can see through the texts which appear in this selection that, even though Galician poetry owes much to Provençal verse, it maintains a distinct personality of its own.

Secular Galician medieval verse lasted from the late twelfth century until 1354, the year of the death of Don Pedro, Count of Barcelos, and the last patron of this type of poetry. In any case, we must bear in mind that a poetic tradition does not vanish overnight, but rather requires a progressive process of disappearance.

In terms of subject matter, three different types of Galician medieval verse can be distinguished: the *Cantigas de amigo* (Songs of Women in Love), *Cantigas de amor* (Songs of Men in Love) and *Cantigas de escarnho e maldizer* (Songs of Ridicule).

The *Cantigas de amigo* have love as their theme, with a female subject (that is, they are placed in the mouth of a woman in love, even though these poems were always written by men). The *Cantigas de amigo* are the most indigenous of the forms of secular Galician verse, bearing a strong influence from popular verse but created artistically in Court under rigorous formal criteria.

In the *Cantigas de amor* we can find the same themes as in the *Cantigas de amigo*, but here the subject is masculine. This male sings of the greatness of an ideal woman, to whom he owes fidelity and at whose service he always places himself. Here there is a strong influence from Provençal verse.

Among the *Cantigas escarnho e maldizer*, the *escarnho* (jibes) make use of hidden meanings while the *maldizerr* (curses) use a much more open form of criticism.

Religious verse stems from an imitation of secular love poetry, and is represented by four hundred and twenty-seven compositions written by King Alfonso X, The Wise, stemming from his passionate devotion towards the figure of the Virgin Mary. Some of these are more of a lyrical style, while others are narrative in approach. As *Cantigas de Santa María* (The Songs of Saint Mary) translate the courtly love of the *Cantigas de amor* to a religious level. In these the poet does not swear fidelity to a *señor*, he swears fidelity to the Virgin and praises her virtues.

Galician medieval prose is usually divided into three generic classifications: hagiographic, historiographic and fiction. Despite the fact that not one of the three contains original creations in the Galician language, being translations or versions from other languages, this does not mean that they represent a cultural episode of no value.

The main protagonist in hagiographic prose in Galician is the apostle Saint James. The main text is *Miragres de Santiago*, (The Miracles of St James), an abridged version of the *Liber Sancti Iacobi*, conserved in a fragmentary codex from the first third of the fifteenth century. For many historians this is the real jewel of our medieval prose.

Prose fiction is derived from the *Roman de Troie*, a text from the second half of the twelfth century. Thus the *Crónica troiana* (Chronicle of Troy) is a version of a French text completed in 1373.

Apart from this text, there are various fragments and loose manuscripts of varying literary value, among which a *Livro de Tristán* (from the Brittany subject matter) stands out, written in the third quarter of the fourteenth century. There are also texts from three sequences – *Livro de José de Arimatea, Merlín e Demanda do Santo Graal* – in which can be found the divided material of the *Vulgata que contén o ciclo artúrico ou materia de Bretaña*.

In the period between the sixteenth and eighteenth centuries, the Dark Centuries, the existence of Galician literature is little more than anecdotical. This is on account of the decadence and political dependence of Galicia – and as such, of Galician letters –, which reached the modern period without a monarch of its own and, above all, without the presence of its own political and social institutions. Even though it was still considered a kingdom, Galicia became part of the crown of Castile, without having any autonomous institution to provide a counter-weight to centralist politics. Quite the opposite, new institutions were created – the General Military Headquarters, the Royal Court – which only served to increase dependence on the Court. Galicia became a mere province which attended, from a marginal position, the emergence of the Spanish monarchy, based in and around the kingdom of Castile. We find, therefore, from the seventeenth century onwards, a Galician language without any body of power to give it support, lacking the prestige of a literature such as that which it had enjoyed during the Middle Ages. Thus literary manifestations became sporadic and lacking the splendour of the past. Compositions from the period include circumstantial poems, Christmas carols, and the odd gem such as "Respice fínem" by Pedro Vázquez de Neira or a text by Xoán Gómez Tonel, "Turbas corran as Agoas, poña luto". From this period comes too the first play we know of in Galician, *A Contenda dos labradores de Caldelas* (1671), written by Gabriel Feixoo de Araúxo, in which we see the conflict between Galicians and Portuguese caused by fishing on the River Miño, and as such the play is known as *Entremés famoso sobre da pesca no río Miño*.

The nineteenth century saw a new interest in literature as part of a search for a local identity. The Peninsular Wars against the French provided an excellent breeding ground for awareness of questions relating to culture and identity and, as the century progressed, it is possible to see a progression and strengthening of identifying features which were translated into the literary text as a strong compromise and criticism of injustice. To aid understanding the period can be divided into three phases: the Early Writings (1808-1840), the Pre-Revivalists (1804-1863) and the Literature of the *Rexurdimento* or Revival.

During the first phase (1808-1840) a large number of texts can be found whose content is more utilitarian and practical rather than strictly literary. These writings were in general strongly linked to the socio-political context of the period, which explains the important role of the war against the French and the conflict between liberals and conservatives. We can also find a new theatrical text in which arranged marriages are criticised: the play by the liberal Antonio Benito Fandiño *A Casamenteira* (1812). There are also some texts of high literary value such as *A alborada* and the *Égloga de Belmiro e Benigno*, by Nicomedes Pastor Díaz.

As of 1840, probably as a result of the direct influence of the political and cultural movement denominated Provincialism, a large number of poems written in Galician appeared and were published in the country's press. One of the main events which took place in the age of the Pre-Revivalists (the writers who preceded Rosalía de Castro, Eduardo Pondal and Manuel Curros Enríquez, the three fundamental figures in nineteenth century Galician Literature) was the publication *of A Gaita Gallega. Tocada polo Gaiteiro, ou Carta de Christus para ir Deprendendo a Ler, Escribir e Falar Ben a Lingua Gallega* (1853), written by Xoán Manuel Pintos and popularly known as *A Gaita Gallega* (The Galician Pipes). This was a collection of narrative and dialogue poetry written in Galician, Spanish and Latin (and with quotes in French) whose main character was a bagpiper who puts his Castilian drummer right about numerous prejudices he has regarding Galicia and the Galicians.

Another important event for Galician Literature in this period was the celebration in A Coruña of the Xogos Florais (1861), a literary competition in which poets participated in both Galician and in Spanish. The really important feature, however, from a literary point of view, was the publication of the prize-winning poems in a volume entitled *Álbum de la Caridad, Seguido de un Mosaico Poético de Nuestros Vates Contemporáneos*. In this book we can find poems by writers of the stature of Francisco Añón, Xoán Manuel Pintos, Alberto Camino, Rosalía de Castro or Eduardo Pondal. Moreover, when we refer to the Pre-Revivalists, we refer to a group of authors with common thematic interests: singers of Galicia and its land-scape, defenders of Galician language and culture, extolling the virtues of customs, of songs of love, of nostalgia, and with a special concern for the political and social situation of Galicia.

The most outstanding writers of the period of the Pre-Revivalists were Vicente Turnes, Marcial Valladares (poet, grammarian and author of the first novel in Galician, *Maxina ou a filla espúrea* (Maxina or the Scorned Daughter) (1880), Xoán Manuel Pintos, the magnificent poet Francisco Añón, Alberto Camino and the brothers Antonio de la Iglesia, author of the important anthology *El idioma Gallego. Su Antigüedad y Vida* (1886), in three volumes, offering as it does the widest selection of linguistic, historical and literary texts from the Middle Ages up to his own time, and Francisco María de la Iglesia, author of the first contemporary Galician play, *A fonte do xuramento* (1882).

If we use the term Revival to denominate the nineteenth century in terms of literature, the full meaning of the term refers to the period which starts with the publication of the book of poems *Cantares Gallegos* (Galician Songs) (1863), by Rosalía de Castro, and the Revival would always be fundamentally concerned with poetry as a genre.

Led by historians, and most particularly by Rosalía de Castro's husband, Manuel Murguía, the Revival was essentially a lyrical movement, given that both narrative and drama in Galician only started to flourish in the 1880s, towards the end of the Revival and at the beginning of the transition towards twentieth-century Galician literature.

It is usually claimed that the writers of the Revival started from nothing, lacking a cultured literary tradition and basing their work on popular literature (the only tradition which these poets recognised). However, in reality, this ought to be put into perspective. If it is true that the writers of the Revival did not know the secular troubadour poetry and most medieval prose, they did know the religious verse and the poetry developed by the Galician-Castilian school. In fact this was one of the most forceful arguments made by the defenders of Galicia at the time, the Regionalists, who were led by Manuel Murguía, the *factotum*, the ideologue for the Galician Literature of the twentieth century.

At this point in time, Galician Literature not only has an identity of its own, but can also boast the social support of the people who felt fully identified with the work of Rosalía de Castro and her *Cantares Gallegos* (1863), clearly defending Galicia and its language in the prologue. The people, customs, characters, social and political grievances are all obvious on reading her work, and moreover there is also a highly intimate personal component which is always present in the works of the author. After this came the more intimate, personal and social concerns, as seen in the publication in 1880 of *Follas Novas* (New Leaves), a work which highlights the personal and social anguish which imprisoned the author and the anxieties and concerns as seen in the social circles of the period. Her work must be read in order to realise that in Rosalía we have the *mater magistra* of our literary and social existence.

The Celtic line, the glorious past of Galicia and the recovery of her identity, spawned by the Pro-Celtic thought of Manuel Murguía, who dreamt of a glorious future for the Galician people, gives life to the highly original poetry of Eduardo Pondal, in his important collection *Queixumes dos pinos* (Lamentations of the Pines) (1886).

The liberal, anti-clerical and most non-conformist line was defended in the poetry of Manuel Curros Enríquez, first in his *Aires da miña terra* (Airs of My Land) (1880) and then in his caustic and critical *O divino sainete* (The Divine Farce) (1888).

An author of great importance who was central to this process of cultural and poetic recovery was the poet, journalist and narrator from Ourense, Valentín Lamas Carvajal, who left an indelible mark on Galician Literature at the end of the nineteenth century. A similar case is that of the poetry of the physician and humanist Manuel Leiras Pulpeiro and the historian and novelist Antonio López Ferreiro, author of three historical novels, *A tecedeira de Bonaval* (The Weaver from Bonaval) (1894), *O castelo de Pambre* (The Castle of Pambre) (1895) and *O niño de pombas* (The Dove's Nest) (1905).

As is apparent in this Anthology, the great period for Galician Literature (in terms of quantity and quality) was, of course, the twentieth century. From this time Galicia possesses a literature which wants to be 'normal', and which struggles against historical, social, political and cultural ups and downs which do not allow normality to be present in the realm of literature, as would be expected within a society which considers itself to be democratic but which, in fact, is full of restrictive linguistic complexes and prejudices. At the beginning of the twentieth century Galician Literature picked up the inheritance of the advances and achievements of the Revival, but the new ideas and new social situation were to modify the literary panorama. A greater awareness by Galician society of its collective work would favour a literature which was further identified with social problems, and also new aesthetic demands in the development of works of literature. This would lend a degree of maturity to the writers of the period.

The writers of the first third of the twentieth century gave a new impulse to Galician culture and brought about the opening of Galician literature to the international literary movements of the time. Galician society underwent unprecedented activity in the first decades of the twentieth century of a kind unknown for many years: the nobility (present since the middle ages) disappeared allowing common people access to land ownership, and a small industrial and financial bourgeoisie began to become consolidated, based around the canning industries, ship-building, cattle ownership and businesses related to emigration. The agrarian movements which defended peasants against exploitation and abuse long suffered under the 'lords of the land' became established. At the same time it is also important to mention the social and cultural organisation of a Galician nationalism which would become the civil, social and cultural backbone of society.

With the writers of the period of the Language League known as the *Irmandades da Fala* (1916), of the *Nós* Group (1920) and of the avant-garde generations, the limits of nineteenth-century Galician literature were surpassed and new literary horizons were opened, as much in the field of poetry as in that of narrative or drama (in 1903 the Regional School of Recitation was founded, and in 1919, the National Conservatory of Galician Art). These writers lent a degree of maturity and literary consolidation to both narrative and theatre, genres which had been largely marginal up to this point within the Galician literature.

And so, after a period of effort and determination to catch the train of modernity in accordance with the new times, the first third of the twentieth century marked the consolidation which started to open up the paths towards normality. In this respect, we can witness the birth of the narrative of Manuel Lugrís Freire or Xosé Lesta Meis, the poetry of Antonio Noriega Varela and the magnificent and pluralistic poetic works of Ramón Cabanillas, but also drama, with names like Antón Villar Ponte and, once again, Ramón Cabanillas.

It would, however, be the writers of *Nós* (from the *Nós* Period) who would create modern Galician prose, developing the essay and, most especially, fiction, with Ramón Otero Pedrayo, Vicente Risco, Alfonso D. Rodríguez Castelao and Rafael Dieste, as representatives of narrative, but also as representatives of the renovation of the theatre, influenced by modern European theatre, particularly the Irish folk-drama learnt from W. B. Yeats and J. M. Synge.

Reinforcing this maturity and renovation, in the same period, there appeared a number of avant-garde poets, or poets who used the atmosphere of the avant-garde with Luís Amado Carballo, the fruitful meeting of tradition and modernity in the neo-troubador works of Fermín Bouza-Brey and the early Álvaro Cunqueiro, or the modernity of Manuel Antonio, as seen in the marvellous *De catro a catro* (Four by Four) (1928).

The Civil War (1936-1939) broke out, however, and Galician language and literature were erased at the stroke of a pen by the fascist authorities. In the summer of 1936 there was a historical and cultural purge in Galicia. It was but a few days from the majority approval by the people of the Autonomy Statute to the military uprising against the democratic government of the Second Spanish Republic, giving rise to the 'long night of stone', as it would so accurately be described by the poet Celso Emilio Ferreiro.

Galician nationalism survived underground until 1950, in terms of cultural activity. In the mid-nineteen-sixties a new form of Galician nationalism would arise, based on political parties which incorporated Marxism into their ideologies.

Galician literature was gagged until Edicións Monterrey and the Editorial Galaxia started, around 1950, slowly, to recover Galician literature.

Numerous authors in exile, however, in spite of the subjection of Galicia and the editorial difficulties there, continued their political and cultural work in favour of Galicia and her identity, with Buenos Aires for years acting as the cultural capital of Galicia. Classic authors of Galician literature were re-edited (Rosalía de Castro, Eduardo Pondal, Manuel Curros Enríquez or Manuel Antonio), new poetry from authors such as Emilio Pita, Lorenzo Varela or Luís Seoane was published, as was the fiction of Ramón de Valenzuela and Silvio Santiago, and drama, in particular that of Manuel Varela Buxán.

In the nineteen-fifties, with a certain climate of normality existing, a new type of literature emerged, which tried to build bridges with the past, but which also stood for the recovery, for recuperation. In the early nineteen-fifties and in the following decades, the sixties and seventies, the generation of 1936 would be dominant, comprised of authors who had started to write during the Second Republic but who wrote most of their work during the post-war period. Among these were the prose writer Ánxel Fole, an author who explored the world of popular culture from a new perspective, the great poet Aquilino Iglesia Alvariño who combined the works of classical writers (Greek and Latin) with great modern poets, the editor, poet, prose writer and playwright Xosé María Álvarez Blázquez, or the poets Xosé María Díaz Castro, Eduardo Moreiras, Miguel González Garcés, Pura Vázquez, María Mariño Carou or Celso Emilio Ferreiro, all of whom produced well-written, demanding works. At this time three fundamental figures of Galician literature were recovered, namely the poets, fiction-writers and dramatists Eduardo Blanco Amor, Ricardo Carballo Calero and Álvaro Cunqueiro.

All these authors form a group of creators who managed to recover for Galician literature the prestige it had lost after the fratricidal war.

Between the nineteen-fifties and sixties the group of men and women writers who made up the first strictly post-war generation started to appear. These were university-educated writers who incorporated new cultural models and new techniques and narrative forms into Galician Literature from the master-narrators of the twentieth century like James Joyce, Franz Kafka, Marcel Proust, John Dos Passos, William Faulkner, Albert Camus, Samuel Beckett or the new French narrative mode of the *Nouveau Roman*.

Just as writers from the *Nós* Group (Vicente Risco, Castelao, Ramón Otero Pedrayo) had incorporated new European cultural tendencies into the Galician Literature of the nineteen-twenties, these new writers attempted to update forms of telling stories and writing techniques. The world of the unconscious, the transformation of reality, social and existential conflict, the absurdity of life, repression and violence; all of these appear time and time again in their fiction.

Finally, a major change in Galician literature occurred after the end of the Franco Dictatorship in 1975. With the change in the political regime from Dictatorship to Parliamentary Democracy, a number of political changes were to take place which would favour Galician Literature. Galician language and literature, after being persecuted for so long, started to be recognised as marks of Galician identity and, as such, were studied and considered to be part of our heritage. The passing of the Autonomy Statute for the Historical Community of Galicia in 1981, gave rise to a number of laws. The Galician language became co-official within Galicia and is now studied at all levels of education. Even, however, while recognising the advances and changes which have taken place over the last few years, the situation has not yet been normalised, and there still exist numerous imbalances which only through time and a firm belief in the possibility of changing the course of things will we be able to overcome these difficulties.

Luciano Rodríguez Gómez

The Galician Language:
An Unfinished Task

Galician is a Romance language, spoken in the north-west of the Iberian peninsula, in a territory which currently occupies the whole of the Autonomous Community (or Region) of Galicia (made up of the provinces of A Coruña, Lugo, Ourense and Pontevedra), plus the western Asturias and the westernmost parts of the provinces of León and Zamora, which both belong to the Autonomous Community of Castilla-León. It is also spoken in a small area of Extremadura (in the municipalities of San Martín de Trebello, Valverde do Fresno and As Ellas) located in the north-west of the province of Cáceres.

The Galician language went through a period of complete normality during the Middle Ages, during which time it was the vehicle of a very important corpus of literary works, above all in the fields of religious and non-religious lyric verse (the Songs of Women in Love, Songs of Men in Love, Songs of Ridicule, Songs of Saint Mary, etc) and in which it was used both for legal documents and for the administration. But during the second half of the fifteenth century its non-literary use was reduced to the area of legal documents, and even this ceased during the sixteenth century, when it was substituted by Castilian Spanish, which, accompanying the centralist aim of forming the Spanish state, gradually established itself in Galicia as the language of administration, education, the Church and in general of all formal relations. Moreover, from the fifteenth century on, Galician began to lose its vitality as a literary tongue, although it continued to be used by almost the whole population in the sphere of the family and informal relations. In the eighteenth century some voices emerge, above all that of Father Sarmiento, denouncing the situation of marginalisation to which the Galician language was subjected, and demanding its reintroduction into education, the administration and religion. But it was not until the nineteenth century that a powerful literary revival took place, with figures of the importance of Rosalía de Castro, Curros Enríquez and Eduardo Pondal, and a demand for its public use through certain political movements, such as regionalism, which also demanded a greater regional autonomy for Galicia. At the beginning of the twentieth century, through the *Nós* Generation and the Seminary of Galician Studies, a nationalist movement would develop more strongly, urging for the rights of the Galician language, this movement eventually resulting in its recognition as having equal official status with Spanish in the Statute of 1936. The Spanish Civil War and the Franco dictatorship held up the process of recognition of the official status of Galician, which would not re-emerge until the return of democracy after Franco's death. During the last quarter of the twentieth century, a process of social normalisation of the Galician language began. Today it is still meeting with great difficulties, even though the most dynamic and progressive forces within Galician society are committed to this process, and in spite of the fact that this recent phase has witnessed the production of literary works of a high quality.

The native language of Galicia is Galician. By this we mean, and as such it is reflected in the Galician Statute of Autonomy, that the result of the natural development of Latin within the present territory of the Autonomous Community of Galicia and other bordering areas is Galician.

In the Galician Statute of Autonomy, apart from this acknowledgement, the official status both of Galician and Castilian Spanish is established, whereby everybody has the right to know and use both of them, and the authorities are urged not only to guarantee the normal and official use of both languages, but also to encourage the use of Galician in all aspects of life, in the public, cultural and information fields. Since the fifteenth century, the presence of Castilian Spanish in Galician has been increasing steadily, due to political, economic and social factors, in which time there has always been a sector of the population who know either Galician or Castilian Spanish, and another minority who know both languages, and who are used to expressing themselves mainly in one of them. This situation is referred to as social bilingualism.

In Galicia, the use of one or another language is frequently related both to social status and to function, and this is why we talk of the existence of "diglossic bilingualism of adscription" and of "functional diglossia".

Galician used to be the language of the least powerful sectors and those with least social prestige, the poor and least educated layers of society, while Castilian was considered the language of power, of the classes with a higher economic and social level. The most powerful and prestigious classes used to be established in the urban world: the town was considered as the centre of power, which explains why the process of de-Galicianisation was much more marked in the urban areas than in their rural counterparts, where only a minority (the teacher, the doctor, the pharmacist, the vet, etc) used Castilian as a sign of social difference, as against the rural and seafaring communities. This code, by which each language was linked to certain layers of the population, has been starting to change in recent years. On the one hand, many parents traditionally in the Galician-speaking sectors of society chose to speak to their children in Castilian, in order to facilitate their advancement in the social scale, and spread the Castilianisation of these sectors which had not been affected until then. On the other hand, in recent years, the rule by which members of certain layers of society (those who enjoyed a higher social, cultural and economic position) should speak Spanish changed: many Galician speakers who had access to a higher social status, resisted Castilianisation; other Galician language speakers, who had given up using their language as a normal means of expression in one period of their lives, took it up again, and it is not unusual to find cases of Galicianisation among those who used to have Castilian as their first language.

The idea that Galician was a language well adapted for use in certain functions, but was not valid in others, was also widespread. Galician was seen as a good means of oral communication within the family, but Castilian Spanish was the written language and the formal oral one. Also, in functional diglossia, significant changes have occurred in recent years, and in some cases an inversion of roles has taken place between Galician and Spanish, whereby Galician has occupied the place as Language A (for more formal acts) and Castilian is Language B, for more informal and colloquial exchanges, such as within the family.

These processes have been taking place at the same time as the development of the process of linguistic normalisation, as a result of the acknowledgement of the official status of the Galician language, the increase in Galician self-esteem and the increasing defence of Galician by political and labour union organisations.

The 1978 Spanish Constitution allowed the recognition of the historical rights of the different peoples within the Spanish state, among which were linguistic rights. This made it possible to begin the process of normalisation of the Galician language, a process in which we are still involved. In this process a series of initiatives and measures were taken, referring both to the social status the language enjoys and to the corpus, which have allowed its unhindered use in contemporary society.

Within the field of the normalisation of its status, important legislative campaigns were carried out, as well as joint action to foster the spread of the Galician language.

Within the legislative initiatives we must highlight the approval of the Linguistic Normalization Act, the General Plan of Linguistic Normalisation, and others referring to the legal recognition of Galician in the EU, and the regulation of the use of Galician in the educational system.

Law 3/1983, dated the 15 of June, known as the Law of Linguistic Normalisation, (which from now on will be referred to as LNL) is a qualitative step forward in the establishment of the legal status of Galician. It consists of 6 sections and an annexe.

Section I, referring to linguistic rights in Galicia, is particularly complex. In the first sub-section it states that Galician is the native language of Galicia, and that all Galician people have the duty to know it and the right to use it. In this declaration, the duties and rights regarding the Galician language were put together very clearly for the very first time. But this declaration of principles was appealed against and returned to the Constitutional Court, who declared the "duty to know" clause in the second paragraph of the first sub-section of this law to be unconstitutional.

In the second section it is stated that both Galician and Castilian Spanish are official languages in all the institutions of the autonomous region, in its administration, municipal administration and in all those public institutions depending on the Autonomous Community, and that administrative acts will be valid and produce the same effect whichever official language is used. Moreover, public organisations are encouraged to promote the Galician language.

Section III is very important, that referring to the use of Galician in education, not only as a subject of study, but as a vehicle of communication. We must not forget that schools were one of the most important ways of contributing to the process of de-Galicianisation, and that it must take prime position in the revival of the language's prestige.

Section IV refers to the use of the Galician language in the media: besides establishing the duty of the Xunta de Galicia (the government of Galicia) to encourage the use of Galician in the media, it must also encourage cultural manifestations and promote books in Galician; it also states that Galician must be the normal language of use on radio stations, television channels and other media of social communication managed by and within the ambit of the Autonomous Community (sub-section 18), and that the government will lend economic and material support to the media not included in the previous sub-section.

Section V deals with the protection that should be provided for Galician, both among the emigrant community abroad and in Galician-speaking territories bordering on the Autonomous Community; while Section VI talks of the responsibility of the Galician government and the municipal corporations in the protection and encouragement of Galician, with a view to the normalisation of its use in all kinds of activities.

There is another annexe which refers to the regulation, updating and proper use of the language, in which the rules of the Royal Galician Academy (RAG) are established as the rightful authority.

The announcement of the LNL was received with different degrees of acceptance, ranging from those who were fiercely critical of it to those who received it enthusiastically. In any case, it was a qualitative step forward in the recognition of the status of the Galician language.

The confirmation that the normalisation of the Galician language was proceeding at an unsatisfactorily slow pace, and the appearance of phenomena that caused great concern regarding its health, led the political parties to consider the necessity of creating a "General Plan of Linguistic Normalisation" (PXNL), passed unanimously by the Galician Parliament on September 24 2004.

The PXNL was devised with the idea of arousing commitment and enthusiasm in Galician society, and aims to associate the Galician language with the concepts of modernisation, progress and the future. Two points about the philosophy of the PXNL are worthy of note: the positive offer or adoption of the Galician language as a language of contact and as the language of choice in the administration and among enterprises and professionals in communicating with citizens; and the informative offer which would allow the idea of the validity, legality and advisability of writing administrative and commercial documents in Galician.

More than 400 specific measures were drawn up, presented in a positive and cordial manner, targeting those seven areas it was intended to include: the administration; education, the family and young people; the media and cultural industries; the economy; health; society; and the external projection of the language. These measures, which aimed to achieve specific goals, were proposed by the different commissions set up for each area, after a detailed analysis of the strengths and weaknesses of Galician within each field.

Apart from these vertical sectors, three horizontal ones were established affecting each of the former: those of language rights, new technologies and updating of the corpus. As far as putting the PXNL into practice is concerned, the government is obliged to present at the beginning of each year, the list of measures it means to implement in the course of that year, the executive organs involved, the cost and the system of assessment; moreover, at the end of each year, it must come to Parliament to give an account of how far the measures taken have borne fruit.

Spain is a state that forms part of the European Union, which also legislates about aspects of language, acting, above all in accordance with certain rules that have important repercussions on the different languages spoken within its territory. The status awarded to Galician within the EU has a lot to do both with its external projection and with the normalization process within Galicia itself.

On 11 May 2004, the Galician Parliament agreed unanimously that the Xunta urge the Spanish government to take the necessary steps so that Galician should be fully recognised as an official language of the European Union, on an equal footing with the official languages of the member states. The PXNL also includes, as one of its aims, that of obtaining official status within EU institutions.

On December 13 2004 the government of Rodríguez Zapatero presented this request before the Council of Europe in order that the co-official languages in the Spanish state should be conceded a statute as official languages of the EU, and worked actively and enthusiastically to this end, bearing in mind:
– the special circumstances of languages in Spain;
– the official nature of these languages within a member state of the EU;
– the necessity for the EU to be approachable by its citizens;
– that the Spanish government would pay for the costs involved in creating this new situation.

The Council of Europe, the only European institution with competence to define linguistic rules within the EU, decided not to concede this co-official status, but agreed to regulate its use. To this end it published (13 June 2005) the Council's Conclusions referring to the use of other languages in the Council, and in turn, in other institutions and organisations of the European Union. In these Conclusions the fields where these languages could be used are determined:

– Acts derived from procedures which were the result of joint decision-making can be translated into Galician, but this translation has no legal standing.

– It will be possible for the institutions to allow the use of these languages in oral sessions. The interpretation will be passive, which means that the only right granted is that of speaking Galician, which will be translated into other official languages. Thus, the translation of other languages into Galician is excluded. These interventions will only be allowed if they are previously formulated, within a reasonable period of time, and provided the necessary means of so doing exist.

– Citizens will have the right to address EU institutions in the Galician language. Even so, according to the Conclusions, this communication will not be direct, but will be made through a mediating organisation named by the national authorities.

On 16 November 2005, the president of the Regions Commission, Peter Straub, signed an agreement in which for the first time the use of Galician, Basque and Catalan are allowed in an EU institution. The European Parliament approved the use of the Spanish co-official languages in citizens' communications with the European Parliament. The agreements also allow the use of Galician in the Council of Ministers of the European Commission.

Citizens who wish to communicate with the European Ombudsman in Galician can also do so, thanks to the application of the agreement between Spain and this European organisation.

The presence of Galician in the Galician educational system is regulated by the Parliamentary Act 124/2007, of 28 June, which deals with both the use of the Galician language in the administration, with the teaching of it as a subject and with its use as a vehicle for the teaching of other subjects. As far as the educational administration in Galicia is concerned, it establishes that educational centres dependent on, and personnel in the service of, the administration are obliged to use the Galician language in general and encourage its oral and written use both in mutual and internal relations, in the relations with Galician regional and local administrations, and with other organisations in Galicia, both public and private, without this infringing on the rights of the teaching staff. It also lays down that internal administrative acts of teaching centres, such as the minutes of meetings, communiqués and announcements should be written, as a rule, in Galician, except in the case of communicating with other autonomous communities and with bodies depending on the State Administration based outside the community, in which case Spanish will be used (Section 2).

As for the number of teaching hours, a balance is sought between Galician and Spanish, with the same number of hours being devoted to the teaching of Galician and Spanish (Section 6). As a vehicle of teaching, in pre-school education, teachers should use the pupil's dominant mother tongue, he or she taking into account the social environment and taking care that pupils acquire knowledge of the other official language of Galicia for both speech and writing, within the limits set by each stage or cycle. Meetings of the staff will decide which is the mother tongue, according to the criteria established in the language plan designed by each centre (Section 7).

Throughout primary education, according to the PXNL, Mathematics; Environmental, Social and Cultural Studies; and Education for Citizenship and Human Rights, will all be compulsorily taught in Galician, and an appropriate level in linguistic competence will be guaranteed in both official languages of the community (Section 8).

In compulsory secondary education the following subjects will be taught in Galician: Natural Science; Social Science; Geography; History; Mathematics; and Education for Citizenship. Apart from the subjects listed above, staff meetings will agree to top up the number of subjects taught in Galician until they reach a minimum of 50% as established in the PXNL. Compulsory secondary education will provide all students with an adequate level of competence in both the official languages so that their use is affected positively (Section 9).

In the last two years of secondary school (Bacharelato) students will receive at least half of their teaching hours in Galician, in the terms established for this stage in the PXNL (Section 10).

In specific professional training, artistic teaching and that aimed at the world of sport, at middle and higher education levels, the parts of the syllabus set aside for students' particular speciality and career guidance within their formation will be taught in Galician, as will those parts of the professional syllabus decided by the management of the centre, after taking into account the opinions of the respective departments involved, and in all must total at least 50% of subjects, as established by the PXNL (Section 11). In all subject areas, students must be informed of their specific vocabulary in the Galician language.

It is laid down that, during two academic years, students from other parts of Spain or from foreign countries whose official language is Spanish, who have been recently incorporated into the Galician educational system, in the fourth year of secondary education or in Bacharelato will be exempt from being graded in tests in Galician. However, attendance in Galician language classes is compulsory, so that they can become integrated, linguistically speaking, and so that they can (by means of a special effort on their part, with specific didactic materials and with continual assistance from teaching staff) master the Galician language adequately by the end of the period of exemption, and continue their studies at the level corresponding to their age, being then able to register in the same conditions as the rest of their classmates.

This law was an important step forward regarding the presence of Galician as vehicle of communication, in that, following the guidelines contained in the PXNL, it is an attempt to guarantee 50% of learning in Galician at most levels of the educational system, and obliges each centre to define clearly which are those subjects to be taught in this language, requiring the inclusion of basic subjects, not only those that could be called fringe ones. The new government elected in 2009 has called this law into question and has already presented a Draft Bill that worsens the official status of the Galician language.

Apart from legislative initiatives, many other steps have been taken to boost the advancement of the Galician language, such as the launching of Galician Radio and Television, the creation of organisations to study the Galician language and others aimed at promoting the language outside the region.

No modern society can consider it possesses a normalised language if it is not used in the media, and particularly in the electronic media. In Galicia, in 1973, the Territorial Centre of Spanish Radio and Television began to use the Galician language in bilingual editions of news bulletins. But it was when democracy arrived, and with the Statute of Autonomy in the middle of its process of development, that the Radio and Television Company of Galicia (CRTVG) was created through the Act of Galicia 9/1984 of 11 July 1984. The CRTVG is a public company which has the vocation and commitment to encourage Galician language and culture by means of radio and television programmes transmitted wholly in Galician.

Galician Radio (RG) started trial broadcasts on 24 February 1985, on the anniversary of Rosalía de Castro's birthday, and started regular transmissions on 24 July 1985, on the eve of the Day of the Galician Homeland, from its studios in San Marcos-Bando (Santiago de Compostela).

Today, Galician Radio and Television are fully consolidated, with reasonably high audience levels when compared with similar audiovisual entities in Spain. Besides, Galician Television (TVG) has two international channels which broadcast to the whole of the EU and America, thanks to the Hispasat satellite. Today, TVG broadcasts with digital technology covering 85% of the population of Galicia, and will reach 90% by the beginning of 2010.

Leaving aside the research done into the Galician language in the universities, where the Galician Language Institute always held, and continues to hold, a prominent position, two other institutions exist with a certain tradition in the study of the Galician language: The Royal Galician Academy (RAG) and the Padre Sarmiento Institute. It was felt to be necessary to create a dynamic research organisation which would respond quickly and efficiently to the strategic necessities called for by the fact that the Galician language now carried out new functions. For this reason, the Ramón Piñeiro Centre and the Scientific and Technical Termin-ology Service (Termigal) were launched.

In 1993, by means of an order of the Department of Education of the Xunta de Galicia, the Ramón Piñeiro Linguistic and Literary Research Centre was created, which would later change its name to Ramón Piñeiro Centre for Research into the Humanities. This is a centre created within the philosophy which led to the creation of state research centres in European countries (CNRS in France, CNR in Italy or CSIC in Spain itself) with the aim of realising research projects of strategic importance for the development of the Galician language, carrying out large-scale projects which, owing to their size, it would be hard to place within public research projects, and to serve as points of reference for research in Galicia within their field of interest.

This Centre performed some very important work in the study and recovery of our cultural heritage. It is also a centre for reference, where fundamental resources are made available for students to carry out linguistic and literary investigation. Projects that have sprung from the spirit that moves this centre are: BILEGA (The Computerised Bibliography of the Galician Language), CORGA (The Corpus of Reference of Modern Galician), The Galician Phraseology Database, CODOLGA (Corpus Documentale Latinum Gallaeciae), Medieval Galician, the Literary Reports, which give an account of the literary output in Galician each year, or the Bibliography of Galician Literature.

But the Ramón Piñeiro Centre is above all a centre which confronts the current and future needs of the Galician language, hence the importance of developments there in linguistic engineering and technologies of speech. Pioneering work developed there included the first text to speech (TTS) converter in the Galician language, the first automatic Galician-Spanish translator, and the systems of automatic labelling and lemmatisation for modern Galician, which will be of great help for encoding texts which make up certain corpora and databases.

In modern societies, specialised communication is becoming more and more important. Never before in human history have so many scientific and technical advances been made at the speed at which they are being produced at the present time. To which we must add the phenomenon of globalisation: information is being transmitted in close to real time from one side of the planet to the other. Languages need to generate resources to label these new realities with which we are being flooded day by day, and the need arose to establish organisations to update terminology, which are especially necessary in languages which do not enjoy the status of absolute normality, because they run the risk of being invaded by a flood of terminology proceeding from other languages which will disfigure their identity. This was the reason behind the creation of TERMIGAL, the Galician Service of Scientific and Technical Terminology, founded in 1996, by means of an agreement between the Xunta de Galicia and the Royal Galician Academy.

In the process of linguistic normalisation, it is necessary to achieve an extension of the social uses of the language within its own territory, but also to make it known abroad; it is necessary for others to know and recognise it. For this reason it is so important to promote the Galician language abroad. In this direction, we must emphasise initiatives such as the Courses of Galician Language and Culture for Foreigners, launched with three main aims:

– The formation of teachers of Galician language and culture in different universities, with the ability to teach these subjects when they are incorporated into university staff.

– Encouraging research about Galicia and its language.

– Encouraging the knowledge of our literature and its translation.

Since 1988, up to the present day, these courses have been held, jointly organized by the Xunta de Galicia, the Royal Galician Academy and the Galician Language Institute of the University of Santiago de Compostela (USC), directed from the start by Professor Manuel González González of the USC.

A large number of teachers of Galician have been trained in these courses, in different universities, and some of the most outstanding pages written by non-Galicians about sociolinguistics have probably been written by students on these courses. For example, the first Galician grammar written in Japanese (by Take Kazu Asaka), an extraordinary anthology of Galician literature translated into Russian (directed by Helena Zernova) of which thirteen volumes have already been published, and the first Galician-Finnish dictionary, to give just a few examples.

Another initiative which contributed enormously to making the Galician language known abroad was the creation of the Galician Centres of Study, whose function it was to teach this language in the world's foremost universities, but also to act as disseminators of Galician culture. The teaching of the Galician language in the most important universities in the world is an important symbolic act which reflects, to an extent, the degree of international recognition attained by a language. About fifty of these centres exist in prestigious universities such as Oxford, Paris III, Tübingen, Saint Petersburg, Sao Paulo, Santa Barbara, and so on, which attempt to transmit the idea that Galicia is a living tongue, a vehicle of expression of a modern active people, rich in literature and possessing a culture thousands of years old.

Within the promotion of Galician abroad we must mention the grants made available by the Ramón Piñeiro Centre each year for foreign researchers who wish to carry out research projects in this Centre, in the fields of literature, language, history, anthropology or any other aspect of Galician culture. The period of time these researchers can stay is between a minimum of three and a maximum of seven months. Most of them are integrated in lines of investigation developed within the Centre itself, and they really play a very important part in it, contributing not only to improving the knowledge of some aspect of our contemporary life or historical reality, but also spreading the knowledge of our culture in their own countries.

Many other initiatives have been made to improve the knowledge of the Galician language abroad, some in collaboration with universities or other types of organisations in other countries with similar interests. This is the case, for example, of the Centre of Studies of Iberian and Pre-Hispanic Languages, or the Library of Galician Letters. The Centre of Studies of Iberian and Pre-Hispanic Languages was presented officially under the name of the House of Languages in 2005, promoted by the Cervantes Institute, the University of Alcalá and the principal linguistic institutions of Galicia, the Basque Country and Catalonia. Its basic aim is the teaching, investigation and transmission of the languages of Spain and Portugal outside their homelands.

The Library of Galician Letters website, linked to the Miguel de Cervantes Virtual Library, has as its objective to facilitate digitalised works of Galician literature from all ages to Internet users, from its first manifestations in medieval times (thirteenth to fifteenth centuries) up to the present day.

The organisation of written Galician into common rules concerning its spelling and morphology is a recent phenomenon, though many ill-fated attempts have been made throughout its history, which failed, either because of the weakness of the proposals or due to the lack of esteem in which the authors were held. We could mention some of these attempts, such as that carried out in 1933 by the Seminary of Galician Studies with the publication of *Some Rules for the Unification of the Galician Language*, which was in fact a proposal for internal use by the Seminary itself. In 1970 the *Orthographical and Morphological Rules of the Galician Language* were published by the Royal Galician Academy, which were nothing but an endorsement of the solutions proposed by the Galaxia publishing house. In 1971 the Galician Language Institute issued the handbook *Galego I,* followed by *Galego II* and *Galego III*, which, though they were not presented as rulebooks as such, offered far more soundly-based proposals concerning spelling and morphology than those made until then. It was clear that the studies carried out in the University of Santiago de Compostela in the nineteen-sixties and seventies regarding Galician speech and literary language were offering, for the first time, a fairly solid foundation for the knowledge of the Galician language. The Galician Language Institute, in these works, basically adopted the rules of the Royal Galician Academy, in a slightly modified way, above all with regard to the selection of certain lexical and morphological variants and the accommodation of learned words (an aspect that hardly appears in the rules of the RAG). But these unimportant, barely perceptible differences of emphasis meant that in society as a whole there were perceived to be two contrasting sets of rules.

In 1976 an attempt was made to overcome the differences between the ILG and the RAG. Intellectuals from all those sectors of society who were committed to the language took part in seminars between December 1976 and June 1977, which would produce the Foundations for the Unification of the Linguistic Rules of Galician. After the fall of the Franco regime, it was felt to be necessary to overcome the differences between the rule systems, above all when the new status of Galician was taken into account (schools, the administration, and so on). In each of these weekly seminars, which took place in the Philology Faculty of the University of Santiago de Compostela, one or more topics were discussed, working from the basis of studies secured from a specialist or committee, which were debated openly until a unanimous or majority agreement was reached. In spite of a previous commitment (made during the first session) to accept and defend the solutions agreed on, the truth is that the agreements were never kept by some, and that others soon failed to keep them as well, with only the ILG really continuing to defend the agreement at all.

The creation of a Linguistic Commission in 1979 could well be described as an utter failure. Its members were designated individually to draw up some *Rules of Spelling for the Galician Language*. It was supposed to devise rules for internal use by the Xunta and for those works published in Galician which needed approval by the Xunta itself. These rules were made public in May 1980 and had no effect at all, probably because they were made without reference to any institutions with any tradition in the study of the Galician language, and because they were drawn up by a commission which was unable to define what model of Galician they wanted. The outcome was a nonsensical text which did not even reflect the agreements of the commission itself, a fact that was denounced by some of its members. This proposal did not receive the backing of any important grouping.

The recognition of the official status of the Galician language required that this situation should be resolved, and to some extent it was this fact that forced an agreement between the ILG and the RAG: a direct dialogue was established between the two organisations, and a commission named to draw up a draft document which would serve as the basis for another technical commission, which was given the task of shaping the final text. This definitive text was approved in a joint session held by the ILG and RAG in the headquarters of the RAG on 3 July 1982. These Rules of Spelling and Morphology of the Galician Language were declared to be official by the Xunta in 1983. But it would be the passing of the Law of Linguistic Normalisation, in which the RAG is the institution charged with establishing the correct model of the language and its future updating, that would give Galician its definitive character as an official language. These rules have undergone two major processes of updating, one in 1995 and a further, more profound, change in 2003. Nowadays, these rules enjoy widespread social acceptance and only a few small groups reject them on ideological grounds.

It was also necessary to make a proposal concerning lexical rules, similar to those which had to do with spelling and morphology. This was partially fulfilled by the *Orthographical Vocabulary of the Galician Language* or VOLGA, which was the first serious proposal for a normalised vocabulary in the Galician language, where a selection is made, priorities determined regarding the forms in the different dialects, Castilian Spanish corruptions and spurious and unnecessary words are weeded out (with the elimination of invented and corrupted words which had been spread via lexicographical works and literature), a proposal is made for the correct spelling of words (regarding the correct use of "b" and "v"; the use of "h"; establishing the proper accentuation of words, and so on) and an updating and modernisation of the lexicon is carried out, in order to respond to the need to express oneself appropriately in today's world.

The VOLGA was published in a provisional edition in the summer of 1990, and jointly edited by the RAG and ILG in 2004, the new edition of the *Dictionary of the Royal Galician Academy* being based on this publication.

A lot has been done to give back to the Galician language its dignity and authority as the native language of Galicia, rights which should never have been lost, but history leaves wounds and consequences which are hard to overcome. The present situation is still far from being one that could be considered normal. It is this fact that made it advisable to make a General Plan for Linguistic Normalization, as, although certain steps forward have been made, there also exist some very worrying phenomena regarding the health of Galician, such as the decline in the transmission of the language within the family, the increase in monolingualism in Spanish, the process of urbanisation, which favours the use of Spanish, the incapacity of schools to gain fresh habitual Galician speakers, the total dominance of Spanish-language media, the continuing idea that Galician is useless or unnecessary, the lack of commitment to Galician of the business community, or the deterioration in the quality of the Galician language, especially within urban society.

The transmission of a language within the family is a fundamental factor in guaranteeing the future of that language, as those who learn a language in their own homes will tend to use it in the future in most situations where communication is necessary. The data available in this respect are most unfavourable for Galician. In the sector of the population aged between 16 and 54, only 20.6% use only Galician exclusively as their initial native language, as against 36.2% who use only Spanish. Even among those who consider both languages to be their native language, the language acquired at home is predominantly Spanish.

As for the language most commonly used, in recent years there has been a great increase in Spanish monolingualism, together with a decrease in monolingualism in Galician. We also find an increase in the preferential use of Spanish and a decrease in preferential use of Galician. This phenomenon affects not only city life, but is taking place to a worrying degree in all types of areas.

In the last decades of the twentieth century there was a significant movement of the population from rural to urban areas. This massive change of habitat was also accompanied, to a great extent, by linguistic change. The act of joining the city also clearly triggered the act of expressing oneself in Spanish, a relatively marked tendency in the second generation and strongly marked in the third.

Schooling meant a huge step forward in linguistic knowledge, especially in the mastery of reading and writing in Galician.

The creation of the Galician radio and television service, with the introduction of Televisión de Galicia and Radio Galega, which was a major achievement, were not enough, however, to counteract the enormous influence of radio and television channels broadcasting regularly in Spanish, even though these may occasionally use Galician. The disproportion between the use of Spanish and Galician in the written media produced in Galicia is scandalous, and does not reflect at all the relative proportion of the two languages' presence in Galician society. The media perpetuate pre-existing models dating from when it was unthinkable that Galician could become a modern language of communication.

There still persists prejudice against the Galician language in Galician society, particularly among young people, prejudices which were thought to have been overcome. Spanish is still associated in our society with progress, innovation and intelligence, while Galician is associated with values frozen or stagnant in time, not useful for climbing socially or for progressing economically.

In spite of a supposedly favourable attitude towards Galician, the truth is that, apart from a few exceptions, the level of commitment among the Galician business community and the principal economic agents in Galician society towards the language is still very low.

The worryingly poor quality of the language used must be added to the above point, especially in urban areas. Galician has never enjoyed such a complex and well-organised corpus as it does nowadays (rules, grammar books, vocabulary, spelling, monolingual and bilingual dictionaries, specialized glossaries and so on) but at the same time Galician has never been used in such poor quality, and with such a high level of linguistic contamination. This is especially worrying in Urban Galician, otherwise known as Neo-Galician, a variety of Galician used by an increasing number of speakers, mainly city-dwellers, mostly having Spanish as their mother-tongue, who use a type of Galician strongly influenced by Spanish, above all in phonology, syntax and phraseology, but also with a very marked influence in their morphology and lexicon.

The return to democracy in Spain, after Franco's death, meant a progressive recognition of the linguistic rights of Catalan, Basque and Galician in their respective communities. Successive Galician governments have encouraged a series of initiatives aimed at the social normalization of the Galician language, and with this aim in mind specific laws have been passed and specific measures have been taken to encourage its use. But the measures taken have not been effective enough, either because they were the wrong ones or because they were applied without much conviction. The truth is that Galician gained ground in social spheres where it had previously been absent (the administration, education, media, and so on) but, paradoxically, lost out in the number of habitual speakers to a degree that has caused great concern, and is less and less transmitted via the family. This delicate situation with regard to its presence in society has been accompanied by a decline in the quality of the language, increasingly contaminated by Spanish. Urgent measures need to be taken to transform this situation, before the arrival of a scenario in which the situation is irreversible.

Manuel González González

Medieval Literature

Secular Poetry

Songs of Women in Love (Cantigas de amigo)

Mendinho (13th century)

Sedíam' eu na ermida de San Simión...

Sedíam' eu na ermida de San Simión
e cercáronmi as ondas, que grandes son.
    Eu atendend' o meu amigo!
    Eu atendend' o meu amigo!

Estando na ermida ant' o altar,
cercáronmi as ondas grandes do mar.
    Eu atendend' o meu amigo!
    Eu atendend' o meu amigo!

E cercáronmi as ondas, que grandes son,
non ei i barqueiro nen remador.
    Eu atendend' o meu amigo!
    Eu atendend' o meu amigo!

E cercáronmi as ondas do alto mar,
non ei i barqueiro nen sei remar.
    Eu atendend' o meu amigo!
    Eu atendend' o meu amigo!

Non ei i barqueiro nen remador,
morrerei eu fremosa no mar maior.
    Eu atendend' o meu amigo!
    Eu atendend' o meu amigo!

Non ei i barqueiro nen sei remar
morrerei eu fremosa no alto mar.
    Eu atendend' o meu amigo!
    Eu atendend' o meu amigo!

I sat in the chapel on the Isle of San Simón...

I sat in the chapel on the Isle of San Simón,
and waves came all around me, how very big they are:
    waiting for my lover,
    waiting for my lover.

I stood in the chapel at the table of the Lord,
and the big waves of the sea came all around me there:
    waiting for my lover,
    waiting for my lover.

The waves came all around me, how very big they are;
I have no boatman with me, nor anyone to row:
    waiting for my lover,
    waiting for my lover.

And the waves of the tall sea came all around me there;
I have no boatman with me, and I don't know how to row:
    waiting for my lover,
    waiting for my lover.

I have no boatman with me, nor anyone to row;
all beautiful I'm going to die in that massive sea:
    waiting for my lover,
    waiting for my lover.

I have no boatman with me, and I don't know how to row;
all beautiful I'm going to die in that tall, tall sea:
    waiting for my lover,
    waiting for my lover.

Pai Gómez Charinho (1225–1295)

As frores do meu amigo...

As frores do meu amigo
briosas van no navío.
    E van-s' as frores
    d'aquí ben con meus amores;
    idas son as frores
    d'aquí ben con meus amores.

As frores do meu amado
briosas van eno barco.
    E van-s' as frores
    d'aquí ben con meus amores;
    idas son as frores
    d'aquí ben con meus amores.

Briosas van no navío
pera chegar ao ferido.
    E van-s' as frores
    d'aquí ben con meus amores;
    idas son as frores
    d'aquí ben con meus amores.

Briosas van eno barco
para chegar ao fossado.
    E van-s' as frores
    d'aquí ben con meus amores;
    idas son as frores
    d'aquí ben con meus amores.

Para chegar ao ferido,
servir-mi, corpo velido.
    E van-s' as frores
    d'aquí ben con meus amores;
    idas son as frores
    d'aquí ben con meus amores.

Para chegar ao fossado
servir-mi, corpo loado.
    E van-s' as frores

d'aquí ben con meus amores;
idas son as frores
d'aquí ben con meus amores.

The flowers of my lover...

The flowers of my lover,
they go eager in the boat.
    And the flowers go
    away from here with all my love.
    The flowers have gone
    away from here with all my love.

The flowers of my darling,
they go eager in the ship.
    And the flowers go
    away from here with all my love.
    The flowers have gone
    away from here with all my love.

They go eager in the boat
to reach the wounded one.
    And the flowers go
    away from here with all my love.
    The flowers have gone
    away from here with all my love.

They go eager in the ship
to reach the injured one.
    And the flowers go
    away from here with all my love.
    The flowers have gone
    away from here with all my love.

To reach one who was wounded
in serving me, fine body.
    And the flowers go
    away from here with all my love.
    The flowers have gone
    away from here with all my love.

To reach one who was injured
in serving me, praised body.

And the flowers go
away from here with all my love.
The flowers have gone
away from here with all my love.

Martín Codax (13th century)

Ondas do mar de Vigo...

Ondas do mar de Vigo,
se vistes meu amigo
   ie ai Deus se verrá cedo!

Ondas do mar levado,
se vistes meu amado,
   ie ai Deus se verrá cedo!

Se vistes meu amigo
o por que eu sospiro,
   ie ai Deus se verrá cedo!

Se vistes meu amado
por que hei gran cuidado,
   ie ai Deus se verrá cedo!

O waves of the sea of Vigo...

O waves of the sea of Vigo,
if only you've seen my lover,
   and, oh God, if only he'd come soon!

O waves of the heaving sea,
if only you've seen my darling,
   and, oh God, if only he'd come soon!

If only you've seen my lover,
the man for whom I'm sighing,
   and, oh God, if only he'd come soon!

If only you've seen my darling,
the man for whom I'm pining,
   and, oh God, if only he'd come soon!

¡Ai Deus, se sab' ora meu amigo...

¡Ai Deus, se sab' ora meu amigo
com' eu senheira estou en Vigo!
    e vou namorada...

¡Ai Deus, se sab' ora o meu amado
com' eu en Vigo senheira manho!
    e vou namorada...

Com' eu senheira estou en Vigo,
e nulhas gardas non ei comigo;
    e vou namorada...

Com' eu en Vigo senheira manho
e nulhas gardas migo non trago;
    e vou namorada...

E nulhas gardas non ei comigo
ergas meus olhos, que choran migo;
    e vou namorada...

E nulhas gardas migo non trago,
ergas meus olhos, que choran ambos;
    e vou namorada...

Oh God, would that my lover knew...

Oh God, would that my lover knew
I'm all alone in Vigo town
    and I'm in love.

Oh God, would that my darling knew
I'm left alone in Vigo town
    and I'm in love.

I'm all alone in Vigo town
and I have no guards with me
    and I'm in love.

I'm left alone in Vigo town
and I have no guards with me
    and I'm in love.

And I have no guards with me
except my eyes, which weep with me,
    and I'm in love.

I have brought no guards with me
except my eyes, which weep together,
    and I'm in love.

Eno sagrado, en Vigo...

Eno sagrado, en Vigo,
bailava corpo velido,
    ¡Amor ei!

En Vigo, no sagrado,
bailava corpo delgado.
    ¡Amor ei!

Bailava corpo velido,
que nunca ouver' amigo.
    ¡Amor ei!

Bailava corpo delgado,
que nunca ouver' amado.
    ¡Amor ei!

Que nunca ouver' amigo,
ergas no sagrad', en Vigo.
    ¡Amor ei!

Que nunca ouver' amado,
ergas en Vigo, no sagrado.
    ¡Amor ei!

In the churchyard, in Vigo...

In the churchyard, in Vigo,
a lovely body was dancing,
    I have a love!

In Vigo, in the churchyard,
a slender body was dancing,
    I have a love!

A lovely body was dancing
that never had a lover,
   I have a love!

A slender body was dancing
that never had a sweetheart,
   I have a love!

That never had a lover
except in the churchyard, in Vigo,
   I have a love!

That never had a sweetheart
except in Vigo, in the churchyard,
   I have a love!

Airas Núnez (13th century)

Bailemos nós ja todas tres, ai amigas...

Bailemos nós ja todas tres, ai amigas,
so aquestas avelaneiras frolidas,
e quen for velida, como nós, velidas,
   se amigo amar,
so aquestas avelaneiras frolidas
   verrá bailar.

Bailemos nós ja todas tres, ai irmanas,
so aqueste ramo d'estas avelanas,
e quen for louçana como nós, louçanas,
   se amigo amar,
so aqueste ramo d'estas avelanas
   verrá bailar.

Por Deus, ai amigas, mentr' al non fazemos,
so aqueste ramo frolido bailemos,
e quen ben parecer como nós parecemos,
   se amigo amar,
so aqueste ramo, sol que nós bailemos,
   verrá bailar.

Let's dance all three, O my friends...

Let's dance all three, O my friends,
under these blossoming hazels,
and whoever's pretty like us, pretty ones,
    if she loves a lover,
under these blossoming hazels,
    will come and dance.

Let's dance all three, O my sisters,
under this hazelnut branch,
and whoever's comely like us, comely ones,
    if she loves a lover,
under this hazelnut branch,
    will come and dance.

By God, friends, we've nothing to do,
let's dance neath this bough of blossom,
and whoever's good-looking as we're good-looking,
    if she loves a lover,
under this bough where we're dancing,
    will come and dance.

Fernand' Esquío (13th–14th century)

Vaiamos irmana, vaiamos dormir...

Vaiamos irmana, vaiamos dormir
nas ribas do lago, u eu andar vi
    a las aves meu amigo.

Vaiamos irmana, vaiamos folgar
nas ribas do lago, u eu vi andar
    a las aves meu amigo.

Nas ribas do lago, u eu andar vi,
seu arco na maão, as aves ferir,
    a las aves meu amigo.

Nas ribas do lago, u eu vi andar,
seu arco na mano a las aves tirar,
    a las aves meu amigo.

Seu arco na mano as aves ferir,
e las que cantavan leixa-las guarir,
    a las aves meu amigo.

Seu arco na mano a las aves tirar,
e las que cantavan non as quer matar,
    a las aves meu amigo.

Let's go there, my sister, let's go there to sleep...

Let's go there, my sister, let's go there to sleep
on the banks of the lake where I once saw him:
    my lover hunting for birds.

Let's go there, my sister, let's go there to rest
on the banks of the lake where I once watched him:
    my lover hunting for birds.

On the banks of the lake where I once saw him,
his bow in his hands for wounding the birds:
    my lover hunting for birds.

On the banks of the lake where I once watched him,
his bow in his hands for shooting the birds:
    my lover hunting for birds.

His bow in his hands for wounding the birds,
but those who were singing he lets them escape:
    my lover hunting for birds.

His bow in his hands for shooting the birds,
but those who were singing he never will kill:
    my lover hunting for birds.

Pero Meogo (13th century)

O meu amig' a que preito talhei...

O meu amig' a que preito talhei,
con vosso medo, madre, mentirlh' ei;
e se non for, assanhars' á.

Talheilh' eu preito de o ir veer
ena fonte ú os cervos van bever;
e se non for, assanhars' á.

E non ei eu de lhi mentir sabor,
mais mentirlh' ei con vossa pavor;
e se non for, assanhars' á.

De lhi mentir nen un sabor non ei,
con vosso med' a mentirlh' averei;
e se non for, assanhars' á.

To my lover, and I'm pledged to him...

To my lover, and I'm pledged to him,
I shall lie, mother, for fear of you,
and if I do not go, he will be angry.

I have pledged to go and see him there
at the spring where the stags go to drink,
and if I do not go, he will be angry.

I shall not lie to him willingly,
and yet I shall lie for fear of you,
and if I do not go, he will be angry.

And I have no wish to lie to him,
but for fear of you I have to lie,
and if I do not go, he will be angry.

Por mui fremosa, que sanhuda estou...

Por mui fremosa, que sanhuda estou
a meu amigo, que me demandou
que o foss' eu veer
a la font' ú os cervos van bever.

Non faç' eu torto de mi lh' assanhar
por s' atrever el de me demandar
que o foss' eu veer
a la font' ú os cervos van bever.

Afeito me ten ja por sandía,
que el non ven, mais envía
que o foss' eu veer
a la font' ú os cervos van bever.

I'm beautiful and so I'm cross...

I'm beautiful and so I'm cross
with my beloved, who's asked me
to go and see him
at the spring where the stags go to drink.

I'm not wrong to be cross with him
for making so bold as to ask me
to go and see him
at the spring where the stags go to drink.

He clearly takes me for a fool:
he doesn't come, but sends for me
to go and see him
at the spring where the stags go to drink.

Tal vai o meu amigo con amor que lh' eu dei...

"Tal vai o meu amigo con amor que lh' eu dei,
come cervo ferido de monteiro d' el Rei.

Tal vai o meu amigo, madre, con meu amor,
come cervo ferido de monteiro maior.

E se el vai ferido irá morrer al mar,
sí fará meu amigo se eu del non pensar".

"E guardádevos, filha, ca ja m' eu atal vi
que se fezo coitado por guaanhar de min".

E guardadevos, filha, ca ja m' eu vi atal
que se fezo coitado por de min guaanhar".

My darling has departed, with love I've given him...

'My darling has departed, with love I've given him,
like a stag that's been wounded by the huntsman of the King.

My darling has departed with love of mine, dear mother,
like a stag that's been wounded by the chief royal huntsman.

And if the stag is wounded it goes to the sea to die;
as will my dearest darling if he's not in my mind.'

'Be careful, though, my daughter, for I've seen such as he
pretending they're grief-stricken to win rewards from me.

Be careful, though, my daughter, for such as he I've seen
pretending they're grief-stricken to win favours from me.'

Ai cervos do monte, vínvos preguntar...

Ai cervos do monte, vinvos preguntar:
fois' o meu amigu' e, se alá tardar,
qué farei, velidas?

Ai cervos do monte, vínvolo dizer:
fois' o meu amigu' e querría saber
qué farei, velidas?

Oh hinds of the mountain, I've come here to ask...

Oh hinds of the mountain, I've come here to ask:
my lover's departed and if he is long
what shall I do, my beauties?

Oh hinds of the mountain, I've come here to say:
my lover's departed and I'd like to know
what shall I do, my beauties?

Levóus' a louçana, levóus' a velida...

Levóus' a louçana, levóus' a velida,
vai lavar cabelos na fontana fría,
leda dos amores, dos amores leda.

Levóus' a velida, levóus' a louçana,
vai lavar cabelos na fría fontana,
leda dos amores, dos amores leda.

Vai lavar cabelos na fontana fría,
passou seu amigo que lhi ben quería,
leda dos amores, dos amores leda.

Vai lavar cabelos na fría fontana,
passa seu amigo que a muit' a amava,
leda dos amores, dos amores leda.

Passa seu amigo que lhi ben quería,
o cervo do monte a augua volvía,
leda dos amores, dos amores leda.

Passa seu amigo que a muito amava
o cervo do monte volvía a augua,
leda dos amores, dos amores leda.

The comely girl rose, the beauteous girl rose...

The comely girl rose, the beauteous girl rose:
she's off to wash her hair in the cold, cold spring.
She's happy in love, in love she is happy.

The beauteous girl rose, the comely girl rose;
she's off to wash her hair in the spring so cold.
She's happy in love, in love she is happy.

She's off to wash her hair in the cold, cold spring;
her lover goes by, who dearly loves her.
She's happy in love, in love she is happy.

She's off to wash her hair in the spring so cold;
her lover goes by, who cherishes her.
She's happy in love, in love she is happy.

Her lover goes by, who dearly loves her;
the stag of the mountain was stirring the water.
She's happy in love, in love she is happy.

Her lover goes by, who cherishes her;
the stag of the mountain was moving the water.
She's happy in love, in love she is happy.

Enas verdes ervas...

Enas verdes ervas
vi andalas cervas,
meu amigo.

Enos verdes prados
vi os cervos bravos,
meu amigo.

E con sabor d' elhas
lavei mias garcetas,
meu amigo.

E con sabor d' elhos
lavei meus cabelos,
meu amigo.

Desque los lavei
d' ouro los liei,
meu amigo.

Desque las lavara
d' ouro las liara,
meu amigo.

D' ouro los liei
e vos asperei,
meu amigo.

D' ouro las liara
e vos asperava,
meu amigo.

Amidst the green grasses...

Amidst the green grasses
I saw the hinds roaming,
my dear.

Amidst the green meadows
I saw the fierce stags,
my dear.

For joy of the hinds
I washed my fair tresses,
my dear.

For joy of the stags
I washed my fair locks,
my dear.

After washing my locks,
I did braid them with gold,
my dear.

After washing my tresses
I braided them with gold,
my dear.

I did braid my locks
and did wait for you,
my dear.

I braided my tresses
and waited for you,
my dear.

Preguntarvos quer' eu, madre...

Preguntarvos quer' eu, madre,
que me digades verdade,
se ousará meu amigo
ante vós falar comigo?

Pois eu mig' ei seu mandado
querría saber de grado
se ousará meu amigo
ante vós falar comigo?

Irei, mia madre, a la fonte
ú van os cervos do monte,
se ousará meu amigo
ante vós falar comigo?

I'd like to ask you, mother...

I'd like to ask you, mother,
and please tell me the truth,
if my lover will dare
to talk to me, with you.

And since I have his message
I'd dearly like to know
if my lover will dare
to talk to me, with you.

I'll go, mother, to the spring
where the mountain stags go
if my lover will dare
to talk to me, with you.

Fostes, filha, eno bailar...

Fostes, filha, eno bailar
e rompestes i o brial.
Pois o namorado i ven
esta fonte seguídea ben,
pois o namorado i ven.

Fostes, filha, eno loir
e rompestes i o vestir.
Pois o namorado i ven
esta fonte seguídea ben,
pois o namorado i ven.

E rompestes i o brial
que fezestes ao meu pesar.
Pois o namorado i ven
esta fonte seguídea ben,
pois o namorado i ven.

E rompestes i o vestir
que fezestes a pesar de min.
Pois o namorado i ven
esta fonte seguídea ben,
pois o namorado i ven.

Daughter, you went; as you danced...

Daughter, you went; as you danced
in that place you tore your skirt.
Since your lover's coming here
follow the course of this spring,
since your lover's coming here.

Daughter, you went; as you played
in that place you tore your dress.
Since your lover's coming here
follow the course of this spring,
since your lover's coming here.

Being there you tore your skirt,
something done in spite of me.
Since your lover's coming here
follow the course of this spring,
since your lover's coming here.

Being there you tore your dress,
something done in spite of me.
Since your lover's coming here
follow the course of this spring,
since your lover's coming here.

"Digades, filha, mia filha velida..."

"Digades, filha, mia filha velida,
porque tardastes na fontana fría?
Os amores ei.

Digades, filha, mia filha louçana,
porque tardastes na fría fontana?"
Os amores ei.

"Tardei, mia madre, na fontana fría,
cervos do monte a augua volvían."
Os amores ei.

Tardei, mia madre, na fría fontana,
cervos do monte volvían a augua."
Os amores ei.

"Mentís, mia filha, mentís por amigo,
nunca vi cervo que volvess' o río.
Os amores ei.

Mentís, mia filha, mentís por amado,
nunca vi cervo que volvess' o alto".
Os amores ei.

'Tell me, my daughter, my lovely daughter...'

'Tell me, my daughter, my lovely daughter:
why did you tarry at the cold spring?
I am in love.

Tell me, my daughter, my beauteous daughter:
why did you tarry at the spring so cold?'
I am in love.

'I tarried, mother, at the cold spring:
those mountain stags were stirring the water.
I am in love.

I tarried, mother, at the spring so cold:
the water was stirred by those mountain stags.'
I am in love.

'You lie, my daughter, lie for your lover:
I've never seen stags stirring the river.
I am in love.

You lie, my daughter, lie for your sweetheart:
I've never seen stags stirring the spring.'
I am in love.

Songs of Men in Love (Cantigas de amor)

Bernal de Bonaval (13th century)

A dona que eu am' e tenho por senhor...

A dona que eu am' e tenho por senhor
amostrade-mi-a, Deus, se vos en prazer for,
    senón dade-mi a morte.

A que tenh' eu por lume destes olhos meus,
e por que choran sempre, amostrade-mi-a, Deus,
    senón dade-mi a morte.

Essa que vós fezestes melhor parecer
de quantas sei, ¡ai Deus!, fazede-mi-a veer,
    senón dade-mi a morte.

¡Ai, Deus!, que mi a fezestes máis ca min amar,
mostrade-mi-a u possa con ela falar,
    senón dade-mi a morte.

That lady whom I love and is my mistress dear...

That lady whom I love and is my mistress dear:
show her to me, O God, if this should be your will,
    if not, put me to death.

That lady who's the light of these my own two eyes,
for whom they always weep, show her to me, O God,
    if not, put me to death.

That lady whom you made the very loveliest
lady I know, O God, show her, let me see her,
    if not, put me to death.

O God, who made me love her more than my own self,
reveal her to me now where I can speak to her,
    if not, put me to death.

Airas Núñez (13th century)

Que muito m' eu pago d' este verão...

Que muito m' eu pago d' este verão,
por estes ramos et por estas flores
et polas aves que cantan d' amores,
por que ando i led' e sen cuidado
et assí faz tod' omen namorado,
sempre i anda led' e mui louçã.

Quand' eu passo per algūas ribeiras,
so bōas árvores, per bōos prados,
se cantan i pássaros namorados
logu' eu con amores i vou cantando
e logo alí de amores vou trobando
et faço cantares en mil maneiras.

Ei eu gran viço e grand' alegría,
quando m' as aves cantan no estío.

How I enjoy these summer months...

How I enjoy these summer months,
with all these flowers on all these branches,
with all these birds that sing of love,
for I walk glad and free of care,
and so does every man in love,
he always goes happy and zestful.

And when I walk on riverbanks
under good trees, beside good meadows,
if birds in love are singing there
then I too sing, for I'm in love,
and then I make ballads of love
and I make songs of every kind.

I feel great pleasure and great joy
when the birds sing to me in the summer.

Johán Zorro (13th–14th century)

En Lixboa, sobre lo mar...

En Lixboa, sobre lo mar,
barcas novas mandei lavrar,
   iai, mía senhor velida!

En Lixboa, sobre lo ler,
barcas novas mandei fazer,
   iai, mía senhor velida!

Barcas novas mandei lavrar,
e no mar as mandei deitar,
   iai, mía senhor velida!

Barcas novas mandei fazer,
e no mar as mandei meter,
   iai, mía senhor velida!

In Lisbon, by the sea...

In Lisbon, by the sea,
I ordered new boats built,
   oh my lovely lady!

In Lisbon, by the shore,
I ordered new boats made,
   oh my lovely lady!

I ordered new boats built
and launched into the sea,
   oh my lovely lady!

I ordered new boats made
and sent into the sea,
   oh my lovely lady!

Johán Airas de Santiago (13th–14th century)

Andei, senhor, León e Castela...

Andei, senhor, León e Castela
despois que m' eu d' esta terra quitei,
e non foi i dona nen donzela
que eu non viss', e máis vos én direi:
quantas máis donas, senhor, alá vi,
tanto vos eu mui máis precei des i.

E quantas donas eu vi, des quando
me fui d' aquí, punhei de as cousir,
e poilas vi, estive cuidando
en vós, senhor, e por vos non mentir,
quantas máis donas, senhor, alá vi,
tanto vos eu mui máis precei des i.

E as que alá maior prez avían
en todo ben, tódalas fui veer,
e cousi-as, e ben parecían,
pero, senhor, quero-vos al dizer:
quantas máis donas, senhor, alá vi,
tanto vos eu mui máis precei des i.

I crossed, my mistress, León and Castille...

Once I had taken my leave of this land,
I crossed, my mistress, León and Castille,
and there was no lady or maiden there
I did not see, and I've more to reveal:
the more ladies, my dear, I went to view,
the more, very much more, I valued you.

And every one of the ladies I saw
after leaving here, I strove to espy,
and, once I'd seen them, my thoughts always turned
to you, my dear mistress, and I'll not lie:
the more ladies, my dear, I went to view,
the more, very much more, I valued you.

And the ladies with the highest renown
for the finest parts, I called on them all,
I perused them, they were good to behold;
and yet, my mistress, I'll say something more:
the more ladies, my dear, I went to view,
the more, very much more, I valued you.

Alfonso X, The Wise (1221–1284)

Par Deus, senhor...

Par Deus, senhor,
enquant' eu ffor
de vós tam alongado,
nunca en mayor
coyta d' amor
nem atam coytado
foy eno mundo
por sa senhor
homen que fosse nado,
penado, penado.

Sen nulha ren
sen vosso ben,
que tant' ey desejado
que ja o ssem
perdí por em,
e viv' atormentado,
ssem vosso ben,
de morrer en
ced' é muy guisado,
penado, penado.

Ca, log' aly
hu vos eu vy,
fuy d' amor afficado
tam muyt' en mi
que non dormí,
nen ouve gasalhado
e, sse m' este mal
durar assy,

eu nunca fosse nado,
penado, penado.

By God, my lady...

By God, my lady,
as soon as I
was very far from you,
never in greater
pains of love
or so struck down with grief
was in this world
for his beloved
any man ever born,
sorrowful, sorrowful.

Bereft of all
without your good
that I have so desired,
it has made me
lose all my sense
and life is agony
without your good;
to die from this
directly would be best,
sorrowful, sorrowful.

Because as soon
as I saw you
I was possessed by love
so deep inside
that I've not slept
and nothing gives me joy;
and if this ill
persists like this
I should not have been born,
sorrowful, sorrowful.

Don Denís (1261–1325)

Quer' eu en maneira de proençal...

Quer' eu en maneira de proençal
fazer agora un cantar d' amor
e querrei muit' i loar mía senhor,
a que prez nen fremusura non fal,
nen bondade, e mais vos direi en:
tanto a fez Deus comprida de ben
que máis que toda las do mundo val.

Ca mía senhor quiso Deus fazer tal
quando a fez, que a fez sabedor
de todo ben e de mui gran valor
e con todo est' é mui comunal,
alí u deve; er deu' lhi bon sen
e des i non lhi fez pouco de ben,
quando non quis que lh' outra foss' igual.

Ca en mía senhor nunca Deus pôs mal,
mais pôs i prez e beldad' e loor
e falar mui ben e rir melhor
que outra molher; des i é leal
muit', e por esto non sei oj' eu quen
possa compridamente no seu ben
falar, ca non á, tra-lo seu ben, al.

I would like, in the manner of Provençe...

I would like, in the manner of Provençe,
to make a song of love without delay,
and in it I shall praise my ladylove
who nothing lacks in merit or in beauty
or in goodness; and I shall tell you more:
God made her so complete in wondrous things
she's finer than all ladies in the world.

God chose to make my lady in such manner,
when he made her, that he made her most wise
in all goodness and of very great worth,
and nonetheless she is most sociable

when this is right, and he gave her good sense,
and furthermore he did her no small good,
deciding no other should be her equal.

For in my lady God never put wrong,
but put there merit and beauty and praise
and very fine speech, and far better smiles
than in any other; what's more, she's true,
and so I know today of no one who
can speak sufficiently of her distinction,
for there is nothing in her but distinction.

Proençaes soen mui ben trobar...

Proençaes soen mui ben trobar
e dizen eles que é con amor,
mais os que troban no tempo da flor
e non en outro sei eu ben que non
an tan gran coita no seu coraçón
qual m' eu por mía senhor vejo levar.

Pero que troban e saben loar
sas senhores o máis e o melhor
que eles poden, sõo sabedor
que os que troban quand' a frol sazón
á e non ante, se Deus mi perdón,
non an tal coita qual eu ei sen par.

Ca os que troban e que s' alegrar
van eno tempo que ten a color
a frol consigu' e, tanto que se fôr
aquel tempo, logu' en trobar razón
non an, non viven qual perdiçón
oj' eu vivo, que pois m' á de matar.

Provençals often make very fine songs...

Provençals often make very fine songs
and, so they say, they do all this with love,
but those who sing in the season of flowers
and in none other, I well know that they
do not feel in their hearts such intense grief
as I know that I feel for my love's sake.

However much they sing and may acclaim
their ladies to the very very best
of their ability, I know full well
that those who sing when flowers are in season,
and never sooner, and may God forgive me,
do not feel the great grief that I do feel.

For those who only sing and go rejoicing
during the season when the flowers are
full of their colour, and who, once that season
is over, have no further need for song,
don't live in the perdition in which I
today do live, and which will be my death.

Fernand' Esquío (13th–14th century)

Amor, a ti me venh' ora queixar...

Amor, a ti me venh' ora queixar
de mía senhor, que te faz enviar
cada u dormio, sempr', e m' espertar,
e faz-me de gran coita sofredor;
pois m' ela non quer veer nen falar,
    ¿que me queres, Amor?

Esta queixume te venh' or dizer,
que me non queiras meu sono tolher
pola fremosa do bon parecer
que de matar home sempre' á sabor;
pois m' ela nen un ben quiso fazer,
    ¿que me queres, Amor?

Amor, castiga-te desto, por én,
que me non tolhas meu sono por quen
me quis matar e me teve en desden
e de mia morte sera pecador.
Pois m' ela nunca quiso fazer ben,
    ¿que me queres, Amor?

Amor, castiga-te daquesto, por tal
que me non tolhas meu sono por qual
me non faz ben e sol me faz gran mal

e mi o fará, desto son julgador.
Poi-lo seu ben cedo coita mi val,
    ¿que me queres, Amor?

O Love, to you I come now to complain...

O Love, to you I come now to complain
about my lady, who keeps sending you,
whenever I fall asleep, to wake me up,
and forces me to undergo great grief.
Since she will neither see nor speak to me,
    what do you want of me, O Love?

So now I come to you with this complaint:
please do not be so keen to spoil my sleep
for the sake of that fine and lovely lady,
always so very eager to kill men.
Since she has never done me any good,
    what do you want of me, O Love?

O Love, please try to learn from this, and so
do not come spoiling my sleep for the one
who tried to kill me and held me in scorn
and will be the sinning cause of my death.
Since never any good has she done me,
    what do you want of me, O Love?

O Love, please try to learn from this, and thus
do not come spoiling my sleep for the person
who never does me good but only harm,
and will do so again, as I well know.
Since what is good for her soon brings me woe,
    what do you want of me, O Love?

Songs of Ridicule (Cantigas de escarnho e maldizer)

Johán García de Guilhade (13th century)

Ai, dona fea, fostes-vos queixar...

Ai, dona fea, fostes-vos queixar,
que vos nunca louv' en meu trobar;
mais ora quero fazer un cantar,
en que vos loarei toda vía;
e vedes como vos quero loar:
dona fea, velha e sandía!

Ai, dona fea, se Deus mi perdón,
e pois avedes tan gran coraçón
que vos eu lôe en esta razón,
vos quero já loar toda vía;
e vedes qual será a loaçón:
dona fea, velha e sandía!

Dona fea, nunca vos eu loei
en meu trobar, pero muito trobei;
mais ora já un bon cantar farei,
en que vos loarei toda vía;
e direi-vos como vos loarei:
dona fea, velha e sandía!

Oh, ugly lady, you went and complained...

Oh, ugly lady, you went and complained
that never do I praise you in my songs,
but now I'm going to make a song for you
with which I'll praise you over and again
so look and see what praise it's going to be:
you're ugly and you're old and you're insane.

My ugly lady, and may God forgive,
since you have such a heartfelt, fond desire
for me to praise you, in the following way
I now will praise you over and again

so look and see what form the praise will take:
you're ugly and you're old and you're insane.

My ugly lady, I have never praised you
in any of my songs, though I've sung much,
but now I'll make a splendid song for you
with which I'll praise you over and again
so look and see how I shall make that praise:
you're ugly and you're old and you're insane.

Martín Soárez (13th century)

Foi un día Lopo jograr...

Foi un día Lopo jograr
a cas dun infançón cantar
e mandoul-lh' ele por don dar
tres couces na garganta;
e fui-lh' escass', a meu cuidar,
segundo com' el canta.

Escasso foi o infançón
en seus couces partir en don
ca non deu a Lopo entón
máis de tres na garganta;
e máis merece o jograrón,
segundo com' el canta.

Jongleur Lopo went one day...

Jongleur Lopo went one day
to sing at the house of a noble,
who sent down as a gift for him
three kicks in the gullet:
a paltry gift, it seems to me,
considering his singing.

The nobleman was niggardly
when distributing kicks,
sending to that jongleur Lopo
just three of them in the gullet:

that joker merits many more,
considering his singing.

Afonso Méndez de Besteiros (13th–14th century)

Don Foão, que eu sei que á preço de livão...

Don Foão, que eu sei que á preço de livão,
vedes que fez ena guerra, daquesto soo certão:
sol que viu os genetes, come boi que fer tavão,
    sacudiu-s' e revolveu-se, al-
      çou rab' e foi sa vía a Portugal.

Don Foão, que eu sei que á preço de ligeiro,
vedes que fez na guerra, d' aquesto son verdadeiro:
sol que viu os genetes, come bezerro tenreiro,
    sacudiu-se' e revolveu-se, al-
      çou rab' e foi sa vía a Portugal.

Don Foão, que eu sei que á prez de liveldade,
vedes que fez na guerra, sabede-o per verdade:
sol que viu os genetes, come can que sal de grade,
    sacudiu-se' e revolveu-se, al-
      çou rab' e foi sa vía a Portugal.

Lord So-and-So, as I know, is famed as a fickle fellow...

Lord So-and So, as I know, is famed as a fickle fellow.
Look what he did in the war, about this I have no doubt:
on glimpsing the Arab horsemen, like an ox stung by a fly
    he shook, turned on his heel, raised tail up al-
      oft and trotted back home to Portugal.

Lord So-and So, as I know, is famed as a flighty fellow.
Look what he did in the war, about this I am convinced:
on glimpsing the Arab horsemen, like a little sucking calf
    he shook, turned on his heel, raised tail up al-
      oft and trotted back home to Portugal.

Lord So-and-So, as I know, is famed for fickleness.
Look what he did in the war, it is absolutely true:
on glimpsing the Arab horsemen, like a dog freed from a cage

he shook, turned on his heel, raised tail up aloft and trotted back home to Portugal.

Afonso Eanes do Cotón (12th–13th century)

Abadessa, oí dizer...

Abadessa, oí dizer
que érades mui sabedor
de todo ben; e, por amor
de Deus, querede-vos doer
de min, que ogano casei,
que ben vos juro que non sei
mais que un asno de foder.

Ca me fazen en sabedor
de vós que avedes bon sen
de foder e de todo ben;
ensinade-me máis, senhor,
como foda, ca o non sei,
nen padre nen madre non ei
que m' ensin', e fiqu' i pastor.

E se eu ensinado vou
de vós, senhor, deste mester
de foder e foder souber
per vós, que me Deus aparou,
cada que per foder, direi
Pater Noster e enmentarei
a alma de quen m' ensinou.

E per i poderedes gaar,
mia senhor, o reino de Deus:
per ensinar os pobres seus
máis ca por outro jajũar,
e per ensinar a molher
coitada, que a vós veer,
senhor, que non souber ambrar.

O Abbess, I have been informed...

O Abbess, I have been informed
that you have knowledge unsurpassed
of all that's good; and so, for love
of God, take pity, please, I beg,
on me, poor man: I'm newly wed,
and solemnly I swear I know
no more than an ass about fucking.

And this is why I have been told
that you possess a fine command
of fucking and of all that's good,
so teach me more, my lady, do,
on how to fuck, for I don't know;
no mother or father have I
to teach me. I'm so ignorant.

And if perchance I go well-taught
from you, my lady, in this art
of fucking, and know how to fuck
thanks just to you, whom God sent me,
each time I'm going to fuck I'll say
a paternoster, and commend
the soul of the lady who taught me.

And thus you will most surely gain,
my lady, the kingdom of God,
by educating his poor creatures,
more than by fasting and all that;
and by teaching any distressed
woman who could well come to you,
not knowing, m'lady, how to screw.

Pero Gómez Barroso (?–c.1273)

Moir' eu aquí de grand' afán...

Moir' eu aquí de grand' afán
e dizen ca moiro d' amor;
e avería gran sabor
de comer, se tevesse pan;

e, amigos, direi-vos al:
moir' eu do que en Portugal
morreu don Ponço de Baián.

E quantos m' est' a mi dit' an
que non posso comer d' amor,
dé-lhis Deus tan gran sabor
com' end' eu ei; e veerán
que á gran coita de comer
quen dinheiros non pod' aver
de que o compr', e non lho dan.

I'm dying here from greatest need...

I'm dying here from greatest need
and they say I'm dying of love;
I'd be very happy indeed
to eat, if I had any bread;
and, my friends, I'll tell you some more:
I die from what, in Portugal,
Don Ponço de Baián died from.

And as for all those who've told me
that it's for love that I can't eat:
may God send them all as much joy
as I feel from it; then they'll see
what a longing for food is felt
by he who can't get any cash
to buy food, and is given none.

Airas Núnez (13th century)

Porque no mundo mengou a verdade...

Porque no mundo mengou a verdade
puñei un día de a ir buscar,
e u por ela fui a preguntar
disseron todos: "Allur la buscade,
ca de tal guisa se foi a perder
que non podemos én novas aver,
nen ja non anda na irmaidade."

Nos moesteiros dos frades regrados
a demandei, e disseron-m' assí:
"Non busquedes vós a verdad' aquí
ca muitos anos avemos passados
que non morou nosco, per bõa fe,
[nen sabemos ond' ela agora esté]
e d' al avemos maiores coidados".

E en Cistel, u verdade soía
sempre morar, disseron-me que non
morava i avía gran sazón,
nen frade d' i ja a non coñocía;
nen o abade outrosí no estar
sol non quería que foss' i pousar
e anda ja fora desta badía.

En Santiago, seend' albergado
en mía pousada, chegaron romeus;
preguntei-os e disseron: "Par Deus,
muito levade-lo camiñ' errado,
ca se verdade quiserdes achar
outro camiño convén a buscar,
ca non saben aquí d' ela mandado."

Since in this world the truth's become so rare...

Since in this world the truth's become so rare
I went to try and search it out one day,
and wherever I asked they all would say,
'You'll have to go and seek the truth elsewhere
because from here it's vanished without trace
and we've no news about it in this place.
The truth is not in this house, anywhere.'

In houses ruled by Benedictine law
I sought the truth, and they responded thus:
'Don't you come seeking the truth among us!
Many long years has it been, to be sure,
since last it had a home with us in here.
Where it's residing now we've no idea,
and other matters concern us much more.'

With Cistercians the truth used to reside
always, but there they told me it had been
a long, long time since it had last been seen.
By no friar could it be identified,
nor would the Abbot, at any behest,
give it permission to lodge as a guest,
and now it has to live its life outside.

As, in Santiago, I began my stay
in my hostel, a group of pilgrims came;
I asked them, and 'By good God's holy name,'
they all declared, 'you've gone badly astray
if it's the truth you're after, for you'll hear
no news about it from anyone here.
You'd better go and seek some other way.'

Other Secular Poetry

Airas Núnez (13th century)

Oí og' eu úa pastor cantar...

Oí og' eu úa pastor cantar
d' u cavalgava per úa ribeira,
e a pastor estava senlheira
e ascondi-me pola ascuitar,
e dizia mui ben este cantar:
    "So lo ramo verd' e frolido
    vodas fazen a meu amigo;
    ¡choran olhos d' amor!"

E a pastor parecía mui ben
e chorava e estava cantando,
e eu, mui passo, fui-mi achegando
pola oir, e sol non falei ren;
e dizia este cantar mui ben:
    "¡Ai estorninho do avelanedo,
    cantades vós e moir' eu e peno,
    e d' amores ei mal!"

E eu oí-a sospirar entón,
e queixava-se estando con amores,
e fazía guirlanda de flores;
des i chorava mui de coraçón
e dizía este cantar entón:
    "¡Que coita ei tan grande de sofrer,
    amar amigu' e non' ousar veer!
    ¡E pousarei so lo avelanal!"

Pois que a guirlanda fez a pastor
Foi-se cantando, indo-s' én manselinho;
e tornei-m' eu logo a meu caminho,
ca de a nojar non ouve sabor;
e dizía este cantar ben a pastor:
    "Pela ribeira do río
    cantando ía la virgo

d' amor.
¿Quen amores á
como dormirá,
ai bela frol?"

Today I heard a shepherdess singing...

Today I heard a shepherdess singing
as I rode along a riverbank
and the shepherdess was all alone
and so I hid to listen to her;
and she was sweetly singing this song:
    'Under the green and flowering bough
    my darling is now being wed;
    my eyes weep with love.'

And that shepherdess did look most lovely
and she was weeping and she was singing,
and little by little I came closer
to listen to her, and I said nothing;
and sweetly she was singing this song:
    'Oh, starling in the hazel-bush,
    you sing and I die and grieve
    and I am lovesick.'

And after this I heard she was sighing,
she was lamenting being in love,
she was making a garland of flowers,
she was weeping from her very heart;
afterwards she was singing this song:
    'What grief so very great I shall suffer,
    loving my dear and not daring to see him!
    And I'll lie under the hazel-bush.'

Once the shepherdess had made her garland
she went away singing, placidly,
and I continued quickly on my way
for I did not want to trouble her;
the shepherdess sweetly sang this song:
    'Along the riverbank
    the maiden went singing
    of love.

She who is in love
how will she sleep,
oh, beauteous flower?'

Johán Airas de Santiago (13th–14th century)

Pelo souto de Crexente...

Pelo souto de Crexente
ũa pastor vi andar
muit' alongada da gente,
alçando voz a cantar,
apertando-se na saia,
quando saía la raia
do sol nas ribas do Sar.

E as aves que voavan,
quando saía l'alvor,
todas d' amores cantavan
pelos ramos d' arredor;
mais non sei tal qu' i 'stevesse
que en al cuidar podesse
senón todo en amor.

Alí 'stivi eu mui quedo,
quis falar e non ousei;
empero dix', a gran medo:
"Minha senhor, falar-vos-ei
um pouco, se mi-ascuitardes
e ir-m' ei, quando mandardes,
máis aquí non 'starei."

"Senhor, por Santa María,
non estedes mais aquí,
mais ide-vos vossa vía;
faredes mesura i,
ca os que aquí chegaren,
pois que vos aquí acharen,
ben dirán que máis ouv' i."

Up on Crescente Hill I saw...

Up on Crescente Hill I saw
a young shepherdess who was roaming
far away from all other people,
and lifting up her voice to sing,
pulling her dress tightly around her
when the beam of the sun came out
on the banks of the River Sar.

And the birds that were in the air
as light of day was dawning there
were all of them singing of love
among the branches all around,
and I don't know if anyone
could have thought about anything
other than about love alone.

And there I stayed quite motionless,
I tried to speak but did not dare;
I managed, full of fear, to say:
'My lady, I will speak to you
a little while, if you will hear,
but I shall not stay in this place
and I shall go when you command.'

'O Sir, for Holy Mary's sake
please don't remain here any more
but do continue on your way;
for that's the prudent thing to do:
anyone coming to this place,
will say, on finding you with me,
that something else has come to be.'

Pero Amigo de Sevilla (13th century)

Quand' eu um día fui em Compostela...

Quand' eu um día fui em Compostela
em romaría, vi ũa pastor
que, pois fui nado, nunca vi tam bela,
nem vi outra que falasse milhor

e demandei-lhi logo seu amor
e fiz por ela esta pastorela.

Dixi-lh' eu logo: "Fremosa doncela,
queredes vós mim por entendedor?
que vos darei boas toucas d' Estela
e boas cintas de Rocamador
e d' outras dõas, a vosso sabor
e fremoso pano pera gonela"

E ela disse: "Eu nom vos quería
por entendedor, ca nunca vos vi
se nom agora, nem vos filharía
dõas, que sei que nom som pera mi,
pero cuid' eu, se as filhass' assí,
que tal á no mundo a que pesaría.

E, se veess' outra, que lh diría,
se me dissesse 'ca per vós perdí
meu amigu' e dõas que me tragía'?
Eu nom sei rem que lhi dissess' alí;
se non foss' esto de que me temí,
nom vos dig' ora que o nom faría."

Dix' eu: "Pastor, sodes bem razõada,
e pero creede, se vos nom pesar,
que nom est oj' outra no mundo nada,
se vós nom sodes, que eu sabia amar,
e por aquesto vos venho rogar
que eu seja voss' ome esta vegada."

E diss' ela, come bem ensinada:
"Por entendedor vos quero filhar
e pois for a romaría acabada,
aquí, d' u sõo natural, do Sar,
cuido-m' eu, se me queredes levar,
ir-m' ei vosqu' e fico vossa pagada."

One day I went to Compostela...

One day I went to Compostela
on pilgrimage, and there I saw
a shepherdess; I've never seen

one as lovely or as well spoken,
and soon I asked her for her love
and wrote this pastoral for her.

I said to her: 'Most beauteous maiden,
will you accept me as your lover?
I'll give you fine hats from Estela,
fine ribbons from Rocamadour
and other gifts, just as you please,
and beautiful cloth for a gown.'

She said to me: 'I do not want you
for my lover: I've never seen you
until today, nor can I take
gifts that I know aren't right for me;
I think that, if I did accept,
there's someone else who'd be displeased.

If a girl came, what would I say
if she declared, "Through you I've lost
my lover and the gifts he brought"?
I know nothing that I could say,
and if it weren't for this I fear,
I wouldn't now be saying no.'

And I said: 'Shepherdess, you're wise,
but trust me, and may this not vex you:
there is no woman in the world
whom I love, except you alone,
and this is why I come to beg you
to have me as your man right now.'

And then she says, shrewd as she is:
'Yes, I will take you as my lover
and, once you've done your pilgrimage,
I think that if you want to take me
from this place, Sar, my native village,
I'll go and be your happy mistress.'

Afonso X, The Wise (1221–1284)

Non me posso pagar tanto...

Non me posso pagar tanto
do canto
das aves, nen de seu son,
nen d' amor, nen de mixón,
nen d' armas – ca ei espanto,
por quanto
mui perigoosas son –,
come dun bon galeón
que mi alongue muit' aginha
deste demo da campinha,
u os alacrães son;
ca dentro no coraçón
sentí deles a espinha.

E juro par Deus lo santo
que manto
non tragerei, nen granhón,
nen terrei d' amor razón,
nen d' armas – porque quebranto
e chanto
ven delas toda sazón –;
mais tragerei ũu dornón,
e irei pela marinha
vendend' azeit' e farinha;
e fugirei do poçón
do alacrán, ca eu non
lhi sei outra meezinha.

Nen de lançar a tavolado
pagado
non sõo, se Deus m' ampar,
aquí, nen de bafordar;
e andar de noute armado
sen grado
o faço, e a roldar;
ca máis me pago do mar
que de seer cavaleiro;
ca eu foi ja marinheiro

e quero-m' oimais guardar
do alacrán, e tornar
ao que me foi primeiro.

E direi-vos ũu recado:
pecado
nunca me pod' enganar
que me faça ja falar
en armas, ca non m' é dado
(doado
m' é de as eu razõar,
pois las non ei a provar);
ante quer' andar sinlheiro
e ir come mercadeiro
algũa terra buscar,
u me non possan colpar
alacrán negro nen veiro.

I cannot be as gratified...

I cannot be as gratified
by songs
of birds or by their melody
or by amours or by ambition,
still less by arms (for these I fear
because
they're dangerous in the extreme)
as by a splendid galleon
to bear me under press of sail
from this devilish La Campiña,
a place all infested with scorpions,
for deep down in my very heart
I have felt their venomous sting.

And by the Holy God I swear
I'll wear
neither cloak nor moustache nor beard
or be involved in any love
or armed conflict (because disaster
and tears
will never fail to come from that),
but instead I will sail a boat
and travel all along the coast,

a seller of oil and of flour;
and I will flee far from the poison
of the scorpion, because I know
no other remedy against it.

Nor does breaking lances in tourneys
here give me
any pleasure, so help me God,
nor does tilting or jousting either;
and venturing out armed at night
is something
I do without joy, like patrolling;
I take more pleasure from the sea
than I do from being a knight,
because I've been a mariner
and from now on I want to stay
away from scorpions, and return
to that earlier career of mine.

I'll make another declaration:
the devil
will never be able to trick me
and make me converse on the subject
of arms, for they are not for me
(it's useless
for me to argue about these,
since I will not be bearing them);
I much prefer to be alone
and take myself off as a merchant
and go in search of any land
where I'm not subject to attack
by scorpions, whether blotched or black.

Religious Poetry

Afonso X, The Wise (1221–1284)

Selection from Cantigas de Santa María (Songs of St Mary)

Cantiga X

Esta é de loor de Santa María, como é fremosa e bõa e ha gran poder.

Rosa das rosas e Fror das frores
Dona das donas, Señor das señores.

Rosa de beldade e de parecer
e Fror de alegría e de prazer,
Dona en mui piadosa seer,
Señor en toller coitas e doores.
Rosa das rosas e Fror das frores
Dona das donas, Señor das señores.

Atal Señor deve home muito amar,
que de todo mal o pode guardar,
e pódelle os pecados perdõar,
que faz no mundo per maos sabores.
Rosa das rosas e Fror das frores
Dona das donas, Señor das señores.

Devémola muito amar e servir,
ca puña de nos guardar de falir
des i dos erros nos faz repentir,
que nós fazemos come pecadores.
Rosa das rosas e Fror das frores
Dona das donas, Señor das señores.

Esta dona que teño por Señor
e de que quero seer trobador,
se eu per ren posso haver seu amor,
dou ao demo os outros amores.
Rosa das rosas e Fror das frores
Dona das donas, Señor das señores.

Song X

This is in praise of Holy Mary, telling how beautiful and good she is and what great power she has.

Rose of roses and Flower of flowers,
Noble of nobles, Lady of ladies.

Rose of beauty and of loveliness,
and Flower of gladness and of joy,
so Noble in her mercifulness,
Lady curing every grief and pain.
Rose of roses and Flower of flowers,
Noble of nobles, Lady of ladies.

All men should dearly love such a Lady,
who can protect them against all evil,
and forgive them the sins they commit
in this world through their evil desires.
Rose of roses and Flower of flowers,
Noble of nobles, Lady of ladies.

All of us should greatly love and serve her:
she strives to stop us from doing wrong,
then makes us repent of evil deeds
that we commit, being sinners all.
Rose of roses and Flower of flowers,
Noble of nobles, Lady of ladies.

This gentlewoman who is my Lady
and whose troubador I wish to be
– if only I can secure her love,
I'll send all other loves to the devil.
Rose of roses and Flower of flowers,
Noble of nobles, Lady of ladies.

Cantiga CIV

Como Santa María fez á moller que quería fazer amadoiras a seu amigo con el Corpo de Jhesu-Cristo e que o tragía na touca, que lle corresse sangue da cabeça ata que o tirou ende.

Nunca ja pode á Virgen home tal pesar fazer,
como quen ao seu Fillo, Deus, coida escarnecer.

E o que o fazer coida, creede aquesto por mi,
que aquel escarno todo ha de tornar sobre si.
E daquesto un gran miragre vos direi, que eu oí
que fezo Santa María; oídemo a lezer:
Nunca ja pode á Virgen home tal pesar fazer,
como quen ao seu Fillo, Deus, coida escarnecer.

Aquesto foi en Galiza, non ha i mui gran sazón,
que ũa ssa barragãa houve un escudeirón
e por quanto se el casara, tan gran pesar houvo entón,
que con gran coita houvera o siso ende a perder.
Nunca ja pode á Virgen home tal pesar fazer,
como quen ao seu Fillo, Deus, coida escarnecer.

E con gran pesar que houve foi seu consello buscar
enas outras sas veziñas, e atal llo foron dar:
que sol que ela podesse ũa ostia furtar
das da eigreja, que logo o podería haver,
Nunca ja pode á Virgen home tal pesar fazer,
como quen ao seu Fillo, Deus, coida escarnecer.

Pois que lle tal ben quería. E ela toste, sen al,
foise a ũa eigreja da Virgen espirital,
que nas nossas grandes coitas nos guarda senpre de mal,
e disso entón que quería logo comoñón prender.
Nunca ja pode á Virgen home tal pesar fazer,
como quen ao seu Fillo, Deus, coida escarnecer.

E o crérigo sen arte de a comungar coidou;
maila ostia na boca aquesta moller guardou,
que per neũa maneira non a trociu nen passou,
e puñou quanto máis pode de se de alí logo erguer.
Nunca ja pode á Virgen home tal pesar fazer,
como quen ao seu Fillo, Deus, coida escarnecer.

Pois que saíu da eigreja, os dedos entón meteu
ena boca e tan toste tiroua ende e escondeu
a ostia ena touca e nada non atendeu,
ante se foi muito agiña por provar esto e veer
Nunca ja pode á Virgen home tal pesar fazer,
como quen ao seu Fillo, Deus, coida escarnecer.

Se lle disseran verdade ou se lle foran mentir
aquelas que lle disseran que lle farían viir
logo a ela seu amigo e ja máis nunca partir
dela se ja podería, e de con ela viver.
Nunca ja pode á Virgen home tal pesar fazer,
como quen ao seu Fillo, Deus, coida escarnecer.

E entrando a ũa vila que dizen Caldas de Rei,
onde aquesta moller era, per como ende eu apresei
aveu én mui gran cousa que vos ora contarei
ca lle viron pelas toucas sangue vermello correr.
Nunca ja pode á Virgen home tal pesar fazer,
como quen ao seu Fillo, Deus, coida escarnecer.

E a gente entón dizía, quando aquel sangue viu:
"Di, moller, ¿que foi aquesto, ou quen te tan mal feriu?"
E ela maravillada foi tanto que esto oíu
assí que nunca lles soube niũa ren responder.
Nunca ja pode á Virgen home tal pesar fazer,
como quen ao seu Fillo, Deus, coida escarnecer.

E pos a mão nas toucas e sentiu e viu mui ben
que era sangue caente, e disso assí porén:
"A mi non me feriu outre senón quen o mundo ten
en seu poder, por grande erro que me lle eu fui merecer."
Nunca ja pode á Virgen home tal pesar fazer,
como quen ao seu Fillo, Deus, coida escarnecer.

Entón contoulles o feito, tremendo con gran pavor,
todo como lle aveera e deron porén loor
todos a Santa María, Madre de Nostro Señor,
e a seu Fillo beeito, chorando con gran prazer.
Nunca ja pode á Virgen home tal pesar fazer,
como quen ao seu Fillo, Deus, coida escarnecer.

A moller se tornou logo á eigreja outra vez,
e deitouse ante a omagen e disse: "Señor de prez
non cates a meu pecado que me o demo fazer fez."
E logo a un mõesteiro se tornou monja meter.
Nunca ja pode á Virgen home tal pesar fazer,
como quen ao seu Fillo, Deus, coida escarnecer.

Song CIV

How, when a woman intended to make love-philtres for her
paramour from the body of Jesus Christ and who had it in her
headdress, Holy Mary made blood flow from her head until she
removed the host.

Nobody can ever cause the Virgin Mary such grief
as anyone who believes he can scoff at God, her Son.

Anyone who thinks he can, you must all believe me now,
will find that the mockery will be turned back in his face...
And concerning this I'll tell you a great miracle I've heard,
performed by Holy Saint Mary: pray hear it now at your leisure.
Nobody can ever cause the Virgin Mary such grief
as anyone who believes he can scoff at God, her Son.

It so happened in Galicia, not so very long ago,
that there was a lusty squire who had his own concubine
and because he had got married, such was her profound distress
that her great worries had caused her to take leave of all her senses.
Nobody can ever cause the Virgin Mary such grief
as anyone who believes he can scoff at God, her Son.

In the deep sorrow she felt, she went to seek the advice
of some others, of her neighbours, and these women gave it her:
if she could but go and steal just one of those holy wafers
that are kept safe in the church, she could hold on to her man,
Nobody can ever cause the Virgin Mary such grief
as anyone who believes he can scoff at God, her Son.

Since he was so dear to her. So, without any delay,
she hurried off to a church of the Blessed Virgin Mary,
who in our great tribulations will always keep us from evil,
and then she said that she wished to take communion forthwith.
Nobody can ever cause the Virgin Mary such grief
as anyone who believes he can scoff at God, her Son.

The priest in all innocence gave her the holy communion;
but that woman then retained the host right inside her mouth,
and she took the utmost care not to swallow or ingest it,
and then rose from where she knelt as speedily as she could.
Nobody can ever cause the Virgin Mary such grief
as anyone who believes he can scoff at God, her Son.

As soon as she left the church, she straightaway put her fingers
into her mouth and removed the wafer from out of it
and hid it inside her headdress and did not tarry one moment
but hurried off at top speed to try the charm out and see
Nobody can ever cause the Virgin Mary such grief
as anyone who believes he can scoff at God, her Son.

If she had been told the truth or if it was lies she'd been told
by those women who had said they would be able to make
her lover come back to her soon and never again leave,
if this was now possible, and for ever live with her.
Nobody can ever cause the Virgin Mary such grief
as anyone who believes he can scoff at God, her Son.

As she walked into a town that they call Caldas de Rei,
which was this woman's home town, as I later was to learn,
something amazing occurred, which I shall now tell you all,
for people saw crimson blood running all over her headdress.
Nobody can ever cause the Virgin Mary such grief
as anyone who believes he can scoff at God, her Son.

And then all the people said, as soon as they saw that blood,
'Tell us, good woman, what's up, who has wounded you so badly?'
She was so very astonished when she heard them say these words
that it was beyond her power to make a reply to them.
Nobody can ever cause the Virgin Mary such grief
as anyone who believes he can scoff at God, her Son.

She put her hand in her headdress and then she felt and she saw
that what was there was warm blood, and so she went on to say,
'Nobody has injured me except one who has the world
in her power, for the sin that makes me deserve this wound.'
Nobody can ever cause the Virgin Mary such grief
as anyone who believes he can scoff at God, her Son.

She told them what had occurred, as she trembled in her fright,
exactly as it had happened, and then they all gave great praise
to the Blessed Virgin Mary, the dear Mother of Our Lord,
and to her most blessed Son, and they wept with immense joy.
Nobody can ever cause the Virgin Mary such grief
as anyone who believes he can scoff at God, her Son.

And the woman now returned immediately to the church,
and then she threw herself down before the image and said,
'Dear Lady, don't heed that sin the devil made me commit.'
And she went off to a convent in order to be a nun.
Nobody can ever cause the Virgin Mary such grief
as anyone who believes he can scoff at God, her Son.

Narrative Prose

From Crónica Troiana, 1373

Agora leixa o conto a falar de Pares et de Elena et del rrey Príamos et de Casandra, et torna a contar cõmo Agamenõ chegou a Parta, et cõmo cõfortou a seu yrmão Menelao et do conssello que lle deu.

Agora diz o conto que, mẽtre este feyto assý passaua, cõmo uos hey cõtado, Agamenõ chegou a Parta, a sseu yrmão Menelao. Et achoo y moy coytado por sua moller, que perdera, et da grã desonrra et do grã mal que auja rreçebudo en sua terra. Et Agamenõ, poyslo veu tã triste, cõfortoo moy ben. Et dýssolle assý:

– Yrmão, seede apreçebudo que nehũ nõ entẽda que uós auedes tã grã coyta, nẽ tã grã maauentura, porla desonrra que rreçebestes, ca os homes que moyto onrrados forõ et gãañaron grã prez, nõ cõquererõ suas onrras cõ lágrimas, nẽ fazẽdo doo. Mays, quando rreçebía desonrra de algũ, logo catauã engẽno et arte cõmo ende fossen vengados. Et assý fazẽ caualleyros que han entẽdemento et que queren gãañar prez en este mũdo. Et esto lles he bõaestança, que cõ a grã coyta que ven ao home, ou cõ gerra, ou cõ proueza, ou desonrramento, lle poden coñosçer pera quanto he, ou quanto ual, ou se he bõo, ou se he mao. Et tódoslos bõos se ensaiarõ ẽnas coytas que sofrerõ, ca todo aquel a que tollẽ sua terra, et rreçebe os grãdes colpes, et sofre as grãdes coytas, et ha de mantẽer as grãdes masnadas, seẽdo proue et mijado, aqueste atal, se o ben passa ou o ben sofre, poja en grã prez et en grã ualor. Et por ende uossa onrra et uosso prez pode poiar en catar maneyra per u haiades vengãça do mal et da desonrra que tẽedes rreçebuda. Et os bõos que ante de nós forõ, assý trouueron sua fazẽda. Poys des oymays nõ soframos a desonrra et o mal que auemos rreçebuda del rrey Príamos et de sua cõpaña, ante façamos juntamento que tomemos ende tal vengãça que seia sabuda per todo o mũdo, et que nossa onrra seia per y arrequẽtada, et que os que agora son et an de vĩjr possan dizer, sen mẽtira, que nũca foy en nehũ tenpo home que tal vengança ouuesse de seu despeyto cõmo nós tomamos do que Pares fezo. Et nõ falemos en esto mays, ante penssemos de enviar nossos mãdadeyros per toda Greçia a tódoslos rreys et condes et duques et prínçepes que y ouuer, que venã todos aparellados de yr sobre Troya a uẽgar nosso despeyto. Et sabede que nõ ha y tal que y moy ledo nõ veña et que nõ seia y cõ quantos mays poder auer. Et depoys que nós todos formos ajuntados et ben gisados de batalla, ben sey que so o çeo nõ ha forteleza nẽ torre nẽ vila nẽ çidade nẽ castelo que sse defender possa a nosso poder. Et quen Pares podesse tomar viuo et o enforquasse cõmo ladrõ. Agora, sen mays tardar, catemos engeño et maneyra per u Troya seia destroýda et cofondida.

From The Chronicle of Troy, *1373*

Now the story stops speaking of Paris and Helen and of King Priam and of Cassandra, and it turns to the subject of how Agamemnon reached Sparta, and how he comforted his brother Menelaus and gave him some advice.

Now the story says that, while this was happening, as I have told you, Agamemnon reached Sparta and his brother Menelaus. And he found him there grief-stricken because of his wife, whom he had lost, and because of the great dishonour and harm inflicted upon him in his own land. And Agamemnon, seeing him so sad, comforted him very warmly. And he said this to him:

Brother, take good care that nobody realizes you are afflicted by such great grief or such great misfortune because of the dishonour inflicted upon you; for the men who have in the past been greatly honoured and have gained great renown did not win their honours with tears or by moaning. Rather, when anyone dishonoured them, they immediately looked for ways and means to be avenged. And this is what is done by knights who have good sense and who wish to gain renown in this world. And this is proper behaviour on their part, for it is in the cares that can come a man's way, with war, poverty or dishonour, that people can know him for what he is, and for what he is worth, and whether he is good or evil. And all good men have shown their mettle in the griefs they have suffered, for anyone whose land is stolen, and takes great blows, and suffers great griefs, and must maintain a great household when he is poor and lacks resources – that man, if he withstands and resists it all well, grows in renown and worth. And therefore your own honour and renown can grow if you seek a way in which to avenge the harm and the dishonour inflicted upon you. And the good men who went before us managed their affairs in this way. So from now on let us not endure the dishonour and harm inflicted on us by King Priam and his company, rather let us gather men together to take such vengeance as will be known throughout the world, so that our honour is restored and those living now and those who will live in the future can truthfully say that never was there any man who wreaked such vengeance for a slight as we wreaked for what Paris did. And let us not discuss this matter any further, rather let us send our messengers throughout Greece to all the kings and counts and dukes and princes there, asking them all to come equipped to attack Troy and avenge the slight we have suffered. And know that there is not one of them who will not be happy to come and join us with all the men he can muster. And once we have gathered and made ourselves ready for battle, I know that there is no fortress or tower or town or city or castle that can be defended against our power. And let us see who can capture Paris alive and hang him as a thief. Now, without delay, we must look for ways and means of defeating and destroying Troy.

Mjragre de Santiago scripto por Papa Calisto, *15th century*

Avẽo así hũu día que, seendo as gardas do altar enno lugar onde he acustumado, trres caualeyros do condado de Peirigol veeron a Santiago en rromaría. Et jazendo ante o altar, poys que fezeron súa oraçón, tornaron contra as gardas, e diséronlle así:

– Este home que aquí ven conosco, ergédeuos a el et rreçebédeo moy ben, ca o apóstolo mostrou el mjragre moi maraujlloso, ca o tirou da forqua onde sía enforquado.

Aquel ome por que eles dizían vẽo alj́ con eles et era moy mançebo. Et andaua vestido de moy nobres panos e paresçía home de gran paragen. Et tragía enno pescoço hũa pértega de caruallo entorta, et chegando ante o altar começou a chamar e dizer así:

– Señor Santiago, aque aquí o teu seruo que tu liuraste do laço da morte.

Entón os que alý estauan preguntáronlle por que rrazón tragía aquela pértega enno pescoço et como lle aviera, et contoulle en esta gisa:

– O señor de hun castelo que eu ora teno ouue dous fillos, et hũu era varón et o outro era fémea. Et esta que era fémea casou con hũu caualeiro, et era moy poderoso et moy mao home. Et despois da morte do sogro demandoume o castelo, que dezía que era seu por parte da moller, a medade del, et quisera enxerdar o outro yrmãao. Eu tina o castelo de mão de seu sogro, et porque entendía que era mayor dereito do fillo varón erdar o castelo, et aquel outro que o quería enxerdar, defendí o castelo o máis que eu pude. O marido daquela dona vío que eu me lle enfestaua con o castelo et quería manteer a fieldade que prometera a seu sogro, queríame por ende mal et nunca em al pensaua senón en como me podería matar, ca coydaua se me matase, que logo coydaría a tomar o castelo. Et andando en esto pensando, vẽo hũu dia a mjn ao castelo et prendeume et, seendo eu en seu poder dáuame moy grandes tormentos. Et sentyme hũa ora del moyto aficado e díxelle: "Tormento que me faças non me pode enpeeçer, ca o señor Santiago me garda de ty et agora che aparesçerá aquí". O caualeyro diso: "Se o teu Santiago te pode liurar de mjñas mãos, esto me veerey eu". Tomou logo hũa pértega de caruallo, esta que me veedes trager, et deytouma enna garganta et enforcoume. Et eu seendo enforcado, enpuxáuame con hũa lança que tiña enna mão, hora a hũu cabo, ora a outro, para morrer máis agína. Et eu seendo asi, vin visiuelemente Santiago, que me desasuxou o laço da garganta et fezme o corpo estar como se estouese sobre hũa escaada. Et pois que se partiron d'alj́ todos os que y foron achegados, mja moller chegou a mjn alj́ hu sía, et vjna deitando as mãaos ennos cabelos e carpyndo moyto et chamándome por nome. Et eu onde sija rrespondylle et díxelle: "Non chores, mais pensa de me tirar d'aquí agina, ca viuo soo et Santiago me ten aquí". Et a moller tornou moyto agina et buscou hũa escaada e despósome da forqua.

Et así contou alý o rromeu que fora liure do laço da morte perlo apóstolo Santiago, et en sinal daquel mjragre leixou alí sóbrelo altar a pértega, que tragia de que fora enforcado. Et con gran alegría tornouse para súa terra.

A Miracle of St James, written by Pope Calixtus, *15th century*

And it happened one day that, when the altar-guards were sitting in their usual place, three knights from the county of Périgord came to St James on a pilgrimage. And as they lay before the altar, after saying their prayers, they turned to the guards and said:

'This man who comes here with us – rise to your feet and greet him warmly, for the Apostle has performed a most marvellous miracle for him, saving him from the gibbet where he had been hanged.'

That man of whom they were speaking came up to them; he was very young, he was dressed in very fine cloth and he seemed like a man of high rank; from his neck there hung a bent oak bar, and approaching the altar he began to cry out and say:

'My Lord St James, here is your servant, whom you saved from the noose of death!'

And then those present asked him why he had that bar hanging from his neck and how it had come to be there, and he told his story thus:

'The lord of a castle of which I am now in charge had two children; one was a boy and the other was a girl. The girl married a knight, and he was very powerful and a very wicked man; after his father-in-law's death he claimed the castle saying that half of it was his, through his wife, and he wanted to deprive his wife's brother of his inheritance. His father-in-law had entrusted the castle to me and, since it was my understanding that the son had the greater right to inherit it, and that the other man wanted to disinherit him, I protected the castle as best I could. That lady's husband saw that I was opposing him in the matter of the castle and that I was determined to keep faith with his father-in-law as I had promised; so he hated me and had thoughts only of killing me, because he believed that if he killed me he would be able to acquire the castle. With ideas such as these he came to me one day in the castle and took me prisoner; and once I was in his power he tortured me terribly, and on one occasion I felt very great duress and I said to him:

"Whatever torture you apply to me will not hurt me, for my lord St James is protecting me against you and will now appear here before you."

The knight said:

"Whether St James can save you from my hands is something we'll soon see."

And then he took an oak bar, this one you see hanging from my neck, and he threw it over my throat and then gibbeted me. And once I was hanging there, he pushed me from side to side with a lance he held in his hands, to make me die all the sooner.

And now I clearly saw St James, who loosened the noose round my throat and positioned my body as if it were propped up on a ladder. Once all those who had come there had gone away, my wife came up to me where I was slumped; she was clutching at her hair and wailing and calling me by my name. From where I was slumped I replied to her and said:

"Do not weep, but take me from here quickly, for I am alive and St James has placed me like this."

And my wife hurried away and found a ladder and took me down from the gibbet.'

And this was how the pilgrim told the story of how he had been freed from the noose of death by the apostle St James, and as a sign of this miracle he left upon the altar the bar he had brought with him, from which he had been hanged. And with great joy he returned to his land.

The Dark Centuries

Anónimo

Cancioneiro de Upsala, *1556*

Mal se cura muito mal,
mais o pouco cando tura
muito máis peor se cura.

O muito mal cando vén
non pode muito turar,
porque teñen de acabar
muito presto a quen lo ten.

Acabar é grande ben
pois o pouco cando tura
muito máis peor se cura.

Songbook of Upsala, *1556*

It is hard to cure a great ill
but a small one, if it lasts,
is much harder to cure.

A great ill, when it comes,
cannot last for long,
because it must soon kill
whoever suffers from it.

Being killed is a great good
because the small ill, if it lasts,
is much harder to cure.

Pedro Vázquez de Neira (16th–17th century)

From Exequias da Raíña Margarida (Exequies for Queen Margaret), *1612*

Respice finem

Morte cruel, esa treidora maña
de roubar de socato a humana vida
¿con qué ollos a puideche ver cumprida
na santa Reina que hoxe perde España?

Se aquel rancor que te carcome e laña
che tiña a mao, para matar, erguida,
¿non deras noutra parte esa ferida
onde non fora a lástima tamaña?

¿Non se torcera aquel fatal costume
e a lei que iguala do morrer na sorte
os altos Reis cos baixos labradores?

Terrible, en fin, é teu poder, oh, Morte,
pois diante de ti, Reis e señores
son néboa, sombra, po, son vento e fume.

Respice finem

Cruel Death: that treacherous trick
of suddenly stealing human life
– how could you have allowed it to be played
on the saintly queen that Spain loses today?

If that hatred that gnaws and rends you
had raised your hand to kill,
could you not have made that wound elsewhere,
where the harm would not have been so great?

Could not that fatal habit have been resisted,
that law that equates in the fortunes of death
lofty kings and lowly peasants?

Terrible, then, is your power, O Death:
before you, kings and lords
are mist, shadow and dust, are wind and smoke.

Xoán Gómez Tonel (17th century)

From Exequias da Raíña Margarida (Exequies for Queen Margaret), *1612*

Turbas corran as Agoas, poña luto...

Turbas corran as Agoas, poña luto
o Aire denso, en melancolía tanta
queime o Fogo a Terra, que sen planta
negue ao fortuno ano seu trebuto

mentras a Porcia do Philippo Bruto
en os ombros da fama sacrosanta
se ergue ao ceo, que súa gloria canta
collendo en flor o xa maduro fruto.

Perdeu, marrando tan ditosa vida,
a Humildá prezo; a Piedade templo
(que derrubou, oh Morte, túa Gadaña);

o Mundo, Reina; o Rei, súa Margarida;
a Fe, columna; a Virtude, exemplo;
a pedra (cuxo engaste foi), España.

Chore nosa montaña,
do gando, leite e novidade espida,
semellando as Abellas no exemplo:

que se súa Margarida,
Reina, Prezo, Columna, Pedra, Templo,
perden Rei, Mundo, Fe, Virtude, España...
tu, que tal perda viche,
¡oh, magoada Galicia!, ¿que perdiche?

Let the Waters run thick, let the dense Air...

Let the Waters run thick, let the dense Air
don mourning, let Fire burn the Earth
into such melancholy that, barren,
it denies its tribute to the turbulent year,

while Brutus of Philippi's Portia,
on the shoulders of sacrosanct fame
rises to heaven, which sings her glory,
plucking that ripe fruit in its prime.

With the passing of such a fortunate life,
Humility has lost esteem; Piety its temple
(which your scythe, O Death, demolished);

the World, a Queen; the King, his Margaret;
Faith, a pillar; Virtue, an example;
Spain (whose setting she was), a precious stone.

Let our mountain weep,
stripped of its sheep, its milk and its crops,
following the example of the Bees:

for if his Margaret, a Queen, Esteem, a Pillar, a Stone, a Temple
have been lost by King, World, Faith, Virtue, Spain...,
you, who witnessed this loss,
O wounded Galicia, what have you lost?

Diego Antonio Cernadas, The Priest of Fruíme (1698–1777)

Berdusido, Berdusido...

En loor do Ilustrísimo Sr. Garrido, bispo de Córdoba, natural do
lugar de Berdusido, no reino de Galicia.

Berdusido, Berdusido,
con todos teus arredores,
non te chames Berdusido,
chámate xardín de flores.

Berdusido, anque un lugar
fuche sempre de proveito,

hoxe con mellor dereito
te podes deso alabar.
Moito che ten que envexar
as terras deste partido,
pois un fillo tan querido
un ser tan novo che dá
que non parece que é xa
Berdusido, Berdusido.

¿Canto outras terras que ves,
que dan bo trigo e bo millo,
darían por ter un fillo
Garrido como ti tes?
Escusas máis corrachés
e xoeles, para pores
raia entre as terras mellores,
porque ningunha acharás
tan guapa como hoxe estás
con todos teus arredores.

Tendo, pois, por fillo un home
de tan gran merecemento
o seu nobre nacemento
basta para darche nome.
Xa ninguén na boca tome
que non es moi coñecido
lugar, pois se o teu Garrido
fruxe do teu terrón é,
non hai razón para que
non te chames Berdusido.

Eu vexo que ese señor é
das vertús un tesouro,
é Garrido como un ouro,
é de Galicia unha flor;
tenlle ós pobres moito amor
é moi sabio antre os doutores,
é un Bispo dos mellores;
e, pois no terruño teu
tal ramallete naceu,
chámate xardín de flores.

Berducido, Berducido...

In praise of the Most Illustrious Señor Garrido, the Bishop of
Córdoba, a native of the village of Berducido, in the Kingdom of
Galicia.

Berducido, Berducido,
with all your surroundings,
you should not be called Berducido:
you should be called a garden of flowers.

Berducido, even though only a village,
you have always been fruitful;
now you have even more right
to boast of this fecundity.
The lands of this district
have much to envy you,
because such a beloved son
gives you such a new self
that it no longer resembles
Berducido, Berducido.

How much would other lands you can see,
growing good wheat and maize,
give to have a son
as splendid as the one you have?
You have no need of any other
jewels or mother-of-pearl
to distinguish you from even the best lands,
for you will find none
as pretty as you are today
with all your surroudings.

Since you have, then, as a son a man
of such great merits,
his noble birth
is enough to give you renown.
Let nobody dare affirm
that you are not a very famous
village, for if your splendid Garrido
is a fruit of your clods,
there is no reason why
you should not be called Berducido.

I can see that this gentleman
is a treasure-house of virtues,
he is as splendid as gold,
he is a flower of Galicia;
he has great love for the poor,
he is very wise among the learned,
he is one of the best bishops;
and, since in your lands
such a fine bouquet was born,
you should be called a garden of flowers

Xosé Cornide Saavedra (1734–1803)

A Filida, *1761*

¿Viche, Filida amada, o paxariño
que arando deses aires nas campiñas
descoidado se achanta polas liñas
que cauto cazador pos no camiño?

¿Viche qué forza fai para soltarse
e levar a bicada ós seus paxaros,
(parte do corazón e fillos caros)
que deixara no niño ó remontarse?

Pois viche a quen che adora pola vida
que, chantado no ichó de un imposibre
cata aquí, cata aló se acha saída

para fuxir, podendo verse libre
e acurruxarse firme no teu seo
en que chocara atento o seu deseo.

To Filida, *1761*

Did you see, dear Filida, that little bird
which, ploughing the fields of those breezes,
carelessly became entangled in those threads
that the prudent huntsman put in its way?

Did you see what efforts it makes to free itself
and take its beakful of food to its young

(a piece of its heart, its dear children)
that it left in the nest when it flew away?

Well, then you have seen the one who adores you
and who, caught in the trap of an impossibility,
looks here, looks there to find a way

to escape, when he could be free
and could nestle down securely on your breast,
where his desire had courteously wept.

The Nineteenth Century

Early Writings

Marcos Parcero (18th–19th century)

Vilancico de Nadal, Catedral de Santiago, *finais do século XVIII*

Un fato de labradores,
que todos somos galegos,
a Belén viñemos xuntos
co noso amigo o gaiteiro,
para ó son dunha alborada
cantar esta mañá cedo,
con moito lecer, aquí
unha tonada a este Neno,
que che está de rechupete
e se non xa o veremos.
A nosa alborada na gaita toquemos,
pois que neste alpendre
Noso Señor vemos. Naceu
para abrirnos as portas do Ceo;
xa vén, endebén,
o noso remedio.
¡Vinde velo todos!
¡Rapaces, ergueivos!
Vinde, vinde axiña;
vinde, vinde ledos;

vinde, vinde axiña;
vinde a velo.

Christmas Carol, Santiago Cathedral, *end of the 18th century*

A bunch of farmers,
from Galicia, all of us,
have come to Bethlehem
with our friend the piper,
to sing here, early this morning,
to the tune of an albada,
and very happy to do so,
a song to this Child,
who's truly gorgeous
–and you'd better not disagree!
Our albada
let's play it on the pipes,
since in this shed
we see our Lord.
He was born to open to us
the gates of Heaven;
our remedy
is on its way, hurrah!
Come see him, all of you!
You youngsters, get up!
Come, come, now, now;
come, come, happily;
come, come, now, now;
come and see him.

Antonio María de Castro e Neira (1771–1826)

Vilancico de Nadal, Catedral de Mondoñedo, *1822*

¡Xesús, e sáltanlle as bágoas!...
Meu amor, ¿qué che faremos?
Toma, unha rosquiña de ovos;
toma, mel e queixo fresco,
manteiga ou leitiño... ¡Nada!
Non quer manxares o Neno;
quer corazós humillados,
quer un amor verdadeiro.

Christmas Carol, Mondoñedo Cathedral, *1822*

Jesus, how his tears do flow...!
My love, what shall we do for you?
Here you are, a clothful of eggs;
here you are, honey and cottage cheese,
butter and milk ... No, no!
The Child doesn't want food;
he wants humble hearts,
he wants true love.

Nicomedes Pastor Díaz (1811–1863)

Égloga de Belmiro e Benigno (fragmentos), *c. 1826–1828*

I

Xa por detrás dos montes se escondía
O rubo pai da luz en carro de ouro;
De nubarrós o ceo se cubría,
Tendía a noite ô lexos manto mouro,
Enterraba o Tesouro
O avaro gardador, medio as escuras,
E pol-as espesuras
Xa non cantaban ledos paxariños;
As ovellas, balando co os filliños,
Pra os curros dos lindeiros escapaban;
O traballo os paisanos xa deixaban
Pra volver xunto as mais dos seus neniños,
E os barcos preparando
Pr- o mar o mariñeiro iba cantando.

II

Cando sentado en unhas altas penas
Que o mar batía con feroz ruxido,
Ardendo en lume vivo as suas venas
Centellándolle os ollos encendidos,
Xamais adormecidos,
Belmiro, labrador, se lamentaba
E os seus gritos alzaba
Ôs ceos dos seus males causadores,
Contándolles ôs aires seus dolores.
Xa tamén revolcándose na area,

Das suas báguas empapada e chea,
Xa âs rocas lles contaba os seus amores,
Xa o triste deliraba
E en semexantes voces se expresaba:

★ ★ ★ ★

XVII

As brillantes estrellas xa se foran
Dos ceos que alborearse comenzaban,
E as flores que o Febeo carro doran
Do oriente as rubas portas franqueaban.
Alegres saludaban
O resplandor primeiro as aveciñas,
Brillaban as gotiñas
Que o rocío nos árboles fixera,
E o grande mar, con maxestad severa,
Bramando, a luz primeira reflectía.
A este augusto espectáculo se erguía
Unha alma boa hacia o Criador da terra.
Todo a Dios anunciaba,
Todo as suas grandezas predicaba.

XVIII

Cando dos seus braciños agarrados
Ás suas casas iban os amigos,
E diante o Ser eterno posternados,
Dos seus votos de paz foron testigos
Os árboles, os trigos,
O mar, as rocas e natura toda,
Xa da cúpula goda
Do templo patrio a punta divisaron.
A esta vista os seus ollos destilaron
Lágrimas de dolor e de ternura
E as ideas do ben e da amargura
No seu peito aún non sano se encontraron.
E, en fin, a aldea viron,
Entraron nela e sempre en paz viviron.

XIX

Don do bondoso ceo, amistá pura
Que endulzas os pesares de esta vida.
¡Case enches o meu seo de dozura!
¡Cánto nos meus dolores me és querida!
Por sempre bendecida
Seas dos corazós que padeceron,
E os que en tí paz tuveron
Ensálcente cen veces e outras cento:
Fuxa amor e o seu fogo violento
Que trai âs almas boas solo males,
E da amistad os goces celestiales
Deixe lugar tan fero sentimento.
¡HOMES DO MUNDO, UN BON AMIGO, UN CAMPO:
HE AQUI A FELICIDAD BUSCADA TANTO!

Eclogue of Belmiro and Benigno (extracts), *c. 1826–1828*

I

The ruddy father of light in his golden chariot
was hiding behind the hills;
great clouds were covering the sky,
far away, night was spreading its dark mantle,
and in the thickets
the miserly guardian, in the half-light,
was burying his Treasure
happy little birds were no longer singing;
sheep, baaing to their offspring,
were making off to the pens in the pastures;
peasants were leaving their work
to return to the mothers of their children,
and the fisherman, making his boats
ready for the sea, was singing.

II

When, sitting on tall rocks
that the sea was battering with a fierce roar,
his veins burning with intense fire
and his eyes ablaze and flashing,
never drowsy,
Belmiro, a farmer, was lamenting
and raising his cries
to the heavens, the cause of all his ills,

telling the breezes of his griefs.
And writhing in the sand,
which was drenched and steeped in his tears,
now he would tell the rocks of his love,
now the wretch, delirious,
would utter these words:

★ ★ ★ ★

XVII

The shining stars had left
the heavens, in which dawn was beginning to gleam,
and the flowers that gild Phoebus' chariot
were passing through the ruddy gates of Orient.
The birds
were joyfully greeting the first radiance,
the drops
that dew had formed on the trees were glistening,
and the great sea, with severe majesty,
roared as it reflected the first light.
Before this august spectacle
a good soul rose towards the Creator of the earth.
Everything proclaimed God,
everything announced his great deeds.

XVIII

When, arm in arm,
the friends were walking home
and, as they lay prostrate before the Lord,
their vows of peace were witnessed
by the trees, the wheatfields,
the sea, the rocks and all nature,
they espied the top
of the Gothic dome of their parish church.
At this sight their eyes flowed
with tears of grief and of tenderness,
and ideas of good and of bitterness
were in their breasts, as yet not healed.
In short, they saw their village,
walked into it and always lived in peace.

XIX

O pure friendship, sent from kindly heaven,
sweetening the sorrows of this life.
You nearly fill my breast with sweetness!
How I love you in my afflictions!
Forever blessed
may you be by hearts that have known suffering,
and may those who have found peace in you
exalt you a hundred times and a hundred more:
may love flee with its violent flame
that only brings ill to good souls,
and may this ferocious sentiment give way
to the celestial joys of friendship.
O MEN OF THE WORLD: A GOOD FRIEND AND A FIELD,
HERE IS THE HAPPINESS THAT IS SO SOUGHT!

The Pre-Revivalists

Xoán Manuel Pintos (1811–1876)

From A Gaita gallega (The Galician Pipes), 1853

Queira Dios que esta Gaita ben tocada...

Alter ejusdem furfuris

Queira Dios que esta Gaita ben tocada
Un recordo lle valla ó bon Gaiteiro,
E que millenta mais unda ó primeiro
Veñan tocar tamén a Gaita amada.
Inda permita Dios que sea soada
Voando muy vistoso o meu prumeiro
Arrolado cos chíos do punteiro
Garrido se mostrando coa alborada.
Avante vaya en tod'as romerías
Levada po las vilas e arredores.
Inda sea a mestra das folías.
Calada nunca estea. E de primores
Inzando os sons preñados, e alegrías,
A busquen homes legos e doutores.

Please God these well-played Pipes...

Alter ejusdem furfuris

Please God these well-played Pipes
bring memories to the good Piper,
and may a thousand more men, where the first one played,
also come to play the beloved Pipes.
May God even permit it to sound out
as my colourful plume flies,
soothed by the chirping of the chanter
as it displays its grace in an albada.
May it lead all festa-processions,
carried through towns and all around them.
May it even be the master of the festivities.
May it never be silent. And, as it fills

its pregnant tones with splendours and joys,
may men both learned and unlearned seek it out.

A fame

Deitouse a fame ó longo nos sembrados
enriba dos centeos, trigos, millos!
Deixou todo-los frutos tan mirrados,
ay nosos fillos!

Perdemos o traballo e a semente
tolleuna o temporal dentro das leiras!
Mais valera que foran co esa enchente
aldeas inteiras!

Antes que o pé da negra fame ver
chegar a porta e ir coa fraca man
palpando a gente que ja está a morrer
por non ter pan!

Alá de onde vimos na montaña
a miseria é tan grande que non pode
a gente se queixar, e a gran fouzaña
da morte acode!

Que un-ha tan fatal calamidade
a sociedá cristiana no estremece!
entre os gentís quizais mais caridade
e virtú crece!

Que triste, santo Dios, que triste praga!
Movede tan siquera a compasión
o rico, que por vós algun ben faga
nesta ocasión.

Non permitás, Señor, que a nai rabiosa
esgaze o fillo tenro que inda mame
como en Jerusalén, e logo o coza
matando a fame!

Ábranse a vez siquera nesta vida
as bulsas e graneiros do avarento!

e médico que cure a gran ferida
sea do famento!

Os pobres cantarán a súa gloria,
faranlle no seu peito hermoso tempro,
verterá ó seu nome pola historia
piadoso exempro!

Que nunca o rico bos alaudos ten
si adora como a Dios a sua riqueza,
e non arría un chavo por ninguén
ri da probeza.

Famine

Famine has lain itself down all along the fields,
over rye, wheat, maize.
It has left the plants so withered,
oh, our children!

We've lost our toil and our seed,
the storm has destroyed it in the furrows!
It would have been better if that flood had done for
whole villages

rather than seeing the foot of black famine
come to the door and go with its gaunt hand
feeling people who are dying
for lack of bread.

Up there in the mountains, where we're from,
destitution is such that people
have no strength to complain, and the great scythe
of death comes.

And such a dreadful calamity
doesn't shock Christian society!
Perhaps among pagans more charity
and virtue grow.

So woeful, holy God, so woeful a plague!
At least move the wealthy to compassion

so that for your sake they do some good
          on this occasion.

Do not allow, Lord, the raging mother
to tear to pieces her tender child, still suckling,
as in Jerusalem, and then cook it,
          to kill hunger.

Let, for once in this life,
misers' purses and granaries be opened,
and let the doctor who heals great wounds be
          the doctor of the hungry.

The poor will sing his glory,
they will make a beautiful temple to him in their breasts,
his name will be spread throughout history,
          an example of charity.

For the rich man is never praised
if he adores his own wealth as if it were God,
and won't let go of a farthing for anyone,
          laughing at poverty.

Francisco Añón (1812–1878)

Á morte de Vesteiro Torres (fragmento), *1876*

II

Era xa media noite, a lúa chea
con arxentada luz a terra inunda,
e da corte na leda barafunda,
polas prazas e rúas serpentea
a xente que vén vindo
de volta dos teatros e paseos,
cochicheando ou rindo
de política, amor e devaneos.

Todo é por fóra deliciosa calma,
imais, ai do triste que alá dentro encerra,
no íntimo da alma,
a máis encarnizada e crúa guerra,
que resistir non pode, malpocado!

No combate interior de cote absorto,
leva no peito o corazón mirrado,
xa para o mundo e seus encantos morto.

Alí vén el con vagaroso paso,
atravesando a plácida corrente
da falangueira xente,
sen sequera facer das lindas caso.
Corre a perderse como o leve esquife
que vai do furacán arrebatado
a escacharse nun áspero arrecife,
ou como o paxariño descoidado,
que atraído da pérfida serpente,
entre as ramas oculta,
aletea xemendo atordoado
e do réptil na gorxa se sepulta...

Alá se foi... perdeuse na revolta...
¡Xa non volverá máis!, porque o vampiro,
que vai tras el con invisible xiro,
á víctima non solta
ata chuparlle o último suspiro.
Da derradeira lúgubre xornada
cubra un denso telón a escena triste
con sangue salpicada.

¡Noite fatal, horrible, malfadada,
de batallar, de dudas e agonía,
que a maxinala a mente se resiste
e na testa o cabelo se arrepía!
O que alí pasaría Diolo o sabe,
que El só ten dos corazóns a chave.

Caeu no chan o valeroso atleta,
cansando de loitar na flor da vida;
por nós pasou cal rápido cometa,
pero deixou na súa despedida
de inextinguible luz un rastro inmenso
que ha de ser cada día máis intenso.

Baixou do ceo á terra
coidando que era esto un paraíso,
mais ó ver que este mundo só encerra

liortas e maldades,
tivo do ceo soidades
e quixo alá volverse de improviso.

Guirnaldas de perpetuas, mirto e flores
con loureiro e ciprés dos nosos hortos
vinde a pór, inspirados trobadores,
do noso bardo sobre os restos mortos.

Vinde axiña, por Dios, ¡xuntos choremos!
As bagullas que alí confundiremos
na súa humilde campa,
serán chuvia de amor que nunca escampa.

On the death of Vesteiro Torres (extract), *1876*

II
It was midnight. The full moon
floods the earth with silvery light,
and, amidst the happy brouhaha of Madrid,
people going back home
from theatres and promenades
wind their way through squares and streets
whispering or laughing
about politics, love and fantasies...

On the outside all is delectable tranquillity,
but alas for he who holds, inside himself,
in the most intimate part of his soul,
the most bitter and cruel war
that he cannot endure, poor wretch!
Daily absorbed in his inner combat,
he carries in his breast a withered heart,
dead to the world and its charms...

Here he comes with uncertain step,
cutting across the calm current
of the exuberant crowd
without even heeding the pretty girls.
He is hurrying to his doom like the light skiff
swept away by a hurricane,
about to be smashed on a rugged reef,
or like the careless little bird

that, attracted by the perfidious snake
hidden among the branches,
flutters and whimpers in bewilderment
and is buried in the reptile's gullet.

There he went... lost round a corner...
He will never return! Because the vampire,
following him invisibly,
does not release its victim
until it has sucked the last sigh out of him.
Let a thick curtain cover the sad scene
of the last doleful day,
spattered with blood...

Fatal, horrible, ill-starred night
of battles, doubts and agony!
The mind shrinks from imagining it
and the hair on the head stands on end.
God only knows what happened there,
for he alone holds the key to hearts.

The brave athlete fell to the ground,
tiring of struggle in the flower of life;
he passed through our midst like a speedy comet,
but, as he bade farewell, he left
an immense trail of inextinguishable light
that will grow ever more intense.

He descended from heaven to earth
thinking that this was some paradise,
but when he saw that this world contains only
conflicts and wickedness
he felt sadlongings for heaven
and suddenly decided to go back there.

Inspired troubadors, come and lay
wreaths of amaranths, myrtle and other flowers
with laurel and cypress from our gardens
over the mortal remains of our bard.
Come quickly, for God's sake; let us weep together!
The tears that we shall mingle there,
over his humble grave
will be a rain of love that never ceases.

The Revival

Marcial Valladares (1821–1903)

From Maxina ou a filla espúrea, *1880*

Aconteceu, pois, que, disposto un baile no teatro, non sabemos por qué empresa, baile de máscaras para o día das candeas, dous de febreiro do ano xa citado, a filla de Sancti-Petri, a rogos dunha desas amigas de súa nai, alcanzou palabra de ir a el e foron ambas, acompañadas do home da mesma amiga, infeliz señor, máis infeliz que a súa señora e de cascos non tan vans. El ía en sinxelo traxe de sala, a muller de máscara e dando o brazo á filla de Sancti-Petri, tamén de sala, pero tan arrebatadora, que ó seu lado diriamos que feas case parecían as máis guapas; así non houbo dandi, máscara alegre nin estudiante que non quixese bailar con ela. A súa amiga, a chaque desto, quitaba o seu partido, divertíase con quen lle daba a gana, bromeaba a Xan e a Pedro, soltaba, en fin, todo o seu xenial bo humor, anque sen nunca abandonar nin perder de vista á que se lle confiara, sempre agarrada a ela, non sendo que bailase. A media noite, cando xa as cabezas andaban quentes, ou trastornadas unhas, co vapor do champaña e demais licores, outras cos incentivos que provocativo amor ostentaba alí, varias, con ambas cousas a un tempo, entra no salón unha comparsa rara, chamada dos magnetizadores, por consisti-las súas bromas en querer magnetizar aquela ou este que tomaban da súa conta. Como o diamante fino e bo loce e se distingue entre tódalas máis preciosas pedras, un dos da comparsa, ó ve-la de Sancti-Petri no salón, dixo, como asombrado e a si mesmo: "¡Otilia aquí! Lindísima magnetizable."

Separouse a pouco da comparsa e, saltando a bromas coa amiga e logo coa de Sancti-Petri, tanto, tanto de magnetismo lles falou, tantas e tantas garatuxas lles fixo, máscara foi tan pegañosa, que a amiga de Otilia, levando a broma do encaretado, prestándose ela mesma a ser magnetizada, incitou a Otilia a que a imitase e, cal paxaros inocentes, fascinados pola boa, sobre todo Otilia, deixáronse entrambas ir e foron ata un gabinete non moi alumeado onde a descoñecida máscara, con estudiada verba e novas garatuxas cloroformizounas as dúas e abusou de Otilia. Pasado un cuarto de hora, en si volveron, miraron unha para a outra espantadas e, sentindo o ruído da música que no salón tocaba, o vocerío desordenado das máscaras que por el cruzaban, críanse nun inferno, refregaban os ollos e trataban de recordar ónde estaban, a qué alí viñeran. Voltas algo máis en si, recoñeceron o sitio, erguéronse das sillas en que a vilá máscara as deixara e soas, enteiramente soas, botan en busca súa, mais en balde, pois nin el nin a comparsa aparecían, marcharan xa e, avergonzadas, corridas case, sentáronse nun recuncho do local onde a topalas chegou entonces o infeliz señor que en busca delas tamén andaba.

From Maxina or the Scorned Daughter, *1880*

It so happened then that the ball was arranged in the theatre by goodness knows what company, a masked ball for Candelmas, the second of February of the year mentioned. Sancti-Petri's daughter had been asked by one of her mother's friends and was told she could go. They went together, accompanied by this friend's husband, an unhappy fellow, much more so than his wife and with less of her vanity. He was dressed in a simple evening suit, while his wife wore a mask and walked arm in arm with Sancti-Petri's daughter who was wearing an evening gown. She was so stunning that at her side even the most beautiful women looked ugly, and there wasn't a single dandy, masked party-goer or student who didn't want to dance with her. Her friend benefited on account of this, having fun with whoever she felt like, laughing with John or Peter and letting loose all her wit and humour, clinging on to her friend except when she was dancing. At midnight, when heads were hot, and some out of kilter from the champagne and other spirits, others with licentious ideas on their minds, and many with both, a strange group in fancy dress entered the room going under the name of the mesmerisers, because their fun was had by trying to mesmerise anyone that took their fancy. Just as a good, fine diamond shines and stands out among all other precious stones, one of the fancy dress party spotted Sancti-Petri's daughter in the ball-room and said to himself in a voice of astonishment, "Otilia here! She is just perfect to be mesmerised!".

A little later he moved away from the group and started joking, first with the friend and then with Sancti-Petri's daughter, speaking so, so much about mesmerising, paying them so, so many compliments. The mask was sticky, and Otilia's friend, playing along with the masked stranger, decided that she was willing to be mesmerised. She encouraged Otilia to go along with her and both of them, especially Otilia, went along like innocent little birds fascinated by a boa constrictor to a well-lit room where the masked stranger with careful words and more compliments chloroformed both of them and took advantage of Otilia. After a quarter of an hour they came around and looked at each other in panic. The music coming from the other room and the mumbled chatter from the masked party-goers created a kind of hell, and the friends rubbed their eyes trying to remember where they were and what they had come for. When they had recovered a bit they recognised the place and got up from the seats where the evil masked stranger had left them alone and went off in search of him. Their search was in vain, for neither he nor any of his group appeared. They had already taken their leave and the two women sat down in shame in a corner of the room where the unhappy gentleman, who had been looking for them was to find them.

Eduardo Pondal (1835–1917)

From Queixumes dos pinos (Lamentations of the Pines), *1886*

"E ti, campana d'Anllóns...

"E ti, campana d'Anllóns,
que vagamente tocando
derramas nos corazóns
un bálsamo triste e brando
de pasadas ilusións.

Alá nos pasados ventos
primeiros da miña vida,
oio os teus vagos concentos,
reló dos tristes momentos
da miña patria querida.

¡Cantas veces te lembrou
o que marchou para a guerra,
cando á súa nai deixou,
e partindo á estraña terra
de Baneira te escoitou!

¡Cantas do mar africano,
cautivo bergantiñán,
oio nun soño tirano
o teu tocar soberano,
aló nas tardes do vran!

Cando te sinto tocar,
campana de Anllóns doente,
nunha noite de luar...
rompo triste a suspirar,
por cousas dun mal ausente.

Cando doída tocabas
polas tardes á oración,
campana, sempre falabas
palabras con que cortabas
as cordas do corazón.

Estabas contando ós ventos
cousas do meu mal presente,
os meus futuros tormentos,
que dabas cos sentimentos
según tocabas doente.

Campana, se polo vran
ves lumiar na Ponte-Ceso
a cachela de San Xoán,
dille a todos que estou preso
nos calabozos de Orán.

E a aquela rula inocente
que me morría de amor
no regazo docemente,
tremendo como unha flor
sobre escondida corrente;

diraslle que unha de ferro
arrastro, rouca cadea,
castigo atroz do meu erro;
e que dentro deste encerro
o seu amor me alumea.

Ei ti, golondrina errante
dos longos campos de Arxel,
se á miña terra distante
te leva o voo constante
dille o meu penar cruel.

Se alguén por min preguntar,
dille que estou en prisións;
e unha noite de luar
iráste unha vez pousar
no campanario de Anllóns."

Así, triste en terra allea,
aló nas prisións de Orán,
cantaba un mozo de aldea;
e nos grillóns da cadea
levaba o compás coa man.

"Oh, nai da miña vida,
adiós, adiós, meu pai;
prenda de min querida,
adiós, oh, miña nai;
sombras dos meus avós,
río da Ponte-Ceso,
pinal de Tella espeso...,
acordávos dun preso
como el o fai de vós:
campana de Anllóns,
noites de luar,
lúa que te pos
detrás do pinar;
adiós...,
adióos...,
adióoos..."

'And you, bell of Anllóns...

'And you, bell of Anllóns,
that faintly ringing
spills into hearts
a sad, mild balsam
of past fond hopes:

away in the long-past
first breezes of my life,
I hear your faint harmonies,
the clock marking the sad moments
of my dear homeland.

How often you were remembered
by the man departing for war,
when he left his mother
and, on his way to a foreign land,
listened to you from Baneira chapel!

How often, a captive of the African sea,
this man from Bergantiños
hears in a tyrannical dream
your sublime chiming
on those summer afternoons!

When I hear you ringing,
mournful bell of Anllóns,
on a moonlit night...,
I burst into sorrowful sighs
because of an absent ill.

When you plaintively rang
to call to evening prayers,
O bell, you always spoke
words with which you cut
the strings of my heart.

You were telling the winds
all about my present ill
and my future torments,
for you chimed in with my feelings
in the mournful way you rang.

Bell, if in summer
you see, glowing in Ponteceso,
the St John's Night bonfire,
tell them all I'm a prisoner
in the dungeons of Oran.

And to that innocent dove
who was dying of love
so sweetly on my lap,
trembling like a flower
upon a hidden current,

you will say that I drag
a rasping chain of iron,
a dreadful punishment for my wrong;
and that in this prison
her love illumines me.

And you, wandering swallow
of the long fields of Algiers,
if to my far-off land
your constant flight takes you,
tell her of my cruel suffering.

If anyone should ask after me,
tell them I'm in prison;
and, one moonlit night,
you will go to perch
on the bell-tower at Anllóns.'

Thus, sad in a foreign land,
away in the prison of Oran,
a young villager sang;
and on the fetters of his chain
he beat time with his hand.

'O beloved mother,
goodbye; goodbye, my father;
goodbye, oh, my mother,
my dearest darling;
shadows of my forebears,
river of Ponteceso,
dense pine-forest of Tella...,
remember a prisoner
as he remembers you:
bell of Anllóns,
moonlit nights,
moon setting
behind the pines;
goodbye...,
goodbye...,
goodbye...'

¡Que barba non cuidada!...

¡Que barba non cuidada!
¡Que pálida color!
¡Que vestido, que longa
noncuranza afeou!
Quezais é algún malvado,
quezais é algún ladrón...
Miña madre, valédeme,
valédeme, por Dios;
quezais é algún minguado
que o xuízo lle mancou;
¡oh! ¡que vista tan brava,
chea de espanto e dor!

Non sei se me dá medo,
se me dá compaixón;
parece un pino leixado do vento,
parece botado do mar de Niñóns.

–Sinxela rapaceta,
non me teñas temor;
non son un vagamundo,
non son ningún ladrón:
xeroglífico ousado
do limo soñador,
vou, e, ignoto a min mesmo,
escuro enigma eu son;
se quezais estou tolo,
estou tolo de amor:
por eso as boas xentes,
pra onde vagante vou,
ó ver meu abandono
din con admiración:
parece un pino leixado do vento,
parece botado do mar de Niñóns.

Pensamentos insomnes,
turbulenta ambición,
propósitos de ferro
o ánimo nobre ousou;
de mil suidades fondas
o túrbido escadrón,
como a Luzbel, privara
do primeiro esplendor.
Son os bardos sapientes
que lei fatal lanzou,
soñadores e vagos,
da súa condición:
por eso eu a min mesmo
non me conozo, non,
e exclaman os camiños
mesmos por onde vou:
parece un pino leixado do vento,
parece botado do mar de Niñóns.

Such an unkempt beard!...

Such an unkempt beard!
Such a pale colour!
Such clothes, so shabby
from long neglect!
Perhaps he's some villain,
perhaps he's some thief...
Dear mother, please help me,
please help me, for God's sake;
perhaps he's some wretch
who's lost his reason;
oh! such a wild look,
full of dread and pain!
I don't know if he fills me with fear
or fills me with compassion;
he's like a pine-tree after a gale,
he's like something thrown up by the sea at Niñóns.

'Guileless young lass,
do not fear me;
I am no tramp,
I am no thief:
a bold hieroglyph
dreaming in the mud
am I, and, unknown even to myself,
I am a dark enigma;
if perchance I am mad,
I am mad from love:
this is why good people,
when they see me so slovenly,
all say in amazement:
he's like a pine-tree after a gale,
he's like something thrown up by the sea at Niñóns.

Sleepless thoughts,
tumultuous ambition,
iron resolves–
the noble spirit ventured on them all;
but the turbid squadron
of a thousand profound sadlongings,
stripped it, as it stripped Lucifer,
of its first splendour.

The bards are sages,
vague dreamers,
that a fatal law cast out
from their rightful place:
this is why I do not
know myself, no,
and the very paths
along which I walk exclaim:
he's like a pine-tree after a gale,
he's like something thrown up by the sea at Niñóns.

Carballos de Carballido...

Carballos de Carballido,
cando era rapaz deixeivos;
vin despois de muitos anos;
    xa vamos vellos.

Pasáronse as alegrías
que trouguera o tempo ledo;
a mocedá foi pasada;
    xa vamos vellos.

Eu teño os cabelos brancos,
vós tendes os gallos secos;
os nosos días pasaron;
    xa vamos vellos.

Oak-trees of Carballido...

Oak-trees of Carballido,
as a lad I left you;
after many years I have returned;
    we are growing old.

They are all over, those joys
that happy times brought;
youth has disappeared;
    we are growing old.

My hairs are all white,
your branches are all withered;

our days have gone by;
we are growing old.

As almas escravas...

As almas escravas
de ideas non grandes,
van pensando mil cousas femíneas,
molentes e infames.

Mil soños forxando,
que o ánimo agobian;
arrastrando infamantes cadeas,
cal brandos ilotas.

Espíritos brandos,
espritos muliebres,
sedentarios, que lenta consome
e mórbida, febre.

Mais a alma do bardo,
enérxica, ousada,
que audaz liberdade
tan só soña e ama,
¡vai pensando en propósitos férreos
que ergueran a patria!

Servile souls...

Servile souls,
who have no great ideas,
ponder on a thousand matters
that are feminine, soft and infamous.

Forging a thousand dreams
that oppress the spirit;
dragging infamous chains
like feeble helots.

Feeble spirits;
womanish, sedentary
spirits, slowly consumed
by sickly fever.

But the soul of the bard,
vigorous, daring,
that boldly loves and dreams
only of freedom,
ponders on iron resolves
that once uplifted our homeland!

¡Oh, quen poidera...

¡Oh, quen poidera
pillarte soa,
no seo amigo
de escura cova!
E como hedra
que cinguidora
branca columna
premente enrosca,
cos brazos darche
mil tenras voltas;
dicirche ó oído
mil tenras cousas;
ie o término atopar da esquiva ruta,
en breve hora!

Oh, if only I could...

Oh, if only I could
catch you alone,
in the friendly depths
of a dark cave!
And, like ivy
winding tight around
a white column,
wrap my arms tenderly
around you over and again,
whisper into your ear
tender things over and again;
and find the end of the elusive way,
quickly!

From Outros poemas (Other Poems), *1917*

Os pinos

¿Que din os rumorosos
na costa verdecente,
ao raio transparente
do plácido luar?
¿Que din as altas copas
de escuro arume harpado
co seu ben compasado
monótono fungar?

–Do teu verdor cinguido
e de benignos astros,
confín dos verdes castros
e valeroso chan,
non des a esquecemento
da inxuria o rudo encono;
desperta do teu sono,
fogar de Breogán.

Os bos e xenerosos
a nosa voz entenden,
e con arroubo atenden
o noso rouco son,
mais só os ignorantes,
e féridos e duros,
imbéciles e escuros
non nos entenden, non.

Os tempos son chegados
dos bardos das idades,
que as vosas vaguidades
cumprido fin terán;
pois, onde quer xigante
a nosa voz pregoa
a redenzón da boa
nazón de Breogán.

Teus fillos vagorosos
en que honor só late,
a intrépido combate

dispondo o peito van;
sé, por ti mesma, libre
de indigna servidume
e de oprobioso alcume,
rexión de Breogán.

A nobre Lusitania
os brazos tende amigos,
aos eidos ven, antigos,
con un punxente afán;
e cumpre as vaguidades
dos teus soantes pinos,
duns máxicos destinos,
¡ouh, grei de Breogán!

Amor da terra verde,
da verde terra nosa,
acende a raza briosa
de Ousinde e de Froxán;
que aló nos seus garridos
xustillos, mal constreitos,
os doces e albos peitos
das fillas de Breogán

que á nobre prole ensinen
fortísimos acentos,
non mólidos concentos
que ás virxes só ben están;
mais os robustos ecos
que, ¡oh, patria!, ben recordas
das sonorosas cordas
das harpas de Breogán.

Estima non se alcanza
cun vil xemido brando;
cal quen requer rogando
con voz que esquecerán;
mais cun rumor xigante,
sublime e parecido
ao intrépido sonido
das armas de Breogán.

Galegos, sede fortes,
prontos a grandes feitos;
aparellade os peitos
a glorioso afán;
fillos dos nobres celtas,
fortes e peregrinos,
loitade plos destinos,
dos eidos de Breogán.

The pines

What say those whisperers
on the greening slope
in the transparent ray
of placid moonlight?
What say the lofty tree-tops
of dark, serrated needles
with their rhythmical
monotone rustling?

'Begirt with your greenery
and with benign stars,
the setting for green hill-forts
and a valorous clan,
do not commit to oblivion
the gross malevolence of insult;
awake from your slumbers,
O home of Breogán!

The good and the generous
understand our voice
and eagerly heed
our harsh sounds,
but only the ignorant
and the brutish and callous,
imbeciles, nonentities,
do not understand us.

The times have arrived
of the bards of the ages,
for your indecision
will come to a full stop;
because everywhere

our colossal voice proclaims
the redemption of the good
nation of Breogán.

Your dilatory sons,
in whom honour alone throbs,
are making their breasts ready
for an intrepid combat;
be, by your own efforts, free
from infamous servitude
and from shameful epithets,
region of Breogán.

Noble Lusitania
stretches forth friendly arms,
beholding its old lands
with pressing desire;
and it fulfils the vague hopes
of your rustling pines
about magical destinies,
O citizens of Breogán.

Love of green land,
of this green land of ours,
fires the spirited race
of Ousinde and Froxán;
and, ill-constrained
in their lovely bodices,
may the gentle white bosoms
of the daughters of Breogán

teach their noble offspring
powerful tones,
not the soft harmonies
only good for virgins;
and also the robust echoes,
that, O homeland! you recall,
of the resounding strings
of the harps of Breogán.

Esteem is not achieved
with a vile soft moan,
like someone begging

with a voice that will be forgotten;
but with a colossal reverberation,
sublime, and similar
to the intrepid sound
of the arms of Breogán.

Galicians, be strong,
be ready for great deeds;
prepare your breasts
for a glorious endeavour;
sons of the noble Celts,
strong wanderers,
struggle for the destinies
of the fields of Breogán.'

A fala

Nobre e harmoniosa
fala de Breogán,
fala boa, de fortes
e grandes sen rival;
ti do celta aos ouvidos
sempre soando estás
como soan os pinos
na costa de Froxán;
ti nos eidos da Celtia
e co tempo serás
un lábaro, sagrado
que ao triunfo guiará,
fala nobre, harmoniosa,
¡fala de Breogán!

Ti, sinal misterioso
dos teus fillos serás
que plo mundo dispersos
e sen abrigo van;
e a aqueles que foran
nunha pasada edá
defensores dos eidos
contra o duro román
e que aínda cobizan
da terra a libertá,
nun pobo nobre e forte,

valente, axuntarás,
ioh, fala harmoniosa,
fala de Breogán!

Serás épica tuba
e forte sen rival,
que chamarás aos fillos
que aló do Miño están,
os bos fillos do Luso,
apartados irmáns
de nós por un destino
envexoso e fatal.
Cos robustos acentos,
grandes, os chamarás,
iverbo do gran Camoens,
fala de Breogán!

Our language

Noble and harmonious
language of Breogán,
good language, of the strong,
great and unrivalled;
you always sound
in the ears of the Celt
as the pine-trees sound
on the coast of Froxán;
you, in Celtic fields,
one day will be
a sacred labarum
guiding us to triumph,
noble, harmonious language,
language of Breogán!

You will be the mysterious sign
of your sons,
scattered over the world
and shelterless;
and all those who were
in a past age
defenders of their fields
against the harsh Roman
and who still long

for the freedom of their land,
you will unite
as a noble, strong, brave people,
O harmonious language,
language of Breogán!

You will be an epic clarion,
unrivalled in power,
calling to the sons
who are beyond the River Miño,
the good sons of Lusitania,
brothers separated
from us by a fatal,
envious destiny.
With your strong, splendid tones
you will summon them,
word of the great Camões,
language of Breogán!

O dolmen de Dombate

Aínda recordo, aínda, cando eu era estudante,
garrido rapacete, que ben rexerse sabe;
cando ía pra Nemiña a estudiar a arte
do erudito Nebrija e do bo Villafañe;
e ía a cabalo, ledo, cal soen os rapaces.

Pasado Vilaseco, lugar batido do aire
no alto da costa de Uces de montesía canle;
pasado Vilaseco, indo pla gandra adiante,
xa vía desde lonxe o dolmen de Dombate.

Deixando Fonte-Fría, cara ao lado de Laxe,
e levando o camiño de San Simón de Nande;
polo chan de Borneiro, de cativos pinales,
cuase pasaba a rentes do dolmen de Dombate.

Quedaba o misterioso, fillo doutras idades,
coa súa antiga mesa, coas súas antigas antes,
no seu monte de terra, no alto e ben roldante,
poboado en redondo de montesío estrame,
de pequenas queiroas e de toxos non grandes,
como calada esfinxe, que sublime non fale;

como náufrago leño, de soberbio cruzamen,
lanzado sobre a praia por potente oleaxe,
que de pasada rota mostre rudas señales,
e mostre aberto o flanco por glorioso combate,
e con linguaxe muda das súas glorias fale.
¡Canto, ai, mudar pode longa e vetusta idade!

Entonces eu deixando ambas rendas flotantes,
penoso ía cuidando, pla Viqueira salvaxe,
nos nosos xa pasados, nos celtas memorables,
nas súas antigas glorias, nos seus duros combates,
nos nosos vellos dolmens e castros verdexantes.

E despois a Nemiña, ou que fose ou tornase,
ao velo desde lonxe indo pla gandra adiante,
sempre ledo exclamaba: ¡O dolmen de Dombate!

Agora que pasano meus anos xogorales,
agora que só vivo de tristes suidades,
que cumpro con traballo meu terrenal viaxe
e que á miña cabeza branquea a grave idade,
aínda recordo aínda, o dolmen de Dombate.

The dolmen of Dombate

I still remember, still, when I was a student,
a fine young fellow, who knew how to look after himself,
when I was going to Nemiña to study the art
of the erudite Nebrija and the good Villafañe;
and I was going on horseback, as young fellows do.

Once past Vilaseco, a village battered by the air
atop Ures Hill in the mountain pass;
once past Vilaseco, pressing on through the wasteland,
from afar I could see the dolmen of Dombate.

Leaving Fonte Fría, over towards Laxe,
and taking the path to San Simón de Nande,
upon Borneiro plain, with its small pine-groves,
I was riding right by the dolmen of Dombate.

This mysterious being, a son of other ages,
still had its ancient top-stone, with its ancient uprights,

on its high mound of earth, a splendid stage,
the ground covered all around by mountain scrub,
by low heather and small gorse bushes,
like a silent sphinx, sublimely speechless;
like a shipwreck with superb rigging
thrown upon the beach by powerful rollers,
showing the rude marks of a past battle,
showing its side cleft open in glorious combat,
and speaking in mute language of all its glories.
How many things, oh!, long years can change.

And then, having dropped both reins,
I was thinking, through wild Viqueira,
of our forebears, the memorable Celts,
of their past glories, of their hard combats,
of our ancient dolmens and our greening hillforts.

And then on to Nemiña; and whether going or coming,
whenever I saw it from afar as I went on through the wasteland,
I would exclaim with joy: O dolmen of Dombate!

Now that my smiling years have passed,
now that I only live on sadlongings,
now that I am completing with great effort my earthly journey
and grave age is whitening my head,
I still remember, still, the dolmen of Dombate.

Os camiños, os matos montesíos...

Os camiños, os matos montesíos,
os garridos ensoños, os lindeiros,
os cantos saudosos, os resíos,
os cómaros, os pinos, os regueiros,
as promesas, os triunfos, os desvíos,
as doces esperanzas, os sendeiros;
todo me dá soidades e triganzas,
todo me trae punxentes memoranzas.

Paths, mountain thickets...

Paths, mountain thickets,
splendid daydreams, pastures,
nostalgic songs, fallow patches,

field-ridges, pine trees, brooks,
promises, triumphs, lapses,
sweet hopes, tracks,
–it all gives me sadlongings and anxieties,
it all brings me pungent memories.

Cando no escarpado Ougal...

Cando no escarpado Ougal
apunta a soa floriña,
anunciando ao cazador
do ano a estación garrida;
cando da doce Fungar
ás curvas praias mariñas
en nó tecido voando
chegan as lixeiras píllaras;
entonces do bardo a alma
que soña entre as uces irtas,
apoiado na súa harpa,
en donde o vento suspira;
mentres que os fillos dos homes
danse ás faenas da vida,
entonces do bardo a alma
visita a melancolía.

When on steep Ougal...

When on steep Ougal
the lone flower appears
announcing to the huntsman
the splendid season of the year;
when over the sweeping beaches
of sweet Fungar,
flying in a tight knot,
the agile plovers arrive:
then the soul of the bard,
who dreams among the tall heather-bushes,
leaning on his harp,
while the sons of men
set about life's toils –
then the soul of the bard
is visited by melancholy.

Rosalía de Castro (1837–1885)

From Cantares gallegos (Galician Songs), *1863*

Campanas de Bastabales...

Campanas de Bastabales,
cando vos oyo tocar,
mórrome de soidades.

I

Cando vos oyo tocar,
campaniñas, campaniñas,
sin querer torno a chorar.

Cando de lonxe vos oyo,
penso que por min chamades
e das entrañas me doyo.

Dóyome de dór ferida,
que antes tiña vida enteira
y hoxe teño media vida.

Solo media me deixaron
os que de aló me trouxeron,
os que de aló me roubaron.

Non me roubaron, traidores,
iay!, uns amores toliños,
iay!, uns toliños amores.

Que os amores xa fuxiron,
as soidades viñeron...
De pena me consumiron.

II

Aló pola mañanciña
subo enriba dos outeiros
lixeiriña, lixeiriña.

Como unha craba lixeira,
para oír das campaniñas
a batalada pirmeira.

A pirmeira da alborada
que me traen os airiños
por me ver mais consolada.

Por me ver menos chorosa,
nas suas alas ma traen
rebuldeira e queixumbrosa.

Queixumbrosa e retembrando
por antre a verde espesura,
por antre o verde arborado.

E pola verde pradeira,
por riba da veiga llana,
rebuldeira e rebuldeira.

III
Paseniño, paseniño,
vou pola tarde calada
de Bastabales camiño.

Camiño do meu contento;
y en tanto o sol non se esconde
nunha pedriña me sento.

E sentada estou mirando
como a lúa vay saíndo,
como o sol se vay deitando.

Cal se deita, cal se esconde
mentres tanto corre a lúa
sin saberse para donde.

Para donde vai tan soya
sin que ós tristes que a miramos
nin nos fale, nin nos oya.

Que se oira e nos falara,
moitas cousas lle dixera,
moitas cousas lle contara.

IV

Cada estrela, o seu diamante;
cada nube, branca pruma;
triste a lúa marcha diante.

Diante marcha crarexando
veigas, prados, montes, ríos,
donde o dia vay faltando.

Falta o dia, e noite escura
baixa, baixa, pouco a pouco,
por montañas de verdura.

De verdura e de follaxe,
salpicada de fontiñas
baixo a sombra do ramaxe.

Do ramaxe donde cantan
paxariños piadores
que coa aurora se levantan.

Que ca noite se adormecen
para que canten os grilos
que cas sombras aparecen.

V

Corre o vento, o río pasa.
Corren nubes, nubes corren
camiño da miña casa.

Miña casa, meu abrigo,
vanse todos, eu me quedo
sin compaña nin amigo.

Eu me quedo contemprando
as laradas das casiñas
por quen vivo suspirando.

★ ★ ★ ★

Vén a noite..., morre o día,
as campanas tocan lonxe
o tocar da Ave María.
Elas tocan pra que rece;

eu non rezo, que os saloucos
afogándome parece
que por min tén que rezar.
Campanas de Bastabales,
cando vos oyo tocar
mórrome de soidades.

Bells of Bastabales...

Bells of Bastabales,
when I hear you ringing
I die of sadlonging.

I

When I hear you ringing,
bells, dear bells,
despite myself I weep again.

When I hear you afar
I think it's me you call
and deep inside I ache.

I ache with wounded pain,
for once I had a whole life
and now I have a half life.

I was left with but a half life
by those who brought me thence,
by those who stole me thence.

I was not stolen away, you traitors,
oh! by foolish loves,
oh! by loves so foolish.

For those loves have fled,
and sadlonging came...
It has consumed me with grief.

II

Early in the morning
I climb the hills
fleet of foot, fleet of foot.
Like an agile goat,

to hear the first chime
of the dear bells.

The first chime of dawn
brought by the breezes
to give me some comfort.

To make me less tearful,
on their wings they bring it,
both playful and plaintive.

Plaintive and trembling
through the green thickets,
through the green woodland.

And across the green meadow
over the flat valley
playful, playful.

III
Slowly, slowly,
I go in the silent evening
towards Bastabales.

Towards my contentment;
and just before the sun hides
I sit on a stone.

And as I sit I watch
how the moon slowly rises,
how the sun slowly sets.

How he sets, how he hides,
while the moon rushes off,
nobody knows where.

Where she's going all alone
without speaking or listening
to us sad ones who gaze at her.

For if she listened and spoke to us,
I'd tell her many things,
I'd tell her many stories.

IV

Each star her diamond,
each cloud a white feather,
sadly the moon goes before them.

Before them she goes lighting
valleys, meadows, hills, rivers,
whence day is departing.

Day departs, and dark night
descends, descends little by little
over green mountains.

Green and full of foliage
scattered with springs
under the shade of the boughs.

Boughs where sing
cheeping little birds
that rise with the dawn.

That fall asleep as night comes
so that the crickets can sing
as they emerge with the shadows.

V

The wind blows by, the river passes by,
clouds blow by, clouds blow by
on the way to my house.

My house, my shelter;
they all go, I am left
without company or friend.

I am left contemplating
the hearth-glow in the houses
for which I sigh.

★ ★ ★ ★

Night comes..., day dies,
far away the bells chime
the tones of the Ave Maria.

They chime for me to pray,
I do not pray, for it seems
that these sobs choking me
must be praying for me.
Bells of Bastabales,
when I hear you ringing
I die of sadlonging.

Eu ben vin estar o moucho...

Eu ben vin estar o moucho
enriba de aquel penedo:
¡Non che teño medo, moucho;
moucho, non che teño medo!

I

Unha noite, noite negra,
como os pesares que eu teño,
noite filla das sombrisas
alas que estenden os medos;
hora en que cantan os galos,
hora en que xemen os ventos;
en que as meigas bailan, bailan,
xuntas co demo pirmeiro,
arrincando verdes robres,
portas e tellas fendendo,
todas de branco vestidas,
tendídolos brancos pelos
contra quen os cans oubean
agoirando triste enterro;
cando relumbrar se miran
antre os toxales espesos,
cal encendidas candeas
ollos de lobo famento;
e os ramallaxes dos montes
antre si murmuxan quedos,
e as follas secas que espallan
os aires da noite inquietos,
en remuíños se xuntan
con longo estremecemento,
indo camiño da igrexa,
soya, cos meus pensamentos,
cabo da fonte da Virxe

pretiño do cimeterio,
dempois de sentir un sopro
que me deixou sin alento:
eu ben vin estar o moucho
enriba de aquel penedo.

II

Arrepuiñadas todas
as carnes se me puñeron,
e os cabelos no curuto
fóronse erguendo direitos;
gotas de sudor corrían
a fío polo meu peito,
e trembaba como tremban
as augas cando fay vento,
na pía da fonte nova,
que sempre está revertendo.
Aquel moucho alí fincado,
cal se fose o mesmo demo,
fito a fito me miraba
cos seus ollos rapiñeiros,
que coidei que me roubaban
non máis que de lonxe velos.
De lume me paresían
e que me queimaron penso;
penso que eran tizós roxos
da fogueira dos infernos,
que polas niñas me entraron
hastra o corazón dreitos.
En él remorsos había
de amoriños pecadentos...
¡Ay, quen ten de eses amores,
non pode hachar bon sosiego!

Chovía si Dios ten augua,
ventaba en tódolos ventos,
e ensarrapicada toda
a camiñar non me atrevo;
que o moucho, fita que fita,
me espera naquel penedo;
mais acordeime da Virxe
que sempre conmigo levo;
résolle un Ave-María,

e cobrando novo alento,
como os páxaros do mare
nadando paso o regueiro;
corro a enriba do valado,
brinco embaixo do portelo,
e dende alí berro entonces
con cantas forzas eu teño:
¡Non che teño medo, moucho;
moucho, non che teño medo!

I saw the owl...

> *I saw the owl*
> *perched on that rock.*
> *I'm not scared of you, owl;*
> *owl, I'm not scared of you!*

I

One night, a night as black
as my sorrows,
a night in league with the dark
wings spread by fears;
a time when cocks crow,
a time when winds moan;
when witches dance and dance
with the original Devil,
tearing up green oaks,
splitting doors and tiles,
all dressed in white,
with their white hair loose,
howled at by dogs
that presage a sad funeral;
when the glow can be seen
among the dense gorse-bushes,
like burning candles,
of the eyes of a hungry wolf;
and all the twigs in the scrub
whisper to each other,
and the dry leaves scattered
by the restless night-breezes
come together in whirls
with a long shudder,
as I walked towards the church,

alone with my thoughts,
by the Spring of the Virgin,
very close to the cemetery,
after I'd heard a blowing
that left me without breath,
I saw the owl
perched on that rock.

II

Goose pimples covered
the whole of my body,
and the hairs on my head
slowly bristled up;
drops of sweat
ran down my breast,
and I shuddered
as water shudders when the wind blows
over the bowl of the new fountain
that never stops flowing.
That owl perched there,
as if it were the Devil himself,
was staring and staring at me
with its thief's eyes
that seemed to steal me away
as I looked at them from afar.
They appeared to be on fire
and I believe they burned me;
I believe they were red firebrands
from the bonfire of hell
that pierced me through my pupils
straight into my heart.
And in my heart was remorse
for sinful loves...
Oh, whoever has such loves
can never find tranquillity!

God was hurling his rain down,
and all the winds were blowing,
and, wet through and through,
I do not dare to walk on;
for the owl, staring and staring,
is awaiting me on that rock;
but I remembered the Virgin,

whom I always carry with me;
I pray an Ave Maria to her
and, gaining second wind,
like a bird of the sea
I swim across the stream,
I run up the fence,
I hop under the gate,
and from there I shout
with all the strength I have:
I'm not scared of you, owl;
owl, I'm not scared of you!

A gaita gallega

Resposta
Ó eminente poeta D. Ventura Ruiz de Aguilera

I

Cando este cantar, poeta,
na lira xemendo entonas,
non sei o que por min pasa
que as lagrimiñas me afogan,
que ante de min cruzar vexo
a Virxen-mártir que invocas,
cos pés cravados de espiñas,
cas mans cubertas de rosas.
En vano a gaita, tocando
unha alborada de groria,
sóns polos aires espalla
que cán nas tembrantes ondas;
en vano baila contenta
nas eiras a turba louca,
que aqueles sóns, tal me afrixen,
cousas tan tristes me contan,
que eu podo dicirche
non canta, que chora.

II

Vexo contigo estos ceos,
vexo estas brancas auroras,
vexo estos campos froridos
donde se arrullan as pombas,
i estas montañas xigantes

que aló cas nubes se tocan
cubertas de verdes pinos
e de froriñas cheirosas;
vexo esta terra bendita
donde o ben de Dios rebota
e donde anxiños hermosos
tecen brillantes coroas;
mais, iay!, como tamén vexo
pasar macilentas sombras,
grilos de ferro arrastrando
antre sorrisas de mofa,
anque mimosa gaitiña
toque alborada de groria,
eu podo dicirche
non canta, que chora.

III

Falas, y o meu pensamento
mira pasar temerosas
as sombras deses cen portos
que ó pé das ondiñas moran,
e pouco a pouco marchando
fráxiles, tristes e soyas,
vagar as naves soberbas
aló nunha mar traidora.
Y iay! como nelas navegan
os fillos das nosas costas
con rumbo á América infinda
que a morte co pan lles dona,
denudos pedindo en vano
á patria misericordia,
anque contenta a gaitiña
o probe gaiteiro toca,
eu podo dicirche
non canta, que chora.

IV

Probe Galicia, non debes
chamarte nunca española,
que España de ti se olvida
cando eres, iay!, tan hermosa.
Cal se na infamia naceras,
torpe, de ti se avergonza,

y a nay que un fillo despreça
nay sin coraçón se noma.
Naide por que te levantes
che alarga a man bondadosa;
naide os teus prantos enxuga,
y homilde choras e choras.
Galicia, ti non tés patria,
ti vives no mundo soya,
y a prole fecunda túa
se espalla en errantes hordas,
mentras triste e solitaria
tendida na verde alfombra
ó mar esperanzas pides,
de Dios a esperanza imploras.
Por eso anque en son de festa
alegre á gaitiña se oya,
eu podo dicirche
non canta, que chora.

V

     "Espera, Galicia, espera."
¡Canto este grito consola!
Páguecho Dios, bon poeta,
mais é unha esperanza louca;
que antes de que os tempos cheguen
de dicha tan venturosa,
antes que Galicia suba
coa cruz que o seu lombo agobia
aquel difícil camiño
que o pé dos abismos toca,
quiçáis, cansada e sedenta,
quiçáis que de angustias morra.
Págueche Dios, bon poeta,
esa esperanza de groria,
que de teu peito surxindo,
á Virxe-mártir coroa,
y esta a recompensa sea
de amargas penas tan fondas.
Págueche este cantar triste
que as nosas tristezas conta,
que soyo ti..., iti entre tantos!
das nosas mágoas se acorda.
¡Digna voluntad de un xenio,

alma pura e xenerosa!
E cando a gaita gallega
aló nas Castillas oyas,
ó teu corazón pergunta,
verás que che di en resposta
que a gaita gallega
non canta, que chora.

The Galician Pipes

Reply
to the eminent poet Don Ventura Ruiz de Aguilera

I

When this song, poet,
you play on your lyre, lamenting,
I don't know what happens to me,
for my tears choke me,
and before me I see passing
the Virgin-martyr you invoke,
her feet pierced with thorns,
her hands covered with roses.
In vain the pipes, playing
a glorious albada,
scatter through the air tunes
that fall into the bobbing waves;
in vain the crazy crowd
dances happily on the threshing-floors,
for those tunes afflict me so,
they speak of such sad things,
that I can tell you:
the pipes don't sing – they weep.

II

Like you I see these skies,
I see these white dawns,
I see these flower-filled fields
where doves coo to each other,
and these giant mountains,
touching the clouds on high,
and covered with green pines
and sweet-smelling flowers;
I see this blessed land,

overflowing with God's good,
where beautiful angels
weave shining garlands;
but oh! since I also see
haggard shadows passing by,
dragging iron fetters
amidst mocking smiles,
even though the tender pipes
play a glorious albada,
I can tell you:
the pipes don't sing – they weep.

III
You speak, and in my mind
I watch the passing
of the shadows in those hundred ports
dwelling at the edge of the waves
and, as little by little they leave,
fragile, sad and alone,
the wandering of the proud ships
away into a treacherous sea.
And oh! since on them sail
the sons of our coasts
on their way to infinite America
that bestows on them bread and death
as naked they beg in vain
for mercy from their fatherland,
even though the poor piper
plays happy bagpipes,
I can tell you:
the pipes don't sing – they weep.

IV
Poor Galicia, you should
never call yourself Spanish,
for Spain forgets you
although you are, oh! so beautiful.
As if you had been born in infamy,
it foolishly feels ashamed of you;
and the mother who despises her child
is called a heartless mother.
Nobody, to help you to your feet,
holds out a kind hand to you;

nobody dries your tears
as you humbly weep and weep.
Galicia, you have no fatherland,
you live alone in the world,
and your prolific offspring
scatters in wandering hordes
while, sad and alone,
prostrate on the green carpet,
you beg hope from the sea,
you implore God for hope.
And so although in their festive way
the pipes might sound happy,
I can tell you:
the pipes don't sing – they weep.

V

'Have hope, Galicia, have hope.'
How comforting is this cry!
May God reward you, good poet,
but it's a crazy hope:
before the time comes
for such good fortune,
before Galicia climbs
with the cross that burdens her shoulders
up that arduous road
that touches the depths of the abysses,
perhaps, weary and thirsty,
she will die of anguish.
May God reward you, good poet,
for that hope of glory
which, issuing from your breast,
crowns the Virgin-martyr,
and may this be the compensation
for such deep, bitter griefs.
May He reward you for this sad song
that tells of our sorrows,
for only you... you among so many!
remember our sufferings.
Worthy decision of a genius,
a pure, generous soul!
And when away in Castile
you hear the Galician pipes,
just ask your heart:

you'll see that it replies
the Galician pipes
don't sing – they weep.

From Follas Novas (New Leaves), *1880*

Diredes d'estos versos, y é verdade...

Diredes d'estos versos, y é verdade,
Que tên estrana insólita harmonía,
Que n'eles as ideas brilan pálidas
    Cal errantes muxicas
    Qu'estalan por instantes,
    Que desparecen xiña,
Que s'asomellan â parruma incerta
Que voltexa n'o fondo d'as curtiñas,
Y ó susurro monótono d'os pinos
    D'a veira-mar bravía.

Eu direivos tan sô, qu'os meus cantares
Asi sân en confuso d'alma miña,
Como say d'as profundas carballeiras
    Ô comezar d'o día,
    Romor que non se sabe
    S'é rebuldar d'as brisas,
Si son beixos d'as frores,
S'agrestes, misteirosas harmonías
Que n'este mundo triste
    O camiño d'o ceu buscan perdidas.

You will all say of these verses, and it's true...

You will all say of these verses, and it's true,
that they have a strange, uncommon harmony,
that in them pale ideas glow
    like floating cinders
    which crackle every so often,
    which soon vanish,
that they're like the fitful mist
which wreathes at the end of cottage gardens,
and like the monotone whispering of the pines
    at the wild edge of the sea.

I shall only tell you that my songs
come out like that, in a muddle, from my soul,
just as there comes, from the deep oak forests
    at the beginning of the day,
      a murmuring, and no one knows
      whether it is breezes frolicking,
flowers kissing,
or rustic, mysterious harmonies
that, lost in this sad world,
    search for the way to heaven.

Un-ha vez tiven un cravo...

    Un-ha vez tiven un cravo
    Cravado no corazon,
Y eu non m'acordo xa s'era aquel cravo,
    D'ouro, de ferro ou d'amor.
Soyo sei que me fixo un mal tan fondo,
    Que tanto m'atormentou,
Qu'eu dia e noite sen cesar choraba
Cal chorou Madanela na Paixon.
    –Señor, que todo o podedes,
    Pedinlle un-ha vez á Dios,
Daime valor par'arrincar d'un golpe
    Cravo de tal condicion.
    E doumo Dios, e arrinqueino,
    Mais... ¿quen pensara?... Despois
    Xa non sentin mais tormentos
    Nin souben qu'era delor;
Soupen sô, que non sei que me faltaba
    En donde o cravo faltou,
E seica, seica tiven soidades
    D'aquela pena... ¡Bon Dios!
Este barro mortal qu'e envolve o esprito
    ¡Quen'o entenderá, Señor!...

Once I had a nail...

    Once I had a nail
    nailed into my heart,
and I no longer remember if that nail
    was of gold, of iron or of love.
I only know it did me such deep harm,

it tormented me so much,
that I wept day and night, unceasingly,
as Mary Magdalene wept at the Passion.
  'Lord, who art all-powerful,'
  once I beseeched God,
'give me strength to tear out
  such a harmful nail, once and for all.'
  And God gave it me, and I tore it out;
  but who would have thought it? Afterwards
  I felt no more torments
  and I knew no more pain;
I only know I missed I know not what,
  where the nail was missing,
and perhaps, perhaps, I felt sadlonging
  for that pain ... Good God!
This mortal clay that enwraps the spirit—
  who can understand it, Lord...!

Oxe ou mañan, ¿quen pode dicir cando?...

Oxe ou mañan, ¿quen pode dicir cando?
  Pero quisais moy logo,
Viranme á despertar, y en vez d'un vivo,
  Atoparán un morto.

O rededor de min, levantaranse
  Xemidos dolorosos,
Ayes d'angustia, choros d'os meus fillos,
  D'os meus filliños orfos.

Y eu sen calor, sin movemento, fría,
  Muda, insensibre á todo,
Así estarei cal me deixare a morte
  Ó helarme c'o seu sopro.

E para sempre ¡Adios, cant'eu quería!
  ¡Que terrible abandono!
  Antre cantos sarcasmos hay,
  Ha d'haber, e houvo,
Non vin ningun qu'abata mais os vivos
Qu'ó d'a humilde quietú d'un corpo morto.

Today or tomorrow, who can say when?...

Today or tomorrow, who can say when?
    but perhaps very soon,
they'll come to awake me, and instead of someone living
    they'll find someone dead.

Around me will be raised
    grief-stricken wails,
cries of anguish, lamentations of my children,
    my little motherless children.

And I without warmth, without movement, cold,
    silent, senseless to everything,
that's how I'll be, as death will leave me
    when it freezes me with its breath.

And for ever goodbye to all I loved!
    Such a terrible parting!
    Of all the sarcasms that exist,
    will exist and have existed,
I have not seen any that depress the living
more than the humble stillness of the dead.

¡Silencio!

      ¡Silencio!
    A man nerviosa e palpitante ó seo,
As niebras n'os meus ollos condensadas,
Con un mundo de dudas n'os sentidos
Y-un mundo de tormentos n'as entrañas;
    Sentindo como loitan,
    En sin igual batalla,
Inmortales deseios que atormentan,
    E rencores que matan,
    Mollo n'a propia sangre a dura pruma
    Rompendo a vena inchada,
Y escribo... escribo... ¿para qué? ¡Volvede
    Ô mais fondo da yalma,
    Tempestosas imaxes!
Ide á morar c'as mortas remembranzas;
Qu'a man tembrosa n'o papel sô escriba
¡Palabras, e palabras, e palabras!

Da idea a forma inmaculada e pura
    ¿Donde quedou velada?

Silence!

            Silence!
    With nervous hand and throbbing breast,
with mists condensed upon my eyes,
with a world of doubts in my senses
and a world of torments in my bowels,
        sensing how a battle is being fought,
        a supreme battle,
between immortal desires that torment me
        and rancours that kill me,
I dip my hard pen into my blood,
        breaking open the swollen vein,
and I write..., I write..., to what purpose? Go back
        to the depths of my soul,
        stormy images!
Go and dwell with my dead memories!
To think that the trembling hand only writes on paper
words, and words, and words!
The immaculate, pure form of the idea –
        where has that been hidden?

Cando penso que te fuches...

    Cando penso que te fuches,
Negra sombra que m'asombras,
Ô pé d'os meus cabezales
Tornas facéndome mofa.
    Cando maxino qu'ês ida,
N'o mesmo sol te m'amostras,
Y eres a estrela que brila,
Y eres o vento que zóa.
    Si cantan, ês tí que cantas,
Si choran ês tí que choras,
Y-ês o marmurio d'o rio,
Y-ês a noite, y ês a aurora.
    En todo estás e tí ês todo,
Pra min y en min mesma moras,
Nin m'abandonarás nunca,
Sombra que sempre m'asombras.

Just when I think that you have gone...

Just when I think that you have gone,
pitch-black shadow that's scaring me,
you come back to my pillow-side,
to taunt me with your mockery.
　　When I imagine that you've left,
in the sun you appear to me,
and you're the star that shines its light,
and you're the wind that hums and drones.
　　There's singing, and it's you who sings;
there's weeping, and it's you who weeps;
and you're the murmur of the brook,
and you're the night, and you're the dawn.
　　You are in all and you are all,
for me and in my self you dwell,
and never will you leave me be,
black shadow always scaring me.

¡Nin as escuras!

I

– Tod'está negro, as sombras envolven á vereda,
E nin o ceu ten ollos, nin o pinar ten lengua.

¡Vamos! D'o que hay oculto, ¿quen midéu as fonduras?
¡Alma n'habrá que sepa!... ¡ven!... á noit'está escura.

– ¿Escura?... mais relumbra non sei que luz traidora...
– É un-ha estrela que brila, n'as auguas bulidoras.

– ¿E non oyes que runxe algo ond'aquel herbal?
– É o vento que anda tolo, corrend'antr'á follax.

– Escoita, sinto pasos, e asoma seica un bulto...
– ¡S'é un vivo, matarémolo! non fala s'é difunto.

Mais aqui ond'este cómaro, hai un-ha cova fonda,
Ven, e santos ou deños, que nos atopen óra.

II

¿A donde irei conmigo? ¿donde m'esconderei?
Que xa ninguen me vexa y eu non veixa á ninguen?

A luz d'o dia asómbrame, pásmame a d'as estrelas.
Y as olladas d'os homes, n'a yalma me penetran.

Y é que ó que dentro levo de min, penso que ô rostro
Me sai, cal sai d'o mare, ô cabo un corpo morto.

¡Houbera, e que saira!... mais non, dentro te levo:
Fantasma pavoroso d'os meus remordementos!

Not even in the dark!

I
'All is blackness, shadows envelop the path,
and neither does the sky have eyes, nor the pine-grove a tongue.

Come on! Who's ever measured the depths of what's hidden?
Not a soul will know...! The night is dark.'

'Dark...? But there's some kind of treacherous light shining...'
'It's a star gleaming in the restless water.'

'And can't you hear something rustling in those grasses?'
'It's the wind running riot amongst the leaves.'

'Listen, I hear footsteps, and I think a shape's appearing...'
'If it's alive, we'll kill it; it won't speak if it's dead!

But here in this ridge there's a deep hollow:
come, and whether saints or devils, let them try and find us now.'

II
Where shall I take myself? Where shall I hide
so that nobody sees me and I see nobody?

The light of day scares me, the light of stars terrifies me,
and men's looks pierce my very soul.

And what I carry within me – I believe it comes out
On to my face, as a corpse is eventually washed up on the shore.

If only, once there, it had come out...! But no: I carry you in me,
horrifying phantom of my remorse!

¡Prá á Habana!

I

Venderonll'os bois,
Venderonll'as vacas,
O pote d'o caldo
Y á manta d'a cama.
    Venderonlle ó carro
Y as leiras que tiña,
Deixarono soyo
C'o á roupa vestida.
    –María, eu son mozo,
Pedir non m'é dado,
Eu vou pó-lo mundo
Pra ver de ganalo.
    Galicia está probe,
Y á Habana me vou...
¡Adios, adios, prendas
D'o meu corazon!

II

Cando ninguen os mira
Vénse rostros nubrados e sombrisos,
Homes qu'erran cal sombras voltexantes
Por veigas e campíos.
    Un, enriva d'un cómaro
Séntase caviloso e pensativo,
Outro, ó pe d'un carballo, queda imóvil
C'o á vista levantada hácia ó infinito.
    Algun cabo d'a fronte reclinado
Parés qu'escoita atento o murmurio
D'augua que cai, e isala ẍordamente
Tristísimos sospiros.
    ¡Van á deixá-la patria!...
Forzoso, mais supremo sacrificio.
A miseria está negra en torno d'eles
¡Ay! iy adiant'está o abismo!...

III

O mar castiga bravamente as penas,
E contr'as bandas d'o vapor se rompen
As irritadas ondas
D'o Cántabro salobre.

Chilan as gaviotas
¡Alá lonxe!... ¡moy lonxe!
N'a prácida riveira solitaria
Que convida ó descanso y ôs amores.
    De humanos séres á compauta linea
Que brila ô sol, adiántase e retórcese,
Mais preto, e lentamente as curvas sigue
D'o murallón antigo d'o Parrote.
    O corazón apértase d'angustia,
Óyense risas, xuramentos s'oyen,
Y as brasfemias s'axuntan c'os sospiros...
¿Onde van eses homes?
    Dentro d'un mes n'o simiterio imenso
D'a Habana, ou n'os seus bosques,
Ide á ver que foy d'eles...
¡N'o eterno olvido para sempre dormen!...
¡Probes nais que os criaron,
Y as que os agardan amorosas, probes!

                    IV
    – Ánimo, compañeiros
Tod'â terra é d'os homes.
Aquel que non veu nunca mais que a propria
A iñorancia o consome.
¡Animo! A quen se muda Dio-lo axuda!
¡E anque ora vamos de Galicia lonxe,
Verés dêsque tornemos
O que medrano os robres!
Mañán é o día grande ¡â mar amigos!
¡Mañán, Dios nos acoche!
    ¡N'o sembrante á alegría,
N'o corazón o esforzo,
Y a campana armoniosa d'a esperanza,
Lonxe, tocando á morto!

                    V
    Este vaise y aquel vaise
E todos, todos se van,
Galicia, sin homes quedas
Que te poidan traballar.
Tes en cambio orfos e orfas
E campos de soledad,
E nais que non teñen fillos

E fillos que non tên pais.
E tês corazóns que sufren
Longas ausencias mortás,
Viudas de vivos e mortos
Que ninguen consolará.

Off to Havana!

I

    They've sold his oxen,
they've sold his cows,
his cooking pot
and the blanket from his bed.
    They've sold his cart
and the plots he owned;
they've left him only
the clothes he wore.
    'María, I'm young,
begging isn't for me;
I'm going out into the world
to try and earn my living.
    Galicia is poor,
and I'm off to Havana...
Goodbye, goodbye, darlings
of my heart.'

II

    When no one is looking,
faces are clouded and dark,
men who wander like aimless shadows
in valleys and meadows.
    One, on a ridge between plots,
sits plunged in brooding thought;
another, under an oak, stands motionless,
his eyes raised towards infinity.
    One man, lying near the spring,
seems to harken to the murmuring
of the falling water, and breathes
sad, sad sighs.
    They are about to leave their homeland...!
An inevitable yet supreme sacrifice.
Penury is black around them,
and before them is the abyss...!

III

The sea batters the rocks,
and against the side of the steamer crash
the angry waves
of the briny Biscay Bay.
　　The seagulls scream
over there, far away...! far, far away!
by the placid, lonely shore
that fosters repose and love.
　　The dense line of human beings
that shines in the sun winds its way onwards,
but closely and slowly it follows the curves
of the old Parrote bastion wall.
　　The heart shrinks in anguish,
laughs are heard, oaths are heard,
and blasphemies mingle with sighs...
Where are these men going?
　　In one month's time, in the vast cemetery
of Havana, or in its forests,
go and see what became of them...
In eternal oblivion they sleep for ever!
How pitiful the mothers who raised them,
and the women who lovingly await them, how pitiful!

IV

　　'Cheer up, my companions!
The whole earth belongs to men.
He who has never seen more than his own land
is consumed by ignorance.
Cheer up! God improves the man who moves!
And even though we're going far from Galicia,
you'll see, when we return,
how much the oak trees will have grown!
Tomorrow's the big day: off to sea, my friends!
Tomorrow, may God prosper us!'
　　On his face, joy;
in his heart, endeavour;
and the harmonious bell of hope,
far away, tolling!

V

　　This man leaves and that man leaves,
and they all leave, every one.

Galicia, you're left without men
who could work you.
Instead you have orphan boys and girls
and fields of solitude,
and mothers who have no sons
and sons who have no fathers.
And you have hearts that suffer
long mortal absences,
widows of live men and of dead men
whom nobody will comfort.

Tecin soya á miña tea...

Tecin soya á miña tea,
Sembrey soya o meu nabal,
Soya vou por leña ô monte,
Soya á vexo arder n'o lar.
Nin n'a fonte nin n'o prado
Asi morra c'o a carráx
El non ha de virm'á erguer,
El xa non me pousará.
¡Que tristeza! o vento soa,
Canta o grilo ô seu compás...
Ferbe o pote... mais, meu caldo,
Soiña t'hey de cear.
Cala rula, os teus arrulos
Ganas de morrer me dan,
Cala grilo, que si cantas
Sinto negras soïdás.
O meu homiño perdeuse,
Ninguen sabe en onde vay...
Anduriña que pasaches
Con él as ondas d'o mar,
Anduriña, voa, voa,
Ven e dime en ond'está.

Alone I wove my cloth...

Alone I wove my cloth,
alone I sowed my turnip-patch
alone I go to the forest for firewood,
alone I watch it burn in the hearth.
Neither by the spring nor in the meadows

– may I die with the fury of it –
will he come to raise me up,
will he come to lay me down.
Such sorrow! The wind thrums,
the cricket sings to its rhythm,
the pot is boiling... and yet, O broth of mine,
all alone I shall sup you.
Hush, dove – your cooing
makes me want to die;
hush, cricket – for if you sing,
I feel dark sadlongings.
My darling man is lost,
nobody knows where he is...
O swallow that went with him
over the waves of the sea;
O swallow, fly, fly to me,
come and tell me where he is.

Vamos bebendo

– Teño tres pitas brancas
    E un galo negro,
Que han de poñer bos ovos,
    Andand'o tempo.
Y hei de vende-los caros
    Po-lo Xaneiro.
Y hei de xuntá-los cartos
    Para un mantelo,
Y heino de levar posto
    No casamento,
Y hei...
        – Pois mira, Marica,
    Vai por un neto
Qu'antramentas non quitas
    Eses cerellos,
Y as pitas van medrando
    C'o galo negro,
Para poñe-los ovos,
    E todo aquelo
do Xaneiro, d'os cartos,
Y o casamento,
Miña prenda da yalma
    ¡Vamos bebendo!

Let's have a drink

'I've got three white chickens
　　and a black cock,
and they'll lay good eggs
　　in due course;
and I'll sell them dear
　　in January;
and I'll save money
　　for a mantilla;
and I'll wear it
　　at our wedding;
and I'll...'
　　　　　　　　'Well look you here, Marica,
　　just go for a jugful,
and while you're getting together
　　all those glad-rags,
and the chickens are growing
　　with the black cock,
to lay eggs,
　　and all that stuff
about January, money
　　and the wedding,
my dearest darling,
　　let's have a drink!'

Conto galego, *1864*

Un día de inverno ó caer da tarde, dous amigos que eran amigos desde a escola, e
que contaban de anos o maldito número de tres veces dez, camiñaban a bon paso
un sobre unha mula branca, gorda e de redondas ancas, e outro enriba dos seus pés
que non parecían asañarse das pasadas lixeiras que lles facía dar seu dono.

O de a pé corría tanto coma o dacabalo, que vendo a suor que lle corría ó seu
compañeiro pola fronte e as puntas dos cabelos, díxolle:

– ¿E ti, Lourenzo, por que non mercas un cometoxos que te leve e te traia por
estes camiños de Deus?, que esto de andar leguas a pé por montes e areais é bo para
os cans.

– ¡Cometoxos! Anda e que os monten aqueles para quen se fixeron, que non é
Lourenzo. Cabalo grande, ande ou non ande, e xa que grande non o podo ter, sen
el me quedo e sírvome dos meus pés que nin comen, nin beben, nin lles fan mester
arreos.

– Verdade é que o teu modo de camiñar é máis barato que ningún, ¡nego de
min!, que agora teño que pagar o portádego só porque vou en besta, e non coma ti,

nestes pés que Deus me deu. Pero ... así como así, gusto de andar as xornadas en pernas alleas para que as dun non cansen, e xa o dixen: debías mercar un farroupeiro para o teu descanso. Mais ti fas como o outro: hoxe o gano, hoxe o como, que mañá Deus dirá. Nin tes arrello nin cousa que o valla; gústanche os birbirichos e as birbiricheiras, o viño do Ribeiro e as ostras do Carril. ¡Lourenzo!, debías casar, que ó fin o tempo vai andando, os anos corren, e un pobre dun home faise vello e cóbrese de pelos brancos antes de que poida ter manta na cama, e aforrar para unha ocasión; e esto, Lourenzo, non se fai sen muller que teña man da casa e garde o diñeiro que un gana.

– Boi solto, ben se lambe.

– ¡O vento!, esas sonche faladurías. Ó derradeiro, ¿para que os homes naceron, se non é para axuntarse coas mulleres, fillo da túa nai? (Lourenzo tose). Seica te constipaches co resío do serán, malo de ti. (Lourenzo volve tusir). Léveme Deus se non é certo, e tanto non tusiras, se agora viñeses á carranchaperna, enriba dun farroupeiro.

– ¡Constipado eu! Non o estiven na miña vida, e penso que agora tampouco. Pero... sempre que se me fala de casar, dáme unha tose que... ¡hem!... ¡hem!... e seica esto non é bo sinal. ¿Non cho parece, Xan?

– O que me parece é que es rabudo coma as uvas de cacho, e eso vénche xa da nacenza, que non polo ben que te estimo deixo de coñecer que es atravesado coma os cangrexos. Nin podo adiviñar por qué falas mal das mulleres que tan ben te queren, e que te arrolan nas fiadas e nas festas, coma a fillo de rei, e sabendo que túa nai foi muller, e que se túa nai non fora ti non viñeras ó mundo coma cada un de tantos.

– Nin moito se perdera anque nunca acá chegara. Que mellor que suando polos camiños para ganar o pan da boca, e mellor que rechinar nas festas e non nas festas con meniñas que caras se venden sen valer un chavo, enganando os homes, estaría aló na mente de Deus.

– ¡Diancre de home!, que mesmo ás veces penso se es daqueles que saúdan o crego só porque non digan. E pois ti es dono de dicir canto queiras, pero eu tamén che digo que me fai falla un acheguiño, e que me vou casar antes da festa, así Deus me dea saúde.

– E permita El-Señor que non súes moito, Xan, anque agora é inverno, que entonces si que inda tusirás máis ca min, cando de casar me falan. E advírtoche que teñas tino de non matar carneiros na festa, que é mal encomezo para un casado, por aquelo dos cornos retortos que se guindan ó pé da porta, e xa se sabe que un mal tira por outro. ¡Deus nos libre!

– ¿E ti queres saber que xa me van parecendo contos de vella, todo eso que se fala de cornos, e da maldade das mulleres?, pois cando nesta nosa terra se dá en dicir que un can rabiou, sexa certo ou non sexa, corre a bóla e mátase o can. Mais eu por min che aseguro que non atopei nunca muller solteira que non se fixese moi rogada, nin casada que ó seu home comigo faltase; e paréceme que aínda non fago tan mal rapaz, anque o dicilo sexa fachenda.

– E que eso vai no axeitarse, e ti seica non acertaches, Xan; que o demais, como un home queira, non queda can tras palleiro. Eu cho digo, non hai neste mundo máis muller boa para os homes, que aquela que os pariu, e así arrenega delas coma do demo. Xan, que a muller demo é, segundo di non sei qué santo moi sabido; e ó demo, ata a cruz lle fai os cornos de lonxe.

– Volta cos cornos.

– É tan sabido que se tanto mal che fai nomealos é porque xa che dan sombra dende o tellado da que ha de ser túa muller.

– ¡Seica me queres aqueloutrare! Pouco a pouco, Lourenzo, que nin debes falar así de quen non coñeces, nin tódalas mulleres han de ter o ollo alegre, que de moitas eu sei por quen se puidera poñer, non unha, senón cen vidas.

– O dito, dito queda, que cando eu falo é con conciencia; e repítoche que sendo muller, non quedo por ningunha anque sexa condesa ou de sangue nobre, como soen dicir, que unhas e outras foron feitas dunha mesma masa e coxean do mesmo pé. Deus che mas libre do meu lar, que agora no lar alleo aínda non as cuspo.

– ¡Ah! ladrón da honra allea, lévete o deño se eu quixera que cuspiñases na do meu, que o pensamento de que quizais terei que manter muller para un rabudo coma ti, faime pór os cabelos dereitos, e o entendemento pensatible. Pero... falemos claros, Lourenzo, coma bos compañeiros que somos. Ti es máis listo ca min, ben o vexo, e por onde andes sabes te amañar que admira, mentres que eu me quedo ó pé do lume, vendo como o pote ferve e cantan os grilos. O conto vai no amaño... pero esto de que as has de botar todas nunha manada, sen deixar unha para min, vállanme tódolos santos que me fai suar. ¡Vaia!, dime que aínda viches mulleres boas, e que non todas lle saben poñer a un home honrado os cornos na testa.

– Todas, Xan ... todas, e para os Xans, aínda máis; que mesmo parece que o nome as atenta.

– ¡Condenicado de min, que seica é certo! Pero meu pai e miña nai casáronse e eu tamén quero casar, que mesmo se me van os ollos cando vexo ó anoitecido un matrimonio que fala paseniño sentado á porta da eira, mentres corren os meniños á luz do luar por embaixo das figueiras.

– ¡O aire, o aire!, e déixate de faladurías. Paseniño, que paseniño tamén se dan beliscos e rabuñadas, e paseniño se fan as figas.

– En verdade, malo me vai parecendo o casoiro, pero moito me temo que a afección non me faga prevaricar; mais sempre que case, casarei cunha do meu tempo, cheía de carnes, con xuízo e facendosa, que poida que neso non haxa tanto mal... ¿Que me dis?

– Que es terco coma unha burra. Ti te-lo deño, Xan, e agora estache facendo as cóchegas co casoiro. Pero ten entendido que non hai volta senón que Deus o mande, que tratándose daquelo da fraqueza das mulleres, todas deitan coma testas, e caen coma se non tivesen pés.

Así falando, Xan e Lourenzo ían chegando a cerca dun lugar; e como xa de lonxe empezasen a sentir berros e choros, despois de subiren a un alto, por saber o que aló pasaba, viron que era un enterro, e a un rapaz que viña polo camiño preguntáronlle polo morto, e respondeulles que era home dunha muller que inda moza quedaba viúva e sen fillos, que nunca tivera, e que o morto non era nativo daquela aldea, pero que tiña noutra herdeiros.

Foise o rapaz, e Lourenzo chegándose a Xan díxolle entonces:

– ¿E ti queres, Xan, que che faga ver o que son as mulleres, que agora a ocasión é boa?

– ¿E pois como?

– Facendo que esa viúva, que non sei quén é, nin vin na miña vida, me dea nesta mesma noite palabra de casamento para de aquí a un mes.

– ¿E ti estás cordo, Lourenzo?

– Máis ca ti, Xan; ¿queres ou non queres?

– E pois ben, tolo. Vamos apostar, e se ganas, perdo a miña mula branca que herdei de meu pai logo fará un ano, e que a estimo por isto, e por ser boa, coma as niñas dos ollos. Curareime entonces do mal de casoiro: pero se ti perdes, tes que mercar un parroufeiro e non volver falar mal das mulleres, miñas xoias, que aínda as quero máis que á miña muliña branca.

– Apostado. Baixa, pois, da mula e fai desde agora todo o que che eu diga sen chiar, e ata mañá pola fresca, nin ti es Xan, nin eu Lourenzo, senón que ti es meu criado, e eu son teu amo. Agora ven tras min tendo conta da mula, que eu irei diante, e di a todo amén.

Meu dito, meu feito.

Lourenzo tirou diante, e Xan botouse a pé, indo detrás, coa mula polas bridas que eran novas así coma os demais arreos, e metían moita pantalla.

Ó mesmo tempo que eles ían chegando ó Camposanto, ía chegando tamén o enterro, rompendo a marcha o estandarte negro e algo furado da parroquia, o crego e as mulleres que lle facían o pranto, turrando polos pelos como se fosen cousa allea, berrando ata enroucar, e agarrándose á tomba de tal maneira que non deixaban andar ós que a levaban.

– ¡Ai, Antón! ¡Antón!, dicía unha, poñéndose coma a Madanela, coas mans encruzadas enriba da cabeza. Antón, meu amigo, que sempre me dicías "¡Adeus, Mariquiña!" cando me atopabas no camiño. ¡Adeus, Antón, que xa non te verei máis!

E outra indo arrastro detrás da caixa, e pegando en si, dicía tamén:

– ¿Onde estás, Antón, que xa non me falas? Antón, malpocadiño, que che fixeron as miñas mans uns calzóns de lenzo cru e non os puxeches. Antón; ¿quen ha de pór agora a túa chaqueta nova e os teus calzóns, Antón?

E a viúva, e unhas sobriñas da viúva, todas cubertas de bágoas, vestidas de loito, e os periquitos desfeitos de tanto turrar por eles, e os panos desatados, berraban aínda máis; sobre todo a viúva, que indo de cando en cando meterse debaixo da mesma tomba, de onde a tiñan que arrincar por forza, dicía:

– ¡Ai, meu tío! ¡Ai, meu tío, bonito coma unha prata, e roxiño coma un ouro, que cedo che vai come-la terra as túas carniñas de manteiga! ¡E ti vaste, meu tío! ¿Ti vaste? ¿E quen será agora o meu acheguiño, e quen me dirá, como me dicías ti, meu ben: "Come, Margaridiña, come para engordar, que o que é teu é meu. Margarida, e se ti coxeas, tamén a min me parece que estou coxo." ¡Adeus, meu tío, que xa nunca máis durmiremos xuntiños nun leito! ¡Quen me dera ir contigo na tomba, Antón, meu tío que ó fin contigo, miña xoíña, entérrase o meu corazón!

Así a viuviña se desdichaba seguindo ó morto, cando de repente, meténdose Lourenzo entre as mulleres cubertos os ollos cun pano, e saloucando como se lle saíse da alma, exclamou berrando aínda máis que as do pranto.

– ¡Ai, meu tío!, ¡ai, meu tío, que agora vexo ir mortiño nesa tomba! Nunca eu aquí viñera para non te atopar vivo, e non é polo testamento que fixeches en favor meu, deixándome por herdeiro de canto tes, polo que eu tanto te choro, que sempre te quixen coma a pai, e esto de que me habías de chamar para despedirte de min e que te hei de ver xa morto, párteme as cordas do corazón. ¡Ai, meu tío! ¡ai, meu tío!, que mesmo morro coa pena.

Cando esto oíron tódalas do pranto, puñeron arredor de Lourenzo, que mesmo se desfacía a uña de tanta dor como parecía ter.

– ¿E logo ti como te chamas, meu fillo? – preguntáronlle moi compadecidas del.

– Eu chámome Andruco, e son sobriño do meu tío, que me deixou por herdeiro e me mandou chamar por unha carta para se despedir de min antes de morrer; pero como tiven que andar moita terra, xa só o podo ver na tomba, ¡Ai, meu tío! ¡Ai, meu tío!

– ¿E ti de onde es, mozo?

– Eu son da terra do meu tío, volveu dicir Lourenzo, saloucando ata córtarselle a fala.

– ¿E teu tío de onde era?

– Meu tío era da miña terra.

E sen que o puidesen quitar desto, Lourenzo, proseguindo co pranto, foise achegando á viuviña, que aínda que por entre as bágoas que a cubrían puido albiscar aquel mozo garrido que tanto choraba polo seu tío. Despois que se viron xuntos, logo lle dixo Lourenzo que era o herdeiro do defunto, e ela mirouno con moi bos ollos, e acabado o enterro, díxolle que tiña que ir con ela á súa casa, que non era xusto parase noutra o sobriño do seu home, e que así chorarían xuntos a súa desgracia.

– Desgracia moita. ¡Ai, meu tío! – dixo Lourenzo –; pero… consoládevos que co que el me deixou conto facerlle dicir moitas misas pola alma, para que el descanse e poidamos ter nós tamén maior consolo acá na terra, que ó fin, ña tía, Deus mándanos ter paciencia cos traballos, e… que queiras que non queiras, como dixo o outro, a terriña cae enriba dos corpiños mortos, e…, ¿que hai que facer?… nós tamén temos que ir, que así é o mundo.

Así falando e chorando, tornaron camiño da casa da viúva, e Xan que ía detrás coa mula, e que nun principio non entendera nin chisca do que quería facer Lourenzo, comezou a enxergar, e pasoulle así polas carnes unha especie de calafrío, pensando se iría perder a súa muliña branca. Anque ó ver a dor e as bágoas da viuviña, que non lle deixaban de correr a fío pola cara aflixida, volveu ter confianza en

Deus e nas mulleres a quen tan ben quería.

– E vós, ña tía, ¿terés un sitiño para meter esta mula e o meu criado, que un e outro de tanto camiñar veñen cansados coma raposos?

– Todo o terei para vós, sobriño do meu tío, que mesmo con vervos paréceme que o estou vendo, e sérveme de moito consolo.

"Dencho coa viuviña, os consolos que atopa", murmurou Xan para si metendo a mula no presebe. "Pero disto a casar – engadiu contento de si mesmo –, aínda hai la mar."

E con esta esperanza púxose a comer con moitas ganas un bo anaco de lacón, que a viúva lle deu mollándoo cunha cunca de viño do Ribeiro que ardía nun candil, e que lle alegrou a pestana; mentres tía e sobriño estaban aló enriba no sobrado, falando da herdanza e do morto cos que os acompañaban.

Desta maneira pasou o día e chegou a noite, e quedaron sós na casa a viúva, Lourenzo e Xan, que desque viu cerrar as portas estivo á axexa, co corazón posto na muliña branca, a alma en Lourenzo, e a esperanza en Deus, que non era para menos. E non sen pena viu como a viúva e Lourenzo foron ceando, entre as bágoas, uns bocados de porco e de vaca que puñan medo ós cristiáns, e uns xarros de viño que foran capaces de dar ánimos ó peito máis angustiado. Pero ó mesmo tempo nada se falaba do particular, e Xan non podía adiviñar como se axeitaría Lourenzo para ganar a aposta que vía por súa.

Ó fin trataron de se ir deitar, e a Xan puxéronselle os cabelos dereitos, cando viu que en toda a casa non había máis que a cama do matrimonio e que a viúva tanto petelexou para que Lourenzo se deitase nela, que aquel tivo que obedecer, indo ela, envolta nun mantelo, meterse detrás dun taboado que no sobrado había.

Xan, coa alma nun fío, viu desde o faiado, onde lle botaran unhas pallas, como a viúva matou o candil e todo quedou ás escuras.

– Seica quedarás comigo, miña muliña branca, e abofé que te vin perdida, exclamou entonces; ó fin as mulleres foron feitas dunha nosa costela e algo han de ter de bo. Sálvame, viuviña, sálvame deste aperto, que inda serei capaz de casar contigo.

Deste modo falaba Xan para si, anque ó mesmo tempo non podía cerrar ollo, que a cada paso lle parecía que runxían as pallas.

Así pasou unha hora longa, en que Xan, contento, xa ía durmir descoidado, cando de pronto oíu, primeiro un suspiro e despois outro, cal se aqueles suspiros fosen de alma do outro mundo; estremeceuse Xan e ergueuse para escoitar mellor.

– ¡Ai, meu tío, meu tío! – dixo entonces a viuviña –; ¡que fría estou neste taboado, pero máis frío estás ti, meu tío, nesa terriña que te vai comer!

– ¡Ai, meu tío, meu tío! – exclamou Lourenzo da outra banda, como se falase consigo mesmo –; ¡canto me acordo de ti, que eu estou no quente e ti no Camposanto nun leito de terra onde xa non tes compañía!

– ¡Ai, Antonciño! – volveu dicir a viúva –, que será de ti naquel burato, meu queridiño, cando eu que estou baixo cuberto, ¡bu, bu, bu!... ¡que frío vai! ¡Tremo coma se tivese a perlesía! ¡bu, bu, bu!

– ¡Miña tía!

– ¿E seica non dormes, meu sobriño?

– E seica vós tampouco, ña tía, que vos sinto tremer coma unha vara verde.

– ¿Como queres ti que durma, acordándome nesta noite de xeada do teu tío, que agora dorme no Camposanto, frío coma a neve, cando se el vivise durmiriamos ambos quentiños nese leito onde ti estás?

– ¿E non podiades vós poñervos aquí nun ladiño, anque fose envolta no mantelo como estades, que entre tía e sobriño é o mesmo que entre nai e fillo, e aínda máis habendo necesidade coma agora, xa que non querés que eu vaia durmir ó chan, que mesmo é capaz de darvos un flato coa dor e co frío, e é pecado, ña tía, tentar contra a saúde?

– Deixa, meu fillo, deixa, que anque penso que mal non houbera en que eu me deitase ó lado dun sobriño coma ti, envolta no mantelo e por riba da roupa, estando como estou tremendo, ¡bu, bu, bu!... quérome ir afacendo, que moitas destas noites han de vir para min no mundo, que se antes fun rica e casada, agora son viúva e pobre, e canto tiven meu, agora teu é, que a min non me queda máis que o ceo e a terra.

– E... pois, miña tía... Aquí para entre dous pecadores, e sen que ninguén nos oia máis que Deus, vouvos dicir que eu sei dun home rico e do sangue do voso defuntiño, que se vós quixerades, tomaríavos por muller.

– Cala, sobriño, e nome falés doutro home... que inda parece que o que tiven está vivo.

– Deixá, miña tía, que así non perderedes nin casa, nin leito, nin facenda, que é moito perder dunha vez; sen contar co meu tío, a quen lle hei de dicir tantas misas coma días ten o ano para que descanse e non vos veña chamar nas noites de inverno. Así el estará aló ben, e vós aquí; e se el vivise, non outra cousa vos aconsellara, senón que tomarades outra vez home do seu sangue, xa que a xente do seu sangue lle deixou o que el e vós comestes xuntos na súa vida.

– E seica tes razón, meu sobriño, pero..., ¿se este era o teu pensamento, Antón, meu tío por qué no me dixeches antes de morrer, que entonces eu o fixera anque fose contra vontade, só por te servir?

– Pola miña conta, ña tía, que se meu tío nada vos dixo, foi porque se lle esqueceu co conto das agonías, e non vos estrañe que a calquera lle pasara outro tanto.

– Tes razón, tes, a morte é moi negra, e naquela hora se esquece. ¡Ai, meu tío, meu tío! ¿Que non fixera eu por che dar gusto? ¡Bu, bu, bu! ¡que frío vai!

– Vinde para aquí, que se non vos asañás, direivos que eu son o que vos quere por muller.

– ¿Ti que me dis, home? Pero a ver que o adiviñe logo, que só un sobriño do meu tío lle quixera cumprir así a vontade...

– Pero a ser, tiña que ser de aquí a un mes, que despois teño que ir a Cais, en busca doutra herdanza, e quixera que antes quedarades outra vez dona do que foi voso. O que ha de ser, sexa logo, que ó fin meu tío hao de estar desexando desde a tomba.

– ¡Ai, meu tío, meu tío, que sobriño che deu Deus, que mesmo de oílo paréceme que te estou oíndo! Pero..., meu fillo..., é aínda moi cedo, e anque ti e mais eu nos volveramos casar coa intención de lle facer honra e recordar o defunto, o mundo murmura... e...

– Deixavos do mundo, que casaremos en segredo e ninguén o saberá.

– E pois ben, meu sobriño, e só porque es de sangue do meu tío, e xa que me dis que se ha de alegrar na tomba de vernos xuntos..., co demais..., ¡ai!, Deus me valla ..., ¡eu queríalle moito a meu tío!, ¡bu, bu, bu!... ¡como xea!

– Vinde para onda min envolta no mantelo, que non é pecado, xa que habés de ser miña muller.

– Pero... aínda non a son, meniño, e teño remorsos... ¡Bu, bu, bu! ¡Que flato me dá pola cabeza e polo corazón!

– Ña tía, vinde, e deixavos de atentar contra a saúde, que se algo pecasedes antes de casar, témonos que confesar.

– Irei, logo..., irei, que necesito un pouco de caloriña.

Entonces sentíronse pasadas, ruxiron as pallas, e a viúva exclamou con moita dor:

– ¡Ai, miña Virxe do Carme que axiña te ofendo!

– ¡Ai, miña muliña branca, que axiña te perdo! – murmurou entonces Xan, con sentimento e con coraxe. E chegándose en seguida á porta do sobrado, berrou con forza:

–¡Meu amo, a casa arde!

–Non arde, home, non, que é rescoldo.

–Pois rescoldo ou lúa, se agora non vindes voume coa mula.

E Lourenzo, saltando dun golpe ó chan, dixo:

–Agarda, logo. ¡Esperaime, ña tía, que logo volvo!

E hai cen anos que foi esto, e aínda hoxe espera a viuviña polo sobriño do seu tío.

A Galician Tale, *1864*

One winter's day, just as evening was falling, two friends, whose friendship went back to their schooldays, but who had now reached the accursed age of ten times three years, were travelling at a good rate. One was on the back of a white mule with broad round flanks while the other was on foot, impervious, it would seem, to their speed.

The one who was on foot was going every bit as fast as the one on the mule who, when he saw the sweat dripping from the other, said:

– Lourenzo, why don't you buy an old nag to carry you? Walking so far on foot over these hills and dales is only good for dogs.

– Nag! These long-ears are only good for those who were born for them, not for old Lourenzo here. A big horse is all that's any good, and as I can't afford a big horse I'm fine with my feet which don't eat, drink or need a harness.

– You're right that it's much cheaper to walk than any other way, for heaven's sake, it's only me that's got to pay a toll because I'm on the back of a mule, while you are on your own two feet. But, truth be told, I do prefer to use the legs of others; that way mine don't get tired. Like I said, you should buy an old mule so you can get a bit of rest. But you're like that, aren't you, here today, gone tomorrow, God will provide. You're always the same, you like cockle-girls, Ribeiro wine and oysters from Carril. Lourenzo, you ought to get married, time is flying past and no one is getting any younger. Soon your hair will turn grey before you can put a blanket on your bed. You need to save for the future, Lourenzo, and you can't do that without a woman to look after the house and save the money that you earn.

– A rolling stone gathers no moss.

– Nonsense, that's just a saying. After all, why are men born if it's not to be with women? (Lourenzo coughs). You must have caught a cold in the cool of the evening, you poor devil. (Lourenzo coughs again). Lord help me if it's not the truth, but you wouldn't be coughing if at least you were straddled over some old nag.

– A cold, me! I haven't had a cold in my whole life, and I don't think I have one now. But – whenever anybody talks to me about getting married, I seem to break out into a cough – hem!, hem! – and that can't be a good sign. What do you reckon, Xan?

– What I think is that you are as stubborn as a mule, and you were born that way, and as much as I like you I have to admit that you are as sneaky as a snake. I can't even guess why you speak so badly about women, what with how much they like you and they always treat you like a prince at dances and festas, and knowing that your mother was a woman and if it hadn't been for your mother neither you nor countless others would have come into this world.

– Not much would have been missed if I hadn't been born. Better than sweating my way along the roads to earn enough to eat, better than grumbling my way through *festas* or whatever with young lasses who sell themselves even though they are not worth a farthing, cheating us men; it would be better to still exist only in the mind of God.

– What a devil you are! I sometimes think you are one of those people who only says hello to the priest so that nobody makes any comments. You are free to say whatever you want, but I'm telling you that I need a little comfort, and I'm going to get married before the Feast Day if the Lord gives me strength.

– And Lord help you not to sweat too much, Xan, even though it's winter now, because then you would cough more than I do whenever someone talks to me about getting married. And I'm warning you that you'd do well not to kill any rams at the Feast, because that's a bad way for a married man to start off, because of the twisted horns that are thrown at the doorway, and you know that one bad thing leads to another. Lord help us!

– You know, all that talk about horns and how bad women are is starting to sound to me like old wives' tales. In this country, as soon as the rumour spreads that a dog has rabies, whether it's true or not, the rumour gets around and they kill the dog. But I can assure you that I have never met a single lass who hasn't played hard to get, or a married woman who has cheated on her husband with me, and I don't think I'm that unattractive a bloke even if I shouldn't say so myself.

– And that comes because you're adapted, and maybe you didn't get it right, and what's more, nobody's safe from a man who's really determined. What I say is that the only good woman for a man is the one who gave birth to him, and I avoid the others like the plague. Xan, women are devils, and according to one very wise saint whose name escapes me, and even the cross can put horns on the devil from a distance.

– Here we go again with the horns.

– It's common knowledge that if it hurts you so much to hear them mentioned that's because they are already casting their shadows from the roof of your future wife's home.

– Are you trying to wind me up? Watch it, Lourenzo, you shouldn't talk like that about someone you don't even know, and not all women have a roving eye and I know a lot who you could live with for not one but a hundred lives.

– I stick by what I said; when I say something I say it because I know what I'm talking about, and I tell you again that all women, even a blue-blooded countess were cast out of the same mould and act the same way. Let the good Lord keep them away from my fireplace because if they're in someone else's house I can't reach them with my spit.

– Oh, you mudslinger – the devil take you if you were to spit on mine, even thinking that I'd have to look after a woman for a brute like you makes my hair stand on end and makes me think. But, let's speak clearly, Lourenzo, like the good mates we are. You are cleverer than I am, I know that, and you know how to handle yourself wherever you are while I stand back watching the kettle boil and the crickets sing. The question is how you settle things, and lumping them all into the same basket without leaving one for me, that really gets up my nose. Come on, at least tell me that you've met some good women, and that not all of them have put horns on an honest man's head.

– They all have Xan, all of them, and for the Xans of this world even more. It even seems as if your name encourages them.

– Damn it, maybe it's true! But my father and mother got married, and I want to get married too. My eyes get all cloudy when I see a married couple sitting outside of an evening, slowly talking together while the children run around in the moonlight under the fig trees.

– Oh the open air, the open air! Stop all this about talking. People bite and scratch each other slowly, and slowly they make the V-sign at each other.

– It's true, it looks bad, but I'm afraid nothing is going to make me change my mind, and when I get married I'm going to get married to someone of my own age, nice and plump, sensible and hard-working, that couldn't be all that bad, could it? What do you reckon?

– You're as stubborn as a mule. The devil is in you, Xan, and now he's tickling your ribs with the idea of marriage. But as I see it nothing happens unless God wills it, and when it comes to the weakness of women, they all lay down readily and fall as if they had no feet.

And so, talking away, Lourenzo and Xan were getting near a village. From far off they started to hear cries and shouts and, on reaching the top of a hill to see what was happening they saw that it was a funeral. They asked a lad who was coming along the road to tell them who it was who had died, and he told them that it was the husband of a woman who had been left a childless widow even though so young. The deceased was not from that village originally, but he had heirs in another village.

The lad moved on and Lourenzo went up to Xan and said:

– Do you want me to show you what women are like, Xan, now that the time is right?

– How do you mean?

– I'll make this widow, even though I don't know who she is and I've never in my life set eyes on her, give me her word tonight that we will get married in a month's time.

– Are you in your right mind, Lourenzo?

– More than you are, Xan. Do you want me to or not?

– Go on then, you fool. Let's make a bet, and if you win I'll loose the white mule I inherited from my father a year ago, which I love because of that and because it's good and the apple of my eye. I'll then be cured of marriage sickness. But if you lose, you have to buy a nag and stop talking badly about women, the beautiful jewels, who I love even more than my little white mule.

– It's a deal. Get off the mule then, and do what I tell you without answering back and until tomorrow evening you are not Xan and I'm not Lourenzo. You are going to be my servant and I'll be your master. Now, walk behind me trailing the mule and I'll go on ahead. And say yes to everything.

No sooner said than done.

Lourenzo walked on ahead and Xan dismounted and walked, leading the mule by the bridle, which was new like the rest of the tack, and they made a splendid sight.

Just as they were reaching the graveyard the funeral procession was also arriving, led by the black, raggedy standard of the parish, the priest and the wailing women, tearing at their hair and screeching until they were hoarse, pulling at the coffin so they didn't allow the pall-bearers to get past.

– Oh Antón, Antón! cried one, as if she was Mary Magdalene, her hands crossed above her head. Antón my friend, you always said to me "Bye Mariquiña" when we met on the roadway. Farewell Antón, I'll never see you again!

And another, draping herself over the coffin, beating her breast, cried:

– Where are you Antón. Why is it you don't you talk to me anymore? Antón, you poor wretch, I made you holland trousers with my own hands and you never wore them. Antón, who is going to put on your new jacket and your new trousers now, Antón?

And the widow, and some of the widows' nieces, all covered in tears, dressed in mourning, their hairpieces in shreds after so much pulling at them, their clothes unfastened, were shouting even more. Especially the widow, who every so often crawled under the coffin from where she had to be extracted by force, saying:

– Oh, my dear! Oh my dear, handsome as a silver plate, burnished like gold, how your buttery flesh is going to be eaten by the earth! And you are leaving, my dear! You are leaving me! Who will comfort me now, and who will say, as you used to say to me, my dear husband, "Eat up, Margaradiña dear, eat up and fatten yourself up, for what is yours is mine. Margaradiña dear, if you limp it seems to me that I limp too". Goodbye my dear husband, with whom I will never again share a bed! What I would give to join you in your grave, Antón, my dear, for with you my darling I bury my heart!

The widow followed the coffin wretchedly in this way until, suddenly, Lourenzo squeezed in amongst the women, his eyes covered by a piece of cloth, weeping as if he was about to lose his soul, shouted out louder than even the mourners wailing.

– Oh, my uncle, my dear uncle! Now I see you dead in this grave! I should never have come here to find you lifeless, and it is not because of the will which you made out in my favour, leaving me to inherit all you own. I am crying so much, for I loved you like my own father. You should have called me to bid my farewells to you. It breaks my heart to find you here dead. Oh, my uncle, my dear uncle! I am going to die from sorrow.

When all the wailing women heard this they gathered around Lourenzo who seemed to be going through so much suffering.

– So what's your name, son – they asked, feeling very sorry for him.

– My name is Andruco, and I am my uncle's nephew. I was left as his heir and he wrote a letter to me asking me to bid farewell to him before he died, but as I had to walk so far I can only see him in his grave, Oh, my uncle, my dear uncle!

– And where are you from, lad?

– I'm from my uncle's land, replied Lourenzo, sobbing until his voice was hoarse.

– And where was your uncle from?

– My uncle was from my land.

And that was all they could get out of him. Lourenzo, still sobbing, made his way towards the widow, who even through her tears could make out the handsome young man who was crying so much for his uncle. When they met he told her that he was the heir of the deceased, and she looked kindly on him and, once the funeral was over she said that he had to come home with her, that it wouldn't be right for her husband's nephew to stay anywhere else, and that there they would be able to cry together.

– So much sorrow. Oh, my dear uncle! – said Lourenzo –; but, but be consoled by the fact that with all he left me I'll be able to pay for lots of masses to pray for his soul, so he can rest in peace and we can be comforted here on earth. For, after all, dear aunt, God tells us to be patient through our trials and, like it or not, as some-one said, the earth falls on the dead bodies and... what can we do about it? We also have to die some time. That's the way of the world.

So talking away and crying, they went back to the widow's house, and Xan, fol-lowing along behind with the mule, and who at the beginning didn't understand a thing Lourenzo was up to, began to cotton on, and a sort of shiver passed through his body at the thought that he might be about to lose his little white mule. The widow's tears, however, which were still running down her cheeks, gave him hope and he trusted in God and in the women who he liked so much.

– And would you, dear aunt, have anywhere I could put up my mule and my servant? They're dead beat after such a long trail.

– Everything I have is at your disposition, nephew, and just looking at you is like looking at him, and that brings me comfort.

"The devil take the young widow, what comforts she finds!", murmured Xan to himself as he put the mule into the stable. "But from that to getting married is a long way", he added, pleased with himself.

And with that hope in his heart he started to eat a nice piece of shoulder of pork which the widow had given him, and which he washed down with a bowl of Ribeiro wine of the very best which cheered him up no end, while the aunt and the nephew sat upstairs talking about the inheritance and the deceased with the people who were with them.

So the day went by and night fell, and Lourenzo and Xan were left alone in the house with the widow. Xan's heart was with his little white mule, his soul was with Lourenzo and his hope lay in God. And it was with a heavy heart that he watched Lourenzo and the widow eating together through tears, huge mouthfuls of pork and beef and jugs of wine that would strike fear into any good Christian. In any case, however, they were not talking about anything in particular, and Xan couldn't work out how Lourenzo would be able to win the bet.

Eventually it was time for bed, and Xan was alarmed to find that the only bed in the house was the couple's double bed, and that the widow was so insistent that Lourenzo should sleep there that he had to obey. She, wrapped in a blanket, went to lie down behind the partition in the upstairs room.

Xan, at his nerve's end, watched from the loft where he had been given some straw, how the widow put out the oil lamp and things went dark.

– Looks like you're going to stay with me, my little white mule, and the truth is I thought I had lost you, he said then; after all women were made from one of our ribs so there must be some good in them. Save me, little widow, save me from this predicament, and I'd even be willing to marry you myself.

Thus spoke Xan to himself, although he was still unable to sleep a wink, and it seemed as if the straw was rustling more and more.

A long hour passed and Xan, pleased, was about to fall asleep without any concern when, all of a sudden he heard first a sigh and then another, sounding like sighs coming from a soul from another world. Xan shuddered and sat up to hear better.

– Oh my dear, my dear! – said the widow. How cold I am on this board, but it's much colder that you are, my dear, in that bitter earth that is going to eat you away!

– Oh my uncle, my dear uncle! – exclaimed Lourenzo, on the other side, as if he was talking to himself – how much I'm thinking about you, I'm here in the warmth while you're in the cemetery in an earthen bed with nobody to keep you company!

– Oh, Antón! – said the widow again – what will become of you in that hole, my darling, while I'm here under cover. Brrr Brrr! It's so cold. I'm shivering as if I had the palsy! Brrr Brrr!

– Aunt!

– Are you not sleeping, nephew?

– No I'm not, and neither are you, aunt, I can hear you trembling like a leaf on a tree.

– How can you expect me to be able to sleep knowing that on this frosty night your uncle is asleep in the cemetery, cold as snow, when if he were alive we would be sleeping together all nice and warm in the bed that you're in just now?

– Why don't you come and snuggle up here on one side of the bed. You can keep your blanket wrapped around you. In any case, an aunt and a nephew is just like a mother and son, especially when there's real necessity like now, since you don't want me to sleep on the floor, but it could even give you heartburn, what with the pain and the cold, and it is a sin, dear aunt, to put your health at risk?

– No don't, son, please don't. I know there would be no harm in me lying down beside a nephew like you, with my blanket wrapped around me over my clothes, especially the way I'm shivering, brrr brrr! But I want to start getting used to it, for many nights like this await me in this world. Before I was rich and married, but now I'm poor and a widow, and all that was mine is now yours and all I have left is heaven and earth.

– Well, aunt, between the two of us, and no one else but God and us, I must tell you that I know of a rich man of your husband's blood who would, if you wanted, like to take you for his wife.

– Hush, nephew, and don't talk to me about another man. It still seems as if the one I had is still alive.

– No, aunt, that way you wouldn't lose your house, nor your bed, nor your property. That's a lot to lose all at once, not to mention your husband, who I'm going to have masses paid for every day so that he can rest in peace and not come calling on winter nights. In that way he will be fine there, and you here, and if he were alive the advice he'd give you would be none other than to find another man of his own blood, people of his own blood left him what he and you ate together during his life.

– You're probably right, nephew, but… If that was what you wanted, Antón, why didn't you tell me before you died, because then I would have done it even against my own will to carry out your wishes?

– As far as I can see, aunt, if my uncle didn't say anything to you it's just because he forgot on his deathbed, which is not in the least surprising, and could happen to anybody.

– Yes, you're right, you're right. Death is a very bad business, and at the time of dying you can forget things. Oh my dear, my dear! What wouldn't I do just to please you? Brrr Brrr! It's freezing here!

– Come over here. So long as you're not going to be angry, I'll tell you that it's me who wants to marry you.

– But what are you saying? Let's see if I get this straight. Only a nephew of my husband's could carry out his will…

– Yes, but it would have to be in a month's time, because after I have to go to Cais where I have to collect another inheritance. Before that I'd like you to own everything that was yours again. What must be must be, because my uncle is wishing for this from his tomb.

– Oh my dear, my dear! What a nephew you were given by God; listening to him is just as if I was listening to you! But son, it's still very soon, and even if you and I were to get married in order to carry out the wishes of the deceased, people talk… and…

– Forget about people! We'll get married in secret and nobody will know.

Alright then, nephew, but only because you are of my late husband's own blood, and because you say he would be happy in his tomb to see us together. For all the rest, what does it matter? I loved your uncle deeply. Brrr Brrr! It's freezing here!

– Come over here wrapped in your blanket. It's no sin, as you're going to be my wife.

– But I'm not your wife yet, dear, and I feel pangs of conscience. Brrr Brrr! How my head aches, what heartburn!

– Aunt, come over here, and stop putting your health in danger. If you commit a sin before we get married we will have to go to confession.

– Alright, I'll come over. I need a little bit of warmth.

Then footsteps were heard, the straw rustled and the widow shouted out in great pain:

– Oh, My Lady, Virgen of the Carmen, how soon I have offended you!

– Oh, my little white mule, how soon I am going to lose you! – murmured Xan then, with feeling and with courage. He went straight to the upstairs door and shouted in a loud voice:

– Master, the house is on fire!

– It's not on fire, it's just the embers.

– Well be it embers or the moon, if you don't come now, I'm heading off with my mule.

And Lourenzo, jumping to the floor with one great leap, shouted:

– Hang on a minute. Aunt, wait a while for me, I'll be right back.

That was a hundred years ago, and still today the widow is waiting for her nephew.

Antonio López Ferreiro (1837–1910)

From A tecedeira de Bonaval (The Weaver of Bonaval), 1894

A Victoria de Fisterra

Ó fin, o que tanto se temía en Galicia e que tanta alarma metera en Santiago, o que tanto receaba o conde de Castro, chegou de súpeto. O día 13 de xullo apareceu nas nosas costas a armada francesa, composta de vintecinco naos ben armadas e equipadas. Veu percorrendo tódolos nosos portos e saqueando o que encontraba á man. Fondeou entre Muros e Fisterra e, entre outras falcatruadas nesta última vila, por non deixar nada atrás ata arramplou con tódalas mantas que había no hospital, facendo o propio noutros portos. O peor foi cando puxo en terra toda a xente de armas, que pasaba de catro mil homes, mentres en toda Galicia a penas había soldados que puidesen chamarse tales, polo poucos e mal armados que en xeral estaban. Causou isto tal alarma que nin no mesmo Santiago se encontraban por seguros da invasión. Ó conde de Castro todo se lle volvía mandar avisos e máis avisos a D. Álvaro de Bazán que, no intre que estaba fóra o emperador, quedara por capitán xeneral do mar océano, e á sazón achábase en Laredo arrombando unha escuadra para mandar a Flandres.

Colleu D. Álvaro con vintecatro naos que lle quedaran, e o 18 de xullo virou a proa en dirección ás costas de Galicia. Daba gloria o ver con qué pompa as nosas naos sulcaban a extensa saba das augas.

Ó amencer do día 25 deu vista a nosa armada á vila de Fisterra. A inimiga achábase diante de Muros dispoñéndose a saquea-lo porto se non lle aprontaban os doce mil ducados que pedían. Os muradáns xa ofrecían oito mil, pero nisto descóbrense as dúas escuadras e o descubrirse e dispoñerse o combate foi todo un. Aquilo non foi combate, foi unha manda de raios que caeu sobre as naos francesas e as desbaratou aínda non en dúas horas. Ó primeiro embiste da nao de D. Álvaro contra a capitana inimiga, foise esta ó fondo con case toda a súa tripulación. Revolveuse logo a nosa capitanía contra outra nave francesa que viña acudirlle á súa e, en pouco tempo, rendeuna e tomouna. Co mesmo arrinque e brío pelexaron as demais naos españolas; así foi que tódalas naos inimigas, menos a que se foi ó fondo e unha que escapou a présa (madia levaba, que ía co pao maior menos) para ir dar noticia, se chegou a tempo, todas elas, repito, e o botín que levaban, caeron en poder dos nosos. Naquela cañeira foron degolados na batalla máis de tres mil franceses e os demais quedaron presos. Dos nosos morreron uns trescentos, sinte os cincocentos que foron feridos.

A primeira cousa en que pensou o marqués de Santa Cruz despois da batalla foi vir a Santiago darlle gracias ó Apóstolo por aquela tan grande victoria gañada no seu día. Deixoulle encomendado o mando da Armada ó seu fillo maior D. Álvaro, mozo de dezaoito anos, e encargoulle que levase a remolque os barcos inimigos e os esperase na Coruña. El veuse dereito a Santiago, onde o esperaba o conde de

Castro, capitán xeneral e gobernador de Galicia, cos oidores da Audiencia. Anque respecto do particular non falan nada as memorias antigas é de supoñer que pousase D. Álvaro no pazo do Arcebispo. O cal, para satisface-los desexos do nobre e valeroso marqués, dispuxo que logo se cantase na catedral un solemne Te Deum en acción de gracias por tamaña victoria. A solemnidade foi tan cumprida como requiría o caso. Asistiu, por suposto, o Cabido e a Audiencia en corpo con tódolos seus oficiais. Cando D. Álvaro puxo o pé na igrexa encontrouse cun gran fato de xente de todas clases que o esperaba cobizosa de ver polos seus propios ollos aquel gran capitán. Ata as bóvedas da catedral parecía que se mostraban fonchas e oufanas de que lles rendese homenaxe un home daquel peito.

Cantado que foi o Te Deum, recorreu o Marqués tódalas estacións que soían visita-los peregrinos. Detívose, en particular, diante do altar maior, que entonces tiña unha forma moi diferente de agora. Era máis sinxelo e non tiña tanto ringo-rrango como o que vemos hoxe. O cal, como foi feito nunha época en que se pensaba que a bonitura consistía en atestar e macizar ben as cousas de figuras, adornos e recovecos na maneira que se ataca e enche un fardo ou un xergón, así está cargado de flores, froitas e feixes de cousas. Parecer, parece un almacén de madeira, se se quere ben traballada pero nada máis. Só dunha vez, viñeron de Deza para a obra da capela maior cento noventa carros de nogueira.

The Victory of Finisterre

In the end, the thing that was so feared in Galicia, which had placed the city of Santiago in a state of such alarm, and which the Count of Castro had been so concerned about, happened all of a sudden. On July 13 the French navy reached our coasts, composed of twenty-five well-armed and well-equipped vessels. It sailed into all of our ports plundering whatever it found in reach. It laid anchor between Muros and Finisterre and, amongst other crimes, in the latter stole all the blankets from the hospital so as not to leave anything behind, an action which was repeated in other towns. The worst came when the soldiers came ashore, more than four thousand men, when in all Galicia there were hardly any soldiers worthy of the name, and the few that existed were poorly armed. Such panic was caused that people did not even feel safe in Santiago itself. The Count of Castro could do nothing but send warnings to Don Álvaro de Bazán who, while the Emperor was out of the country, was Captain General of the Seas and who at that time was in Laredo putting a squadron together to send to Flanders.

Don Álvaro de Bazán took the twenty-four ships he had left and, on July 18 set sail for the coasts of Galicia. It was wonderful to see how our vessels soared through the wide open waters.

On the morning of the 25th our navy was spotted off the coast of Finisterre. The enemy was off Muros ready to sack the port if they were not given the twelve thousand ducats they had asked for. The people of Muros had offered eight thousand, but then the two fleets found each other and no sooner had this happened did they get ready for combat. It was much more than a battle. It was a shower of lightning bolts which fell on the French fleet and destroyed it in less than two hours. During the first onslaught by Don Alvaro's ship against the French captain's vessel it was sent to the bottom with all its crew. Our captain then turned around and attacked another French ship which had come in support of its flagship and in no time it was defeated and taken. The rest of the Spanish ships fought with the same vigour and resolve, and all the enemy ships were captured and their booty taken, except for the ones which were sunk and one which managed to escape (without its mainsail) to spread the news if it got back in time. In the massacre more than three thousand French were killed and the rest taken prisoner. About three hundred of our men died and some five hundred were wounded.

The first thing the Marquis of Santa Cruz thought about after the battle was to head for Santiago to give thanks to the Apostle for such a great victory which had been won on his day. He left the fleet in the hands of his eldest son Don Álvaro, a lad of eighteen, and ordered him to tow the enemy boats and wait for him in A Coruña. He went straight to Santiago where the Count of Castro was waiting for him with the Captain General, the Governor of Galicia and local dignitaries. Although nothing is written in the old annals we can presume that Don Álvaro was lodged in the Archbishop's palace. Then, in order to carry out the wishes of the noble and illustrious Marquis, a solemn Te Deum was said in the Cathedral as an action of thanksgiving for such a great victory. The solemnity required by such an occasion was maintained. The Council and the Court, of course, were in attendance with all their officials. When Don Álvaro entered the church he found a huge number of people from all classes, who were anxiously waiting to see this great captain with their own eyes. Even the vaults of the Cathedral seemed proud that such a brave man was paying homage to them.

After the Te Deum was over the Marquis went round all the stations of the cross usually visited by pilgrims. He stopped, in particular, before the High Altar, which was then very different from how it is now. It was simpler and did not have so many adornments as we can see nowadays. This was done in a time when it was thought that beauty consisted in stuffing and filling up things with figures, adornments and nooks so that they were attacked and filled like bundles or sacks, and so it is covered in flowers, fruit and bundles of things. It looks like a wooden warehouse, well-wrought, but nothing else. One time a hundred and ninety carts full of walnut were brought from Deza to decorate the main Chapel.

Valentín Lamas Carvajal (1849–1906)

From Gallegada, *1884*

Os graxos da Burga

Pasaron moitos anos; esquecéronse moitos recordos; desapareceron os máis dos vellos costumes de Ourense; pero non se varreu da memoria das xentes o recordo nin os costumes dos *graxos da Burga*. Inda hoxe a sona que deixaron esténdese polas vilas e aldeas de toda Galicia, pois o mesmo que a sombra ó corpo, vai esta nomeada seguindo ós fillos de Ourense por onde camiñan.

¿Que estudiante non escoitou aló en Santiago dos vermellos labios da costureira a quen cortexaba, as frases de "non me fío que es dos *graxos da Burga*"? ¿Que fillo de Ourense non se lembra dos receos con que foi mirado polas mozas nas romaxes da nosa terra, e dos contratempos con que tivo que loitar denantes de se facer dono do seu corazón, só por ser *dos da Burga*, como nos chaman?

¿Que pai, por deixado da man de Deus que andase, foi de boas a primeiras gustante en que a súa filla falase cun de Ourense, sendo como son *graxos da Burga*, e polo mesmo considerados polos labregos, sen que se dean de conta da razón que teñen para xulgalos así, como ós mozos de menos lacha e máis sabidos en picardías que andan polo mundo?

Como nos tempos da Inquisición era para os relaxados *o sambenito*, así é para os ourensáns inda hoxe a nomeada de *graxos da Burga*.

Outros a fixeron, e como se se tratase dun foro ou dunha renda perpetua, vímola pagando nosoutros, sen que nos valla axuntar cartos para redimir esa gabela que nos botaron ó lombo denantes de que nacesemos.

Para que todos coñezan o que eran os *graxos da Burga* e para que se convenzan de que desapareceu a caste, e de que non é xusto que xulguen ós ourensáns como os xulgan, vouvos contar a causa desa pauliña.

Aló polo ano de 1834, despois de que botaron ós frades dos conventos, dous orfos de dezasete anos que non tiñan oficio nin beneficio nin quen lles dese de comer, nin sitio onde acollerse, cansos de andar langraneando por esas rúas, gañándolle a volta ós serenos para se librar dunha malladura de costelas, axuntáronse baixo da costa da Alameda, onde os vagabundos debían xogar ó parar, se non mente aquela cántiga:

Ai, Baltar,
non xogues ó parar
na costa da Alameda
debaixo do hospital,

e sentados ó pé daquel gruñeiro que debeu ser plantado no tempo de María Castaña, puxéronse a parrafear, ocupándose da súa sorte e do seu porvir, cicais pola vez primeira.

Non contan as crónicas o que falaron; mais sábese de certo que oito días despois daquel parrafeo estableceran os dous galafates o seu lar nun cavouco feito polos homes, e que servía de rexistro, como punto medio da Burga de Arriba e da Burga de Abaixo.

A *fundación*, como tódalas cousas novas, foi adiante e chegou a ter moitos adictos. Tódolos vagos e moitos fillos de familia, que sen selo, andaban chalados da casa, tiñan alí o seu agarimo, os seus compañeiros, o seu modo de vivir.

No inverno polas noites durmían ó quente; no verán polas tardes, cando a raxeira do sol contiña os veciños nas casas, eles saían ás arrasadeiras, e polas noites cando se depercataban de que os serenos prenderan no sono, nin máis nin menos que se fosen grilos, saían do burato para cantar e toma-lo fresco.

Non pasaron catro meses e xa tiñan lembradía en sete légoas á redonda: o cavouco chamábase *Casino*, os seus habitadores eran coñecidos co nome de *graxos da Burga*. Os sete primeiros socios, os máis ilustres graxos, os lexisladores daquela sociedade aventureira e nómade, os que botaron as bases daquela congregación de nugalláns, os enxeñeiros, arquitectos e traballadores a un mesmo tempo, que trazaron, dirixiron e fixeron as obras do *Casino da Burga*, foron o *Mourón*, o *Pachete*, o *Portela*, o *Redes*, o *Carruxo*, o *Oso* e o *Cancheiro*. Eran sete coma os sabios de Grecia.

Para ser *graxos da Burga* a ninguén se lle pedía patente, nin cuota, nin certificación de boa conduta, nin sequera o nome de pía, nin os apelidos de pai e nai. Con dicir: "Eiquí estou", tíñase feita a presentación en forma. O bautismo facíanllo despois sen cerimonias, cunha nomeada da que ninguén se esquecía, como se a gravasen en letras de ouro no medio e medio da praza. O regulamento por que se rexían, sen ser escrito nin publicado, cumpríase ó pé da letra, pola contra dos que se poñen en letras de molde e se publican, que nunca se cumpren.

A lei social dos *graxos da Burga* encontrábase nesta frase espida de retóricas: "Todo é de todos." Naquela comandita non había ganancias nin perdas, nin capital nin traballo. Se un tiña a fortuna de arrapañar algunha cousa boa nunha taberna da vila, disfrutábana todos en amor e compaña, e pobre do graxo que denantes de chegar ó Casino se atrevese a petiscar no que afanara; fose pan, fosen sardiñas, tal como se collera contra a vontade do seu dono, plantábase no chan que facía de mesa e servíase por iguais anacos a tódolos socios. Non había hora fixa de xantar, porque moitos días non había de que. Os estómagos dos graxos da Burga, semellándose ós corpos, estaban afeitos a non traballar a diario. Cando pasaba un día sen comer e ós máis deles se lles abría moito a boca, non levaban a ela as mans por mor de que non as pagasen cunha dentada por ser as causantes da fame que corría.

Tampouco andaban moi sobros de roupa: para os sete non tiñan máis que tres mudas, compostas de tres pantalóns, tres chalecos, tres chaquetas e tres gorras escalazadas; e nada ten de estraño que a esto lle chamasen mudas, porque o seu traxe era feito polo xastre e do mesmo pano co que vestiu Adán no Paraíso; quero dicir que dos sete, catro andaban en coiro, pois o turno para mudarse non chegaba máis que a tres.

Os que andaban de roupa nova tiñan que facer o servicio por fóra; os demais quedaban de sentinela gardando a entrada e saída do Casino por mor de que ninguén se coase por el embaixo, cousa que sucedeu poucas veces, e cando sucedeu, sen que os graxos lle batesen, o que tal fixo levou que rascar para unha tempada.

Cando algún graxo se puña ó sol e se entretiña en matar polo sistema de *uñate* a cochumillada que lle proía no corpo, non faltaba compañeiro que lle advertise o dano que estaba facendo, nestas ou parecidas palabras:

– Deixa as uñas para mellor acasión; non trates tan mal eses exércitos que nos defenden e gardan sen que coman rancho nin pidan plus, e que sen lles pasar revista de comisario teñen o armamento tan corrente que non hai quen se atreva a chegar onda nosoutros.

Os graxos da Burga tiveron as súas malas épocas, e non deixaron de pasar os seus traballos.

Na Burga de Arriba, no cume da fonte había unha pedra longa dende a que podía guiparse o que pasaba ó longo do Casino. Os rapaces de Ourense descubriron aquela clase de pena-vixía, lembrada *Santardós*, e para atentar ós graxos armábanse de pedras e dende alí acantazábanos, berrando a todo berrar: "¡Luz ó Casino!"

Aquela pedrea chegou a facer a delicia dos rapaces que andaban na escola do Rebolo, os que denantes que chegase a hora de entre lusco e fusco, xa andaban axuntando municións e xente que lle fose dar luz ó Casino.

Para se librar dos cantazos, tiveron os graxos da Burga que facer unhas obras de reparación e defensa. Abriron uns buratos na parede e neles se metían engruñándose namentres que os pelouros estrondaban e rolaban pola cova embaixo.

As panadeiras da Barreira queixáronse ó alcalde señor Lebrón de que os graxos lles roubaban as broas enteiras, e da noite para a mañá, co pensamento de que os serenos puidesen collelos mellor, por orde da autoridade, un ferreiro púxolle unha reixa ó burato que daba saída á Burga de Arriba.

– Pecháronnos unha porta e non hai chave que faga nela – dixeron os graxos –, mais non por eso deixaremos de face-las nosas escapatorias.

Vendo o alcalde que non daba resultados a cazapeira, anoxouse e mandou que puxesen outra reixa no burato da Burga de Abaixo. Escomezou a traballar o ferreiro, anuncióuselles que se non saían quedaban alí pechados para sempre; mais como se tal cousa, os graxos, denantes de se render ó inimigo, acordaron morrer alí xuntos, imitando así, sen coñecer a Historia nin polo forro, o heroico exemplo dos fillos de Numancia.

Os graxos da Burga tiñan o corazón a proba de desgracias. Dunha vez armáronlle a un deles unha trampa nunha viña: puxéronlle unha gran rateira de ferro, feita de encarga para o caso. Caeu un nela e tronzóuselle unha perna. Os graxos da Burga, lonxe de ter mentes de se vingar do feito, exclamaron case choromicando: "Trátannos coma ós zorros, pero non hai que facerlle. Xa teremos tino de manter a ese coitado compañeiro que quedou impedido para o *traballo*."

Nas noites de inverno tiñan iluminado o Casino cos faroles que afanaban nos patios das casas; mais nin con luz chegaron os serenos a collelos descoidados.

Cando un sereno metía a cabeza polo burato, como se fose por bruxería, as luces apagábanse e o Casino quedaba ás escuras, e se houbo algún que anoxado pola burla se resolveu a entrar a tentas, nunca deu cun deles nin por moito tentar, pois nestes casos á voz de "ratos ós buratos", ían os graxos da Burga a poñerse como se tivesen o corpo de goma, nas estreitas e altas rendixelas das paredes, dicindo con sorna morna despois que o sereno pasara diante do escondrixo en que estaban engruñados: "¡Coloumau!"

A máis dun dependente da alcaldía que se viu no allo ouvinlle contar que non sabe como non perdeu o xuízo ó verse tan abouxado ó sentir falar tan preto de si e mais non lle poder botar as gadoupas a un daqueles *paxaros* que voaban sen ter ás.

Por este xeito viviron ata o ano de mil oitocentos corenta e seis, en que, coa chegada do provincial de Ourense, desapareceron os graxos da Burga, que se converteron en tambores e cornetas despois de resistir un sitio posto en toda regra por un piquete de soldados.

Dende entón non quedou dos graxos da Burga máis que a relembranza, anque algún deles despois de que lle deron a absoluta, se ben non pretendeu establecer a escola de novo, practicou aqueles costumes, viviu naquela vida e morreu en opinión de *graxos da Burga* enxebre.

Quedounos tamén ós fillos de Ourense, que dito sexa sen ánimo de gabarnos, nin facemos como facían nin pensamos como pensaban, a condenada sona de graxos da Burga, pola que somos lembrados e coñecidos nas vilas e aldeas da nosa terriña, sen xustiza e sen razón para elo, como se ve polo que deixo dito.

The Rascals from the Burga

Many years have gone by; many memories have been long forgotten; most customs of Ourense have been lost; but nothing has been able to wipe from the remembrance of the people the memory and the customs of the rascals from the Burga. Even today the reputation they left is still remembered in the towns and villages of all Galicia because, as sure as the shadow goes with the body, this name follows the sons of Ourense wherever they might roam.

What student never heard in Santiago from the red lips of the seamstress he was courting sentences like "I don't trust him, he's one of the rascals from the Burga"? What son of Ourense does not remember the distrust with which he was looked at by the girls during the festas in our country, and of the setbacks he had to overcome before winning the heart of someone, just because, as they said, he came from the Burga?

What father, poor as he might be, would really like his daughter to chat with a lad from Ourense, knowing what the rascals from the Burga are like? All the farmers know, without realizing why, that they are considered to be the most shameless and the craftiest lads in the world.

Just as during the times of the Spanish Inquisition the blame was put on those with loose morals, so people from Ourense are still blamed for everything as the rascals from the Burga.

Others might have done it, but as if it were part of a charter, a rent which has to be paid for perpetuity, we have to pay this price, and we are not even allowed to save enough money to pay off this tax which we have been forced to bear since before we were even born.

In order that everyone can understand what the rascals from the Burga were like, and so that everyone can realize that this group has disappeared, and that it is unfair that those of us from Ourense are judged in this way, I'm going to tell you the reasons behind this slander.

Round about 1834, after the friars had been expelled from the monasteries, two seventeen-year-old orphans who were unemployed and had no money to live on, no food to eat, nowhere to sleep, tired of wandering aimlessly through the streets trying to steer clear of the night watchmen in order to avoid a beating, got together under the Alameda hill where tramps used to play or stay, in the words of the old song:

Oh, Baltar,
Don't play or stay
On Alameda hill
Below the hospital

And seated under that blackthorn bush, which must have been planted in the times of María Castaña, they started to talk, concerned about the state they were in and their future, perhaps for the first time.

The chronicles don't tell us exactly what they talked about, but we do know for certain that eight days after that talk the two rogues started to live in a man-made cave half way between the Upper Burga and the Lower Burga.

The foundation, like all new things, went ahead and soon had many supporters. All the layabouts and quite a few sons of good family, or who seemed to be, and who spent their time out of their homes, found refuge, friends and a way of life there.

On winter nights they would sleep in the warmth; on summer afternoons when the heat of the sun kept people indoors, they would creep about, and at night time when they saw that the watchmen were asleep, they came out of their hole like crickets to sing and take the air.

After only four months they were known for seven leagues around: the hole became known as the casino, and its inhabitants were called the rascals from the Burga. The first seven members, the most distinguished rascals, the legislators of that adventurous, nomadic society; those who set the tone for the rest of the rogues, the engineers, architects and labourers all at once, those who drew up, directed and carried out the projects of the Casino da Burga were the Mourón, the Pachete, the Portela, the Redes, the Carruxo, the Oso and the Cancheiro. There were seven of them, like the sages of Greece.

No one was asked for any licence, any entrance fee, any good behaviour certificate in order to join the rascals from the Burga. They weren't even asked their Christian names, nor the surnames of their mothers and fathers. It was enough just to say "Here I am" in order to be accepted. They were then baptised without any ceremony, with a christening which no one would forget, as if it were written in letters of gold in the middle of the square. The rules they obeyed, though unwritten and unpublished, were carried out to the letter, unlike rules which are written and published and which are never obeyed.

The social law of the rascals from the Burga could be summed up in a single phrase, free of all rhetoric: "Everything belongs to everyone". In that commandment there was no profit or loss, no capital or labour. If you had the good fortune to pinch something good from one of the taverns in the town, everybody was welcome to it, and woe betide the rascal who dared to take a bit of it before arriving at the Casino. Be it bread, sardines or whatever, it was laid out on the floor which took the place of a table and served out equally, whether its owner liked it or not, among all the members. There was no set time for lunch, because many days there was nothing to eat. The rascals' stomachs, like the rest of their bodies, were not used to working every day. When they had gone a day without eating, and most of them had their mouths wide open, they dared not raise their hands to their mouths for fear of biting them as they were the cause of the lack of food.

They weren't too well off in terms of clothes either. Between the seven of them they only had three changes of clothes, consisting of three pairs of trousers, three waistcoats, three jackets and three knitted caps. Not really much of a change of clothes, but there was nothing strange about this, as they usually dressed in clothes made by the same tailor and of the same cloth as that used by Adam in the Garden of Eden. In other words, of the seven of them, four ran about in the nude because there was only a change of clothes for three.

Those who wore the new clothes had to take care of the outside service, while the other kept watch on the entrance to the Casino to make sure that nobody got in underneath, something which happened rarely but, even if the rascals didn't beat them up, whoever tried it was itchy for a good time after.

Whenever one of the rascals went out into the sun and started to delouse himself using the technique of sticking his fingernails into his scabs, there would always be someone to tell him the harm he was doing to himself in these or similar words:

– Leave your fingernails for more important tasks: Don't treat them so badly, these armies that defend us and protect us without ever asking for any meal or for a bonus, and without having to go to the police station provide such good weapons that nobody dares to come against us.

The rascals from the Burga went through hard times and never stopped doing their work.

In the Upper Burga, at the top of the fountain there was a long rock from which it was possible to spit on anyone who was passing by the Casino. The lads fom Ourense discovered that sort of lookout rock called the Santardós, and as a means of attacking the rascals they would arm themselves with stones and throw them down on them, shouting "light up the Casino!".

This rock throwing was great fun for the lads who went to the Rebolo school who spent the twilight gathering weapons and people to go and light up the Casino.

In order to escape from the blows from the stones, the rascals from the Burga had to repair their defences. They opened up a couple of holes in the wall and crawled into them while the rocks hit the area around the tunnel and rolled away down.

The bakers from Barreira Street complained to the mayor, Mr Lebrón that the rascals were stealing whole loaves of bread, and overnight, thinking that the watchmen would be able to catch them more easily, the authorities ordered an ironmonger to put up some railings around the hole which gave out onto Upper Burga.

– They've shut our door, and there's no key that can open it, said the rascals, but that's not going to stop us making our escapes.

When the mayor saw that his mesh was not doing any good, he got angry and ordered more railings to be put up over the hole in Lower Burga. The ironmonger started to work and told them that if they didn't get out now they'd be trapped there forever, but the rascals, before giving into the enemy agreed to die there all together imitating, without any knowledge of history, the heroic example of the sons of Numancia.

The rascals from the Burga were well used to misfortune. Once one of them was caught in a trap in a vineyard. A huge iron mousetrap, especially built for the purpose. The rascal was caught and his leg was cut. The rascals from the Burga, far from thinking about revenge, exclaimed almost as one: "They treat us like foxes, but nothing can be done about it. We'll make sure we look after and care for our companion who has become disabled and unable to work".

On winter nights they lit up the Casino with lamps they took from the courtyards of houses, but even with the light the watchmen were never able to catch them unawares. Whenever a watchman stuck his head into the hole, as if by art of witchcraft the lights would go out and the Casino would be left in darkness. And if anybody was annoyed by this trick and tried to crawl in, he was never able to find them no matter how hard he tried, because that is when the cry of "rats in the holes" went up and the rascals from the Burga slid through the high narrow cracks in the walls as if their bodies were made of rubber, saying later in an ironic tone that the watchman had passed right in front of where they had been hiding: "He got my hand!".

More than one municipal employee was to wonder how he hadn't gone mad when he had been bewildered by hearing them speak so close to him but unable to get his hands on one of these birds which flew even though they didn't have wings.

In this way they survived on up until the year eighteen forty-six when, with the arrival of the Provincial of Ourense, the rascals from the Burga disappeared, becoming drummer boys and buglers after resisting a full-scale siege by a squad of soldiers.

Since then all that is left of the rascals from the Burga is their memory, although some of them when they were discharged, even though they didn't intend to set up the school again, did carry out the old customs, living and dying like true rascals from the Burga.

And with no intention of praising them, and not that we do what they did nor think as they thought, we sons of Ourense have also been left with the damning accolade of rascals from the Burga, the name by which we are known and remembered in the towns and villages of our land, unfairly and with no reason, as you can see from what I have said.

Manuel Curros Enríquez (1851–1908)

From Aires da miña terra (Airs from my Land), *1880*

Introducción

Escribir nada máis pra onha provincia
ou, como os pobos árcades fixeron,
escribir sobre a casca dos curtizos,
cáxeque todo ven a ser o mesmo.

A nosa vos, na soledá perdida,
morrerá sin deixar xiquera ise eco
que a brisa malencónica do outono
deixa na copa azul dos ameneiros.

Non pode ser tampouco doutra sorte:
pasaron xa, pra non volver, os tempos
en que a lenguaxe era unha cifra máxica
fácele sólo ó sacerdote hebreo.

As xentes tristes que no verbo humano
percuran os ideales que entreveron,
cando ó vate interrogan, novo Oráculo,
queren revelaciós, que non misterios.

I escribir nunha lengua conecida
daqueles sólo que onda nós naceron,
¿que é sinón responder a esas perguntas
en revesgados xeroulifos pérxicos?

Todo tende á unidá, lei, de entre todas,
a máis ineusorabre do Progreso;

i el que de cen naciós un pobo fixo,
un idioma fará de mil dialeutos.

Como paran no mar tódolos ríos,
como os raios do sol paran nun centro,
tódalas lenguas han de parar nunha,
que hemos de falar todos, tarde ou cedo.

¿Por que botar ó púbrico este libro
si a división dialéutica condeno?,
diredes, con razón, os que leades,
si as ledes, estas páxinas. – Diréivolo:

Cando tódalas lenguas o fin topen
que marca a todo o providente dedo,
e cos vellos idiomas estinguidos
sólo unha fala universal formemos;

Esa fala pulida, idioma úneco,
máis que hoxe enriquecido, e máis perfeuto,
resume das palabras máis sonoras
que aquelas nos deixaran como en herdo;

Ese idioma, compendio dos idiomas,
como onha serenata pracenteiro,
como onha noite de luar docísimo,
será, – ¿que outro sinón? – será o gallego.

Fala de miña nai, fala armoñosa,
en que o rogo dos tristes rube ó ceo
i en que dende a prácida esperanza
ós afogados e doridos peitos.

Fala de meus abós, fala en que os parias,
de tréboa e polvo e de sudor cubertos,
piden á terra o grau da cor da sangue
que ha de cebar á besta do laudemio...

Lengua enxebre, en que as ánemas dos mortos
nas negras noites de silencio e medo
encomendan ós vivos as obrigas
que, ¡malpocados!, sin cumprir morreron.

Idioma en que garulan os paxaros,
en que falan os ánxeles ós nenos,
en que as fontes salouzan e marmullan
entre as follosas álbores os ventos;

Non, ti non morrerás, céltica musa,
nada da Suevia nos chouzales pechos,
últemo amor do páledo Macías,
atravesado o corazón cun ferro;

Fecundo nume do úneco rei sabio
que no solio de España tivo asento,
arpa imortal da doce Rosalía,
do infortunado Añón, himno postreiro:

Ti non podes morrer... ¡Eso quixeran
os desleigados que te escarneceron!
mais ti non morrerás, Cristo das lenguas,
¡non, ti non morrerás, ou Nazareno!

Apóstol teu, anque o máis ruín de todos,
pra onde quer levarei teu Evanxelio,
o fatelo vistindo de inominia
que pra mofa nas costas che puseron.

No teu nome, por terras e por mares,
ofercerei paz e salú ós enfermos,
falareilles da patria ós desterrados,
de libertade e redención ós servos.

Anunciarei o día do teu trunfo
por cibdades e vilas e desertos,
e si por te anunciar me apedrearen,
¡inda ó morrer te mentarán meus beizos!

Introduction

Writing for but one province
and, as the peoples of Arcadia did,
writing on the bark of cork-oaks,
come to much the same thing.

Our voices, lost in emptiness,
will die without even leaving that echo
that the melancholy breeze of autumn
leaves among the blue crowns of alders.

Yet it cannot be otherwise:
they have passed now, never to return, those times
when language was a magic cipher
only readily understood by the Hebrew priest.

The sad people who in the human word
seek the ideals they have glimpsed
want, when they question the bard, that new oracle,
revelations, not mysteries.

And writing in a language known
only by those born where we were born
– what is it but replying to those questions
in topsy-turvy Persian hieroglyphs?

Everything tends to unity, the most inexorable
of all the laws of progress;
and he who made one people out of a hundred nations
will make one language from a thousand dialects.

Just as all rivers flow into the sea,
just as the rays of the sun flow from one centre,
all languages must flow into one
that we shall all speak, sooner or later.

Why give this book to the world
if I condemn linguistic division?
you will say, rightly, those who read
these pages, if you do read them. I shall tell you:

when all languages find the destiny
that the finger of providence marks for everything
and, with the old languages extinct,
we form one universal language,

that elegant tongue, that sole language,
richer than now and more perfect,
summary of the most sonorous words
that those other languages bequeathed to us,

that language, compendium of languages,
as pleasurable as a serenade,
as delightful as a moonlit night,
will be – what other? – the Galician language.

Language of my mother, harmonious language
in which the pleas of the sorrowful rise to heaven,
and in which tranquil hope descends
to choking, grief-smitten breasts;

language of my forebears, language in which pariahs,
covered in shadow and dust and sweat,
beg earth for the blood-coloured grain
that will fatten an animal – the lord of the manor.

Pure language of ours, in which the souls of the dead,
during black nights of silence and fear,
charge the living with the duties
that they, poor wretches, died without discharging.

Language in which birds sing,
in which angels and children speak,
in which springs sob and in which
winds murmur among leafy trees.

No, you shall not die, Celtic muse
born in the dense scrublands of Suebia,
the last love of pale Macías,
his heart transfixed by an iron shaft;

fecund muse of the only wise king
who ever sat on the throne of Spain,
immortal harp of sweet Rosalía,
last hymn of ill-fated Añón;

you cannot die... That is what
the disloyal sons who mocked you would like!
But you shall not die, Christ of languages;
no, you shall not die, O Nazarene!

As your apostle, even though the very wretchedest,
I will take your Gospel far and wide,
wearing the ignominious mantle
that they draped over your shoulders to mock you.

In your name, over land and sea,
I will offer peace and health to the sick;
to exiles I will speak of the homeland,
to slaves of liberty and redemption.

I will announce the day of your triumph
throughout cities and towns and deserts,
and if, for announcing you, I am stoned,
even as I die my lips will name you!

O maio

Aquí vén o maio
de frores cuberto...
puxéronse á porta
cantándome os nenos;
i os puchos furados
pra min estendendo,
pedíronme crocas
dos meus castiñeiros.

Pasai, rapaciños,
calados e quedos,
que o que é polo de hoxe
que darvos non teño.
Eu sónvo-lo probe
do pobo gallego:
ipra min non hai maio,
pra min sempre é inverno!...

Cando eu me atopare
de donos liberto
i o pan non me quiten
trabucos e préstemos,
e como os do abade
frorezan meus eidos,
chegado habrá entonces
o maio que eu quero.

¿Queredes castañas
dos meus castiñeiros?...
Cantádeme un maio

sen bruxas nin demos;
un maio sin segas,
usuras nin preitos,
sin quintas, nin portas,
nin foros, nin cregos.

The May-garland

Here comes the May-garland,
covered with flowers.
The children, all singing,
stood at my door;
and then, as they held out
their ragged caps,
they begged for dried chestnuts
from my chestnut trees.

Come in, my dear children,
but keep quiet and calm,
because at this moment
I've nothing to give.
You see, I'm the pauper,
the people of Galicia:
for me there's no Maytime,
for me it's always winter...!

As soon as I find that
I'm free of landlords,
and my bread is not taken
by taxes and debts,
and my fields flourish
like the priest's fields,
then the Maytime I want
will have arrived.

So you want some chestnuts
from my chestnut trees?
Well, sing of a Maytime
with no witches or demons;
no reaping in Castile,
no loan sharks or lawsuits,
no press-gangs or food-taxes
or land-rents or priests.

Na chegada a Ourense da primeira locomotora

I
Velahí vén, velahí vén avantando
cómaros e corgas, e vales, e cerros.
¡Vinde vela, mociños e mozas!
¡Saludaina, rapaces e vellos!

Por onde ela pasa
fecunda os terreos,
espértanse os homes,
florecen os eidos.

Velahí vén, velahí vén tan houpada,
tan milagrosiña, con paso tan meigo,
que parece unha Nosa Señora,
unha Nosa Señora de ferro.

Tras dela non veñen
abades nin cregos;
mais vén a fartura
ii a luz i o progreso!

II
Catedral, demagogo de pedra,
dun pobo fanático erguida no medio,
repinica esas chocas campanas
en sinal de alegría e contento.

Asocia esas voces
ó són dos pandeiros,
ias santas surrisas
de terras e ceos!

E ti, río dos grandes destinos,
que os himnos ensaias dos trunfos ibéricos,
requeimáda-las fauces de sede
ven o monstro a beber no teu seo.

Bon samaritano,
dálle auga ó sedento;
que a máquina é o Cristo
dos tempos modernos.

On the arrival in Ourense of the first railway engine

I

Look, here she comes, here she comes
past field-ridges and paths and valleys and hills.
Come and see her, lads and lasses!
Come and see her, young and old!

Wherever she passes
she makes the lands fertile,
men awake from their sleep,
fields burst into bloom.

Look, here she comes, here she comes
so lofty, so miraculous, with such a magical step,
that she's like an Our Lady,
an Our Lady of iron.

Behind her don't come
priests or clerics,
what does come is plenty
and light! and progress!

II

Cathedral, stone demagogue
standing in the midst of a fanatical people,
chime those cracked bells of yours
as a sign of happiness and joy.

Unite those tones
with the sound of the tambourines,
and with the holy smiles
of lands and skies!

And you, river of great destinies,
rehearsing the hymns of Iberian triumphs:
with her jaws burnt with thirst,
the monster is coming to drink from your depths.

Good Samaritan,
give water to the thirsty,
for the machine is the Christ
of modern times.

¡Ai!

¿Como foi?... – Eu topábame fora
cando as negras vixigas lle deron;
polo aramio súa nai avisoume
     i eu vinme correndo.

¡Coitadiño! Sintindo os meus pasos,
revolveu cara a min os seus ollos.
Non me viu... e chorou... ¡ai!, xa os tiña
     ceguiños de todo.

Non me acordo que tempo me estiven
sobre o berce de dor debruzado;
sólo sei que me erguín co meu neno
     sin vida nos brazos...

Volvoreta de aliñas douradas
que te pousas no berce valeiro,
pois por el me perguntas, xa sabes
     qué foi do meu neno.

Oh!

How did it happen?... 'I was away
when the terrible blisters appeared;
his mother told me by wire
     and I came as fast as I could.

Poor little thing! Hearing my steps
he turned his eyes towards me.
He couldn't see me... and he wept...
     oh! they were sightless.

I don't remember how long I was
prostrate upon that bed of pain;
I only know that I stood up with my child
     dead in my arms...'

Butterfly with golden wings
settling on the empty cot,
you ask for him, and now you know
     what happened to my child.

Cántiga

No xardín unha noite sentada,
ó refrexo do branco luar,
unha nena choraba sin trégolas
os desdés dun ingrato galán.

I a coitada entre queixas dicía:
"Xa no mundo non teño ninguén,
vou morrer e non ven os meus ollos
os olliños do meu doce ben".

Os seus ecos de malenconía
camiñaban nas alas do vento,
   i o lamento
   repetía:
"¡Vou morrer e non ven ó meu ben!"

Lonxe dela, de pé sobre a popa
dun aleve negreiro vapor,
emigrado, camiño de América
vai o probe, infelís amador.

I ó mirar as xentís anduriñas
cara a terra que deixa cruzar:
"Quen puidera dar volta – pensaba –,
quen puidera convosco voar!..."

Mais as aves i o buque fuxían
sin ouír seus amargos lamentos;
   sólo os ventos
   repetían:
"¡Quen puidera convosco voar!"

Noites craras, de aromas e lúa,
desde entón ¡que tristeza en vós hai
prós que viron chorar unha nena,
prós que viron un barco marchar!...

Dun amor celestial, verdadeiro,
quedou sólo, de bágoas a proba,
   unha cova
   nun outeiro
i on cadavre no fondo do mar.

Song

As she sat in the garden one evening
in the lustrous white light of the moon,
a young maiden was weeping and weeping
for her lover's ungrateful disdain.

Amidst sighs the poor girl was declaring,
'In this world I have nobody now,
I shall die and my eyes do not gaze at
the sweet eyes of my dear darling man.'

And those echoes of deep melancholia
travelled forth on the wings of the wind;
    it repeated
    her lamenting:
'I shall die and they don't see my dear!'

Far away from her, up on the poop-deck
of a steamship perfidious and cruel,
stands an emigrant bound for America:
that young maiden's unhappy, dear love.

As he gazed at the elegant swallows
on their way to the land he had left,
'Oh, if I could but turn back,' he pondered,
'if I only could fly back with you.'

But the birds and the boat both were fleeing;
they heard none of his bitter laments;
    and the breezes
    just repeated,
'Oh, if I could but fly back with you!'

O clear nights of aromas and moonlight:
ever since, what deep sadness you've held
for all those who once saw a girl weeping,
for all those who once saw a ship sail!...

Of a love that was true and celestial,
no more trace now remains except tears,
    and a grave, up
    on a hilltop
and a corpse in the depths of the sea.

Na morte da miña nai

Doce malencolía, miña Musa,
do meu esprito noiva feiticeira,
déixame que hoxe no teu colo dorma
    isono de pedra!

Nunca, reiciña, nunca como agora
falla fixéronme os teus bicos mornos:
choveu por min chuvia de sangue e traio
    frío nos ósos.

Quéntame ti, que tiritando veño,
ti, que do peito curas as feridas,
amiga xenerosa dos que sofren,
    ¡melancolía!

Tope miña alma, á sombra dos ciprestes
que os tristes ermos das túas illas cobren,
o esquecemento que en ningures hacho
    prás miñas doores.

Fai que ó rumor dos teus regueiros, brando,
se adormezan meus tristes pensamentos.
¡Son un orfo!... Agarímame ó teu colo...
    Xa outro non teño.

Xa outro non teño en que pousa-la frente,
polas agurras do pesar sulcada;
xa outro non teño que a amargura enxugue
    ¡das miñas bágoas!

Nai, ¡adorada nai!, mártir escura,
branca pombiña, arruladora e tenra,
¡ai! si souperas como me deixabas...
    non te morreras.

Dende que te perdín, a terra, o ceo,
todo é pra min da mesma cor da morte.
O sol non me alumea, nin os campos
    pra min tén frores.

Cal sobre os condenados a pauliña
caíu sobre miña alma eterno loito;
todo me amarga, hastra o aire que respiro;
dáname todo.

Do corazón fuxiume esa alegría
que é nas frores aroma e vos nos páxaros,
i andan por dentro do meu peito os corvos
arrevoando.

¡Como recordo aquelas noites craras
en que ó fulgor da prateada lúa
me arrulába-lo sono, dos teus cantos
coa doce música!

¡Como recordo aquelas tardes tristes
en que os tronos sentindo, rezabamos
porque Dios leve ós probes mariñeiros
a porto salvo.

Polos necesitados camiñantes,
polos vellos sin pan e sin abrigo,
polos nenos sin pai..., abandonados...,
¡coma os teus fillos!

¡Ai! Eu tamén rezar quixera agora
por ti, de tanto amor en xusto pago;
mais dende que te fuches, miña rula,
¡teño un cansacio!...

Malenconía, Musa dos doentes,
do meu esprito noiva feiticeira,
¡déixame que hoxe no teu colo dorma
sono de pedra!

On the death of my mother

Sweet melancholy, my muse,
bewitching ladylove of my spirit,
let me sleep today upon your lap
    a sleep of stone!

Never, my sweetheart, never as I do now
have I needed your warm kisses:
a rain of blood has rained on me and I am
    cold to my bones.

Warm me, for I am shivering,
you who cures wounds of the heart,
O melancholy, generous friend
    of those who suffer!

May my soul find, in the shade of the cypresses
that cover those sad wastelands, your islands,
the oblivion that I can nowhere find,
    the refuge from my griefs.

Make my sorrowful thoughts fall asleep
to the soft murmur of your brooks.
I am an orphan! Caress me upon your lap...
    I have no other now!

I have no other on which to rest my brow,
furrowed by deep lines of woe,
I have no other to dry
    my bitter tears!

Mother, adored mother, dark martyr,
white dove, cooing and tender,
oh, if you knew in what straits you were leaving me...
    oh, you would not have died.

Ever since I lost you, the earth, the sky,
everything is the very colour of death.
The sun does not shine on me, nor do the fields
    have flowers for me.

As excommunication falls upon condemned men,
so eternal mourning fell upon my soul;
all is bitter for me, even the air I breathe;
    everything hurts me.

From my heart fled that happiness
that is perfume in flowers and song in birds,
and inside my breast the crows
    are hovering.

How I remember those clear nights
when, by the light of the silver moon
you sang me to sleep with the sweet music
    of your songs!

How I remember those sad afternoons
when, hearing thunder, we prayed
that God might take poor sailors
    to a safe port;

and prayed for travellers in need,
for the old without bread or shelter,
for children without parents..., abandoned,
    like your children!

Oh! I too would pray now
for you, as just recompense for so much love;
but ever since you went away, my sweet,
    I have felt so weary!

Melancholy, muse of those who suffer,
bewitching ladylove of my spirit,
let me sleep today upon your lap
    a sleep of stone!

Nouturnio

Da aldea lexana fumegan as tellas;
detrás dos petoutos vai póndose o sol;
retornan prós eidos coa noite as ovellas,
tiscando nas beiras o céspede mol.

Un vello, arrimado nun pau de sanguiño,
o monte atravesa de cara ó piñar.
Vai canso; unha pedra topou no camiño
e nela sentouse pra folgos tomar.

   – ¡Ai! – dixo –, ¡que triste,
  que triste eu estou! –
  I on sapo, que o oía,
  repuxo: – ¡*Cro, cro*!

¡Ás ánemas tocan!... Tal noite como esta
queimóuseme a casa, morreume a muller;
ardeume a xugada na corte, i a besta,
na terra a semente botouse a perder.

Vendín prós trabucos bacelos e hortas
e vou polo mundo de entón a pedir;
mais cando non topo pecháda-las portas,
os cans sáinme a elas e fanme fuxir.

   Canta, sapo, canta:
  – ¡Ti i eu somos dous!...
  I o sapo, choroso,
  cantaba: – ¡*Cro, cro*!

Soliños estamos antrambos na terra,
mais nela un buraco ti alcontras i eu non;
a ti non te morden os ventos da serra,
i a min as entrañas i os ósos me ron.

Ti, nado nos montes, nos montes esperas,
decote cantando, teu térmeno ver;
eu nado entre os homes, dormento entre as feras,
e morte non hacho si quero morrer.

   Xa tocan... Recemos,
  ¡que dicen que hai Dios!...
  El reza, i o sapo
  cantaba: – ¡*Cro, cro*!

A noite cerraba, i o raio da lúa
nas lívidas cumes comeza a brilar;

curisco que tolle nos álbores brúa
i escóitase ó lexos o lobo oubear.

O probre do vello, cos anos cangado,
ergueuse da pedra i o pao recadou;
virou para os ceos o puño pechado
e cara ós touzales rosmando marchou...

Cos ollos seguíndoo
na escura estensión,
o sapo quedouse
cantando: – ¡*Cro, cro*!

Nocturne

The tiles of the far-distant village are smoking;
behind craggy mountains the sun slowly sets;
with nightfall the sheep return home to the farmsteads
and nibble the grass that lies soft by the track.

An ancient, propped up on a stick made of buckthorn,
is plodding through scrub to the forest of pine.
He's weary; he comes to a rock by the wayside,
and on it he sits to recover his breath.

He said, 'Oh, unhappy,
unhappy am I!'
A toad, when it heard him,
responded: 'Croak, croak!'

'They're ringing for prayers! ... On a night just like this one
my house was burnt down and my wife perished there,
my oxen both died in the stable, my horse too,
the seed that I'd planted was spoilt in the ground.

To pay tolls and taxes I sold fields and vineyards,
and ever since then I have wandered and begged;
but when I don't find all the doors locked and bolted
the fierce dogs attack me and force me to flee.

Oh sing, toad, oh sing, for
we're two of a kind...'

The toad, sad and tearful,
was singing: 'Croak, croak!'

'The two of us live all alone on this planet,
but you find a hole in it and I do not;
the winds from the serra don't bite at your body:
they gnaw at my bowels and they chew on my bones.

You, born in the wilds, in the wilds are expecting,
while ceaselessly singing, to come to your end;
I, born among humans, half-sleep among wild beasts,
and I cannot find death if I want to die.

The bells ring ... Let's pray, for
they say God exists!...'
He prays, and the toad went
on singing: 'Croak, croak!'

The night closes in, and the beams of the moonlight
begin to shine down on the mauve mountain-tops;
the wind of the north that dismantles trees bellows,
the howls of the wolf in the distance ring out.

The poor beggarman, from the years bent and weary,
rose up from the rock and took hold of his stick;
he raised his clenched fist and he shook it at heaven
and, muttering, into the wastelands he went...

And watching him walk through
that gloomy expanse,
the toad, left alone there,
was singing, 'Croak, croak!'

¡Crebar as liras!

Por sobre a barafunda
de escarnios e pauliñas
que as cántigas dos servos
por ondequer suscitan,
espaventada, atóneta,
a virxe Poesía
clamou desalentada:
"¡Vates, crebade as liras!"

¡Crebar as liras cando
se fai temer aínda
a maza de Xan Dente
por vara de Xusticia!
¡Cando nos nosos Códigos
non val dun home a vida
os sete vis escudos
en que a tasou *Molina*!

¡Calar!... ¡Que non se escoite
o patuxar das vítimas
no mar de inxofre e sangue
da escravitú caídas!
¡Calar!... ¡I as maus cravadas,
i a túnica cinguida,
i a intolerancia abaixo,
i a intolerancia arriba!

Non. Feita está a pormesa
i é menester cumprila.
A patria morre. ¡Malia
o fillo que a non mira!
¡E malia quen lle negue,
por tedio ou covardía,
os himnos que a amortaxen,
o sangue que a redima!

¡Crebar as liras diante
da libertá que espira
baixo a gadoupa férrea
do dogma que a asesina!...
¡Inda goberna Claudio!
¡Inda Seiano priva!
¡Inda os proscritos choran
e triunfa Mesalina!

¡Non a crebés, poetas!
Templaina en ódeo, en ira,
hatra que dela saian
as esplosiós das minas;
hatra que cada nota,
coma onha espada fira,

coma un andacio, barra
as vellas teogonías.

Gustoso esnaquizara
e resignado a miña,
si neso do meu pobo
a sorte consistira;
mais, mentres orfo e triste
os meus consolos pida,
crebala... ina túa testa
tan sólo, tiranía!

Smash your lyres!

Over the uproar
of mockery and excommunication
that the songs of slaves
arouse on all sides,
virgin Poetry,
terrified and astonished,
cried dejectedly,
'Bards, smash your lyres!'

'Smash your lyres' when
people are still made to fear
the cacique's club
in the form of a magistrate's mace!
When according to our Laws
the life of a man is not worth
the seven vile escudos
at which *Molina* valued it!

'Keep quiet!'... So that no one hears
the splashing of the victims
of slavery fallen
into the sea of sulphur and blood!
'Keep quiet!'... With hands nailed down
and wearing the holy tunic,
and intolerance below,
and intolerance above!

No. The promise has been made
and it must be kept.

Our homeland is dying. Accursed be
the son who does not look to her!
And accursed be he who,
from tedium or cowardice,
denies her hymns to enshroud her,
blood to redeem her!

'Smash your lyres' in the presence
of liberty, expiring
under the iron talon
of the dogma that kills her!...
Claudius still rules!
Sejanus is still powerful!
The proscripts are still weeping!
Messalina still triumphs!

Do not smash them, poets!
Tune them to hatred, to wrath,
until from them come
explosions of land-mines;
until each note
wounds like a sword
and like a plague sweeps away
the old theogonies.

Happily and with resignation
would I break mine into pieces
if the fortunes of my people
depended upon it;
but so long as, orphaned and sorrowful,
they beg for my consolation,
I will smash it... only
on your head, tyranny!

A Virxe do Cristal (fragmento)

O día crarexaba;
do sol, que a relumbrar encomenzaba,
unha franxa marela
polos altos petoutos se estendía;
a brisa nas silveiras rebuldaba,
i alá no ceio – pendurada estrela –
chilraba aletexando a cutuvía.

    Do lado de Levante
de sombra e lume pavillón flotante,
vai correndo mainiña, mainamente,
tapando os hourizontes, negra nube,
e dela por didiante
trévoa de fogo ardente
esparxe húmedo cheiro a terra quente.

    Martiño camiñaba
máis triste cada ves, a toda présa.
¡Cantas bágoas choraba
por aquel camiñiño da devesa!

    "Querer unha rapaza hermosa e pura;
pedila por muller con cortesía;
ir forrando prá voda e mais pró cura;
gardarlle lei un día i outro día;
respetala, adorala con loucura;
pegar por ela choutos de alegría;
e cando un está lévedo, ceguiño
pola amorosa febre,
escoitar unha noite nun camiño:
"Non te cases, Martiño,
si non queres levar gato por lebre..."

    "Traballar toda a vida;
andar bregando sempre co esta aixada
pra conservar sin lixo, ennobrecida,
a limpa fama de meus pais herdada;
e de pronto escoitar de boca allea
unha mañá, no medio dun camiño:
"Mira o que fas, Martiño,
que che se rin de ti por toda a aldea..."

    "¡Ai, coestes comparados,
nada os tormentos son dos condenados!
¿Será verdá, Xan de Ventraces? ... ¡Dimo!
¡Ten piedade de min, destas bagullas,
deste inferno en que ximo,
devorado por dentes coma agullas!
Eu non sei si te crea,
pero ... ¡Virxe María!,

si dixeses verdade, eu morrería...
¿Sera-lo demo? ... ¡Arrenegado el sea!"

Así dicindo o mísero labrego,
sin calma nin sosego,
meteuse na devesa de contado,
e do seu sacho armado
comenzou sen refolgo o seu trafego.

The Virgin of the Crystal (extract)

Day was dawning;
a yellow band
of the sun, which
was beginning to shine,
spread over the high crags;
the breeze was frolicking among the brambles
and high in the sky, a hanging star,
the lark fluttered and warbled.

Towards the east
a black cloud,
a floating pavilion of shadow and light,
advances calmly, calmly, hiding the horizon,
and before it
a thunderstorm of burning fire
sends out a damp smell of hot earth.

Martiño was walking,
sadder and sadder, at top speed.
How many tears he shed
along that path to the grazing-grounds!

'You love a pure, beautiful girl;
you ask courteously for her hand;
you save for the wedding and the priest's fees;
you stay faithful to her day after day;
you respect her, you madly adore her;
you give jumps of joy for her;
and when you're head over heels in love, blinded
by the fever of love,
you hear one night on a path:

"Don't marry, Martiño,
unless you want to be sold a cat for a cony..."

You work all your life;
you're always toiling with this mattock
to keep undefiled and ennobled
the pure repute inherited from your parents;
and you suddenly hear from someone's mouth
one morning, in the middle of a path:
"Look what you're doing. Martiño,
they're laughing at you all over the village..."

Oh, compared with these torments,
the torments of the condemned are nothing!
Can it be true, Xan de Ventraces...? Tell me!
Take pity on me, on these tears,
on this hell in which I groan,
devoured by needle-teeth!
I don't know whether to believe you,
but... by the Virgin Mary!
if it were the truth you've told me, I'd die!
Might it be the devil's work?... Curse him!'

Thus speaking, the wretched farm-labourer,
restless and uneasy,
went off into the grazing-grounds
and, armed with his mattock,
not pausing to catch his breath, set about his work.

From O divino sainete (The Divine Farce), *1888*

Entrei no vagón, e diante...

Entrei no vagón, e diante
de min presentouse a escena
máis atroz e repunante.

Montón de frades noxentes,
ouscenos, crasos, cebados,
de longas uñas e dentes,

con rudo ranxer de moas
botan a parva, engulindo
cal torpes serpentes boas.

Chocoume da xente aquela
a feroz voracidade,
que ergue o estómago de vela.

I espricarma non sabía,
cando oín que un dos viaxeiros,
convidándome, dicía:

– ¿Querme acompañar? Sin gana
cómeselle esto. – ¿E que é eso?
– Un pouco de carne humana,

mesmo de xunto á rileira,
nunca saio sen un toro
de Murguía na fiambreira.

– Mercé, non levo apetito.
– Matámolo a paos nantronte,
ii élle bocado esquisito!

Non ben houbo iste acabado
saltou outro: – Ó señor halle
de gustar máis o pescado.

Se así for, por sorte, apreixe
un bocadiño siquera
de Manuel Ánxel... – ¡Bon peixe!

– Da Cruña caieu na praia:
úsanse alí unhas traíñas
de onde non se ergue o que caia...

I así, pra min estendendo
anacos do seu almorzo
todos fóronme ofrecendo

con crianza e fidalguía
talladas de Oxea, Vicetto,
Lamas, Pondal, Rosalía...

Mirando aquiles horrores,
vendo qué trato merecen
os artistas i escritores,

suspirei con triste xesto:
"¡Pardiola! ¡Non val a pena
de amar a patria pra esto!"

Atento Añón ó meu dito,
– Ten conta – ouservou –, ten conta
con non alzares o grito;

que se esta xente soubera
quen eres ti, que a censuras...
¡non che arrendo a que che espera!

¿Coidabas outra caricia
outer da que outemos todos,
dos críticos de Galicia?

Pois, meu amante, vai vendo...
– i Añón amostroume un frade
que iba os meus ósos roendo.

I entered the compartment...

I entered the compartment, and before
me was the most atrocious
and repugnant scene.

A crowd of loathsome friars,
obscene, crass, bloated,
with long nails and teeth,

coarsely champing away,
are having a snack, devouring
like clumsy boa constrictors.

The ferocious voracity
of those people astonished me;
it turns the stomach to see it.

And I did not understand,
when I heard that one of the travellers
was saying as he invited me:

'Will you join us? No need for an appetite
to enjoy this.' 'And what is it?'
'A bit of human meat.

From around the kidneys,
I never travel without a slice
of Murguía in my luncheon-box.'

'Thank you, I am not hungry.'
'We beat him to death the day before yesterday,
and it's an exquisite morsel, you know!'

No sooner had this one finished speaking
than another came out with: 'The gentleman
will no doubt prefer fish.

If this is so, perchance, take
at least a little nibble
of Manuel Ánxel... a real fishy character!

He was caught off the Corunna coast:
they have such fine long-boats there
– whatever falls into them does not rise.'

And in this way, holding out
pieces of their breakfast,
they all in turn offered me

with good manners and chivalry
slices of Oxea, Vicetto,
Lamas, Pondal, Rosalía...

Contemplating these horrors,
seeing what treatment is given
to artists and writers,

I sighed sorrowfully:
'For God's sake! It isn't worthwhile
loving the homeland if this is the result!'

Añón, hearing what I'd said,
observed, 'Take care, take care
not to raise your voice:

if these people knew
who you are, and that you're finding fault with them...
I wouldn't want to be in your shoes!

Were you expecting to receive
any caress other than the one we all receive
from the censurers of Galicia?

Well, my dear fellow, now you see...'
And Añón pointed to a friar
who was gnawing my bones.

From Poemas soltos (Other Poems), *1885*

A Rosalía

Do mar pola orela
mireina pasar,
na frente unha estrela,
no bico un cantar.
E vina tan sola
na noite sin fin,
¡que inda recei pola probe da tola,
eu, que non teño quen rece por min!

A Musa dos pobos
que vin pasar eu,
comesta dos lobos,
comesta se veu...
Os ósos son dela
que vades gardar.
¡Ai, dos que levan na frente unha estrela!
¡Ai, dos que levan no bico un cantar!

To Rosalía

At the edge of the sea
I saw her pass by.
On her forehead a star,
on her lips a song.
And I saw her so lonely
in the endless night

that I prayed for that poor mad woman,
I, with no one to pray for me!

The Muse of the people
whom I saw passing by,
was eaten,
eaten by wolves...
The bones are hers
that you will keep.
Alas for those with a star on their forehead!
Alas for those with a song on their lips!

Manuel Leiras Pulpeiro (1854–1912)

From Cantares gallegos (Galician Songs), *1911*

Voume prá beira do río...

Voume pra a beira do río,
que consola ouvil-a yauga;
porque a yauga vai dicindo:
¡Todo pasa, todo pasa!

★ ★ ★

Fun de romaxe ô Conforto
donde tantos se consolan.
E, cal eu fun, tal volvín
Co-as miñas peniñas todas.

★ ★ ★

¡Ai, Morte, canto xa tardas
en me levares contigo!
¡Ben se ve que non te doyes
d'as dôres d'os coitadiños!

I'm off to the river bank...

I'm off to the river bank
for it's comforting to hear the water;
because the water is saying:
All flows past, all flows past!

* * *

I went as a pilgrim to O Conforto,
where so many find consolation.
And as I went so I returned
with all my many sorrows.

* * *

¡Oh, Death, how long you take
to carry me away with you!
It's easy to see that you don't feel
for the pains of those who suffer!

From Obras completas (Complete Works), *1930*

¡Bagallos d'o mar bruantes...

¡Bagallos d'o mar bruantes,
quen non se pasme de vervos
non sabe sentil-o grande!

* * *

Antes

¡Vaite, noite, correndo e pasade,
auga e pedra, que teño n-os agros
o panciño que piden os meus nenos
que levan, de fame, seguido xa un ano!

Despois

¡Vente, noite, correndo e volvede,
auga e pedra, e levaime con todo;
que, apedradol-os os agros, non queda
pra nós outra cousa que o fondo d'un pozo!

Roaring rollers of the sea...

Roaring rollers of the sea,
whoever's not amazed to see you
cannot feel grandeur!

★ ★ ★

Before

Go, night, quickly; and begone,
rain and hail, for in the fields I have
the bread that my children beg:
they've been hungry a whole year!

After

Come, night, quickly; and return,
rain and hail, and carry me and everything away:
with my fields battered down, there's nothing
left for us but the bottom of a well!

The Twentieth Century

The First Thirty Years

Manuel Lugrís Freire (1863–1940)

From **Asieumedre (Mayiprosper),** *1916*

Conto

Don Constante era un avogado de moita sona na Coruña. Pasaba o verán nun pazo da parroquia de Moruxo, preto da vila de Betanzos. A horta non tiña semeadura de abondo, e ademais, polo fondal faltáballe un bon pedazo para ser cadrada. Lindaba por este lado cunha leira de Bastián, que non quería de ningunha maneira vender o cacho de terreo que cobizaba don Constante.

Un día presentouse Bastián na Coruña, no despacho do noso avogado, e díxolle:

– Señor, poño no seu coñecemento cómo lle cadrou en sorte ao meu fillo Pedro, que é o meu brazo dereito, ir servir ao rei. Non sei qué vai ser de min, pois xa estou moi velliño e non podo traballar a miña pobre facenda.

– Tes razón, amigo Bastián.

– E polo mesmo, eu víñalle rogar que me emprestase algún diñeiro sobre da leira que está a carón do fondal da horta do seu pazo de Moruxo.

– ¿En que condicións? – preguntou entón don Constante cheo de alegría porque por fin ía redondea-la horta.

– Señor, como vostede queira. Vender non lla vendo, porque me doe moito desfacerme dos bens que foron de meus pais; así é que se lle parece ben, tomareille o diñeiro en pacto de retro.

– Ben, home, ben... – respondeu o avogado relambéndose de gusto por dentro.

– Como a miña leira é moi grande, hipotecarei namais que a metade.

– Conforme, amigo Bastián, sempre que a parte que hipoteques linde coa miña horta.

– Deso non debemos falar. Así se fará.

Fixeron a escritura de pauto de retro, e Bastián largou co diñeiro a redimir a Perucho, que volveu aquel mesmo día para a súa casa máis contento que un cuco.

Ía cumprir un ano despois desto. A véspera do vencemento da hipoteca, presentouse Bastián en compaña de tres veciños seus, para que lle servisen de testigos, no despacho de don Constante.

– Meu amo e señor – dicíalle Bastián cunha cara de tristeza que mesmo partía as cordas do corazón; eu sonlle home perdidiño. Este ano caeron enriba de min moitas desgracias. Non collín maínzo ningún, as viñas inzáronse de feluxe, apodreceron as patacas no celeiro e deume moita perda a venda do gando. Inda que lle levei en maio tres cacholas e tres pernís de cocho ao beato Frei Pedro Manzano, afogoume un bacoriño e rompeu unha perna un cuxo... ¡Non lle podo pagar, meu amo! ¡Doume por perdidiño!

– ¿E daquela?

– ¿Daquela? ¡Ai, meu señor don Constante, que lle estou empeñadiño de todo, e non me queda outro remedio, para saír de apuros, que hipotecarlle a outra metade!

– ¡Vállanos Deus! Para que vexas que te trato ben, e que non abuso da túa situación, dareiche a mesma cantidade pola outra parte da leira.

– Os homes coma vostede teñen no ceo un lugar escolleito a la diestra de Dios padre... Fixeron a escritura, e cando Bastián tiña os cartos nas mans, dixo, póndose máis teso e serio que un cacique en días de eleccións:

– Agora, meu señor, quero deshipotecar a outra metade, que vence mañá. Aquí ten o diñeiro; e os presentes sexan testigos de como fago a entrega.

– Mira, meu amiguiño – respondeulle don Constante dándolle unhas palmadiñas no lombo –, agora queda a miña horta sen completar, e terei que poñer unha ponte, se me deixas, para pasar á outra banda que agora me hipotecas. Ti non tiveches necesidade de ir a Santiago a aprender leis. Coa retranca que Deus che deu tes dabondo para xiringar a calquera letrado como me xiringaches a min.

Tale

Don Constante was a well-known lawyer in Coruña. He spent the summer in the parish of Moruxo, near the town of Betanzos. The garden did not have much planted in it and furthermore at the bottom there was a good bit missing for it to be fully square. On this side it bordered a field owned by Bastián who under no circumstance wanted to sell this little bit of land which Don Constante wanted.

One day Bastián turned up in Coruña, in the lawyer's office, and he said:

– Sir, I 'm here to let you know that it has fallen upon my son Pedro, the apple of my eye, to have to go and serve the king. I do not know what is going to become of me because I am now too old to be able to work my poor little piece of land.

– You're right, Bastián my friend.

– That's why I've come to beg you to lend me some money on the land of mine which is beside your garden in Moruxo.

– Under what conditions? – asked Don Constante, happy because he was at last going to be able to square off the garden.

– Sir, just as you wish. I'm not going to sell it to you, because it pains me to do away with things I've inherited from my parents so, if you don't mind, I'll take the money in a repurchase pact.

– Well, well... replied the lawyer, licking his chops with pleasure.

– As my field is very big, I'll only mortgage half of it...

– Alright, Bastián, as long as the part you mortgage is the part which borders my garden.

– We needn't talk about that. That's how it'll be done.

They wrote out the deed for a repurchase pact, and Bastián went off with the money in order to buy his son out of the army. Pedro came back home that same day as happy as a lark.

A year was about to pass since this had happened. On the day before the mortgage was due, Bastián appeared in Don Constante's office with three of his neighbours to act as witnesses.

– Sir, sir – said Bastián, with a heartbreaking sadness visible in his eyes, I'm a broken man. So many misfortunes have befallen me this year. I couldn't harvest any maize, my grapes were infected, my potatoes have rotted in the shed and I've lost money selling cattle. I took two pig's heads and two shoulders of pork to the good Friar Pedro Manzano in May, but even so one of my piglets drowned and one of my calves broke a leg. I can't pay you back, sir! I'm a broken man!

– And so?

– And so? Oh, Don Constante, sir, I owe everything to you, and there's nothing left for me to do but to mortgage the other half to you!

– Dear lord! Just so you can see that I treat you well and I'm not taking advantage of the situation, I'll give you the same amount for the other half of your field.

– Men like you have a place in heaven sitting at the right hand of God... They wrote out the deed, and when Bastián had the money in his hands he said, looking more serious and upright than a party boss on election day:

– Now, sir, I would like to buy back the mortgage on the other half which is due tomorrow. Here's the money, and these people are witnesses that I have handed it over.

– Look here, friend – answered Don Constante, patting him on the back, – now my garden is unfinished, and I'll have to build a bridge, with your permission, in order to cross over to the other side which you've mortgaged out to me. You didn't have to come to Santiago to study law. With the craftiness God gave you, you've got enough to beleaguer any lawyer like you've beleaguered me.

Antonio Noriega Varela (1869–1947)

From Do ermo (Of the Wasteland), *1920*

Laverquiña

Laverquiña que te axotas
das degaradas gaivotas
oíndo o salvaxe berro;
musa que a mariña estrañas,
olla as azules montañas
desde as praias do desterro.

Esquece o mar, lembra o gado
miúdo e o regalado
vivir, as tumbadas festas
e as cantigas dos pastores,
que fan grilandas coas flores
amareliñas das xestas.

Little lark

Little lark, scared
of the voracious seagulls
as you hear their savage screams;
muse, a stranger in the coastlands,
look up at the blue mountains
from the beaches of your exile.

Forget the sea, remember the small
animals and the good
life, the far-famed festas
and the songs of the shepherds,
who make garlands
with the yellow broom flowers.

Ora é unha abedoeira

Trocouse en arboriña (foi noutrora)
e aparece nos ermos orballada
porque gusta das lágrimas da aurora
xoíñas fulgurantes... A isolada

ora é unha abedoeira, mais xa fora
Ninfa tal vez, ou Princesiña, Fada
ou a Meiga máis linda e argalladora
que inquietou ós brañegos de Labrada.

Trocouse en arboriña, e entre abrollos
esmeraldas perdera: os claros ollos,
dous astros milagrosos... Mais non perde

súa esvelteza, prodixio de finura,
seu vestido, milagre de brancura
e unha ondeante mantilliña verde.

Now she is a birch tree

She turned into a tree (it was another time)
and she stands in the wastelands bedewed
because she likes the tears of the dawn,
gleaming jewels... That lone woman

is now a birch tree, but once she was
perhaps a Nymph, or a Princess, or a Fairy
or the prettiest and most scheming Sorceress
who ever perturbed the highlanders of Labrada.

She turned into a tree, and amidst thistles
she lost emeralds: her bright eyes,
two miraculous stars... But she does not lose

her slimness, a wonder of delicacy,
her dress, a miracle of whiteness,
or a flowing green mantilla.

Unha breve pucharquiña

É unha breve pucharquiña
sobre un enorme penedo.

Sen fatuidade urbana
míranse naquel espello
as floriñas dun carpazo,
a ramaxe dun esvedro,
linda pastora de Anaigo
e as estreliñas do ceo.

É unha breve pucharquiña
sobre un enorme penedo.

A little puddle

It's a little puddle
on a vast rock.

With no urban fatuity,
into that mirror look:
the flowers of a rockrose
the branches of a strawberry tree
a pretty shepherdess of Anaigo
and the stars of the sky.

It's a little puddle
on a vast rock.

Saben as ilusións miñas

Saben as ilusións miñas
dun carreiriño brañego
entre orballadas espiñas.

Despértamo a luz febea
e a través dos piñeirales
devagariño serpea.

Ó pé dun Cristo se enrosca
onde a queiroguenta serra
é máis ourizada e fosca.

E por un ermo se estende,
que dun sabugo se ufana
e a rosmaniño recende.

Con moitos predios a bravo,
meu pazo ideal vos brindo
do carreiriño no cabo.

My dearest hopes know

My dearest hopes know
of a path in mountain pastures
between thorn-bushes.

Phoebus's light rouses it for me
and through the pine-groves
it slowly winds.

By a Crucifix it twists and turns
where the heathery serra
is most rugged and harsh.

And it stretches through a wasteland
that boasts of one elder-bush
and is scented with rosemary.

Surrounded by untilled fields,
my ideal mansion I offer you
at the end of this path.

Ramón Cabanillas (1876–1959)

From No desterro (In Exile), *1913*

A Basilio Álvarez

¡Sementador! O trigo dos beirales
mostra as espigas mestas e douradas,
e as segadoras fouces, afiadas,
teñen tráxico brillo de puñales.

O teu verbo, estalante nos pinales,
troca, ó chegar ás chozas das valgadas,
os salaios das gorxas abafadas
en ruxidos guerreiros e triunfales.

A aldea ergueuse co claror da aurora
agardando o sinal, e non sosega
en axexo de loita vingadora.

¡Xa a luz do sol do mediodía cega,
sementador! Sementador, xa é hora
de dá-lo berro e comeza-la sega!

To Basilio Álvarez

Sower! The wheat in the fields by the river
shows its ears, thick-packed and golden,
and the sharp sickles, as they reap,
have the tragic sheen of daggers.

Your word, exploding in the pine-groves,
transforms, as it reaches the hovels in the valleys,
sobs in choking throats
into triumphal, warlike roars.

The village rises with the light of dawn,
watching for the sign, and it is restive
as it lies in wait for the vengeful struggle.

By now there's a blinding midday sun,
O sower! Sower, it is now time
to give the shout and start the reaping!

Na taberna

Os mozos mariñeiros da fiada
lémbranse rindo alleos de coidados,
cheira a aceite e pemento requeimados
rustrido de xurés en caldeirada.

Conta o patrón nun corro a treboada
do ano setenta – historia de afogados –
e empuxándose, inando, entran mollados
os homes dunha lancha de enviada.

Pasa de man en man a xerra roiba
de albariño, e namentres cae a choiva
e o vento fai tremer a casa enteira,

detrás do mostrador clarexa o ceo
nas trenzas de ouro, no mirar sereo,
no sorriso de luz da taberneira.

In the tavern

The sailor lads, laughing, carefree,
recall the festa by the water-mill;
the dressing for a horse-mackerel stew
smells of burnt oil and red pepper.

The landlord tells a group of customers about the storm
of 1870 – a story of drowned men –
and, jostling each other, panting,
the crew of a longboat comes in, soaking wet.

The red jug of albariño wine goes
from hand to hand and, as the rain falls
and the wind shakes the whole building,

behind the bar the sky grows clear
in the golden plaits, in the serene gaze,
in the smile of light of the landlord's wife.

From Rosa de cen follas (Rose with a Hundred Petals), *1927*

¡Amor, eterna inquedade!

I
¡Amor, eterna inquedade,
pon nos meus beizos doídos
o cáliz da Saudade!

¡Dáme a divina tristeza
da nave que vai sen rumbo
sobre do mar da incerteza!

¡Dáme o segredo choído
de ser roseira sen rosas
e cantiga sen sonido!

¡Dáme o doce desespero
de non saber se me quere
morréndome do que a quero!

¡Dáme a sagra vaguidade
de ir tecendo a miña vida
con soños de eternidade!

Love, eternal restlessness!

I

Love, eternal restlessness,
place between my aching lips
the chalice of sadlonging!

Give me the divine sorrow
of the ship drifting
on the sea of uncertainty!

Give me the locked-away secret
of being a rose-bush without roses,
and a song without sound!

Give me the sad despair
of not knowing if she loves me
as I die from my love of her!

Give me the sacred uncertainty
of weaving my life
with dreams of eternity!

From Terra asoballada (An Oppressed Land), *1917*

Diante dunha cunca de viño espadeiro

¡O espadeiro! ¡Acios mouros, cepas tortas,
follas verdes, douradas e vermellas,
gala nas terras vivas de Castrelo
nos Castelos de Oubiña e nas areas
de Tragove e Sisán, do mar de Arousa
e o Umia cristalino nas ribeiras!

¡O espadeiro amante! ¡O viño doce!
¡Alegría de mallas e espadelas,
compañeiro das bolas de pan quente
e as castañas asadas na lareira!

¡O espadeiro! ¡O resolio que louvaron
en namorantes páxinas sinxelas
os antigos abades do mosteiro
de Xan Daval, na vila cambadesa,
aqueles priores leigos e fidalgos,
mestres na vida, na virtú e na ciencia,
que sabian – ¡ouh tempos esquencidos! –
canta-la misa, escorrenta-las meigas,
acoller e amparar orfos e pobres,
rir coas rapazas, consella-las vellas,
darlles leito e xantar ós peregrinos,
pechar por foro as portas da súa igrexa
á xustiza do Rei, cobra-los dezmos
e dispoñer vendimas e trasegas!
¡O espadeiro morno! ¡O roxo viño,
sangue do corazón da nosa terra,
que arrecende a mazás e a rosas bravas,
quence os peitos e as almas alumea,
e sabe a bicos de mociña nova,
aldeana e trigueira!

¡Como canta ó caír nas brancas cuncas
desde as pintadas e bicudas xerras!
¡Como latexa e brilla ó coroalas!
¡E como loce e ri cando as adreza,
asemellando fíos de rubises,
cun rosario de escumas sanguiñentas!

★ ★ ★ ★

Espadeiro! ¡Espadeiro! ¡Ledo viño
das noites mozas! Claridá de estrelas.
O aturuxo zoando nas quebradas...
Mozos... Pandeiros... Un amor que empeza...
Aromas das carqueixas e do trevo...
De man en man, a bota carreteira...
Unha cantiga ó pé dunha ventana...
¡Detrás dos vidros, Ela!

¡Ouh, espadeiro amante! ¡Ouh, roxo e quente
sangue do corazón da nosa terra!
¡Acende os corazóns dos apoucados!
¡Prende lume nas almas, viño celta!

Before a cup of Espadeiro wine

O espadeiro! Dark bunches of grapes, twisted vine-stocks,
leaves green, golden and red,
gala dress of the living lands of Castrelo,
the Castles of Oubiña and the sands
of Tragove and Sisán, Arousa Bay
and the banks of the crystalline Umia!

O delicious espadeiro! O delectable wine!
Cheer of threshings and of scutchings,
companion of hot bread rolls
and of chestnuts roasted on the hearth!

O espadeiro! O ambrosia praised
in simple beguiling pages
by the old abbots of the monastery
of Xan Daval, in the town of Cambados,
those masters of life, of virtue and of knowledge
who knew – O forgotten times! –
how to sing mass, drive witches away,
welcome and succour orphans and paupers,
laugh with young lasses, advise old women,
give pilgrims bed and food,
lock their church doors, backed by rights and privileges,
against the King's authorities, collect tithes
and organize grape-harvests and wine-rackings!

O warm espadeiro! O red wine,
blood of the heart of our land,
redolent of apples and wild roses,
which warms breasts and lights souls,
and tastes of the kisses of a young lass,
an auburn-haired village-girl.

How it sings as it falls
from the mottled, beaked jugs into the white wine-cups!
How it trembles and glistens as it traces its crown inside them!

And how it sparkles and chuckles as it decorates them
with a rosary of bloody foam
like strings of rubies!

★ ★ ★ ★

Espadeiro! Espadeiro! Happy wine
of youthful nights! Starlight.
The joycry echoing through the gorges...
Young men... Tambourines... A love beginning...
Aromas of broom and of clover...
From hand to hand, the wineskin...
A song under a window...
Behind the glass, Her!
O delicious espadeiro! O warm red
blood of the heart of our land!
Fire the hearts of the poor-spirited!
Set light to souls, wine of the Celts!

From **Na noite estrelecida (In the Starry Night)**, *1926*

O Cabaleiro do Santo Grial (fragmento)

Galahaz, derradeiro, colle estreita vereda
que se adentra no monte, inquedante e segreda.
Sen espora nin lanza, sen escudo ni'espada,
alma e vida nun soño e no ceo a mirada,
sen coidar de malfado, dragón ni'encantamento,
o cabelo loiriño como airón dado ó vento,
escollido e chamado, vai ridente e lanzal,
que garda o corazón puro e limpo de mal.

Na escura corredoira cinguida de silveiras
escoitou voces irtas, medosas e tristeiras,
asubíos e ouveos, e chirridos de dentes
e pasadas de lobos e fungar de serpentes,
e veu brillar, ó paso de chouzales espesos,
uns ollos sanguiñosos, enmeigados e acesos
que o axexaban firente dende furos sombrizos.
Mais Galahaz non treme de agoiros nin feitizos.
E de alí a tres xornadas de longo camiñar,
san e salvo, atopouse na ribeira do mar.

Mainiño, maino, o vento a rosas recendía
e o mar ía espellado e o ceo estrelecía.
E acaeceu que ó tempo que Galahaz chegaba,
unha barca, senlleira, no areal atracaba,
cáliz de ouro garnido na brancura da vela,
a cruz roxa no pao e na proa unha estrela.
Galahaz, puro e limpo, entrou nela arelante,
e a nave naquel punto fixo rumbo a Levante
e alonxouse da praia, a vaivén compasado
coma berce dun neno dunha fada arrolado.
E con auga en repouso e o luceiro a brillar,
un camiño de prata relucía no mar.

E nos ollos azuis unha sagra visión,
florecidos os beizos nun rondel de oración,
Galahaz vai levado, nun soñar caricioso,
dunha espranza divina e un relembro saudoso.
E a barquiña envolveita nun claror de luar,
vai avante, en silencio, de vagar... de vagar...

Ó romper novo día, a barca milagreira
atracou antre as laxes dunha nova ribeira.
Unha brétema escura desfacíase en bágoas
no curuto das pedras e no limpo das ágoas,
e zarraba o camiño á terra de arribada
como forte parede por xigantes labrada
ó longo da ribeira, impoñente penedo
sen rubida ni'asalto nin buraco segredo.

Galahaz colleu terra levado do destino,
o corazón escravo dun mandado divino,
e mentres desparece o escuro neboeiro
e a barquiña se alonxa guiada do luceiro,
ollou, dunha raiola de sol dependurada,
descer dos altos ceos brillante e longa espada
que abrindo no rochedo unha fonda ferida,
ficou nel encravada, deica o puño afundida.

Á vista do milagre, o baril cabaleiro
aceso nunha sagra fervenza de romeiro
e no peito unha arela que maior non podía
que lle acorra e lle valla pregou Santa María.
E chegándose á pedra, de ánimo esforzado

botoulle man á espada e cinguiuna ó costado.
O penedo, a tal intre, foi por medio fendido,
deixando aberto e franco un camiño florido
que corría unha terra verdecente e mimosa
na que os pinos erguían a súa voz maxestosa,
eran gloria dos ollos rebrillos dos orballos
nas herbiñas das leiras e as follas dos carballos,
un río de augas limpas, azuis e sereas
durmíase nun leito de douradas areas,
recendo de fiúnchos enchía o vento mol
e as lavercas voaban en circos cara ó sol.
E Galahaz trunfante e cheo de ledicia
entrou camiño adiante nas terras de Galicia.

The Knight of the Holy Grail (extract)

Galahad, last of all, takes a narrow path,
fearsome and secret, that leads into the mountain.
Without spur or lance, without shield or sword,
his soul and his life in a dream, and his gaze on heaven,
without a thought for misfortunes, dragons or spells,
his hair blond like a crest fluttering in the breeze,
chosen and called, he rides tall and smiling,
for he has kept his heart pure and free from evil.

From the dark path wreathed in brambles
he heard harsh, fearful and sad voices,
whistling and howling and gnashing of teeth
and pacing of wolves and hissing of serpents;
and as he passed dense scrublands he saw, shining out,
bloody, bewitched, burning eyes
that spied on him stabbingly from shadowy holes.
But Galahad is not afraid of omens or spells.
And after three long days' riding,
safe and sound, he found himself on the shore of the sea.

The soft, soft wind had a perfume of roses
and the sea was a mirror and the sky was shining its stars.
And it happened that, at the time Galahad arrived,
a sole boat was grounding on the sandy beach,
with a golden chalice adorning the white of its sail,
the vermilion cross on its mast, and a star at its prow.
Galahad, pure and free from evil, went aboard eagerly,

and at that very moment the boat headed for Levant
and sailed away from the beach, rolling rhythmically
like a child's cradle rocked by a fairy.
And, with water in repose and evening star shining,
a road of silver glistened in the sea.

And, in his blue eyes a sacred vision,
his lips flowering in a rondeau of prayer,
Galahad is being carried forward, in a tender dream,
by a divine hope and a remembrance of sadlonging.
And the boat, wrapped in bright moonlight,
sails on, in silence, slowly... slowly...

As a new day broke, the miraculous boat
reached land among the rocks of a new shore,
A dark mist was dissolving in tears
on the tops of the stones and in the clear waters,
and the way to land was closed off,
like a strong wall built by giants
the length of the shore, by an imposing cliff
with no secret crannies for climbing and storming it.

Galahad rode ashore borne by destiny,
his heart enslaved to a divine command,
and, while the dark mist disappeared
and the boat departed, guided by the star,
he watched as, hanging from a sunbeam,
a great gleaming sword came down from the high heavens
and, opening a deep wound in the cliff,
was left embedded in it, buried to the hilt.

Before the miracle, the excellent knight,
burning in the holy frenzy of a pilgrim
and in his breast a supreme desire,
begged Holy Mary to help and succour him.
And reaching the cliff, with his spirit strengthened,
he took hold of the sword and girded it to his side.
The rock, now, was cleft in twain,
leaving, open and clear, a flowery path
that ran to a verdant and endearing land
where the pines raised their majestic voice,
where it was glory to see the glistening of the dew
on the grass in the fields and the leaves of the oaks,

where a river of clear, blue, serene water
slept on a bed of golden sand,
where the aroma of fennel filled the gentle breeze,
and where skylarks soared in circles towards the sun.
And Galahad, triumphant and full of joy,
rode on along the road into Galicia.

Xosé Leista Meis (1877–1930)

From Estevo, 1927

Antes de chegar a Triscornia, que está no alto do monte da Cabaña, Estevo botou a vista atrás. Viu a Habana chea de luces. Os tranvías moi alumeados, a correr dun sitio para outro, semellaban xogos de luces que ían e viñan polo aire para facer bonita a cidade. Estevo non vira un tranvía nin sabía como eran. Naquel tempo inda non os había na Coruña. Quedou admirado. Na súa alma volveu nacer a ilusión da fermosura da Habana que tiña na aldea. E como non a puido ver máis que dun vistazo, porque había que seguir para adiante, foi máis grande o efecto que lle produciu. Xa deu por ben empregado todo o que pasara na viaxe. Agora, inda que lle ofreceran levalo a Galicia non ía. Primeiro quería ver ben como era a Habana.

Cando chegaron fixéronos lavar a todos de todo o corpo. Facíalles boa falta. Despois deitáronse. Había departamentos para homes e mulleres. Eran de madeira. Estaban limpiños e alumeados que daba gusto velos.

Ó outro día déronlles de almorzar pan con café. Ás once, ou así, xantaron. Ían en fatos, porque todos dunha vez era imposible, ós comedores, que eran grandes, onde xa estaban os pratos en fila, todo ó longo das mesas, cheos dunha potaxe de arroz con fabas, garavanzos e anacos de touciño. Ó pé de cada prato había un boliño de pan. Era unha boa ración, non había queixa. A xente non tiña máis que sentarse e poñerse a comer. Canto máis pronto acabaran mellor, porque así poderían vir máis axiña os que estaban agardando. E ó que non lle chegara un prato podía recuncar, sen ter que pedilo. Xa poñían en cada mesa uns poucos máis da conta para que botase man quen quixera. O ourensán sempre recuncaba.

– Hai que enche-la barriga para poder incha-lo fol – dicíalle a Estevo.

O primeiro día Estevo comeu pouco. Inda lle duraba o malestar da viaxe. Pero ó outro día deixou o prato limpo. E despois comía canto lle deran. Poñíase coma un aro. Desde o día que embarcou na Coruña ata daquela non comera tanto nin que lle gustase tan ben. Os aires frescos de Triscornia abríronlle as ganas. Pasáballe diante ó ourensán.

Triscornia non lle causou tan mal efecto como lle fixeran crer. Era un terreo grande, todo cerrado con aramios de picos. Dentro estaba moi ben, tiña árbores, flores, campos verdes coma os de Galicia, porque lles botaban auga tódolos días; sitios para pasear, con area e todo, coma as hortas dos señores. Ó lonxe víase o mar por onde veñen os barcos que van de aquí. Despois, aquel entrar e saír arreo de xente.

Os días pasábanlle sen moita aquela. E co ourensán que quitaba as angurias, mellor. E non digo que ben porque alí non se gañaba nada, senón que se gastaba aínda; e ademais como non se tiña a certeza de cando se ía saír, nin para onde nin para que clase de traballo, porque alí os axentes din unha cousa e despois resulta o que eles queren que sexa, están os ánimos algo esvaídos, baixo o sufrimento dun porvir que non se ve nada claro por moito que un mire. Polo demais, xa digo, os días alí eran levadeiros. Tamén era o que tiña. Os arredores son feos. Monte pelado, da cor da cinza, sen nada verde.

Tódolos días polas mañás, e algún tamén polas tardes, viñan capataces e axentes buscar homes para traballar. Levaban a cincuenta e a máis. Cando chegaban á oficina saía un empregado a avisar a grandes berros. Pero non facía falta. Xa se poñían tódolos emigrantes ben á man para colle-lo mellor sitio, a fin de que os viran. O malo era que o axente non se agarraba ós primeiros que vía. Escolmaba os que tiñan máis corpo e parecían máis fortes. Eles pedían todos a unha:

– ¡Léveme a min! ¡Léveme a min!

From Estevo, *1927*

Before reaching Triscornia, at the top of the Heights of Cabaña, Estevo looked back. He could see all the lights of Havana. The trams were lit up and, as they moved from one place to another, they looked like fireworks coming and going, making the city look beautiful. Estevo had never seen a tram, nor did he know what they were. In those days they didn't have any in A Coruña. He was amazed. In his soul he felt once again the wonder of the beauty of Havana he had felt in his village. And as he could only look at it once, as he had to keep going forward, it seemed all the more impressive. He thought that all he'd gone through on the journey had been worth it. Now, even if someone offered to take him to Galicia, he wouldn't go. First he wanted to see what Havana was like.

When they arrived they were made to wash their whole body. It was very necessary. Then they went to bed. There were rooms for men and women. They were made of wood. They were clean and well-lit, and a pleasure to see.

The next day they were given bread and coffee for breakfast. At around eleven o'clock they had lunch. They went in groups, because it would have been impossible for them all to go at once, to the dining rooms where the plates were already lined up along the tables, full of soup made with rice, beans, chick peas and pieces of bacon. Beside every plate was a little loaf of bread. They were good portions, and nobody complained. All everyone had to do was to sit down and eat. The sooner they finished the better, because that meant that those who were still waiting could get theirs quicker. If anyone didn't have enough they could get a second helping without having to ask. A few more plates had been placed on every table so that anyone who so wanted could eat them. The lad from Ourense always had seconds.

– You need to fill up your belly in order to fill up the bellows – Estevo was told.

The first day Estevo didn't eat very much. He was still feeling unsettled after the journey. But the next day he left his plate clean. And then he ate whatever he was given. He started to put on weight. Since the day he set sail from A Coruña until then he hadn't eaten so much, and hadn't enjoyed his food so much. The fresh air of Triscornia opened up his appetite. They blew past the lad from Ourense.

Triscornia wasn't as bad as he had been led to believe. It was a large area of land, closed in by barbed wire. Inside it was fine, with trees, flowers, green fields like the ones in Galicia, because they were watered every day. There were places for walking, with sand and everything, just like the gardens of the rich. In the distance you could see the sea, where the boats sailed away. Then, the steady coming and going of people.

The days went by without many incidents. And apart from the worries, this was fine for the lad from Ourense. I'm not saying this was good, because there you couldn't earn any money, rather you still had to spend. What is more, there was still some uncertainty about whether he was going to get out and what sort of work he might get, because the agents there said one thing and then it turns out that they just did as they wanted, so morale was pretty low, under the suffering of an uncertain future which did not seem at all clear no matter where you looked. But apart from that, as I said, the days were bearable. That was what there was. The surrounding area was ugly. Bare mountains, ash-coloured, with no sign of any greenery.

Every morning, and sometimes in the afternoon, foremen and agents came to look for men to go and work. The most they took was fifty men. When they got to the office a clerk came out and let everyone know at the top of his voice. But this wasn't necessary. All the immigrants tried to get the best possible spot to be seen. The worst thing was that the agent didn't choose the first ones he saw. He chose the biggest and the ones who looked strongest. They all shouted:

– Take me! Take me!

Xosé Crecente Vega (1896–1948)

From Codeseira, *1933*

Anoitecer

Vai o sol na furada. Os sapos preguiceiros
cansados baixo as pedras de estar acochadiños,
saen tocar a frauta ás beiras dos camiños
e escóitanse nas regas os grau grau barulleiros

das ras. Pasan zoando por entre os maciñeiros
os roncós. E parellas de ledos paxariños

agrúchanse, piando, na quentura dos niños
entre a follaxe espesa de silvas e loureiros.

Unha nena onda a fonte cun rapaz parrafea.
Enchendo as corredoiras vén a habenza prá casa.
Ei, marelo, pra adiante – un labrego que pasa.

Toca ás Avemarías a campana da aldea...
E no curral seus rezos murmuran dúas veciñas
e lámbense dúas vacas tocando as campaíñas.

Nightfall

The sun is in its grotto. Lazy toads,
weary of lying hidden under stones,
come out to play their flutes beside the paths,
and in the brooks sound out the noisy croaks

of frogs. Stag-beetles buzz as they advance
through orchards. Pairs of happy little birds
huddle together, chirping, in warm nests
in the thick foliage of the bays and brambles.

A girl next to the spring chats to a lad.
Filling the lanes, the sheep are coming home.
Brownie, walk on – a farmer passing by.

The village church sounds out its evening peal...
Two women in the yard murmur their prayers
and two cows lick each other, clanking bells.

Fiction of the Nós Period

Vicente Risco (1884–1963)

O lobo da xente. Lenda galega, *1925*

O sucedido que vou referir, contáronmo como certo. Dixéronme ónde foi, que foi preto de Trives; vive aínda quen mo contou, e que, cando era novo, coñeceu a tódalas persoas que andaron na historia, porque tampouco non hai tanto tempo que pasou: haberá coma cincuenta ou sesenta anos. Mais entre aquel tempo e o noso hai moita máis distancia cá que eses sesenta anos representan: hai toda a que poñen a soberbia e a pseudo cultura.

Dígoo porque agora que andan os sabios abesullándose para esculcaren unha chea de feitos desta clase, o vulgo letrado das vilas non quere dar creto a estas historias por máis que llo aseguren persoas asisadas e verdadeiras. Eu teño para min que os antigos sabían disto moito máis do que nós podemos sospeitar tan sequera, e que moito do que sabían os antigos aínda o sabe o vulgo iletrado das aldeas.

Mais imos ó conto.

Era polo castañar. O tempo era revolto e outonizo, chovía por veces e facía tan escuro, que era noite pouco despois de xantar. Ía un tempo coma de día de defuntos, e a tristura do mes das ánimas espallábase xa empardecendo o ceo por toda a banda.

O Ánxel andaba nun souto, onda o río da Cabalar. Era nativo de Sobrado e inda non chegara ás quintas. Tiña o cabelo claro, os ollos azuis, as meixelas roxas. Tiña un gran peito e brazos fortes, e era coraxoso e valente. Estaba termando dun sequeiro e saíra nunha escampada a apañar folla no souto.

Non sei que ten a natureza nestas encanadas fondas onde o sol entra pouco, que semella que se recolle en si mesma e fica calada, embora muda e todo, estea falando decote a tódolos sentidos do home...

O souto onde andaba o Ánxel era pecho e sombrizo, cuberto o chan de herba verde entre a que medraban gamóns, estraloques, póutegas e chouparros, flora das terras húmidas...

Os soutos teñen un cheiro de seu. O cheiro dos soutos é un cheiro especial, e non é o da amenta acochada non sei onde, nin do fiollo, nin das escornacabras; eu coido que é a sombra dos castiñeiros a que cheira a fresco, cheira a silencio encalmado... É un silencio onde se oen cae-las follas secas, como hai un mes se oían cae-los ourizos regañados...

As chancas do Ánxel, ó tripáren esmagando as follas cobrizas e douradas, molladas no chan, facían un ruído apagado. Andaba xuntando as follas ás moreas para estercar de que estivesen curadas.

Un veciño pasou aló enriba pola verea, e berroulle dende o valado:

– Ai, Ánxel, ¿seica estás a seca-las castañas?

– Estou.

– Pois recóllete pronto e atranca ben, non che vaia vi-lo lobo da xente.

Había tempo, desapareceran algúns nenos dos que ían co gando ó monte. Un camiñante aparecera medio comido no camiño real. Ó pouco, aconteceulle igual a unha costureira que andaba a coser polas aldeas... Despois, un criado da casa da Mata. Un neniño deitado no rolo, diante da porta da casa, un día de sol, desaparecera tamén. Logo os casos repetíranse. Principiaron a dicir que era un lobo, que, de que se afán a comer carne de cristián, xa non queren comer doutra, porque seica lles sabe mellor, que hai quen di que é unha carne doce, e outros aseguran que é imitante á do marrán, mais como ninguén a probou, non se sabe de certo... Mais outros dicían que debía ser un home, un facinoroso, unha sorte de sacaúntos. Aínda os había que pensaban que era un home que se volvera lobo...

E aínda pasaron máis cousas, e dicían que unha das veces viran as pisadas do lobo, mais dun lobo moi grandísimo... Por fin a moita xente xa lle non collía dúbida pois por dúas veces, homes que ían de viaxe, atacounos un lobo tremendo, que non sei como puideron fuxir. Dunha das veces, un disparoulle e o lobo coma se nada.

O medo correu por toda aquela terra, e a xente non quería saír fóra despois de empardecer, e aínda se non quería desviar moito da casa no día claro. A sona do lobo da xente collía ata Maceda por unha banda, e ata Quiroga e Valdeorras por outra, e aínda chegaba a Viana..., había quen xuraba que lle entrara na casa; outros que o atoparan indo para tal sitio ou para tal outro. Uns que era brancazado e vello. Outros que era mouro. Que se tiña os dentes de tal xeito ou de tal outro, nunha ringleira ou en tres, que se tumba que se taramba; o que se apalpaba era o medo...

O certo é que o lobo é cousa de temer. Ningunha outra fera arrepía ós homes coma o lobo. El algo ten... O lobo ten ollar magnético; os seus ollos reluman coma brasas de noite: na noite pecha, sen estrelas, pode un ter a carón seu o sinistro paseante nocturno, e non verlle o vulto, mais as dúas flamiñas acesas dos seus ollos anuncian que alí está. É un ollar que traspasa a un coma unha espada, e detén o sangue nas veas e deixa a un coma a neve...

Non cómpre tan sequera velo: abonda sentilo ouvear medoñento para que lle pase a un por todo o corpo o arreguizo astral, igual ó que se sente cando un atopa unha ánima en pena, ou cando lle dan unha labazada no medio da noite silandeira unhas mans invisibles...

Nin que o lobo fose cousa do outro mundo... E mais algo debe ter que ver con iso, e se cadra, os antigos algo souberon do seu misterio; imais agora os homes esqueceron tanta cousa!

O Ánxel era un mozo doutro tempo, e era un pouco medrán. Mais saber, sabía o que tiña que facer. Así que, de que escureceu, meteuse no sequeiro, pechou ben a porta e polo si polo non, botou dúas trancas, asegurou a bufarda, pillou unha machada e pousouna no banco da lareira, ben á man. Despois puxo uns guizos no rescoldo e soprou nas brasas ata que levantou a lapa; entón foi partindo máis guizos botándoos no lume. Así que o lume se ergueu ledo e danzarín, enchendo o sequeiro de claridades e de sombras estrañas, sacou un cacho de touciño, e foino comendo co pan pouco e pouco. Rematou. Aínda había un grolo de viño na gamela; escurrichouno, limpou os beizos co revés da man e ficou un pedazo mirando para o lume.

Non se oía máis que arde-la leña, escacha-la casca das castañas na caniceira, e algunha vez o aire fóra, que andaba coas follas secas. Algo tamén, moito menos, o río da Cabalar, aló para abaixo.

Principiaba a topenear, o Ánxel, cando lle pareceu que sentía así coma se andasen rañando na porta... Púxose a espreitar un pouco inquedo, reparando ben: non sentiu ren. ¡Boh!, ¡que ía ser! Como lle viñese o xuncras do Mateo falando do lobo da xente... E mais... agora si... agora si que era certo; agora andaban rañando na porta...

– Que me leve o demo se non anda aí – pensou o Ánxel.

E anque cheo de medo, ergueuse caladiñamente e apañou a machada... A cousa ía de veras: agora trequeneaban na porta, e con forza. Con forza que estralaban as táboas. O Ánxel meteuse atrás do lume...

De súpeto, o arreguizo astral correulle dende as unllas dos pés ó coiro da testa, e tódolos cabelos se lle puxeron de punta: na porta había unha fendedela, e por ela pasaba a pata dianteira dun lobo grandísimo. Unha pouta negra, grande, con unllas afiadas que relucían.

O Ánxel non quixo ver máis. Caladiñamente agatuñou pola parede, e foise acochar riba da caniceira. Dende alí miraba para a porta morto de medo.

Pola porta apareceu un fociño longo, con dentes brancos que en poucos instantes fixeron salta-las táboas, e polo burato, coouse no sequeiro o lobo da xente.

O Ánxel vira o lobo moitas veces; xa dixen que era un mozo doutro tempo. Mais lobo coma aquel, tan negro, tan peludo, tan espantosamente grandísimo, con aqueles ollos sanguiñentos e relucentes, que escintilaban máis có lume da lareira, con aqueles dentes brancos e afiados coma navallas, aquel fociño mouro, lixado de sangue fresco, aquelas poutas grandes coma as dun oso, coma aquel nunca, endexamais outro vira na vida. O Ánxel, acochado na caniceira, tremía coma unha vara verde, mais non rebuliu.

O lobo da xente foise chegando ó lume coma con receo. Andou cheirando o banco, a machada que o Ánxel deixara no chan, a navalla e o pan riba do banco, e logo ficou quedo un pedazo. O Ánxel sentíao alentar, coma un can cando vai canso.

Despois, aquela si que foi: o lobo da xente principiou a rebulir, foi soltando a pelexa, e apareceu de súpeto transformado nunha rapaza fermosa coma un caravel recén aberto. Non levaba máis cá camisa, e os cabelos escuros con reflexos dourados estaban despeiteados e soltos e chegábanlle moito máis abaixo do medio corpo.

Sentouse no banco, a rente do lume, e púxose a quentar. Debía vir aterecida, e o Ánxel que lle non quitaba os ollos, viu que pola face, branca coma a dun defunto, lle coaban regueiros de bágoas. Logo tapouna coas mans e estralou saloucando e chorando tan amargurada, que ó Ánxel se lle partía a alma.

Mais nisto, alumouse cunha idea toda a conciencia do rapaz. Non sei quen lla inspiraría: a alma da caste, que vive en nós e que o sabe todo, sería, se cadra. O caso foi que pegou nun varal que había na caniceira, e sacando un brazo, pillou co varal a pelexa do lobo da xente, que a rapaza tiña ó pé dela, e botouna no lume.

A rapaza pegou un berro adoecido:

– ¡Ai, pel, váleme! ¡Váleme, miña pel querida!

A pelexa revoltábase enrabexada para fuxir do lume, e tiraba por irse para onde a moza, mais o Ánxel tíñaa presa co varal e non a deixaba escapar. E a pelexa rebulía e asubiaba, mais ó fin foise queimando ata que ardeu toda.

Entón a rapaza ergueu os ollos verdes, onde escintilaban palliñas de ouro, e díxolle ó mozo docemente:

– ¡Baixa, baixa, que me libraches; non teñas xa medo de min!

O Ánxel baixou da caniceira e veuse sentar onda ela. El díxolle:

– Foi a miña nai quen me botou a fada, mais ti quitáchesma.

Preguntou o rapaz: – ¿E como foi para che bota-la fada?

– Pois verás. Eu son filla do señor Farruco da Navea, que Deus teña en gloria; era eu neniña pequecha cando morreu meu pai, e a miña nai casou cun de San Clodio, e viñeron para a casa. De principio non me daba tino ningún, nin me falaba. Eu sacaba a facenda ó monte, cociñaba para eles, cociñaba para os porcos, ía á roza e ás patacas; eles ían ás festas, e deixábanme soa na casa, levaban empanadas e viño... Mais de que fun medrando, inda que a miña nai non levaba ben que eu fose, o home principiou a me querer levar con eles ás festas, e aínda lle dixo unha vez a ela que se ela non quería vir, que iámo-los dous, el e mais eu... E dar dábame máis agarimo ca a mi madre... Mais ó fin, un día, andando na roza, achegouse a min, e eu que lle coñecín a intención porque lle vin os ollos, e que non tiña quen me puidese valer, defendinme e leveille unha man co foucíño. Cando o trouxeron ferido para a casa, a miña nai púxose enrabechada coma un can doente; botouse a min, que se a non collen as veciñas, alí dá conta da súa filla, de rabiosa que estaba, e como non me puido bater, volvíase tola e berraba:

– ¡Vaite da casa, mala muller! ¡Mala filla! ¡Filla dun lobo! ¡Loba! ¡Permita Deus que te volvas loba e que andes arrastrada polo monte coma os lobos, mala filla!

Fada que me botou, fada que me saíu... Fuxín onda a miña tía, a señora Fermina da Pousa, que é irmá do meu pai, que está viúva e vive a pobriña soa, que non ten fillos. Mais aquela noite xa tiven moita quentura. Sentía unha cousa estraña andarme polo corpo, que eu non sabía ben o que era, e ó mesmo tempo un medo que me aterrecía...

Para o outro día non quixen comer cousa ningunha, por máis que fixo a miña tía para que comese, nin tan sequera un bocado lle quixen probar... Eu tiña medo de que chegase a noite, porque pensaba que era cando me ía pasa-lo que me tiña que pasar á forza, que eu non sabía o que era nin imaxinaba que fose a fada... Aquilo que me rebulía no corpo, arrimóuseme á cabeza e púxoseme aquí, por riba da fronte, coma se tivese alí unha pedra pesando e doíame ó tocala...

Non sei que me deu aquela noite que me puxen coma tola: esgacei a saba coas unllas e triceina cos dentes, e principiei a berrar e ouvear coma un lobo...

A miña tía foi onda unha veciña que era entendida. Veu a veciña, e referinlle todo. Entón ela dixo:

– Esa é a fada que túa nai che botou. Se cha botou de mala intención, a non ser que Deus mande outra cousa, que é o que pode todo, tenche que saír... Mira o que lle pasou ó fillo da Rosa da Porteliña, que lle dixeron que había morrer na guerra e por máis que librara do servicio, na guerra foi morrer... Se eu tivese a reliquia que tiña o Salgueiros, o que marchou para o Barco... Mira, filla: a fada non a pode quitar nin o mesmo que a bota, anque logo se arrepinta. Éche igual có aire cativo, e o mal ollado, e o meigallo. Todo che vén do mesmo lado. É unha forza que, de que un a colle, pode face-lo que queira con ela, como un sexa entendido; mais ás veces tamén se colle por casualidade, como é cando un bota unha fada. E ti has andar polo monte, con pel de lobo, namentres non pasen os anos que teñen que pasar, ou namentres non pérda-la pel de lobo, mais entón, o mellor é que a queimen, que se non, estea onde estea, non has parar ata que a volvas coller.

E así foi. Aquela noite, que era a terceira non sei que me pasou pola testa, que me fun da casa e non volvín. E andei perdida, cumprindo a miña fada, ata hoxe, que dei contigo. ¡Deus cho pague que me volviches á vida dos cristiáns!

Non hai para que dicir: o conto remata referindo que o Ánxel e maila moza casaron.

The Werewolf. Galician Legend, *1925*

The following was told to me as being the truth. They even told me where it took place, near Trives. The person who told it to me still lives there, and when he was young, he knew all the people who appear in the story, because it is not such a long time since it happened, some fifty or sixty years. There is, however, a lot more distance between then and now than these sixty years represent. There is the distance caused by pride and pseudo-culture.

I mention this because now that the learned are sniffing around trying to find out lots of things like this, the educated townspeople do not want to give any credit to these stories, even if they are told by people who assure us that they were present at the events and declare them to be true. I reckon that the people in the olden days knew a lot more about this than we can even begin to suspect, and a lot of what the people of the olden days knew is still known by the uneducated common people in the villages.

But to our tale.

It was the season for picking chestnuts. The weather was unsettled and autumnal, it was raining on and off and getting dark early, and not long after lunch it was like nigh-time. The weather was like Halloween, and the sadness of the month of November was spread out right across the sky.

Ánxel was in a thicket near the Cabalar river. He was from Sobrado and hadn't yet been called up for military service. His hair was fair, his eyes blue and his cheeks red. His chest was broad and his arms strong, and he was brave and courageous. He was building the supports on a drying shed and went out during a dry spell to spread leaves on the ground.

I don't know what it is about nature in these deep glens where the sun hardly gets through, but it seems to be wrapped up in itself and to remain still, silent, and everything always seems to be talking to all the human senses…

The thicket where Ánxel was working was closed-in and shady, and the ground was covered in green grass through which white asphrodels, foxgloves and other flowers which needed wet soil grew…

These thickets had their own smell. The smell of the thickets is a special smell, and is not that of mint, nor of fennel, nor of terebinth; I think that it is the shade of the chestnut trees which smells fresh, smells of calm silence… It is a silence in which you can hear the dry leaves fall, just like a month or so ago you could hear the open chestnut burrs dropping to the ground…

Ánxel's clogs made a muted sound as they stepped over the coppery and golden leaves which lay damp on the ground. He was gathering the leaves into heaps to use as manure when they were ready.

A neighbour passed by the path above and shouted down to him from the fence:

– Hey, Ánxel, Is that you drying the chestnuts?

– That I am.

– Well gather up your things quickly. You don't want the werewolf to be coming.

Some time ago some children who went with the cattle up into the hills had disappeared. Someone who had been walking had been found half-eaten on the Royal Highway. Shortly after the same thing happened to a seamstress who had been out sewing from village to village. Then a servant from the Mata house. A baby lying in a cradle, just beside the door to the house, one sunny day disappeared too. And these cases continued. People started to say that it was a wolf which, having eaten Christian flesh, didn't want any other type because it was tastier, it was, some said, a sweeter meat. Others said that it tasted like pork, but as nobody had tried it, no one knew for sure… Others said that it must be a man, a criminal, a type of thug. But there were others who thought it was a man who had turned into a wolf…

Even more things happened, and one time people said they had seen the paw prints of a wolf, of what must have been a huge wolf… Eventually there seemed to be no doubt about it for many people because on two occasions men who were travelling said they had been attacked by a giant wolf and didn't know how they had been able to escape. One of these times the man shot the wolf but the wolf was completely unharmed by his shot.

Fear spread throughout the countryside and people didn't want to leave home after dark nor move far from home at daytime. The story of the werewolf was known from Maceda on one side to Quiroga and Valdeorras over on the other, even spreading as far as Viana… some even swore it had gone into their houses. Others said they had seen it coming or going from one place to another. Some said it was white and old. Others that it was dark coloured. That its teeth were like this or like that, in one row or in three, that it did one thing or the other. Fear was felt everywhere…

It is true that a wolf is something to be scared about. No other wild animal could frighten a man like a wolf. It has something… the wolf has a magnetic gaze, its eyes burn like embers in the night. On a dark, starless night, you can have a sinister being beside you and not be aware of a thing, but then its two flaming eyes let you know that it is there. Its look goes through you like a sword, stops the blood I your veins and leaves you as cold as ice… You don't even have to see it: just to feel it sends a fear through your whole body like an astral shiver, the same way you feel when you find a poor lost soul, or when invisible hands hit you in the middle of a silent night…

It's not as if the wolf were something out of this world… But it must have something to do with this, and perhaps the ancients knew something about its mystery, but nowadays mankind has forgotten so much.

Ánxel was a lad from another time, and he was a bit timid. But he knew what he had to do. So, when it got dark he went inside the hut, shut the door well and placed two bars across the door, closed the window, took an axe and placed it on the bench beside the fire, close at hand. Then he put some wood on the fire and blew on the embers until the flames rose. Then he broke up some more wood and put it on the fire. When the flames started to burn away merrily, filling the hut with light and strange shadows, he took out a piece of salt pork and ate it slowly with a piece of bread. He finished eating. There was still a drop of wine left and he drained it before drying his lips with the back of his hand. He watched the flames for a while.

All that could be heard was the firewood burning, the crackling of the chestnuts as they dried and, at times, the wind outside, blowing the dry leaves. You could also hear, much less though, the Cabalar river down below.

Ánxel had started to drop off when he heard what seemed to be something scratching at the door… Warily he looked and listened, but could hear nothing. In any case, what was it going to be? As boring old Mateo had come talking to him about the werewolf. But wait. Now here's something. Now there is definitely something scratching at the door…

– The devil take me if there's not something out there – thought Ánxel.

Even though he was filled with fear, he got up slowly and picked up the axe… This was serious: something was banging on the door. The door was being hit so hard now that the wood was shaking. Ánxel got behind the fire.

Suddenly, the astral shiver ran through his body from his head to his toes and all his hair stood on end. There was a hole in the door now, and through it poked the front paw of a huge wolf. It was a big, black paw, with sharp shiny claws.

Ánxel didn't want to see any more. He quietly crawled up the wall and hid above the chestnut pot. From up there he watched the door with fear in his heart.

A long snout appeared through the doorway with white teeth which quickly bit their way through the wood and through the hole the werewolf made its way into the hut.

Ánxel had seen a wolf many times before. As I mentioned earlier, he was a lad from another time. But a wolf such as this one, so hairy, so fearfully huge, with such bloodshot, shiny eyes which burned brighter than the fire in the hearth, with huge white fangs as sharp as razors, its dark snout covered in fresh blood, paws as big as those of a bear, a wolf like this he had never, ever seen in his whole life. Ánxel, hiding behind the chestnut pot, tremble like a leaf, but he did not make a move.

The werewolf crept warily up towards the fire. It sniffed at the bench, at the axe which Ánxo had left on the floor and the knife and the bread ontop of the bench, and then it stopped still. Ánxel heard it breathe like a tired dog.

Then, after that, the werewolf started to move, and started to shed its skin, and all of a sudden it turned into a beautiful girl like a newly opened carnation. She wore nothing more than a shirt, and her dark hair with blonde highlights hung loose right down her back.

She sat down on the bench beside the fire and started to warm herself up. She must have been frightened, and Ánxel, who couldn't take his eyes off her, saw that tears were running down her face which was as white as a corpse. Then she covered her face with her hands and burst into tears again, crying with such sadness that Ánxel's heart was broken.

That was when an idea occurred to the lad. I don't know what inspired him, maybe it was in his blood. In any case he pulled a stick out of the chestnut pot and sticking out his arm he managed to pick up the werewolf's skin which the girl had beside her and tossed it into the fire.

The girl let out an anguished cry:

– Oh, my skin! My dear skin!

The skin flew around angrily as if trying to escape from the fire, trying to get back beside the girl, but Ánxel was quick with he stick and wouldn't let it get away. And the skin flew around and hissed, but it ended up burning until it was completely swallowed up by the flames.

Then the girl raised her green eyes, where golden flashes glittered, and said to the lad sweetly:

– Come down, come down now. You've freed me, you don't need to be scared of me.

Ánxel came down and sat beside her. She said:

– It was my mother who put the spell on me, but you have broken it.

The lad asked: – And why did she cast a spell on you?

– Well, you see, I'm the daughter of Mr Farruco de Navea, may God rest his soul. I was just a little girl when my father died, and my mother remarried to a man from San Clodio who came to live with us. At first he paid no attention to me whatsoever, he wouldn't even talk to me. I took my work up into the hills, I cooked for them, I cooked for the pigs, I worked with the crops and with the potatoes. They went out to the fiestas and left me at home, they took wine and pies with them… As I grew up, however, even though my mother was against it, he started to want to take me to the fiestas, and he even told her once that if she didn't feel like going the two of us would go, he and I… And the truth is he was a lot sweeter to me than to my mother… But eventually, one day when I was in the fields he came up to me, and I knew what he had in mind because I could see it in his eyes. I had no one to look out for me, so I defended myself and cut off his hand with my sickle. When they brought him back home wounded my mother got as angry as a mad dog and threw herself at me. If the neighbours hadn't pulled her off she would have killed me, so angry she was, and as she couldn't get at me to hit me she went mad and shouted:

– Get out of this house, you evil girl! Evil daughter! Daughter of a wolf! She-Wolf! I hope God turns you into a wolf and you have to lope around the hills like a she-wolf, evil daughter!

She had cast her spell on me, and that spell took effect… I ran away to the house of my aunt, Mrs Fermina da Pousa, my father's sister, who is a widow and lives all alone, poor thing, she doesn't have any children. Later that night I felt a strange heat. I felt something strange crawl over my body. I didn't know what it was, and at the same time a great fear came over me.

The next day I didn't feel like eating a thing, even though my aunt tried to get me to eat, and I couldn't eat a single mouthful. I was scared of the night falling, because I thought that was when whatever was going to happen would happen to me. I had no idea what it was, nor did I imagine it was a spell. That thing which was stirring in my body moved up to my head and stopped here, on my forehead; it was as if I had a stone there which hurt whenever I touched it…

I don't know what happened to me that night that made me go so mad: I ripped the sheets with my nails and tore them to shreds with my teeth, and I started to howl like a wolf…

My aunt went to see a neighbour who knew about these things. The neighbour came, and I told her everything. Then she said:

– That was the spell your mother cast on you. If she cast it with evil intention then only God, who can do anything, would be able to stop it… Look what happened to Rosa de Porteliña's son. He was told that he would die in a war, and even though he managed not to get called up it would be in a war that he was to die. If I had the relic that Salgueiros had, the one that went off to O Barco… Look, love, the spell can't be taken back, not even by the person who cast it, not even if she is sorry for having cast it. It's the same with curses or whatever. They all come from the same place. It is a power which, once someone has it, they can do what they want with it. Sometimes people have that power by chance, though, like when a spell is cast. You have to wander the hills in the skin of a wolf until the years that have to pass have passed, or until you lose the wolf's skin. When you do, the best thing to do is to burn it, because if you don't you won't be able to stop until you get it again.

And that is what happened. That night, the third, I don't know what got into my head, but I left home and didn't go back. I wandered lost, carrying out the spell, until today when I met you. May the Lord pay you for bringing me back to a Christian life!

There is no need to say it: the story ends with Ánxel and the lass getting married.

From O porco de pé, *1928*

Deu volta e encamiñouse ó Casino deserto arestora. Subiu á sala de lectura e pillou o primeiro boletín que atopou. Era o diario local de máis sona, un diario que o Alveiros lía case sempre, polo interese extraordinario da primeira páxina, onde entremedias de novas aterradoras sobre da Cheka e do Presidente Calles, de centos de bispos e milleiros de frades fusilados, de igrexas profanadas, de conventos queimados e calamidades sen conto que as loxas masónicas desencadeaban no mundo, viñan artigos de alta filoloxía, onde porfiaban se se había dicir Alcalda ou Alcaldesa, Concellala ou Concellal, sobre do correcto emprego do pretérito plus-cuamperfecto de subxuntivo nas oracións de xerundio, e contra o penoso e tristeiro espectáculo dos galicismos que emporcan a pureza da fermosa fala castelá; noticia de inventos prodixiosos, chamados a transtorna-la face da orde planetaria: camas automáticas, rateiras con música, paraguas-escopeta, impermeables eléctricos e agullas para coser sen fío; longas poesías de columna e media dedicadas A Ella, acontecementos extraordinarios dos Estados Unidos: a viaxe que proxecta un Profesor de Harvard ó planeta Marte; o roubo dun tren enteiro, máquinas, vagóns e todo, realizado por dous ladróns montados nunha motocicleta con side-car, os cales esconderon o tren nunha caseta de cazadores de bisontes preto do Canadá; un millonario que lle regalou á noiva dous xigantescos baobabs da África, plantados en macetas de bronce; reseña da festa da Árbore en tódolos concellos da provincia, cos discursos do escolante, o crego, o alcalde e os himnos cantados polos nenos das escolas; artigos encamiñados a defende-la decencia no vestir e a combate-la moda de levaren as donas ó len as extremidades torácicas, parte considerable das abdominais e a parte superior do tórax; reseñas de vodas, bautizos e necroloxías de persoas moi coñecidas na súa casa á hora de comer, confeccionadas por algún dos seus familiares; *Rápidas* de escritores locais, e artigos de fondo da superproducción estandarizada de Prensa Asociada. En realidade, era prodixioso aquel xornal que saía a cotío feito e dereito, sen a máis pequena intervención do Director nin de ningún dos redactores.

From The Standing Pig, *1928*

He turned round and went back to the now-deserted Casino. He went upstairs to the reading room and took the first paper he could find. It was the best-known local newspaper, a paper that Alveiros almost always read because of its highly interesting front page where, between terrifying news about the Cheka and President Calles, of the hundreds of bishops and thousands of friars who had been shot, about the churches which had been desecrated, the convents burned down and the countless disasters started by Masonic Lodges throughout the world, there were articles of great philological interest. These would debate on whether we should use Mayoress or Lady Mayor, Madam Councillor or just Councillor, about the correct usage of the subjunctive of the pluperfect tense in gerundive phrases and about the disgraceful and sad use of Galicianisms which spoiled the beauty of pure, pristine Spanish. There was also news about great new inventions which would surely change the face of the earth, such as automatic beds, musical mouse-traps, shotgun-umbrellas, electric raincoats and needles which could be used to sew without any thread. There were poems one and a half columns long dedicated To Her, extraordinary events from the United States such as the journey by a Harvard professor to Mars; the theft of an entire train, engine, wagons, the lot, car-ried out by two thieves riding a motorcycle and side-car who hid the train in a bison hunters' hut near Canada; a millionaire who gave his girlfriend two giant African Baobabs planted in bronze pots. There was also a report on the Day of the Tree in all the towns in the Province with the speeches by the local schoolmasters, by the priests, by the mayors and the hymns sung by the school-children. There were articles defending the need for decency in dressing which deplored the fash-ion of ladies showing part of their naked limbs, abdomen and upper thorax, reports from weddings, christenings and the obituaries of people unknown outside their own families written by members of said families. There were quick pieces written by local journalists and in-depth articles in the standardized super-production for-mat of the Press Association. It really was a remarkable newspaper, which appeared on a daily basis without the slightest intervention of either the Editor or any of the Subeditors.

Alfonso D. Rodríguez Castelao (1886–1950)

From Retrincos (Remnants), *1934*

Sabela

Cando eu andaba no estudio era un mozo das romarías, bailador e divertido. Non había festa na vila, nin nos arredores, onde non aparecese danzando como un trompo esgarabelleiro. ¡Ai, aqueles valses, aquelas mazurcas, aquelas polcas e aque-las habaneras!

Entón o agarradiño aínda era un pecado venial, e bailabamos con tino, para que os vellos non refungasen.

As mozas acoirazaban o corpo con xustillos e non consentían o arrimo; pero arrecendían a roupa gardada con mazás e a carne lavada con xabrón de rosas. Os mozos bailabamos por darlles gusto ás pernas, e contentabámonos co cheiro...

Había na vila unha rapaza do meu tempo, xeitosa de corpo, feitiña de cara, leda de xenio, traballadora de condición, pescantina de oficio e limpa de conducta, pero picante nos dicires.

As súas verbas tiñan o labio salgado dos mariscos. Os dicires escintilaban con-tentamente, e nos seus arredores non podía medra-la tristura. A risa facíalle goios de amor nas fazulas, poñíalle pintiñas de malicia nos ollos e brillo de nácar nos dentes. Os andares, arfados e velaíños, facían no aire ronseis de gracia. Andaba descalza, e os engados da súa carne non tiñan segredo para os ollos de ninguén. Os pés lenes, as pernas brancas, os brazos redondiños. O corpo era un gran corazón plisado. Cantaba como un xílgaro e bailaba como un argadelo.

Era a rapaza máis fermosa da vila, e dábase conta do seu poderío. Escarolábase, burlona, cando os señoritos forasteiros lle facían a rosca e revíase, compasiva, cando os mozos do seu igual criaban o pasmo.

Ela gustaba de contar na ribeira os perigos en que se metía, e as pescas estordegábanse de risa cos ditos da rapaza, que descubría, de miúdo, tódalas súas enchoiadas amorosas. Ela gustaba de acender fogueiras e logo apagalas, e nos seus feitizos de serea morrían os fumes dos señoritos e as olladas dos mozos mariñeiros. Era dona de si e viviu sempre ceibe de murmuracións.

Nos días de festa parecía outra. A saia longa, a chambra de flores, o pano de oito puntas. Unha lazada verde na trenza do pelo. A cara con certo remilgo de señoritinga. Os andares contados, por mor dos zapatos... Ata bailar tres veces non xurdía na súa face a risa escachada dos días soltos. No retorno da festa entraba na casa cunha cantiga nos beizos e cos zapatos na man.

A primeira vez que bailei foi con ela.

Eu dedicábame, nos meses de vacacións, á vida de gandaia, e cando me fixen mozo quixen ser un tunante; pero non sabía bailar de modo. Eu reloucaba por aprender ben o agarradiño e lucirme nas romarías; pero non lles daba xeito ás pernas.

Unha noite atrevinme:

– ¿Queres que botemos esta polca?

– ¿E ti sabes?

– Imos ver.

A rapaza comprometeuse a ensinarme, e eu pagáballe coa miña ledicia de estudiante. Empecei dando voltas á dereita. Ela levábame... "Agora dous pasiños de lado." "Agora outra volta." "Dálle máis aire ó corpo." "¡Non saímos do sitio!" "¡Ai, que burro!" "Así, home, así." "Agora vai ben."

Pouco a pouco fun aprendendo, e non tardei en bailar valses e mazurcas con certa mestría. Despois xa me fixen bailador e aproveitaba tódalas tocatas; pero afeito á miña compañeira non tiña gusto en bailar con outras. De remate os dous fixemos unha das mellores parellas.

A rapaza e máis eu estabamos unidos polo baile. Ela seguía burlándose dos namorados, e eu ríame, a cachón, dos seus ditos. Queriámonos ben; pero non sentiamos desacougos amorosos. Se chegase a poñer ollo na súa fermosura burlaríase de min coma dos demais.

Con todo a miña nai reprendíame:

– Ti non es para comparar coa Sabela. ¿Por que non bailas con todas? ¡Sempre coa mesma, sempre coa mesma! Pois nin ti lle fas favor a ela nin ela cho fai a ti.

– Baila moi ben ¿sabe, miña nai?

– Bailará; pero ela é unha pesca e ti es un estudiante. O baile é cousa do demo e Sabela é unha boa rapaza. Pobre de ti como non a respectes.

Miña nai, coma tódalas nais, coidaba que o seu fillo era un Tenorio; pero a honradez de Sabela gardábase detrás de catro muros de cantería.

Marchei da vila cargado cun título universitario, e as preocupacións do meu vivir arredáronme das troulas. Perdín a mocidade, fíxenme home; o baile chegou a parecerme cousa de parvos, e hai moitos anos que nin tan sequera vexo bailar.

Do tempo de estudiante non gardei un recuncho para as lembranzas de romaría, e Sabela esvaéuseme da memoria.

Cando se proclamou a República lanceime á política e saín deputado das Constituíntes. A miña vila quixo agasallarme e alá fun eu.

Desembarquei baixo o estrondo das bombas e entre o entusiasmo dos vellos amigos, que acugulaban o peirao e a ribeira. O azougamento non me deixaba camiñar, e se sodes sentimentais comprenderéde-la miña emoción, porque a vila natal non é coma tódalas vilas.

Cheguei á casa de meus pais, e na beira da porta vin unha muller. Era gorda de ventre, de pernas e de brazos; a cara inflada e vermella; a boca sen dentes; a postura de regateira.

Miroume, fite a fite, cos ollos mergullados en bágoas, e ó pasar a carón dela sioume con voz estremecida estas verbas:

– ¡Meu bailador!

Sabela

When I was a student I was one of those lads who enjoy parties, dancing and fun. There wasn't a party in the town or the surrounding area where I couldn't be found dancing around like a dervish. Oh, the waltzes, those mazurkas, polkas and habaneras!

Close-dancing was then a deadly sin, and we danced with moderation so the old folks wouldn't get annoyed.

The girls armour-plated themselves with bodices and wouldn't allow us up too close to them, but their clothes were scented with apples and they washed their skin in rose-water. We lads danced to give our legs something to do, and we were happy enough with just a whiff…

In the town there was a girl of my age with a beautiful figure, sweet face, cheerful character; who was hard-working, a fisher-lass by trade who was of impeccable conduct but saucy when she spoke.

Her words carried the salty tang of shellfish. Her speech twinkled joyfully and around her there could be no sadness. Her laughter left her dimples in her cheeks, malicious glints in her eyes and the shine of mother-of-pearl in her teeth. Her floating and soft footsteps made graceful waves in the air. She walked barefoot, and the charms of her skin held no secret for anyone. Her naked feet, her white legs, the curve of her arms. Her body was a great folded heart. She sang like a goldfinch and danced like a spinning top.

She was the most beautiful girl in the village, and she was aware of her own power. She was haughty with the outsiders, young gentlemen who tried to woo her, and came to life again sympathetically when the lads she knew believed the wonder.

On the riverbank she liked to talk about the dangers she got herself into, and the fisher-lasses laughed themselves silly with what she said, when she unfolded, piece by piece, her amorous adventures. She liked to light fires and then put them out, and in her mermaid's spells the conceit of the young gentlemen and the stares of the sailor lads were quickly put down. She was always her own mistress, and she lived free from all murmurs.

On feast days she seemed like another person. With a long skirt, a floral blouse, and a kerchief with eight points. A green ribbon in the braid of her hair. A slightly ladylike look in her eye. Her footsteps careful, on account of her shoes. Not until she had three dances did the usual laughter appear. After the party she would go back home with a song on her lips and her shoes in her hands.

The first time I ever danced it was with her.

During the holidays I worked with the cattle, and when I was a young lad I fancied myself as a bit of a musician, but I couldn't dance very well. I was dying to learn how to dance slowly and be able to show off at the dances, but my feet just didn't seem to match.

One night I drew up the courage.

– Would you like to dance a polka?

– Do you know how to?

– Let's see!

The lass agreed to teach me, and I paid her back with all the pleasure of a student. I started turning to the right. She led me… "Now two steps to the side". "One more time around". "Give yourself more room". "Don't leave your space!". "Oh, what an ass!". "That's it, that's it". "Now you're doing it".

Little by little I learned, and before long I was dancing waltzes and mazurkas with some skill. Then I became a real dancer, and took advantage of every chance I got, but I was attached to my partner and didn't want to dance with anybody else. We ended up becoming one of the best couples dancing.

The lass and I were joined together by dancing. She still made fun of all her pretenders and I laughed out loud at all the things she said. We liked each other a lot, but we didn't feel any romantic notions towards each other. If I had started to admire her beauty she would have laughed at me like she did with all the others.

In any case, my mother told me off:

You're not like Sabela. Why don't you dance with all the girls? Always with the same lass, always with the same lass! You're not doing yourself nor her any favours.

– But she dances really well, mum.

She might well do, but she is a fisher-lass and you are a student. Dancing is the devil's business and Sabela is a good lass. Heaven help you if you don't respect her.

My mother, like all mothers, thought her son was a Casanova, but Sabela's honour was safe behind four walls.

I left town with a University degree and the worries of life put an end to my parties. I grew up and became a man, and dancing seemed to be something for idiots, and for many years I didn't even see a dance.

From my student days I didn't even spare a little corner in my memory for the village dances, and Sabela vanished from my mind.

When the Republic was proclaimed I became involved in politics and was elected as a Deputy in the Constitutive Assembly. My town wanted to congratulate me so I went along.

I disembarked to the sound of fireworks and the cheers of old friends who lined up on the pier and on the riverbank. The throngs wouldn't let me through, and if you are of the sentimental type you'll be able to understand my emotions, because your home town isn't any old town.

I got to my parents' house and, by the door I saw a woman. She had a fat stomach, a round red face, toothless mouth and stood awkwardly.

She looked at me her eyes wet with tears and, as I walked by she whispered in a shaky voice these words to me:

– My dancer!

From Cousas (Things), *1926–29*

O pai de Migueliño

O pai de Migueliño chegaba das Américas e o rapaz non cabía de gozo no seu traxe festeiro. Migueliño sabía cos ollos pechados cómo era o seu pai; pero denantes de saír da casa botoulle unha ollada ó retrato.

Os americanos xa estaban desembarcando. Migueliño e a súa nai agardaban no peirao do porto. O corazón do rapaz batíalle na táboa do peito e os seus ollos esculcaban nas greas en procura do pai ensoñado.

De súpeto avistouno de lonxe. Era o mesmo do retrato, ou aínda mellor portado, e Migueliño sentiu por el un grande amor, e canto máis se achegaba o americano, máis cobiza sentía o rapaz por enchelo de bicos. Ai, o americano pasou de largo sen mirar para ninguén, e Migueliño deixou de querelo.

Agora si, agora si que o era. Migueliño avistou outro home moi ben traxeado e o corazón dáballe que aquel era o seu pai. O rapaz devecía por bicalo a fartar. ¡Tiña un porte de tanto señorío! Ai, o americano pasou de largo e nin tan sequera reparou en que o seguían os ollos angurentos dun neno.

Migueliño escolleu así moitos pais que non o eran e a todos quixo tolamente.

E cando esculcaba con máis anguria fíxose cargo de que un home estaba abrazando a súa nai. Era un home que non se parecía ó retrato; un home moi fraco, metido nun traxe moi frouxo; un home de cera, coas orellas fóra do cacho, cos ollos encoveirados, tusindo...

Aquel si que era o pai de Migueliño.

Migueliño's Father

Migueliño's father was coming back over from the Americas, and the young lad was as pleased as punch dressed up in his best clothes. Migueliño could picture his father with his eyes closed, but just to make sure he took another quick look at the picture before leaving the house.

The Americans were disembarking. Migueliño and his mother waited on the quay in the harbour. The young lad's heart was beating like a drum and his eyes scanned the crowds looking for the father he had so often dreamed about.

All of a sudden he could see him in the distance. He was just the same as in the picture, or even better, and the nearer the American got to him the more the lad wanted to cover him in kisses. But the American just walked straight past without looking at anyone, and Migueliño stopped loving him.

Here he is, here he is now! Migueliño saw another man, well-dressed, and his heart told him that this was his father. He was dying to kiss him. He looked so noble! But no, the American passed by without even noticing the anguish in the boy's eyes following his steps.

Migueliño chose a lot of fathers that way, none of whom were his, but all of them he loved madly.

And when his suffering was at its greatest he realised that a man was hugging his mother. This man looked nothing like the picture: a skinny man dressed in a loose-fitting suit; a man made of wax with sticking-out ears, hooded eyes, coughing away. Yes, that was Migueliño's father.

Se eu fose autor...

Se eu fose autor escribiría unha peza en dous lances. A obra duraría dez minutos nada máis.

Lance Primeiro

Érguese o pano e aparece unha corte aldeá. Enriba do estrume hai unha vaca morta. Ó redor da vaca hai unha vella velliña, unha muller avellentada, unha moza garrida, dúas rapaciñas bonitas, un vello petrucio e tres nenos loiros. Todos choran a fío e enxoitan os ollos coas mans. Todos fan o pranto e din cousas tristes que fan rir, ditos paifocos de xentes labregas, angurentas e cobizosas, que pensan que a morte dunha vaca é unha gran desgracia. O pranto debe ter unha gracia choqueira, para que estoupen de risa os do patio de butacas.

E cando se farten de ri-los señoritos baixará o pano.

Lance Segundo

Érguese o pano e aparece un estrado elegante, adobiado con moito señorío. Enriba dunha mesa de pés ferrados de bronce hai unha bandexa de prata, enriba da bandexa hai unha almofada de damasco, enriba da almofada hai unha cadeliña morta. A cadela morta semellará unha folerpa de neve. Ó seu redor choran unha fidalgona e dúas fidalguiñas novas. Todas elas fan o pranto e enxoitan as bágoas con paniños de encaixe. Todas van dicindo, unha a unha, as mesmas parvadas que dixeron os labregos diante da vaca morta, ditos tristes que fan rir, porque a morte dunha cadela non é para tanto.

E cando a xente do galiñeiro se farte de rir a cachón, baixará o pano moi amodiño.

If I Were an Author ...

If I were an author I would write a play in two acts. The work would last only ten minutes.

First Act

The curtain rises on a country cow shed. A dead cow lies on a bed of hay. Around the cow stand an old, old woman, an oldish looking woman, a handsome maid, two pretty young girls, a dignified-looking man and three blonde children. All of them are crying aloud and drying their tears with their hands. They are all weeping and say sad things which would make you laugh, the uncouth things that sad, envious country people say, people who think that the death of a cow is a huge disaster. The weeping should be funny in a clownish sort of way, so that the people in the stalls fall about laughing.

Second Act

The curtain rises on a smart stand, elegantly adorned. On top of a table with bronze legs lies a silver tray. On top of the tray is a damask rug, and on top of the rug is a dead puppy. The dead puppy looks like a snowdrop. Around it stand a noblewoman and two young noble girls. All of them are crying aloud and drying their tears with their lace handkerchiefs. They are all saying, one after the other, the same silly things that the country folk were saying around the dead cow, sad things which would make you laugh, because the death of a puppy is no big deal.

And when the people in the gods stop laughing out loud, the curtain will go down very slowly.

O Rifante era un mariñeiro...

O Rifante era un mariñeiro que gañaba pesos a moreas e que na súa bolsa gardábanse talmente como auga nunha peneira. En terra o Rifante non tiña caletre ningún; en canto poñía o pé no seu barco trocábase nun sabio. Tiña moitos fillos e moitos netos e todos a gastar porque o mar daba para todo.

Ninguén lle negou o creto de bo patrón e de bo cristián que tiña; mais ás veces parecía ter tratos co demo. Habían de largar o aparello outros mariñeiros e non habían de coller ren; chegaba o Rifante e collía unha fartura de peixe.

O Rifante era farturento de seu. Estando a pique de morrer afogado ofreceuse a Nosa Señora e regaloulle un manto de seis mil reás, ademais da misa cantada, música, foguetes, traxes novos e comida a fartar.

O Rifante tiña fe na súa fada. Unha vez enfermou e fixo de patrón o fillo máis vello. En canto volveu do mar, o fillo achegouse ó leito do pai e tatexando de medo contoulle que o aparello quedara trabado nunhas pedras. O Rifante dixo simplemente: "Non teñas medo, Ramón; o mar levouno, o mar dará para outro." E despois calou e virouse cara á parede.

¡Que confianza tiña o Rifante no mar!

Pero tanta fartura minguou de súpeto e a fame foi entrando en tódolos fogares. Tal aconteceu cando as traíñas mataron o xeito.

O Rifante apareceu un día diante do meu pai, amigo seu dende nenos e ademais conselleiro.

– ¿Sabes unha cousa? – dixo –. Hai fame, ¡fame! na casa do Rifante. Ti xa sabes que nunca pedín nada a ninguén; mais agora veño petar na túa porta para que me emprestes mil reás. Quero botarlle un balcón novo á miña casa, ¿sabes?, e así a xente que vexa que ando en obra non pensará que os meus non teñen que levar á boca.

Meu pai, que percorreu moito mundo, aseguroulle que a fame cúrase con pan; mais o Rifante púxose teso e volveu falar.

– A vergonza é peor que a fame.

E seguro meu pai de non convencer en terra a un home que soamente ten intelixencia no mar, abriu a gabeta e colleu mil reás; pero o Rifante atallouno:

– Non, agora non mos deas; xa virei por eles.

Na noite daquel día velaí se sentiu unha tropa na nosa casa. Era o Rifante que viña coa muller, os fillos, os xenros, as noras cos netos todos en procura dos mil reás.

A patulea do Rifante encheu a casa toda e daba medo pensar cómo formarían roda demandando pan ó seu patriarca.

O Rifante, coa gorra encachada até as orellas, pediulle os cartos a meu pai, e, ó recibilos das súas mans, descubriuse relixiosamente e amosándollos a todos dixo con solemnidade:

– Miña muller e meus fillos: Se morro xa sabedes que se lle deben cincuenta pesos a este home.

E sen dicir outra verba tapou a cabeza e foise diante de todos, escaleira abaixo.

Rifante Was a Sailor...

Rifante was a sailor who made a lot of money which he kept in his pocket like water in a sieve. On land Rifante was nobody at all, but as soon as he set foot on his boat he was turned into a sage. He had many children and a lot of grandchildren and a lot of money to spend because the sea had enough for everybody.

Nobody denied that he was a great skipper, or that he was a good Christian, but at times he seemed to have made a deal with the devil. Other seamen would lay out their nets and catch nothing, while Rifante would arrive and fill his up with fish.

Rifante was also very generous himself. Once when he was on the point of drowning he made an offering to Our Lady and bought an altar cloth which cost six thousand reals, as well as paying for a mass, music, fireworks, new clothes and enough food to feed a regiment.

Rifante had faith in his lucky star. One time he was ill and his eldest son took over as skipper. When he came back ashore the son went up to his father's bedside and trembling with fear told his father how the nets had been tangled up in some rocks. Rifante just said "Don't be scared, Ramón; the sea takes away, but the sea will provide for more". Then he went silent and turned towards the wall.

Rifante really had a lot of confidence in the sea!

Such generosity had a limit though, and things got bad and hunger came in through many doors. That's what happened when the sardine fishing boats ruined the traditional way of fishing.

Rifante appeared at our house one day to talk to my father, who had been his friend since childhood and to whom he still turned for advice.

– Do you know what? – he said – We are hungry, famished in my house. You well know I never asked anything from anybody, but now I've had to come to ask you to lend me a thousand reals. I want to put a new balcony up in my house, you know, so that people will see me up working on it and that way they won't think that my family has nothing to eat.

My father, who had seen a lot of the world, told him that hunger could be cured with bread, but Rifante went tense and spoke again:

– Shame is worse than hunger.

My father was sure he wouldn't be able to convince on land a man who was only intelligent at sea, opened a drawer and took out a thousand reals. Rifante, however, stopped him:

– No, don't give them to me now. I'll come and get them.

That same evening the noise of people was heard outside my house. It was Rifante, who had come with his wife and children, his sons and daughters in law and his grandchildren to get the thousand reals.

Rifante's whole tribe packed the house, and it was frightening to think of them all surrounding their father begging him for bread.

Rifante, cap pulled down over his ears, asked my father for the money and, once it was in his possession, solemnly doffed his cap and said:

– Wife and children: If I die, you know that fifty pesos are owed to this gentleman.

And without another word he put his cap back on and led them all downstairs and out of the door.

Ramón Otero Pedrayo (1888–1976)

From Entre a vendimia e a castiñeira (Between the Grape Harvest and the Chestnuts), *1957*

A revolta de Casdenón

Na estrada dos Chaos, a revolta de Casdenón é, como denantes, a máis vistosa. Dá xenio, no outono, ó se ergueren as néboas dos riachos e lourear o sol nos penedos, botar un pito alí, denantes de seguir camiñando.

Á dereita, pola encosta, inzáronse bastos os piñeiros. Aínda son novos. Inda non podreceron os tocóns dos vellos.

Poucos se lembran hoxe, pois bolen os novos rumbos do mundo, do vinculeiro da casa de abaixo, chamada así por estar entobada no fondal da ribeiriña. Era en seis parroquias en roda alcuñado o Bicho polo moito ben, a moita influencia e o non pouco medo que puña. Medio fidalgote, medio patrón labrego, non se bulía cunha area de sal na parroquia sen o seu mandado. De mozo tivera sona de destemido. De vello, con dous cabaceiros ateigados, noventa moios nas cubas, ducia e media de cabezas de gando e un montón de obrigas na gabeta, tampouco tiña grimo e non había rapaz que se atrevera a choutarlle no pomar... Foise pondo groso, e por primeira vez da súa vida, saía de a paseo, sen obxecto ningún, por consello dos médicos, desconfiados da operación do porco cotián, os enxaugos de augardente mañanceira para espaventar a neboeira, a xerra dos seis netos... Non seus paseos collía para a revolta de Casdenón pola alegría da boa vista. Tanta larganza e tan ben disposta, case lle parecía ben seu ó Bicho, por ter nela, e á vista, boas pezas de arada, e touzas, e muíños...

Aconteceu que por causa dunha serventía houbo cuestión entre o Bicho e o seu veciño, do mesmo tempo do que el, o señor Estevo dos Inxertes. Foi este un patrón rexo, francote, bo prosas, asisado, orfo, pois endexamais quixera casar.

Entrambos eran tercos. Foron ó avogado, andaron regalos e metéronse homes. Por un chisco se non agarran os dous no adro, saíndo da misa. Ganou o Bicho, perdeu o dos Inxertes e non se falou máis do choio... Era pouca cousa, na comparanza co afundimento da casa de Vilerma, que alá foi como unha ponte río abaixo, ou coa morte da vella Prisca, que inda hoxe se non sabe se lle deran, a mantenta, a fariña dos ratos, ou foi ela quen tivo culpa, pois co frío, soidade e pobreza, dábase á pinga da augardente...

O vello dos Inxertes non tiña dúbida. Non foi raro que se aledasen ó velo derreado do pao xudicial a pesar de ter o Bicho, por rico, máis envexosos. O dos Inxertes puña medo pola lingua e pola sabenza e gran memoria das cousas da aldea. Quixeron moitas persoas herdalo con afagos e mimos. El ben os vía chegar, ría nos fociños dos pretendentes, e só tiña lei a un mozo, o Etelvino, chegado pola porta. Era rexo, calado, e capaz de botarse de capitón ó río polo seu amo. Ademais de agradecerlle o bo trato, admirábao. Figurábaselle fóra de razón que un home sabido de letras, engaiolador, cos seus contos, dos homes ó domingo na taberna, patrón de respecto cando levaba o pendón nas procesións arredor do adro, fora tripado por un bazuncho pipoteiro, aforrón, de vista baixa, de falar roufeño, que collía media estrada cando paseaba ó sol cara ós Chaos.

Polo seu xenio, o rapaz houbéralle polo menos acantazado o tellado ou posto lume ás medas. Non se atrevería a dicilo. O amo ata falaba co Bicho – que entón facíase con el moi compracente e cortés – e semellaba non lle doer a ferida.

Pero Etelvino entendeu ben o risco na fronte do amo, cando viña do eido da serventía ou era nomeado dediante del. Co tempo, ensañábase a chaga. Tiña medo á noite, polo recordo vergoñoso.

– Vou vello – dicía para si –, ¡que se non!

O Etelvino agardaba unha palabra. Non viña, nin viría. Decorría o terceiro outono. Houbo precisión de cartos na casa. Pensou o señor Estevo nos piñeiros que tiña na encosta sobre a revolta de Casdenón.

Foi alá co mozo. Este tallaría os pineiños. Non pasaban de dezaoito ou vinte. Altos, escuros de frouma e rouca voz ó vento. Pola encosta era doado botalos a rolar deica a estrada despois de tronzados. Na estrada, recolleríaos o camión.

O Bicho sempre, no seu paseo – eran días de sol febreiriño, ventando o marzal – ollaba para os piñeiros. Un serán, cruzándose co señor Estevo, díxolle:

– Valen boa presa de cartos: agora mellorará o estrume.

Houbo unha rouca resposta do vello, e unha ollada de lume do Etelvino.

Só quedaban tres altos piñeiros cando amo e criado, ollando a encosta e o vulto do Bicho adiantando a modo pola estrada, tiveron o mesmo pensamento.

O vello durmiu pouco, o mozo espertou con outro enxergar. Semellábanlle as horas camiñar a paso de boi. Despoixa do compango e dunha gotiña, camiñaron para o monte.

Non se decataban, non se podían decatar, por que aquel día eran máis amigos un do outro, falándose menos, e sen se mirar ós ollos.

Ó pasar diante do camiño que baixa para a casa do Vinculeiro, tivo o señor Estevo a idea de procurar outro traballo. Había moito que facer... Mais non se atreveu, como se entre os dous houber algún xuramento.

Non había ninguén polos eidos, nin pola estrada. O sol non era moito. Levantábase un ventiño livián e fino. Xostreaba como un vimbio... Houbera desexado o vello calquera parolada. Ás veces había convidadas. A xente acougaba nas bodegas, outra na feira.

O Etelvino calcaba o vieiro do monte como o fío do peirao quen se embarca co perigo de afogar. Xa estaban os derradeiros piñeiros tronzados. Só faltaba un. As toradas rexas, redondas, pesadas, só agardaban un rempuxón para rolar monte abaixo. Era femoso velas baixar. No primeiro tercio da encosta, de pelo de lobo, un saínte de laxe pizarreña dáballe nova forza para baixar choutando... Paraban as máis no foxo... Denantes o Etelvino enxergaba se viña xente ou gando.

Só había tres toradas e un piñeiro sen tronzar no chan. O Etelvino, con menos présa do que outras veces, recadou o tronzador. O vello fixo un pito. Ollouno estrañado e contento o mozo... Non se miraron cando o Bicho apareceu, coma sempre, paseniño, máis groso e pousón, considerando a modiño o val, os terreos, co colo da zamarra ergueito...

O cálculo foi operación perfecta no cerebro de entrambos. Decorreu un minuto coma unha cobra. Ó rempuxar o Etelvino, ó vello non lle tremeu o pito na man. Tivo medo do que lle viría enriba se a torada non baixaba a tempo. Pero a ollada e a man do mozo eran de seguranza matemática... Non houbo un iai! Non miraron para abaixo, descenderon as outras toradas con menos forza... Dispuxérase o rapaz a meter o tronzador, cando se ouvíu xente e berros... Ninguén sospeitou nada. O vello foi ó enterro, deu responsos, e deixou herdeiro ó Etelvino, que inzou familia na parroquia.

The field at Casdenón

On the road to Chaos the field at Casdenón is now as it was then the most striking one of all. It is beautiful to stop and light up a cigarette in autumn, when the mists rise up from the streams and the sun shines golden over the crags, before carrying on your journey.

To the right, up the hill, there are large numbers of pine trees growing. They are still young. The remains of the trunks of the old ones haven't yet rotted away.

Nowadays few remember, with all the changes in the world, the old owner of the house down below, so called because it is situated right down in the valley beside the banks of the stream. He was known in six parishes as The Beast for all the good he did, all the influence he had and not less for all the fear that he inspired. Part landowner, part farmer, not a grain of salt was boiled in the parish unless he had ordered it to be done. As a youth he was known for his daring. As an old man, with two full pumpkin fields, ninety full barrels, a dozen and a half heads of cattle and a whole lot of obligations he was still a frightening figure and not a single lad would dare to cross him. He had started to get fat and, for the first time in his life and on the advice of his doctors, who were concerned about the daily portions of pork, the morning glasses of liquor to clear the mists away, the jars of his six grandsons, he went for a walk with absolutely no objective. On his way he went around the field at Casdenón to gladden his eyes. He was in such a good mood it almost seemed to the Beast that it all belonged to him, as he had, in sight, good ploughing land, groves of trees and mills...

It so happened that because of a right of way there existed a dispute between the Beast and his neighbour, a man of his age, Don Estevo dos Inxertes. He was a strict master, frank, well-spoken, formal and all alone in this world, as he had never wished to get married.

Both of them were stubborn. They went to see a lawyer and blows were nearly exchanged. Luckily they were both held back in the atrium on their way out of church. The Beast won, Inxertes lost, and nothing more was said... It wasn't that big a deal, in comparison with the fall of the house of Vilerma, which was like a bridge downstream, or the death of old Prisca; even today no one knows whether she was fed rat poison on purpose or whether it was her fault, because with the cold weather, poverty and loneliness she liked a drop or two of home-distilled liquor…

The old Inxertes man had no doubt about it. It wasn't strange for people to be glad that he had been beaten at Court, even if the Beast, because he was richer, had more people envious of him. People were scared of the Inxertes because of their tongues, their wisdom and their vast knowledge of and long memory for village affairs. A lot of people wanted to inherit from him and sucked up to him because of that. He could see them coming for miles, and he laughed in the face of anyone who tried to impress him. He only had time for one lad, Etelvino. He was strong, silent and was willing to do anything for his master. As well as being grateful for his kindness towards him, he admired him. It seemed incredible to him that someone as wise, as charming, well-respected both in the bar on Sundays and when he was standard bearer at the processions around the church, could be trampled on by such a mean, worthless, rough-talking oaf who took up half of the road when he walked out in the sunshine towards Chaos.

Because of his nature, the lad would at least have thrown stones at his roof or set fire to his haystacks. He didn't dare to tell him. His master even spoke to the Beast – who was then being most indulgent and polite to him – and didn't seem to be hurt by the wound.

But Etelvino well understood the danger on his master's brow when he came from the servant's quarters or came face to face with him. With time the wound started to show. He was afraid at night because of the shameful memory.

I'm getting old – he said to himself –, oh yes I am.

Etelvino was waiting for a word from his master. It didn't come, nor would it. The third autumn came. Money was needed at home. Mr Estevo thought about the pine-trees he had on the hill up by the field at Casdenón.

He went up there with the lad. The lad would cut down the pines. There were only about eighteen or twenty. Tall and dark, with their leaves and needles blowing in the wind's murmur. On the slope it was easy to roll the trunks downhill towards the road once they'd been cut. A lorry would pick them up from the road.

The Beast, whenever he was out walking – in these sunny February days, with a slight March-like wind – liked to look at the pine-trees. One evening, when he met Mr Estevo, he said to him:

– That's worth a lot of money: now the manure will be better.

The old man gave a hoarse reply, and Estelvo gave him a fiery look.

Only three tall pines were left when master and servant, looking at the hill and the large figure of the Beast heading quickly down the road, had the same idea.

The old man slept very little, and the young man awoke with a fresh idea. The hours seemed to drag by at the speed of oxen. After eating and having a drink or two, they headed for the hill.

They didn't realize, nor could they have known, why they were better friends than ever that day, speaking less and not looking each other straight in the eyes.

When they walked past the road leading down to Vinculeiro's house, Mr Estevo had an idea of how to get more work. There was a lot to be done, but he didn't dare. It was as if there was a kind of oath between them.

There was nobody in the fields or on the road. There wasn't a lot of sunshine. A light, easy wind was blowing. He was shaking like a willow... He would have been grateful for any conversation. Sometimes there were guests. People got together in the wine cellars or at the fairs.

Etelvino walked carefully along the hillside as if he were on the edge of a quay-side in danger of drowning. The last pines had been cut. The heavy round logs just needed a push to roll down the hill. It was wonderful to see them roll down. On the first part of their descent a sharp protruding rock of slate-stone gave them a new impulse to carry on rolling down. Most of them came to a halt in the ditch at the bottom. Before Etelvino watched to see if any people or cattle were about.

Only three logs and a pine-tree which hadn't been cut up were left. Etelvino, less quickly than on other occasions, picked up the saw. The old man rolled a ciga-rette. He looked, surprised and happy, at the young man... They didn't look at each other when the Beast appeared, slowly as usual, looking in a leisurely fashion at the valley, the fields, his jacket collar turned up...

Both of them calculated perfectly. A minute slid by like a cobra. When Etelvino pushed, the cigarette didn't even tremble in the old man's hand. He was afraid that he'd be seen at the top of the hill if the log didn't roll down in time. But the young man's look and the sureness of his hand were mathematical... There wasn't a sin-gle shout. They didn't look down, and rolled the other logs down less forcefully. The young lad was getting ready to use the saw when they heard people shouting. Nobody suspected a thing. The old man went to the funeral, paid his respects and left his inheritance to Etelvino who raised his family in the parish.

From Arredor de si, 1930

Na aldea da outra banda badalan as campás. Un instante paran as angueiras labre-gas, e vai correndo polo val a nova: don Bernaldo está a morrer. A procesión do viático baixa polas canellas do lugar. O mordomo do enfermo, o señor Pascual, tan vello coma el, vai coa testa núa, cos ollos mollados tocando a campaíña. As salas e os corredores da casa énchense dunha multitude axeonllada. Dona María ten todo dispostiño: brancos panos sobre as mesas, acendidas as lámpadas das imaxes. O día figura máis raiolante, máis fondo e puro o azul do ceo. Cantan os paxariños coma aqueles que están engaiolados na dourada capela do Cristo de Ourense.

Cando el Señor chegou á alcoba, tódalas caras se baixaron ó chan e no silencio oíase o tremer dos corazóns: o velliño desfeito e caducado, tan pretiño da morte, tirouse do leito sen que houbese forzas para retelo; botáronlle por riba un vello manteo e axeonllado no medio da estancia, cos brazos en cruz, comungou santa-mente. Dona María choraba nun recuncho. Logo, don Bernaldo sentiuse mellor. Bendiciu longamente a dona María e ó Xacobe. Trazou no aire unha cruz coa man enrugada e serena. Aquela bendición voaba como unha pomba sobre o río e íase pousar na testa murcha da irmá tolleitiña. Cando falou foi para preguntar polo Adrián.

Decorreron cerca de dous días, calados fondos, atentos ó máis pequeno movemento do doente. Dona María só deixaba a casa para ir un instante bicar á velliña. Contábualle piadosos enganos. Ata lle dixo que don Bernaldo desexaba un dociño de guindas, que había na casa. Dona María fitaba, fría e decoñecida, ó Xacobe sen lle dicir palabra.

Anoitecendo o segundo día, chegou Adrián da estación. Viña máis fraco, desfeito da viaxe. A nai, refuxiándose no seu peito, chorou por fin bágoas consoladoras. Fuxía a derradeira inquietude da cara do doente e a súa man acariñaba a testa do sobriño axeonllado. Na noite ficaron sós. Entón o doente faloulle ó Adrián:

– Meu fillo, vai ó despacho e descolga aquel mapa grande... Quero velo antes de morrer...

O sobriño coa axuda do señor Pascual trouxo á alcoba o mapa de Fontán. Penduráronoo da parede. Os ollos do enfermo reviviron. A man figuraba sinalar horizontes. Unha pura alegría animaba a cara murchiña e branca. Adrián, cunha vela na man, ía alumando os lugares que o vello dicía con voz lonxana: Corme, Laxe, Caramiñas, Niñóns... Adrián non sabía sempre atopar os sitios. O enfermo falaba:

– Non, á dereita, á esquerda, un pouco ó norte.

A vela alumou longamente un nome e o sitio de Compostela. Adrián lía nomes de montes, de ríos, de aldeíñas, de ermidas. A luz ía seguindo os trazados dos camiños.

Naqueles instantes estraños e fondos figuraban lucir no mapa agras marelas de centeo, ermos vestidos de flores de toxo e de piorno, serras penedosas, campanarios barrocos, xente que vai polos carreiros ós muíños e ás feiras, verdeceres de camposantos, fuxir de augas, praias douradas, galgar de ondas nos cons, velas que saen roselando o mar, orballeiras sobre as arboredas mestas, rúas de vellas cidades, soidades de esquecidos mosteiros.

Adrián sentíase conmovido ata o máis fondo do seu ser. Treméndolle a man foi alumado todo o camiño de Santiago, a terra de Ourense, as dúas aldeíñas xémeas do val onde eles estaban; parou un instante como un cirio funeral no nome da aldeíña na que morría D. Bernaldo e logo foi percorrendo todo o debuxo das fronteiras e costas da Galicia. Don Bernaldo xa non falaba. Sorría. Grosas bágoas queimaban as fazulas do Adrián. Tivo que saír á sala e liberar os seus saloucos na fiestra, cara á noite. Logo, atendendo ós signos do doente, púxolle o crucifixo nas mans. Xa non o afastaba dos beizos.

Chegaba dona María co abade. Un feble suspirar fuxía axiña do leito. O crego murmuraba as oracións de agonía. Un rumor como o da derradeira auga dunha fonte que se enxoita. Don Bernaldo morría docemente, e unha negra sombra corría sobre o mapa da Galicia.

From About Oneself, *1930*

In the village on the other side the bells were tolling. In just a moment the agricultural winds stop blowing and the news spreads quickly throughout the valley: Don Bernaldo is dying. The procession moves down the village streets. The sick man's servant, Señor Pascual, as old as his master himself, is bare-headed, damp-eyed as he rings the bell. The rooms and the corridors of the house fill up with a disconsolate multitude. Dona María has everything ready: white cloths over the tables and the lamps around the religious images are alight. The day seems more radiant, the blue of the sky somehow deeper and purer. The birds sing like the caged birds in the golden chapel of the Christ of Ourense.

When the Lord arrived in the bedroom, all of the faces were lowered and in the silence the beating of every heart could be heard: the old man, so discomposed and ancient, so close to death, threw himself from the bed and nobody was able to stop him. They covered him in an old blanket and kneeling in the middle of the room with his arms in the form of a cross he received Holy Communion. Dona María was crying in a corner. Then Don Bernaldo started to feel better. He gave a long blessing to Dona María and Xacobe. He made the sign of the cross in the air with his hand, withered but serene. This blessing flew over the river like a dove and landed on the emaciated head of his crippled sister. When it spoke it asked about Adrián.

Two days past, days of deep, solemn silence, awaiting even the slightest movement of the patient. Dona María only left the house for an instant to go and give the old lady a kiss. She told her white lies. She even told her that Don Bernaldo had asked for a dozen of the cherries that she had in her house. Dona María stared at Xacobe, cold and unknown, without saying a word.

At nightfall of the second day, Adrián arrived from the station. He was slimmer, worn out after the journey. His mother, burying her head in his chest, at last let loose her comforting tears. The final concern left the dying man's face and his hand caressed the head of his nephew who knelt before him. At night they were left alone together. It was then that the dying man said to Adrián:

– Son, go to my office and take down the big map… I want to see it before I die…

His nephew brought the map of Fontán into the bedroom with the help of Señor Pascual. They hung it from a wall. The dying man's eyes came alive. His hand seemed to point out the horizons. His withered, pale face was filled with pure joy. Adrián, with a candle in his hand, lit up the places that the old man named with his faraway voice: Corme, Laxe, Caramiñans, Niñóns… Adrián didn't always know how to find the places. The sick man spoke:

– No, to the right, left a bit, a bit more to the north.

The candle lit up the name of Compostela for a long time. Adrián read the names of mountains, hills, villages, hermitages. The light followed the roads.

In such strange and profound moments the map seemed to show yellow fields of barley, hills covered in gorse and whin, rocky mountain ranges, baroque church steeples, people going along the roads to the mills and the fairs, the green church-yards, rushing waters, golden beaches, the crashing of the waves on cliffs, sails that stand out amidst the sea, drizzle falling in the woods, streets in the old towns, the solitary, ancient monasteries.

Adrián was moved to the depth of his soul. With trembling hand he lit up the length of St James' Way, the land of Ourense, the two little twin villages in the val-ley where they were. He stopped for a moment like a funeral candle when he came to the name of the village where don Bernaldo was dying and then went on to trace all the coasts and borders of Galicia. Don Bernaldo had stopped talking. He smiled. Huge tears burned Adrián's face. He had to get out of the room and wipe away his tears by the window, into the night. Then, following the signs of the sick man, he placed the crucifix in his hands. He didn't move it away from his lips.

Dona María came with the abbot. A weak sigh still came from the deathbed. The priest murmured the dying prayers. A sound like the final drops of water from a fountain that had gone dry. Don Bernaldo died peacefully, and a black shadow fell over the map of Galicia.

From Os camiños da vida (The Paths of Life), *1928*

Os señores da terra (fragmento)

Xa entrado o século, o morgado morreu. Nos derradeiros anos teimaba deixar o privilexio do seu nacemento e camiñar a Sant-Iago para estudiar a Teoloxía. A pesar da febleza do corpo, gastaba moitas noites en oración. Daba xenio ouvilo falar en latín cos cregos. Don Xosé María sentiu de corazón ó irmán. A morte do morgado axiña levou á cova á nai doente, envellecida. Con poucos meses de espacio foron enterrados no adral da Colexiata, pois por humildade non quixeron usar da sepul-tura familiar nas naves da igrexa. O pai, parviño, pasaba a vellez nunha silla poltrona rindo como un neno. Fóronse gastando as rendas da casa; os terreos apenas pro-ducían unha miseria. Ademais, don Xosé María pouco tiña de administrador. Tiña un xenio ledo e gozaba coas enredadelas. Moitas mañás cabalgaba para chegar de boa hora á ribeira de Vigo, deténdose cos amigos, cregos ou fidalgos, de camiño. Baiona íaselle facendo noxenta. Só cando chegaba o outono paseaba polo adral da Colexiata, ollando a herba verdecente riba das pedras dos seus. Consolaba logo nas farras da ribeira de Vigo; unha pesca loira tíñalle chuchado os miolos. Namorouse da picardía daquel andar coas saias recachadas, o pisar dos peíños miúdos sobre a area da praia do Areal. Estaba rindo con ela despoixa dunha noite de amor, marisco e viño branco, cando entraron na praza os franceses. Fuxiu deseguida para o pazo do val Miñor. Os ratos esburacaran as alacenas, as pingueiras do teito apodrecían os pisos. Entón decidiu escoitar prudentes consellos e tomou estado. Ela era unha fidalga veciña. Xa estaban coas admonicións cando o baril erguemento da terra de Vigo. O morgado acudiu deseguida ó chamamento do abade de Sobroso, o seu grande amigo. Quedou admirado do entusiasmo da xente. Pois alí andaba o alférez

Morillo, en quen todos ollaban un gran porvir na milicia. Tiña ambición e sabía empregar o seu valor nas ocasións. Vigo forte figuraba un inimigo sañudo. ¿Que farían os amigos de dentro? Viu oficiais de grande uniforme ollando cun rir de bigotes loiros os ataques dos paisanos. Nunha saída, don Xosé María vendimou a un granadeiro francés coma se fora un coello: de vello representábase coma se fora onte a escena, a corredoira, os loureiros lixados co sangue daquel home que parecía un xigante. Todos estaban impacientes polo asalto, como os lobos. El esquecérase do matrimonio e só arelaba entrar para bicar á pesca graciosa. Ollou a Cachamuíña na porta da Gamboa. Despois da rendición foi de présa a casar, unha mañá cediño, na Ramallosa. O mesmo día voltou ó seu posto na División do Miño. Cruzaron ledas terras para se situaren co corpo dos paisanos no paso de Ponte Caldelas. Houbo alí poucos tiros. Admirou a elegancia dun húsar francés, xa vellote, esguío, que chegaba coma se tal cousa ó pé do río para tentear o vao. Polo val rubía o estrondo dun gran combate. Era a acción da Pontesampaio.

Rematada a guerra de Galicia tivo vagar para pensar no porvir. A casa estaba ben derrotada. O capital da dona non abondaba para mandar cantar un cego. Entón recibiu cartas das tías de Trasouto: só quedaba unha e reclamaba a presencia do seu herdeiro. A casa de Baiona e as terras e pazo do Miñor, despoixa de satisfeitos os débitos, pasaron ás irmás. Unha, casada cun curial, outra, freira. Don Xosé María decidiuse a probar novo vivir na montaña ourensá.

Lords of the Land (extract)

Well into the century the eldest son and heir died. Towards the end of his life he thought about renouncing his birthright and going to Santiago to study theology. Despite the weakness of his body, he spent a great many nights in prayer. It was wonderful to hear him talking to the priests in Latin. Don Xosé María felt for his brother with all his heart. The death of the eldest son soon led his sick, aging mother to her grave. Within the space of a few short months they were buried in the atrium of the Collegiate Chapel, as out of humility they did not want to use the family tomb inside the church. The father who had gone mad spent his old age sitting in an easy chair laughing away like a child. The household income was quickly spent, and the lands produced very little. Moreover, Don Xosé María was not much of an administrator. He was of a happy disposition and enjoyed having fun. Many a morning he would ride early towards the shore at Vigo, and he would stop on the way to chat to his friends, priests or landlords. Baiona was becoming distasteful for him. Only when autumn came did he walk around the atrium of the Collegiate Chapel, smelling the green grass that grew over the tombs of his family. He would take comfort in the parties on the shore at Vigo: one blonde fisher-lass had tickled his fancy. He fell in love with the naughty way she lifted up her skirts to walk on her dainty feet over the sand of Areal beach. He was laughing with her after a night of love, shellfish and white wine, when the French arrived in the square. He fled immediately to the palace at Val Miñor. The mice were gnawing holes in the cupboards, while water leaked through the roof rotting the floorboards. It was then that he decided to listen to the sage advice and get married. She was a local landowner. They were in the middle of the banns when the good uprising took place in the area of Vigo. The eldest son went straight away when called by the abbot of Sobroso, a good friend of his. He was astonished by the people's enthusiasm. There, it seemed, was the Lieutenant Morillo, who everybody assured had a great future in the militia. He was most ambitious and knew how to use his courage should the occasion so require. The tough city of Vigo seemed a powerful enemy. What would his friends being doing there inside? He saw uniformed officers laugh through their blonde moustaches at the attacks by his countrymen. On a sortie, Don Xosé María caught a French grenadier as if he were a rabbit. As an old man he remembered the scene as if it were yesterday, the path through the woods, the laurels stained with the blood of that man who seemed like a giant. Everyone waited impatiently for the attack, like a pack of wolves. He forgot all about his wedding and could only think about going to kiss his beautiful young fisher-lass. He saw Cachamuiña in the doorway of the Gamboa. After the surrender he went off to get married, one early morning in the Ramallosa. That same day he returned to his post in the Miño Brigade. They crossed pleasant lands until they arrived at the pass at Ponte Caldelas where they joined the main group of their army. Few shots were fired there. He admired the elegance of an aging French hussar who came up along the river as if it was nothing, trying to try out the vanguard. The roars of a great battle came up from the valley. It was the battle of Pontesampaio.

When the war in Galicia ended he was in no hurry to think about his future. The house was in ruins. His wife's finances were hardly enough to pay for anything. Then he received word from his aunts in Trasouto. Only one was left alive and she requested the presence of her heir. The house in Baiona and the lands and Palace of Val Miñor, riddled with debts, were passed on to his sisters. One was married to an ecclesiastical clerk, the other a nun. Don Xosé María decided that he try out a new life in the mountains of Ourense.

Rafael Dieste (1899–1981)

From Dos arquivos do trasno (The Leprechaun Files), *1926*

O neno suicida

Cando o taberneiro rematou de ler aquela nova inquedante – un neno suicidárase pegándose un tiro na sen dereita – falou o vagamundo descoñecido que acababa de xantar moi pobremente nun curruncho da tasca mariñeira, e dixo:

– Eu sei a historia dese neno.

Pronunciou a palabra neno dun xeito moi particular. Así foi que, os catro bebedores de augardente, os cinco de albariño e o taberneiro calaron e escoitaron con xesto inquiridor e atento.

– Eu sei a historia dese neno – repetiu o vagamundo –. E, tras dunha solerte e ben medida pausa, encomezou:

– Alá polo mil oitocentos trinta, unha beata que despois morreu de medo viu saír do camposanto florido e recendente da súa aldea a un vello moi vello en coiro. Aquel vello era un recén nacido. Antes de saír do ventre da terra nai escollera el mesmo ese xeito de nacencia. ¡Canto mellor ir de vello para mozo que de mozo para vello!, pensou sendo espírito puro. A Noso Señor chocoulle a idea. ¿Por que non face-la proba? Así foi que, co seu consentimento, formouse no seo da terra un esqueleto. E despois, con carne de verme, fíxose a carne do home. E na carne do home aformigou a caloriña do sangue. E como todo estaba listo, a terra-nai pariu. Pariu un vello en coiro.

De como despois o vello topou roupa e mantenza é cousa de moita risa. Chegou ás portas da cidade e como aínda non sabía falar, os ministros, despois de lle botaren unha capa enriba, leváron diante do xuíz coma se tivesen sido testigos: Aquí lle traemos a este pobre vello que perdeu a fala coa tunda que lle deron uns ladróns mal entrañados. Nin roupa lle deixaron.

O xuíz deu ordes e o vello foi levado a un hospital. Cando saíu, xa ben vestido e mantido, dicíanlle as monxiñas: Vai feito un bo mozo. Ata parece que perdeu anos.

Daquela xa aprendera a falar algo e fíxose esmoleiro. Así andou moitas terras. Alá en Lourdes estivo dúas veces; da segunda tan amozado que, os que o coñeceran da primeira, coidaron que fora milagre da Virxe.

Cando adquiriu experiencia de abondo pensou que o mellor era manter secreta aquela estraña condición que o facía máis mozo cantos máis anos corresen. Así, non o sabendo ninguén – non sendo un ou dous amigos fieis – podería vivir mellor a súa verdadeira vida.

Traballou de vello e fíxose rico para folgar de mozo. Dos cincuenta ós quince anos a súa vida foi a máis feliz que se pode imaxinar. Cada día gustaba máis ás mozas e andou enleado con moitas e coas máis bonitas. E ata disque unha princesa... Pero diso non estou certo.

Cando chegou a neno encomezou a vida a se lle ensarillar. Dáballe medo a sorpresa con que o vían entrar tan ceibe nas tendas a mercar lambetadas e xoguetes. Algún rateiro de viseira calada teno seguido ó longo de moitas rúas tortas. E algunha vez ten comido as súas lambetadas a tremer de anguria, coas bágoas nos ollos e o almibre nos beizos. A derradeira vez que o topei – tiña el oito anos – andaba moi triste. ¡Pesaban, ademais, tanto no seu espírito de neno os recordos da súa vellice!

Logo encomezou a lle escaravellar día e noite unha obsesión tremenda. Cando pasasen algúns anos recolleríano en calquera calexa extraviada. Quizais algunha señora rica e sen fillos. Despois... ¡Quen sabe o que pasaría despois! A lactancia, os paseos nun carriño, cunha sonalla de axóuxeres na manciña tenra. E ó remate... ¡Ou! O remate poñía espanto. Cumpri-lo seu sino de home que vive ó revés e refuxiarse no seo da señora rica – poida que cando ela durmise – para ir alí devecendo ata se trocar primeiro nunha sambesuga e despois en arumia e logo en pequenísima semente...

O vagamundo ergueuse moi pensabundo, coas mans nos petos, e deu algúns paseíños todo amargurado. Ó cabo dixo:

– Explícome, si, explícome que se chimpase un tiro na sen o pobre rapaz.

Os catro bebedores de augardente, crían. Os cinco de albariño, sorrían e dubidaban. O taberneiro negaba. Cando todos desortían máis enfervoadamente, o taberneiro ergueuse de súpeto nas puntas dos pés e púxose a mirar todo arredor cos ollos moi abertos. O vagamundo desaparecera sen pagar.

The Suicidal Child

When the innkeeper finished reading out that disturbing piece of news – a child had committed suicide shooting himself in the right temple –, the unknown tramp, who had just eaten badly in a corner of the fisherman's inn, spoke. He said:

– I know the story of that child.

He said the word "child" in a very peculiar way. For that reason, the four liquor drinkers, the five who were imbibing albariño wine and the innkeeper became silent and listened with inquisitive and attentive looks.

– I know the story of that child – the tramp repeated –. And after a sly and well-measured pause, he began:

– Around 1930 a goody-goody who afterwards died of fear saw a very old man in the nip leaving the flowery, sweet-smelling cemetery in her village. That old man was a new-born baby. Before leaving the womb of Mother Earth he himself had chosen that type of birth. How much better to go from being old to young than from young to old!, he thought, when he was still pure spirit. Our Lord was struck by the idea. Why not try it? That is why, with His permission, a skeleton was formed in the bosom of the earth. And afterwards with worm flesh human flesh was made. And in the human flesh the warmth of blood tingled. And as all was ready Mother Earth gave birth. She gave birth to an old man in the nip.

How afterwards the old man found clothes and sustenance is something to make you split your sides. He arrived at the city gates and, as he still did not know how to speak, the ministers, after covering him with a cape, took him to the judge as if they had been witnesses:

– We're bringing you here this poor old man who lost the power of speech due to the beating he was given by some hard-hearted thiefs. They didn't even leave him his clothes.

The judge gave some orders and the old man was taken to a hospital. When he left, well-dressed and well-fed, the dear nuns said to him:

– You're looking lovely. It even seems as if you've got younger.

By that time he had learnt to speak a little and he became a beggar. So he travelled to many lands. He went over there to Lourdes twice; the second so rejuvenated that those who knew him from the first time thought that the Virgin Mary had performed a miracle.

When he had acquired sufficient experience he thought that the best thing was that that strange matter that made him younger the more years that passed should be kept secret. In that way, if nobody knew anything – except one or two faithful friends –, he could live his real life better.

He worked as an old man and became rich enough to rest when young. From 50 to 15 his life was the happiest that could be imagined. As each day passed young girls liked him more and he was involved with many and the prettiest. They say that even with a princess… But I'm not so sure about that.

When he became a child his life got mixed up. The surprised looks when he went into a shop by himself to buy sweets and toys frightened him. Sometimes a petty thief, with his cap pushed down on his head, followed him down many twisted streets. And sometimes he ate his sweets trembling with anxiety with tears in his eyes and syrup on his lips. The last time I met him – he was eight years old – he was very sad. The memories of his old age weighed down his childish spirit so much!

Afterwards a tremendous obsession began to bore into him. When some years had passed he would be found in some lost alley. Perhaps a rich lady with no children. And after that… Who knows what would happen after that! Breastfeeding, the outings in pram, with the rattle held in the baby hand. In the end… Oh! The end was horrible. To fulfil his destiny as a man whose life goes in the opposite direction and take refuge in the womb of the rich lady – maybe when she was sleeping – to go there slowly shrinking until he becomes first a leech then a flea and then a tiny seed…

The tramp got up very pensively with his hands in his pockets and walked some steps very downheartedly. At last he said:

– I have explained why the poor boy plugged himself in the temple.

The four liquor drinkers believed him. The five albariño drinkers smiled and doubted him. The innkeeper didn't believe him. When all of them were arguing most hotly, the innkeeper got up suddenly on tiptoe and began to look all around with his eyes wide open. The tramp had gone off without paying.

O vello moreno

Non me podo lembrar en que taberna de que porto foi. Só sei que a cortina da entrada era vermella e que se enchía como unha vela co vento noitego. Debeu de se-lo rapaz de abordo (sempre andaba con nós, fumaba en pipa e chiscaba o ollo) quen ó ve-la cortina daquel xeito dixo que iamos en popa. Outro dixo que estaba empreñada. E outro que era unha bailarina. Moura…, engadiu; razón, supoño, de que non lle visen as pernas. Este xa trasvariaba, e no pulo de ir namora-la bailarina desapareceu.

Bulía a marusía das conversas con ese ledo barullo en que xa non sabe un quen fala e quen escoita. Nalgún intre paréceme que se falou dos chineses… duns que ateigaban grandes ríos coas casiñas boiantes; e por entre eses chineses apareceron uns ingleses, e xa de seguida estaba outro lembrándose dunha noiva que tivera en Cardiff e do bonito que era oíla coma quen oe a un paxaro, facendo que entendía (yes, yes…), para que ela rise e garulase máis. Sobre mulleres, como son, como convén tratalas, case que todos tivemos algo que dicir. Cousas, por certo, de moi pouco peso.

Fóranse algúns dos máis trouleiros, e aínda se lles oíu cantar, desafinando polo fino, ó virar por algunha venela cara ós diques, cando o Vello Moreno, deica entón moi calado, arregañou os dentes (non podo xurar que aquilo fose un sorriso) e dixo ollando para min e, máis de esguello, para outros que estaban por alí, preto da súa mesa:

– ¡Parvadas!

Cando lle quixen dá-la razón, sen saber ben aínda a que parvadas afitaba, xa estaba el rosmando cousas que non entendín, como disposto a se pechar de novo nos seus pensamentos.

– Si, lerias... – dixen eu non obstante, na teima de acertar –. Coidan que en catro retrousos caben tódolos casos e misterios do mundo.

Entón espabilouse:

– ¡Os casos do mundo!... Eu sei dunha muller que aínda hoxe agarda polo seu home... ¡Mais agarda en balde!

Arregañou os dentes outra vez. Se era dor ou sorriso, ou tenreza ou furia, eu non o sei. Era el así, o Vello Moreno. Polo xeito de acariña-lo vaso, xa baleiro, que un mociño espelido acudiu a encher e que el esbicou, pareceunos que ía contar algunha cousa, algún raro exemplo. Todos calamos e escoitamos.

– Ela coidou que ninguén o había de saber... – rompeu a dicir despois dun intre de silencio que, para todos nós, era parte do conto –; e como se sentía, digo eu, moi enlevada por aqueles ollos de entendido en mulleres que a percorrían paseniño de pés a cabeza, deixou primeiro abertas as orellas, parándose a oí-lo que non debía, e despois as portas... ¡A modiño, a modiño! Non espertar ós nenos...

O narrador fixo unha pausa ollando para nós. Nas caras de todos viu que si, que entendiamos ... Podía seguir.

– ¡Malpocada! – dixo como considerando o caso moi delicadamente –. En segredo, en segredo, fórono sabendo todos, tódolos que nas vilas saben estas cousas... E o raposiño aquel, viaxante, por máis señas, e do que non se soubo máis nada algún tempo despois, deixou dicir cousas moi churrusqueiras a catro lampantíns que trincaban á súa conta. Deixounas dicir, sentindo as cóchegas. El a sorrir, moi reservado... Máis ou menos de esguello, falouse do home dela, que andaba lonxe, a navegar. E foi cando el dixo (aínda agora se conta): ¡Disque é un toscalleiro, pero soubo escoller! Dígovolo eu... E baixou unha punta do bigote para desafogar, mordéndoa, algún degaro súpeto que lle gabearía polo corpo. Non sei por que me entreteño neses detalles...

– Os contos hai que adornalos – dixo algún dos presentes.

– Si, hai que adornalos, moi ben adornadiños – fungou o Vello Moreno. Bebeu un pouco, apartou de si o vaso e seguiu xa de corrido –: Un día soubo que o seu home viña xa de volta. Que estaba preto, na cidade... Soubo que podía chegar axiña, no intre insospeitado, e encomezou a arranxa-la casa para recibilo con agarimo. Disque ata mercou algunha roupa nova... E velaí que o home non remataba de chegar. Chegaron en troques dous deses baúis que chaman mundos. E aínda outro despois. E, nunha letra, os miles para o desempeño. E de seguida outra que dobraba á primeira. Mais del, do home, ninguén daba razón. Soamente preguntas das veciñas. ¿E logo, cando vén? Mañá, mañá... As abesulladoras viron como se miraba nun espello, como poñía aquí, alá, o retrato del, co seu marquiño de cunchas e cara-muxos... Mañá, mañá. Os picariños non se fartaban de remexer nas pechaduras dos mundos, ou de andar arredor. Ó cabo puideron abrilos, porque da cidade chegou o máis vello amigo do navegante e deulles unhas chaves... E mentres eles remexían, o forasteiro falaba moi baixiño coa nai.

Do seo dos mundos encomezaron a saíren adobíos de neno, feitucos e charra-manduscos, lambetadas, un trenciño, moedas estranxeiras, bólas de vidro, azuis, moradas, cor da prata, do ouro, do lume ... E deberon de se quedar moi aglaiados cando llas mostraron á nai, e viron que ela rompía a chorar ... E ben, esa muller é a que agarda en balde. Hai quen di que lle quería ó seu home.

Calou un intre. Parecía de pedra; unha pedra na que fosen deixando tremulentas escumas, vindo de moi lonxe, unhas escuras ondas. Dicía agora:

– Si, dende fóra, en falas e consellos, é moi doado ter bos ollos e boas entrañas. As entrañas demóstranse... Por exemplo, non tendo trato, anos arreo, con muller ningunha. Talmente un frade, deses antigos, dos desertos, mais acudindo a tesar un cabo, ou a empuxar vultos na estiba ou ó que cadre, que os brazos aínda rexen; e hai nun deles un nome floreado que non se desborra. Un bo traballo, feito por eses chineses que falabades. Si, hai quen di que lle tiña lei ó seu home, hai quen o di... ¡Mais a min, a min, non haberá quen teña cara a mo dicir!

E de súpeto o Vello Moreno, que tiña a man a tremer no cinto, arrandeou no aire o seu coitelo e espetouno na mesa. Longo tempo quedou o coitelo a abanear.

Seica fun eu quen preguntou despois dun silencio:

– ¿Hai moitos anos que foi...?

O Vello Moreno pasou a man pola branca testa rapada e dixo:

– Moitos.

Non quixen preguntar máis, e falamos do semblante do tempo.

The Dark Old Man

I can't remember in what inn in what port it was. I only know that the curtain in the entrance was red. And that it filled up like a sail with the night wind. It had to be the boy on board (he always went around with us, smoking a pipe and winking his eye) who, on seeing the curtain like that said that we were on the stern side. Another said that it had to be pregnant. And another that it was a dancer. A Moorish girl…, he added; due to the fact, I suppose, that he couldn't see any legs. He was getting out of control and during his impulsive dash to court the dancer he disappeared. The undercurrent of the conversations shook with that happy noise in which one doesn't know who is talking and who is listening. It seemed to me that at a certain moment there was talk about the Chinese…, of some who filled big rivers with floating houses; and in the middle of those Chinese there were some

English people, and then another began to reminisce about a girlfriend he had in Cardiff and how nice it was to hear her like hearing birdsong, pretending that he understood her (yes, yes...), so that she would laugh and be even noisier. About women, what they are like, how one should treat them, we nearly all had something to say. Things, actually, which are not very important. The most dedicated revellers had gone and you could still hear them sing very much out of tune on turning into one of the alleys that led to the quays, when the dark old man, until then very silent, showed his teeth (I can't swear that that was a smile) and said, looking at me and out of the corner of his eye at others who were there, near his table:

– Rubbish!

When I wanted to agree with him, without yet knowing well what rubbish he was referring to, he was already murmuring things that I didn't understand, as if he was ready to sink into his thoughts again.

Yes, nonsense... – I said, nevertheless wanting to be right –. They think that all the events and mysteries in the world will fit in four witticisms.

Then he came to life: – All the events in the world!... I know of a woman that even today still waits for her husband... but she is waiting in vain!

He showed his teeth again. If it were pain or a smile or tenderness or anger I don't know. He was like that, the dark old man. From the way in which he caressed his glass, now empty, which a sharp-looking boy came to fill, and which he took to his mouth, it seemed to us that he was going to tell us something, a strange thing. We all shut up and listened.

– She thought that nobody knew about it – he said at last after a momentary silence that for all of us was part of the story –; And how she felt, I mean, flattered by those eyes of an expert in women that looked her over bit by bit, she firstly left her ears open, stopping to hear what she shouldn't, and after the doors... slowly, slowly! Don't wake the children...

The narrator paused, looking at us. On everybody's face he saw that, yes, we understood... He could go on.

– Poor woman! – he said as if he considered her story gently –. In secret, in secret, they all found out soon, those that in small towns find these things out... and that wretch, a travelling salesman no less and of whom nothing else was known some time after, let fall some vulgar things to four barefaced people who drank at his expense. Letting them fall tickled him. Smiling discreetly... More or less as if aside, he spoke of her husband who was far away at sea. And it was when he said (it is still said nowadays):

– They say he is rough, but he knew how to choose! I assure you...

He pulled down a corner of his moustache to relieve himself of some sudden desire that crawled through his body by biting it. I don't know why I give these details...

– You have to spice up stories – one of those present said.

Yes, one has to spice them up, well spiced up – the dark old man growled. He drank a little, he pushed the glass away and he went on with the story –. One day she found out that her husband was coming back. That he was near, in town… She knew that he could turn up at any minute, at the moment he was least expected, and began to tidy up the house to receive him warmly. They say that she even bought some new clothes… And can you believe it! He never arrived. Two of those big trunks arrived instead. And still one more after and another after that. And in a letter a lot of money to pay off debts. And then another that doubled the first amount. But about him, about the man, nobody knew anything. Only the neighbours' questions. And so, when is he coming? Tomorrow, tomorrow… The gossips saw how she looked at herself in the mirror, how she hung in this place or that his picture in its frame made of shells and barnacles… Tomorrow, tomorrow. Her children never got tired of picking the locks of the trunks or of being around them. Finally, they were able to open them because the sailor's oldest friend came from town and gave them keys… And while they were picking, the stranger whispered to the mother.

Children's trinkets began to appear from inside the trunks, baubles, fripperies, sweets, a little train, foreign coins, glass balls, blue, purple, silver, gold, the colour of fire… And they must have been quite amazed when they showed them to their mother and saw her burst into tears… Well, that is the woman that is waiting in vain. Some people say she loved her husband.

He stopped for a moment. He seemed to be made of stone; a stone in which dark waves, coming from far away, left sparkling foam. He now said:

– Yes, seeing it from outside, talking and commenting about it, it is very easy to be well-disposed and kind-hearted. Good-heartedness is shown… for example, in not having anything to do with women for many years. The same as a friar, one of those from long back in the deserts, but pulling a rope tight, or pushing big weights on the docks, or whatever, and one's arms still can do it; and on one of them a name surrounded by flowers that can't be removed. A good job, done by those Chinese you were talking about. Yes, there are those who say she was faithful to her husband, there are those who say it… But nobody would have enough cheek to say that to me, to me!

And suddenly the dark old man with his hand trembling at his belt, moved his knife in the air and stuck it in the table. The knife vibrated for a long time.

I think it was me who asked after a silence:

– Did it happen many years ago… ?

The dark old man passed his hand over his white shaven head and said:

– Many.

I didn't want to ask him any more questions and we spoke about how the weather was.

Nova York é Noso

O neno tiña algo que lles dicir ós outros nenos que andaban a enredar con el na beiramar. Tiña algo que lles dicir, pero non remataba de dicilo. Por veces poñía cara de malo, cheo como estaba daquel orgullo que non certaba a deixar ceibe. Ata lle rabuñou a outro, así nun pronto, a lle brincar na caa os lampos dunha íntima fogueira. Esbandallaba tódolos xogos con aquel seu desacougo, mesmo como de gato alporizado por veciñanza de treboada. Era un raro rebuldar o seu, con súpetos enlevos.

Seu pai chegara aquel mesmo día de Nova York e os demais nenos non lle preguntaban nada, nin lle facían máis mimos e respetos que outros días. Quizais por iso, porque a pregunta non chegaba, foi polo que rabuñou a quen el coidaba que calaba adrede.

Sacou dun peto un asubío noviño, de forasteira feitura e moito rebruñido, e púxose a chifrar cheo de coraxe. Non o quixo emprestar a ninguén e gardouno outra volta no peto, domeándose moito ó enfonda-la man para demostrar un peto fondo, coma os petos en que se gardan as mellores cousas. Arredor dos seus ollos bulía unha surrisa dubidosa, ninguén sabe se mala ou suplicante. Mais non lle preguntaron nada.

Seu pai chegara de Nova York aquel mesmo día. Vírao desembarcar no peirao vello. Traxe azul. Viseira de carei. A cara forte coma unha proa. Branco e grande o dentamio. E nos ollos, afeitos a longanías e grandes rumbos, ningunha fachenda.

Houbo un intre en que o fillo do navegante andou a rentes de chorar. E as súas bágoas dispararíanse como frechas quentes e coraxudas. Pero non chorou. Ergueuse con máis cara de malo aínda, o peito en arco, a manciña pechada, os labres a tremer. Ergueuse así, garboso, o neno e dixo soamente:

– ¡Nova York é noso!

New York is Ours

The boy had something to tell the other boys mucking around with him on the beach. He had something to tell them, but he did not come out with it. Sometimes he looked spiteful, full as he was of that pride which he could not manage to express. He even scratched one of the others, in a fit of temper, as the flames of the fire inside him jumped to his face. He ruined all the games with his nervousness, like a cat made uneasy by a nearby storm. It was a strange restlessness, interrupted by moments of ecstasy.

His father had come back from New York that very day and the other boys weren't asking him anything about it, nor were they being nice to him or respecting him any more than on other days. Maybe because of this, because that question was not forthcoming, he scratched the boy he thought was keeping quiet on purpose.

He took from his pocket a brand new whistle, of foreign make and highly polished, and began to blow it furiously. He wouldn't lend it to anyone and he put it back in his pocket, reaching right down as he plunged his hand into what he revealed to be a deep pocket, one of those pockets in which the best things are kept. Around his eyes a doubtful smile played, whether malicious or imploring nobody could tell. But they didn't aske him anything.

There was a moment when the sailor's son was close to tears. And his tears would have shot out like hot, fierce arrows. But he did not cry. He rose up with an even more spiteful look on his face, his chest thrust forward, his little hand clenched, his lips quivering. Thus rose, in pride, the boy, and said only this:

"New York is ours!"

The Avant-Garde

Luís Pimentel (1895–1958)

From Sombra do aire na herba (The Shadow of Air on the Grass), *1959*

Paseo

De sotaque sorprendín a mañá
entrando na vila
cantando da man da fina chuvia.
Cos pés espidos e mollados
viña dos camiños verdes, profundos.
Dedos de vento transparentes, baleiros,
en brunidas bandexas.
Scherzo de zoca na acera.
Leda canción.
E debaixo do mantel de liño fresco
a muller do obreiro leva as doce campanadas.
Unha canción que se cae e se levanta.
O polvo nas alas e tamén o ceo.
Unha canción tan lonxana e lene
como a sombra do aire sobre a herba.
Ata min chega tan solo en anacos;
mais eu enténdoa exacta e enteira,
como a sombra do aire sobre a herba.

A walk

Suddenly I surprised the morning
walking into town
singing hand-in-hand with the fine rain.
With naked, wet feet
she came from the green, deep paths.
Transparent, empty toes of wind
on polished trays.
Scherzo of clogs on the pavement.
Happy song.
And under the cloth of fresh linen
the worker's wife carries the twelve chimes.

A song that falls and rises.
Dust on the wings and also the sky.
A song as distant and gentle
as the shadow of air on the grass.
To me it comes only in fragments;
but I understand it, exactly and completely,
like the shadow of air on the grass.

Manuel Antonio (1900–1930)

From De catro a catro (Four by Four), *1928*

Intencións

Encherémo-las velas
coa luz náufraga da madrugada
Pendurando en dous puntos cardinais
a randeeira esguía
do pailebote branco
Coas súas mans loiras
acenan mil adeuses as estrelas

Inventaremos frustradas descubertas
a barlovento dos horizontes
pra acelerar os abolidos corazóns
dos nosos veleiros defraudados

Halaremos polo chicote
dun meridiano innumerado

Na illa anónima
de cada singradura
esculcaremos o remorso da cidade
Ela noctámbula desfollará
como unha margarida prostibularia
a Rosa dos Ventos do noso corazón

Encadearemos adeuses de escuma
pra tódalas praias perdidas
Xuntaremos cadernos en branco
da novela errante do vento

Pescaremos na rede dos atlas
ronseles de Simbad

E cazarémo-la vela
sobre o torso rebelde das tormentas
pra trincar a escota dunha ilusión.

Intentions

We will fill the sails
with the shipwrecked light of early morning
Hanging from two cardinal points
the long narrow swing
that is the white pilot-boat
With their pale hands
the stars signal a thousand farewells

We will invent frustrated discoveries
on the weather side of the horizons
to invigorate the abolished hearts
of our disappointed sailing boats

We will haul on the rope
of an unnumbered meridian

On the anonymous island
of each day's run
we will watch the city's remorse
Sleepwalking she will pluck
like a marguerite in a brothel
the petals from the Compass-Rose of our hearts

We will link farewells of foam
for all the lost shores
We will collect blank log-books
of the errant novel of the wind
We will catch wakes of Sinbad
in the net of the atlases

And we will unfurl the sail
over the rebellious torso of the storms
to make fast the sheet of an illusion.

A fragata vella

Te-los ollos distantes
decorados de rostos xoviais
que os vellos mariñeiros
permutaron polos climas antípodas

Levas no leme
un pulo de brazos tensos
que retorceron os largacíos
horizontes do mar

O vento
atortorando
desfollou dos velamios
outonos de mocidades

Mercabas colares circunmeridianos
nos bazares das estrelas
Amarrabas faros dispersos
co simblador calabrote do ronsel
Floreciches no Mar
primaveras amargas
de foulas e escamallos

Inda que o vento encalme
tremela nas túas velas
unha rafega de transmigracións

Nese teu corazón innumerábel
tamén enchen e devalan
as mareas do meu corazón

The old frigate

You have the distant
decorated eyes of jovial faces
that the old sailors
bartered in antipodean climes

On your rudder you carry
a striving of tense arms
that twisted the long
horizons of the sea

The wind
          torturing
    plucked from your sails
autumns of youthfulness

    You bought circummeridional necklaces
in the bazaars of the stars
    You moored scattered lighthouses
with the vibrating cable of your wake
    You brought into flower on the Sea
bitter springtimes
of foam and fish-scales

    Even if the wind dies down
    in your sails there flutters
a gust of transmigrations

    In your innumerable heart
    there is also a rise and a fall
of the tides of my heart

Os cóbados no varandal

    Atopamos esta madrugada
    na gaiola do Mar
    unha illa perdida[1]

    Armaremos de novo a gaiola
    Vai saír o Sol
improvisado e desorientado

    Xa temos tantas estrelas
e tantas lúas submisas
que non caben no barco nin na noite

    Xuntaremos paxaros sen xeografía
pra xogar coas distancias
das súas ás amplexadoras

---

[1] O mar adentro é unha illa d'auga ·
    rodeada de ceo por todas partes

E os adeuses das nubes
mudos e irremediábeis

E armaremos unha rede de ronseis
pra recobrar as saudades
coa súa viaxe feita
polos océanos do noso corazón.

Elbows on the rail

Early this morning we found
in the bird-trap of the Sea
a lost island[1]

We shall set up the trap again
The Sun is about to rise
extempore and disorientated

By now we have so many stars
and so many submissive moons
that there is no room for them in the boat or in the night

We shall collect birds without geography
to play with the distances
of their enveloping wings

And the farewells of the clouds
mute and incurable

And we shall spread a net of wakes
to retrieve sadlongings
with the journey completed
over the oceans of our hearts.

[1] Out-to-sea is an island of water
surrounded on all sides by sky

Sós

> Fomos ficando sós
> o Mar o barco e mais nós
>
>   Roubáronnos o Sol
>   O paquebote esmaltado
> que cosía con liñas de fume
> áxiles cadros sen marco
>
>   Roubáronnos o vento
>   Aquel veleiro que se evadiu
> pola corda frouxa do horizonte
>
>   Este océano desatracou das costas
>   e os ventos da Roseta
> orientáronse ao esquezo
>   As nosas soedades
> veñen de tan lonxe
> como as horas do reloxo
>   Pero tamén sabemos a manobra
> dos navíos que fondean
> a sotavento dunha singradura
>
>   No cuadrante estantío das estrelas
> ficou parada esta hora:
>   O cadáver do Mar
> fixo do barco un cadaleito
>
>   Fume de Pipa   Saudade
>   Noite   Silencio   Frío
>   E ficamos nós sós
>   sen o Mar e sen o barco
>   nós.

Alone

> We were gradually left alone
> the sea the boat and us
>
>   The sun was stolen from us
>   The lacquered packet-boat
> that sewed with threads of smoke
> nimble unframed pictures

The wind was stolen from us
That sailing boat which slipped away
beyond the tightrope of the horizon

This ocean sailed away from the shores
and the winds of the Rosette
found their bearings absent-mindedly
Our solitudes
come from places as distant
as the hours on the clock

But we also know the manoeuvres
of the ships that drop anchor
on the weather side of a day's run

In the stationary quadrant of the stars
this hour stopped:
The corpse of the sea
turned the boat into a coffin

Smoke from a Pipe   Sadlongings
Night   Silence   Cold
And we were left alone
without the Sea and without the boat
us.

From Poemas soltos (Uncollected Poems), *no date*

Elexía ao capitán Roald Amudsen que se perdeu no Polo Norte

Oh captain! My captain!
Walt Whitman

PAISAXE:
Ninguén puido encontrar entre a neve
eses beizos xeados
que se lle perderon ao silencio
E as lonxedades
ceibes
descinguiron a soedade
No remuíño
da derradeira ráfega de vento

foise toda esperanza
e o Sol apagado.
Ningunha voz poderá destemerse
sen caer morta aos pés da neve
coma un paxaro novo.
Oh, Capitán! Meu capitán!

Elegy to Captain Roald Amundsen, lost at the North Pole

Oh captain! My captain!
Walt Whitman

LANDSCAPE:
Nobody could find among the snow
those frozen lips
that he lost to silence
And the remotenesses
free
ungirded the solitude
In the whirl
of the last gust of wind
all hope departed
and the Sun was extinguished.
No voice will be able to lose its fear of itself
without falling dead at the feet of the snow
like a young bird.
Oh, Captain! My captain!

Manuel Luís Acuña (1900–1975)

From Fírgoas (Crevices), *1933*

Nin branco nin preto...

Nin branco nin preto.
Iso.
Sen tremores de ríos
sen badaladas de paxaros.
Sen ritmo de astros
nin estraligos de noite medoñenta,
sen ouveo de lobos
cando o vento galga por cómaros e crebadas.

Sen salaios de árbores
cando asulagan rosas nos remuíños do solpor.
Periférico.
Sen cerne nin miola.
Chairo.
Sen apertas de curvas nin adeuses de penedías.
GRIS.

Neither white nor black...

Neither white nor black.
Exactly.
Without quaking of rivers
without chiming of birds.
Without rhythm of stars
or crashings in fearful night,
without howls of wolves
when the wind races over field-ridges and through gorges.
Without sobs of trees
when roses are drowned in the whirlpools of sunset.
Peripheral.
Without tree-heart or bone-marrow.
Flat.
Without embraces of curves or farewells of crags.
GREY.

Luís Amado Carballo (1901–1927)

From O galo (The Cock), *1928*

S-6

A súa queixa no brañal
debulla con luz de prata
a fonte nunha sonata
no clavecín de cristal,
e a rentes dunha silveira
monea no violón
con triste e pesado son
unha abella aventureira.
Aló nun souto remoto
un grilo ben afinado

trema un fadiño miñoto
"muito ben repinicado..."
e o concertista pimpín
rebuldante polos matos
acompáñao en pizzicatos
do seu vesgo violín.

O xílgaro máis alá
con voz de tiple barata
comete unha fermata
de ópera italiá,
e o cuco no piñeiral
con gran degaranza proba
na fauta do trinque nova
toda a escala natural.

Entran "a tempo" facendo
os piñeiros violinistas
en compaña dos solistas
un sentimental crescendo,
e como na Pastoral
ten un canto realista
de emoción oitocentista
o rego entre o salgueiral.

S-6

The spring in the wetland
unravels with silvery light
its lament in a sonata
on its crystal harpsichord,
and by a bramble-bush
an adventurous bee
grates on the double bass
a sad and tedious sound.

Over in a distant grove
a well-tempered cricket
quavers a north-Portuguese fado,
'most authentically ornamented',
and the chaffinch, that maestro,
hopping through the thickets,
accompanies him with pizzicatos
on his cross-eyed violin.

Further away, the goldfinch,
in the voice of a cheap soprano,
attacks a fermata
from an Italian opera,
and the cuckoo in a pine wood
tries out, with great gusto,
the entire natural scale
on his brand-new flute.

The violin-playing pines
come in *a tempo*, rising,
together with the soloists,
to a sentimental crescendo,
and, as in any pastorale,
the brook among the willows
sings a realistic canto
of eighteenth-century emotion.

From Proel (The Prowman), *1927*

O cruceiro

O xesto monacal de pedra
benzoa o acougo da aldea...

Axeónllanse os camiños
abrazados ao cruceiro
nunha azul eternidade
de pedra e ceo.

A agonía do solpor
conmove o pranto da terra
e a paisaxe persígnase
con santas cruces de pedra.

A campaíña de prata
do día
latexa un ángelus
de epifanía.
E o sol agoniante
vén encravarse na cruz
abrindo os marelos brazos
como o salvador Xesús.

The cross

The monkish stone gesture
blesses the peace of the village...

The lanes kneel,
embracing the cross
in a blue eternity
of stone and sky.

The agony of the sunset
moves the earth to tears,
and the countryside makes the sign
of holy stone crosses upon itself.

The silver bell
of day
throbs an angelus
of epiphany.

And the dying sun
comes to be nailed on the cross
opening its yellow arms
like the saviour Jesus.

Fermín Bouza-Brey (1901–1973)

From Nao senlleira (Solitary Ship), *1933*

Gándara

Naquel biduído dos bidos louzanos
o páxaro sol non pía os seus raios
e morre de amor.

Naquel biduído dos lanzales bidos
o páxaro sol non criba os seus píos
e morre de amor.

Non criba os seus ritmos, non pousa os seus raios
e albean de frío os albres delgados
e morre de amor.

Non ceiba os seus raios, non tece os seus fíos
e albres e mámoas albean de frío
coa poldra que morre no mato cativo.

Wasteland

In that grove of lush birches
the sun-bird does not chirp its rays
and it dies of love.

In that grove of slender birches
the sun-bird does not winnow its chirps
and it dies of love.

It does not winnow its rhythms, it does not perch its rays
and the thin trees whiten from cold
and it dies of love.

It does not send forth its rays, it does not weave its threads,
and trees and dolmens whiten from cold
with the filly that dies in the low scrub.

Galician Literature in Exile

Emilio Pita (1909–1981)

From Jacobusland, *1942*

Semente

A Castelao

Albas fazulas, azos esmorecidos
nos beizos sulagado o sorriso, abrente
de esperanza. Abalan as mans de lume:
enterran semente.

Sangue da Terra; sangue vivo revivo,
sangue do sangue, pérola ourilucente
de esperanza. Abalan as mans de lume:
enterran semente.

Mariñeiros do sol; ceibe proel da nao
pola mar verdosiña dun soño quente
de esperanza. Abalan as mans de lume:
enterran semente.

Seed

To Castelao

White cheeks, broken spirits,
smothered on lips the smile, dawn
of hope. The hands of light sway back and forth:
they bury seed.

Blood of the Earth; living reliving blood,
blood of blood, glittering pearl
of hope. The hands of light sway back and forth:
they bury seed.

Sailors of the sun; free prowman of the boat
through the green sea of a dream warm

with hope. The hands of light sway back and forth:
they bury seed.

Luís Seoane (1910–1979)

From Fardel de exiliado (An Exile's Knapsack), *1952*

Building castles in Spain

En New York morreu fracasado, trinta e tres anos de América, Ramón Rodríguez
Iglesias
que tiña traballado todos eses anos no porto da cidade,
na colleita de mazás en California
nas minas de Pensilvanya
na sega do trigo en Minnesota
indo dun estado a outro soñando, asentado
coas pernas fóra, nas portas dos vagóns de carga dos ferrocarrís
pra ter, era o seu soño, un castelo ergueito sobre rochas cubertas
de argazos, de percebes, de patelas, de nécoras
sobre dunha mar fonda, de polbos pretos,
na costa atlántica galega.
Un castelo cavilaba envolto en cincentas néboas e altas vagas
e que, sen sabelo, Ramón Rodríguez Iglesias tiña herdado había moitos anos.

Cando morreu, ao seu sobriño descoñecido, Dalmacio da Coruña,
quedáronlle do tío de América uns poucos dólares
e tamén o castelo ergueito sobre de rochas, broslado de escumas de mar
que o tío americano tiña soñado
nas minas de Pensilvanya, no porto de New York, nos trigais de Minnesota,
nos pomareiros de California.

Building castles in Spain

In New York, Ramón Rodríguez Iglesias died a failure, thirty-three years in
America,
having worked all those years in the city's port,
in the apple harvest in California,
in the mines of Pennsylvania,
in the wheat harvest in Minnesota,
going from one state to another dreaming, seated
with legs dangling from doors of goods waggons on railways,
to own, this was his dream, a castle rising above rocks covered

with seaweed, with barnacles, with crabs of many kinds,
and above a deep sea, with its dark octopuses,
on the Galician Atlantic coast.
He was musing upon a castle wrapped in ash-grey mists and high waves,
one which, unawares, Ramón Rodríguez Iglesias had inherited many years
                                                                earlier.

When he died, the nephew he did not know, Dalmacio from Corunna,
was left a few dollars by his uncle,
and also the castle rising above rocks, embroidered with sea-foam,
that his uncle in America had dreamed about
in the mines of Pennsylvania, in the port of New York, in the wheatfields of
                                                                Minnesota,
in the orchards of California.

Ramón de Valenzuela (1914–1980)

From Era tempo de apandar, *1980*

Saín e ós poucos pasos encarei de súpeto cun compañeiro de facultade vestido de falanxista con enseñas de xefe local.
  – ¡Ola!
  – ¡Ola!
  – ¿Aínda vives?
  – Pois parece que si.
  – A min paréceme que non debías de vivir.
  – A opinión dos que me xulgaron foi outra.
  – ¿Que viñeches facer aquí?
  – ¿É un interrogatorio?, díxenlle serio.
  – Contesta o que che pregunto, dixo imperativo coas mans nas pistolas. Outros dous falanxistas puxéronse a pouca distancia de nós.
  – Veño de viaxante de comercio. Dos Laboratorios Nor-Occidentales. Vendo raticida.
  – ¿Como podo saber que di-la verdade?
  – Pregúntalle a Ismael, el mercoume algo. Ademais teño unha credencial.
  – Ven comigo. Eu non me fío de credenciais que poden ser falsas.
  Os dous falanxistas achegáronse algo máis. Non tiña opción de me negar. Entramos no establecemento de Ismael e axiña chegou, con cara sorrinte, o mesmo que me atendera antes. A miña situación era claramente de arrestado, máis que nada pola seriedade e dureza de vista na cara do meu arrestador.
  – ¿Que pasa? ¿Ocorre algo?, dixo o comerciante virándose serio tamén.
  – ¿Ti mercácheslle algo a este?

– Pois si, merqueille un raticida. ¿Que problema hai?

– ¿E sabes quen é este?

– Paréceme telo visto nalgunha ocasión, mais, en realidade non sei.

– Por se non o sabes voucho dicir eu. Este é un roxo separatista, deses que andaban á beira de Castelao e non entendo por qué o ceibaron da cadea.

Ollou súpeto para min como para se baleirar unha xenreira contida. Despois fitou para o comerciante case que coa mesma severidade, pegou un taconazo erguendo a man e fíxolles aceno ós compañeiros para que saísen con el a asaltar outra trincheira.

Quedei fronte a fronte co dono. Agardaba que falase el pero el non tiña cousa que me dicir e ficaba serio para min. Fixen propósito de non iniciar eu a conversa e estivemos así unha chea de tempo.

From It Was a Time for Putting up with Things, *1980*

I went out, and after taking a few steps, I suddenly met someone I had known at the University, dressed in the fascist uniform with badges that showed he was a local boss.

– Hello!

– Hello!

– Are you still alive?

– Well, it appears so.

– It appears to me that you shouldn't be alive.

– The opinion of those who tried me was different.

– What have you come here to do?

– Is this an interrogation?, I asked him seriously.

– Answer what I asked you, he said imperiously with his hands on his pistols. Two other fascists were at a short distance from us.

– I have come here as a travelling salesman. From NorthWestern Laboratories. I sell rat poison.

– How do I know you are telling the truth?

– Ask Ismael. He bought something from me. Moreover, I have credentials.

– Come with me. I don't trust credentials that might be false.

The two fascists came a bit closer. I couldn't refuse. We went into Ismael's shop and he appeared immediately, smiling. In the same way he had served me before. It was clear that I was under arrest, especially because of the seriousness and harshness in the expression of the one who had arrested me.

– What's up? Is there something wrong?, the shopkeeper said becoming serious too.

– Did you buy something from this one here?

– Well, yes, I bought rat poison from him. Where's the problem?

– And do you know who this is?

– I think I saw him once, but I'm not really sure.

– If you don't know, I'm going to tell you. This is a red separatist, one of those who went around with Castelao and I don't understand why they left him out of jail.

He looked at me suddenly as if he wanted to release contained hate. Afterwards, he stared at the shopkeeper with almost the same severity, he clicked his heels as he raised his hand and gestured to his companions to leave with him so as to assault some other trench.

I was left face to face with the owner. I was waiting for him to speak but he had nothing to say to me and stood seriously in front of me. I purposely did not want to start a conversation with him and we were like that for a long time.

Lorenzo Varela (1916–1978)

From Lonxe (Far), *1954*

I

Dourados peixes, flores amarelas
coronarios do monte, tremoeiras do mar:
¿onde verei a lúa das eiras que gardades,
ou serea das ondas, ou fada das lamelas?
¿Onde meus carros, miñas dornas, onde
ouvirei no meu peito enguedellado
a cántiga do merlo nos outeiros,
na baixamar o tremecer da auga?
¿Onde terei na man a man fidalga dela
debaixo dun castiro de ponlas enxoiadas?
E este meu corazón, ¿o meu corazón onde
acougará sen vós, levándovos adentro?
¿Onde, meus peixes, miñas flores, onde?

II

Dourados peixes, flores amarelas:
lonxe de vós, ¿onde deixa-los ósos?,
¿onde deixar a morte que vos debo?
¿Que queredes de min, que me chamades
e despois vos marchades sen levarme?
¿Onde me agardaredes, compañeiros?
¡Xa veu o tempo de que as flores falen,
xa veu o tempo de que os peixes digan!

III

Dourados peixes, flores amarelas,
cando soño con vós nácenme verdes,
azuis carballeiras que me arrolan
nun alto estrelecer sobre da noite
nunha neve romeira tras a vida.
E vou, lonxe de vós, inda máis lonxe,
pra vos lembrar mellor, máis docemente,
o mesmo que un pandeiro que caíra,
baixara dando tumbos
desde o berce do monte alboreado
ao cadaleito, xa sen fin, do mar:
lonxe de vós, inda máis lonxe. Lonxe. Lonxe.

I

Golden fishes, yellow flowers,
arteries of the hills, movers of the sea:
where shall I see the moon of the threshing-floors you guard,
or the mermaid of the waves, or the fairy of the fields?
Where my carts, my boats, where
shall I hear in my tangled breast
the song of the blackbird on the hillocks,
at low tide the quivering of the water?
Where shall I hold in my hand her noble hand
beneath a chestnut tree with bejewelled boughs?
And this heart of mine, where will my heart
find peace without you, since it carries you within itself?
Where, my fishes, my flowers, where?

II

Golden fishes, yellow flowers,
far from you, where shall I leave my bones,
where leave the death I owe you?
What do you want of me, calling me
and then going away, leaving me behind?
Where will you await me, companions?
It's time for flowers to talk,
it's time for fishes to speak!

III

Golden fishes, yellow flowers,
when I dream about you, green
and blue oak-groves are born in me, lulling me

in a high starring above the night,
in a pilgrim snow beyond life.
And I go, far from you, even further,
to remember you better, more sweetly,
like a tambourine falling,
bouncing down
from the cradle of the dawn hills
into the now endless coffin of the sea:
far from you all, still further. Far. Far.

The Recovery

Eduardo Blanco Amor (1897–1979)

From A esmorga, *1959*

E sen saber cómo, atopámonos na rúa do Instituto. Ao lonxe, por en medio dela, víase vir vindo un municipal, a paso vagaroso. A rúa estaba alampada de luar e non podiamos atravesala sen ser ollados. Conque fómonos deixando ir, dun en fondo, apegados á parte sombriza, e ao chegar fronte ao adral da igrexa de Santa Eufemia, vimos que estaba aberta e metémonos nela coma ratos...

O altar maior lucía todo aceso de candeas, que moito me chamou a atención que a tales horas da noite isto sucedese. Estaban aló, a carón, dúas ou tres ducias de cabaleiros, pois mulleres non se vían, todos axeonllados, oíase o besbellar dos rezos a pouca voz, e todos moi xuntos e rezando a eito, coma se estivesen botando unha ladaíña, desas das misións ou das rogativas... Eu non sabía como trepar co raio das chancas ferradas para que non fixesen estrondo nas laxes. Un daqueles cabaleiros algo debeu de apercibir porque se voltou para abesullar, pero xa nós estabamos acochados tras dunhas columnas, descontra un confesonario.

Nestas, renxeu un pouquiño a porta e vimos ao municipal, que por certo era o tío Sardiña; metía o morro un pouco, pero non pasou de aí. Anque non nos podía ver onde estabamos, por se acaso metémonos no confesonario no mesmo instante en que de novo nos tentaba aquela fodida risa. O tío Sardiña fitou un instante e logo foise, arrimando a porta a modiño. Ficamos un pouco sen saír, agardando a que se afastase por se lle daba por voltar a meter os fociños, e mentres tanto encetamos a segunda garrafa da augardente que estaba tan baril coma a primeira e que semellaba ter algún engado con aquel seu xeito de pórnos tan ledos.

"Estes son os que lles din da Adoración Nocturna, que rezan soamente de noite", dixo o Milhomes que as sabía todas.

Despois dun pouco, asomámonos a axexar para ver se era o instante de poder-mos saír. E foi aí cando nos asegundou a condenada da risa, pero esta vez con boa causa, pois vimos que todos aqueles cabaleiros xa non estaban axeonllados senón case debruzados, coas nádegas erguidas e as cabezas baixas, case rente ao chan, botando todos xuntos unha cántiga coma se a rosmasen polo nariz.

O Milhomes foi o primeiro que escomezou a ceibar aquela risiña de soleta que, como xa había un bo anaco que a estaba aturando, subiulle de seguida a cacarexo. E coma se o seu riso fose quen para abrirse o cachón dos nosos, isandiós!, aquilo foi un esboiro de gargalladas que ata me deu un punto nas illargas que non me deixaba alentar; e un pouco co rir e outro pouco coa bebida, case non atinabamos coller para o lado da porta. E por se fose pouca toda esta perdición, o Bocas, que entre as súas animaladas tiña sona de peidorreiro, ao chegar preto da porta, botou un deses seguidos que arrematan cun estrondo, con perdón da súa cara...

–

– Déixeme rir, señor, que algo divertido me tiña que vir ás mentes polo entremedio de tantas cousas feas e tristeiras desa noite do carafio.

–

– ¿E que máis feitos quere, señor? Os feitos son estes, un por un e tal como sucederon. O remate deles foi porque outras cousas foron pasando denantes. Se non tiveran pasado, o remate sería doutro xeito do que foi. Porque a verdade é que cada cousa que faciamos non era das que se vían decote nas esmorgas, que ao fin todas son cousas de diversión e trastadas que teñen remedio... Nós iámolas facendo de tal xeito coma se as fixesemos sen darnos conta, ao menos polo tocante a min, para que logo non tivesen remedio, coma quen vai fechando portas tras de si e guindando coas chaves, como para non querer voltar, tal coma se adrede camiñásemos á nosa perdición.

From The Binge, *1959*

And without knowing how, we found ourselves in the street where the secondary school was. In the distance, in the middle, one could see a policeman coming with slow steps. The street was lit by the moon and we couldn't cross it without being seen. So we went ahead in single file on the dark side and, when we got to the courtyard of Saint Euphemia church, we saw that it was open and we went in like mice...

The main altar shone, completely lit up by candles, and I was surprised that, at that time of night, this was so. There were two or three dozen gentlemen at the side, all kneeling, but no women were to be seen; muttered prayers in low voices were heard, and they were all very close together and praying copiously, as if they were saying a litany, like those in the missions or in rogations... I didn't know how to walk in my damn iron-soled clogs without making noise on the stones. One of those gentlemen must have heard something because he turned around to pry, but we were already hidden behind some pillars in front of a confession box.

At that moment, the door creaked a little and we saw the policeman who, by the way, was Uncle Sardine; he poked his nose in a little but not any farther than that. Although he couldn't see us where we were, we went into the confession box just in case, in the same instant that that fucking desire to laugh took hold of us. Uncle Sardine stared a moment and then went away, pulling the door to slowly. We remained inside without leaving, waiting until he went away in case he decided to nose about again, and meanwhile we began the second carafe of liquor that was as great as the first and that seemed to be charmed, the way it was able to make us so happy.

"These are those who are called Night-Worshippers, who only pray at night", a Thousand-Men said, who knew everything about it.

After a while we got out to spy to see if we could go away. And it was there when that damned laughter came back to us again, but this time it was justified, as we saw that all those gentlemen were not on their knees anymore but were almost falling on their heads, with their bottoms lifted and their heads down, almost touching the ground, singing a hymn together as if through their noses.

A Thousand-Men was the first to burst into that shameless giggle that, as he had been holding it in a long time, quickly became a cackle. And it was as if his laugh was able to open the floodgate of ours, Jesus Christ!, that was an explosion of guffaws that even gave me a stitch in my side that left me breathless; and what with laughing and drinking we were almost not able to find our way to the door. And if all this hullabaloo was not enough, Big-Mouth, who amongst all his madnesses was well-known for being farty, on getting near the door let off one of those long ones that end in thunder, if you will excuse me....

–

– Allow me to laugh, sir, something funny had to come to my mind in the middle of so many ugly, sad things that happened that fecking night.

–

– What more facts do you want, sir? The facts are these, one by one and just as they happened. They came to their end because other things took place before. If they hadn't happened that way, the end would have been different to what it was. Because, to tell the truth, the things we did weren't what were usually seen in binges but are things which, in the end, are all ways of having fun and making mischief that can be made up for… We were doing them in such a way as if we did them without knowing what we were doing, at least speaking for myself, so that afterwards there was no solution, like someone who closes doors behind him and throws the keys away, as if he didn't want to come back at all, in a way as if we were walking on purpose towards our ruin.

From Xente ao lonxe, *1972*

O gremio de carpinteiros acordou que non fosen á Ursaira, ou mellor dito que non voltasen, os seus afiliados. O Quintín Amor, tívoos que procurar, en número que dobraba aos outros, no Centro Católico de Obreros que o bispo vello fundara para coutar o avance do Centro de Sociedades Obreras, de orixe socialista.

Saíron en tres coches ao romper o día. En total eran catorce homes. De véspera xa saíra un carromato de seis mulas con escaleiras, aparellos de roldaina e táboas de andamio. Todo ía previsto para rematar o máis axiña posible; polo menos deixar o baldaquino, e partes duns altares que tamén se propuñan traeren, en disposición de acarrexo para o día seguinte.

De noite aínda, saíra tamén un piquete formado por dez números de acabalo con máuser e cornetín de ordes, ao mando do tenientiño...

Xa de véspera se correra por A. que esta forza ía por orde do gobernador e "consentida" polo señor bispo.

Era, supúxose, o acostumado despregue dos medios de coacción que se adoitaban para as grandes manifestacións e folgas de traballadores nas cida des e zonas industriais, e non se acertaba a supor qué se propuñan facer dez homes con dez fusís de guerra fronte a aquela desaxeitada xuntanza de labregos, que sobraba a presencia, supúxose, dunha parella de a pé para esparexelos sen máis trámites.

Os que coñecían estes procedementos, sabían ben que chegaba un intre en que, por entremedias dos vivas, dos morras, dos cantos e das inocentes vociferacións, ouvíase de sócato o agoniante ouvear do cornetín de ordes, deixando os outros bruídos, e incluso a acción, callados un instante no ar e pondo á xente en ánimo acorado e fuxidío.

Dicíase que toda a noite estivéranse a ver os fachóns acesos por camiños, congostras e vereas, en dirección ao planaltiño de Ursaira. Ao lonxe ouvíanse, xa dende o mencer, as campás das parroquias co longo son do toque de tronada. Algúns que saíran de A. para ver "o que pasaba" foran detidos no empalme de Cea e obrigados a voltar.

Cando chegaron o Quintín e os seus homes, atoparon unha mesta multitude de homes, inmóbil, enchendo o adral, e greas de mulleres e rapaces no limiar das portas da igrexa. O lugar, o día de festa, as roupas de gardar e os panos rechamantes e ledos das mulleres dábanlle a aquelo un ar de romaxe muda e estantía.

Os xendarmes, co tenientiño á fronte, fixeron algúns algareos e trotes dos caballos arrincando faíscas coas ferraduras nas lousas do grande adro do Mosteiro.

Como a xente non se movía nin semellaba pórlles moita atención aos alardes, o tenientiño sacou o sabre e todos sacaron os sabres, e puxéronse en posición e quedaron quedos como se os foran retratar; e uns "americanos" do lugar de Coirós, que estaban axexando na cima da torre con cariz de rexouba, puxéronse a aplausar.

O tenientiño fíxolle aceno ao cornetín, e o toque de atención rachou o cristalino ar de xuño. Todo moi propio e cabal, como un ledo e vello xogo de rapaces.

Agardaron outro pouco e como ninguén se movía, os xendarmes co tenientiño á fronte, meteron os cabalos entre o xentío pero ninguén abalou e deixáronse caer sentados.

Entón o Quintín Amor e a súa xente fóronse dando un rodeo e entraron por unha porta do costado, pero resultou que dentro da igrexa había outros homes e fixéronos saír pola porta principal aos arrempuxóns.

Sen máis toques de cornetín, os cabalos galoparon por enriba da xente; logo recuaron, sempre co tenientiño a carón; botaron pé a terra e fixeron dúas descargas...

From People in the Distance, *1972*

The carpenters' guild agreed that its members wouldn't go to Ursaira, or to be more exact, that they weren't to go back there. Old Quintín Amor had to go to look for them, a number which was double the others, in the Catholic Workers' Centre that the old bishop had founded to bring a stop to the Social Workers' Centre, which was socialist.

They went in three cars at the break of day. There were fourteen men altogether. The day before a wagon with six mules had already left with ladders, pulleys and scaffolding. Everything was calculated to end as soon as possible; at least to leave the canopy and parts of some altars that they were thinking of bringing, ready for transport the next day.

When a picket also left, made up of ten on horse with mausers and a bugler under the command of a little lieutenant, it was still night...

The day before the rumour had already been spread in A. that this group had been formed by the Governor and "consented to" by His Lord, the Bishop.

It was supposed that it was the usual deployment used as a means of coercion on big demonstrations and workers' strikes in cities and industrial areas, and it wasn't easy to understand what ten men with ten rifles were meaning to do with that disorganised group of farm labourers, because it was supposed that a pair of men on foot were more than enough to break them up without more ado. Those who were familiar with this way of proceeding knew well that a moment came when, in the middle of the "long lives", "deaths to", songs and innocent vociferations, one suddenly heard the annoying yell of the bugler, making the other sounds, even the action, mute in the air for an instant and making the people feel afraid and wanting to run away.

It was said that all night torches could be seen in the paths, narrow cart tracks and trails in the small plateau of Ursaira. In the distance the parish bells had been heard since dawn ringing with the long sound used as a warning for thunderstorms. Some who had left A. to see "what was happening" had been detained at the junction at Cea and forced to go back.

When old Quintín and his men arrived, they found a closely-packed group of men, standing still, filling up the courtyard, and flocks of women and children on the threshold of the church door. The place, the holiday, the clothes for best wear, and the brightly-coloured and cheerful dresses of the women gave all that a feeling of a silent and dumbfounded "fair".

The policemen, with the little lieutenant at the head, made some threats of charging at them, with their horses trotting, snatching sparks with their shoes from the stones in the big courtyard of the monastery.

As the people didn't move and didn't seem to pay much attention to the display, the little lieutenant took out his sword and all the others took out their swords too, and got into position and they stayed as still as if they were going to have their photograph taken; and some "Americans" from Coirós village, that were looking on from the top of the tower and who were in the mood for joking, started to applaud.

The little lieutenant made a sign to the bugler and the bugle call broke the crystalline June air. All very suitable and exact, like a happy and old child's game.

They waited another while and as nobody moved, the policemen, with the little lieutenant at the head, took their horses into the middle of the group of people, but nobody got out of their way and they sat down.

Then old Quintín Amor and his people went off making a detour and went in through a door at the side, but it happened that inside the church there were other men who pushed them out the main door.

Without any more bugle calls, the horses galloped over the people; then they retreated, always with the little lieutenant around; they dismounted and fired twice …

From Os biosbardos, *1970*

Chegamos de volta a Auria sendo eu de once anos despois de finar mi padre, que sairamos de alí sendo eu moi cativo, que eu non nacera en Auria senón en Ponte Barxas, na raia seca de Portugal, sendo meu pai carabineiro como o foi ata o cabo dos seus días; a miña irmá Alexandrina, si, que aló quedou, aos sete, das vixigas en Calahonda, e meu irmán Alixio, tamén, que era o meirande e fuxiu cos xitanos, que se o levaran ou se fuxiu nunca se soubo, e non voltou.

Conque mi madre con sete duros da viuvez que non chegaban a un dente púxose aínda máis a cismar na volta a Auria, que lle quedara unha cachoupiña cun resío de horta preto da Ponte dos Pelamios, a criar pitas e un marrello para cebote, que endexamais se afixera en Madrid, nin en Alxeciras, nin en Alcántara (e aínda menos en Ceuta, onde chorou a cotío ano e medio), como se non houbese pitas nin marraus nas outras bandas do mundo, e cando acadou telos aquí deixou de nifrar por mi padre e de falar do Alixio, como se tivese nacido de novo, e púxolles ás pitas nomes de cristiáns e ao porquiño chamáballe Algabeño, e ao galo, Canalejas.

Segundo me dicían os rapaces de Auria, eu resultara falando o andaluz polo moito que contrapeaba a miña fala coa súa, e facíanme falar e coñeábanse de min sen o aparentar, anque eu dábame conta, e tamén de que xa non falaba andaluz senón madrileño, que se me apegara despois: "anda la osa, nos ha jodío, vaya leche, oye, Ninchi", e eu non tiña culpa, polo cuio facíanme xudiadas, puxéranme "Ninchi" de alcume, e a miña nai dábame chapadas na boca cando chegaba da rúa dicindo porcalladas sen o saber, na fala do país, que mas aprendían os rapaces con nomes trabucados, "dille á túa nai que che dea un pataco para mercar c…, xa verás que ricas." E rachábanme os peóns e afundíanme os puñetes na res xogando a la una anda la mula, e facíanme regañetas de m… cando iamos nadar na Sila, con dous ou tres nós tan apreixados con auga na camisa que non se podían desfacer sen botarlle os dentes.

Eu ben me decataba de que todo aquilo tiña que pasar e pasaría, que xa noutros sitios me pasara, e tiña que pandar e pandaba ata non lle coller o xeito ás cousas e aos ditos de rapazada de Auria. E cando xa ía para catro meses:

– Oes, Ninchi, ímoste levar á pesca dos biosbardos, que xa estamos vendo que es bo rapaz.

– Non sei pescar – eu sabía pescar, que me tiñan levado meu pais ao peirao de Alxeciras, e díxenlles que non porque ventaba a burla.

– Pois aí está o caso. Para os biosbardos ten que ser un novo aquí.

– Hai outros máis novos.

– ¿Cales?

– O fillo do dos queixos de Villalón, o Bósimo, que chegou despois ca min.

– Non serven todos, hom, anque sexan novos. Se servisen todos encheriámonos todos de cartos, porque non sei se sabes que os biosbardos son de moito aprecio, aínda máis cás troitas e as lampreas, e páganos de moita hostia nas casas dos ricos, para que saibas – seguía a barallar Pepe o Melondro, que era o que mandaba, non porque fose algo máis vello, senón porque tiña a voz grosa, de home, que tamén lle chamabamos o Roncollo.

– Porque tes que saber que os biosbardos non veñen ao reclamo se non se é novo, e que só pasan dúas veces ao ano, que se non fose iso todos gañariamos duros ás mancheas só con chamalos e pillalos. Pois nin con rede nin con anzol; hai que chamalos polo nome e veñen e métense no fardel. E se ti te prestas imos á parte, que nós pomos o sitio, que non todos os sitios do río serven para se facer con biosbardos dos bos, pois os ruíns semellan peixes.

– ...

– Porémoste no sitio xusto e farémosche compaña afastados alí de preto, que nós non podemos estar, que non somos novos, e para que non teñas medo, que a algúns dálles cagana ao vérense sós alí, de noite.

– Non, non quero, buscade outro.

– Que non o hai, home, que a máis de novo ten que cadrar en verso. ¿Non te chamas Leonardo?

– Si.

– Pois aí tes, Leonardo biobardo. Con iso e con ser novo, cousa feita. Vaia unha sorte que tes, seres novo aquí e chamáreste Leonardo. A saqueta ten que ser de tascos de liño, se non non serve, bueno, anque non sexa de tascos ten que ser branca e ben limpa – o Melondro era moi listo, semellaba saber todas as verbas do mundo e telas dispostas en ringleira tralos dentes para ceibalas sen alentar no seu xusto intre.

– E ten que ser mañá sen falta, porque váisenos a lúa e logo non se pode, que esta é a lúa de Santiago, e van como barbas e colleremos a saqueta chea e ogallá poidas traer dúas.

Aquela noite ao deitarme decateime de que a lúa ía vella encol de Santa Ladaíña, cofeándose no cumio do monte, e tardei en coller o sono.

A miña nai botouse a rir e chamoume lambón e díxome que todo eran argalladas dos rapacetes de Auria, os peores do mundo: e que eu non sabía por non terme criado alí, e que xa llo tiñan feito a moitos e que algúns quedaran pensativos da burla durante un tempiño arredándose da xente, así como aloleados, polo cuio cando alguén se aparvaba, fose polo que fose, a xente dicía que andaba a pensar nos biosbardos. Con todo, deume a saqueta onde trouxera unhas fabas que lle deran os parentes de Vilar de Astrés. Conque era o rigor do verán e mi madre quedaba a velar ata a mañanciña cosendo pantalóns de gambrona para o Demetrio que tiña un "roupasfeitas" na Ferreira, e como o sobrado onde dormiamos estaba inzado de chinches á miña nai tanto lle daba, no tempo quente, que viñese cedo ou tarde.

Agardábanme no fielato da Ponte Vella pouco denantes da medianoite e baixamos calados ao río. O río aínda collía uns anacos de lúa vella, de lúa podre, de anaco de cabazo podre que se despenaba, de manteiga amarela, de luz pegañosa, polas restrebas escorrendo a se derreter por embaixo dos piñeiros de Santa Ladaíña a retrincos aínda máis vermellos, como cando vin o ferro vivo na fundición de Malingre ou o ferro na fragua do Catapiro no primeiro instante da auga, agora sen chiar, alumando de preguiza, sen renxer, manseliño polas restrebas; todo tépedo, calado, arrecendendo a río do verán, á espesidume do cheiro do verán, ás pozas mornas do verán, a cabazo podre, a lúa morta fermentada do verán, escorregando ata os enchoupos do brión, cos retrincos de luz amarela, morredía, na auga encol dos cachóns mudos do verán, e tantas ras na espesidume do seu canto no cheiro da lama do verán, e a luz vermella nas pozas e limos apegadizos, e nos coiñais dunha soa cor na espesidume dos seixos, e os grandes ocos mouros na espesidume do ar do verán e as sombras medrando medrando, afundíndose, estendéndose sen se ver xa a outra beira do río, xa con présa como apagándose todo de contado, e puña medo.

Deixáronme só no remate da Pena dos Afogados e agacháronse non lonxe, tralas cepas da Ponte Vella, outros apoleirados nos grandes ameneiros. A voz do Melondro púxose a me chegar trocada, medoñenta, coma dos profundos, aínda máis grosa que de home cumprido, e chegaba polo ar encol do moe-moe das ras, e eu abrín o fardel e xa o tiña aberto e sostido con entrámbalas mans, co podre lume amarelo nas mans que viña a rentes cortando as cousas polo medio, e eu púxenme a repetir os dictados do Melondro, ollando para enriba co fardel ben teso entrámbalas mans:

– "Son Leonardo."
– Son Leonardo.
– "Ti es biobardo."
– Ti es biobardo.
– "Biobardo vente ao saco que eu te agardo e son Leonardo."
– Biobardo vente ao saco que eu te...

Pasoume, de socato, un ventiño pola fronte, polo nariz, polos beizos, entroume nos ollos coma rachadela de luz, e caeu no fardel un peso coma de pedra.

– "Son Leonardo."
– Son Leonardo.

Surtiu de novo a luciña da auga, alabeando no ar, faiscante, seguida, e o fardel acadou máis peso, e escomecei a suar polas tempas.

– "Vente ao saco."
– ...ao saco. E outro, e outro, por máis que o Melondro bulise a berrar e eu a ecoarlle.

– "Ti es biobardo."
– Biobardo... e o brillo choutando do redondel da auga para a curva do ar, alabeado no ar un instantiño, coma venablo, faiscante, seguido, un instante na mourenza, e os choutos do seu paso pola bris na miña fronte, no nariz, nos beizos.

– ¿Cantos tes? – berrou o Melondro máis de preto, coa voz retranqueira unha

miga insegura. Oíanse nas árbores risiñas abafadas, imitanzas do axóuxere do moucho, do chío da curuxa.

– Non sei, ao menos unha ducia ou máis. – Eu mantiña o fardel a pulso, con
esforzo, nun recanto de lúa xa rastreira, a carón do penedo.

– ...ou quizais dúas. Xa non podo con eles.

Saíron de onde estaban agachados e quedaron máis de preto, calados; e, a pouco,
escacharon a rir a eito. O Melondro achegouse un pouco máis sen chegar de todo.

– ¿E logo, que botaches no fardel? Porque o fardel estar está cheo, dixo para os
outros, que pararon de rir e recuaron.

– Eu non botei nada, encheuse só, un cada vez que berrabamos... Viñan do río,
brincaban polo ar, afundíanse pola boca da saqueta.

– ¡Me caso en sandiós...! Vírate para aquí... O fardel está cheo e reloce.

Vireime para onde saían as voces, sostendo malamente o fardel. O Melondro
adiantou outro pouco.

– Me caso no carano, teno ateigado e non se moveu do sitio... ¡Baléirao na pedra,
carano! Tremáballe a voz e puxéraselle máis rouca.

Deille a volta ao fardel; e denantes de o devorcar xa perdera todo o peso.
Soamente escoou na pedra unha luz poeirenta, azul e movediza coma cando se
mollan os mistos.

From Haggis Hunting, *1970*

We came back to Auria when I was eleven, after my father had died, well, we had
left there when I was very young, well, I wasn't born in Auria but in Ponte Barxas,
on the frontier with Portugal, my father being a carabineer as he was until the end
of his life; my sister Alexandrina died there, at seven, in Calahonda, because of
smallpox, and my brother Alixio stayed there too, who was the oldest and ran off
with the gypsies but if they had taken him or he did run off was never known, and
he never came back.

So my mother with the few pennies from her widow's pension, that wouldn't
feed a church mouse, started to think even more about going back to Auria,
because she had a small cabin left there, with a patch of orchard close to Pelamios
bridge, to raise hens and a piglet to fatten, because she had never got used to
Madrid or to Algeciras or Alcántara (and even less to Ceuta, where she cried every
day for a year and a half), as if there weren't hens or pigs or other parts of the world,
and when she finally got them here, she stopped wailing for my father and talking
about Old Alixio, as if she had been born again, and she gave the hens Christian
names and she called the piglet Algabeño, and the cock Canalejas.

According to what the boys from Auria told me, I was noticeable for speaking
with an Andalucian accent because my way of speaking was very different from
theirs, and they made me talk and they pulled my leg without letting on, although
I knew and also that I spoke not with an Andalucian but with a Madrid accent,
which I picked up afterwards: "look yez, we're fucked, it's only brutal, Ninchi",

and it wasn't my fault, for all that they played dirty tricks on me, they gave me the nickname "Ninchi", and my mother hit me on the mouth when I got home saying dirty things without knowing it, in the language of the country, because the boys taught me them with the wrong words, "tell your mother to give you a penny to buy c… you'll find out how nice they are". And they broke my spinning tops and they hit me with their fists in the back playing leapfrog and when we went swimming in the Sila, they made two or three damn knots in my shirt, made so tight by being wet that they couldn't be untied unless you used your teeth.

I knew perfectly that all that had to happen and that it would happen, because it had happened to me in other places, and I had to put up with it and I did so as not to become used to the things they did and the sayings of the lads from Auria. And when four months had gone by:

– Listen here, Ninchi, we're going to take you fishing for haggis, because we can see that you're a good fella.

– I don't know how to fish – I knew how to fish because my parents had taken me to the port in Algeciras, but I told them I didn't because I suspected that they were having me on.

– That's just why. For the haggis it has to be someone new here.

– There are others who are newer.

– Who?

– The son of the cheese people from Villalón, old Bósimo, who came after me.

– Not all will do, lad, even if they are new. If they did, we'd all be rich. Because I don't know if you know that haggis is a delicacy, even more than trouts and lampreys, and they give a shit load of money for them in the houses of the rich, if you want to know – Pepe the Melondro went on mixing things up, he was the boss, not because he was the oldest but because he had the deep voice of a man, for which we called him Bassy too.

– Because you should know that a haggis doesn't come to a decoy unless it is someone new, and that they are only here two times in a year, well, if it weren't for that, we'd all earn piles of money only by calling them and catching them. Because neither with a net nor a hook; you have to call them by their names and they come and jump into the sack. And if you're willing we'll go halves, well, we'll find the place, because not all places on the river are suitable to find good haggis, because the bad ones are like fish.

– …

– We'll put you in the right place and we'll keep you company a bit away but not far, because we can't be there as we're not new, and so that you won't be afraid, as some wet their pants with fear being alone there at night.

– No, I don't want to, find someone else.

– There's no one else, lad, as apart from being new it has to rhyme. Aren't you called Travis?

– Yes.

– Well, there you have it, hunting the haggis Travis. With that and with being new, the thing is sewn up. How lucky you are to be new here and to be called Travis. The sack has to be made of linen; if not it won't do; well, even if it isn't linen, it has to be white and very clean – Old Melondro was very clever, he seemed to know all the words in the world and to have them all lined up behind his teeth to release them without breathing at the right time.

– And it has to be tomorrow and no other day, because the moon won't be out and after you can't do it because this is Santiago's moon and there are loads then and we'll bring the sack home full up and with a bit of luck two.

That night when I went to bed I realized that the moon was going down above Santa Ladaíña rubbing against the top of the mountain, and I couldn't get to sleep for a while.

My mother burst out laughing and she called me greedy and she told me that it was all a trick on the part of the lads from Auria, the worst in the world, and that I didn't know because I wasn't raised there, and that they had done the same to many a one and that some had remembered the joke for a while after, keeping away from everybody, as well as being dazed, so that when someone was bewildered, for whatever reason, people said that they were thinking of the haggis. In spite of all that, she gave me a sack in which some relatives from Vilar de Astrés had brought beans. So it was the hottest part of the summer and my mother stayed up until dawn sewing trousers made of sacking for old Demetrio who had a draper's in Ferreira, and as the loft where we slept was full of bugs, during the heat it was all the same to my mother if I came in late or not.

They were waiting for me at the inspection point in Ponte Vella a bit before midnight and we went down to the river in silence. The river still caught pieces of the moon going down, the rotting moon, a piece of rotten pumpkin that fell headlong, a piece of yellow lard, a piece of sticky light, dripping on the stubble left from the crops, melting under the pines at Santa Ladaíña, at times even redder, like when I saw the red-hot iron at the foundry in Malingre or the iron at old Catapiro's forge when first they put it in water, now without hissing, illuminating lazily, without creaking, tamely through the stubble; all was lukewarm, silent, with the aroma of summer river, of the thickness of summer smells, of the warm pools of summer, of rotten pumpkin, of a dead fermented summer moon, slipping as far as the sprinkling of the moss, with the remnants of yellow light, dying in the water on the mute summer bubbles, and so many frogs in the thickness of their croaking in the heat of the summer mud, and the red light in the pools and sticky slime, and in the rocky places all the same colour in the thickness of the stones, and the big black emptiness in the thickness of the summer air and the shadows growing, growing, sinking, spreading out until one couldn't see the other bank of the river, now in a hurry, as if everything were being switched off quickly, and it was frightening.

They left me alone at the bottom of the Rock of the Drowned and they hid not far away, behind the vines at Ponte Vella, and others up on the branches of big alders. Old Melendro's changed voice began to reach me, fearful, as if from the deepest depths, even deeper than the voice of an adult, and it reached me through the air above the murmur of the frogs, and I opened the sack and when I had it open then I caught it with both hands, with the rotten yellow light on my hands that came cutting things in half, and I started to repeat the instructions of Old Melondro, looking up with the sack stretched tight in both hands:

– "I'm Travis".

– I'm Travis.

– "You're a haggis".

– You're a haggis.

– "Haggis come to Travis, waiting Travis".

– Haggis come to Travis…

Suddenly a breeze brushed my forehead, my nose, my lips, it went into my eyes like a fissure of light, and a weight like a stone fell into the sack.

– "I'm Travis".

– I'm Travis.

A light came out of the water again, marking a curve in the air, sparkling, continuous, and the sack became heavier, and beads of sweat formed on my temples.

– "Come to Travis".

– to Travis. And another, and another, even though Melondro continued shouting and I answered him like an echo.

– "You're a haggis".

– Haggis… and the brightness jumping from the circle of water towards the sphere of the air, marking a curve in the air for a brief moment, like a lance, sparkling, continuous, an instant in the darkness, and the leap of the breeze in my forehead, my nose, my lips…

– How many have you? – Old Melondro shouted nearer to me, in an ironic tone but a bit unsure of himself. Smothered giggles were heard in the trees, imitations of an owl's rattle, and of the screech of a barn owl.

– I don't know, at least a dozen or more. – I held the sack by sheer strength, with effort, in a corner lit by the moon going down, beside the boulder.

– …Or maybe two. I can't hold it anymore.

They came out from where they were hidden and came close silently and a bit afterwards they burst their sides laughing. Old Melondro came still closer without getting there completely.

– Eh! But what did you put in the sack? For the sack is full – he said to the others who stopped laughing and edged away.

– I didn't put anything in, it filled up by itself, one every time we shouted… They came from the river, they jumped in the air, they disappeared into the sack.

– Jeepers…! Turn round here… The sack is full and it's shining.

I turned towards where the voices came from, lifting the sack with difficulty. Old Melondro advanced towards me a bit more.

– Jeepers creepers, it is full to the top and he didn't budge… Empty it on the stone, cripes! His voice shook and it had become hoarser.

I turned the sack upside down and before doing so it had lost all its weight. Only a dusty light dripped on the stone, blue and unsteady like damp matches.

A medosa Blandina, *1974*

Versión radiofónica
Persoaxes:
BLANDINA, 25 anos, costureira, moi andada e soleta.
ULPIANO, 18 anos, algo túzaro.
Piñeiral montesío na outa noite do vran. Ao lonxe rumores de folión, como fondo de todo o diálogo.
BLANDINA *volta pra o seu lugar na compaña de* ULPIANO. *El baril, forte, pro meio zouma e inxel, ao menos nas aparencias. Ela, lerchona, lista como un allo, collida pola aboiante concupiscencia da romaxe.*

BLANDINA Foi unha sorte atoparte, Ulpiano. Si non foras ti, e non tivera a miña nai algo doente, leve o demo si me estrevería a voltar pra a casa, e menos atallando por estes piñeirais tan medoños.

ULPIANO Verdadeiramentes non se ve nin ouce alma viva... Nin os mortos se aventurarían por estas trebas...

BLANDINA ¡Santismo sacramento! Non fales de mortos, hom... Ai, Jasús, co témera que eu son...

ULPIANO ¿E como te aventuraches a vir soia a máis de dúas horas de camiño do teu lugar?

BLANDINA Toleas... ¿Como ía vir soia, home? Viñen co meu irmán Calros e máis co siñor Fuco o Cerralleiras, a xantar a casa do párraco, que, como se sabe é tío noso... Pois pescaron unha tranca tan escedida que aínda non anoitecera e xa estaban os dous trousados e tirados no curro da reitoral coma marraus, fóra a alma. ¡Concencia negra! E agora eu soia por estes piñeirais dúas légoas de camiño, esposta a quen sabe cantos riscos e perigos...

ULPIANO Non, o que é por iso podes ir tranquía... Conózote ben, conócense as nosas xentes, somos de lugares pertos... E a máis deso...

BLANDINA Pois nin por esas... Pódesme crere que non me chega a camisa ao corpo; porque, ao fin, ti eres home, e unha é muller, e como di o dito, o home é iesca e a muller estopa: vén o diaño e sopla...

ULPIANO

Parvaxolas.

Aquí non sopla máis que esta nordesía do Rodicio que mete a friax na cana dos ósos aínda estando na canícula.

BLANDINA Serache a ti porque o que é a min... Agora mesmo, millor dito xa dende fai un istantiño, ¡ai!, sinto unhas alfas de calore que me ruben acoxegando polas costas até ensaríllanseme no corpo todo; e máis no peito, millor dito nos peitos, como si os tivese contrapeándoseme do frío ao lume, coma cando unha ten callentura.

Arrepiándose.

¡Huiii! Si non fora o escuro veríasme os cachetes ardendo, mesmamente ardendo.

ULPIANO ¿Non será un estérico?

BLANDINA Vaia home, pensei que eras máis comprido. Ese é mal das vellas ou das que van quedando pra a desfeita. Eu aínda son moza, e coma tal o sangue ándame ás veces a bulir nas veas do corpo, tanta nas de afora coma nas de adentro que son as piores.

ULPIANO Pois serache o viño.

BLANDINA ¿O viño? Malia si grolo del bebín, que nin me gosta nin me presta. Todo o máis foron dúas copas de anís escarchado que me fixo beber coasi á forza meu tío, e onde van elas; foi ao saírmos da misa... É o medo, Ulpiano, o medo.

ULPIANO ¿Pro medo de que, muller?

BLANDINA Boh, déixame en pace hom... ¿E de que ha sere? ¿E logo non che poden vir á cachola algunhas malas ideias, aquí nesta mourenza, tan desapartada dos lugares? ¿Non te podía tentar o demo, non? Pois de palla no has sere, tan home como campas ou aparentas, que te estiven a considerare todo o día, que até parez que che se vai a romper a roupa coa forza das carnes... Que hastra os ollos che brilan na noite coma si foran de raposo, Deus me dea...

ULPIANO   *Alpabarda.*

¡Vaites, vaites...! Pois déixaos que brilen, que os ollos non apalpan e o ollar non lle fai mal a ninguén.

BLANDINA Pois has saber que polos ollos comenza todo, os amores e máis as xenreiras. ¿Nunca viches unha cobra fitando fixamentes a un paxariño até que lle cai no papo?

ULPIANO   *Desentendéndose.*

Boeno, boeno; anda muller anda, que nin eu son cobra nin ti carriza. ¡Tendes cada cousa as mulleres! ¿Non te decatas que con esas pantesías váichese acuartando o paso, que si un fose malpensado aínda daría que pensar si o fas adrede? Temos camiño pra máis de hora e meia. Non penses en trapalladas, fecha o peteiro que así rende máis o tempo e a andadura...

Camiñan un tempiño calados. Zoan máis fortes as rachas do vento. Supitamente BLANDINA *ceiba do peito un arrepío que semella un brado de ferida.*

BLANDINA ¡Huuuuiiii!

ULPIANO ¡Asús, que susto me deches! ¿Que che dou, Blandina?

BLANDINA As alfas outra vece que me ruben polas costas coma lume viva dunha fogueira.

ULPIANO ¿Non comerías algo que non che asentou?

BLANDINA

          Cun tono menos queixoso, coasi natural mais un pouco despeitado.

¡Bueno, puñés, pareces parvo! ¿Non che estou a decir que todo é medo? I encima pídesme que cale...

ULPIANO Entón falemos.

BLANDINA Agora fala ti que eu xa dixen o meu.

ULPIANO Pois, pois...

BLANDINA ¿Pois que?

ULPIANO ... pois que estes de San Verísimo de Rebordechao fan unhas romerías que arden nun candil. Coido que no folión de arestora han ter gastado máis de, ¡que sei eu!, só nos foguetes de luceiría portuguesa. E xa verás ao saír da misa as bombas de estrondo; porque téñoche que decir un segredo, con tal que non o contes logo.

BLANDINA

Achegándoselle moito, anceiosa.

Que, que...

ULPIANO

Tamén de moi perto.

Pois que... as bombas pásanas de contrabando pola raia seca de Chaves.

BLANDIN

Estentórea.

¡Aiiiiiii!

ULPIANO ¡Arrenégote, muller! ¿Véñenche as alfas, de novo?

BLANDINA

Coa voce crebada.

As alfas, si; pro agora, ademais, tiven unha visión.

ULPIANO ¿E que viches?

BLANDINA Propiamente unha visión non foi, senón unha figuración...

ULPIANO Déixate de andrómenas e apreta o paso que xa falta pouco pra salirmos do piñeiral.

Siguen outro pouco calados. Brúa, lene, o vento nos piñeiros e fungan os paxaros nocturnios.

BLANDINA

Como falando pra si.

¿E non hei ter medo, e non me han vir figuracións? ¡Ai, Jasús, Jasús! Ir soia cun mozo por este atallo do piñeiral e polas congostras fondísimas que aínda fallan por percorrer; afastados do mundo, sin ninguén que me valia nun caso de apuro... ¿E que podería eu facer, que? ¿Que sería de min si che acometese un ramo de tolicie, deses que lle dan aos mozos, indo soios cunha indefensa muller, de noite, lonxe da xente toda...? Agora mesmo o pensaba cando te me arrimaches pra contarme esa parvada das bombas... Ai, Dolcísimo Nome, as cousas en que unha se ve...

ULPIANO ¿Que vas baduando, muller, que nin sei o que falas?

BLANDINA ¿De que hei falar, prosma, de que hei falar? Tal como vou tremando de medo coma un vimio, cicais nin me podería defender por máis que quixese... Ai, Señor San Verísimo, cando penso que si me tocases cun dedo, aquí mesmo cairía redonda, coma unha morta, sin poderme valer... Nin as pernas me valerían que cando penso neso xa se me eivan sin que me toques.

ULPIANO Boeno, muller boeno. Eres boa plepa ti, coma todas as mulleres... Morra o conto... ¿Pensas que non vos conozo, a ti coma a todas as outras? Aquí onde me ves, que somello unha estoa, seiche ben o terreo que piso... Moito latricar, que si esto que o outro, que si tal e que sei eu, que si tumba que dalle, pra veres o que dou de min... Pro seguro estou que si... boeno, boeno... pegarías un berro que se ouviría en dúas légoas darredor...

BLANDINA   *Lerchísima.*

¿Quen, eu? ¡Búscala berradora...! Ademais, dende fai un istante, estoume a quedar ronca coma un pito...

Fearful Blandina, *1974*

Version for radio

Characters

BLANDINA , 25, a seamstress, worldly-wise and forward.

ULPIANO , 18, somewhat churlish.

A remote pine forest late on a summer night. In the distance sounds of a festa, as a background to the entire dialogue.

BLANDINA *is returning to her village in the company of* ULPIANO. *He, hale and hearty, but rather dull and simple, apparently, at least. She, cheeky, as bright as a button, caught up in the buoyant concupiscence of the festa.*

BLANDINA It was a stroke of luck coming across you, Ulpiano. If it weren't for you, and my mother wasn't under the weather, the devil take me if I'd have dared to go back home, still less cutting through this fearsome pine forest.

ULPIANO Truly there's not a soul to be seen or heard... Not even the dead would risk coming into these shadows...

BLANDINA By the Holy Sacrament! Don't talk about the dead, don't... Oh Lord, and me such a jittery character...

ULPIANO And how did you pluck up the courage to come alone, more than a two-hour walk from your village?

BLANDINA You're crazy... How could I have come alone? I came with my brother Carlos and Señor Fuco the odd-job man, to have lunch at the priest's house – as you know, he's our uncle... Well they got so legless, night hadn't yet fallen and there they were the two of them, after spewing their guts up, lying like pigs in the yard of the priest's house, dead to the world. The inconsiderate creatures! And as a result, a two-league walk for me, all on my own, through this pine forest, exposed to goodness knows what risks and dangers...

ULPIANO No, you needn't worry about all that... I know you well, our people know each other, we come from neighbouring villages... And on top of that...

BLANDINA Well even so... Believe you me, I'm feeling jittery; because when all's said and done you are a man and one is a woman and, as the saying goes, man is tinder and woman is oakum: along comes the devil and blows...

ULPIANO

                                        Stupefied

All that blows around here is this northeaster from O Rodicio that chills you to the marrow of your bones even at midday.

BLANDINA You speak for yourself... Right now, or rather ever since a moment ago, oh!... I've been feeling tickly waves of heat coming up my back until they wind themselves round my whole body, and in my breast, or to be more exact in my breasts, it's as if they were freezing one moment and burning the next just like when one has a fever. *Shivering.* Ayyy! If it wasn't for the dark you'd see my cheeks burning, really burning.

ULPIANO Mightn't it be the hysterics?

BLANDINA Dear me, I did think you were more polite than that. That's an illness of old women or of women who're only fit for the knacker's yard. I'm still a young girl, and so my blood sometimes rushes through the veins of my body, both the outer ones and the inner ones, and they're the worst.

ULPIANO Well it must be the wine.

BLANDINA The wine? The devil take me if I had so much as a sip of it – I don't like it and it doesn't like me. All I had was two glasses of sweet anisette that my uncle made me drink almost by force, and that was ages ago, just after coming out of church. It's fear, Ulpiano, fear.

ULPIANO But fear of what, woman?

BLANDINA Bah, leave off, won't you... What do you think? Couldn't some wicked ideas get into your nut, here in this darkness, so far from anywhere? Couldn't you be tempted by the devil? Well you can't be made of straw, such a man as you look or seem to be – I've been watching you all day long, anyone would say your clothes are about to burst open with the power of your flesh... And your eyes even shine in the night as if they were a fox's eyes, by God.

ULPIANO

In a daze.

Goodness gracious...! Well just let them shine, eyes don't touch and looking does nobody any harm.

BLANDINA Well just let me tell you everything starts with eyes, both loves and hates. Haven't you ever seen a snake fixing a little bird with its gaze until it's got it in its jaws?

ULPIANO

Wanting nothing to do with this.

All right, all right; come off it, woman – I'm not a snake and you aren't a wren. What ideas you women do get! Don't you realize that all those fantasies of yours are making you slow down, and a suspicious person could think you're doing it on purpose? We've got more than an hour and a half's walk in front of us. Don't be thinking about silly things, shut your trap – that way we'll make better use of our time and our energy...

They walk for a while in silence. The gusts of wind howl more loudly. Suddenly BLANDINA *lets out a cry that sounds like the scream of one wounded.*

BLANDINA Aaaaayyyy!

ULPIANO Good Lord, what a fright you gave me! What's up, Blandina?

BLANDINA Those hot waves again, coming up my back like the very flames on a bonfire.

ULPIANO Mightn't you have eaten something that didn't agree with you?

BLANDINA

In a less fretful tone, almost normal yet still a little peevish.

Come on, sod it, you're like a simpleton. Aren't I telling you it's all fear? And on top of that you ask me to keep quiet...

ULPIANO Let's talk, then.

BLANDINA Now you talk, I've said my bit.

ULPIANO Well, well...

BLANDINA Well what?

ULPIANO ... well these people in San Verísimo de Rebordechao organize fantastic festas. I think that on this one they must have spent more than, I don't know how much, on the Portuguese rockets alone. And after mass tomorrow you'll see what firecrackers; for I must tell you a secret, so long as you don't let on.

BLANDINA

Coming very close, eagerly.

Yes, yes...

ULPIANO Well, they... smuggle the firecrackers across the border at Chaves.

BLANDINA

Strident.

Ayyyyy!!!!!

ULPIANO Damn you, woman! Are the waves coming, again?

BLANDINA

In a broken voice.

Yes, it's the waves; but now, on top of that, I've had a vision.

ULPIANO And what did you see?

BLANDINA It wasn't exactly a vision, but something I imagined...

ULPIANO Stop all these silly ideas and get a move on, not far now and we'll be out of the pine woods.

They walk on a little further in silence. The wind growls among the pine trees and the night birds hoot.

BLANDINA

As if talking to herself.

How can I not feel frightened, how can I not imagine things? Oh good Lord, good Lord! Walking alone with a young lad along this short cut through the pine woods and along those deep, secluded paths ahead; far from the world, without anyone to help me if I'm in trouble... And what could I do, what could I do? What would become of me if you were seized by a fit of madness, one of those fits that young lads have, when alone with a defenceless woman, at night, far away from everyone...? I was thinking this just now when you came up close to tell me that nonsense about the firecrackers... Oh, sweet name of Jesus, such a jam I'm in...

ULPIANO What are you babbling about, woman, I can't tell what you're saying.

BLANDINA What can I say, you dimwit, what can I say? Trembling as I am like an aspen leaf, maybe I wouldn't even be able to defend myself however much I wanted... Oh, by the holy Saint Verísimo, when I think that if you touched me with one finger, I'd fall flat right here, like a dead woman, unable to help myself... My very legs would be useless, when I think about that they go all weak without you touching me.

ULPIANO All right, woman, all right. You're a right nuisance you are, like all women .. Enough of all that... Do you think I don't know you, you and all the others? I know it might not look like it, and that I seem a fool, but let me tell you I know very well the ground I'm on... Lots of blather, on and on and on, again and again and again, with this that and the other, just to see what I'm good for. But I'm certain that if... if I... you'd let out a yell that'd be heard two leagues away...

BLANDINA

Brazenly

Who, me? I'm a fine yeller I am...! What's more, just a moment ago I went as hoarse as a chicken...

Ánxel Fole (1903–1986)

From Á lus do candil (By the Light of a Candle), *1953*

Os lobos

Moitas veces ouvín dicir que os lobos non atacan as persoas. E isto non é certo. O secretario de Caldas foi comido por eles cando voltaba da feira de Viana. Algúns dixeron que o mataran por roubalo, e que despois o comeran os lobos: mais a dous-centos metros de onda o comeran foi atopado un lobo morto coa gorxa afuracada por unha bala.

Aqueles días viran os pastores unha manda de dez cunha loba con tres lobecos. Era tempo de neve, e baixaran da serra da Moá. Ó parecer, despois de esgotados os cartuchos, quixo subir a unha árbore, mais non puido. Alí estaba a seu carón, o revólver con seis cartuchos baleiros no bombo. Era un bo revólver americano. Ó sentirse feridos algúns lobos, todos se botaron riba del. Se tivera un bo foco eléctrico quizais se salvara. Ó lobo se non se lle fere de morte é peor. Eu matei un con dous tiros de postas. Foi morrer tres cantos máis aló de onde o asegundara. Atináralle na testa e no fociño, e ía deixando un regueiro de sangue. Arrincaba cos dentes os cañotos das xestas. Quizais non se me arrepuxo porque era de día.

De noite médralles o corazón e son moi valentes. Non vos riades. Tamén lles pasa iso ós lobicáns. O señor cura de Peites tiña un. De noite íase ó monte e chamaba ós lobos. Viñan con el. Din que abría os tarabelos das cortes coma unha persoa. Unha noite velouno o señor cura. Era un gran cazador. Tiña un rifle de dez tiros que lle trouxera un sobriño de California. Meteulle dous tiros seguidos no entrecello ó galgar un pasadelo. O crego estaba na xanela da rectoral cun foco, e o lobicán voltaba do monte, polas tres da mañá, acompañado dos lobos. Abrírono e esfolárono axiña, e viron que tiña o corazón inchado...

¿Sabedes cando se atreven os lobos cos homes? Cando teñen moita fame, ou cando se decatan que lles teñen medo. Por iso case que nunca atacan a tres ou máis xuntos. Cando atopan un home só pola serra, pónense a traballalo. Teñen moito distinto... Xa veredes como o traballan. De primeiro, acompáñano; despois, pónenselle diante; máis tarde, chéganlle a zorrega-las pernas cos rabos... Así, pouquiño a pouquiño. Vén un intre en que o home xa non pode máis. O medo alporízalle os cabelos. Parécelle que lle cravaran arames na testa. Váiselle a voz, perde o sentido. Xa está perdido. Bótanse os lobos enriba del e esnaquízano. Cada vinte anos ou menos, dáse por estas terras un caso deses. Desaparece un home. Crese que o mataron ou que fuxiu para as Américas. Ó cabo de dous ou tres anos ninguén fala del. Un cazador atopa nunha xesteira unha caveira. ¿De quen sería? Así lle aconteceu ó Pastrán de Vesuña, hai moitos anos. Mais se o home non perde a coraxe, non se atreven con el.

Todos coñecedes coma min ó Emilio, o castrador de Rugando. Atendede ben e xa saberedes que é certo todo canto levo dito sobre os lobos. E vostedes tamén, señoritos...

Non habería rapaz coma el se non fora tan xogantín. Xogaba ata a camisa. Unha vez, na cantina da Cruz, xogou a besta con tódolos arreos, e perdeuna. Tivo que andar a pé castrando ranchos dende Leixazós a Pacios, ou de Bustelo a Vilañán. Era home moi botado para adiante, e o primeiro nas liortas.

Se non me trabuco, fora pola Santa Lucía cando lle aconteceu o que vos vou contar. Por ese tempo todos sabedes que non traballan os capadores. O bo do home dedicábase á farra. Había pouco que casara cunha moza de casa forte. Xa estaba en tratos cun xateiro da Ermida para mercar un cabalo.

Queríano moito en tódolos sitios onda capaba ranchos, e convidábano sempre á mata. Aquel día xantara en Arnado. Xa se sabe como son eses xantares da mata. Empezan ás doce, poño por caso, e rematan ás cinco. O fígado asado con aceite e pemento, os roxóns e o raxo. Viño nunca falta. Tempo de fartura. Xantara aquel día en cas do Rulo. Enchéranse de néboa os cavorcos. Non se vía un burro a tres pasos, dispensando.

O Rulo díxolle que pasara a noite na súa casa.

– Andan os lobos – advertiulle – moi bastos. Con esta néboa tan mesta pódeste esfragar. Non che pase coma ó Bieito de Corga, cando ía para Ferramolín, que se derrubou polo canto do Mazo e foi dar ó río. Alí quedou defunto cos cadrís partidos por testalán, pois teimou coma ti por saír de Vilarbacú unha noite coma a de hoxe.

Mais o capador había pouco que casara, como vos dixen, e non houbo xeito de facelo quedar. Nin tan sequera quixo levar algúns fachucos de palla para o camiño. E alá se foi o Rugando tan só cunha cachaba de freixo e a súa navalla no peto para se defender. Gracias a Deus que coñecía ben o camiño. Xa levo dito que era home valente. El mesmo mo contou en Santa Cubicia de Quiroga, na tasca do Avelino.

Polas primeiras horas todo foi ben. Non viu amosas de lobos por ningures. Parouse a acender un pito denantes de chegar á lindeira da devesa de Bonxa. Mais de alí a un pouquichiño oíu patuxar nun trollo. Xa sabedes que é terreo fondal onde se encora a auga. Unha migalliña despois oíu un longo ouleo. E outro lle respondeu da outra banda da valgada. Tamén sentiu unhas carreiriñas polos dous lados do camiño. Os lobos seguían chamándose os uns ós outros. Por sorte para el, había moitos seixos no camiño. Encheu tódolos petos de croios. Non me dixo que empezara a ter medo, mais eu coido que si...

Dous lobos grandísimos fórono acompañando. Ían sempre de par del, ás dúas mans. Case que parecían dous cans que foran co seu amo. Se el se paraba, tamén eles se paraban. Algunhas veces púñanselle diante. Entón, o capador guindáb*a*lles un coio. E batíalles... Os lobos apartábanse. No máis fondal dunha congostra tivo que pasar un pontigo. Esgotara as pedras que trouxera nos petos. Xa lle quedaban poucos fósforos. Do outro lado do pontigo viu unhas luces coma de vagalumes. Acendeu un fósforo. Non había pedras no camiño. Tivo que coller bulleiro coas mans e tirarllo ós lobos, ó mesmo tempo que berraba moi forte. Ergueuse un e deixouno pasar. Quizais foran seis. A todos lles relucían os ollos. Un deles botoulle os dentes á cachaba e arrincoulla da man. Íanse metendo nel cada vez máis. Ata lle fustrigaban as pernas cos rabos. Acendeu, un tras outro, os tres fósforos que lle quedaban. Gracias a isto puido coller un coio. Atinoulle a un lobo no peito. Regañaban todos os dentes coma cando se van botar sobre as ovellas. Xa sentía que lle esmorecían os pulos, que se ía quedando sen forza. Os lobos seguían a chamarse uns ós outros. Tremaba coma un vimbio. Xa non os podía escorrentar nin sequera berrar. Íalle estoupar o corazón. Unhas cantas alancañadas máis e xa estaría na casa. ¿Podería dalas? De sutaque, viu tremelar unhas luces na tébrega; ladraban uns cans ó lonxe. Meteu os dedos na boca e asubiou. Chamábano de lonxe. Estourou un tiro de escopeta.

– Anda Rabelo, anda Sultán – oíu que dicían.

Diante el había tres fachucos de palla ardendo. Seus tres cuñados dábanlle fortes apertas.

– Andabámoste buscando – dixo un –. Chegaron o Sultán e o Rabelo brincando ó seu redor e dando ouveos de ledicia.

Entraron na casa. As mulleres estaban na cociña. Na gran lareira había un bo lume.

– Traédeme auga – dixo o capador.

E caeu estalicado no chan.

Todos se alporizaron. Houbo moitos berros e prantos. Máis de dúas horas estivo sen sentido. Leváronno ó leito. A forza de fretas volveulle o acordo.

– Se non sairades a buscarme, tan só se me atoparían os ósos. Xa non podía resistir máis – dixo o bo do home.

Para que vexades como traballan os lobos á xente.

Wolves

I have often heard it said that wolves don't attack people. And this is not true. A secretary in the Town Hall of Caldas was eaten by them when he was coming back from the fair in Viana. Some said that he had been killed so as to steal from him and that the wolves ate him afterwards; but two hundred metres away from where they had eaten him a dead wolf was found with his throat torn open by a bullet.

At that time some hunters had seen a pack of ten with a she-wolf and three wolf cubs. It was snowy weather and they had come down from the Moá mountain range. It seems, after using up all the cartridges, he wanted to go up a tree but couldn't. There, at his side, was the revolver with six empty cartridges in its barrel. It was a good American revolver. When some wolves sensed that they were injured they dashed at him. If he had had a good electric lamp perhaps he might have saved himself. It's worse if a wolf isn't wounded to death. I killed one with two slugs. He went off to die three cock's steps from where he had been injured. I had got him in the head and the nose, and he went away leaving a trail of blood. He rooted out broom with his teeth. Perhaps he didn't face up to me because it was daytime.

At night their hearts grow bigger and they become braver. Don't laugh. That also happens with wolfish dogs. The good priest at Peites had one. At night, he went to the mountains and called to the wolves. They came to him. They say that he could open the locks on the stables as if he were human. One night the good priest watched him. He was a great hunter. He had a rifle that his nephew had brought him from California. He put two shots into him, one after the other between the eyes as he went through a narrow pass. The clergyman was at the window of the presbytery with a lamp, and the wolfish dog was coming back from the hills at about three in the morning accompanied by the wolves. They opened him and skinned him, and they saw that his heart was swollen…

Do you know when wolves face up most to men? When they are very hungry or when they realize that they are afraid of them. That's why they never attack three or more together. When they find a man alone in the mountains they work on him. They have a good instinct… You'll see how they work on him. First, they accompany him; then they go ahead of him; afterwards they whip him on the legs with their tails… So, little by little. A time comes when the man can't take anymore, fear makes his hair stand on end. It is as if they had driven wires into his head. He becomes mute, he loses consciousness. He's lost. The wolves dash at him and tear him to pieces. Every twenty years or so something like that happens around here. A man disappears. He is believed to have been killed or to have run away to America. After two or three years nobody talks about him anymore. A hunter finds a skull among some brooms. Whose is it? That's what happened to Pastrán de Vesuña, many years ago. But if men didn't show fear they wouldn't face up to them.

You all know Emilio, the gelder from Rugando, as well as I do. Listen well and you will see that it is all true what I have said about wolves. And you too, sirs…

There would have been nobody equal to that lad if he hadn't been a gambler. He even gambled his shirt. One time in the "Cruz" canteen he gambled his mount with the harness and he lost it all. He had to go around on foot castrating piglets from Leixazós to Pacios or from Bustelo to Vilañán. He was very daring and the first to start a fight.

If I'm not wrong it was around St. Lucia's day when what I'm going to tell you happened to him. At that time, as you all know, gelders weren't in much demand. The good man gave himself up to having a good time. Not long before he had married a girl with a lump of money. He was already negotiating with a cattle-dealer from Ermida to buy a horse from him.

He was very much liked in all the places he went to castrate piglets. And he was always invited to pigkillings. That day he had eaten in Arnado. You know what those meals are like at pigkillings. They start at twelve, for example, and finish at five. Roast liver with oil and peppers, fried crackling and gammon steak. Wine is never lacking. A time to stuff yourself. That day he had eaten at Rulo's house. The hollows had filled with mist. You couldn't see your nose, excuse the expression.

Old Rulo told him he could stay at his home.

– The wolves – he warned him – are everywhere. With this thick mist you crash into everything. Don't let what happened to Bieito de Corga, when he was going to Ferramolín, happen to you, he fell headlong from Mazo rock and ended up in the river. He lay there dead with his lower back broken all because he was muleheaded, because he insisted, like you, on leaving Vilarbacú on a night like this.

But the gelder had got married a short time before as I already told you, and there was no way to make him stay. He didn't even want to take straw torches for the journey. And off went Rugando with only an ash stick and with his knife in his pocket to defend himself. Thanks be to God that he knew the way. I already said that he was a brave man. He himself told me so in Santa Cubicia de Quiroga in Avelino's tavern.

For the first few hours everything went fine. There were no wolf tracks anywhere. He stopped to light a cigarette before getting to the hedge in Bonxa meadow. But a bit after he heard splashing in the mire. You know that type of thick soil where water dams up. A little afterwards he heard a long howl. And another answered him from the other end of the gulley. He also heard running on both sides of the path. The wolves continued calling one to the other. Luckily for him there were a lot of stones on the path. He filled all his pockets with pebbles. He didn't tell me that he was beginning to be afraid but I think that he was…

Two really big wolves accompanied him. With him, on either side. They almost seemed to be two dogs walking with their master. If he stopped, so did they. Sometimes they went in front of him. Then the gelder threw a pebble at them. And he hit them… The wolves moved away. At the lowest part of a cart track he had to cross a little bridge. He had used all the stones in his pockets. He only had some matches left. From the other side of the little bridge he saw some lights like glowworms. He lit a match. There were no stones on the path. He had to pick up mud in his hands and throw it at the wolves at the same time as he screamed. One of them got up and he let him pass. Perhaps there were six. All of their eyes shone. One of them bit his stick and tore it out of his hand. They were getting closer and closer. They even whipped his legs with their tails. He lit the three matches he had left one after the other. Thanks to that he could pick up a pebble. He hit a wolf on the chest. They all bared their teeth like when they attack sheep. He felt his nerve leaving him, that he was losing strength. The wolves continued calling one to the other. He shook like a willow. He couldn't drive them away anymore, he couldn't even shout. His heart felt like it was going to explode. A few more strides and he would be at home. Would he make it? Suddenly, he saw some lights twinkle in the darkness; a few dogs were barking in the distance. He put his fingers in his mouth and whistled. They called him from far away. A shotgun fired.

– Come on, Rabelo, come on, Sultan – he heard them say.

He saw three straw torches burning before him. His three brother-in-laws embraced him tightly.

– We were out looking for you – one of them said –. Rabelo and Sultan came up jumping around him and howling with joy.

They went into the house. The women were in the kitchen. There was a roaring fire in the fireplace.

– Bring me water – the gelder said.

And he fell flat on the floor.

Everyone got a fright. There was a lot of shouting and crying. He was unconscious more than two hours. They put him to bed. Thanks to massages he came to.

– If you hadn't gone out looking for me you'd have found only my bones. I couldn't have held out any longer – the good man said.

So you see how wolves work on people.

María Mariño Carou (1907–1967)

From Verba que comenza (Words that Begin), *1990*

Está caíndo a folla i en min nace primavera...

Está caíndo a folla i en min nace primavera.
¿Como digo onte sendo hoxe?
¿Quen entenderá este mar vello?
¡Como farto a miña verba do nacer que xa pasou!
¡Como reino nas migallas onde medrei un bon día!
¿Como piso forte sendo branda?
¿Como digo si se o non está escoitando?
¿Quen entenderá este mar vello?
Medro, medro e non sei parar.
Presa xa e ceguiña no cume,

lévame,
lévame ó chan a verba.

Queda hoxe o chan soio
muxindo a pegada do tempo.
Mesturadas terras peneiran, peneiran fariña,
fariña que non fai masa,
Rebélanse as ondas ós mares.
os ríos afogan a pradeira seca,
os camiños non se atopan.
¿Quen entenderá este mar vello?
É outono i en min nace primavera.
¿Quen o entenderá?

Leaves are falling and in me spring is born...

Leaves are falling and in me spring is born.
How can I say yesterday when it's today?
Who can understand this old sea?
How I fill my words with the birth that's past!
How I reign among the crumbs where I grew up one fine day!
How can I tread firmly being soft?
How can I say Yes if No is listening?
Who can understand this old sea?
I grow, I grow and I can't stop.
A prisoner now and blind on the peak
I'm carried,
I'm carried to the ground by words.

The ground is left alone today
milking the footsteps of time.
Mixed lands sieve, sieve flour,
flour that does not make dough.
The waves rebel against the seas,
the rivers drown the dry meadow,
the paths are nowhere to be found.
Who can understand this old sea?
It's autumn and in me spring is born.
Who can understand?

Aquilino Iglesia Alvariño (1909–1961)

From Corazón ao vento (Heart in the Wind), *1933*

As altas horas

Finouse a miña alma no colo desta hora
de azucenas, que pasa para os ermos da aurora...

Na cama do luar, branquiña e perfumada
recóstase a durmir a erma penascada.

A noite, agruchadiña no colo do horizonte
é unha pastora imbele que adormeceu no monte.

Un rebaño de cirros, coma ovelliñas brancas,
anda pacendo a lúa nas celestes caivancas.

The small hours

My soul expired in the lap of this hour
of lilies, which moves on towards the wastes of the dawn...

In the bed of moonlight, white and perfumed,
the craggy wasteland lies down to sleep.

Night, curled up on the lap of the horizon,
is a frail shepherdess who fell asleep in the wilds.

A flock of cirrus, like white sheep,
is grazing the moon on the celestial river-banks.

From Cómaros verdes (Green Field-Ridges), *1947*

Nos curros de Aldoar

Non na cama de hexámetros virxilianos
con Deiopea. Nos curros de Aldoar
durmiu esta noite o vento coa Oreade.

Os seus bicos sabían a queirogas,
a rosadas e xestas do Valiño

con flores e niños de xemexeme.
Traguía nas súas mans un soño ledo

de aloumiñar centeos e liñeiras.
E a súa voz era moi noviña
de falar coas loias no camiño no sol.

Vento pagán de ollos verdes,
tu n'afundiche frotas nemigas no Tirreno!

Nese teu mar de grañas infinitas
arrempuxas os pailebotes claros
dos cantares das leiras.

In the pastures of Aldoar

Not on the bed of Virgilian hexameters
with Deiopea. In the pastures of Aldoar
the wind slept tonight with the Oread.

His kisses tasted of heather,
of dew and broom of O Valiño
with flowers and dunnocks' nests.

He brought in his hands a joyful dream
of caressing rye and flax fields.
And his voice was very young
from talking to the skylarks on the way to the sun.

Pagan wind with green eyes,
you never sank enemy fleets in the Tyrrhene sea!

In your sea with its infinite scrublands
you blow along the bright pilot-boats,
the songs in the fields.

From Nenias, *1961*

Polos vellos poetas que foron

Houbo un tempo feliz
no que o silencio escuro con ollos sempre abertos
dos negros bronces das Insuas

alcendía os pulsos e as chincheiras
dos meus amigos,
os vellos poetas do mar e do vento,
os que cantaron as crinas fermosas dos cabalos de Asia
e as proas das negras naos.

Cando estes poetas morreron,
naceulles no oco do seu peito un silencio harmonioso
de moi finas herbas de olor
e longuísimo vento da mar.

Os outros amaron xa os días breves coma vasos
e os vasos ben colmados
dun viño louro coma o sol.

Son os meus amados poetas do Mediterráneo,
os finos amadores dos pazos brancos de África,
e os outros,
os ledos feireantes das louras frautistas de Lidia.

Mais estes inda non morreron,
que no fondo dos grandes vasos do porto, á media noite,
cantan os seus versos de ouro
a alegría das pernas finas, e áxiles, e fortes,
a das gargantas lisas coma cera,
que treman de chuchas
e unha música que non sei de cristal coma lume.

Tamén amaron cousas belas
os poetas aqueles das cidades novas e fráxiles como vidros
e brancas pombas ó mencer.
Tamén amaron cousas belas.
Mais a súa alma estaba chea de medos
e de longuísimas noites sen amor nin viño,
e de lonxanas princesas de tempos idos, mortas,
doces saudades de neve derretida.

Cando mármores e bronces
resucitaron a luz fermosa da súa noite,
os poetas amaron outra vez
o viño roxo e as pombas,
e as mozas ledas e fortes.

Despois viñeron outros poetas e outros.
E aínda os poetas sen sorte, meus avós tan tristes,
os que soñaban con mortes moi tremendas,
con asfixias sen consolo nos cuartos do hotel,
cos ollos fondos das pistolas de gatillos negros.

¡Ai, que alta e lonxana
vai xa a súa voz escura, son amigo!
¡Ai, que saudade das súas mans, pálidas coma a cera,
e das súas cabezas ladeadas docemente!

Mais, ¿que vaga ternura enche aínda o silencio
que abriron os seus versos como alas?

For the old poets of the past

There was a happy time
when dark silence with the ever-open eyes
of the black bronzes of the Islands
would kindle the pulses and the brows
of my friends
the old poets of the sea and the wind,
those who sang the lovely manes of the horses of Asia
and the prows of the black boats.

When these poets died,
in the hollows of their breasts was born a harmonious silence
of delicate aromatic herbs
and long, long sea wind.
The others loved the days as brief as wineglasses,
glasses brimming
with a wine as golden as the sun.

These are my beloved poets of the Mediterranean,
the urbane lovers of the great white houses of Africa,
and the others,
the happy traders in blond girl-flautists of Lydia.

But these have not died yet,
for at the bottom of the great glasses of port, at midnight,
their verses of gold sing
the gaiety of slim, agile, strong legs,
of throats as smooth as wax

that pulsate with kisses,
and a music that I do not know of crystal, like light.
They too loved beautiful things,
those poets of the new cities, as fragile as windows
and doves at dawn.
They too loved beautiful things.
But their souls were full of fears
and of long, long nights without love or wine,
of distant princesses of times gone by and dead,
sweet sadlongings for melted snow.

When marbles and bronzes
revived the beautiful light of their night,
the poets once again loved
red wine and doves,
and happy, strong girls.

Then came other poets and others still.
And even the luckless poets, my sad, sad forebears,
those who dreamed about most dreadful deaths,
about uncomforted asphyxiations in hotel rooms,
about the deep-set eyes of pistols with black triggers.

Oh, how high and remote
is their dark voice now, that friendly sound!
Oh, what sadlongings for their hands, as pale as wax,
and for their heads, sweetly inclined!

But what vague tenderness still fills the silence
opened by their verses like wings?

From Lanza de soledá (Lance of Solitude), *1961*

Muro final

Non deixar ningún rastro e morrer todo enteiro!
Racine

Co que vai vir no seu durmir alerta.
Un oco escuro por detrás do lume
dos seus ollos. En todo, a servidume
do ser mortal, que, ó trevelar, desperta.

Despedíranse entón. E nesa aperta
final que nun suspiro se consume
– a noite no horizonte, o demais fume –
foran un, nunha bágoa, os dous ben certa.

Pero, ¿que importa amor, lobo que ouvea
no ermo en soledá, e afán que alea
un intre nada máis e varre o vento?

O certo. O que non marra. O que non erra
é xa sabe-la boca chea de terra,
muro final que abate o pensamento.

Last wall

Not to leave any trace and to die whole! Racine

What will come keeps him alert in his sleep .
A dark hollow behind the light
of his eyes. In everything, the servitude
of the mortal being who, as he falls asleep, awakes.

So they had said goodbye. And in that final
embrace that is over in a sigh
– night on the horizon, the rest smoke –
the two had been one, in a just tear.

But what matters love, a wolf that howls
alone on the wasteland, and a desire that flutters
for a moment and is swept away by the wind?

What is just. What does not fail. What does not err
is knowing that one's mouth is already full of earth,
the last wall to be demolished by thought.

Ricardo Carballo Calero (1910–1990)

From Salterio de Fingoi (The Fingoi Psaltery), *1961*

Demasiado duro es pra contigo...

Demasiado duro es pra contigo.
Con todos demasiado duro.
Perdóalos a eles de contado.
En troques
de amor, dáslles perdón.
É porque non os amas.
Mais a ti mesmo
endexamais perdoas.
Porque tampouco te amas a ti mesmo.
E o teu perdón e a túa crueza
son o xeo que esvara
do teu callado corazón.
Con eles tes de ser menos brandido;
as pérolas guindadas
aldraxan aos que as collen
sen procuralas afincadamente.
Contigo has ser máis xeneroso.
Sempre o reo odia ao xuíz.
Se paz arelas ter contigo mesmo,
sé máis benévolo pra ti.
Cando a te perdoar xa teñas aprendido,
aprendido terás a amar, a amarte;
e mentres te non ames
non amarás os máis.
Daquela,
o teu perdón pra os máis terá valor,
pois o teu propio amor terá de dalo
e será sacrificio. Agora, non.

Nada val o que aos outros dás.
Nada val o que a ti te negas.
Négalles algo. Outórgate algo.
Se non tes pra ti lume que te quente,
o río dos teus dons aos que te aldraxan
será glaciar que non poidan beber.

You're too hard on yourself...

You're too hard on yourself.
Too hard on everybody.
Them you forgive straight away
Instead
of love, you give them forgiveness.
It's because you don't love them.
But you never
forgive yourself.
Because you don't love yourself, either.
And your forgiveness and your cruelty
are the ice that slithers out
of your congealed heart.
With them you must be less prodigal;
pearls cast down
affront those who pick them up
without working to obtain them.
With yourself you must be more generous.
The accused always hates the judge.
If you long to be at peace with yourself
be kinder to yourself.
When you've learnt to forgive yourself
you'll have learnt to love, to love yourself;
and so long as you don't love yourself
you won't love others.
And then
your forgiveness of others will be of value,
because your love of yourself will have to give it
and it will be a sacrifice. Not now.

What you give others is worth nothing.
What you deny yourself is worth nothing.
Deny them something. Grant something to yourself.
If you have no fire to warm yourself,
the river of your gifts to those who affront you
will be a glacier that they cannot drink.

From Futuro condicional (Future Conditional), *1982*

Elexía veneciana

Podedes me borrar do Libro de Ouro,
meus compatricios.
Hai tempo que non coido se o Turco rube ou baixa,
e os meus buques están ancorados no molle.

Non me tenta ocultar a miña calva
baixo a tiara de dogo.
Un corno e un roupón non me preservarían
dos arrañóns de tantos senadores.

Que outro celebre as súas nupcias co mar.
A boca desa esposa é demasiado amarga.
Prefírome solteiro, ceibo de tal beleza,
que abala como quer e atraizoa aos seus homes.

Ti, Fóscari; ti, Dándolo; ti, Loredano, olládesme
sen dúbida co horror con que a un irmán perdido.
Quizá teño algún sangue dun Otelo ignorado,
e o meu torgo non é enxebre de Aquilea.

Non me retratarán Bellini nen Tiziano;
escuro morrerei, pobre gallo esquecido.
Mais ollo o mar rillar as pedras de Venecia,
e atopo triste o antroido da vella Serenísima.

Venetian elegy

You can erase me from the Book of Gold,
my fellow-countrymen.
For some time now I have not cared whether the Turk comes or goes,
and my ships are anchored in the dock.

I am not tempted to hide my bald head
under the tiara of the doge.
A horn and a robe would not protect me
against the scratching of so many senators.

Let another man celebrate his marriage to the sea.
That wife's mouth is too bitter.

I prefer to be a bachelor, free from such a beauty
who ebbs and flows as she pleases and betrays her men.

You, Foscari; you, Dandolo, you, Loredano, regard me
no doubt with the horror with which a lost brother is regarded.
Maybe I have some of the blood of an undetected Othello,
and my stock is not the pure stock of Aquileia.

Neither Bellini nor Titian will paint a portrait of me;
I shall die in obscurity, a poor forgotten fighting-cock.
But I watch the sea gnawing at the stones of Venice,
and carnival in the old Serenissima seems sad to me.

Álvaro Cunqueiro (1911–1981)

From Merlín e familia e outras historias (Merlín and Family and Other Stories), *1955*

O reloxo de area

Estaba eu xogando aos bólos co fillo do Arnegueiro, e o pai, o señor Antón da Arnega, viña tódolos anos por Santos a zoquear a Miranda e facía nunha semana cantas zocas se precisaban nun ano na casa nosa, e ao pequeno, que era algo xorobeta e chamábase Florentino, traíao para face-la tinta e tinguir as zocas, e o máis do tempo andaba atrás de min, e quería que lle amosase os xílgaros que tiña, xogase con el aos bólos, e lle ensinase historias; estaba, digo, xogando aos bólos co Florentino, cando se nos entrou por portas don Felices, cantor que fora na Igrexa de Santiago, home de moitos misterios, e no tocante ás súas virtudes, cabaleiro moi cortés e afeito ao augardente de Portomarín. Viña na súa mula meiresa, co aquel seu montar escarranchado, reclamando de mi amo a compostura dun reloxo de area que nunha bulsa de terciopelo negro, atada con cordón roxo, na súa man traía. Lémbrome, como se o estivera mirando, dos seus ollos chispos, vivos e faladores do acabalado nariz colorado, a boca de finos beizos moi franca de corte, cantimais que era risoña, e os longos brazos e grandes mans, que chocaban en home de poucas medras coma aquel, que por aí se andaría pola talla de quintas.

– Este que aquí ves, díxome o señor Merlín namentres don Felices metía a mula na corte, que non me deixaba a min ese labor que era besta dada a roer e espantadiza; este que aquí ves, é home moi sabido, e en bota-las cartas a Salamanca de Galicia. Somos amigos vai para moitos anos, e pasmo facendo memoria das cousas que lle vin adiviñar, tanto polas cartas coma pola fariña, que se chama esta adiviñación alfitomancia e é moi secreta, e sobre todo no que toca a tesouros amoedados, xentes que van na América, amores de viúvas e mortes violentas. Destas podo dicirche que mesmo as ve retratadas.

Chegou pois don Felices co seu reloxo de area, que era unha peza moi requintada de arte toledano, con dúas cobras por asas, o cristal do vaso rosado, os pés catro cabezas de anxeliños, as columnas semellando viñas mui abondosas en acios, e todo o coroaba un espello como a uña do meñique, montado nunha onza de ouro de El-Rei don Carlos III. O arranxo que pedía don Felices era que ao espelliño voláraselle o azougue cando lle estaba adiviñando na feira de Viana do Bolo, a querenda dunha moza ao señorito de Humoso.

A compostura non era auga de maio, que facía falta azougue italiano serenado, e xa metidos en obras e gastos conviña mudarlle tamén a area ao reloxo. Non era cousa de dous nin de tres días, e nos que pasou don Felices con nós, tomando sempre de parva papas de arrandas e chanfaina asada, fíxenme seu amigo. Toda a fachenda del eran fibelas de prata: traía unha na cinta verde do sombreiro, catro por botóns na chambra, outras catro no tabardo, dúas por cada liga, ie que xarretes gordos tiña!, e en cada zapato a súa, e eu limpáballas cada mañá con sal de preste, e por iso estábame moi agradecido. O máis do día dábao por gastado don Felices en falar con mi amo de "Da mántica variationibus", do demo que en alemán se chama Hornspiegel, que se amosa por "espello do corno" e andaba en Sevilla facendo moita piñata nas casadas; do galo que en Soria puxo un ovo de ouro por dediante de notario, de cales eran as siñás do "Dies illa", de quen matou a Prim e de como era a máquina do tren, e tamén dunha consulta que traía, e que tiña revoltas as capelas das igrexas, de se os que tocan frauta, clarinete ou oboe e fiscorno non poden polo Dereito canónico, e esta era sentencia do Cabido de Tui, comer guisantes e fabas, comidas que engordan o alento e trougan o son dos instrumentos. Polo serán subía a botar diante de dona Ginebra as cartas, por saber que fora de toda a cabalería de Bretaña, de se casara na casa dona Galiana, se aparecera o camiño de Cavamún, cantos fillos tiña o neto de don Amadís, se daquela estaría ou non chovendo na Habana, e de se quedara empreñada do zar de Rusia a Belle Otero. Don Felices gozaba sonsacándolle as novas ás cartas, e cando pillaba unha que sorprendía a dona Ginebra ou a mi amo, sorría humildoso, dicindo como para si:

– Nun ano, esta nova non vén no papel.

Tamén a min botoume as cartas unha noite, trala cea, primeiro de como dicen "á capa solta", despoixas "al torneo", e aínda máis, como chaman "co pano diante", que é o tal pano unha estola de crego, e hei dicir que todo me adiviñou, ata que eu andaba coas faldras de Manoeliña de Carlos, e que se seguía apedrando nela, para a Candeloria de tres anos que vén teriamos bautizo. Dixo que como pintaba a corda de bastos comezando por enriba, acaíase soa a sota de ouros, e viña de cabeza por entre carreiros de espadas o catro de copas,

cuatro copas al heredero, y
la espada al cintulero,
primero y delantero,

que era seguro que sería neno. Eu alalei mirando as catro copas coloradas, e aquel letreiro que lles pon Heraclio en Vitoria e que dice "Clase opaca." Ao seu tempo, e porque quen trebella, trebella, e eu seguíalle ensinando a Manoeliña a cuspir caguñas, dispensando, e en anoitecendo saímos por maio a tornar das niñadas á denonciña, naceu Ramonciño. Moitas veces o mirei cando o andaba anainando, e nunca puiden dar en min qué fíos ían e viñan daquel catro de copas, clase opaca, a aquela bulidora baluguiña de manteiga. ¡Moito sabía don Felices!

Amañoulle mi amo o reloxo, e alá se foi don Felices coa súa mula meiresa, e levaba présa por chegar á feira de Cacabelos, que quería troca-la mula por outra máis mansa e mellor comedora. Ramonciño vai no ceo, que aos cinco anos cumpridos pola Candeloria, un martes lardeiro levouno unha calentura que lle quedou do xarampón. Xa estaba eu casado daquela coa Manoeliña, e viviamos en Pacios, e eu era o barqueiro que levaba á xente na barca, da ribeira de Trigás á Mourenza.

– ¡Moito sabe don Felices!, dicíalle eu a mi amo vindo de despedir aquela Salamanca.

– ¡Todo o que non se ve!, respondíame don Merlín, namentres levaba ao nariz, moi fino coas puntas dos dedos, un chisco de rapé.

The Hourglass

I was playing skittle with Arnegueiro's son, and his father, Mr. Anton da Arnega, came every year to Miranda on 1 November to make clogs and in a week he made as many clogs as were necessary for us for the whole year, and he brought a kid, who had a bit of a hunchback and was called Florentino, to make the dye and dye the clogs, and the best part of the time he spent running after me, and he wanted me to show him the goldfinches I had, to play skittle with him and to teach him stories. I was, as I was saying, playing skittle with Florentino, when Don Felices came in the door. He had been a psalm-singer in St. Santiago, a man full of mystery, and, with reference to his virtues, a very polite gentleman and used to the liquor from Portomarín. He came on his mule, with that bow-legged style of riding, asking my boss to fix an hourglass for him that he brought in a black velvet bag tied with a red cord. I remember him as if I were looking at him now, his lively sparkling, talkative eyes above his big red nose, the thin-lipped mouth with its naive shape and moreover smiling, the long arms and big hands that were out of place in such a small man that was near the minimum height to be allowed to do military service.

– This which you see here, – Mr. Merlín told me as Don Felices put the mule in the stable, well, he didn't leave that job to me, well, the beast was an animal very given to biting and nervous –; this which you see here is a man who is clued-up and on reading cards he is the "Salamanca" of Galicia. We've been friends for many years and I'm flabbergasted by the things I've seen him predict, as much from cards as from flour, and this sort of prophecy is called flouristry and it's very secret and most of all with reference to treasures made up of coins, people who go to America, widows' love affairs and violent deaths. Of these last I can tell you that I have seen pictures of them.

Then Don Felices came in carrying his hourglass which was a superior piece of artwork from Toledo, its two handles were in the form of serpents, the glass was pink, four little angels' heads serving as legs, the columns like vines full of vine leaves and all of it was crowned by a mirror like a nail on your little finger, mounted on a gold coin from the time of King Charles the Third. The repair which Don Felices wanted was to fix the little mirror which had lost its coating of silver when he was foretelling a girl's love for a young master from Humoso in the fair at Viana do Bolo.

The mending wasn't plain sailing, because tempered Italian silver coating was needed, and, if one were set on spending and repairing, the sand in the clock should also be changed. It wasn't going to be done in two or even three days, and during the days Don Felices spent with us, always eating gruel and cheap stew, I became his friend. He took greatest pride in his silver buckles: He had one on the green band in his hat, four like buttons on his shirt, another four on his tabard, two for each garter, and what fat calves he had!, and on each shoe a buckle too, and I cleaned them every morning and he was very grateful for that. Don Felices spent most of the day talking to my boss about "Da mántica variationibus", the devil that in German is called *Hornspiegel*, that means "hornmirror" and went around Seville kicking up a row amongst married women; of the cock that laid a golden egg in the presence of a notary in Soria, what were the signs of "Dies illa", who killed Prim and what a train engine was like, and also about a consultation he made, and he had those in the chapels in the churches all in a fuss over it, about whether those who play the flute, clarinet, oboe and cornet can't, according to canonical law, and this was the decision of the chapter in Tui, eat peas and beans, food that makes breathing difficult and weakens the sound of the instruments. In the evening he went up to read cards for Lady Guinevere to see what had happened to all the knights of Britain, if Lady Galiana had got married at home, if the way to Cavamún had been discovered, how many children Don Amadís's grandson had, if it were raining or not then in La Havana, and if the Belle Otero had become pregnant by the Czar of Russia. Don Felices enjoyed getting the news out of the cards, and when he found something that was a surprise to Lady Guinevere or my boss, he smiled humbly, saying as if to himself:

– Until next year this won't be in the papers.

He showed me the cards one night too after supper, first clubs, then diamonds and last hearts, and I have to say that he foretold everything for me, even that I liked Manoeliña de Carlos, and that if I went on insisting, for Candlemas Day in three years' time there would be a baptism. He said that, as the clubs appeared on top, the jack of diamonds was really all right alone and the four of hearts fell headlong between spades:

For the heir hearts four, and
the spade for more
First and fore,

which meant that it was sure to be a boy. I hummed with joy looking at the four red hearts and that label carrying the trademark of Heraclio from Vitoria and that says "first class". When the time came, he who tries and tries again succeeds and because I continued showing Manoeliña a few dirty tricks, if you will excuse me, at twilight in May we went to a fair and after Ramonciño was born. Many times I looked at him when I was fondling him, and I could never understand what threads of mine came and went from that four of hearts, first class, to that nervous little ball of fat. What Don Felices knew!

He fixed the hourglass for my boss, and Don Felices went away with his mule, in a hurry to get to the fair in Cacabelos, as he wanted to change the mule for a tamer one which ate more. Ramonciño is in heaven, because after his fifth birthday about the time of Candlemas, one Shrove Tuesday a fever took him which he had after the measles. At that time I was married to Manoeliña, and we lived in Pacios, and I was the boatman who took people from Trigás shore to Mourenza.

– What Don Felices knows! I said to my boss, after saying goodbye to that "Salamanca".

– Everything that can't be seen! Don Merlín answered me, while he brought to his nose, very elegantly between his fingertips, a pinch of snuff.

From As crónicas do sochantre, 1956

A historia que vou contar – comezou a dicir monsieur de Nancy póndose de pé, e el era un esqueleto máis ben mirriaque e inquedo –, non sería moi propia para que ouvise algúns dos seus comentos madame de Saint-Vaast se estivese viva, pero non importa estando morta, que xa pois non a acicato coas miñas novidades nin é verdade que chufe nela, no que vou contar da miña primeira mocidade, de armas eróticas. Miña nai, que viñera a Dijon dende o Hospicio de Baune, colocada para remontar bragas nos capuchinos de Saint-Maximien, tras variados amores rematou de pupila nun tapadillo que na vila ducal tiña un peinador marsellés, por tras do repeso da carne. Nacín eu, e non se soubo de quen, que daquela non tiña miña nai cortexo fixo, e o peinador marsellés dicía que eu sería de calquera pobre pousafoles, pero ela trebellaba en que eu debería de ser dun vello taberneiro que se achegara por alí unha noitiña de chuvia e aínda perdera unha capota de dobre ala, e arbulaba miña nai con que dende aquel día quedáralle, dispensando, un sofoco vespertino con mareos, co que foi o decatarse de que estaba engrave. O taberneiro, se fose só bebedor de viño ou mozo, quizabes non acreditase nos prospectos que mo acertaban por pai pouco menos que escriturado, pero como era gustoso de augardentes e retafias, xa ía vello cáncamo, e a muller que tivera deixárao por un cabo dragón de Metz, atestándolle que non lle cumpría o débito conxugal...

– Que en Lorena é causa remisoria – apuntou o escribán de Dorne –. Con permiso da concorrencia, o texto romano di: *Nox plaena in hebdomada*, que se traslada por "unha vez por semana" cando menos.

– Ao taberneiro, digo – proseguiu o verdugo lorenés –, pareceulle doado crer naquel mérito de facerme nunha tardiña de outono e con tan pouca alarma, e dixo que si, que sería, e ata me recoñecía o pelo que eu traía, tan mouro e mesto, imitante nun todo ao dun irmán que tivo que detentara por nove anos a praza de monsieur de Nancy, por conta do Leito de Lorena, e que era mui prezado por ser festivo, que sempre que aforcaba a alguén na praza, dende a trabada que se erguía facía señas aos coñecidos e algunha gracia ás señoras da nobreza. Como a miña nai lle saíra o partido dun ambulante alemán que andaba amosando a novidade dunha lanterna xorda polas vilas de Borgoña, deixoume na taberna co taberneiro, que inda non dixen que se chamaba Colet, por mal nome Caldeiro, quen me criou moi axiña, espabilando os meus biberóns cun tercio de tinto e as miñas papas con mediana copia de moscateis, e poñíame derriba da barrica de ratafia de Besançon, e amosábame á clientela, baixándome as bragas, e el berraba: ¿E non está pistoleiro o meu bonetiño? Esto era moi celebrado, e aproveitaba así Colet, dito Caldeiro, para poñer de presente, por intermedio das miñas vergonzas, que el non fora tan capón como a muller dixera, que alí estaba o herdado, e de onde non hai non se quita. E deste paso era do que denantes dixen que non se me tomase por chufón.

Monsieur de Nancy procurou na caixiña unha toma de rapé, e esta vez sen ofrecer, que quizaves non lle quedase, ou estivese tan embeito nas rafegadas da súa vida que se lle fose, sorbeu en tres tempos, e co pano na man atendeu ao espurro. Veulle este moi cómodo e espaciado, e limpouse, pasando tamén o pano pola cachola, coma se suase: costumes que sempre quedan da vida.

– Tiña eu, contando a ollo, sobre dezasete anos, e axiña me puxera garboso, cando unha mañá amenceu na taberna un que parecía gran señor, que viña na posta de Lyon con dous criados, e presentouse coma substituto en Lorena de meu tío, o irmán de meu pai Colet, a quen, no entretanto, ensináranme a chamarlle putativo un sancristán das terciarias clarisas de Santa Leocadia. O novo monsieur de Nancy traíalle a meu pai Colet un reloxo de prata, un bastón estoque e a lámina cos nós das forcas reais, debuxo este de moito tento, e co que meu señor tío, que tamén digo sería putativo, gañara o emprego, e que cun can que se chamaba Mistère, e doce libras flamengas que estaban emprestadas a unha condesa sobre dun aviso que lle viña de Pondichery das Indias, era toda a herdanza que quedaba libre de empeños. Chorou Colet, que sempre se chora máis a gusto nas familias polos que chegaron alto, e non viu reparo en que me fose eu co novo monsieur a Nancy, canto por estar a carón da condesa devandita cando lle chegasen cartos frescos, canto porque o señor verdugo, que era home moi cortesán, me aseguraba de aprendiz remunerado. Axiña puido descansar en min, que o máis do tempo el gustaba de pasalo lendo o Gil Blas e calcetando medias, e saíanlle moi medidas, con gracias de flores e paxariños bordados, e por aquel tempo, e co gallo dunhas sospeitas duns velenos houbo moito traballo, e eu aprendín o oficio moi livián, e admiráronse dende o primeiro día do solto que andaba para o público na trabada, e aplaudiuse moito unha invención na que din, que cunha cana de Malaca afumada que me dera por galano a condesa do aviso dos cartos, libraba o ferro da trampa, namentres miraba para o ceo, e sen quebrar cintura. Amoloume algo meu amo, que me puxo de mentecato vaidoso. Eu ía pola casa da condesa das doce libras flamengas, e véndome tan feliz en facer os nós da lámina de meu tío, e máis outros que eu inventaba, pedíame que llos ensaiase nas súas roupas menores, xa fose enagua, corsé, xustillo bomba e todo o máis que vai por embaixo e se aperte con cordón ou fita; axudaba, pois, a vestir á condesa, que era gorda e apeitugada, moi branca, e tiña moitas cóxegas, e usado para vestila, axiña pasei a ser usado para espila, que para que houbese que chamarme a altas horas adobiaba eu uns nós que ninguén sabía desfacer. Adoeceu daquela monsieur de Nancy dunha tos escatimada, e non podía deixar o leito, no que pasaba grandes apuros de hipo e flegma. Cando finou, sen máis quedei titulado no seu posto. ¡Cando saín da Cámara de coller as testemuñais, dei gracias a Deus que en tan pouco tempo, e tan solazadamentes, me tiña feito un home de proveito!

Ficou monsieur de Nancy un algo pensativo, e tendendo a man esquerda á luzada do farol, buscando nela, comentou:

– Do anel de ferro coas armas lorenesas que me deron, quedoume algo orinado un ósiño deste dedo.

O escribán de Dorne foi o único que se interesou por aquel enferruxe, advertindo que el nunca levara nos seus dedos nada que non fose de ouro contrastado.

– Eu, polo meu oficio, señor escribán, viña obrigado. Pasei a vivir nunha casiña na praza da Lanterna, e non téndolle chegado á señora condesa, naqueles catro anos derradeiros, o aviso dos cartos de Pondichery de Indias, non viu inconveniencia ningunha en vir comigo de ama de chaves, que de casarme, como me pedía, non lle quixen ouvir ren, porque era moi dominante no trato. ¡Tamén se chego a presentarme no tapadiño do peinador marsellés de condés alcuñado, preguntando pola Blanca, que era miña nai, non habería pouco alborozo! Pero todo o sosego en que eu estaba na miña casa, herdado, para máis, do defunto Colet, dito Caldeiro, torceuse axiña. El foi que colleron en Bar-le-Duc a un que dicían que era o Xudeu Errante, o que se soubo porque levaba moedas de Nerón na bolsa, pintado todo o corpo con letras de cábala, e nunha grande caixa traía cousas para empregos secretos: un espello co que se podía falar en lingua hebraica polas noites, e esto atestouno un prelado que veu de París nunha mula xorda, moi regalada de paso e que se chamaba Catalina; unha tesoura coa que habería que cortarlle a perrera ao derradeiro rei que houbese en Francia, o que era grande traizón presuposta, porque con esto dicíase que a Coroa acababa, e tiña a tesoura unha seña que dicía Fun de Xudas Iscariote, e tamén traía candeas que se acendían soas, e bálsamos penetrantes para facer ouro a escuso. Todo foi mui propalado. Colleron, digo, ao Xudeu Errante e pasou as cuestións da auga, do lume e da mancorda, e declarou moi pintados os seus crimes, tal e tal, e que pasaba anos sen comer nin beber, que andaba vintesete leguas nun día e que poñendo o ollo do cu nunha parede, baixadas as bragas, ouvía o que pasaba nas casas. Esto, coido eu, foi o que máis anoxou aos señores de Lorena, porque daba o acusado señas de todos eles en panos menores, e se tiñan pezas de quita e pon. A forca, pois, víñalle como anel ao dedo, e após de aforcalo, aínda, por traizón a El-Rei, había partilo en catro. Pero esto derradeiro – engadiu monsieur con noxo – non era cousa miña.

– Pois é oficio de patente real coma outro calquera – dixo o escribán.

– En Ruán asubiábales aos cabalos, cando partían a algún por tiro, o señor vizconde de Kerjean, e a familia do morto tiña por fineza que este cabaleiro acudise.

Sempre o regalaban – atestou Coulaincourt de Bayeux.

– Eu estaba no meu – proseguiu Nancy –. Foi que catro días denantes do aforcamento veu unha señora de visita á nosa casa, tratando de quitar a Ashavero daquel compromiso, pagando en ouro contante o cambialo por outro, e xa pensara nun bohemio que tiña un falcón, co que andaba por Borgoña e Lorena gañando a vida, que o ceibaba para cazar pombas de trapos que colgaba en veledas, e que durmía, bébedo sempre, baixo a ponte de Brille. El, como á miña marquesa non lle viñan avisos de Pondichery de Indias, e coa filosofía que daquela se falaba xa se vía que se acercaban anos de escaseza para as miñas mañas, e xa se murmuraba dun médico que inventara unha grande coitela que caía con moita gravidade sobre do pescozo do penado, deixeime tentar do saquetiño de ouro, que mo botaban mesmo cantando na miña mesa.

– ¿E el en qué viña? – perguntou curioso o escribán.

– En doblas de Hungría, que é moeda que non admite desprezo. Todo saíu do mellor: merquei a un sarxento da policía, e unha noite de farra na garda do castelo, a conta do meu bolsillín, puxemos ao bohemio onde estaba Ashavero, que despoixas das cuestións en que se probara xa non era coñecido, nin de carnes nin de cor, e veu a mañanciña da xustiza e sacámo-lo bohemio para a praza grande, cunha caperuza cubríndolle a cara, e era de pano merino, e é franqueza que teñen en Lorena os que morren na forca, pagando, eso si, por ela ao verdugo. E xa colgaba morto o bohemio, cando se amosou voando na praza, que estaba menos que mediada de xente pola chuvia, o falcón do bohemio, do que nos tiñamos esquecido, e foise para onde se abaneaba seu amo, e dunha agarrada quitoulle a caperuza, e voou con ela. Outros bohemios estaban ao pé da forca por mercar en poxa as roupas do defunto, e coñeceron ao seu nacional, que estaba alí de randeeira, e botáronse a berrar a trampa, e aínda que a min me gardaban os granadeiros do Real Auvernia, acertáronme cun coitelo na caluga, e afociñei contra o chan. Estaba morto... O meu traballo é que teño de andar por aí deica ese Ashavero pase a Roma, onde vai poñer unha tenda de espellos, e el non é o propio Xudeu Errante, senón un curmán del, que era afiador de fouciños en Jericó e tíñalle emprestado uns cartos, e anda tralo Xudeu Errante verdadeiro, e cada sete anos descansa outros sete, máis que nada para botar a conta do montante de capital e réditos, nos que é moi relixioso. Cando pase a Roma, que será para o ano que vén, eu poderei volver á miña cova, pero por agora teño de servirlle de testemuña co Xudeu Errante de que este é o curmán, e que non foi aforcado en Nancy, que o verdadeiro Ashavero está en que si, que o foi, e que xa a débeda vai remitida. O meu afiador é un home moi cumprido. Sáeme aos camiños e dáme saquetadiñas de rapé de Lyon. Eu sempre fun moi palaciano de trato, e ando amolado agora, que é sabido que os verdugos, en canto morren, teñen veda de rir. ¡Quen mo ía dicir a min, este prohibitus, co tentado que eu era da risa nas outras alamedas da vida!

From The Choirmaster's Chronicles, *1956*

The story that I'm going to tell – Monsieur de Nancy began, standing up, and he was a weak, nervous skeleton –, it wouldn't be quite right that Madame de Saint-Vaast heard some of his comments, if she were alive, but it doesn't matter because she's dead, as I won't do her any harm with my news and neither is it true that I'm mocking her with what I'm going to tell about my adolescence, about erotic warfare. My mother, who had arrived at Dijon from the Baune Hospice, worked mending underpants for the Capuchins in Saint-Maximien, after several love affairs, ended up as a prostitute in a brothel in disguise that a hairdresser from Marseilles had in the town behind a butcher's shop. I was born, and nobody knows who my father was, as at that time my mother didn't have a regular lover, and the hairdresser from Marseilles said that I was the son of some poor tramp, but she insisted that I must be the son of some old innkeeper who had arrived there one rainy night at sundown, and moreover had lost a two-tiered cape, and my mother supposed so because from that day on she had had, if you'll excuse me, a suffocating sensation in the evenings, with dizziness, so that she realized that she was pregnant. The innkeeper, if he were only a wine drinker or young, perhaps wouldn't figure in the documents that certified that he was my father, almost legalized, but as he liked liquor and other stuff, he was an old fogey, and his wife left him for a corporal in the dragoons from Metz, arguing that he didn't carry out his conjugal duties...

– That in Lorraine is a justified cause – the scribe from Dorne remarked –. With the permission of the audience, the Roman text says: *Nox plaena in hebdomada*, that can be translated as "once a week" at least.

– The innkeeper, I say – the executioner from Lorraine continued –, found it easy to believe in his own merit which caused my conception on an Autumn evening and with so little alarm, and said yes, it was him, and he even recognized that I had the same hair so dark and thick, very like a brother he had that had occupied a post that had belonged to Monsieur de Nancy, for nine years, paid by Lorraine, and was very much respected for being a character, for when he hung someone in the square, he always made signs to his acquaintances from the gallows and a joke now and then for the aristocratic ladies. As my mother had found a good catch in a German travelling salesman, who went around showing the novelty of a blind lantern in the towns in Burgundy, she left me in the inn with the innkeeper, I haven't said yet that he was called Colet, nicknamed Tin, who brought me up quickly, adding fuel to my milk bottle with a third part of red wine and mixing in a poor imitation of moscatels in my baby food, and he put me up on the barrel of liquor from Besançon, and showed me to the customers, taking down my knickers, shouting: Hasn't my beauty got a pistol?" This caused a lot of laughs, and so Colet, alias Tin, took advantage of this to show, through my privates, that he hadn't been such a eunuch as his wife had made out, as there was that which I had inherited from him, and that couldn't have come from nowhere. And it's because of this anecdote that I said earlier that I shouldn't be taken for vain.

Monsieur de Nancy looked for a dose of snuff in his snuff box, and this time without offering any, because maybe he had none left, or he was so absorbed in his memories that he forgot; he sniffed three times and with his handkerchief in his hand he waited to for the sneezes to come. These came very comfortably and with intervals between, and he cleaned his nose, wiping his head with the handkerchief as well as if he were sweating: customs which always remain with one in life.

I was, more or less, seventeen, and had become a dashing boy, when one morning someone appeared in the inn who seemed to be an important gentleman. He had come in the coach from Lyon with two servants, and introduced himself as my uncle's replacement in Lorraine, that is the brother of my father Colet who, meanwhile, a sacristan of the Poor Clares in Santa Leocadia had taught me to call a putative father. The new Monsieur de Nancy brought my father a silver watch, a sword stick and a picture of the different knots in the king's nooses, a drawing which was very well-done and with which my dear uncle, whom I also call putative, had earned his living, and, with a dog called Mistère, and with twelve Flemish pounds that were loaned to a Countess through a notice that came from Pondichery of the Indies, was all the inheritance he had that was not pawned. Colet cried because one always cries better in one's family for the winners and he didn't see any problem in my going to Nancy with the new Monsieur, as much for being with the before-mentioned Countess when the fresh money arrived as because the honourable executioner, who was a very highly-connected man, found me a paid apprenticeship. He could rely on me immediately because he liked to spend most of his time reading Gil Blas and knitting stockings, and he made them well, with flower decorations and embroidered birdies; and at that time, because of the suspicion of some poisonings, there was lots of work, and I learnt the trade very quickly and from the first day everybody was impressed by my confidence on the scaffold, and they applauded an invention of mine very much, as with a blackened Malaca rod, that the Countess of the money had given me as a present, I let go of the iron in the trap door, while I looked at the sky without having to bend down. My boss annoyed me a bit because he called me a vain idiot. I used to go to the house of the Countess of the twelve Flemish pounds and, seeing that I was so happy making the knots in my uncle's pictures and others that I invented, she asked me to try them out in her underclothes, in her petticoat, in her corset, her vest and everything else that goes under and that is tied with laces or ribbons; so I helped to dress the Countess, who was fat and busty, very white, and very ticklesome, and as I served to dress her, I soon served to undress her, well, so that she had to call me in the small hours, I prepared some knots that nobody knew how to untie. At that time Monsieur de Nancy became sick with a bad cough, and he was confined to bed where he had attacks of hiccoughs and was choked with phlegm. Without more ado I took over his job when he died. When I left the courthouse after collecting my credentials, I gave thanks to God that in so little time, and so happily, I had become a successful man!

Monsieur de Nancy became a bit thoughtful and, extending his left hand towards the light of the lamp, looking at the former, he commented:

– Because of the iron ring with the arms from Lorraine which they gave me, a little bone in this finger is a bit rusty.

The scribe from Dorne was the only person interested in that rust, claiming that he never wore anything that was not pure gold on his fingers.

– I, Mr. Scribe, was forced to do it in my profession. I went to live in a little house in Lamp Place and, as the notice of the money from Pondichery of the Indies hadn't come to the Countess in the previous four years, she didn't see any harm in coming to work for me as a housekeeper, because I didn't want to hear anything about marrying her, as she asked me, because she was very dominant. And if I were to go to the brothel in disguise that belonged to the hairdresser from Marseilles as a Count, asking for Blanca, who was my mother, wouldn't there be a flutter! But all the tranquility I had at home that came to me from the deceased Colet, alias Tin, came to an end. It happened that they trapped in Bar-le-Duc one who said he was the Wandering Jew, which was clear because he had coins from Nero's time in his pockets, all his body was painted with letters from the cabala and in a big box he had things for secret uses: a mirror with which one could speak Hebrew at night, and a prelate who came from Paris on a deaf donkey testified to this, and a very pleasant donkey it was who was called Catalina; a scissors with which one had to cut the fringe of the last king that there was in France, which was supposed to be great treason, because it was said that if this was done there would be an end of the monarchy, and the scissors had marks which said "I belonged to Judas Iscariot"; and he also had candles which lit up by themselves and penetrating balsams to make gold in secret. It was the talk of the town. They trapped, as I was saying, the Wandering Jew and he was made to undergo the tests of water, fire and the rack and he confessed to his crimes with all sorts of details, this and that, that he had lived whole years without eating or drinking, that he had walked twenty-seven leagues in one day and that, his hole against a wall, with his underpants down, he heard what was going on inside. This, I think, was what most annoyed the Lorraine gentlemen, because the accused gave information about them in their underwear, and that they had members which could be taken on and off. The rope, therefore, fitted him like a glove and after hanging him for treason to the king, he still had to be quartered. But this last – Monsieur added with disgust – had nothing to do with me.

– Well, that's a profession with a royal licence like any other – the scribe said.

In Rouen the Viscount de Kerjean whistled at the horses to tear someone to pieces, and the dead man's family thought it a privilege that this man came. They always gave him presents – Coulaincourt de Bayeux declared.

– I stuck to what I knew – Nancy continued –. It happened that four days before the hanging a woman came to visit our house, trying to free Ahasuer from that difficult situation, paying gold in cash to change him for another, and she had thought of a bohemian with a falcon, with which he went around Burgundy and Lorraine to make a living, so he released it to hunt pigeons made of rags that he hung on weather vanes, and he slept, always drunk, under the bridge at Brille. As no news came to my Marquess from Pondichery of the Indies, and because of the philosophical talk which was then popular I saw that lean years were coming for my skill, and as it was rumoured that a doctor had invented a big knife that fell heavily on the prisoner's neck, I allowed myself to be tempted by the little bag of gold which they threw on my table, almost singing.

– And what coins were used? – the scribe asked with curiosity.

– Hungarian doubloons which is money not to be spitted at. Everything worked out perfectly: I bought a sergeant in the police, and one night when the guard on the castle was on the binge, in exchange for the little bag, we put the bohemian in Ahasuer's place who, after the trials to which he had been submitted, was not recognizable, neither in flesh nor in colour, and the morning of the hanging came and we took the bohemian out to the big square with a hood over his head, and it was made of merino wool, and it is a privilege for those who are hung in Lorraine, paying the hangman for it, of course. And the bohemian was already hanging dead when, flying into the square, which was only half full due to the rain, came the bohemian's falcon, which we had forgotten about, and he went to where his master was swinging and with his claw he pulled off his hood and flew away with it. Other bohemians were at the foot of the scaffold raffling the dead man's clothes, and they recognized their fellow countryman who was swinging there, and they started to shout out the trick, and although the grenadiers from the Royal Auvergne protected me, they got me with a knife in the back of the neck, and I fell flat on the ground. I was dead… My job is that I have to go from here to there until that Ahasuer goes to Rome, where he will open a shop which will sell mirrors, and he isn't the real Wandering Jew, but his cousin, who was a grinder of sickles in Jerico and he had lent him some money, and he was after the true Wandering Jew, and every seven years he rests another seven with the idea of calculating the amount of the interest, about which he is meticulous. When he gets to Rome, which will be next year, I'll be able to go back to my grave, but for now I have to bear testimony to the Wandering Jew that he is his cousin, and that he wasn't hung in Nancy, well, the real Ahasuer thinks he was, and the debt has been cancelled. My grinder is a very urbane man. He meets me on the road and he gives me little bags of snuff from Lyon. I have always been very polite, and I'm annoyed now, well, it is well-known that the hangman, when he dies, is forbidden to laugh. Who would have told me about this prohibitus, with my great inclination always to laugh in all walks of life!

From Escola de menciñeiros (School of Bonesetters), *1960*

Melle de Loboso

Un tal Melle, veciño de Loboso, partido de Mondoñedo, decidiu cando xa cumprira setenta anos, aprender a ler e a escribir, e en menos dun mes o mestre houbo de dalo por útil. Ós que lle preguntaban a qué viña tomarse aquel traballo ós seus anos, contestaba que ó mellor podía mandar algún recado dende o outro mundo, e entón sempre sería mellor por escrito que de palabra. Para que non houbese dúbida de que era el quen mandaba novas, deixaría denantes de morrer unha amosa de letra en papel de barba. E mandou Melle que cando morrese, que lle meteran no peto da chaqueta papel, sobres, e lapis tinta.

Loboso é o máis alto de Pastoriza, e fai honra ó nome: montes avesíos, xesteiras ata carón das casas, hortas pobres, folgados costentos nos que malmedra o centeo, brañas isoladas e o lobo vagante. A xente de Loboso é alta e roiba, e o pelo dourado das mozas é a única flor en toda aquela soidade.

Finou Melle, e enterrárono co recado de escribir que pedira, e o lapis tinta afiado polos dous cabos, e aínda lle meteron no peto unha navalliña por se quebraba puntas, que apertaba moito ó escribir... Pasou o tempo e non chegaba recado ningún de Melle e a xente de Loboso íase esquecendo da ocorrencia. Pasaron dous longos invernos e dous ledos e pequenos veráns. Un sobriño de Melle, por Pascua, mercou na feira de Meira un par de galiñas, unha negra castelá e outra do pescozo pelado, e ó soltalas na eira miroulles o ovo, e esta derradeira viña con el na punta, tanto que o puxo deloutro día, cediño, e cacarexouno ben. Era un ovo longo, longo, coa casca mourenta e manchada. O sobriño de Melle pensou que traería dúas xemas, e antollóuselle de almorzo unha torreznada, e cando xa se engurraban os liscos na tixola, partiu o ovo nun prato para batelo, e o ovo, por dedentro, estaba baleiro de clara e xema, e soamente gardaba un sobre, no que estaba escrito con letra de lapistinta – letra comprobada do finado Melle – esto: "Amañai la chimenea. Tu tío que lo es Vitoriano Melle." E so o nome, un solemne rubricado. E ben se vía que o Melle tiña mollado a punta do lapis máis de dúas veces escribindo o recado.

Deu a nova o sobriño a voces, acudiron os veciños e foi lido cen veces o sobre. Cando o sobriño foi ó galiñeiro a busca-la galiña do pescozo pelado, atopouna morta. E o aviso do finado chegara a tempo se fora atendido, que dúas noites despois un vendaval que viña tolo, levou a cheminea dos Melle.

E isto é todo. Os Melle de Loboso conservan a carta do tío. Hai veciños de seu que din que inda recibiron outras, e todas por ovos ou camiños máis secretos aínda, pero que esas cartas non as amosan porque tratan de intereses e consellos en preitos.

Melle from Loboso

A certain Melle, from Loboso, in Mondoñedo, decided, when he was sixty years old, to learn to read and write, and in less than a month the schoolmaster had to give him a pass. To those who asked him why he took on this task at his age he answered that maybe he could send some message from the other world and so it would always be better in writing rather than spoken. So that there would be no doubt that it was he who sent the messages, he was going to leave a sample of his handwriting on handmade paper before death. And Melle ordered that, when he died, paper, envelopes and a pencil be put in the pocket of his jacket.

Loboso is the highest part of Pastoriza, and it lives up to its name: sombre mountains, broom right up to the houses, meagre orchards, sloping meadows in which stunted rye grows, isolated sodden pastures and the wandering wolf. The people from Loboso are tall and fair, and the golden hair of the girls is the only flower in all that solitude.

Melle died, and they buried him with the writing utensils which he had asked for, and the pencil sharpened at both ends, and they even put in his pocket a little knife in case he broke the point because he leaned heavily when he wrote … Time passed and no message came from Melle and the people from Loboso started to forget about his idea. Two long winters passed by and two happy, short summers. At Easter, a nephew of Melle's bought a couple of hens in the Meira fair, one was a Castilian black and the other had no feathers on her throat, and on releasing them he looked at their eggs, and the latter came with it almost coming out, so much so that she laid it early the next day, she announced it well. It was a long, long egg, with a brown, speckled shell. Melle's nephew thought it would have two yolks and took a fancy to having it with bacon for his breakfast and when the slices were curling in the frying pan, he broke the egg in a plate to beat it, and the egg, inside, was empty of white and yolk and there was only an envelope there, on which there was this written in pencil – handwriting which the nephew checked out as being the same as the deceased Melle's –: "Fix the chimney. Your uncle, sincerely, Vitoriano Melle". And only the name, a solemn paraph. One could see well that old Melle had wet the point of the pencil more than twice writing the message.

The nephew shouted the news, the neighbours arrived and the envelope was read a hundred times. When the nephew went to the henhouse to get the hen with no feathers on her throat, he found her dead. The dead man's warning would have come in time if it had been attended to, as two nights later a mad wind took off Melles' chimney.

And that's all. The Melles from Loboso keep the uncle's letter. There are neighbours that say that they received more later on and all of them through eggs or even more secret ways, but they don't show those letters because they deal with interests in or advice on lawsuits.

From Xente de aquí e de acolá (People from Here and There), 1971

Louredo de Hostes

A Louredo coñecino, como a tanta outra xente, na barbería do meu amigo Pallarego. Podía eu contar moitas cousas de Louredo, pero o que me interesa agora é o caso dos seus anteollos, mercados en Valencia na praza ou na rúa de Jaume I. Pasaba que Louredo non soñaba. Facía o servicio militar no rexemento de cabaleiría da Raíña Victoria Eugenia, e tiña un sarxento que tódalas mañás formaba o escuadrón e contáballes aos soldados o que soñara aquela noite. ¡Que tío soñando! As máis das veces soñaba unha viaxe ás Filipinas, ou que lle tocaba a lotería e deixaba o exército e ía a Madrid, e estaba sentado nun teatro. E contaba o asunto da peza que representaban, con moita moza guapa, e denantes de que caese o pano chamábano para que subise ao escenario, e subía de uniforme de gala, con morrión, e levaba á primeira actriz aos baños de Archena, de onde era natural. Louredo doíase de non soñar. Nin coa súa aldea nin coa romaría de Santa Mariña. Como era mediano de estatura e pernas tortas e un ollo manchado, o que lle gustaría soñar é que era alto, e que se chiflaba por el unha valenciana, alta, branca, os ollos mouros, que se deixaba quedar coma as galiñas, e Louredo aloumiñaría nela moi afinado. Louredo, respectuoso, foise onda o sarxento Granero.

– Con permiso, mi sargento. ¿Que hay que hacer para soñar?

– ¡Cómprate unos anteojos, gallego!, respondeulle, burlón.

Louredo tomou a resposta moi a serio, e non parou ata atopar en Valencia quen lle vendese uns anteollos para soñar, uns anteollos que Louredo dicía que eran nubrados, cunha armazón de prata. A primeira noite que durmiu con eles postos, soñou unha película enteira, pero tan rápido todo, que non entendeu o asunto. A única cousa que lle quedou gravada foi que el saía de cabo, e que unha señora gorda lle daba un caramelo de café con leite.

– ¿Guapa ou fea?, preguntáballe eu.

– Home, para se-la primeira vez que soñei unha muller, aínda saía ben decente, cunha blusa colorada.

Dende aquela, con tal de durmir cos anteollos postos, Louredo soñaba tódolos días, e grandes triunfos, cunha pequena que bailaba, e cunha negra que tiña un canario nunha gaiola, e regalábanlle o cabalo mellor do rexemento. Todo ía ben, menos cando xantaba sandía, que entón soñaba que subía a un tellado, e arrempuxábano e caía á rúa... Morreu solteiro e deixóulle-los anteollos aos sobriños, para que soñasen por turno. Os sobriños ríanse do tío e deixáronlle ao señor cura de Baroncelle que levase para a rectoral os anteollos. ¡Sabe Deus o que soñaría o reverendo don Daniel Pernas Nieto coa axuda deles, qué valencianas brancas, qué viños tintos, qué troitadas, qué festas, naquelas longas e frías noites de inverno, cando acinsan coa xeada as ponlas núas das bidueiras!

Louredo from Hostes

I met Louredo, like many other people, in my friend Pallarego's barber's shop. I could tell many things about Louredo, but what interests me now is the story about his glasses, bought in Valencia in Jaume I Place or Street. It happened that Louredo didn't dream. He was doing his military service in the cavalry regiment of Queen Victoria Eugenia, and he had a sergeant that every morning lined up the soldiers and told them what he had dreamed the night before. What a fellow for dreaming! Most of the times he dreamed about a trip to the Philippines, or that he won the lottery and left the army and went to Madrid, and that he was sitting in a theatre. And he described the play that was on, with a lot of pretty girls, and before the curtain came down they called him to come up on stage, and he went up wearing his dress uniform, with his shako, and he took the leading actress to the spa in

Archena, where he was from. Louredo was sorry that he couldn't dream. Not about his home village nor about the festivities at Santa Mariña. As he was of middling height with short legs and with a fleck in his eye, what he would like to dream was that he was tall, and that a tall, white, dark-eyed girl from Valencia was crazy about him, and let herself be loved like hens do, and Louredo would caress her very skilfully. Louredo, respectfully, spoke to Sergeant Granero.

– If I may, Sergeant. What do you have to do to dream?

– Buy some glasses, Galician! , he answered sarcastically.

Louredo took the answer very seriously, and he didn't stop until he found someone in Valencia who would sell him glasses that would make him dream, glasses that Louredo said were cloudy, with silver frames. The first night that he slept with them on he dreamed a whole film, but everything went so fast that he didn't understand anything. The only thing that he was sure of was that he was in it from beginning to end, and that a fat lady gave him a coffee sweet.

– Was she good-looking or ugly?, I asked him.

– Well, as it was the first time I dreamed about a woman, she turned out fairly all right, with a coloured blouse.

From then on, if he slept with his glasses on, Louredo dreamed every day, and dreamed about great triumphs, about a little girl that danced, about a black woman with a canary in a cage, and about how they gave him the best horse in the regiment. Everything was fine, except when he ate watermelon, because then he dreamed that he went up on a roof and that he was pushed and fell into the street below… He died a bachelor and left his glasses to his nephews, so that they could dream by turns. The nephews laughed at their uncle, and they allowed the priest at Baroncelle to take the glasses to the presbytery. God knows what Reverend Daniel Pernas Nieto dreamed with their help, about what white girls from Valencia, what red wines, what feast of trouts, what parties, in those long, cold winter nights, when the naked branches of the birches turn the colour of ashes because of the frost!

From Cantiga nova que se chama ribeira (New Lay Called Waterside), *1933*

Hai unha illa louvada...

Hai unha illa louvada
alá no fondal do mar.
Ten bois da color do tempo
e pastoras de cristal.

Ten un río de paxaros
que desemboca en canción.
Paxaros mornos de illa
con os seus niños no sol.

Ten lúa nova e crecente
e ollos pra dicir iai la!
A boca tena pechada
para vendimas de sal.

E ten un cabelo novo,
iai, amor! qué pelo ten.
Cheiro profundo de alga
e sabor limpo de mel.

There is a much-praised island...

There is a much-praised island
down in the depths of the sea.
It has oxen the colour of time
and crystal shepherdesses.

It has a river of birds
that flows into song.
warm island birds
with their nests in the sun.

It has a new waxing moon
and eyes for saying La, la!
It keeps its mouth closed
for grape harvests of salt.

And it has new hair,
oh, my love! what hair it has.
Deep smell of seaweed
and clean taste of honey.

Se miña señor á alba da Arousa bailar...

Se miña señor á alba da Arousa bailar
poñereille, belida, un ventiño no mar.
¡A dorna vai e vén
que meu amor ten!

Poñereille unha frauta e mais un reiseñor
e unha longa soidade coma a do mar maior.
¡A dorna vai e vén
que meu amor ten!

Na illa Cortegada poñereille un galán
por pastor das mareas co seu remo na man.
¡A dorna vai e vén
que meu amor ten!

Poñereille unha gaita no bico da ría
e unha abelaneira no medio do día.
¡A dorna vai e vén
que meu amor ten!

If my lady dances at the dawn of Arousa Isle...

If my lady dances at the dawn of Arousa Isle
I will give her, that lovely one, a breeze on the sea.
The little boat comes and goes
carrying my love!

I will give her a flute and a nightingale
and a long solitude like that of the Great Sea.
The little boat comes and goes
carrying my love!

On Cortegada Island I will give her a gallant
as a shepherd of the tides with his oar in his hand.
The little boat comes and goes
carrying my love!

I will give her bagpipes in the mouth of the bay
and a hazel-bush in the middle of the day.
The little boat comes and goes
carrying my love!

From Dona do corpo delgado (Lady with the Slender Body), *1950*

Derradeira elexía a Manoel Antonio

Diríamos que pedra para a túa fronte fría
– para a túa alma mar e vento duro.
Ti si poeta, fenecido de algas verdes
o teu único corpo, silencioso e breve.

Agora escoita aí, nese outro lado,
onde ás mareas e a Deus e á sombra toda
coma o Norés se repite, fondo estraño,
viaxeiro antergo, gaivota no teu sangue.

Nós non choramos. Finamentes tristes
desconsolado ouvido inacabábel somos.

Last elegy to Manoel Antonio

We would say stone for your cold brow
– for your soul sea and harsh wind.
True poet you, dead from green seaweed
your only body, silent and brief.

Now listen there, on that other side
near the tides and God and all shadow,
how the Northeaster blows again, strange depths,
ancient traveller, seagull in your blood.

We do not weep. Delicately sad,
we are a disconsolate interminable ear.

Rondeau das señoras donas pintadas no ouso do Vilar...

Rondeau das señoras donas pintadas no ouso do Vilar,
no século XIV, cheirando unha flor

LE VERSE

Ese vento de seda é o tempo que pasa.
¿Soñades a doce primavera de antano
nesa flor que reflexa o seu van no negro pozo dos vosos ollos?

Le temps s'en va!

– Esas bolboretas que abanan a raiola do sol
son as súas toucas cobixando as pálidas frontes.
¿Soñaredes aínda no ouso do Vilar os soñares do tempo pasado?

Le temps s'en va!

¡Ese enorme silencio cristalino e dourado!
Se vós agora falardes, miñas donas amigas,
¿a vosa voz enchería, como unha fonte de agua, o vaso do silencio?

Le temps s'en va!

¡Ei, donas do Vilar! Erguede os finos rostros e sorride,
que andan galáns de corte con saudades de vós!
Agás que prefirades velos morrer de amor.

Le temps s'en va.
Le temps s'en va,
mes dames!

L'ENVOI

De tódolos amores o voso amor escollo:
Miñas donas Giocondas, en vós ollo
tódalas damas que foron no país,
unhas brancas camelias, outras flores de lis.

Le temps s'en va! Ou dádesme ese bico
que cheira a rosas de abril do Mil e Pico
ou finarei chorando na miña soedá,
namentres envellezo: Le temps, le temps s'en va!

Rondeau of the fine ladies painted in the apse of the church of O Vilar...

Rondeau of the fine ladies painted in the apse of the church of O Vilar in the fourteenth century, smelling a flower

LE VERSE

That silken wind is time passing.
Do you dream of the sweet spring of yesteryear
in that flower that reflects its waist in the black well of your eyes?

Le temps s'en va!

'Those butterflies that fan the sunbeam
are their headdresses sheltering their pale foreheads.'
Might you still be dreaming, in the apse of O Vilar, the dreams of
times past?

Le temps s'en va!

That vast silence, crystalline and golden!
If you spoke now, my ladies, my friends,
would your voices fill, like a fountain of water, the glass of silence?

Le temps s'en va!

Hey, ladies of O Vilar! Raise your delicate faces and smile,
for gallants at court have sadlongings for you!
Unless you prefer to see them die of love.

Le temps s'en va.
Le temps s'en va,
mes dames!

L'ENVOI

Of all loves I choose your love:
My ladies, Giacondas, in you I see
all the ladies there have been in this country,
some white camellias, others fleurs-de-lys.

Le temps s'en va! Either you give me that kiss
that smells of April roses of the year one thousand odd
or I die weeping in my solitude,
as I grow old: Le temps, le temps s'en va!

From Herba aquí ou acolá (Grass Here Or There), *1980*

Ricorditi di me

Siena mi fe. Pro non da pedra súa
nin do seu aire frío nin da súa luz.
Fíxome do semen que se amosaba aos ollos
dos que abrían de golpe as fiestras para ollarme.
As súas olladas ían e viñan polo meu corpo
como o rulo sobre da masa de pan, á que afina.

Disfemmi la Maremma. Púxome Nello dei Paganelli
na punta dun coitelo, coidando que eu non era virxe.
E érao, aínda que luxada pola cobiza
dos sieneses ollos virís.
Cortado fun antes de tempo,
eu que quixen ser lirio e pasei por puta
e o que sabía de bicar era por libro.
Nello foise, co falcón na luva,
sen agardar a que cantase a rula.

Ricorditi di me

Siena mi fe. But not its stone
nor its cold air nor its light.
It made me from the semen that showed itself in the eyes
of the men who used to throw windows open to stare at me.
Their stares passed to and fro over my body
like the turtle-dove over pastry on which it has set its sights.

Disfecemi Maremma. Nello dei Paganelli had me
at the tip of a knife, thinking I was not a virgin.
And I was one, even though sullied by the lust
of virile Siennese eyes.
I was cut too soon,
I who wanted to be a lily and was taken for a whore,
when what I knew about kissing came from books.
Nello went away, his falcon on his glove,

not waiting for the she-dove to sing.

O poeta escolle abril

De quen fuximos? Quizabes, dime, a cinza
non rexeita a garrida mocidade e o sangue?
En abril e maio non hai cinza, dicen.
Fiquemos, amigo, sob das azas de abril.

Que fuxan o río, a rosa colorada,
beba deica o final a chama a estela, o titaque o reló,
procuren un lonxe ou un ningures os camiños onde morrer.
Á par que foxe, leve o río o cadáver de Ofelia e as margaridas da ribeira.

Pro nós, amor, temos os cans fieis das verbas.
Dicimos cinza e é po agora mesmo o que foi chama.
Ofelia, dis, e un sorriso alerta a túa memoria
e os ollos teus, rula, nena e suave terciopelo.

Temos a verba, amor, para dicir: abril.
Sob as súas azas florecerán os días.

The poet chooses April

What are we fleeing from? Tell me, does not ash, perchance,
reject resplendent youth and blood?
In April and May there is no ash, they say.
Let us remain, my friend, under the wings of April.

Let the river flee, and the red rose too,
let the star drink its flame to the last, the clock its tick-tock,
let the paths look for a far away or a nowhere in which to die.
As it flees, let the river carry off Ophelia's corpse and the daisies on
                                             the bank.

But we, my love, have words, those faithful dogs.
We say ash and what was flame at once is dust.
Ophelia, you say, and a smile alerts your memory
and your eyes, my dove, girl and soft velvet.

We have the word, my love, to say: April.
Under its wings the days will flower.

Alma, coma no concerto

Alma miña, coma no concerto de Vivaldi
con violino principale e altro violino per eco,
eu quixera que foses
esa voz que in lontano
dende os outeiros eternos devólvenos
a canción de cada día.

Vas camiñando atente
deica chegar onde o violín dá o eco
pro sempre está máis lonxe
dos teus pasos e dos camiños,
– da túa vida, do que ti recordas
das primaveras e das mortes
e dunha muller preñada acobadada nunha cancela
mirando sen ver pra unha lagoa verde.
¡Como viaxar a Carcasona!

Ata que te decatas
de que o violín que dá o eco in lontano
eres ti mesmo, entón a vida
coma un pano bordado téndese diante de ti,
escoitas o vento e a túa voz de neno
o canso tusir da nai, as andoriñas que retornan
e as primeiras verbas de amor, e aquel verso
no que dabas a alma vestida de violetas
pechando os ollos por se te morrías
diante dun espello polo que ía e viña
unha sorrisa
e agora xa sabes
por un eco lonxano
en que perdiche a vida sen saber que a vida
xa non volve, nunca, endexamais.
A vida mesmo é o eco dun soño
que agora sabes que o tiveches, por un eco.

O soul of mine: as in the concerto

O soul of mine: as in the concerto by Vivaldi
con violino principale e altro violino per eco,
I wish you were
that voice that in lontano

from the eternal hills gives back to us
our daily song.

You are walking on, alert,
until you reach where the violin sounds its echo,
but it is always beyond
your steps and the paths
– your life, what you recall
of springtimes and deaths
and a pregnant woman with her elbows on a gate
looking sightless at a green lake.
Like travelling to Carcassonne!

Until you realize
that the violin in lontano
is you yourself, and then life
like an embroidered cloth stretches before you,
you listen to the wind and your voice when a child,
your mother's weary coughing, the returning swallows
and the first words of love, and that verse
in which you yielded your soul dressed in violets
shutting your eyes in case you died
before a mirror over which flitted
a smile
and now you know
because of a distant echo
on what you wasted your life not knowing that life
does not return, never, ever.
Life is the echo of a dream
that you now know you dreamt, because of an echo.

Celso Emilio Ferreiro (1912–1979)

From O soño sulagado (The Drowned Dream), *1954*

Ollaime ben

Ollaime ben, eu son unha arbre triste
feita de escura terra.
Un segredo de outonos e de lúas
pola raíz me chega.
Un agoiro de páxaros durmidos
nas miñas ponlas medra.

Vede estas mans de ventos e solpores,
vede cómo latexan.
Son os froitos acedos
dunha antiga colleita
de medo e soidá. Sobre min choven
as soidades amargas das estrelas.

Ollaime ben, eu son unha arbre triste
afincada na orela
dun río interminábel, misterioso,
de muda voz coma o falar das pedras.
Estou pechado en min. Alá por fóra
os homes viven, morren, sempre a cegas
camiñan apalpando a longa noite,
namentres o bon Deus, calado, espreita.

Look at me hard

Look at me hard, I'm a sorrowful tree
made of dark earth.
A secret of autumns and moons
reaches me through my roots.
A portent of sleeping birds
grows among my branches.

See these hands of winds and sunsets,
see them throb.
They're the acrid fruit
of an ancient harvest
of fear and loneliness. Upon me rain
the bitter solitudes of the stars.

Look at me hard, I'm a sorrowful tree
standing on the bank
of an endless, mysterious river,
with a mute voice like the speech of the stones.
I'm shut into myself. Out there
men live, die, always blindly
they grope their way through the long night,
while the good God, silent, lies in wait.

From Longa noite de pedra (Long Night of Stone), *1962*

O teito é de pedra...

No meio do caminho tinha uma pedra
tinha uma pedra no meio do caminho
tinha uma pedra
no meio do caminho tinha uma pedra
Carlos Drummond de Andrade

O teito é de pedra.
De pedra son os muros
e as tebras.
De pedra o chan
e as reixas.
As portas,
as cadeas,
o aire,
as fiestras,
as olladas,
son de pedra.
Os corazóns dos homes
que ao lonxe espreitan
feitos están
tamén
de pedra.
E eu morrendo
nesta longa noite
de pedra.

The roof is stone...

No meio do caminho tinha uma pedra
tinha uma pedra no meio do caminho
tinha uma pedra
no meio do caminho tinha uma pedra
Carlos Drummond de Andrade

The roof is stone.
Stone are the walls
and the black shadows.
Stone the ground
and the window-grilles.

The doors,
the chains,
the air,
the windows,
the glances,
are stone.
The hearts of the men
who lie in wait in the distance
are made
also
of stone.
I too, dying
in this long night
of stone.

Non

Se dixese que si,
que todo está moi ben,
que o mundo está moi bon,
que cadaquén é cadaquén...
Conformidá.
Admiración...
Calar, calar, calar,
e moita precaución.
Se dixese que acaso
as cousas son así,
porque si,... velaí,
e non lle demos voltas.
(Se aquel está enriba
e aqueloutro debaixo
é por culpa da vida.
Se algúns van de porta en porta
cun saco de cinza ás costas
é porque son uns docas).
Se dixera que si...
Entón sería o intre
de falar seriamente
da batalla de flores
nas festas do patrón.
Pero non.

No

If I said yes,
that everything's fine,
that the world's fine,
that every man's his own master...
Acquiescence.
Admiration...
Keep quiet, quiet, quiet,
and take great care.
If I said that maybe
things are like that
because that's the way they are... you see,
and better not bother any more.
(If that man's on top
and that other man's underneath
it's life's that's to blame.
If some go from door to door
with sacks of ashes on their backs
it's because they're lazy so-and-so's.)
If I said yes...
Then that would be the time
to talk seriously
about the floral battle
waged during our town festas.
But no.

Deitado frente ao mar

Lingua proletaria do meu pobo
eu fáloa porque si, porque me gosta,
porque me peta e quero e dáme a gana,
porque me sae de dentro, alá do fondo
dunha tristura aceda que me abrangue
ao ver tantos patufos desleigados,
pequenos mequetrefes sen raíces
que ao pór a garavata xa non saben
afirmarse no amor dos devanceiros,
falar a fala nai,
a fala dos avós que temos mortos,
e ser, co rostro erguido,
mariñeiros, labregos da linguaxe,
remo e arado, proa e rella sempre.

Eu fáloa porque si, porque me gosta
e quero estar cos meus, coa xente miña,
preto dos homes bos que sofren longo
unha historia contada noutra lingua.
Non falo pra os soberbios,
non falo pra os ruíns e poderosos,
non falo pra os finchados,
non falo pra os baleiros,
non falo pra os estúpidos,
que falo pra os que aguantan rexamente
mentiras e inxustizas de cotío;
pra os que súan e choran
un pranto cotián de bolboretas,
de lume e vento sobre os ollos núos.
Eu non quero arredar as miñas verbas
de tódolos que sofren neste mundo.
E ti vives no mundo, terra miña,
berce da miña estirpe,
Galicia, dóce mágoa das Españas,
deitada frente ao mar, ese camiño...

Lying before the sea

Proletarian language of my people,
I speak it because I do, because I like to,
because that's how I feel and I want to and I have an urge to,
because it comes from inside me, from the depths
of a bitter sorrow that takes hold of me
when I see so many disloyal jackanapes,
rootless little good-for-nothings
who, once they don their ties, forget
how to affirm themselves in the love of their ancestors.
To speak our mother tongue,
the tongue of our dead forebears,
and to be, with heads held high,
sailors and farmers of language:
oar and plough, prow and share always.
I speak it because I do, because I like it
and I want to be with those who are mine, with my people,
close to the good men who for long have suffered
a story told in another language.
I do not speak for the proud,
I do not speak for the vile and powerful,

I do not speak for the puffed-up,
I do not speak for the empty,
I do not speak for the stupid,
because I speak for those who stoutly endure
lies and injustices day after day;
for those who sweat and weep
a daily lament of butterflies,
of fire and wind over naked eyes.
I will not distance my words
from all those who suffer in this world.
And you live in this world, land of mine,
cradle of my race,
Galicia, sweet sorrow of the Spains,
lying before the sea, that road...

From Onde o mundo se chama Celanova (Where the World Is Called Celanova), *1975*

Xaneiro, 1972, II

Cando quero vivir
digo Moraima.
Digo Moraima
cando semento a espranza.
Digo Moraima
e ponse azul a alba.

Cando quero soñar
digo Moraima.
Digo Moraima
cando a noite é pechada.
Digo Moraima
e ponse a luz en marcha.

Cando quero chorar
digo Moraima.
Digo Moraima
cando a anguria me abafa.
Digo Moraima
e ponse o mar en calma.

Cando quero sorrir
digo Moraima.

Digo Moraima
cando a mañá é clara.
Digo Moraima
e ponse a tarde mansa.

Cando quero morrer
non digo nada.
E mátame o silencio
de non dicir Moraima.

January 1972, II

When I want to live
I say Moraima.
I say Moraima
when I sow hope.
I say Moraima
and the dawn turns blue.

When I want to dream
I say Moraima.
I say Moraima
when the night is black.
I say Moraima
and the light starts moving.

When I want to weep
I say Moraima.
I say Moraima
when anguish stifles me.
I say Moraima
and the sea is calm.

When I want to smile
I say Moraima.
I say Moraima
when the morning is bright.
I say Moraima
and the afternoon is quiet.

When I want to die
I say nothing.

And I am killed by the silence
of not saying Moraima.

Alma da Terra

Lonxana Celanova vinculeira,
torre ebúrnea da miña mocidade,
cando te lembro sae da súa toqueira
coma un furón de soños a saudade.

Unha chuvia monótona e tristeira
cae decote na miña intimidade,
e sinto que unha sombra silandeira
coma un solpor, o meu esprito invade.

Quero voltar a ti, nai garimosa,
colo natal, arxila rumorosa,
para acalar esta anguria que me berra

dende o fondo da noite estrelecida,
pedindo amor, pregando fe de vida
pra ser eternamente alma da terra.

Soul of my land

Distant, firstborn Celanova,
ivory tower of my youth,
when I remember you, out of its den comes,
like a ferret of dreams, nostalgia.

A monotonous and sorrowful rain
falls daily on my inmost being,
and I feel that a shadow, as silent
as a sunset, invades my spirit.

I want to return to you, loving mother,
maternal lap, whispering clay,
to quieten this anguish screaming at me

from the depths of the starry night
asking for love, begging for proof that I am alive
to be eternally soul of my land.

From A fronteira infinda (The Infinite Frontier), 1972

Mi pana bulda

Candelario era un home pacífico e por bo non tiña feito carreira na milicia. Recén incorporado ás forzas armadas destináronó ao campo de concentración de Guasina, no delta do Orinoco, onde o dictador de turno mandaba aos seus inimigos para que morresen comestos polo clima, as doenzas, os mosquitos, o esgotamento e as cóbregas. Alí viu cousas horrendas e foi testemuña de escenas espantosas de degradación e de sadismo. Os prisioneiros traballaban sobor de terra encharcada de auga, atados a unhas carretas nas que transportaban pedras da mañá á noite, nun labourar totalmente inútil. De noite durmían amontoados nuns galpóns, de piso mollado arreo polas medras do río. Os homes parecían estatuas de lama movéndose lentamente polos lameiros, carrexando pedras coas que formaban montóns que despois desfacían para levar as pedras a outro lugar da pequena illa. Cansos, esfameados, febrís, durante o día, ademais do traballo forzado, tiñan que soportar os golpes e aldraxes dos gardas; e de noite aguantar a praga de mosquitos zancudos, jejéns, pousándose coma unha brétema viscosa e irritante sobre os seus corpos. E os castigos especiais: durmir atado á carreta; permanecer varios días inmóbil, coa cabeza descuberta baixo o sol de fogo, e o peor de todos, o castigo da cela, unha cova natural na orela das terribles anacondas, unhas serpes acuáticas capaces de apresar e arrastrar a un home ata o fondo do río, para esmigallalo entre os seus potentísimos aneis e despois gandilo. O repugnante espectáculo daqueles homes, asoballados e ofendidos polos verdugos a xornal, tiña provocado en Candelario un singular estado de ánimo que lle facía vivir como coutado por un muro de desleixo, algo así coma un non-quero-saber-nada-do-que-estápasando. "Todo isto non é máis que merda – dicía –, ¿e por que hei de estar a fozar e cheirar nesta porcallada, se non podo evitala?"

Candelario endexamais maltrataba aos prisioneiros e sempre se negaba a colaborar en calquera forma de abuso. "Eu non son un caimán, son un soldado." Esta actitude neutra tiña a Candelario descualificado perante os xefes, e por iso non puido acadar máis que os galóns de distinguido. Semellaba que a inadaptación de Candelario ao medio tíñase trocado nunha irresistible voracidade sexual de macho sempre disposto, cunha resistencia física inesgotable. A súa sona correu polas dúas orelas do Orinoco e foi o semental indiscutible daquelas terras. Corpachudo, fraco, de ósos fortes, os ollos profundos cheos dunha estraña luz nocturna, Candelario non abusaba da súa forza nin da metralleta. Tumbaba mulleres como moscas, pero sempre polo aloumiño e convencemento. Unha vez descalabrou a planazos de machete a un soldado do seu pelotón ao que sorprendeu intentando abusar dunha nena. "Pero Candelario, se é muller; fíxate que tetiñas tan ben postas ten", dicía o indigno entre planazo e planazo. "Cala, bocallón dexenerado, que te estripo", berraba Candelario coa súa voz de treboada.

Aos dous anos da súa chegada a Guasina, máis de cen meniños de ambos sexos, esparexidos polos casaríos, rancherías e aldeas de ambas orelas, levaban a súa marca de fábrica. Pero dun xeito ou doutro, a vida sempre cobra estas débedas, e Candelario pagounas pouco despois en Porto Cabello, onde tiña ido para escoltar un grupo de prisioneiros destinados a Guasina. Entón coñeceu a unha mesoneira que lle sorbeu sentido e sexo. Era unha muller de cor suave, dourada, coma unha folla de carballo no outono. Expelía un estraño perfume de animal lascivo, e o seu andar cadencioso semellaba estar envolto nunha invitación á intimidade. Chamábase Lesbia. Era un ser nacido para o pracer, un animal de cama, coma os cabalos de pura raza son animais de carreira. En canto viu a Candelario, Lesbia soubo que era da súa mesma especie e que, fatalmente vencellaríase a ela por sentimentos de paixón profunda. Non precisou insinuarse. Deixouse levar polos feitos que favoreceran o seu encontro e, durante os tres días que durou a estadía de Candelario na cidade, viviron unha longa batalla de amor. Non coñeceron máis tregua que a das lívidas albas, cando, cansos, espidos, quedaban durmidos sobor do leito revolto mentres pola fiestra entraba o resplandor do mencer e os cantos dos paxaros. "Quero irme contigo", díxolle Lesbia. "Quero ser a túa soldadeira."

Asentouna nun rancho abandonado na orela dereita do río ao pé dunha enorme ceiba de flores vermellas e brillantes, que o encubría coa súa sombra protectora. Candelario traballou dúas semanas arreo para facer un pouco máis cómodo o rancho. Restaurou o teito, afianzou madeiras e trabes; construíu unha chousa arredor, para evitar as incursións dos bichos, e co machete desbrozou unha trocha para camiñar ata o río.

A chegada da mesoneira foi coma o estoupido dun foguete no medio da pequena guarnición da illa. Os que a viron fixéronse linguas da súa beleza. Ao seu redor naceu coma un mito de Venus traída polo gran río. O xefe do destacamento militar un miserable con grao de capitán, díxolle un día a Candelario: "¿Por que escondes a túa fermosa soldadeira, cónchale? Podes traela á illa cando queiras, que será ben recibida. Os soldados facían chistes procaces e organizaban bromas á conta da parella, ata que unha tarde, dempois da retreta, Candelario, sen alterarse, sen ira, sen mirar a ninguén, colleu o fusil, moveu o cerrollo para pór unha bala na recámara, e friamente dixo: "Esa muller non está en poxa; é miña nada máis." Xa nunca voltaron a embromalo.

Lesbia foi dúas veces á illa e voltou magoada pola vida infrahumana dos prisioneiros. "Eu tiña noticias de que isto era horrible, pero non tanto." Nunha das ocasións, Candelario sorprendeuna perto dos barracóns espreitando cara ao lugar onde estaban os presos traballando. Tiña os ollos cheos de bágoas. "Non quero que volvas aquí – comentou Candelario –, pois este é un prato moi forte para o teu estómago." Na realidade era un pretexto, pois o que verdadeiramente preocupaba a Candelario era a evidencia de que, tarde ou cedo, tería problemas co Capitán, aquel canalla que, ademais de dono de vidas e facendas, críase dono do dereito de pernada. "Un día calquera – pensaba Candelario – procurará afastarme, dándome un servicio, para intentar deitarse con ela; o fracaso fará que se volte en contra de min e non me deixará atravesar o río na lancha da xefatura."

Pasar o río a nado era un intento suicida. Anque a distancia non era moi grande, debaixo da pel sucia daquel semovente xigantesco, velaba a morte en forma de pirañas, anacondas, babas... Entón, prevendo calquera contratempo futuro, dispúxose a construír con présa unha curiara coma as dos indios. Levoulle máis dun mes tumbar unha corpuda árbore, troceala e desbastala ata deixala oca e lista para navegar. Atracouna atada á orela do río, e, xa sosegado e tranquilo, deixou seguir a súa historia de amor, agardando que, en calquera intre, o esperado problema co Capitán o forzaría a usar a curiara como nave de comunicación entre a illa e o seu fogar. O problema xurdiu ás dúas semanas xustas, mais non precisamente co Capitán, senón cun preso que desapareceu da illa coma se o río o houbese tragado. Cando Candelario, canso da infructuosa procura do prisioneiro, voltou ao rancho, Lesbia e a curiara tiñan tamén desaparecido. Na porta do rancho, cravado cun alfinete, un papeliño explicaba todo. "Síntoo moito, perdóame."

Un consello de guerra acusou a Candelario de "cómplice por neglixencia culposa" e foi condenado a perder os galóns de "distinguido" e voltar á condición de soldado raso por tres anos, nun cuartel do interior do país. Candelario non sentiu carraxe contra de Lesbia. Comprendía que a fermosa mesoneira usárao como instrumento para levar a cabo un deliberado e ben tramado plan de fuga do prisioneiro de Guasina, quizais o seu marido, quizais o seu amante, ou tal vez só un camarada. Pero, ao mesmo tempo, non deixaba de coidar que o feito implicaba un heroico sacrificio, de valorosa e audaz entrega a unha causa que, en todo caso, era nobre. Supoñía que o encontro con Lesbia en Porto Cabello non fora ao chou, senón intelixentemente preparado. Estaba disposto a admitir que o frechazo amoroso que ela mostrou ao comezo, era unha pura finxición. Pero custáballe crer que todo o de despois, nos tres meses longos de convivencia na orela do río, fose unha comedia que Lesbia representaba ata extremos non precisos. "O noso amor foi coma unha transfusión de sangue", dicíase a sí mesmo. Aferrábase á hipótese de que Lesbia, fervoenta idealista, prestárase a facer aquelo sen outra razón que a obedencia á súa militancia política. Entón era posible que o amor, finxido ao comezo, rematara sendo verdadeiro ao final. Non podía ser doutro xeito. ¿Cómo, senón, aquela tenrura expresada en doces e misteriosas palabras que ela lle dicía ás veces no mesto silencio da noite, cando supuña que Candelario estaba durmindo? "Mi pana bulda", dicíalle amodiño, e todo o rancho se ateigaba de luz e paxaros da amencida.

– ¿Vostede comprende?, dicíame "mi pana bulda", ¿dáse conta?

– Non – contestille a Candelario, despois de escoitarlle a súa historia.

– Ela nunca me quixo dicir o sentido daquelas fermosas palabras. Agoriña hai unha semana, viñen a saber o seu significado na fala dos baixos fondos de Caracas. Quere dicir "o meu mellor amigo", ¿vostede dáse conta? Eu sei que a toparei un día calquera. Agora estou pagando polas moitas saias que erguín e as moitas mulleres que tiven, sen amor, entre os brazos.

– É posible – comentei –, a vida non dá nada de balde.

– Cando remate o castigo, atopareina. "Mi pana bulda", ¿vostede comprende?

My Pana Bulda

Candelario was a quiet man and because he was so good he hadn't been promoted in the militia. On recently entering the armed forces, he was sent to Guasina concentration camp, in the Orinoco delta, where the dictator of the moment sent his enemies to die consumed by the climate, disease, mosquitos, exhaustion and snakes. He saw terrible things there and he was witness to awful scenes of humiliation and sadism. The prisoners worked on the earth swamped with water, tied to wagons in which they transported stones from morning to night, totally useless work. At night they slept, piled up in sheds, the floor saturated because of the flooding of the river. The men looked like clay statues, moving slowly around the mire, carrying stones with which they made heaps which they later took apart to take the stones to another part of the small island. Tired, hungry, feverish, apart from the forced labour, they had to put up with beatings and outrages from the guards during the day; and at night suffer the scourge of the long-legged mosquitos, jejens, posing like a viscous and irritating mist on their bodies. And the extra punishments: sleeping tied to the wagon; staying several days without moving, bareheaded under the burning sun, and the worst of all, the punishment cell, a natural cave on the bank of the river inhabited by terrible anacondas, aquatic snakes capable of capturing a man and dragging him to the bottom of the river to crush him, encircling him with their extremely powerful bodies, to eat him afterwards. The disgusting sight of those men, vexed and offended by hired executioners, had caused Candelario to be in a singular state of mind that made him live as if protected by a wall of apathy, something like I-don't-want-to-know-anything-about-what-is-happening. "All this is nothing but shit – he said –, and why do I have to root in and smell this filth, if I can avoid it?"

Candelario never ill-treated the prisoners and he always refused to collaborate in any type of cruelty. "I'm not an alligator; I'm a soldier". This neutral attitude disqualified Candelario in the eyes of his bosses, and for that reason he never achieved a high rank in the army. It seemed that Candelario's inability to adapt to his circumstances had been transformed into the irresistible sexual voracity of an ever-ready male, with tireless physical resistance. His reputation spread to both sides of the Orinoco and he was the indisputable stud of the area. Strong, thin, with heavy bones, with deep eyes full of a strange dark light, Candelario did not use either his strength or his machine gun badly. Women fell before him like flies, but he always won them by affection and conviction. Once he gave a terrible beating with the handle of his machete to a soldier from his troop that he surprised trying to abuse a little girl. "But Candelario, it's a woman; look at her nice little tits", the wretch said between blows. "Shut up you degenerate big mouth, or I'll rip your guts out", Candelario shouted, with his voice like thunder.

Two years after his arrival at Guasina, more than a hundred little children of both sexes, spread around among country houses, ranches and villages on both banks, carried his trademark. But, in one way or another, life always recovers these debts, and Candelario paid them a little afterwards in Porto Cabello, where he had gone to escort a group of prisoners going to Guasina. Then he met a female innkeeper who captivated him sensually and sexually. She was a woman with soft-coloured skin, golden, like an oak leaf in the Autumn. She gave off the strange perfume of a lascivious animal, and her swaying walk seemed to be enveloped in an invitation to intimacy. She was called Lesbia. She was a being born for pleasure, a bedroom animal, like purebred horses are meant to be racehorses. When she saw Candelario, Lesbia knew that he was of the same species as her, and that he would be bound fatally to her by feelings of a profoundly passionate kind. She did not need to ingratiate herself. She let herself be carried away by the facts which brought about their meeting and, during the three days that Candelario was in the city, they experienced a long war of love. They knew no other truce except the white dawns when, tired, naked, they fell asleep on the dishevelled bed while through the window the brightness of the sunrise and birdsong entered. "I want to go with you", Lesbia said to him. "I want to be your camp follower".

He settled her in an abandoned ranch on the right bank of the river, at the foot of an enormous ceiba with bright red flowers, that covered it with its protective shade. Candelario worked hard for two weeks to make the ranch a bit more comfortable. He fixed the roof, fastened planks and beams; he built a fence around it, to prevent the incursion of animals, and with his machete he cut an opening in the undergrowth so as to be able to walk to the river.

The arrival of the innkeeper was like the explosion of a rocket in the little island garrison. Those who saw her spoke of her beauty. A myth about her of a Venus brought by the river started. The boss of the military detachment, a wretch with the rank of captain, said to Candelario one day: "Why do hide your beautiful camp follower, cónchale? You can bring her to the island when you want, she will be very welcome". The soldiers made dirty jokes and messed about at the pair's cost, until one afternoon, after retreat, Candelario, without any sign of being disturbed, without anger, without looking at anybody, got his rifle, opened the lock to put a bullet in the chamber and said coldly: "That woman is not up for sale; she belongs to me only". They never joked about him again.

Lesbia went to the island twice and came back upset by the subhuman conditions in which the prisoners lived. "I had heard that this was horrible but not like that". On one of those occasions, Lesbia found herself near the living quarters spying at the place where the prisoners were working. Her eyes were full of tears. "I don't want you to come back here – Candelario said –, this is too much for you to stomach". It was really a pretext, for what actually worried Candelario was that it was evident that, sooner or later, he would have problems with the Captain, that swine that, apart from controlling lives and properties, thought that he had the right to droit de seigneur. "One of these days – Candelario thought – he'll endeavour to get me away from here, making me go on service so that he can try to go to bed with her; his failure will make him turn on me and he won't let me go across the river in the launch from the headquarters".

To swim across the river was suicidal. Although the distance was not great, under the dirty skin of that giant living thing, death waited in the form of piranhas, anacondas, babas… Then, foreseeing any possible future setback, he started to build quickly an Indian canoe called a curiara. It took him a month to fell a big tree, chop it up and hollow it out so as to be ready to sail. He moored it on the river bank and, then quietly and calmly continued with his love life, waiting for the moment when, at any time, the expected problem with the Captain would force him to use the curiara as a means of transport between the island and his home. The problem arose just two weeks after, not exactly with the Captain, but with a prisoner that disappeared from the island as if the river had swallowed him up. When Candelario, tired of the fruitless search for the prisoner, went back to the ranch, Lesbia and the curiara also had disappeared. Pinned to the doorway of the ranch was a bit of paper that explained everything. "I am really sorry; forgive me".

A court martial accused Candelario of being "a guilty accomplice due to negligence" and he was condemned to lose his stripes and to go back to being an ordinary soldier for three years in a barracks in the middle of the country. Candelario didn't hate Lesbia. He understood that the beautiful innkeeper had used him as a way of carrying out a deliberate and well-thought out escape plan for the prisoner in Guasina, perhaps her husband, perhaps her lover, or maybe only a friend. But, at the same time, he still believed that it all meant a heroic self-sacrifice which was a brave and audacious surrender to a cause that was noble anyway. He supposed that his meeting with Lesbia in Porto Cabello was not by chance but had been intelligently prepared. He was prepared to admit that her apparent falling in love with him at first was pure pretence. But he found it hard to admit that everything that came afterwards, in the three long months they lived together on the bank of the river, was a farce which Lesbia put on with such unnecessary detail. "Our love was like a blood transfusion", he told himself. He held on to the hypothesis that Lesbia, an ardent idealist, would have done all that without any other reason except obedience to some political convictions. So it was possible that the love, which was feigned at first, ended up being real. It couldn't be any other way. How, if not, could one explain that tenderness expressed in the sweet and mysterious words that she said to him at times in the dense silence of the night, when she thought Candelario was asleep? "My pana bulda", she said to him slowly, and all the ranch filled up with light and birds of the dawn.

– Do you understand?; she called me "my pana bulda"; do you know what I mean?

– No – I answered Candelario after listening to his story.

– She never wanted to tell me the meaning of those beautiful words. A week ago I discovered their meaning in the slang used in the Caracas underworld. It means "my best friend"; do you understand? I know I'll meet her some day. Now I'm paying for the many skirts I lifted and the many women I held, without love, in my arms.

– It's possible – I told him –, life gives nothing for nothing.

– When I finish my punishment I'll find her. "My pana bulda". Do you know what I mean?

Xosé María Díaz Castro (1914–1989)

From Nimbos (Haloes), *1961*

Polpa dorida

¡Ei, Terra Verde e Mar de Orballo,
polpa dorida se as hai!
¡Ás túas portas perdín todo
cheiro alleo de terra ou mar
e agora, ó caer no teu colo
oio pacer canto hai!

Sore flesh

Hey, Green Land and Sea of Dew,
sore flesh, as sore as it comes!
At your gates I lost all
foreign smells of land or sea
and now, as I fall into your lap,
I hear everything grazing!

Coma brasas

Poeta ou non, eu cantarei as cousas
que na soleira de min mesmo agardan.
Alumarei con fachas de palabras,
ancho herdo meu, o mundo que me deron.

Aí están, coma brasas contra a noite,
as vellas cousas, cheas de destinos.
Ollos que piden, de famentos nenos.
Ollos que esperan, dunha adolescente.

¡Galiza en min, meu Deus, pan que me deron
leite e centeo e sono e luz de aurora!
Longa rúa do mar, fogar da terra,
e esta cruz que nos mide de alto a baixo
Con este alento, eu lles darei ás causas
o drama cheo que lles nega a vida:
dareilles rostos, pra que se conozan,
palabras lles darei pra que se entendan...

Like embers

A poet or not, I shall sing the things
that on the threshold of my self are waiting.
I shall light with torches made of words
the world I was given, this my broad inheritance.

There they are, like embers in the night,
the old things, full of destiny.
Eyes that beg, of hungry children.
Eyes that wait, of an adolescent girl.

Galicia in me, my God, bread I was given
by milk and rye and sleep and dawn light!
Long street of the sea, the homeland hearth,
and this cross that measures us from top to toe.
Thus inspired, I shall give our causes
the full drama that life denies them:
I shall give them faces, to recognize each other,
words I shall give them, to understand each other...

Penélope

Un paso adiante e outro atrás, Galiza,
e a tea dos teus soños non se move.
A espranza nos teus ollos se espreguiza.
Aran os bois e chove.

Un bruar de navíos moi lonxanos
che estrolla o sono mol coma unha uva.
Pro ti envólveste en sabas de mil anos
e en sonos volves escoitar a chuva.

Traguerán os camiños algún día
a xente que levaron. Deus é o mesmo.
Suco vai, suco vén, ¡Xesús María!,
e toda cousa ha de pagar seu desmo.

Desorballando os prados coma sono,
o tempo vai de Parga a Pastoriza.
Vaise enterrando, suco a suco, o Outono.
¡Un paso adiante e outro atrás, Galiza!

Penelope

One step forward and another step back, Galicia,
and the fabric of your dreams does not budge.
The hope in your eyes gives itself a sleepy stretch.
The oxen plough, it rains.

A bellowing of distant ships
crushes your sleep, as soft as grapes.
But you wrap yourself in thousand-year-old sheets
and in your sleep keep listening to the rain.

The roads will one day bring back
the people they took away: God is the same.
A furrow here, a furrow there, by Jesus!
and all must pay their tithes.

Undewing the meadows like sleep,
time moves on from Parga to Pastoriza.
Autumn is buried, furrow by furrow.
One step forward and another step back, Galicia!

Eduardo Moreiras (1914–1991)

From Nordés, *1992*

Esperanza

O meu destino
foi amar a luz
no espacio nidio da vida entregada
na gloria dun ceo virxe
ata morrer.

Lume do día puro
na música inmorrente.

Crear ás cegas
formas do espírito
que ninguén recordará.

Vencer a resistencia
nun inútil esforzo.

Esquecerei aos do meu sangue
que me deron mágoa
mentres me dura a vida.

Que apodreza o seu rastro
na vida pasada.

Aínda
apousa unha pomba
nos bosques misteriosos de Irlanda.

Ela e ti
sodes o meu amor.

Hope

My destiny
was to love the light
in the clear space of a dedicated life
in the glory of a virgin sky
until death.

Light of the pure day
in deathless music.

Blindly creating
forms of the spirit
that nobody will remember.

Defeating resistence
in a useless effort.

I shall forget those of my blood
who gave me pain
as long as my life lasts.

May their trail rot
in the life of the past.

Still
a dove rests
in the mysterious forests of Ireland.

She and you
are my love.

Xosé María Álvarez Blázquez (1915–1985)

From Canle segredo (Secret Channel), *1976*

Canle segredo

Canle segredo hei ser
prá fervenza da auga manantía
que enxurre as nosas vidas, cando nada
falle do que che eu teño prometido.
Xeneroso leito
de derramada anguria;
terra de terra, aberta pola eixada
do afán e o amor para a semente limpa;
eira de pan
           lareira
                    fondo pozo,
gardador do misterio que nos cingue;
penedía
cara ós ventos da sorte;
albre senlleiro
na chaira dos miñatos...

¡Ti ben sabes
todo o que o meu amor manda que eu seña!

Secret channel

A secret channel I shall be
for the cascade of the flowing water
that will leave its silt on our lives, when
everything I've promised you is fulfilled.
A generous bed
of deposited anguish;
earth of earth, opened up for the clean seed
by the mattock of zeal and love;
threshing-floor for wheat
           hearth
                    deep well,

keeper of the mystery that surrounds us;
a cliff-face
against the winds of fortune;
a solitary tree
on the plain of the buzzards...

You well know
all the things that my love tells me to be!

Miguel González Garcés (1916–1989)

From Nas faíscas do soño (In the Sparks of the Dream), *1972*

A bóveda do mundo esfargallada...

A bóveda do mundo esfargallada,
case cascullo.
Unha cismeira ollada desde a cúpula
penetra formiguexante.
Ser home é ficar só. Só árbore.
Enguedellada sombra pola hedra,
esvarante asubío,
perfume de terror.
Máis témero é non ser. E nova angustia.
Só árbore debaixo da outra cúpula.
¿Por que aquí e agora? ¿E esta selva?
¿E esta hedra feroz? ¿E aquela ollada?
Na beira do meu mar sopeso as horas,
soño soños dos ventos e mais berro.
Berro agora na area do meu nome
en mesta sombra azul de moura brétema.
Ronsel da miña sede. O mar. Silencio.
E a bóveda a renxer esfarelada.

The vault of the world shattered...

The vault of the world shattered,
little more than rubble.
An obsessive look from the dome
breaks in like teeming ants.
To be a man is to be alone. Just a tree.
Shadow enmeshed in ivy,

slithering whistle,
perfume of terror.
It is more terrible not to be. And a new anguish.
Just a tree beneath another dome.
And why here and now? And this forest?
And this fierce ivy? And that look?
On the shore of my sea I weigh the hours,
I dream dreams of the winds and I scream.
I scream now on the sand of my name
in dense blue shadow of dark mist.
The wake left by my thirst. The sea. Silence.
And the vault creaking in ruins.

Pura Vázquez (1918–2006)

From Orballa en tempo lento (Dew Falls In Tempo Lento), 1995

Idade idoira onte

Foi unha idade idoira. Presentía
abrochar desvaríos. Lumes fondas.

Baixo a sombra da espiga. Dos trigais
collía peitaliños de mapoulas.
Alardeaba en leiras do acendido
amaranto. Das prímulas luxosas.
Da camelia brillando sen recendos.
Da doncelez fulgúrea das magnolias.

Cando medrei fun repasando mundos.
Pisei veludos prados lamacentos
e lascivas, suavísimas alfombras.
Lameiros florescentes. As espadas
frescas das herbas. As maduras froitas.

Andei polas follaxes derrotadas.
Os limpos seixos beirarríos. Dondas
florciñas de colores. Celmes astros
alumáronme os vougos da memoria.

Nun curruncho de min houbo unha nena.
Paxaro ceibe remontando as horas.

Enredei cos cristais. Coas xebras verdes.
Coa fluente brisa. As mariñeiras ondas.

Bebín a luz no colo dos abrentes.
Durmín baixo a orballada das auroras.

Fleeting time yesterday

It was a fleeting time. I presaged
extravagancies being buttoned up. Deep fires.

In the shade of the wheat-ear. From the wheat-plots
I picked poppy petals.
In fields I flaunted the burning
amaranth. Luxurious primroses.
The camellia, shining without aromas.
The resplendent girlhood of the magnolias.

When I grew up I went surveying worlds.
I trod on velvety, miry meadows
and lascivious, smooth carpets.
Flowering mires. The fresh
swords of the grasses. The ripe fruit.

I strolled through the defeated foliage.
The clean riverside pebbles. Soft
little coloured flowers. Sweet stars
lit the deserts of my memory.

In a corner of me was a little girl.
A free bird soaring over the hours.
I amused myself with crystal. With green seaweed.
With the flowing breeze. The waves of the deep.

I drank the light on the lap of daybreak.
I slept under the dewfall of the dawns.

From Desmemoriado río (Unremembering River), *1997*

Desmemoriado río o da memoria

En distancias de soles. En macios universos
pérdeseme a memoria. Na faz apouvigada
onde as palabras floran como un mundo sen ecos.

Son aluadas feridas que perderon as rotas.
Espaventadas cinzas nun boligante vento
onde se ispen lizgairas. Son misterios leviáns
de petunias e anémonas ou de lotos efémeros.

Morren nos fríos sámagos de espellos sen imaxe.
Séganlle as transparencias un gume de coitelos.
No esplendor dese cosmos onde o olvido alborece
choutan os labirintos de escurecidos ceos.

Nos pórfiros vermellos dos exilios sen volta,
nas longuras, apáganse como se apaga o senso.
Perdéronse os fulgores e as teimosías fondas
nesta gran desmemoria de crepúsculos lentos.

Unremembering river of memory

In distances of suns. In pale universes
my memory is lost. In the calmed face
where words flower like a world without echoes.

They are moonstruck wounds that have lost their way.
Frightened ashes in a bustling wind
where they lightly undress. They are small mysteries
of petunias and anemones or ephemeral lotuses.

They die in the cold cores of imageless mirrors.
Their transparencies are cut down by a blade of knives.
In the splendour of that cosmos where oblivion is dawning
the labyrinths of darkened skies are at play.

In the red porphyries of endless exiles,
in the longnesses, they fade away as sense fades away.
The flares and the deep pertinacity have been lost
in this great unremembering of slow dusks.

The New Writers of the Sixties

Antón Tovar (1921–2004)

From Non (No), *1967*

O que teño

Teño merlos de sombra nas pólas da canseira,
e ceos a choveren sobre un río de carne;
non teño máis terreos, só teño esa orballeira,
unha cántiga triste sobre os prados e as árbores.

Levo ás costas saudade mesturada de anceios,
saudade como néboa na lama das congostras;
un acio de silencio no que se pousa o medo
como se pousa o mar dos náufragos nas costas.

Vou nun leito de toxos co meu corpo ferido,
o sangue esparexido polas veas do vento,
o pulso dunha arela a latexar camiños,
e a cántiga da angustia que me colleu ben cedo.

Puiden ser unha nube como as alas dun anxo,
ou un grilo, unha rosa, unha xestiña leda,
non cheguei máis que a sombra e néboa, bágoa, pranto
bolboreta da morte coas dúas alas nas tebras.

Teño longos salaios durmiñando na lúa,
teño ríos de bágoas que baixan dos curutos,
teño fíos de sangue que o corazón anúa
e nel un océano de mergullados pulos.

Teño unha lúa vella pra seiturar recordos
e agadañar angustias ermas coma penedos.
Non teño máis fouciña que a que me deu o soño
nin sego máis cancións que as que seguei no tempo.

What I have

I have blackbirds of shadow on the branches of weariness,
and skies raining down on a river of flesh;
I have no more lands, but only that drizzle,
a sad old song upon the meadows and trees.

On my back I carry sadlongings mixed with wishes,
sadlongings like fog in the mud of the lanes;
a grape-bunch of silence on which fear settles
as the sea of the castaways settles on the shores.

I go on a bed of gorse with my wounded body,
my blood scattered through the veins of the wind,
the pulsing of a desire throbbing through paths
and the old song of anguish that took hold of me soon.

I could have been a cloud like the wings of an angel,
or a cricket, a rose, a happy little broom-bush,
I never became more than shadow and mist, tears, weeping,
moth of death with its two wings in the shadows.

I have long sobs dozing on the moon,
I have rivers of tears that flow down from the heights,
I have threads of blood that my heart knots together
and in it an ocean of drowned aspirations.

I have an old moon for cutting down memories
and for scything anguishes as barren as rocks.
I have no other sickle than the one dreaming gave me
nor do I reap any songs other than those I reaped in Time.

Luz Pozo Garza (1922–)

From Códice Calixtino (Codex Calixtinus), *1986*

Chovía en Compostela

O ar semellaba unha camelia branca
que se tornase en chuvia en sombra en pura ausencia.
Sombras escuras.
Columnas primordiais con volume románico.
Mais non estabas ti...

Mirei a tarde.
Liña espiral da chuvia na memoria.
Unha estación de incenso pranto mirra
abisal. Salgueiros partituras.
As fontes fican soas.
Unha especie de bafo de camelias unxidas.
Chove gris Compostela. Un cálice de chuvia.
Mais non estabas ti...

A nosa historia pertence á cripta dos crepúsculos
camiño de Santiago.
Unha longa coroa de cúpulas
xeadas
a facer o milagre polas pontes de Roma.
A nosa historia hase ler baixo a lámpada pura
na noite dos pazos abertos coma un códice.
Na noite debruzada
sobre panos de seda catedrais pechadas
aras de perpiaño.
Nun dolmen presentido perto de Compostela.
Biquei a tarde nos altares.
Mais non estabas ti...

Á procura do tempo
rachei as partituras do Codex Calixtinus
no Pórtico da Gloria.
Unha casulla azul polo pranto e a ausencia
derrubouse sen ruído.
Desprovista das verbas que nivelan os cálices
fiquei a contraluz.
As lousas escribían a paisaxe obstinada.
Despois chegou a noite. Chovía en Compostela.
Mais non estabas ti...

It was raining in Compostela

The air was like some white camellia
that had turned into rain in shadow in pure absence.
Dark shadows.
Primordial columns with Romanesque volume.
But you weren't there...

I looked at the evening.
A spiral of the rain in my memory.
A station of incense, weeping, myrrh,
from the depths. Willows sheets of music.
The fountains are all alone.
A spice: the whiff of anointed camellias.
It rains grey Compostela. A chalice of rain.
But you weren't there...

Our story belongs to the crypt of the dusks
on the Way to Santiago.
A long crown of domes
frozen
making the miracle on the bridges of Rome.
Our story will be read beneath the pure lamp
in the night of the grand houses open like a codex.
In the night, face down
on silken cloths closed cathedrals
altars of parpen.
In a dolmen sensed near Compostela.
I kissed the evening on the altars.
But you weren't there...

In search of time
I tore the music-sheets from the Codex Calixtinus
in the Pórtico da Gloria.
A chasuble, blue from weeping and absence,
collapsed soundlessly.
Deprived of the words that level chalices
I stood against the light.
The flagstones wrote the obstinate landscape.
Then night came. It was raining in Compostela.
But you weren't there...

Manuel Cuña Novás (1926–1992)

From Fabulario novo (New Fable-Book), *1952*

Día de defuntos

Caen e roldan as follas arredor da auga
como se fora o seu dicir: chorade.
Tanguen as campás silencio sen amparo
como se fora o seu tanguer: chorade.

Chorade os ancorados na sombra e na morte;
os nus asolagados na terra lividosa;
a súa mestura fiel escorre manseniña
extinguíndose ao tacto da corpórea presencia.

Unxe o moucho a esperma ardiga
que acende a dubidosa chama marela do recordo.
Agoiran os cans a profunda verdá dos cadaleitos
e o seu ouvido ecoa a nocturna servidume dos mortos.

Agora o vento recende a flores murchas,
a coroas de mirto que desfixo o tempo
e apalpo na outra luz do desamparo
altas verbas xeadas do agoiro derradeiro no intre inexpresable.

Náusea cristalina ensombrecendo a fronte
é esa podredume
que flúe nun leitoso carreiriño de vermes.

Eses abandonados ás poutas da terra
que estiveron a rente da luz que aluma as noites
tornan traspasando os muros,
corpos deshabitados na orfa culpa da terra,
e buscan docemente acobillo ao desamparo.

¿Quen chama nos cristais da fiestra con ademán escuro e estrañable?
esa voz de ningures, que ten de ir?

Pasou un anxo, un anxo
e o silencio ceifa un cabelo de anxo
e a alma ten callada unha pinga de sangue do anxo que pasou,

do anxo que xeou a miña entraña
coa súa ollada doce dende a tebra.
E é un ronsel de tebra anguriante o paso do anxo,
é a dor dos mortos ensumíndose na sombra ardente da tebra,
é a morte, Señor, que ancorou na miña entraña,
na entraña do neno que se fai na placenta
envolto en panos de sangue, aloumiñado na tebra.

As sombras choran; as sombras din: chorade
cheos de horror e loito
os ancorados na vida da morte eternamente.

Quen agora
non tente para os seus pés baixo do mundo
longas filas de morte horizontable,
negará para sempre o que é chama e silencio.

All Souls' Day

The leaves fall and blow around the water
as if what they said were: weep.
The bells chime a defenceless silence
as if what they chime were: weep.

Weep for those anchored in shadow and in death;
those naked and submerged in the livid earth;
their faithful mixture slips softly along
vanishing at the touch of the corporeal presence.

The owl is anointed by the sterile sperm
that lights the hesitant yellow flame of memory.
The dogs sense the profound truth of the coffins
and their howling echoes the nocturnal servitude of the dead.

Now the wind smells of withered flowers,
of myrtle wreaths that time has pulled to pieces
and I feel in the other light of defencelessness
for lofty frozen words of the last omen in the inexpressible moment.

Crystalline nausea overshadowing my brow:
such is that rottenness
that flows along a milky path of worms.
Those abandoned to the talons of the earth

who have been close to the light that shines at night
return passing through the walls,
uninhabited bodies in the destitute guilt of the earth,
and they mildly search for protection from defencelessness.

Who knocks on the glass of the window with a dark and strange motion?
Is it that voice from nowhere, which must go away?

An angel passed by, an angel
and the silence cuts a strand of angel-hair
and my souls holds, congealed, a drop of the blood of the angel that
passed by,
of the angel that froze my very bowels
with its sweet glance from the gloom.
And it is a ship's wake of agonizing gloom, the passing-by of the angel,
it is the grief of the dead being consumed in the burning shadow of
the gloom,
it is death, Lord, which has anchored in my very bowels,
in the bowels of the child that is made in the placenta
wrapped in bloody cloths, caressed in the gloom.

The shadows weep; the shadows say: weep,
full of horror and mourning,
you who are eternally anchored in the life of death.

Anyone now
who does not procure for his feet under the world
long lines of horizontable death
will forever deny what is flame and silence.

Xosé Neira Vilas (1928–)

From Memorias dun neno labrego, *1961*

Eu son...
Balbino. Un rapaz da aldea. Coma quen dis, un ninguén. E ademais, pobre.
Porque da aldea tamén é Manolito, e non hai quen lle tusa, a pesar do que lle acon-
teceu por causa miña.

No verán ando descalzo. O po quente dos camiños faime alancar. Magóanme as
areas e nunca falta algunha brocha para espetárseme nos pés. Érgome con noite
pecha, ás dúas ou tres da mañá, para ir co gando, restrebar ou xuntar monl-
los.Cando amañece xa me doe o lombo e as pernas. Pero o día comeza. Sede, sol,

moxardos.

No inverno, frío. Ganas de estar arreo ó pé do lume. Muíños apeados. Faladurías de neves e lobos. Os brazos son coma espeteiras para encolgar farrapos. Murnas, feridas, dedos sen tentos.

¡Que saben desto os nenos da vila!

Eles ignoran o que eu penso mentres boto ó corpo un gurrucho de caldo con broa. Ou o que sinto cando estou no monte pingando, aterecido, vendo por entre a chuvia unha pantasma bretemosa en cada árbore.

A aldea é unha mestura de lama e fume, onde os cans ouvean e a xente morre "cando está de Deus", como di a madriña. Os rapaces somos tristes. Enredamos, corremos tras dos foguetes e ata rimos, pero somos tristes. Temos a pobreza e os trafegos da terra aniñados nos ollos.

Eu quixera andar mundo. Ir por mares e terras que non coñezo. Nacín e crieime na aldea pero agora síntoa pequena, estreita. Coma se vivise nun cortizo. Teño pensamentos que non lle podo contar a ninguén. Algúns non me entenderían e outros chamaríanme tolo. Por eso escribo. E despois durmo como unha pedra. Quedo desatafegado, libre, coma se me quitasen de enriba un bocoi. ¡Cousas miñas! E tamén de Smith, o capitán que estivo na guerra e cando voltou para a casa púxose a escribir todo o que lle acontecera. Así está nun libro que me trouxo o Landeiro.

¡Se eu fixese un libro! Nin falar. Ogallá que non me atopen o caderno. Daríame vergoña. E non é para menos. Porque nel deborco todo o que sinto. Moi pouca xente o fai. Todos abren o peteiro para dúas cousas; para dicir a verdade ou para arredarse dela.

Na miña casa non me comprendían. E outro tanto acontéceme na do Landeiro. Eso é o peor que lle pode suceder a un, pero a moita xente non se lle dá.

Eu non sei se desvarío. Vexo o mundo darredor de min e adoezo por entendelo. Vexo sombras e luces, nubeiros que viaxan, lume, árbores. ¿Que é todo esto? Ninguén me di, poño por caso, para qué serven as estrelas, nin onde morren os paxaros. Sei de certo que moitísimos anos antes de nacer eu xa había sol e penedos e fuxía a auga polo río. E estou seguro de que todo seguirá igual despois de que eu morra. Virá máis xente, e máis, tripando uns nos outros, esquecéndose adrede dos que morreron, coma se non houbesen vivido.

Escribir nun caderno – iquen o diría! –, é coma baldeirar o corazón. Parece un milagre, pois ó fin de contas non pasa de ser unha conversa comigo mesmo. Pero para min é milagre todo. Dende as pingueiras da chuvia ata o canto do grilo.

Aínda que se me ocorrese facer un libro, como fixo Smith, de pouco valería o que conte. Smith estivo na guerra, e eu son apenas "o neno", como me chaman na casa. Son Balbino. Un rapaz da aldea. Un ninguén.

From Memories of a Country Boy, *1961*

I am…

Balbino. A village boy. As one might say, a nobody. And, moreover, poor. Even though Manolito is from the country as well, but nobody would lay a finger on him, in spite of what happened to him because of me.

In the summer I go around barefoot. The hot dust on the roads makes me take big strides. The sand hurts me and there's never a nail but it will pierce my feet. I get up when it's dark, at two or three in the morning, to go with the cattle, to plough or to gather dry grass. When dawn comes my back and my legs are already aching. But the day begins. Thirst, sun, mosquitos.

In the winter, cold. Wanting to be by the fire all day. Mills stopped. Stories about snow and wolves. One's arms like racks used to hang rags off. Red from the fire, hurting, numb fingers.

What do town children know about this!

They know nothing about what I think while I put some broth with corn bread inside me. Or what I feel when I'm out on the hills drenched, frozen, seeing the trees through the rain as if they were cloudy ghosts.

The village is a mixture of mud and smoke, where the dogs howl and the people die "when God wants", as my godmother says. For boys, we're sad. We play tricks, we run after rockets and we even laugh, but we're sad. We have poverty and hard labour nesting in our eyes.

I'd like to get around. To go to seas and lands that I don't know. I was born and bred in the country but now I find it small, narrow. As if I were living in a beehive. I have thoughts which I can't tell anyone about. Some wouldn't understand me and others would call me mad. So that's why I write. And after I sleep like a log. I feel relieved, free, as if a barrel were taken off me. I'm like that! And also Smith, the captain who fought in a war and, when he came home, started to write down all that had happened to him. That's what's in a book that old Landeiro brought me.

If I could write a book! Not a chance. I hope nobody finds my copy book. It would embarrass me. And I'm not exaggerating. Because I write down there all that I feel. Not many people do it. Everyone opens their mouths for two things; to tell the truth or to put a distance between them and it.

They didn't understand me at home. And the same is true in Landeiro's. That's the worst that can happen to somebody, but it doesn't matter to a lot of people.

I don't know if I'm talking nonsense. I look at the world around me and I try to understand it. I see light and shadow, clouds that travel, fire, trees. What is all this? Nobody tells me, for example, what the stars are for or where birds die. I know for sure that a long time before I was born the sun and rocks existed and the water ran in the rivers. And I'm convinced that it will go on in the same fashion after I die. More people will come, and more, stepping on each other, forgetting, on purpose, those who died, as if they had never existed.

To write in a copy book – who'd think it? – is like emptying one's heart. It's like a miracle, because in the end it's nothing more than a conversation with myself. But for me everything's a miracle. From the drops of rain to the cricket's song.

Although if I were to write a book, like Smith did, what I'd tell wouldn't be of any importance. Smith fought in a war, and I'm just "the kid", as they call me at home. I'm Balbino. A village boy. A nobody.

From Xente no Rodicio (People in the Paddle Wheel), 1965

Todo para Carme

A fonte, e o marelo, e a moza que berraba. ¿Por que espertei outra vez? Non fago máis que soñar estangurriadas. Cousas que non veñen ao caso. ¿Ou si? Está xeando. E o frío roe en min. Non hai mantas nin farrapos que cheguen. E Carme non acaba de vir. Agora está co mozo na solaina. Eles dous sós, no escuro. Falan e falan, baixiño, sen que se lles entenda. En veces quedan calados. O outro día pareceume que xemían. Non sei... O rato segue roendo no faiado. De cote co mesmo renxer. Antes sentía noxo del, pero xa non. Cando esperto, co frío ou despois dun soño medoñento, escoito o seu relar. Entretenme e faime vir outra vez o sono. Gustaríame ir ó faiado e velo no seu trafego. Pero é seguro que fuxiría, como foxen sempre os ratos. Ramón, o tolo, corre tras deles pola eira adiante, cun baloco, cando se arredan os primeiros monllos das medas do centeo, e liscan os que hai debaixo. O rato do faiado... Tremo co frío. ¿Por que o frío fai bater os dentes? Dou voltas, engrúñome, renxen as carochas no xergón, pero sigo aterecida; son moi frienta. Mañá estará todo branco: os tellados, as viñas, o agro. Coma se guindasen unha saba derriba do mundo. E o regueiro terá vidros. Irei enredar con eles nin ben me erga... ¿Por que berraría a moza na fonte? ¡Sóñase cada cousa! Carme non acaba de entrar. Voltarei a durmir cando ela veña. Chegará cos ollos ledos e as fazulas rubias, coma sempre. Cando se deite ha de arretegarme contra de si e quecerei deseguida. Ela é boa. Sempre que o mozo lle trae algunha lambetada, comparte comigo. O outro lerio é cousa da nosa nai. Quere que Carme se case. Fala das mozas solteiras e das rapazas pequechas. Dío por Carme que ten dezaoito anos, e por min, que fixen nove no mes de Santiago. Di que o tempo foxe e despois non hai quen queira á miña irmá. Cavila neso día e noite. Os ovos e a tona do leite son para Carme. E tamén o azucre e a roupa nova e o xabrón de recendo. Somos pobres. O pouco que se pode xuntar vai para ela. Así o dispón a mamai. ¡Teño unhas ganas de chegar a moza! Agora ando chea de remendos, cos zocos escalazados. Ninguén fai caso de min; nin as lendias me sacan. Amais deso, fanme erguer con estrelas, e aturar no monte ou no agro o que caia, sarabia ou raxeira. Toda a comenencia é pra Carme. E eu aturo os privamentos e o traballo máis amolado. Todo para que ela estea lucida e ridente e se poida casar... ¡Que friaxe! Teño os pés entalados. E Carme segue na solaina, co mozo. Os demais, dormen. Debe ser media noite. Todo está quedo, coma se a morte tivese chegado á aldea. Non pasan carros, nin aturuxa ninguén, nin sequera ouvean os cans. O rato, si. El non deixa de relar. E eu... Xa me vén o sono outra vez. O marelo na fonte, e a moza... Somos pobres. Carme... Todo para ela. O rat...

Everything for Carme

The fountain, and yellow, and the girl who shouted. Why did I wake up again? I'm always dreaming strange things. Things that are irrelevant. Or are they? It's freezing. And the cold is biting into me. There are no blankets nor anything to cover myself with. And Carme hasn't come yet. Now she's with her boyfriend in the gallery. Those two, alone in the dark. They talk and talk, in low voices, so that you can't understand them. Sometimes they stop talking. The other day I thought I heard them groaning. I don't know… The mouse is still gnawing in the lumber room. Each day with the same grinding noise. It disgusted me before but not anymore. When I wake up, because of the cold or a dream that frightens me, I hear him chewing away. It amuses me and makes me fall asleep again. I would like to go to the lumber room and see him at it. But he would definitely run away as mice usually do. Ramón, the madman, runs after them in the fields, with a stick, when the first sheaves of rye are gathered and those that are underneath run off. The mouse in the lumber room… I shiver with the cold. Why does cold make your teeth chatter? I turn in the bed, I crouch, the woodwormed bunk creaks, but I'm still numb from the cold; I'm a girl who feels the cold a lot. Tomorrow everything will be white: the roofs, the vines, the countryside. As if someone threw a sheet over the world. And the stream will have ice in it. I'll go to poke it as soon as I get up… Why would the girl at the fountain shout? One dreams such things! Carme still hasn't come back. I'll go back to sleep when she comes. She'll come with happy eyes and colour in her cheeks, as usual. When she goes to bed she'll squeeze me and she'll get warm straight away. She's good. If her boyfriend brings her sweets she shares them with me. The other problem has to do with our mother. She wants Carme to marry. She talks about single girls and small children. She says it because of Carme who's eighteen and because of me. I turned nine in July. She says that time flies and then there won't be anyone who'll want my sister. She thinks about that day and night. The eggs and cream are for Carme. And the sugar also and new clothes and the perfumed soap. We're poor. The little that we can get together is for her. That's what Mammy tells us to do. I really want to become a grown up! Now my clothes are full of patches and with misshapen clogs. Nobody pays attention to me: they don't even kill the lice in my hair. Besides that, they make me get up in the dark and to put up with everything outside, hail or heat. Everything good is for Carme. And I put up with hardships and hard work. It's all so that she looks good and happy and can get married… It's so cold! My feet are stiff. And Carme is still in the gallery with her boyfriend. Everybody else is asleep. It must be midnight. Everything is quiet, as if death had arrived in the village. Carts don't go by and nobody yelps, not even the dogs howl. The mouse goes on. He continues with his chewing. And me… I feel sleepy again. The yellow in the fountain, and the girl… We're poor. Carme… Everything for her. The mou…

Víctor Campio Pereira (1928–)

From O ar que nos leva (The Breeze That Carries Us Away), 1987

Prólogo

Se chego no solpor, se por degaro
de incanxeable luz chego a deshora
e me poño a cantar coma quen chora
pranto de noite pecha en día claro;

se chego no solpor, se me declaro
eivado vagaxeiro nesta hora
de encandecida lúa delatora
serodio corazón, triste paxaro;

se chego, digo, no solpor, e veño
manco de luz, perdido, a este recanto,
e me poño a cantar, é porque teño

no corazón a mar xa presentida.
Mais non me importa que se perda o canto.
Tanto me ten. A luz xa está perdida.

Prologue

If I arrive at sunset, if through longing
for irreplaceable light I arrive late
and I start singing like someone weeping
a lament of deep night in clear day;

if I arrive at sunset, if I declare
I am a crippled tramp at this hour
of a frozen all-revealing moon,
a tardy heart, a sad bird;

if, as I say, I arrive at sunset, and I come
bereft of light, lost, to this nook,
and I start singing, it will be because

I have presaged the sea in my heart.
But I am not concerned if my song is lost.
It doesn't matter. Light is already lost.

Manuel María (1929–2004)

From Advento (Advent), *1954*

Versos dunha terra amarga

¿Por que sempre quedo ancorado
na choiva silenciosa de Santiago
esperando eternamente un anxo mouro
que volte o meu soño neve ou pedra?

Unha arela imprecisa que é saudade
encerra o meu silencio verdecido
de lonxanías brancas ou salaios.
(A alma revoa polo vento atormentada).

E os ollos pasan, fulguran na distancia;
e o corazón envellece de palabras;
e unha estrela é rula xadeante
da miña vida rota e descravada.

A miña sede de mar inmaculado
queda coutada por unha estrofa de auga;
poeta sen loureiros. O ceo das campás
murcha os veludos pagados.

Soamente un puro anceio de ser nardo,
ou chaga sen finura, ou alma...
(Alma dunha noite de lúa e de cristal
con flores e silveiras enloitadas).

Verses from a bitter land

Why am I always anchored
in the silent rain of Santiago
eternally waiting for a dark angel
to turn my dream into snow or stone?

An imprecise idea that is sadlonging
encloses my greened silence
of white distances or sobs.
(My soul flutters, tormented, in the wind.)

And the eyes pass by, they flash in the distance;
and my heart grows old with words;
and a star is the panting turtle-dove
of my broken, unnailed life.

My thirst for an immaculate sea
is confined to a stanza of water;
poet without laurels. The sky of the bells
fades the complacent velvets.

Only a pure desire to be a spikenard,
or an indelicate wound, or a soul...
(Soul of a night of moon and crystal
with flowers and brambles in mourning.)

From A Primavera de Venus (The Springtime of Venus), *1993*

Despedida da primavera

É tempo xa de que me despida, Primavera.
Queda lonxe aquela idade na que
eran irmáns nosos os menceres:
    Flora poñía
un lume abrasador nas nosas veas, Venus
mostrábase propicia, as Tres Gracias
agasallábannos con cancións, danzas,
sorrisos e poemas que alegraban ao mundo
e facían xurdir un tempo novo e ledo:
agromaban rosas, camelias, caraveles,
a vida tiña unha esencia musical
a cuxo máxico son corrían os ríos,
danzaban, rumorosas, as florestas
e ordenaba o seu curso o universo.
De ti me despido pra sempre, Primavera.
Sei que o tempo é irreversíbel
e non vale de nada andar laiando.
Ameite fondamente e de verdade.
    Sempre

levarei o teu sorriso no sombrizo
e escuro pozo dos meus ollos.
　　Só che pido
unha raiola de sol e de alegría pra aquecer
a este meu triste corazón, vello e cansado.

Goodbye to spring

Now it's time for me to say goodbye, Spring.
It's far away, that time when
the dawns were our brothers:
　　Flora put
a burning fire into our veins, Venus
showed herself to be propitious, the Three Graces
regaled us with songs, dances,
smiles and poems that cheered the world
and made a new and happy time emerge:
roses, camellias, carnations were in bud,
life had a musical essence
to whose magical sound the rivers ran,
the flower-gardens danced, rustling,
and the universe ordered its course.
I say goodbye to you for ever, spring.
I know that time is irreversible
and it's no good going around moaning.
I loved you deeply and truly.
　　Always
I shall carry your smile in the shadowy
and dark well of my eyes.
　　I only ask of you
a ray of sunlight and of happiness to warm
this sad, sad heart of mine, old and weary.

Uxío Novoneyra (1930–1999)

From Os eidos (The Fields), *1952*

Courel dos tesos cumes...

¡Courel dos tesos cumes que ollan de lonxe!
Eiquí síntese ben o pouco que é un home!

Courel of proud peaks...

Courel of proud peaks that look down from afar!
Here one does feel how petty is a man!

¡Cousos do lobo!...

¡Cousos do lobo!
¡Cavorcos do xabarín!
¡Eidos solos
onde ninguén foi nin ha d'ir!

¡O lobo! ¡Os ollos o lombo do lobo!

Baixa o lobo polo ollo do bosco
movendo nas flairas dos teixos
ruxindo na folla dos carreiros
en busca de vagoada máis sola e máis medosa...

Rastrexa,
párase e venta
finca a pouta ergue a testa e oula
coa noite na boca...

Hunting-grounds of the wolf!...

Hunting-grounds of the wolf!
Gorges of the boar!
Solitary lands
where no one has ever been or ever will go!

O wolf! The eyes the back of the wolf!

The wolf comes down through the eye of the forest
stirring the branches of the yews
rustling the leaves on the tracks
in search of a more solitary and fearful valley...

It seeks scents,
it stops and sniffs the air,
it tenses forelegs raises head and howls
with night in its maws...

From Elexías do Courel (Elegies to O Courel), *1966*

Do Courel a Compostela, 1966

Os que así nos tein
só tein noso os nosos nomes no censo,
que astra a nosa suor sen alento se perde na terra.

GALICIA, ¿será a miña xeración quen te salve?
¿Irei un día do Courel a Compostela por terras liberadas?
¿Non, a forza do noso amor non pode ser inútil!

From O Courel to Compostela

Those who've got us like this,
all they've got of ours is our names on the census,
because even our dispirited sweat is lost in the earth.

GALICIA, will it be my generation that saves you?
Shall I go one day from O Courel to Compostela through liberated
lands?
No, the strength of our love cannot be useless!

Xosé Fernández Ferreiro (1931–)

From Agosto do 36, *1991*

Gregorio era republicano. Iso era polo menos o que dicía o crego, don Xenaro. "Non pode ser outra cousa sendo, como é, un Xirandón. Lévano no sangue. Xente aguda e de boa madeira, pero as ideas fanos camiñar por onde non deben."

– ¿Non dirá que Gregorio é unha ruín persoa? – preguntábanlle cando tal afirmaba.

– Non – respondía –. Eu non digo iso. Eu só digo que as ideas o traizoan. E iso xa lle ocorría ó seu pai.

Unha vez, Gregorio discutira iradamente co crego por cuestións políticas, na taberna de As Fontiñas, cando estaban a xogar unha partida de tute. "Vostedes os cregos son uns viva la Virgen (disque lle dixo sen recato ningún) que non fan máis ca enganar á xente contándolle mentiras desde os altares e púlpitos, en lugar de lle dici-las verdades e abrirlle os ollos. Claro que a vostedes, e a outros coma vostedes, interésalles máis que o pobo siga cego e analfabeto, pois así, coma os bois capados, é máis manexable."

A cousa fora moi sonada. Algúns non o podían crer. Pero os homes que estaban presentes na taberna cando o altercado, e mailo propio taberneiro, xuraron que si: que era certo que Gregorio lle dixo tales palabras ó crego. E aínda máis, dicían que o mestre erguera o puño, se ben as testemuñas non eran coincidentes neste punto, como tampouco na orixe da liorta. Polo visto seica fora don Xenaro quen o aguilloara por causa das súas ideas políticas, acusándoo, entre outras cousas, de comunista.

De seguro que o mestre había estar bébedo. Todos sabemos que lle gusta a pepereta – opinaban uns.

– Pois ó crego non lle gusta menos – replicaban outros –. E se non está ben que beba un mestre, peor é que beban os que levan sotana.

Para algúns era unha herexía que Gregorio lle dixese tales cousas a don Xenaro, mais para outros estaban moi ben ditas. Aqueles dicían: "É un arroutado coma o pai. Un anticristo." E estes: "Por fin o crego atopou quen llas cante ben cantadas. Xa está ben de que ninguén lle contradiga os seus sermóns e de que nos trate coma ovellas." No que todos estaban de acordo, desde logo, era en que Gregorio (alto e de ollos claros e moi brillantes, que cando bebía algo máis da conta ou se alporizaba mesmo semellaban saírlle das cuncas) era o vivo retrato do pai, o único home da parroquia que xa daquela se permitía discutir co crego e dicirlle de cando en vez algunhas verdades gordas. Incluso na taberna, xogando ás cartas, cousa esta que asemade era criticada por uns e tolerada por outros.

Anque había opinións para tódolos gustos, as simpatías eran máis a prol do mestre que do crego. "A Gregorio queriámoslle máis, non só porque era de aquí e todos o coñeciamos desque naceu, senón porque (como tamén fora xa o seu pai), pese ás súas rarezas e ás súas arroutadas, e a falar sen pelos na lingua, era un home moi servicial e nada interesado. El tiña a casa sempre aberta para todos. Nunca lle negou un favor a ninguén e tíñaos feito a moreas."

Don Xenaro, en cambio, anque levaba moitos anos na parroquia non era alá moi querido pola xente. Era moi interesado. E o seu comportamento durante a guerra deixou moito que desexar. "Por exemplo o crego de Armariz, naqueles anos, salvou a máis dun de ser paseado, para o que tiña que dar moitas voltas e facer viaxes á capital para entrevistarse coas autoridades. Don Xenaro, de sermos sinceros, máis ben fixo do revés. Ou non fixo nada."

Claro que aínda que falaban mal un do outro, non se privaban por iso, de cando en vez, de botar unha partida de tute na taberna das Fontiñas, a mesma onde tivera lugar o altercado por cuestións políticas. Quixesen ou non, nin un nin o outro atopaban máis doada compaña para xogar e discutir nin con tempo libre para tales mesteres.

– Hai que botar man de ti anque non se queira – dicíalle o crego ó mestre, sorrindo mentres barallaba –. Xa me pasaba isto co teu pai. Era raro, pero era intelixente. E xogaba moi ben. Ti eslle cuspidiño, non hai máis que verte e oírte. Incluso te-la súa mesma voz e as súas propias maneiras... Claro que a intelixencia mal empregada pode levar a un ó inferno.

– Xogue, don Xenaro, xogue – respondíalle Gregorio sen lle facer caso –. Non me veña a min con sermóns nin me fale do inferno. Amais que as tabernas non son lugares propicios para semellantes discursos. Para iso xa están as igrexas. ¿Non lle parece?

E nisto estalou a guerra e desatáronse os odios e as vinganzas. A todos nos entrou un gran temor e un gran desacougo no corpo. ¿Que ía pasar? Moitos mozos foron chamados a filas. Axiña comezaron a chegar aquelas estrañas noticias que falaban dos paseos e dos cárceres.

Unha tarde apareceron en Abades os falanxistas. Era a primeira vez que os viamos. Entraron na taberna de Lázaro a tomar algo e a facer preguntas que el nunca revelou. Pero sábese que o nome de Gregorio saíu na conversa. Despois colleron o camiño das Fontiñas e visitaron ó crego na rectoral. Cando cerca da anoitecida regresaron a Santo Estevo, por Abades, Manuel, o de Santos, o fillo do Garabís, que formaba parte do grupo, saudou a algúns veciños. Víase máis empoleirado ca nunca, coa súa pistola ó cinto e o fusil ó lombo. Logo, ó marcharen, soltou aquilo que tanto nos preocupou a todos:

– Imos limpar España de herexes e comunistas.

From August 1936, *1991*

Gregorio was a republican. That was what the priest, Don Xenaro, said at least. "He can't be anything else being, as he is, one of the Xirandóns. It's in their blood. Sharp and decent people, but their ideas take them where they shouldn't go".

– You aren't saying that Gregorio is bad? – they asked him when he said this.

– No – he answered –. I'm not saying that. I'm only saying that their ideas give them away. And the same happened with their father.

One time Gregorio had argued violently with the priest about politics in a tavern in As Fontiñas, when they were playing cards. "You, the priests, are thoughtless (it seems he said this straight out) you do nothing else but pull the wool over people's eyes telling them lies from the altars and pulpits, instead of telling them the truth and opening their eyes to it. Of course you, and others like you, are more interested in keeping people blind and uneducated as, in that way, like castrated oxen, they're easier to manage".

This was talked about a lot. Some people couldn't believe it. But those who were present in the tavern when the argument took place, and the owner, swore it had happened: that it was true that Gregorio said all that to the priest. Even more than that, they said that the schoolmaster had put up his fist, although the witnesses did not coincide on this point, nor did they agree on the origin of the disagreement. It seems that it was Don Xenaro who had provoked the schoolmaster because of his political ideas, accusing him, among other things, of being a communist.

For sure the schoolmaster was drunk. Everybody knows that he likes his drop – some claimed.

– Well, the priest likes it too – others replied –. And if it isn't all right for a schoolmaster to drink, it's worse if it's someone who wears a clerical collar.

For some it was considered blasphemous that Gregorio said such things to Don Xenaro, but for others he hit the nail on the head. The former said: "He's excitable like his father. An antichrist". And the latter: "At last the priest found his match. And it's about time that somebody contradicted what he says in his sermons, not letting him treat us like sheep". On what everyone agreed, certainly, was that Gregorio (tall, with blue, bright eyes, when he drank more than usual or he got angry they even seemed to fall out of their sockets) was the image of his father, the only man in the parish that, even in those times, was not afraid to argue with the priest and tell him a thing or two. Even in the tavern, playing cards, something that was criticised by some and tolerated by others.

Although there were varying opinions, people felt more sympathy for the schoolmaster than for the priest. "We liked Gregorio more, not only was he from here and everybody knew him since he was born, but also because (his father had also been), in spite of his oddness, his outbursts and speaking his mind, he was a very obliging man and not self-seeking at all. His house was open to everybody. He never refused to do anyone a favour and he had done a load of them".

Don Xenaro, on the other hand, although he had been many years in the parish, wasn't very much liked by the people. He was very selfish. And his behaviour during the war left a lot to be desired. "For example, the priest at Armariz in those years saved more than one from being taken away to be shot, for which he had to go out of his way quite a lot and go to the capital to speak with the people in power. Don Xenaro, to be sincere, actually did the opposite. Or he did nothing".

Of course, although they spoke badly of each other, that didn't stop them, from time to time, from playing cards in the tavern at Fontiñas, the same one where the argument had taken place about political matters. Whether they wanted to or not, neither one nor the other found better company for playing and arguing or anyone who had time to do so.

– One has to ask you even if one doesn't want to – the priest said to the schoolmaster, smiling while he shuffled. This happened to me before with your father. He was odd, but intelligent. He played very well. You're his spitting image, one only has to see you and hear you, you even have his same voice and gestures … Of course intelligence badly used can take one to hell.

– Play, Don Xenaro, play – Gregorio answered without paying much attention to him –. Don't start now with your sermons and talk about hell. Besides, taverns aren't suitable places for such stuff. That's what the churches are for. Don't you agree?

And then the war broke out and hate and revenge were set loose. All of us were very afraid and anxious. What was going to happen? Many young men were enlisted. Immediately strange news came about being taken away to be shot and the prisons.

One evening the Falangists appeared in Abades. It was the first time we saw them. They went into Lázaro's tavern to have a drink and to ask questions that he never answered. But it was known that Gregorio's name cropped up in the conversation. Afterwards, they took the road to Fontiñas and they visited the priest in the presbytery. When, very close to nightfall, they were returning to Santo Estevo through Abades, Manuel de Santos, Garabís's son, who was part of the group, greeted some locals. He was more full of himself than ever, with his pistol in his belt and his rifle on his back. Next, when they were leaving, he let fall that which was worrying us all:

– We are going to rid Spain of heretics and communists.

Camilo Gonsar (1931–2008)

From Cara a Times Square, *1980*

Os tolos gozan hoxe de boa prensa; son publicamente admirados case como homes que chegaron a un estado superior, desde o que poden ver ata onde a vista dos cordos non alcanza, e tamén son publicamente compadecidos como víctimas inocentes da crueldade da nosa organización social. Eu non nego nada disto; o que si nego é que, en xeral, as historias feitas ou protagonizadas por tolos me gusten, porque nada teño que ver, nin tan sequera como amateur, coa cura ou a investigación da loucura, nin, a verdade sexa dita, me inspiran os tolos ningunha simpatía especial.

Certo que hai outros tolos, como D. Quixote ou o capitán Ahab, xustamente elevados á categoría de símbolos permanentes da humanidade; pero eran falsos tolos, ou eran tolos só segundo a opinión de xentes ou de mentes vulgares.

Total, o que lle quero dicir é que a historia que lle vou contar nada ten que ver co mundo da loucura. Noutro caso, non se me tería ocorrido sometela á súa consideración.

Pero xa é tempo de ir sen máis ós feitos:

Eu pasara aquela tarde bebendo whisky en diferentes bares do Greenwich Village cun vello inmigrante amigo meu.

Os dous eramos do mesmo país – un deses pequenos e desgraciados países que levan séculos desangrándose, vertendo ríos de emigrantes nos portos americanos.

Ó Greenwich Village, de ordinario, relacionámolo con mozos rebeldes, bohemios, artistas, turistas e demais, e non con vellos inmigrantes. Pero dábase o caso de que o meu compañeiro fora propietario anos atrás dun restaurante ou algo así neste barrio e era, polo tanto, un experto nel, un coñecedor de tódolos seus segredos e da súa vida subterránea.

Eu, pola miña parte, durante a miña estada en New York, case non deixaba pasar nin un só día sen coller un autobús para o Village.

Unha vez alí, todo canto necesitaba para pasar unha tarde interesante era deambular polas rúas, descansando de vez en cando nun café calquera.

Un dos membros da chamada Beat Generation que vivira polo Greenwich Village – como a maioría dos seus camaradas, supoño – di, segundo lin anos despois de que sucederan os feitos aquí relatados, que lle parecía que o Village tiña, en certos momentos, todo o engado dun Utrillo. Supoño que hai ironía nesta observación, porque, non sen fundamento, para os norteamericanos París é sagrado e incomparable, pero a verdade é que eu encóntroa francamente certeira.

Outro dos meus praceres baratos consistía en sentarme en Washington Square. Non deixaba de ser un descanso no medio de todo o rebumbio de Manhattan. Pero a miña querencia por Washington Square aínda dependía doutra razón: a novela con este título de Henry James, que lera eu había moito, sendo estudiante nun medio social moi diferente. Xustamente nesta novela afírmase que o ideal dun retiro tranquilo e doce atopábase para os habitantes de New York, en 1835, en Washington Square. Todo canto podo dicir é que eu atopei o mesmo cento vintecinco anos despois; non sei se foi cuestión de sorte.

O dono do derradeiro bar onde tomaramos uns whiskies era tamén un vello inmigrante, un veterano camarada, por así dicilo, do meu amigo, e paisano de nosóutro-los dous. Había varios meses que non se vían; de xeito que falaron de vagar, o meu amigo e mais el, de lembranzas comúns e, sobre todo, da situación actual, feliz ou non, doutros paisanos, vellos coma eles ou máis novos, e camaradas deles tamén na dura aventura da inmigración – a miúdo ilegal – nos Estados Unidos.

O caso é que, tan logo como saímos do bar aquel, o meu amigo, que vivía non moi lonxe, concretamente na W 12th St8, se mal non recordo, deu en dicir que xa era moi tarde e que tiña que volver para a casa de inmediato e, sen tan sequera despedirse de min, marchou case correndo e deixándome, en certa maneira, abandonado.

Xa era, efectivamente, ben tarde.

Metinme por rúas case desertas e seguín camiñando sen rumbo na noite co propósito de despexarme un pouco. Finalmente, resolvín determe diante dunha parada de autobús.

Mellor dito: pareceume unha parada de autobús. Pode que non a fose, penso agora, e que o meu erro, se tal erro houbo, se debese, en parte, ó whisky.

De todas maneiras, eu desconfiaba de que seguisen pasando autobuses por alí, en vista da hora. Debo sinalar que tiña aínda ideas moi confusas (a verdade é que as sigo tendo) sobre os horarios deste transporte de superficie de Manhattan, onde era aínda pouco menos que un recén chegado. Pero decidín agardar ata que a evidencia de estar perdendo o tempo me pesase demasiado.

Principiei a pasear pola beirarrúa sen afastarme nunca demasiado da suposta parada.

Acababa de da-la volta despois de completar un dos meus paseos cando me encontrei diante doutro camiñante, aínda novo.

From Towards Times Square, *1980*

Mad people have a good reputation nowadays; they are admired in public almost as if they had reached a higher state from where they can see what sane people can't, and they are also sympathized with publicly as innocent victims of the cruelty of our social organisation. I don't deny any of this; what I don't admit, generally speaking, is that I like stories told by or about mad people, because I have nothing to do with a cure for or research into madness, not even as an amateur, nor, to say the truth, are mad people especially attractive to me.

It is true that there are other mad people, like Don Quijote or Captain Ahab, justly elevated to the category of permanent symbols of humanity; but they were false madmen, or they were madmen only according to the opinion of people or vulgar minds.

All in all, what I'm saying is that story that I'm going to tell has nothing to do with madness. If it were so I wouldn't have thought of submitting it for your consideration.

But now it's time to get down to the facts:

I had spent that evening drinking whiskey in different bars in Greenwich Village with an old emigrant friend of mine.

The two of us were from the same country – one of those small, unfortunate countries that have been bled white for centuries, spilling rivers of emigrants in American ports.

Greenwich Village is usually associated with young rebels, bohemians, artists, tourists and the like, and not with old emigrants. But it happened that my companion had been proprietor years before of a restaurant or the like in this area. And he was, as a result, an expert on it, who knew all its secrets and underground life.

I, for my part, during my time in New York, hardly let a day go by without taking a bus to the Village.

Once there, everything I needed to spend an interesting afternoon was found in rambling through the streets, resting from time to time in any sort of café. One of the members of the so-called Beat Generation, who had lived in Greenwich Village – like the majority of his companions, I suppose – has been known to say, as I read years after what I'm going to tell here happened, that he thought that the Village had at certain times all the charm of an Utrillo. I suppose this to be an ironic observation, because, not without foundation, for Americans Paris is sacred and without comparison, but the truth is I find his observation to be totally correct.

Another of my cheap pleasures consisted in sitting in Washington Square. It was a rest in the middle of the uproar of Manhattan. But my affection for Washington Square was also due to another reason: the novel by Henry James of the same name, that I had read a long time ago, when a student in very different social circumstances. Precisely in this novel it is said that the ideal of a quiet and sweet retreat for the inhabitants of New York in 1835 was found in Washington Square. All that I can say is that I found the same one hundred and twenty-five years later; I don't know if it was just luck.

The owner of the last bar where we had had some whiskeys was also an old emigrant, a veteran comrade, to put it that way, of my friend, and countryman of the two. They hadn't seen each other for some months; so my friend and he took their time to talk to each other of their common memories and, above all, of the current state of affairs, happy or not, of other countrymen, old like them or younger, and their comrades also in the hard adventure of emigration – often illegal – in the United States.

So it was that on leaving that bar, my friend, who didn't live far away, to be precise in W 12th St8, if my memory serves me right, said that it was late and that he had to go home immediately and, without even saying goodbye, he went away in a half run, abandoning me in a certain way.

In fact, it was quite late.

I went down almost deserted streets and continued walking without any purpose all night trying to clear my mind a little. Finally, I decided to stop at a bus stop.

Or to be more accurate: a bus stop appeared before me. It might be that it wasn't, I now realize and that my mistake, if it was one, was due, in part, to whiskey.

Anyway, I wasn't sure that buses were still running, keeping in mind the time of night. I should point out that I still had very confused ideas (the fact is I still have them) about the timetables of this means of transport in Manhattan, where I could still be considered as almost a recent arrival. But I decided to wait until the evidence that I was wasting my time became too much for me.

I began to walk up and down the pavement without leaving the supposed bus stop too far behind.

I had just turned after one of my walks when I met another pedestrian, still young.

Xohana Torres (1931–)

From Estacións ao mar (Stations to the Sea), *1980*

A noite cría soños incompletos por riba da vila. Esta é a miña casa; este o aleiro a onde soben as sombras

Ás altas horas
hai un coro puntual de voces, remusmuses,
confusión ideal para os poemas;
formas, escadas, signos, residencias
ás que transbordaremos sen remedio.

Ás altas horas
desvariamos tendidos longamente
no devalo da noite: Tal é así
coma imitamos máis aos mortos.

Ás altas horas
os feitos adquiren un sentido letal:
Escribiremos cartas
que nunca chegarán ao correo;
saber cómo se reza;
arrepentirnos de algo;
amarse coma tolos.

Ás altas horas
hai un lobo terrible que devora os recantos
e hai un tren imposible que pasa e non se vai.

Certeza tanta: Saber
máis sinxela a verdade,
máis aguda a ferida,
máis grave o óso.
Cada noite é cruzar
a soidá do tempo,
dar algo por perdido,
apagar unha lámpada.

Decaemos no escuro. Somos infelices.
Sentinelas sombrías: cans e vellos.

Tamén queda
a irreparable lúa
que deixamos detrás.

**Night rears incomplete dreams above the town. This is my
house; this the gable up to which shadows rise**

In the small hours
there is a punctual choir of voices, a murmuring,
an ideal confusion for poems;
forms, stairs, signs, residences
to which we shall irremediably transfer.
In the small hours
stretched at full length we lose our senses
in the wane of the night: This is how
we best imitate the dead.

In the small hours
facts acquire a lethal sense:

We shall write letters
that will never reach the post;
understand how people pray;
repent of something;
love each other like mad things.

In the small hours
there is a terrible wolf that devours nooks and crannies
and an impossible train that passes by and does not go away.

So much certainty: To know
the truth to be more simple,
the wound more acute,
the bone heavier.
Each night means crossing
the solitude of time,
giving up something for lost,
switching off a lamp.

We decline in the dark. We are unhappy.
Guards in the shadows: dogs and old men.

There also remains
the irreparable moon
that we have left behind.

From Tempo de ría (Ria Weather), *1992*

Vaise a calma da dorna...

Vaise a calma da dorna.
Inaccesible xira a espiral
de lontana tormenta.
Bandadas de andoriñas apousan
nos fíos do telégrafo.
O vento cabalga polas follas
e ti, pai, ergueito, serio,
Illa tamén a onde acudimos nós.

Xa nin me lembro do número de pontes,
antigamente xuntos e da man.
Nada houbese podido con tanta fe,
no camiño ninguén me adiantaría.

Algunha vez recobro memoria do misterio:
aquí está a vila da miña leda infancia
tendida pola bruma que sobe ata o Brión.

Delata outono a paciencia dos días
e un sol serodio que se detén
na túa fermosísima fronte.

Calm leaves our little boat...

Calm leaves our little boat.
Inaccessible spins the spiral
of a distant storm.
Flocks of swallows perch
on the telegraph wires.
The wind rides on the leaves
and you, father, erect, serious,
an Island, too, to which we turn.

I can't even remember the number of bridges,
in olden times together and hand-in-hand.

Nothing could have contended against such faith,
nobody would overtake me on the road.

Sometimes I regain memory of the mystery:
here is the town of my happy childhood
lying in the mist that rises to Brión Hill.

Autumn is betrayed by the patience of the days
and a late sun that pauses
over your beautiful forehead.

Bernardino Graña (1932–)

From Profecía do mar (Prophecy of the Sea), *1966*

O gato da tasca mariñeira

Aquí non hai silencio porque hai homes
falan os homes falan
aquí non pasa o vento esa fantasma
os homes falan falan
e fórmase outro vento outro rebumbio
unha fantasma feita de fume
este fumar sen tino estas palabras
e pasa un suave gato que é da casa.

Beben viño coñac
berran discuten contan chistes mascan
un pouco de xamón tal vez chourizo
o gato ulisca cheira mira agarda
vai á cociña vense ao mostrador quixera
un anaquiño de boa carne un chisco
de tenrura algún queixo unha migalla.

Aquí non hai vagadas nin roncallos
non se ven os cabezos nin as praias
o taberneiro bole saúda cobra serve fala
cambea mil pesetas chama á muller a berros
e contesta ao teléfono ás chamadas
e os homes berran moito cheos de ira
e rin e danse a man e nada pasa.

O gato calandiño ergue as orellas
tan maino tan suavísimo sen gana
cruza por entre as pernas entre as botas
altas botas de caucho contra as augas co seu rabo
arriquichado e duro e tan en calma
e aquí non hai silencio que hai vinte homes
e están ben lonxe os mares que arrebatan.

Se acaso o gato mira os ollos do home
guicha en suspenso escoita en paz agacha
unha orelliña aguda e indiferente

lambe teimudo e calmo unha das patas
e se acaso durmiña e abre un ollo
e ve que os homes beben fuman discuten moito non se cansan
de ensaladilla callos mexilóns anchoas
e viño e viño e viño tinto e branco en tantas tazas
e esgarran cospen entran saen empuxan brindan cantan
e a radio está acendida e óese música
e o gato pasa indemne comprendendo ten costume son os homes
non se espanta.

The cat in the harbour bar

In here there is no silence there are men
they talk the men they talk
in here the wind that phantom does not blow
the men they talk they talk
another wind is made another row
a phantom that is formed of all this smoke
of all this crazy smoking all these words
and a smooth house-cat wanders here and there.

They drink their wine their brandy
they shout they argue they tell jokes they chew
a slice of ham or maybe of chourizo
the house-cat sniffs the air smells watches waits
it goes off to the kitchen comes back to the bar fancies
a morsel of nice meat a little bit
of tenderness some cheese or just a scrap.

In here there are no waves there are no rollers
sandbanks and beaches nowhere to be seen
the landlord rushes greets takes money pours drink chats
changes a banknote yells out to his wife
picks up the phone replying to the calls
and the men shout and shout in all their anger
and they laugh and shake hands nothing bad happens.

Without a sound the cat pricks up its ears
so tame so very smooth indifferent
it strolls between the legs between the boots
long boots of indiarubber to keep the water out
its tail is raised and stiff and still as still

here is no silence here are twenty men
the seas that snatch and steal are far away.

Perhaps the cat looks man full in the face
it peeps in peace it hears in silence folds
down an acute uninterested ear
it licks a leg with calm tenacity
and if it dozes opening an eye
and sees that the men drink smoke argue endlessly don't tire
of Russian salad tripe mussels anchovies
and wine and wine and wine red and white in so many cups
and hawk spit come in go out push drink toasts sing
and the radio's on and music's blaring out
and the cat strolls round unscathed it understands it's used to it
                                                        they're the men
it isn't scared.

From Se o noso amor e os peixes... (If Our Love and the Fish...) 1980

¿Como hei vivir mañá sen a luz túa?

Case morto vivín sen coñecerte
aló na chaira seca por absurdas rúas
onde ninguén me soubo dar mornura.

Foi soedade desconforme adentro
e a semente a caír en terra dura.
¿Como hei vivir mañá sen a luz túa?

Erguinme e vinte ao regresar á terra
como se fora todo aquelo un soño
pesado e ti xa foras sempre miña.

Foi outra vez materno en aloumiño
o bico teu na lingua.
E foi de novo corazón adentro
comprender a existencia e a dozura.
¿Como hei vivir mañá sen a luz túa?

Pero hoxe mesmo o día abriu en medo
entrou na fiestra un sol estraño inmenso
e deixáchesme o leito en mantas frías.

Está a volver agora corazón adentro
a soedade o podre a agonía
a me pinchar as cousas en millóns de pugas
cada minuto en séculos de agullas.
¿Como hei vivir mañá sen a luz túa?

How shall I live tomorrow without your light?

As good as dead I lived not knowing you
away on the dry plain in absurd streets
where nobody could give me any warmth.

It was unwilling loneliness inside
and the seed falling on the stony earth.
How shall I live tomorrow without your light?

I rose and saw you when I came back home
as if all that had been a bad nightmare
and you were now to be forever mine.

It was again maternal in caresses,
your kiss upon my tongue.
It was once more deep down inside my heart
to understand existence and affection.
How shall I live tomorrow without your light?

But this very day today dawned in fearfulness
in through the window came a strange vast sun
and you left me the bed in coldest blankets.

It all comes back now deep down in my heart
the loneliness the rottenness the agony
things piercing me with millions of augers
every minute in centuries of needles.
How shall I live tomorrow without your light?

Manuel Álvarez Torneiro (1932–)

From Luz de facer memoria (Light for Remembering), *1999*

De camiño

Son o que pasa:
visitante e de paso polos bosques talados.

Son o que pasa
con demorado acento de despedir.

Ó Sur quedan as horas abrigosas,
ó efémero lugar da eternidade.

Gardade vós as tardes compartidas,
a palabra-navío na que facer viaxe,
algún froito absoluto dos que queiman nas mans.

Mentide unha clareira cara a alba imposible,
unha magnolia morna,
un fósforo marítimo
para anima-la estampa desolada.

Sede teimosamente inéditos na rosa,
primeirizos no amor que violenta,
contranúmero.

Un tacto de galerna para os neutrais que dormen
ó pé dos horizontes.
Un título de neve.

Un segredo obstinado na arquivolta.

Xa vexo a luz que cae.
Novembro trae avisos.
Cítanme no xardín os fantasmas amados.

Escribo na fronteira.

On the road

I am the one passing by:
a visitor on my way through the felled forests.

I am the one passing by
with delayed tones of farewell.

The sheltered hours have been left in the South,
in the ephemeral place of eternity.

You must all keep the shared afternoons,
the word-boat in which to journey,
some absolute fruit, one of those that burn the hands.

You must feign a clearing over towards the impossible dawn,
a warm magnolia,
a match struck at sea
to enliven the desolate scene.

You must be stubbornly unprecedented in the rose,
novices in the love that violates,
counternumber.

The touch of a northwester for the neutrals who sleep
at the foot of the horizons.
A title of snow.

An obstinate secret in the archivolt.

I see the light that falls.
November brings warnings.
I have a date in the garden with the beloved ghosts.

I write on the frontier.

Salvador García Bodaño (1935–)

From Tempo de Compostela (Time of Compostela), *1979*

Compostela é unha rúa longa

Compostela é unha rúa longa
na memoria
onde vagan os nomes
e as horas
que cadaquén recorda.

Tempo de eternidade nas sombras
case vougas
a caer polos días
e as cousas
maino como unha choiva.

Van no libro da vida as follas
xa sen volta
pasando sobre o atril
das lousas
sen que un se dea conta.

E as lembranzas igual cás ondas
veñen soltas
dende o fondo de nós
e todas
fan un mar que se alonxa...

Compostela is a long street

Compostela is a long street
in the memory
and in it wander the names
and the hours
that everyone remembers.

Time of eternity in the shadows
that are almost empty,
falling on the days
and on the things
as soft as a shower of rain.

In the book of life the pages
are flicking over
never to return, on the lectern
upon the tiles
and one does not notice.

And the memories like the waves
come freed
from the depths of us
and they all
make a sea that flows away...

Antón Avilés de Taramancos (1935–1992)

From As torres no ar (The Towers in the Breeze), 1989

Na outra banda do mar...

Na outra banda do mar constrúen o navío:
o martelar dos calafates resoa na mañá, e non saben
que están a construír a torre de cristal da miña infancia.
Non saben que cada peza, cada caderna maxistral
é unha peza do meu ser. Non saben
que no interior da quilla está a medula mesma
da miña espiña dorsal; que no galipote a quencer
está o perfume máxico da miña vida.
Que cando no remate ergan a vela, e a enxarcia
tremole vagarosamente no ar
será o meu corazón quen sinta o vento,
será o meu corazón.

On the other side of the sea...

On the other side of the sea they are building the ship:
the hammering of the shipwrights rings out in the morning, and
　　　　　　　　　　　　　　　　　they do not know
that they are building the crystal tower of my childhood.
They do not know that each part, each rib
is a part of my being. They do not know
that inside the keel is the very marrow
of my spine; that in the pitch being heated
is the magic perfume of my life.

That when they finally hoist the sail, and the rigging
sways softly in the air,
it will be my heart that feels the wind,
it will be my heart.

From Cantos caucanos (Cantos of Cauca), *1985*

Primeiro canto (fragmentos)

I

Era o clamor universal:
gorxeaban os astros o seu canto,
e o río imenso
esfarrapaba a vaxina froital do mundo
no ámbito do Cauca.

Un deus sinxelo apacentaba os aerolitos
ao pé das criaturas inocentes
– branco corazón de guanábana –.

(Aínda o ferro non coñecía
a súa paixón máis terríbel,
e no taller escuro do espanto
un garañón a gargallada aberta
artellaba a morte total dos séculos
– doce territorio da vida –.)

IV

Non hai regreso, avoa,
nunca
regresa o mesmo home
ao mesmo sitio.
O lobo do deserto
perdeu a túa voz,
e a auga clara da túa man
non apaga a saudade revertida.
Todos os rumbos, todos os navíos
lévanme ao grande río a renacer:
No ámbito do Cauca.

First canto (extracts)

I

It was the universal clamour:
the stars were warbling their song,
and the immense river
was tearing apart the fruit-vagina of the world
in the region of Cauca.

A simple god was grazing on the meteorites
by the side of the innocent creatures
– a white heart of soursop fruit.

(Iron still did not know
its most terrible passion,
and in the dark workshop of dread
a stallion in full guffaw
was planning the total death of the centuries
– sweet territory of life.)

IV

There is no return, grandmother,
never
does the same man return
to the same place.
The wolf of the wasteland
has ravaged your voice,
and the clear water in your hand
does not quench endless sadlongings.
All bearings, all ships
carry me to the great river to be reborn:
in the region of Cauca.

Xosé Luís Franco Grande (1936–)

From Entre o si e o non (Between Yes and No), *1967*

Ás veces entro en min...

Ás veces entro en min
por ver se atopo aquilo meu que eu son
e sempre vexo que non dou comigo
e que son eu quen se me vai das mans.

E sempre volvo a procurarme a min
e nunca vou parar alí onde eu son
aquilo que é máis meu
que debo ser eu...

Ás veces penso que xa estou comigo,
cáseque no meu eido,
e despois vexo que aínda falta máis,
máis alá, un pouco máis...

Eu vou metido en min
coma quen garda o único que ten
e esguizo os velos que non deixan ver
o eido onde eu atobo e onde eu son.

Quén dera estar tan só
que un xa non fora máis que aquilo que é;
quén dera estar así
e ser aquilo que non son aínda...!

A min deixaime así: perdido en min,
esquencido,
    sen eido,
    sen ninguén!

Sometimes I go into me...

Sometimes I go into me
to see if I can find that of mine which is me
and I always see that I do not discover me
and that it is me that slips through my fingers.

And I always try again to search for me
and I'm never going to reach where I am,
that which is most mine
that should be me...

Sometimes I think that at last I am with me,
almost in my garden,
and then I see that there's still further to go,
further on, a little further...
I am inside me as I go,
like one who guards the only thing he owns,

and I tear away the veils that conceal
the garden where I hide and where I am me.

If only I could be so alone
that I was no more than what I am;
if only I could be like that
and be what as yet I am not...!

Leave me like this: lost in me,
forgotten,
    without a garden,
    without anybody!

Xosé Luís Méndez Ferrín (1938–)

From Con pólvora e magnolias (With Gunpowder and Magnolias), *1976*

Señoras do pasado

Mon prince on a les dam's du temps jadis qu'on peut
Georges Brassens

E quíxenvos moi tristemente a todas
as que forades rapidamente eu (un pouco).
Unha lus nos lugares do estremecemento
e tardes coma rodas de bronce, interminábeles.
Poderosas mañáns de rexurdimento e ollos no chan, de amor outido.
E quíxenvos moi escasamente a todas
porque nas regandixas de eu caben ourizos e sufrir é amor
e nada para o tempo que destrúe os ourizos.
E quíxenvos (queréndome) coma un río que fose
dos meus ollos a vós, as tidas e perdidas,
limítrofes do amor, esquencidas pra sempre.
E quíxenvos autente, e case non vos quixen
antre tanto artefauto, construcción, mala pedra,
que nos ten envisgados
nas cousas, coma lentos navíos que mainamente esbaran.
Chamo por vosoutras, nomes apenas tatuados
no baleiro e no fume, e reclamo ese espacio
que deixáchedes e que cecais é globo (de lume e desespero).

Señoras do pasado, damas investigadas a través dos ensoños
sobre cabalos nidios, inmóbiles no outono de antano,
sen bris mesmo,
merci por un crepúsculo, ou acaso algún beixo,
ou polos poderosos erguementos do sangue,
ou por sorrisos líquidos a carón da magnolia.

Quíxenvos lenemente, e mesmamente fúchedes
capaces da captura dun anaco de sombra de min,
e fiquei menos.

Inútil esta ollada por derriba do tempo que me outorga silencio,
escamas, arruínas, borralla, meus ronseles.
Quíxenvos fuxidío, oh amigas de antonte,
meu espantoso espello neste solpor que vence

Ladies of the past

Mon prince on a les dam's du temps jadis qu'on peut
Georges Brassens

And very sadly did I love you all
who had been quickly me (a little).
A light in the places of the shaking
and evenings like bronze wheels, interminable.
Powerful mornings of revival and eyes on the ground, of love obtained.
And very sparely did I love you all
for in the crevices of me there is room for sea-urchins and suffering
is love
and nothing stops time which destroys sea-urchins.
And I loved you (loving myself) like a river running
from my eyes to you, those I had and those I lost,
bordering on love, forgotten for ever.
And I loved you with prudence, and I almost did not love you
amidst so many artefacts, constructions, bad stone,
that keep us limed
on to things, like slow ships that smoothly slip along.
I call out to you all, names barely tattooed
on the void and on smoke, and I claim that space
that you left and that is perhaps a balloon (of fire and despair).

Ladies of the past, ladies investigated in daydreams
upon clear horses, immobile in the autumn of yesteryear,

without the slightest breeze,
merci for a twilight, or perhaps for some kiss,
or for the powerful lifting of the blood,
or for liquid smiles by the magnolia.

I loved you sweetly, and you were even
able to capture a piece of shadow of me,
which was my loss.

Useless this glance over time that gives me silence,
resentment, ruins, ash, my ship-wakes.
I loved you elusively, O lady-friends of the distant past,
my fearsome mirror in this conquering sunset.

From Poesía enteira de Heriberto Bens (The Complete Poetry of Heriberto Bens), *1980*

¡Terra de proseguir e non dar nada...!

... y no hallé cosa en que poner los ojos...
Quevedo

¡Terra de proseguir e non dar nada,
despaciosa Galicia que nos levas
acochados en ti! ¡Lento veleno
que pon nos ollos unha cousa verde!
¡Língoa que me enche a boca enteiramente
e coma un río interno me asolaga!
Quero dicir teu nome e digo a penas
xente de terra, homes lentamente
un por un devecendo e sendo nada.
¡Galicia coma un río que se estiña,
terra de esmorecer, patria do vento!
Quero dicir teu nome e digo dorna
baleira, mergullada dorna negra,
grande arado sen bois, feira sen xente,
noite que vén, enorme noite fría...

Quixera alzar meu canto coma un puño
e pór na miña voz teu nome ergueito
pero non hai ninguén para escoitarme.

Land of pushing on and giving nothing...

... y no hallé cosa en que poner los ojos...
Quevedo

Land of pushing on and giving nothing,
tardy Galicia who carries us
wrapped up in you! Slow poison
that places something green inside our eyes!
Tongue that fills my mouth
and like an inner river floods me.
I want to say your name and barely say
people of earth, men slowly
fading away one by one and being nothing.
Galicia like a river drying up,
land of failing spirits, homeland of wind!
I want to say your name and I say empty
little boat, submerged black boat,
great plough without oxen, fair without people,
night that is coming, vast cold night...

I wish to raise my song like a clenched fist,
place in my voice your proudly standing name
but there is nobody to listen to me.

From O fin dun canto (The End of a Song), *1982*

A un meu fillo

Heureux qui, comme Ulysse,
a fait un beau voyage,
ou comme celui-là qui conquit la toison,
et puis est retourné, plein d'usage et raison,
vivre entre ses parents le reste de son age!
Joachim du Bellay

Cando regreses a Vilanova dos Infantes
despois de visitares terras sen número
recoñecerás que as cousas son máis pequenas e encolleitas
do que ti lembrabas
pro o teu cor moito máis grande porque nel entrara o mundo.

Cando regreses a Vilanova dos Infantes
despois de que o teu esprito tivera amado

co vigor azul veludo do papilio manchaon e outras grandes bolboretas
e nos teus ollos se cebara o ferrete dos mil velenos inimigos,
atoparás irónico o xesto do Castromao, do Furriolo e outras
montañas que encadran a túa patria coa fidel constancia
de quen é manso, tutelar e interno.

Cando regreses a Vilanova dos Infantes
e entres na casa que fundaron os teus antergos
con lucidez e traballo imprecisábel,
notarás a benvida dunha brétoma insidiosa
a velar cada obxecto como visto entre bágoas;
música haberá nas escadas, olas, pipas, lámparas ou espellos ou ecoar
de labores que hai cen anos alí houbo e nun repente
prorrompen nos teus ollos alapeados.

Cando regreses a Vilanova dos Infantes
e os canastros, a profundidade das adegas,
o terror dos subterráneos onde son as trabes de ouro e de alquitrén,
a derrota das murallas no Arrabaldo, o agurgullo
da Fonte de Baixo, a morte enguedellada en cada corredor
derruído, acheguen a ti a man pálida dos antanos amantes,
na tua res domeada polo peso do sentido
choutará un alustre de namorada tristura
como que alumea un facho de luz verde e arcaica.

Cando regreses a Vilanova dos Infantes
tremeranche os xeonllos
do corazón e na alta noite a inmensa lua chea
iluminará pra ti a clave do labirinto
e o teu pai sorrirá dende o frío sepulcro
porque terás conquerido o que ti es
e poderás cantar en Tra-la Cerca como cantou o poeta
dos antanos de Francia:

"Feliz aquel que, tras de percorrer, como Ulises,
as mil aventuras dos mares do mar
e dos mares da paixón vermella arrebatada;
ou aqueloutro que, navegando o Ponto na percura procelosa,
máis que un Año de Ouro, acadou a ledicia innumerábel
da Misión e da Viaxe comprida:
tras cortar incidentes coma rosas
retorna a Vilanova dos Infantes completo de sabiduría."

To a son of mine

Heureux qui, comme Ulysse,
a fait un beau voyage,
ou comme celui-là qui conquit le toison,
et puis est retourné, plein d'usage et raison,
vivre entre ses parents le reste de son age!
Joachim du Bellay

When you come back to Vilanova dos Infantes
after visiting lands without number
you'll realize that things are smaller and more shrunken
than you remember
but your heart much bigger because the world will have come into it.

When you come back to Vilanova dos Infantes
after your spirit has loved
with the blue velvet vigour of the papilio manchaon and other great
                                                                butterflies
and the sting of the thousand enemy poisons has satiated itself on
                                                                your eyes
you'll find ironical the gestures of O Castromao, O Furriolo and
other
mountains that frame your homeland with the faithful constancy
of those who are gentle, tutelary and internal.

When you come back to Vilanova dos Infantes
and walk into the house that was founded by your forebears
with lucidity and unthinkable labour,
you'll notice the welcome of an insidious mist
veiling each object as if seen through tears;
music there'll be in stairs, pots, barrels, lamps and mirrors or the
                                                                echoing
of work done there a hundred years ago that all of a sudden
breaks into your burnt eyes.

When you come back to Vilanova dos Infantes
and the maize-garners, the depths of the wine-vaults,
the terror of the cellars where there are beams of gold and of tar,
the path by the town walls in the Arrabaldo quarter, the bubbling
of the Fonte de Baixo, death entangled in every ruined passage,
all hold out the pale hand of loving long-agos,
through your back, bowed by the weight of perception,

will thrill a lightning-flash of enamoured sadness
like the glow of a green, archaic torch.

When you come back to Vilanova dos Infantes
you'll feel a trembling in the knees
of your heart and in the dead of night the immense full moon
will light for you the key of the labyrinth
and your father will smile from the cold grave
because you'll have conquered what you are
and you'll be able to sing in Tra-la Cerca corner as once sang the poet
of the long-agos of France:

'Happy he who, after ranging, like Ulysses,
through the thousand adventures of the seas of the sea
and of the seas of ardent red passion;
or he who, sailing through the Hellespont on his turbulent quest,
gained, more than a Golden Ram, the innumerable joy
of the Mission and the Journey accomplished:
after cutting incidents like roses
returns to Vilanova dos Infantes complete in wisdom.'

From Estirpe (Stock), 1994

Acougo

Feliz aquel que deixa a aldea sen fechar a porta
do seu domicilio e cabalga deica os vales en que o labrego
ara nas leiras e diversa fincabilidade prende a súa besta
nunha argola da vella tenda de ultramarinos recada
o caxato corvo e pilla as calzadas que o levarán aos planaltos
de touzas poboadas de rulas e fugazmente transitadas
polas estrelas azuis da pega-marza
e alí asenta nun tocón apodrecido de aciñeira
internamente percorrido polas larvas dos escornabois e varios
                                                    vermes
completamente cegos olla ao seu redor porque é verao
a raxeira fai roxir a chicharrada e decátase de que un mundo
de besbellos circenses fan ximnástica nos bicos das gramíneas
resequidas ponse ledo porque na viciña corga xa canta o grilo
a súa balada acolá a corga aquela corga verdegal
na que nin latrica unha meada magra de fíos de auga entre carriza
e o señor bido de traxe mariñeiro dispón no cucuruto da bulsa
pendular do ouriol nota que non ten ansias e anseia telas menos

o peito non llo entolda o desexo de nada amalloa ben os tenis
volta ao camiño para repousar outra volta agora pé
dos loureiros e déitase nunha grama coas follas inmortais
a coroarlle a testa e canta polo baixo as habaneras
en canto o sol devala sobre os cotos da serra incorpórase
dun chouto tan innecesario como precipitado corre
rousa cando o camiño torce e entra na chan alta dos toxos pilla
os subeiros do animal pisa torrón negro ergueito polo fuciño
do porco bravo e cando as sombras can e o sol deixara xa de ser
un rubio farol comproba que no baldío non hai cousa humana
toda escuridade cobra forma de sólido e a cara dun xigante
de fariña vai xurdindo tralos petoutos e decide daquela fechar
os ollos e non ter pensamentos.

Quietude

Happy he who leaves his village without shutting the door
of his domicile and rides to the valleys where the farmer
ploughs his fields and diverse real estate tethers his horse
to a ring on the old grocer's shop picks up
his bent walking-stick and finds the lanes that will take him to the
                                        tablelands
of oak-woods populated with turtle-doves and fleetingly traversed
by the blue stars of the jay
and there sits on the rotten stump of a holm-oak
internally overrun by the larvae of stag-beetles and various worms
that are completely blind looks around because it is summer
the sunbeam makes the cicada colony buzz and notices that a world
of circus grasshoppers are doing gymnastics on the tips of the dried
                                        gramineous plants
rejoices because in the nearby gully the cricket is already singing
its ballad that gully over there that green gully
where there is no babbling from a mean skein of threads of water
                                        amongst moss
and lord birch in a sailor suit is arranging the cone the hanging
                                        pocket
of the golden oriole notices that he has no yearnings and yearns to
                                        have fewer of them
his breast does not conceal his desire from him at all laces up his
                                        trainers tight
goes back to the path to rest again now by
the laurels and lies down on some grass with the immortal leaves
crowning his head and quietly sings slow wistful habaneras

as soon as the sun sinks over the peaks of the serra rises
with a leap as unnecessary as it is hurried runs
creaks when the path twists and enters the high plain of the gorse
                                 bushes finds
animal tracks treads on a black clod raised by the snout
of the wild boar and when the shadows fall and the sun has stopped
                                 being
a yellow lamp realizes that in this wasteland there is no human thing
all darkness takes the shape of a solid and the face of a giant
of flour gradually rises behind the crags and decides at this point to
                                 close
his eyes and not have any thoughts.

From Crónica de nós(Chronicles About Us), *1980*

Xeque-mate

Era o mil oitocentos corenta e a néboa asolagara Ouréns. O cabaleiro embozado, baixo o chapeu enorme que lle asombraba os ollos, endereitaba o cabalón normando contra da Barreira. Pé da Burga, rumorosa de rosmidos de mendigos bébedos, os vapores mesturábanse ao bruar da cidade, algodonoso e amatado. Cheiro de cousa antiga e mesmo interior invadiulle os miolos ao cabaleiro embozado, sinalándolle que era na noite ourensá onde el entraba. Estalaban as ferraduras contra a rúa encoiñada, esvarando secas. Os lampións de gas amosábanlle o camiño da Praza da Constitución. Camiño deserto, frío, inhóspito. Algún graxo dáballe ás canelas baixo os soportais, embrullado cecais nun cobertor astorgán, e as chancas arrincaban unha certa ledicia a aquela desolación romántica. Ingresou na Praza, alumada por un reverbero central e vermellas cadeiras amantes en cada canto, e detivo un intre a súa cabalaría. Dirixiu o embozado a penumbra da súa ollada á banda do Espolón. Cinco fiestras ardían e prometían un interior tépedo e fastuoso. Era o Casino. O cabaleiro desceu da montura e, adestrándoa, achegouse ao pé da escalinata de Santa María a Madre. Moles de pedra negra, entre as que albeaba a grave palidez dalgúns mármores lonxanos, abatéronselle derriba da súa testa. Gargalladas e violíns chegábanlle aos ouvidos. Amarrou a rédea a un remate de ferro e fixo golpexar, seguro, os tacóns pesados no paseo deserto, logo nas esqueiras do vello pazo. Máis adiante a porta de cristais cedía á presión enérxica da man que abrolla dos pregues dunha capa e o cabaleiro esvara por un vestíbulo alfombrado de vermellos. Os risos, a luz dos candelabros, a música, arrodéano amorosos. Abandonaba unha man rápida polos cabelos rizos, axustaba mecánicamente o frac azul sobre as costelas e lanzaba nas mans de adustos lacaios capa e chapeu, pasaba unha ollada lateral á lámina do grande espello coroado de cornucopias carolinas, o que fora cabaleiro embozado. Un intre só, para confirmarse no segredo e displicente culto de si mesmo. O fitar esborrallado e pardo, enmarcado polas inmensas olleiras violáceas, demostrouse teimoso; como a mandíbula cortada e agresiva, e a fronte bombeada;

como a gravata branca que, moitas voltas dando ennobeláballe o pescozo de toro de abidueira; como a boca, trazo esguío e contracto onde os houbese; como as sólidas pernas embutidas en botas á Chantilly, de volta clara baixo os xeonllos, e calzóns de viaxe en gris abrancazado. O cabaleiro entraba xa no salón nobre do Casino e parábase un intre na porta, cunha man na cadeira e todo o peso gravitando nunha perna. O baile de lanceiros, baixo a luz cegadora de mil boxías, ofrendoulle o espectáculo das sedas brancas das mociñas, en contraste co casaco preto dos pollos e o fasto multicolor dos uniformes militares. Sen alterar o seu xesto, o cabaleiro espetou a ollada inerte no vello presidente do Casino que, de calzón curto e fibela no zapato, dáballe a benvida cunha sobria reverencia e presentáballe ao coronel Carrasco, ao maxistrado Ugarte, ao cóengo Bedoya; aos señoritos de Casardomato, das Eiroás e da Penalba, aos que estreitaba firmemente as mans o cabaleiro, recibindo dalgún deles francmasónicos signos inequívocos. Atacaba a orquestra un ledo cotillón, cando o grupo abandonaba o serán e ingresaba na sáa de lectura. Lombos de libros, pardos de coiro e marelos de pergameo, chegaban deica o teito e, pé da estufa, nunha mesiña, descansaba o taboleiro de xadrez coas pezas en desorde por derriba. Devecido, minúsculo, nervoso, paseaba polo cuarto Sandro Fioravanti que, nun ponto, chantábase fronte ó cabaleiro que debuxa un sorriso enigmático ó se deixar beixar en ambas meixelas. Da penumbra dun canto, xorde a masa harmoniosa de Carlota, Carlota Fioravanti, envolveita en veos pretos, cun corazón de brillantes sobre o escote de mármore. O cabaleiro, inclinándose sobre a man enmitonada de granate, mermuraba un comprimento e daba o fogo dos seus labres á cálida neve que se lle ofrecía en cada dedo garnido de sortellas de ouro branco e raras pedras sen brillo. Os presentes ocuparon sofás, cadeiras, mouchos dispostos arredor da estufa. Acendéronse vegueros, coa venia de Carlota, que quedaba de pé cos ollos perdidos na ringleira do *Teatro Crítico*, tal vez saudosa dunha *Enciclopedia* ou dunha *Historia Natural* do Conde de Buffon. O cabaleiro considerou un intre o rosto de cotovía do xogador profesional, a ollada servil e o riso pronto de que se valía, as mans rápidas e aneladas de ópalos e cousas grandes e eclesiásticas. Cun xesto macizo, o cabaleiro sinalou unha cadeira fronte á mesa. Fíxose o silencio. Ouvir ouvíase, unha vez sentados e dispostas as pezas do xadrez no taboleiro, o ruxir dos cirios ó queimarse, o arfar xordo do bandullo da estufa, sospiros dalgún señor alí presente. Escomezaron a partida. O cabaleiro desencolgouse do mundo circundante, e tamén o fixo Sandro Fioravanti. Este levaba as brancas, e a súa xogada central foi un gambito de centro. Os cerebres arderon coma fachos nunha noite cega. Sandro Fioravanti tiña na mente un sistema perfecto de posibilidades. Fechado en si mesmo, o seu xadrez dotábase de elementos limitados e sometidos a unha orde abarcábel. Harmónica xeada, xeométrica, era a súa unha estructura inmóbil. Ostentaba a beleza pedante das casuísticas morais de Port Royal e o abafante matematicismo da capela estucada de Monroy. Ser sería a metódica de saídas que Feixoo ou que Voltaire xogasen nas noites dos pazos, castelos e tertulias, latexantes de inquedanza e de futuro. Perante o seu contrario, o noso cabaleiro apoiaba o cóbado no banzo de madeira da cadeira inglesa e descansaba a súa fazula na cunca dunha man. Despregaba coas pezas unha acción intrépida e selvaxe. Os ollos arrubiánbanlle e entreabría un pouquín os beizos finos. Rápido coma un chicotazo nas respostas, aproveitaba os longos intervalos de meditación de Fioravanti pra espeta-los ollos nos ollos incendiados de Carlota. Amáronse en silencio. O cabaleiro sentía vértigos na virilla e o desexo navegá balle nas veas. Arrebatado, xogaba coma nunca o fixera. Era un xogo suicida, desartellado e histriónico, que facía conmover ao público de cada movemento insólito. Carlota sabía qué signos de paixón lle eran destinados no torbeliño doido dos trebellos negros, e recibía a mensaxe coas manciñas suadas apertando un longo, rendado pano branco de Manchester. Espavorida, quixo abandonar a sáa máis dunha vez, en procura de limonada no serán. A ollada do cabaleiro chantábaa no seu posto, queda. Por primeira vez, despois de longos anos de exercicio, o cabaleiro notou noviñas, inéditas, as pezas. Xa non tiñan aquel valor constrinxido que el herdara de cen mestres devanceiros. Un arreguizo máxico proíalle na res. Sen saber ben por que, iluminacións espantosas dictábanlle o sacrificio dunha peza con propósitos tácticos que só despois lle eran desvelados. As mans do cabaleiro movíanse co imperio dun tirador de pistola. Mobilizados por Fioravanti os peóns contra as defensas do cabaleiro, este entregaba á morte as súas pezas cun sorriso displicente pra, logo despois, infiltrar polos lenzos derrubados da muralla victoriosas mesnadas. Por un intre, Fioravanti pareceu recupera-lo leme e o cabaleiro agardou impertérrito o fatídico xeque-mate. Unha ollada a Carlota, a visión dos seus espléndidos ollos tapados cunha man asustada, devolveulle o control da batalla e, nun apaixonado frenesí, apurou as xogadas até a victoria. Derrotado Fioravanti, o cabaleiro ergueuse ao tempo que tiraba un xaruto do peto do chileque rameado. Non tivo tempo de acendelo, pois Carlota, cun berro arrastrado e rumoroso, precipitábase a el, puña os seus beizos febrentos na boca do cabaleiro, que acariñou os crespóns do seu van esplendente. Mesmamente, as candeas dobraron o resplandor e cegaron ós presentes. O brazo de Don José María Bedoya ergueu o manteo até os ollos nun aceno de horror. O señorito de Casardomato escachou nunha infernal gargallada de bulra. Os máis calaron e agacharon as piadosas testas lexitimistas, mentres Fioravanti ao porse en pé derrubaba a cadeira. O bico foi longo e contiña a frebe do imposíbel, o anseio que gobernara a partida coma un deus de carne xenital e bárbara. Bágoas escoaron polas meixelas de Sandro Fioravanti, que non ousou moverse cando o cabaleiro se desprendeu da aperta de Carlota e, moi solemne, saíu taconeando de cara o salón con ela encolgada do brazo. Dandys, oficiais e damiselas, abríronlle camiño, sen saber, e os novos amantes gañaron o vestíbulo. Recuperou o cabaleiro o seu chapeu; axustou as luvas; permitiu que as esporas lle foran calzadas depositando un e outro pé no escabelo carmesín da portería. Acendeu o veguero con calma; enlazou a Carlota polos ombros, amparándoa coa gran capa; saíron ambos ás neboas de Ouréns, á friaxe. Estreitamente, abrazáronse sobre o palafré de camiño. Xusto ao pasaren os amantes a Fonte do Rei e a pousada vella do camiño de Reza, entraba Fioravanti no retrete do Casino e alí se enchía coa pistola Lefaucheux os miolos de chumbo.

Checkmate

It was eighteen forty and the mist had flooded Ourense. The muffled-up horseman, under the enormous hat that darkened his eyes, rode the big Norman horse
towards Barreira. At the Burgas, noisy because of the grunts of drunken beggars,
the steam mixed with the sounds of the city, a bit woolly and muted. A smell of old
things and even stuffiness invaded the muffled-up horseman's brain, indicating to
him that he was entering into the Ourense night. The horseshoes cracked on the
rough-hewn, stony street, slipping drily. The gas lamps showed him the way to the
Praza da Constitución. A deserted, cold, inhospitable way. Some rascal took to his
heels in the arcades, perhaps wrapped in a blanket from Astorga, and his clogs
extracted a certain cheerfulness from that romantic desolation. He entered the
square, lit by a lamp in the middle and red seats in each corner, and he stopped his
horse for a moment. The muffled-up man directed his darkened look towards the
corner of Espolón. Five windows burnt with brightness and promised a warm and
magnificent interior. It was the Liceo. The horseman dismounted and, leading his
horse, he went up to Santa María steps. Masses of black stone, between which the
grave paleness of distant marble whitened, flew over his head. He heard peals of
laughter and violins. He tied the reins to an iron and, very sure of himself, he made
noise with the heels of his shoes in the deserted alley and afterwards on the steps of
the old palace. A bit further on the glass doors gave way to the strong pressure of a
hand that sprouts from the pleats of a cape and the gentleman moves on slowly
through a hall carpeted in red. The laughs, the light from the candelabrums, the
music surround him lovingly. He left a rapid hand go through his curly hair, he
adjusted his blue dress coat mechanically over his ribs and he sent off his cape and
hat to the hands of the severe footmen; the no-longer muffled-up gentleman
glanced at the plate of the big mirror crowned with Caroline cornucopias. Just a
moment to confirm himself once more in the secret and disdainful worship of
himself. The drab, turbulent look, framed by the immense violet-coloured bags,
was obstinate; just like his strong and aggressive jaw, and his domed forehead; like
his white scarf that, with many knots, wrapped his bull neck; like his very thin, slim
mouth; like his solid legs crammed into boots in the Chantilly style, with a turn up
in a lighter colour under his knees, and travelling trousers in light grey. The gentleman then entered into the principal room in the Liceo and he stopped a moment
in the door, with a hand on his hip and all his weight resting on one leg. The
lancers' dance, under the blinding light of a thousand candles, offered him the
spectacle of the white silk of the young girls, in contrast with the dark frock coats of
the boys and the many-coloured pomp of the military uniforms. Without altering
his gesture, the gentleman fixed his dead look on the old president of the Liceo
that, with knee breeches and buckled shoes, welcomed him with a sober reverence
and presented him to Coronel Carrasco, to the Magistrate Ugarte, Canon Bedoya,
and to the gentlemen from Casardomato, the Eiroás, and the Penalba, with whom
the gentleman shook hands firmly, receiving from some of them unmistakable
Masonic signs. The orchestra was attacking a happy cotillon, when the group aban-

doned the ball and entered the reading room. Spines of books, in drab leather and with yellow pages, reached up to the ceiling. And, at the stove, on a table there was a chess board with the pieces in untidy disorder. Shrunken, tiny, nervous, Sandro Fioravanti walked around the room and in a moment stood in front of the gentleman who had an enigmatic smile on his face when allowing himself to be kissed on both cheeks. From a dark corner, the harmonious bulk of Carlota, Carlota Fioravanti, emerges, wrapped in black veils, with a diamond heart on her marble décolletage. The gentleman, inclining towards the hand covered in a deep red glove, murmured a compliment and gave the fire of his lips to the warm snow offered him in each finger covered with rings in white gold and unusual stones that did not glitter. Those present sat on sofas, chairs, stools arranged around the stove. They lit cigars, with Carlota's permission, who stayed standing with her eyes lost in the row of books in the *Teatro Crítico*, perhaps missing an encyclopedia or a *Natural History* by the Count of Buffon. The gentleman examined for a moment the bird face of the professional player, the servile look and his laugh that came easily, the rapid hands full of opals and big, ecclesiastical rings. With a firm gesture, the gentleman pointed to a chair in front of the table. Silence fell. Well, one did hear some things, once they were sitting down and the pieces were ready on the chess board, the growl of the candles burning, the deaf crackle in the stove's stomach, the sighs of some man who was there. They began the game. The gentleman absented himself from the surrounding world and Sandro Fioravanti did the same. The latter played with white pieces and his principal move was a central gambit. Their brains burned like torches in the blackest night. Sandro Fioravanti had in mind a perfect system of possibilities. As it was closed, his chess depended on limited elements and submitted to an inclusive order. Like a harmonious, geometric frost, his was an unmoveable structure. It manifested the pedantic beauty of the casuistic morals of Port Royal and the stifling mathematics of the stuccoed chapel of Monroy. It would probably be the opening move that Feijoo or Voltaire played in the nights in palaces, castles, literary circles, throbbing with anxiety and future. In front of his opponent, the gentleman leaned his elbow on the wooden arm of the English chair and rested his cheek in the hollow of his hand. He developed an intrepid and savage action with the pieces. His eyes got red and he half opened his thin lips. Quick as the lash of a whip in his answers, he took advantage of the long intervals of meditation of Fioravanti to fix his eyes on the burning eyes of Carlota. They loved each other in silence. The gentleman felt vertigo in his groin and desire sailed through his veins. In a passion, he played as he had never done before. It was a suicide game, disjointed and histrionic, that moved the spectators with each unusual move. Carlota knew what signs of passion were meant for her in the painful whirlwind of the black devices, and she received his message with her little hands sweating, gripping a long, white, lace cloth from Manchester. Very frightened, she wanted to leave the room more than once that evening to look for lemonade. The gentleman's look nailed her to her seat, frozen. For the first time, after long years of practice, the gentleman felt the pieces to be brand new, unused.

They no longer had that restriction that he had inherited from a hundred masters before him. A magical shudder stung him in the back. Without quite knowing why, terrible visions ordered the sacrifice of a piece with tactical purposes which were only revealed to him later. The gentleman's hands moved with the authority of a gunfighter. The pawns were moved by Fioravanti against the gentleman's defence, the latter sent his pieces to death with a scornful smile to later infiltrate victorious troops through the broken walls of the rampart. For a moment, Fioravanti seemed to take charge of the game once more and the gentleman waited without fear for the fatal checkmate. A look at Carlota and the sight of her splendid eyes covered with a frightened hand gave him back control of the battle and, in a passionate frenzy, hurried his moves on to victory. Once Fioravanti was defeated, the gentleman stood up, taking a cigar out of a pocket of his flowery waistcoat. He didn't have time to light it, as Carlota, with a long, loud shout, ran at him and put her fevered lips on the gentleman's mouth, who caressed the crape of her splendid waist. In that precise instant, the candles increased in brilliance and blinded those who were present. Don José María Bedoya's arm lifted his cape to his eyes with a horrified gesture. The gentleman from Casardomato broke out into an infernal jeering laugh. The majority stayed quiet and hid their devout heads, while Fioravanti, standing up, knocked the chair over. The kiss was long and contained the fever of the impossible – the longing which had governed the game like a god with genital, barbarian flesh. The tears rolled down Sandro Fioravanti's cheeks. He did not dare to move when the gentleman freed himself from Carlota's embrace and, very solemn, left for the assembly room with her on his arm. Dandys, officials and little misses let him by, without knowing anything, and the new lovers reached the hall. The gentleman picked up his hat, fitted on his gloves and allowed his spurs to be put on, putting one foot and then the other on the red footstool at the door. He lit a cigar calmly; embraced Carlota's shoulders, sheltering her with his big cape; Both left for the mists of Ourense, for the cold. They hugged closely on the steed as they went on their way. Just as the lovers were passing by the Fonte do Rei and the old inn on the way to Reza, Fioravanti went into the toilet in the Liceo and filled his brain with lead with a Lefaucheux pistol there.

From Arraianos (Border People), 1991

Medias azuis

Levabamos os cabalos co paso de andadura. El, o criado de Xixín, sabía o sitio. Era unha choupana triste, co solpor dándolle pola parte de atrás. Posta a casa no meo dos piñeiros, semellaba un animal derrubado. No cumio, brillaba unha aiga de folla de lata. Relocía a aiga e, de lonxe, viña o fragor do Arnoia escachándose en caneiros e cenzas indecisas. Ningún can latía. O camiño que nos trouxera pasaba arrentes da casopa. Era feito de pedras grandes e antigas, aquel camiño. Pouco antes de chegarmos, o camiño demorárase nun relanzo no que as pedras amosaban carrís labrados por eternidás de carro, e calcamos unha ponte altísima na que os nosos cabalos facían soar ecoares secos, toscos, estreitos, de mil anos.

Nada – dixera días antes o criado de Xixín. Nada, que temos que ir ás mozas a onde eu sei. Que son dúas irmás, teño eu ouvido falar. Que son boas mozas, e roxas do pelo. Brancas, brancas – dicía o criado de Xixín e ao prenuncia-la verba brancas abría a boca con vezo e gula, e locíalle no dentro un cuspe pecadento, coma escuma de mar.

O criado de Xixín era arloteiro. Puxera axóuxeres na canela do poldro que lle confiara o amo. Convenceume, e fomos.

Entón locía un sol derradeiro, de setembro. Lateral e displicente, aquel soliño aloumiñaba a casopa e facíaa amigábel. E así chegamos, o criado de Xixín e mais eu, e puxemos pé a terra enleando el o ronzal e eu as rédeas nas ponlas baixas dun piñeiro. Lembro que os cabalos, que eran amigos como eramos o criado de Xixín e mais eu, deron en se cofear testa contra testa.

O caso é que teñen sona de meigas – dixérame o día antes o criado de Xixín.

E eran orfas. E vivían soas, aquelas mozas ás que nós iamos, por Tras da Chaira. Habitaban unha terra irta, montesa, fría, na que corría o corzo e se movían arrebaños de pericas, coma nubes soltas. Terra fría non dá pan. Por unha corga embaixo, cruzada polo carreiro mallado do lobo, caía o camiño pedrado en plácidos relanzos. Logo estaban as casas da aldea. Por fin, nunha tomada de piñeiros do país, figuraba a casa delas, soa. Seica eran algo meigas.

Entramos polo eixido, o criado de Xixín e mais eu, facendo soar cada un súa espora, que levabamos firme, atada contra o leggin e a bota. Tamén facía tilín a onza de ouro da miña leontina, galano recente do papai – que me empurraba así a ilo substituíndo nos negocios de empréstimo e contrabando de vacas piscas.

Mozas eiquí, mozas eiquí – berraba o criado de Xixín, e eu ría a cachón e veña de petar cos cotobelos na porta verde. Veu un silenzo, e coido que chiou a aiga do tellado. Logo, deseguida, houbo risos dentro, que era todo negro xa, na tardiña. Risos de rapariigas frescas, como nós eramos mozos curros, e acendéronse un, logo dous guizos, e chantáronse nas paredes de cachote. E o lume da lareira foi aumentado. Pasen, pasen – dixeron as gorxas lindas. Senten, senten – insistían elas. E aínda veu unha e prendeu un candil de carburo e púxoo derriba da artesa.

A luz azul dominou aquela cociña de teito, trabes e muros negros coma o alcatrán. Vémolas loiras, lavadas, claras, co pelo tirante e as trenzas sobre o peito. Os panos foran retirados e cobríanlles a penas o pescozo, deixando libres as testas, ambas coma cascos de ouro.

Estaban proparadas, cos avantais e as camisas limpas. Coma se estivesen agardando por nós. E iso que non era o día de mocear. Se chega ser quinta feira (riu unha) habían ver Vustés a maravilla de mozos á espera, no mazadoiro da aira, para teren parrafeo connosco. Non nos atuaban, se cadra por gastarmos espora os dous visitantes, e, eu, leontina de ouro no chileque. Pro, engorde engordiño, foron elas ceibándose francas ao tu por tu.

Habían de ser xémeas dun parto. Nun intre, certa sombra silente apousou nun dos escanos de onda a lareira. Gache, gache – axotaron elas. E o gato negro lanzounos unha ollada de ouro vello antes de dar un pincho e fuxir polas fonduras do fregadeiro de pedra. Dicía o criado de Xixín seren elas meigas. Cáseque se non distinguían, fóra que unha delas tiña unha mancha marrón no ollo esquerdo. O gato puxéranos frío nas res.

E así foi pasando a notiña e parte da noite. Nó-los catro ás apalpadelas. Cada parelliña nun escano, notando o lume que nos queimaba as partes de baixo. Eran dadas. Eran dadas e a cara arrecendíalle a fiúnchos e tomelos, caras de rosa rica. E riabamos coma meniños. Olla que boas mozas non foramos ir topar aló naquel confín de alén do Arnoia, de Tras da Chaira. Case adormeceramos, cando rinchan fóra os cabalos e elas dixeron, de socato moi serias, que nunha légua en rodopío da casa non entraba lobo nin xabariño. Hai, entón, outro silencio no meo do cal renxeu algo entre as tellas, e había ser a aiga do cumio. Fitei para o criado de Xixín, e noteille medo. El descansaba a cara vermella no peito da súa moza. Pasou pola cociña unha cousa dura, sen corpo nin cheirume, que nos puxo encolleitos aos dous valentes moceadores.

O lume esmorece – rosmou unha das raparigas presentindo se cadra un certo lazo en nós outros. Foi a outra apañar un mangado de candeas dunha morea que alí estaba, onda o lar. Agachouse. Levaba saia curta. O criado de Xixín e mais eu abrimos moito os ollos por lle ver os coxotes. A moza gastaba medias azuis de la, até lle cubriren os xeonllos. Curvou máis ela o lombo e as nádegas subíronlle moito a aba do vestido. A carne, despoixa das medias, non era branca, como esperabamos cobizosos. Era renegrida. Tiña cotra.

Murriña, carro de merda – berrou o criado de Xixín. Sen nos pór de acordo botámonos a rir. Eu zorregueille un couce á rapariga, tal que a guindei de capitón no monte de frouma. A súa irmá voltouse contra miña coma unha gata de Algalia e arrabuñoume unha meixela. Eu pilleille o pulso e tirei con ela no lume. Érguese unha entre moxenas e a outra coa cabeza e o dengue cheos de paúlo, que semellaba un ourizo-cacheiro. Botaban foguetes polos ollos, as fillas do Inimigo. Berraban verbas que se enrolaban e se disparaban en espiral, como fan as cóbregas majá para atacar ao individo humano. Abrían os brazos e parecían o voar en esquina do morcego, ou se cadra o desoutra serpe con asas que vai polo airo a morrer na parte de Babilonia. Nós ter tiñamos medo pero riabamos delas ás gargalladas. Chamabámoslles carrañosas, medas de esterco. Elas aldraxábannos con maldicións, e abrían as pernas e erguían as saias. Viámoslles ás dúas idénticas medias azuis, e as coxas cotrañentas, e o becho peludo. Mesmo eu sentín vir aos meus narices, desde aquelas parroquias de cinta a abaixo, un fedor húmido e craso.

Malditos sexades – dixo unha polo baixo e cos ollos case fechos de raiba. Así vos coma a noite – agoirou a outra nun chío que prolongou o gato negro desde o alto da trabe nun miaiar xordo e duradoiro.

Corremos aos cabalos e marchamos de alí ao trote señorito, ceibando risadas até nos doer o bandullo e o van. Deixamos atrás o piñeiral e collemos verea adiante cara a nosa terra, todos felices e contentes, a nos gabar da gambernia que alá deixaramos liada. Xolda coma ela non se tiña falado na miña aldea, nin no lugar de Xixín, e aquela mesma noite habiamos de lla contar ben contada a toda a xente do fiadeiro, ai iso si, e habiamos facer rir a casadas e solteiras, ho, e se tal inda lle ía caír a máis de catro unha moxegada ou unha loita ao lle referirmos como abranguerámo-las meigas na cociña de seu.

¿E el serían? – preguntou de pronto o criado de Xixín. ¿Que? Meigas, meigas. Eu encollín os ombreiros e pecheime nun mutismo que enchía de temores estraños, aquel mesmo intre, o bruído dos cascos dos cabalos ao batuxar nunha parte enlamigada do camiño, camiño que de contado entrou nas bouzas de Auguela, para caír en doces revoltas polos sitios, fondos de bidos e frescura, de Ardeúva e Santa María de Rebordechao.

Ocorreu entón que o mundo familiar e sabido polo que cabalgabamos, estoupou e desfíxose coma un globo de xabrón. No cruceiro das Sete Espadas vimos saír voando (negraz) a curuxa-do-souto de riba da mesa dos defuntos, onde ela estaba a matar un leirón que, malferido, aínda choutou chiando nas ribas do mato para se ir perder entre carrascas. Vin nun instante o resplandor vermello de Marte. Máis grande ca a nunca eu vira, vai esa estrela das disgracias e da guerra – dixen eu en alta voz. O criado de Xixín non me respondeu e sinalou unha néboa mesta e suxa que viña contra nós, coma un pano, e que xa estaba a ocupar todo o arredor, e a cruz de pedra, nun sospiro, deixouse de ver. Axiña o neboeiro nos ocultou a lúa, e mailo planeta de sangue e ira. Por alí – dixo o criado de Xixín –, e seguimos un anaco polo pavimento pedrado da calzada, cara ás nosas casas.

Perdémo-lo camiño. Extraviámonos. Por touzas imprecisas, por toxeiras que ora si ora non recoñeciamos ou criamos sernos familiares, pasabamos a carreiros nos que os cabalos ourizaban as crinas e tremían coas catro patas chantadas en terra, coma se ventasen feras do monte.

Pensabamos nós, sen nos falar, que as irmás eran meigas e que nos desviaran a rota. A min soábame nas orellas a fada que nos botara aquela que tiña a mancha marrón nun ollo. Maldizoados sexades e que vos coma a noite. Comíanos a noite.

Nun certo ponto foise a néboa e caíu sóbor de nós un ceo tacholado de estrelas, entre as que chamaba a atención unha grande, vermella. Atopabámonos nunha gándara alongada e cha. A lúa permitíame consulta-lo reloxo, que marcaba as horas derradeiras da noite. Lonxe, por tras duns píncaros coroados de pedras ergueitas contra o ceo de leite, tal vez pedras sagras dos antigos, viña potente resplandor. Non sabiamos cal era aquel sitio e rachamos a chorar a un tempo, o criado de Xixín e mais eu. Aquela luz roxenta era, sen dúbida, unha cidade, podia que de Portugal. Pro axiña voltou de novo a néboa a tapar o mundo de ao redor. E as nosas cabalerías, cansas, esmaiaban e non querían máis andar. Non querían mais, chegados a non se sabe onde, e voltaron a trepar nunha verea vella e, como coñecéndoa, animaron o seu paso.

Aquel camiño era feito de pedras grandes e antigas e demorou nun relanzo no que o chao amosaba, a unha nova luz que penetraba o neboeiro, carrileiras labradas por eternidás de carro e logo despois calcamos unha ponte altísima na que os nosos cabalos facían resoar ecoares secos, toscos, estreitos, de mil anos.

Veu o día.

Rachou de todo a néboa coa raiola do mencer. Pararon de seu os nosos cabalos e notamos o arreguizo na res, o criado de Xixín e mais eu, porque estabamos perante unha choupana triste, co albor dándolle pola parte de diante. Posta a casa no meo dos piñeiros, semellaba un animal derrubado. No cumio, brillaba unha aiga de folla de lata. Relocía a aiga e, de lonxe, viña o fragor dun río, inequivocamente xa o Arnoia, escachándose en caneiros e cenzas indecisas. Ningún can latía. O camiño que nos trouxera pasaba a rentes da casopa da que partira a maldición, o castigo de medias azuis.

Blue Stockings

We rode the horses at walking pace. He, the servant from Xixín, knew the place. It was a sad cabin, with the sunset lighting it from behind. The house, placed in the middle of the pines, seemed to be a fallen animal. A tin eagle shone on the roof. The eagle gleamed and from afar the clamour of Arnoia river came, crashing against dams and hesitant pools. No dog barked. The way led us by the hut. That way was made with big, old stones. A bit before we arrived, the way slowed into a series of bends in which the stones showed the marks of eternal tracks, and we crossed a very high bridge in which our horses made dry, coarse, narrow, thousand-year-old echoes.

Nothing – the servant from Xixín had said days before. Nothing, we have to go to the girls where I know. Well, they're two sisters, that's what I've heard. They're fine girls and redheads. White, white – the servant from Xixín said and, on saying the word white, he opened his mouth eagerly and greedily, and showed his sinful saliva, like foam on the sea.

The servant from Xixín was a rascal. He had put bells on the leg of the colt that his boss had lent him. He convinced me to go with him.

At that moment an end-of-September sun shone. That low, disagreeable, weak sun lit the hut and made it seem pleasant. And thus the servant from Xixin and myself arrived and got down from the horses, he tied the halter and I the reins to the low branches of a pine. I now remember that the horses were friends, like the servant from Xixín and myself, and they began to rub their heads together.

They have a reputation for being witches – the servant from Xixín had told me the day before.

And they were orphans. Those girls towards whom we were heading lived alone around Tras da Chaira. They inhabited rough, mountainy, cold land, in which deer ran free and there were flocks of lambs that moved around like clouds. Cold earth does not provide bread. By a cart track, a rocky way that went down in placid curves, which was crossed by a trail worn by wolves. After that came the village houses. At last, on a piece of ground full of indigenous pines, their house appeared, alone. I think there was something of the witch about them.

The servant from Xixín and myself entered by the common, each of us making our spurs sound, which we wore tight, tied to leggings and boots. The gold coin on my watchchain also clinked, a recent present from my father – in this way he pushed me into substituting him in his moneylending and cow smuggling.

Girls here, here – the servant from Xixín shouted and I broke my heart laughing and we knocked on the green door with our knuckles. A silence followed, and I think that the eagle on the roof screamed. Immediately afterwards, laughing inside was to be heard, when it was already dark, in the evening. Young, sprightly, girlish laughs, like we were lively boys, first one and then another torch lit up and they were stuck on the walls in a moment. And the fire in the chimney began to get hotter. Come in, come in – said their pretty voices. Sit down, sit down – they insisted. And one of them even came and lit an oil lamp and put it under the kneading trough.

A blue light dominated that kitchen with roof, beams and walls as black as tar. We look at these clean, fair blondes, with their hair tied back and falling in plaits on their breasts. They had taken off their kerchiefs, which hardly covered their necks, uncovering their heads, both like gold helmets.

They were ready, with their clean blouses and aprons. As if they were expecting us. And it wasn't even courting day. If it was Thursday (one of them laughed) you'd see a great number of boys waiting on the threshing floor wanting to talk to us. They didn't address us in intimate terms, perhaps because we, the two visitors, wore spurs, and I wore a gold chain on my waistcoat. But, little by little, they began to feel more at home and to address us more informally.

They must have been twins. In a moment, a certain silent shadow fell on one of the benches in front of the fire. Get away, get away – they said. And the black cat shot us a look of old gold before jumping off and disappearing into the depths of the stone sink. The servant from Xixín said that they were witches. You could hardly tell them apart, except that one had a brown mark in her left eye. The cat had made shivers run down our spines.

And in this way we spent the evening and part of the night. The four of us in the dark. Each couple on a bench, feeling how the fire burnt the lower part of our bodies. They were at ease. They were at ease and their faces smelt of ferns and thyme, pretty rose faces. We laughed like children. What do you think, what nice girls we found there, in that out-of-the-way place, beyond the Arnoia river and Tras da Chaira. We are almost asleep when the horses neigh outside, and they said, suddenly very serious, that neither wolves nor wild boars came within a league of the house. Then there is another silence in the middle of which something creaked in the roof tiles, and it must have been the eagle on the roof. I looked fixedly at the servant from Xixín and I noticed his fear. He was resting his red face on his girl's chest. A hard thing without body or smell went through the kitchen, and it left us two brave ladies' men really scared.

The fire is going out – one of the girls murmured, perhaps with a presentiment of a certain coldness in us. The other went to get an armful of wood from a heap that was beside the chimney. She bent down. She was wearing a short skirt. The servant from Xixín and myself opened our eyes wide so as to see her thighs. The girl used blue, woollen stockings that covered her up to her knees. She bent her back more and her buttocks lifted up the skirt of her dress. Her flesh, above the stockings, wasn't white, as we anxiously wished. It was blackened. It had a crust of dirt on it.

Pig, cart of full of shit – the servant from Xixín shouted. Without agreeing to beforehand, we burst out laughing. I gave the girl such a kick that I threw her head-first into the heap of firewood. Her sister flew at me like a Kilkenny cat and she scratched my cheek. I caught her wrist and threw her into the fire. One gets up among the sparks and the other, with her head and kerchief so full of sticks that she looked like a hedgehog. Their eyes were on fire with anger, the daughters of the Enemy. They shouted words that were tangled and shot out in spirals, like Cuban cobras do when they attack men. They opened their arms and seemed to fly like bats or maybe like that snake with wings that goes through the air to die some-where in Babylonia. We were afraid but roared with laughter at them. We called them pigs, manure heaps. They abused us with curses, and they opened their legs and pulled up their skirts. We saw that the two were wearing the same blue stock-ings, and with dirty legs, and their hairy things. I even noticed in my nose a wet, heavy stink, from those places below the waist.

Damn you – said one of them in a low voice and with her eyes almost closed in anger. I hope the night eats you up – the other prophesied in a shout that the black cat prolonged from the beam above in a long, muffled miaow.

We run to the horses and we leave there in a jogtrot, guffawing until our sides ached. We leave behind the wood full of pines and get onto the road home, both very happy and satisfied when we think about how we are going to boast about the good time we had. Nobody had ever told of having a good time like that in my home nor anywhere in Xixín, and that same night we were going to tell everybody in our group about it, with a lot of details naturally, and we would make the spin-sters and the married women laugh, eh, and even four or more were going to get bitten or get into a tussle when we told how we had caught hold of the witches in their kitchen.

And are they? – the servant from Xixín asked of a sudden. What? Witches, witches. I shrugged my shoulders and fell into a silence that, in that same instant, filled up with the sound of the horses' hooves as they went through a muddy part of the road, crowding my mind with strange fears, a road which immediately entered into Auguela, to fall into sweet turns through the villages in Ardeúva and Santa María de Rebordechao, full of birches and freshness.

It happened then that the familiar and well-known world through which we rode exploded and burst like a soap bubble. At the Seven Swords cross we saw a (dark) owl flying by from the dead man's table, where he was killing an injured dormouse that, even so, jumped screaming into the scrub, disappearing amongst the small oak trees. In an instant I saw the bright red light of Mars. That star of mis-fortune and war was bigger than I had ever seen it, I said aloud. The servant from

Xixín didn't answer me and pointed out a dense, dirty fog that came towards us like a cloth and that was already occupying everything around, and the stone cross was suddenly lost to sight. Immediately the clouds hid the moon and the planet of blood and rage. Over there – said the servant from Xixín –, and we went on for a while on the stone road towards our home.

We lost our way. We were led astray. Through unsafe terrain, through a place with a lot of furze bushes that, at times we thought we recognized or thought was familiar and at times we didn't, we got to roads where the horses' manes went stiff and their four legs shook, sticking into the ground, as if they had a premonition of wild mountain creatures.

We thought, without saying it to one another, that the sisters were witches and they had made us lose our way. The curse that the one with the brown stain in her eye had made rang in my ears. Damn you and may the night eat you up. The night was eating us up. At a certain moment the mist disappeared and we saw a starry sky above us where a big, red star caught our attention. We were in a long, flat waste ground. The moon allowed me to consult my watch, which told me that it was late. Far away, behind summits crowned with straight rocks that stood out against the milky sky, perhaps sacred stones from ancient times, there was a blinding brilliance. We didn't know what that place was and the servant from Xixín and myself burst out crying together. That reddish light was, without doubt, a city, may be in Portugal. But immediately the fog came down again to cover the world around and our tired horses were weak and didn't want to go on any longer. They didn't want to any longer after getting to who-knows-where, and they went back up through an old path and, as if they knew it, began to go more quickly.

That way was made from big, old stones and it slowed down into a bend in which the ground showed, thanks to a new light that penetrated through the clouds, cart tracks sculpted by eternities of carts, immediately after we went over a very high bridge in which our horses made dry, coarse, narrow, thousand-year-old echoes.

Day came.

It broke the fog completely with the rays of dawn. Our horses stopped completely and the servant from Xixín and myself noticed the chills running down our spines, because we were in front of a sad cabin with the red sky shining on its front. The house, placed in the middle of the pines, seemed to be a fallen animal. A tin eagle shone on the roof. The eagle gleamed and from afar the clamour of Arnoia river came, crashing against dams and hesitant pools. No dog barked. The way which had brought us there passed beside the hut from which the curse had come, the punishment of the blue stockings.

María Xosé Queizán (1939–)

From A orella no buraco, *1965*

Excluíndo os intres da trastenda, as horas trascorridas na tenda eran monótonas, soamente alteradas por algún coñecido folgazán, que pasando por alí, púñase de leria comigo, ou ben pola entrada na tenda dalgún forasteiro, que presentara un pequeno problema coa súa demanda pouco común. Unha destas veces, sucedeu un caso curioso, que puido facerme rico: Un home con grosos lentes escuros e aspecto de estranxeiro, tras ter observado atentamente, e durante algún tempo, o queixo calado da vitrina, entrou na tenda e preguntou moi seriamente, de quen era aquela moderna escultura, e se tiña un prezo moi elevado. Contesteille que o seu autor eran os ratos. O ar de despiste que lle daban as gafas, acentuouse ao preguntar:

– ¿Como di?

– Dos ratos.

– ¿É o nome de alguén, ou é que pretende tomarme o pelo?

– Nin unha cousa nin outra. Ese queixo, porque se trata dun queixo, ¿sabe?, está aí desde hai bastantes anos. Pola noite os ratos veñen e o furan e rillan ao seu antollo.

O estranxeiro baixou a testa nun xesto de desilusión.

– ¡Vaia! É pena. Era francamente fermoso.

– ¿É que agora xa non llo parece? Ólleo. É o mesmo que cando vostede o apercibiu por primeira vez, e admirouno, coidando que era a obra dalgún famoso escultor. A beleza que vostede lle atopou é a mesma; soamente variou o autor, pero a obra segue aí, e sexa cal fora a súa orixe, continúa sendo unha obra de arte.

O das gafas case que non me deixou findar a miña perorata. Negou, firme e animadamente.

– Non. Segundo a súa teoría, terían que levar aos museos as pedras de formas agradabeis e bonitas cores, as árbores estrañas, cuxas pólas se enroscasen en formas superartísticas, os penedos que a erosión traballou a través do tempo, e lle deu forma, as conchas de unha e mil facetas... Estas e outras moitas cousas que a natureza posúe fermosas. E non embargantes, non ocorre así.

E rematou categoricamente:

– O home é o único ser capaz de crear arte. Ese queixo pode ser máis ou menos artístico, pero non ten arte. A min fastidioume un pouco aquel desprezo pola miña obra de arte, recén descuberta, e continuei, teimoso:

– Pois eu continúo sen entender qué diferencia habería en que isto o fixeran os ratos ou un home.

El tardou máis en contestar, esta vez. Fixo como se enviara algo pola gorxa. Deume a impresión de que se estaba provendo de paciencia. Logo comezou, lentamente, co mesmo ton dun mestre que trazara de meterlle na testa do seu alumno algo difícil, pero deixando entender, no arrastre irónico das súas palabras, que estaba empapado na materia, que non puña nada en dúbida.

– Explicareillo. Se "iso" – e alongou a palabra dándolle un acento despectivo – estivera feito por un home, implicaría a vontade e a liberdade dun ser que se propuxo facer unha obra, e o conseguiu cun esforzo e un traballo máis ou menos esgotador. Pero, o seu queixo é unha casualidade e, como tal, non ten interese ningún.

Eu non quixen seguir a discusión, pero, antes de findar, quixen probar a sinceridade – aparentemente evidente – do curioso estranxeiro.

– Bueno – díxenlle –, como queira. Regálolle o queixo.

O forasteiro sorriu por primeira vez, contraendo a súa face inverosimilmente en mil enrugas profundas, escondendo o nariz baixo os lentes. O seu sorriso, aparentemente, traizoábao. Parecía, máis ben, un aceno de choro. Respondeu cos labios fruncidos:

– Gracias, pero será mellor que se quede onde está. Non estaría ben deixar aos ratos sen comida. ¿Non cre?

E desapareceu sen sequera botarlle unha derradeira ollada á obra de arte.

A partir deste momento, empreguei boa parte do meu moito tempo libre, en me informar un pouco sobre escultura e escultores actuais, e agora, atópome xa dabondo capacitado para endosarlle o queixo ao próximo amante da arte que apareza na miña tenda, aínda que probabelmente ao final non o fixera, soamente por ver a cara que poñía ao preguntar:

– ¿Dos ratos?

From The Ear in the Hole, *1965*

Excluding the moments in the back room, the time spent in the shop was monotonous, only broken by some idle acquaintance who turned up there and chatted to me, or by the entrance of some unknown person who was a problem due to his unusual request. One of these times, something strange happened, that could have made me rich: A man with thick dark glasses and the look of a foreigner about him, after having observed with attention and for some time the cheese full of holes in the window, came in and asked very seriously by whom that modern sculpture was and if it was expensive. I answered him that the artists were the mice. The absent-minded air that the glasses gave him became more accentuated when he asked:

– What?

– It's the mice.

– Is it somebody's name, or are you pulling my leg?

– Neither one thing nor the other. That cheese, because it's a piece of cheese, do you know that?, has been there for many years. At night the mice come and they fill it full of holes and chew it as they wish.

The foreigner bowed his head with a disappointed air.

– Oh! It's a pity. It was frankly beautiful.

– And it isn't now? Look at it. It's the same as when you discovered it for the first time, and admired it, believing that it was the work of some famous sculptor. The beauty that you found in it is the same; only the artist changed, but the work is the same, and whatever its origin, it is still a work of art.

The man with the glasses almost didn't let me finish my speech. He denied it firmly and animately.

– No. According to your theory, one should take to museums stones with nice shapes and beautiful colours, strange trees, whose branches twine in superartistic forms, the stones that erosion worked on throughout time and gave them form, seashells of one or a thousand forms... these and other many beautiful things that Nature creates. And, nevertheless, they are not there.

And he finished emphatically:

– Man is the only being capable of creating art. That cheese may be more or less artistic but it isn't a work of art.

His lack of respect for my recently-discovered work of art annoyed me a little, and I insisted stubbornly:

– Well, I still don't understand what difference there is between this, done by a mouse, or by a man.

He took longer to answer this time. He seemed to send something through his throat. He gave the impression that he was trying to keep his patience. Then he began, slowly, with the same tone as a teacher that tries to drum something difficult into his student's head, but showing, in the irony of his words, that he was well-up on the subject, that he had absolutely no doubts.

– I'll explain it to you. If "that" – he drew the word out scornfully – were done by a man, it would imply the free will and liberty of a being who put to himself to create a work, and achieved it with an effort and labour more or less exhausting. But your cheese is made by chance and, as such, it has no interest at all.

I didn't want to go on with the argument, but, before finishing, I wanted to try out the sincerity – apparently evident – of the strange foreigner.

– Well – I said to him – , as you wish. I'll give you a present of the cheese.

The stranger smiled for the first time, shrinking his face in an unreal way into a thousand deep wrinkles, hiding his nose under his glasses. His smile, apparently, betrayed him. As a matter of fact it appeared as if he were crying. He answered with his lips puckered:

– Thanks, but it were better if it stayed where it is. It wouldn't be right to leave the mice without food, would it?

And he disappeared without even looking for a last time at the work of art.

From that time on, I employed a good part of my generous free time in finding out about modern sculpture and sculptors, and now I am sufficiently informed to lumber the next art lover that appears in my shop with the cheese, although in the end I probably wouldn't do it only to see his face when he asks:

– It's the mice?

Carlos Casares (1941–2002)

From Vento ferido (The Hurt Wind), *1967*

Como lobos

Agora pasou xa e non hai paragüeiro que o arranxe e é mellor calar por se acaso, por se volven e te untan e che din veña vostede connosco, que cho poden dicir, e te levan, que te poden levar, e métente alí naquel cuartiño e pregúntanche ¿onde estaba vostede o sábado ás dúas da mañá?, eso por che preguntar algo, e ti non sabes qué dicir e sóltanche unha viaxe e aguantas porque aínda que non queiras, aguantas, Eduardo, aguantas ou te perdes, aguantas como aguantan todos, anque despois os amigos che digan ti non tes o que ten que ter un home, porque se mo fan a min mórdolles o corazón, que todo o mundo é moi valente, todo o mundo, pero xa se viu que cando entraron na taberna e preguntaron polo Roxo, ninguén se atreveu a defendelo e eso que todos eran amigos del, pero cando lle dixeron Roxo, veña vostede connosco, ninguén protestou. E agora o Roxo está podrecendo e o mal foi del, que morreu por se meter onde non debía, que o tiñamos ben avisado, que lle tiñamos ben dito mira, Roxo, que vas acabar mal, mira que vas por mal camiño, pero el era teimudo e non fixo caso, porque volta con que todos os homes somos iguais e que temos dereitos, home si, eso sabémolo todos, me cago na puta, tamén o sei eu, pero non se pode falar, que non, home, que non se pode e hai que aguantar e deixar os dereitos e as valentías a unha beira e se mexan por ti, deixa que mexen, que para o que han levar... E de nada che vale que vaias alí e lle digas aquí estou eu que son irmán do Roxo e veño a lles preguntar qué fixeron do meu irmán, que lle como o fígado ao desgraciado que fose, que non che vale de nada e vanche dicir que eles non saben, que alá o xuíz e ao mellor cóllente e mañá apareces ti tamén tirado nun foxo. E ao que te acirre e che diga que non es home, que non es merecente de ser irmán do Roxo, dille que cale, que a vida é así e o que manda, manda e o que non, non manda nada, dígocho eu, Eduardo, dígoche de corazón que a ti non te nomearon para nada, para nada, Eduardo, para nada, porque o meu fillo é testemuña de que lle dixeron ten que vir connosco para arranxar un asunto, e o teu irmán díxolles que non ía, que el estaba bebendo e que non tiña ningún asunto que arranxar fóra de alí e entón eles sacaron as pistolas e xa non falaron máis e o Roxo mirou para os compañeiros e preguntoulles ¿é que xa non hai homes? e eles calaron como mortos pois outra cousa non se podía facer se non querían morrer todos alí e naquel instante chegou a Sara e díxolles ¿onde levan ao meu home?, pero non lle contestaron nada, que eu penso que eles ían cocidos, que o Roxo era moito home e tiñan medo que se lles repuxese. Mandárono subir á camioneta branca e marcharon con el cara ao monte do Sarnadoiro. O demais xa o sabes ti. Apareceu morto dun tiro na cabeza. Agora xa pasou. E é mellor calar. Tamén calou o médico cando lle levaron ao fillo. Sonche cousas da vida e dos homes, que somos como lobos uns para os outros, como lobos, Eduardo, dígocho eu, como lobos.

Like Wolves

Now it's done and there isn't nothing to mend it and it's better to be quiet just in case, in case they come back and get you in a mess and they say to you come with us, that's possible, and they take you away, that's possible too, and they put you there in that little room and they ask you where were you Saturday morning at two o'clock?, so as to ask you something, and you don't know what to say and they give you a clout and you put up with it because, although you don't want to, you put up with it, Eduardo, you put up with it or you're lost, you put up with it like everybody else, although afterwards your friends say that you don't have what it takes to be a man, because, if they do it to me, they're in a big fix, everybody is very brave, everybody, but it was clear that when they went into the tavern and asked for Red, nobody dared to defend him, and they were all his friends, but when they said to him Red, come with us, nobody protested. And now Red is rotting and the fault is his, he died for poking his nose where he shouldn't, we had warned him enough times, we had made it clear to him, look, Red, you're going to end up badly, you're going wrong, but he was stubborn and didn't listen, because one more time all men are equal and we have rights, men yes, we all know that, fuck it, I know it too, but you can't talk, no, for goodness' sake, no, and you have to put up with things and leave the rights and bravery to one side and if they piss on you, let them, for what they achieve with that… And it's not worth going there and saying here I am I'm Red's brother and I've come to ask what you did to my brother, the bastard whoever he is will have to deal with me, that's not worthwhile and they're going to tell you they don't know anything, that's up to the judge and maybe they'll arrest you and tomorrow you end up lying in a ditch. And the one who annoys you and says you're not a man, that you're not up to being Red's brother, tell him to shut up, that that's life and those on top are on top and those who aren't don't count, that's what I think, Eduardo, I'm telling you sincerely that they didn't name you at all, Eduardo, because my son is witness that they told him you have to come with us to fix something up, and your brother said he wouldn't go, that he was drinking and that he had nothing to fix outside of that and then they took out their pistols and they didn't talk anymore and Red looked towards his companions and asked them are there no men left? and they were as quiet as mice and well they couldn't do anything else if they didn't all want to die there and in that moment Sara arrived and she said to them where are you taking my husband?, but they didn't answer at all, as I think they had a skinful, and that Red was too much man for them and they were afraid he would resist. They ordered him to get up into the white van and they went off with him up to Sarnadoiro mountain. The rest you know. He turned up with a bullet in his head. Now that's over and done with. And it's better not to say anything. The doctor didn't say anything either when they took away his son. Those are things that happen in this life and to men, we are like wolves they way we treat each other, like wolves, Eduardo, that's what I think, like wolves.

From Ilustrísima, *1980*

A ilimitada paciencia de Ilustrísima empezaba a rebordar dos límites xenerosos da sua redonda humanidade. Ao final do informe que viña de ler, inquietante e riguroso, aínda se lle engadía a lapis aquela noticia disparatada que non facía senón aumentar a xorda irritación que desde había un par de meses empezaba a sentir polo seu fámulo. Por eso quixo comer só. Apurou o consomé, protestou delicadamente porque o bistec estaba demasiado feito, pediu a cambio un par de magras de xamón, fixo unha mestura de mazás con queixo a modo de postre e deu ordes de que o café llo servisen no Salón de San Ignacio.

Era o seu recuncho preferido nos días de verán, sobre todo para descabezar un soniño despois do xantar e antes da xornada de estudio, que iniciaba ás catro en punto de cada tarde. As tupidas cortinas de veludo vermello evitaban ter que entornar as contras para se defender do sol e os amplos sillóns, os máis confortables de toda a casa, invitaban ao sono alí mesmo, sen necesidade de pasar pola incomodidade para el invencible de se meter na cama a aquelas horas. Soamente os enxames de moscas que se xuntaban naquela parte, quizais atraídas pola presencia próxima dos cabalos, que tiñan a corte xusto debaixo, impedían que aquel agradable salón fora todo o perfecto que Ilustrísima desexaba.

Estaba xa impaciente por que chegaran co café. A saída do doméstico e o suave golpe da pesada porta de castiñeiro ao se pechar detrás del eran o sinal para se poñer cómodo. Desabotoaba a sotana, afrouxaba os cordóns dos zapatos e cubría a calva cun pano branco para se defender das moscas. Despois apoiaba a cabeza na man dereita, estiraba as pernas todo canto podía e deixábase arrolar polos ruídos familiares que subían desde a rúa. Así permanecía, agradablemente adormecido, durante máis dunha hora.

Pero aquela tarde non conseguía pegar ollo. Como un balbordo de palabras enfurecidas renxíalle na cabeza a lembranza do informe de don Xenaro. Desde que ao italiano Pietro Barbagelatta se lle ocurrira instalarse cun cinematógrafo na cidade, Ilustrísima non tiña acougo. Primeiro foron as xestións coa alcaldía para que lle negaran o permiso e que rematarán no fracaso que el prevera de antemán. Despois viñeron as presións sobre o dono do local para que non o alugara e que resultaran igualmente infructuosas. Agora aquela insinuación desatinada e antievanxélica, que xuraba para si non ía permitir pasara o que pasara.

From His Grace, *1980*

The unlimited patience of His Grace began to overflow the generous limits of his plump person. At the end of the unsettling and rigorous report he had just finished reading someone had even added in pencil that absurd news that did nothing but increase the dull irritation that for some months he had begun to feel towards his servant. For that reason he wanted to eat alone. He finished up the consomé, he protested delicately because the meat was burned, he asked for a few slices of ham instead, and he made a mixture of apples with cheese as a sort of sweet and ordered that the coffee be served in the Saint Ignatius drawing room.

It was his favourite place in the summer, especially to have a nap after lunch before his evening study, that began at four o'clock precisely each afternoon. The thick red velvet curtains meant that he did not have to pull the shutters to protect himself from the sun, and the big armchairs, the most comfortable in all the house, were an invitation to fall asleep there, without needing to suffer the discomfort, for him unsurmountable, of getting into bed at that time of the day. Only the swarms of flies that were found there, perhaps attracted by the closeness of the horses, as the stable was just below, meant that that pleasant drawing room could not be as perfect as His Grace wished.

He was already impatient because they came in with the coffee. The exit of the servant and the soft thud of the heavy oak door behind him were the signs that he could make himself comfortable. He unbuttoned his cassock, he loosened his shoelaces and he covered his bald head with a white handkerchief to protect himself from the flies. Afterwards, he leaned his head on his right hand, stretched his legs as far as he could and allowed himself to be lulled to sleep by the familiar sounds that came from the street. He stayed that way, pleasantly dozing, for more than an hour.

But that afternoon he couldn't get to sleep. Like an uproar of furious words the memory of Don Xenaro's report screeched in his mind. Since it had occurred to the Italian Pietro Barbagelatta to set up a cinema in the town, His Grace had had no peace. First it was the negotiations with the Mayor not to give him a license and that had ended up in the total failure that he had foreseen beforehand. Then came the pressures on the owner of the place not to rent it and that had been equally unsuccessful. He now swore that he was not going to allow that ill-advised and anti-evangelic suggestion whatever happened.

From Os escuros soños de Clío (Clio's Dark Dreams), *1979*

Frei Luís de Morgade, curador de Carlos II o Enfeitizado

Recentemente, a revista inglesa de estudios históricos *Past and Present* deu a coñecer un extenso traballo do profesor William A. Griffit sobre un interesante persona-xe galego, Frei Luís de Morgade, de quen a penas se un par de ducias de lectores saberán o nome e algo menos de tres ou catro terán noticia cumprida sobre a súa atraente personalidade. O traballo de Griffit (William A. Griffit, The spanish 18th century. "A biography of Fray Luís de Morgade", en *Past and Present*, nº 97, decembre de 1976) vén encher un pequeno oco na nosa aínda escasa historiografía do século XVIII.

Frei Luís de Morgade foi frade campaneiro no convento franciscano do *Bon Xesús*, en Trandeiras, fábrica hoxe derruída como consecuencia da voracidade bur-guesa e inculta desatada pola Desamortización. Naquel apracible recinto sagro serenaron os seus espaventados ollos na tranquilidade gris celeste das augas da Lagoa de Antela catro bispos franceses fuxidos da Francia revolucionaria de 1789. Menos de cen anos antes, reinando nas Españas don Carlos II o Enfeitizado, Trandeiras e o seu convento andaron en linguas por razón de Frei Luís de Morgade, pois este humilde fillo de San Francisco foi chamado a substituír ao famoso frade Antonio Álvarez de Argüelles, de Cangas de Narcea, como mediador entre o Ilustrísimo Inquisidor Xeral, o cardeal de Córdoba, e o Demo.

Como é sabido, o frade asturiano fracasara no meritorio propósito de liberar a El-Rei do meigallo. Dixéralle o Maligno, en conversa nocturna habida na súa cela, que a causa do mal de don Carlos estaba nun chocolate que lle deran cando tiña catorce anos, e no que a Raíña Nai, dona Mariana de Austria, mandara disolver a sesada dun defunto. Requiriu entón detalles o Inquisidor, e por boca de Frei Antonio respondeu o Demo que non se sabía o nome do defunto, pero que deixara viúva, unha tal Casilda Pérez que vivía na rúa de Herreros, na Vila e Corte. Por máis que a policía buscou e rebuscou, a dita rúa non apareceu por ningures, sen que se soubera tampouco se a rúa existira antes e fora borrada polo Demo para confundir, ou se simplemente fora o propio Demo o que enganara a Frei Antonio co propósito de impedir a curación de El-Rei. O caso é que este incidente supuxo a eliminación do frade de Cangas de Narcea como intermediario entre o lado de alá e a Inquisición.

Mentres tanto El Rei non conseguía verse aliviado do seu mal. Continuáballe tremendo o corpo tódalas noites a pouco de encetar o sono, a voz collíalle tonos de frauta cada vez máis acusados, o pouco que sabía de letras e de números íaselle varrendo do sentido a resultas das moitas pócimas que lle daban... Arredor del todos eran a querer curalo. A Raíña aplicándolle as súas artes amatorias de gata francesa, o Inquisidor tratando de volver entrar en relación co Outro, os físicos untándoo de aceite bendito por dentro e por fóra, o goberno francés roubándolle uns calzoncillos para que os cirurxiáns da Sorbona de París dictaminasen se don Carlos podía ter ou non ter descendencia...

Nestas favorables circunstancias apareceu Frei Luís de Morgade no horizonte real. Despois de enviar cartas ofrecéndose, un día chegou o frade galego a Madrid reclamado polo Santo Tribunal. Viñera andando en sinal de penitencia, desde o seu amado convento de Trandeiras, de onde saíra case dous meses antes. Levaba consigo cartas do Provincial da orde e do bispo da diocese. Desde terras de Castela recibiu escolta por mandado do propio monarca, que devecía por ver diante ao que xa se anunciaba como o seu seguro curador. Por fin, o 2 de febreiro de 1700, polas portas do real Alcázar entraba o frade galego. Era grande e groso e vestía de saco. Un runrún de saias aloucadas e pasos nerviosos quentou o silencio húmido e frío dos longos andares da augusta mansión. El-Rei agardaba na capela, en oración, co Inquisidor, a Raíña e alto personal da casa. Frei Luís entrou paseniño, percorreu con lixeireza a distancia que o separaba de don Carlos e caeu de xeonllos diante da súa presencia. Despois celebrou con moito recollemento e fervor, deu a comuñón ás reais persoas e ao remate retirouse non sen certa teatralidade misteriosa ao seu aposento, onde tivo un aparte co cardeal.

Alí mesmo lle dixo que eran dezaseis e non sete, como se pensaba ata entón, os demos que se paseaban por dentro de El-Rei, e que os había que ir botando fóra un por un e con certo tento, sen demasiada présa, para lle dar tempo ao enmeigadiño de se ir afacendo ao seu novo ser, pois don Carlos fora embruxado xa nos dentros da súa nai, e que nunca vivira sen ter polo menos cinco demos consigo e que uns ían chamando polos outros.

Cando estaba no medio da plática, veu abaixo un anaco do teito da habitación, que feriu lixeiramente ao cardeal nunha orella, o que de seguida se contabilizou na conta do Malo, que ao se sentir descuberto empezaba a pór dificultades. Aínda poría máis os días que seguiron. A Raíña caeu dun cabalo, El-Rei amenceu unha mañá sen fala pero con sentido, o cardeal apañou unhas labazadas de mans invisibles cando estaba na cama facendo as derradeiras oracións do día, á Raíña Nai queimoulle a lingua a sagrada hostia ao tempo de comungar, o físico preferido de don Carlos empezou a facer de vento con tanta forza e ruído e tal frecuencia que tivo que ser relevado do seu servicio, pois provocaba un riso tan grande na Súa Maxestade, que lle comía as poucas forzas que aínda lle quedaban.

A diferencia de Frei Antonio Álvarez de Argüelles, Frei Luís non falaba co Malo, senón co profeta Elías, que era quen o aconsellaba. E o primeiro consello que lle deu foi que El-Rei durmira lonxe da francesa, non fora que algún demo novo se infiltrara cara a dentro por vía de canos. O segundo, que a Raíña Nai quedara a pan e auga durante tres semanas. Despois, que o cardeal xexuara de chocolate e durmira sobre duro, e que o confesor engadira tres racións diarias de corda ás disciplinas nocturnas...

Unha noite, o confesor de El-Rei foi despertado por unha ledicia afogada que desde algún recuncho do Alcázar se lle metía como unha tentación no interior da súa alcoba. Saíu para averiguar de onde procedían as voces do pecado e os murmullos e os salaios leváronno dereito ao cuarto de Frei Luís, que cando se abriu a porta aínda trepaba por riba das carnes brancas da moza que con el estaba. Antes de que o abraiado confesor tivera tempo de averiguar se os espidos eran demos ou persoas, xa Frei Luís corría coa sotana na man e o cu ao aire polos escuros andares reais camiño da rúa.

Saíron homes de armas atrás del e collérono nun palleiro, preto de Toledo. Foi conducido a Madrid, a pé e atado, e sometido a proceso. Queimárono na Praza Maior o día 7 de febreiro de 1700. Aquela mesma noite o seu espírito meteuse na cama de El-Rei e estivo mallando nel sen descanso e chamándolle lambón ata o romper do día.

Brother Luís de Morgade, Faith-healer to Carlos the Second the Spellbound

Recently, the English journal of historical studies, *Past and Present*, published a long work by Professor William A. Griffith about an interesting Galician personage, Brother Luís de Morgade, of whom just two dozen readers will know his name and a bit less than three or four will have heard of his attractive personality. Griffith's study (William A. Griffith, "The Spanish Eighteenth Century. 'A Biography of Fray Luís de Morgade'", in *Past and Present*, no. 97, December 1976) fills a gap in our still scant eighteenth-century historiography.

Brother Luís de Morgade was the bell-ringer in the Holy Jesus monastery, in Trandeiras, a construction that is now in ruins as a consequence of the greed of the ignorant middle-class let loose by the sale of Church lands. Four French bishops, who had escaped from revolutionary France in 1789, calmed their frightened eyes in the bluish grey waters of Antela lake in that peaceful sacred enclosure. Less than a hundred years earlier, when King Carlos the Second the Spellbound reigned, Trandeiras and its monastery were on the lips of everyone due to Brother Luís de Morgade, as this humble son of Saint Francis was called on to substitute the famous friar Antonio Álvarez de Argüelles, from Cangas de Narcea, as a mediator between His Grace the General Inquisitor, Cardinal of Córdoba, and the devil.

As is known, the Asturian friar had failed in the worthy goal of freeing the king from the spell. The Evil One had told him, in a conversation that took place in his cell at night, that the cause of King Carlos's malady was some chocolate they had given him when he was fourteen, and in which the Queen Mother, Queen María of Austria, had ordered that the brains of a dead person be dissolved. The Inquisitor asked for more details then and, through Brother Antonio, the devil answered that he did not know the name of the dead person, but that he had left a widow, a so-called Casilda Pérez, who lived in Herreros Street, in the capital. Even though the police searched and searched again, that same street was not to be found, and it was not even clear if the street had existed before and that it was made to disappear by the devil to confuse everybody, or if it was simply the same devil who had deceived Brother Antonio to impede the King's cure. The fact is that this incident meant the dismissal of the friar from Cangas de Narcea as mediator between the other side and the Inquisition.

Meanwhile the King was not relieved of his malady. His body still trembled every night just after falling asleep, his voice sounded more and more like a flute, the little that he knew of literature and arithmetic was erased from his brain as a result of the many potions that they gave him... Everyone around him wanted to cure him. The Queen, applying her amatory arts of French cat to him; the Inquisitor, trying to communicate with the Other; the physicians, spreading him inside and outside with holy oils; the French government, robbing his underpants so that the surgeons in the Sorbonne in Paris would be able to say whether King Carlos could or could not have children...

In these favourable circumstances Brother Luís de Morgade appeared on the royal horizon. After sending letters offering his services, one day the Galician friar arrived at Madrid, having been called by the Holy Court. He had come on foot as a penance from his dearly-loved monastery in Trandeiras, from where he had left almost two months before. He had with him letters from his Superior and from the bishop in his diocese. From Castille on he was allowed an escort sent by his monarch, who was anxious to have before him someone thought to be sure to cure him. At last, on the 2 of February 1700 the Galician friar entered through the doors of the royal Alcázar. He was big and fat and dressed in sack cloth. A buzz of crazy habits and nervous steps heated the damp, cold silence of the long corridors in the august mansion. The king was waiting in the chapel, praying, with the Inquisitor, the Queen, and the ministers in the palace. Brother Luís entered little by little, quickly crossing the distance that separated him from King Carlos and fell on his knees before him. Afterwards he celebrated Mass with a lot of concentration and fervour, gave communion to the royals and on finishing retired to his quarters, not without a certain theatrical mystery, where he had an aside with the Cardinal.

There he told him that there were sixteen and not seven devils, as was supposed up until then, living inside the king, and that they had to be expelled one by one and with a certain care, without hurry, to give time to the poor possessed one to get accustomed to his new self, because King Carlos had been bewitched inside his mother, and had never been without five devils inside him and that they had called on others to come in.

When he was in the middle of the conversation, a bit of the ceiling in the room fell, injuring the Cardinal slightly on his ear, which immediately was added to the account of the Evil One, who on seeing himself discovered began to make trouble. He would make more in the following days. The Queen fell from a horse, the King woke up one morning dumb but conscious, the Cardinal received blows from invisible hands when he was in bed saying the last prayers of the day, the Queen Mother's tongue was burnt by the host when she was taking communion, King Carlos's favourite physician began to break wind with such force, noise and frequency that he had to be substituted, as it caused His Majesty to laugh so much that it took away the little strength he had left.

Unlike Brother Antonio Álvarez de Argüelles, Brother Luís did not talk to the Evil One but to the prophet Elijah, who advised him. The first piece of advice he gave him was that the King should sleep far apart from the French Queen, in case a new devil infilitrated inside through the conduits. The second that the Queen Mother should be put on bread and water for three weeks. Next that the Cardinal should eat only chocolate and should sleep on a hard board, and that the confessor should add three rations of flagellation each day to the nightly penances…

One night, the King's confessor was woken up by a muffled merriment that from some corner of the Alcázar came into his sleeping compartment as a temptation. He went out to discover from where the voices of sin came and the murmurs and sighs took him straight to Brother Luís's room who, when he opened the door, was still climbing over the white flesh of the girl with him. Before the amazed confessor had time to discover if the naked couple were devils or people, Brother Luís ran off with his habit in his hand and his backside bare through the dark royal passages on his way to the street.

Armed men went after him and they caught him in a straw rick near Toledo. He was taken to Madrid bound and on foot and was sent to trial. They burnt him in the Plaza Mayor on the 7 of February 1700. That same night his spirit got into the

King's bed and hit him unceasingly and called him a sweet-toothed greedy gut until daybreak.

Arcadio López-Casanova (1942–)

From Mesteres (Ancient Songs), *1976*

Mester da profecía

Non hai regreso

É ora a hora da lámpara da maxestá,
candil de mortos
na sombra,
    toda unha vida, toda
unha vida pra non voltar nunca.

Eis qué Noite é a noite,
o que tes
e o que ves,
    ollos de ancianidá contra o solpor da Casa,
mar aínda de ondas contra os xeonllos da lamentación,
soleira
de tebras,
    ti soio, ti
soio,
qué Noite é a noite cando despois da vida pechas as portas pra chorar,
e deitas corpo de alcoba entre os ramos do incenso sen perdón,
e pisas esparto de mármore co cáliz entre as mans,
ora que non hai regreso
poisque nunca puideches voltar,
    nunca
puideches voltar,
    ti soio, ti soio na mañá dos altos acios,
vellez nos ollos que foron mocedá,
pés de orela, areal no que as augas xa non bautizan nin redimen,
exilio pra ficar como ferro de chaves contra as columnas caídas,
vida non tes,
morte non tes,
nada tes e tes todo ora na hora de chegar e non chegar nunca,
cando sen sabedoría ollas esta terra de luz, búcaros de laranxos,
    arume,

lume
das tentaciós,
corpo teu tendido sobre do liño,
fuso de anos tecendo a sombra dos fíos do solpor,
noite
tras noite
fíos de solpor sen amor, xabre de sempre contra a mar das
penitencias,
Casa do Dío – oh, Paternal –
caíndo, caída,
abalar, bazar dos soños das horas, soedá
baixo o teito de pedra e loito...

Eres ora ti mesmo,
corda
de servidume,
noite tras noite na alcoba de tódolos defuntos,
portas pechadas
pra chorar,
ora, ora que a sabencia é viño de cristal na cunca de fillo,
e o pan é mantencia,
e as mans de xuventú limpan o forno,

ti soio, ti

soio,
poisque nunca, nunca puideches voltar,
nin ollar, nin calar.
Día de luz na terra e o mar que anainan o teu desterro,
ti soio
cando peta unha voz contra as táboas do medo
e non ouves...!

Ancient song of prophecy

There is no return.

It is the hour of the lamp of majesty,
lamp of the dead
in the shadows,
a whole life, a whole
life never to return.

The truth is that Night is the night,
what you have
and what you see,
    eyes of old age towards the sunset of the House
sea still of waves towards the knees of lamentation,
threshold
of gloom,
    you alone, you
alone,
for Night is the night when after life you close the doors to weep
and you lay out a body in a bedchamber among the bouquets of the
                            incense unforgiven,
and you tread on esparto-grass of marble with the chalice between
                            your hands,
now that there is no return,
because you never could return,
    you never
could return,
    you alone, you alone in the morning of high grape-bunches,
old age in the eyes that once were youth,
feet at the water's edge, beach on which the waters no longer baptize
                            or redeem,
exile to be left like iron from keys against the fallen columns,
you have no life,
you have no death,
you have nothing and you have everything now at the hour of
                            arriving and never arriving,
when without wisdom you look at this land of light, pots of orange-
                            trees,
    pine-needles,
    fire
of tempations,
your body stretched out on the linen,
spindle of years spinning the shadows of the threads of sunset,
night
after night
threads of sunset without love, the same old putty against the sea of
                            penances,
Casa do Dío – oh, Paternal –
falling, fallen,
the shaking, bazaar of the dreams of the hours, solitude
beneath the roof of stone and mourning...

You are now yourself,
cord
of servitude,
night after night in the bedchamber of all the dead,
doors closed
to weep,
now, now that wisdom is wine of crystal in the son's cup,
and bread is sustenance,
and the hands of youth scour the oven,

you alone, you

    alone,
for you never, never could return,
or look, or keep quiet.

Day of light on the earth and the sea that lull your exile,
    you alone
when a voice knocks on the boards of fear
and you do not hear...!

From the Seventies to the Present Day

Marina Mayoral (1942–)

From Querida Amiga (My Dear Friend), 1995

Estimada señora

Estimada señora:

Estrañarase de recibir esta carta porque vostede non me coñece e eu tampouco a vostede, e non a coñecería nunca se non fose porque vin á miña muller escondendo un libro e picoume a curiosidade de ver o que era. Nada máis empezar a lelo, decateime de qué ía o asunto e, para que vostede se faga cargo axiña e comprenda de que se trata, direille que eu son o sarxento da Garda Civil que casou coa montañesa guapa.

Non sei de onde sacou vostede o que conta. Seguramente foi a miña muller quen llo contou, pero a min paréceme que un escritor serio non pode dar creto ó primeiro que chega con contarallas. Polo menos nestas cousas hai que oír ás dúas partes, digo eu.

A min non me importa gran cousa o que vostede escribiu, unha porque non di nomes e só se decatarán os que estiveron no allo do asunto e coido que deses poucos o lerán, e outra porque vostede non é como don Camilo e outros escritores que fan películas cos seus libros. Se así fose, máis preocupado estaría porque a miña muller é capaz de presentarse no cine dicindo que ela é a chica da historia. ¡Sempre lle foi moi pintureira e moi amiga de facer teatro! Pero de todas as maneiras amólame un pouco que vostede pense que eu son un brután e un aproveitado ou un pailán que non se decata do que lle pasa por diante dos fociños. Pois, escoite: o parvo e o aproveitado era o fillo do capador, que en paz descanse. Se quería casar coa miña muller, ¿quen llo impedía? ¿Que lerias son esas de que eu o deixei sen permiso naquel Nadal? Eu era sarxento da Garda Civil, que entón, con tanta fame que había, era un bo posto, pero non era ninguén para manexar un asunto así. Non foi vela porque non quixo ou porque fixo algo moi gordo para telo arrestado todas as vacacións. Pero o máis seguro é que estivera con outra moza. Os pais, dende pequeno, levaban machacando con que tiña que ser veterinario. Veterinario, non albeite, ¿decátase?, e que tiña que casar cunha señorita da vila, como en efecto fixo. Esas cousas, dende neno, vano marcando a un, e o tipo estaba feito un lío coa miña muller. Porque "V.", como vostede lle chama, era unha muller de bandeira, xa de noviña, e de moito carácter, e traíao a mal traer. Se se coñecían dende nenos, ¿por que el non lle pediu que fose a súa moza? Ela mesma lle contou que foi ela quen se lle declarou; se non chega a facelo, o tipo non era quen de dicirlle nada, por moitas ganas que tivese. Pero cando unha muller coma ela lle bota a un os brazos ó pescozo e lle di quérote, non hai home baixo o sol que se resista. Así que gustar, gustábale, a quen non, pero de casar pouco, e cando aparecín eu, deu a espantada.

Se el tivese intención de casar, ¿pensa que me deixaría o campo libre daquela maneira? Porque o que pasou no coche na noite vella non era para romper un compromiso. ¿A que rapaza guapa non lle deron un apreixón algunha vez? E se a xente falaba, que falase. Ben lles tapei eu a boca a todos, demostrándolles que ela fora tan virxe á igrexa como a que máis. Non sei como ela non o entendeu.

O que pasa é que a miña muller encaprichouse con el porque era precisamente o único que lle escapaba. Todos esgarecían porque lles dixese dúas palabriñas e a ela apetecíalle o que se lle resistía. E non era que a el non lle gustase, diso estou certo, senón que non se quería comprometer e verse obrigado a facer algo que ía en contra dos seus intereses e do que os seus pais agardaban del. O que tiña era labia para ir sacando o que podía da situación sen pasar a maiores. Xa llo dicía neses versos que tanto lle gustan a ela, que o seu amor era imposible e que se lembraría sempre dela. Eu pregúntome e pregúntolle a vostede, ¿por que un rapaz de dezasete ou dezaoito anos considera imposible casar cunha rapaza solteira e sa e boa como era ela? Pois porque quere ser veterinario e casar cunha señorita que non lle gusta, pero que ten cartos e sabe comportarse en sociedade. E non hai máis volta que darlle.

En canto a min, eu decateime en seguida da situación. Aínda que era novo, xa levaba percorrido bastante mundo e tiña máis coñecementos que aqueles ignorantes. ¿Que fixen valer que un parente deles andaba fuxido? En realidade fíxenlles un favor impedindo que os levasen ó cuarteliño para interrogalos, como a outros. Nunca os ameacei nin lles fixen chantaxe, de modo que era lóxico que a familia me estivese agradecida. E a ela, á miña muller, dinlle o que estaba buscando sen saber que o buscaba. Era unha rapaza moi nova e sen ningunha experiencia, inocente nese sentido, pero moi apaixonada, acendíase con só rozala. Poucas mulleres vin así. E se non houbo nada co fillo do capador, con tantas oportunidades que tiveron, foi porque el era unha ave fría e porque tiña moito coidado de non comprometerse.

E estou seguro de que foi esa actitude a que mantivo o interese da miña muller por el. Iso, e que non volveu velo, e ficoulle aquela imaxe da súa xuventude. Se chega a casar con el, seguro que o deixa, que se aburre, porque ela valía moito máis ca el e habíase fartar de arrastrar a aquel mormizo que, sen dúbida, non sabería compracela. Porque comigo, por máis que ela lle diga que quixo sempre ó outro, comigo foi feliz, pasouno ben, ¿comprende?, que esas cousas non poden finxirse e eu de mulleres entendo un pouco. Ela necesitaba un home, e un home con forzas onde hai que telas, dígollo eu, que non era muller que se contentase con palabras bonitas. Moito ler aqueles versos e bicar nas cartas, pero a quen se abrazaba na cama polas noites era a min, e asegúrolle que non viña obrigada, que moitas veces me buscaba ela, aínda que me estea mal o dicilo, pero amólame que vostede e todos os que lean o que escribiu pensen que eu a levei á forza toda a vida, e non foi así.

Fixo sempre o que lle apeteceu, porque ten moito carácter e man esquerda cando quere. Saímos do val por darlle gusto e porque eu comprendín que quería ver mundo e parecíame xusto. Tivemos os fillos que ela quixo e, cando se aburriu de estar sen facer nada, pedín un préstamo e púxenlle un bar de comidas e despois ampliamos, tal como ela lle dixo, e montamos un hotel, pero nada de luxo, que tamén iso o contou á súa maneira.

Se non volveu ver ó fillo do capador, foi porque non lle deu a gana, porque nestes tempos que corren e dispoñendo de cartos e tempo como ela ten, ¿quen lle quitaba de ir á aldea cando sabía que el estaba? Ou mesmo a Barcelona. Lista como é e disposta, xa atoparía a ocasión. Pero non quixo, prefería que a el lle chegasen as noticias por terceiros, que sempre esaxeran, e máis os da aldea. Ela sabía que lle habían dicir: "Estache guapísima, igualiño que cando vivía aquí, non pasa un día por ela, e tan elegante, se vises que roupa trae; fóronlle moi ben as cousas, gaña cartos coma un toureiro, ten casas por toda España, e alterna con xente importante..."; que todo iso dicían, e ela ría e dicía que non, que non, coa boca pequena, así que todos estaban convencidos de que era millonaria e que trataba ós ministros de ti ou pouco menos. Porque a xente é así: primeiro criticábana a ela porque era pobre e o fillo do capador rico, e despois disfrutaban refregándolles ós outros polos fociños os cartos e a boa situación que ela tiña. E ela disfrutaba tamén con iso, e mesmo os favores que fixo á xente da aldea, en parte eran para darse importancia, para facer papel. Sempre lle gustou moito presumir e o seu empeño polo fillo do capador no fondo debíase a que era un dos ricos da aldea. Se chega a ser fillo dun labrego ou dun peón, nin olla para el. E se en vez de veterinario dunha vila de Barcelona, chega a ser un personaxe importante, xa amañaría ela para velo, porque o certo é que el ficou en nada, nin sequera vivía na capital senón nunha aldeíña dos arredores. Por iso non tiña maior interese en volver velo; sabía que, por ben que ela se conservase, os anos non pasan en balde e preferiu que el a recordase coa imaxe da xuventude, xa que, ademais, el non tiña entón nada que ofrecerlle. Eu iso entendíao, era unha pequena vinganza polo desprezo que os pais lle fixeran e pola covardía del, pero que non me veña agora con que sempre estivo namorada do fillo do capador.

De min di, como facéndome un gran favor, que non son un mal home nin un mal marido. ¿E logo que quería? Na aldea, desaparecido o outro, só ficaban paiolos e brutáns, niso tiña razón. E os señoritos da vila non casaban con montañesas pobres coma ela, por guapas que fosen. Eu non a obriguei de ningún modo, casou comigo porque quixo e porque non atopou ninguén mellor, non me fago ilusións.

Eu entón, na forza da vida e co posto que tiña, podía escoller entre moitas mulleres, mesmo das señoritas da vila, que lle aseguro que non me facían noxos cando me achegaba a elas. Pero tamén eu me emperrenchei en conseguila. Ela díxome que non estaba namorada de min, pero cando eu a bicaba apertábase contra min, e pensei que co tempo se lle irían aquelas fantasías da cabeza. Porque son fantasías, sabe, non lle hai tal amor. Amor é estar xuntos día a día, e aguantarse e ver que pasa; non escribir cartas nin facer versos, que igual nin eran del.

Fómonos da aldea porque sempre quixo saír de alí e fomos para o sur porque lle gusta o sol; ¿que gaitas son esas de "toda a terra de España entre o meu noivo e eu?" A distancia a Barcelona é a mesma, pero ela quería marchar, pediumo e eu cumprinlle ese gusto, como todos os que estiveron na miña man. Máis dunha vez tiven que aguantar os celos de vela falar e rir con outros homes e nunca lle dixen nada, porque confiaba nela, no que me dicía de que para ela xa non había máis home no mundo ca min.

E cando xa pensaba que tiña esquecido todas aquelas quimeras, agora sae vostede con esta historia... Claro que vostede non ten culpa, fala polo que lle contaron, polo que ela lle dixo. Pero non é xusto nin é verdade. Se tanto desexase ir con el, teríase ido. Ela non é muller que pare en escándalos, dígollo eu que a coñezo ben, e máis que vivimos tempos nos que o divorcio está á orde do día; sen ir máis lonxe: unha das nosas fillas está separada. Así que, se non marchou, foi porque non lle compensaba.

É certo que, dende que el morreu, está deprimida, pero iso é porque lle falta aquel pulo, aquel aguillón de que o outro soubese o ben que lle ían as cousas. Era máis un inimigo que un amor, dígollo eu. Pero era tamén unha parte da súa xuventude, que desaparece con el. E iso tráea tristeira.

Saír no seu escrito gustoulle, e, aínda que do nome só leve a inicial, iso abonda para que a xente que a coñece se decate de que está falando dela. Xa llelo deu a ler a varias amigas, pero só ás de aquí, ás que non saben a historia completa. E ela anda lendo nel ás agachadas para que eu non a vexa; seguro que o aprende de memoria igual que os versos daquel tipo, porque o que máis lle gusta no mundo é que falen dela e que lle digan cousas bonitas. Por desgracia eu non o sei facer, o único que fixen, e coido que non mal, foi querela toda a vida. Se o mira ben, nesta historia o único amor que durou foi o meu por ela. Se eu soubese escribir, diríallo por escrito, porque parece que iso é o único que ela estima. Pero non sei, e así seguiremos: ela lendo a historia do seu amor e despois apertándose contra min pola noite, e eu cumprindo, como cumprín sempre, porque esa é a miña maneira de querela, de demostrarlle que sigo queréndoa. Agora xa imos vellos os dous, pero eu aínda me atopo con forzas, e tendo cartos no peto non me faltan rapazas novas de carnes duras e pel suave para pasar un rato; pero a min gústame ela, e téñolle lei e non a cambio por ningunha.

E máis nada. Pídolle desculpas por facerlle perder o seu tempo escoitando a un pailán coma min, pero eu tamén necesitaba desafogarme. Aínda que non sexa vostede tan coñecida como Cela e outros, coido que escribe moi ben; mesmo a min se me puxo un nó na gorxa lendo o conto. Foi lástima que non soubese a historia completa. E agora si que nada máis. Reciba un respectuoso saúdo de

O sarxento da Garda Civil

Dear Madam

Dear Madam,
You will be surprised to receive this letter because you do not know me nor do I know you, and I would never have known you had I not observed my wife concealing a book and my curiosity been aroused to see what it was. Once I began to read it, I realized what was the subject matter and, so that you may understand my position without delay and know my reasons for writing, let me tell you that I am

the Garda Civil sergeant who married the pretty mountain girl.

I do not know where you obtained the story that you relate. No doubt it was my wife who informed you, but it seems to me that a serious writer cannot place his trust in the first person who comes along with tittle-tattle. At the very least, in such matters both sides have to be heard, or so I should have thought.

I am not very concerned about what you wrote, firstly because you do not give any names and the only people who will make connections are those who were involved and I imagine that few of them will read it, and secondly because you are not like don Camilo Cela and other writers who make films out of their books. If you were, I would be more worried because my wife is capable of appearing at the cinema and announcing that she is the girl in the story. She has always been fond of the limelight, and fond of play-acting! But at all events it was rather annoying to think you might imagine I am a brute and an opportunist or a peasant who does not realize what is happening under his nose. So listen: the fool and the opportunist was the gelder's son, God rest his soul. If he wanted to marry my wife, what was preventing him? What nonsense is all that about my stopping his Christmas leave? I was a sergeant in the Garda Civil, which in those days when many went hungry was a good job, but I had no power to fix something like that. If he did not go to see her it was because he did not want to go or because he had done something really serious that got him arrested for the whole holiday. But what is most likely is that he was with another girl. Ever since he was little his parents had been harping on about how he must become a veterinary surgeon. A veterinary surgeon, not an animal healer, mind you. And marry a young lady from the town, which is what he did. Things like this, going on ever since childhood, make their impact, and the fellow had got himself embroiled with my wife. Because 'V.', as you call her, was a fine figure of a woman, even when she was young, with a strong character, and she was leading him a merry dance. If they had known each other since childhood, why did he not ask her to be his girlfriend? She herself told you that she was the first to declare her love; if she had not done so, that character would not have been capable of saying anything to her, however much he wanted to. But when a woman like that throws her arms round your neck and says I love you, there is no man under the sun who can resist. So yes, he did like her, who didn't? – but he did not much like the idea of marrying her, and when I appeared on the scene he made good his escape.

If it had been his intention to marry, do you think he would have given me free rein like that? Because what happened in the car on New Year's Eve was no reason to break an engagement. What pretty girl has not been given the occasional cuddle? And if people were gossiping, well let them gossip. I shut all their mouths effectively enough, showing them that she went to the church as much a virgin as the best of them. I do not know why she could not understand this. The fact of the matter is that my wife became infatuated with him precisely because he was the only one who was slipping away from her. All the men were longing for her to say a couple of sweet nothings to them, and she fancied the one who resisted. And it was not that he did not like her, of that I am sure, but rather that he did not want to be under any obligation and find himself committed to doing something that went against his interests and what his parents expected of him. He used his smooth talk to get what he could out of the situation without letting things become serious. He had already said so in those poems she likes so much – that his love was impossible and he would always remember her. I ask myself and I ask you, why would a lad of seventeen or eighteen consider it impossible to marry a girl who was single and healthy and good, as she was? Well, because he wants to become a veterinary surgeon and marry a young lady who he does not like, but who has money and knows how to behave in society. And that is all there is to it.

As for me, I understood the situation straight away. Although I was young, I had been around and I had more savvy than those ignoramuses. I made use of the fact that one of their relatives was a fugitive? The truth is that I did them a favour by preventing them from being taken to the barracks to be interrogated, as happened to others. I never threatened or blackmailed them, so it was natural for the family to feel grateful to me. And to her, to my wife, I gave what she was looking for without knowing it. She was a very young girl, without any experience, innocent in that sense, but very passionate, just brushing against her was enough to arouse her. I have known few women like that. And if nothing happened with the gelder's son, with all the opportunities they had, that was because he was a cold bird and because he took great care not to put himself under any obligation.

And I am sure that attitude is what kept my wife's interest in him alive. That, and the fact that she never saw him again, so the image of her youth stayed with her. If she had married him, she would certainly have left him, she would have become bored, because she was a much finer creature than him and would have tired of dragging through life that undersexed weakling who would not, for certain, have been capable of satisfying her. Because with me, however much she tells you that she always loved the other man, with me she was happy, she had a good time, do you see what I mean? – because such things cannot be feigned, and I know something about women. She needed a man, a man with power in his engine, I'm telling you, for she was not a woman to be kept happy with pretty words. Always reading those poems and kissing those letters, but the one she clung to in bed at night was me, and I assure you that nobody made her, often she was the one who came looking for me, even though I should not say so, but it would annoy me if you and all those who read what you wrote thought I have always controlled her by force, and it was not like that.

She has always done as she has wanted, because she has a strong character and sharp wits when needed. We left the valley to please her and because I realized that she wanted to see the world, and this seemed fair enough to me. We had as many children as she decided and, when she was bored of doing nothing, I asked for a loan and set up a café for her and later we extended it, as she said, and established a hotel, but without any luxury, because that was something she told in her own way, too.

If she didn't see the gelder's son again that was because she chose not to, for in this day and age and with money and time to spare as she has, who was stopping her from going to the village whenever she knew he was there? Or even to Barcelona. Bright as she is, and on the ball, she could easily have found an opportunity. But she decided not to, she preferred news to reach him via third parties, who always exaggerate, specially in the village. She knew they would tell him: 'She's looking gorgeous, just like when she lived here, she looks as young as ever, and so elegant, if only you could see the clothes she wears; things went well for her, she's coining money like a bullfighter, she owns houses all over Spain, and rubs shoulders with important people...'; because all that was what they did say, and she laughed and said no, most certainly not, puckering her lips, so they were all convinced she was a millionairess and on familiar terms with government ministers. For people are like that: first of all they criticized her because she was poor and the gelder's son was rich, and then they amused themselves by rubbing each others' noses in her money and her good position. And she enjoyed this, too, and even the favours she did to the villagers were meant, in part, to make her feel important, play a leading role. She's always loved showing off, and her obsession with the gelder's son was based on the fact that he was one of the rich villagers. If he had been the son of a farmer or farmhand she would not have so much as looked at him. And if instead of being a vet in a little town near Barcelona he had been an important personage, she would soon have worked out how to see him, because the truth is that he came badly down in the world, he didn't even live in the city but in a village on its outskirts. That is why she was not very interested in seeing him again; she knew that, however well preserved she was, the years do not pass in vain, and she preferred him to remember her with the image of youth since, what was more, he had by then nothing to offer her. I understood all this, it was some small revenge for the way his parents had disdained her and for his cowardice, and she has no business to be going around saying she was always in love with the gelder's son.

Of me she says, as if she were doing me some great favour, that I am not a bad man or a bad husband. So what was she hoping for, then? In the village, once that other man had disappeared, all that was left were peasants and brutes – in this she was right. And the young gentlemen in the town did not marry poor mountain girls like her, however pretty they were. I did not force her in any way, she married me because she wanted to and because she could not find anyone better, I'm under no illusions about that.

In the prime of life and with the job I had, I could have taken my choice among many women, even the young ladies in town, because I assure you they did not turn their noses up when I approached them. But I had got it into my head that it must be her. She told me that she was not in love with me, but whenever I kissed her she pressed up against me, and I thought that in time those fantasies would fade away from her mind. Because they are fantasies, you know – that kind of love simply does not exist. Love means being together day after day, and putting up with each other and seeing what happens; not writing letters or making up poems, which very possibly were not even his own work.

We left the village because she always wanted to get away from there and we went down south because she likes the sun; what is all this blather about 'the whole of Spain between my boyfriend and me'? It's the same distance to Barcelona, but she wanted to leave, she asked me if we could and I complied with her wish, as I did with all those that were within my power. On more than one occasion I had to repress my jealousy when I saw her talking and laughing with other men and I never said anything to her, because I trusted her and believed her when she said that for her there was no other man in the world but me.

And just when I thought she had forgotten all those illusions, out you come with this story of yours... Of course you are not to blame, you say what you were told, what she told you. But it is not fair, and it is not true. If she wanted so much to go with him, she would have gone. She is not a woman to be stopped by the fear of scandal, I can tell you that much and I know her well, even less in these times when divorce is an everyday occurrence; there is no need to look far for an example, one of our daughters is separated from her husband. So if she did not leave me, it was because it did not suit her to.

It is true that ever since he died she has been depressed, but that is because she misses that incentive, that stimulus of wanting him to know how well things were going for her. He was more of an enemy than a love, I am telling you. But he was also a part of her youth, which has disappeared with him. All this makes her miserable.

She was pleased to figure in what you wrote, and even though only her initial appears there, that is enough for the people who know her to realize that you are talking about her. She has given it to various friends of hers to read, but only to friends here, who do not know the whole story. And she keeps reading it on the quiet so that I cannot see her; no doubt she is learning it by heart like that other fellow's poems, because what she likes more than anything else in this world is for people to talk about her and say nice things to her. Unfortunately I do not know how to do this – all I have done, and not too badly I think, has been to love her always. If you think about it, in this whole business the only love that has lasted has been mine for her. If I knew how to write, I would say so to her in writing, because apparently that is the only thing she appreciates. But I do not know how, and this is how we shall carry on: she, reading the story of her love and then clinging to me by night, and I doing my duty as a husband, as I have always done, because this is my way of loving her, of showing her I still love her. Now we are both getting old, but I still have some power in my engine, and with money in my pocket there is no lack of young girls with firm flesh and smooth skin to pass the time of day; but she is the one I fancy, and I am fond of her and I would not change her for any other.

And that is all. Please excuse me for having made you waste your time listening to a peasant like me, but I too needed to get it all off my chest. Although you are not as well known as Cela and others, I think you write very well; even I felt a knot in my throat reading the tale. It was a shame you did not know the whole story. And now that really is all.

The Garda Civil sergeant

X. M. Martínez Oca (1942–)

From A chamada escura dos cavorcos, *1982*

Unha cabalgada de valquirias retumbaba sobre a miña cabeza. Soaban ó lonxe as trompas, batía o tamborileo poderoso dos cabalos; fungaba ameazador o vento, e ían e viñan as pólas dos bidueiros, dos ameneiros, dos freixos, paralizados todos os rumores cativos do bosque.

E o ecoar que esvaraba polas encostas do monte concretouse nun trono que estoupou sobre a miña vertical, e logo perdeuse a retumbar na fenda aberta pola que baixaba o río. A esvaecer paso a paso nos cavorcos que se perdían ó lonxe. A se esgazar nos picoutos que punteaban os confíns do horizonte.

E empezaron a caer grosas as primeiras pingadas, o, aire lento, preguizoso, a me apegar contra a herba na que acordara deitado.

Revireime con traballo para me erguer e busquei un cocho no que resgardarme da tormenta. Ó volver o rostro atopei un ollar de fauno, cun sorriso desdentado sobre min. O bocio do Manuel tremaba silandeiro, preñado coma o ceo tormentoso, lustrado pola chuvia que lle batia de esguello.

– ¿Seica te perdiches pola noite? – díxome o meu veciño

Mirei para unha banda e para outra e pouco a pouco lembrei a noite pasada. O meu camiñar polas tebras, perdido, sen unha estrela para me guiar. Acordeime das palabras do vellote da taberna que me acompañara ata o regueiro: un home coma min non debía andar de noite polos camiños do monte.

– Estiven agardando por ti moito tempo para botarmos unha parola e acabei por pensar que quedaras a dormir en Corvillón. Pero este non é o camiño de Corvillón...

¿Tamén o Manuel andaba de brincadeira comigo? Erguinme e pasei os dedos pola cabeza, a alisar o cabelo. As pingadas da chuvia empezaban a medrar, un novo trono estoupou por riba dos tesos, facendo retremar o mundo. O Manuel seguía a ollarme cun aire de humildade raposeira.

– Ven por acá – dixo –. Aí adiante, no muíño, poderémonos gardar un pouco da chuvia.

Seguino sen dicir palabra ata o pardiñeiro esbarañado da beira do río. ¡E pensar que pouco máis ou menos por alí me deixara o petrucio de Eirasvellas pola noite! Debera pasar horas e horas a dar voltas arredor do mesmo lugar. E uns cantos metros máis arriba, medio quilómetro escaso, a miña tenda de campaña e o meu saco de durmir.

Dendes da porta do muíño, o Manuel e máis eu asistimos en silencio á apoteose da tormenta. Os tronos resoaban cunha forza que semellaba querer abrir a montaña en dúas. Cen regueiros desfiachados caían de pedra en pedra, de raíz en raíz, a engrosar o cauce do río. Unha cortina mesta de auga esfuminaba os contornos dos bidueiros, das nogueiras, dos castiñeiros, que aguantaban o chaparrón a pé firme pola encosta.

Despois a tormenta empezou a amainar. Aínda escintilaron uns lóstregos de despedida pola baixada do río. E o aire semellou mais fresco e nós sentímonos máis lixeiros, libres dunha carga que estivera a pesar sobre os nosos ánimos mentres durou o trebón.

De camiño costa arriba cara ó Souto puxémonos coma pitos, case peor que se tiveramos aguantado a tormenta ó descuberto, pero nin a Manuel nin a min nos importaba moito. Eu agardaba polas súas palabras, sabía que o vello devecía por me preguntar algo; pero el seguía en silencio, sen perder o seu sorriso faunesco, a chapuzar cos zocos nos regos que baixaban en pequenas fervenzas polas revoltas do camiño.

– ¿Como foi que deches comigo? – preguntei, para animalo a falar.

Pero el encolleuse de ombreiros.

– Baixo ó río todas as mañás... – dixo. E volveu calar.

Xa na súa casoupa meteu unhas achas na estufa e prendeulle lume. Eu descalceime e quitei os pantalóns. El nin se preocupou en desatar os amallós do zocos.

– Seica non te recibiron alá moi ben en Corvillón... – aventurou.

Fitei para el; pero xa non bailaba ningún sorriso no seu rostro.

– O mozo que estivo aquí neses invernos de atrás tamén pasaba pola taberna de Eirasvellas antes de se vir deitar...

– ¿Xa te enteraches de que estiven na taberna...?

– Home... é un supoñer. Por ese camiño, ¿de onde podías vir? E aínda che cheira un pouco o alento a viño

– ¿Non pensarás que me emborrachei...?

– ¿E se o fixeses, que mal tiña...? Non sei o que hai na xente esa dos Penedos de Corvillón...

¿E que relación podía gardar unha cousa coa outra? Sentinme amocado por deixar transparentar no meu rostro a mala acollida que me fixera Ilda. Anque ¿por que tiña que considerar aquela unha mala acollida? ¿Non fora natural? O caso é que eu fora imaxinando outra cousa, un recibimento de brazos abertos, unhas mostras de amor que á rapaza lle debían estar vedadas naquel ambiente. A serra non era o hospital. Pero ¿é que realmente me dera outras mostras no hospital? Si, si que mas dera. E alí ata o Celso parecía tamén outro, como a me incitar á aventura coa irmá. ¿Que tería pasado ó voltar á casa para se enemistar co pai?

From The Dark Call of the Hollows, *1982*

The ride of the Valkyries resounded over my head. Trumpets sounded afar, the powerful drumming of the horses hammered; the wind whistled threateningly, and the branches of the birches, alders, ash trees came and went, all the tiny sounds of the wood were paralysed.

And the echo that slipped down the sides of the mountains became apparent in a roll of thunder that broke over my head and afterwards disappeared, rumbling in the open crevice down which the river passed. Vanishing little by little in the hollows lost in the distance. Ripping itself on the peaks that were points on the horizon.

And the first heavy drops began to fall, and the slow lazy air pushed me against the grass in which I had been lying when I awoke.

I turned with difficulty to get up and looked for a shed in which to shelter from the storm. On turning my face I met the look of a faun, with a toothless smile, on me. Old Manuel's goitre trembled silently, pregnant like the stormy sky, shining from the rain which hit him obliquely.

– So you got lost during the night? – my neighbour said to me.

I looked from side to side and little by little I began to remember the night before. My way through the shadows, lost, without even a star to guide me. I remembered the old timer's words in the bar, who had accompanied me as far as the stream: a man like me shouldn't be walking at night on the mountain.

– I was waiting for you a long time for a chat and I ended up thinking that you had stayed overnight in Corvillón. But this isn't the way to Corvillón…

Was Old Manuel pulling my leg too? I stood up and passed my fingers over my head, straightening my hair. The drops of rain were becoming more frequent, a new clap of thunder broke over the low hills, making the world shake. Old Manuel was still looking at me with an air of humble craftiness.

– Come here – he said –. There ahead we can shelter in the mill.

I followed him to the ruined building by the side of the river without saying a word. And to think that it was there, more or less, that the old man from Eirasvellas had left me last night! I must have spent hours and hours walking around the same place. And a few metres ahead, at just half a kilometre, my tent and my sleeping bag.

From the door of the mill, Old Manuel and myself were witnesses to the apotheosis of the storm. The thunder resounded with a force which seemed to want to open the mountain in two. A hundred unravelled streams fell from stone to stone, from root to root, making the river bigger. A dense curtain of water clouded the outlines of the birches, walnut and chestnut trees, that stood up to the shower holding their ground on the mountain side.

Then the storm began to go away. Some lightning still was in the sky down river as if to say goodbye. The air seemed fresher and we felt lighter, free from a load that had been on our spirits while the tempest lasted.

On the way uphill to Souto we got soaking wet, almost worse than if we had been outside during the storm, but it didn't matter either to Manuel or to me.

I waited for him to speak, I knew that the old fellow was anxious to ask me something; but he continued in silence, without losing his faunish smile, splashing with his clogs in the channels that went down in little waterfalls through the turns in the path.

– How did you find me? – I asked, to get him to talk.

But he shrugged his shoulders.

– I go down to the river every morning… – he said. He became silent once more. And then in his cabin he put some logs in the stove and lit them. I took off my shoes and trousers. He didn't even bother to untie the laces on his clogs.

– I believe you didn't get a good reception in Corvillón... – he hazarded.

I stared at him; but there wasn't the trace of a smile on his face.

– The boy that was here the last few winters also went to the tavern in Eireasvellas before coming to go to bed...

– So you knew that he was in the tavern...?

– Well, I supposed it. On that path, from where would you be coming? And your breath still smelling of wine.

– You don't think that I was drunk...?

– If you had been, what's the problem...? I don't know what's up with those people from Penedos de Corvillón...

And what relationship was there between one thing and the other? I felt annoyed for showing so clearly how badly Ilda had treated me. Although why should one think that that was being badly treated? Wasn't it to be expected? The fact is I had gone there expecting something else, that I would be received with open arms, a demonstration of her love which the girl probably wasn't allowed to give me in that place. The mountains weren't the hospital. But had she really given me a different treatment in the hospital? Yes, she had. And there even Old Celso seemed to be very different, as if he were encouraging me to have a romantic affair with his sister. What did happen when he came home and found that he was estranged from his father?

Alfredo Conde (1945–)

From Xa vai o grifón no vento, *1984*

O Durance trae as augas do Verdon, acaso do Lac de Sainte Croix; de certo que son azuis, cando menos nesta hora da tarde na que unha grea de coches e acentos invaden as súas ribeiras e corpos novos e estraños se citan novamente dediante do milagre da auga.

Non saben moi ben os estudiantes o porqué da súa presencia alí. Ben cerca está o mar, as praias, mesmo as piscinas de Aix; sen embargo eles están aquí, nesta ribeira de coios e árbores escasamente doces. Hai unha vella mansión abandonada e medio derruída, pola que os rapaces entran intempestivamente percorréndoa en toda a súa extensión, en toda a súa vetustez.

O que mellor se conserva son as antigas cortes nas que vellos arcos de cantería sosteñen unhas bóvedas coas que o tempo e os desastres non puideron. Trátase dunha estraña mansión con catro torres cilíndricas aínda ergueitas, que puido ser pousada ou mosteiro, fortaleza ou misión de fronteira: está a carón do río e aquilo non ten xeito de ser terra de labor; aínda que acaso o fose nalgún tempo.

Lucille, responsable directa do curso e do desprazamento ata tan sinalado e inhóspito lugar, axudada das súas acólitas, dispón fogóns de butano, cazolas e insípidas salchichas de carne branca, grosas salchichas co único mérito de seren picantes e de turraren do viño, o que, quente como ha de estar e coa calor que vai será máis ben contraproducente. Trátase, polo que se ve, dun *pique-nique* universitario. Os estudantes están a se bañar.

O río está cheo de coios e ata ten un cachón polo que a auga colle un pouco de velocidade, moi pouquiña, pero que fai que os alumnos se resistan a se meter nel, deixándose levar pola corrente. O profesor visitante recorda, entón, os cachóns do Pai Miño; aquelas mañás de maio nas que se botaban a andar, ausentes que estaban das horas de clases, pola ribeira arriba, oito, dez, doce quilómetros, ata que o sol dicía que era xa moito hora de regresar abaixo, á Oira que amaba Don Vicente, e entón mergullábanse na auga e deixábanse levar por ela, felices na inconsciencia, lixeiros coma plumas. O río baixaba rápido e, ó chegaren os cachóns, había que endereitarse cara ó sitio indicado, polas aceas que desaugaban nos muíños, a carón delas, sempre por onde a auga escorregase sen romper. Se non lográba-lo camiño axeitado podía vi-la morte ou a resurrección, no medio de tanta e tanta escuma, co corpo tolleito de golpes e de emocións de abondo fortes. Pero se ías polo camiño axeitado velocidades de vágado e tolemia levábante río abaixo coma un lampo de luz, acaso coma un biobardo, que o Eduardo albiscaría antes de que fose noite, o corpo ben estarricado, toda a súa lonxitude ben acadada. Baixabas así, preso de emoción e medo, temendo sempre bater cos xeonllos nos coios porque a auga estaba baixa logo do cachón, e a vías pasar por embaixo túa, coma se fosen eles os que se movesen e ti sentises tan só no teu corpo aquela lixeireza material que só a auga comunica.

O visitante, o máis vello de tódolos profesores visitantes, o máis retraído de todos eles, non resiste a tentación e vaise indo, paseniño, cachón arriba, remontando o río, ata que chega a cen metros do encoro, onde a auga empeza a coller forza. Houbo quen viu aquel se aproximar por riba dos coios da ribeira, difícil e lento, e ridículo nos equilibrios, disfrutando das viravoltas que o vello escritor ía dando; gozando das forzadas posturas que adoptaba, das catro patas nas que andar tivo por máis dunha ocasión; e que agora observa alporizado que aquel toleirán se introduce no río e nada, case se diría que maxestosamente, cara a onde a auga colle forza. E avisa. Os máis ousados dos rapaces tensan os seus corpos e dan conta de que están dispostos a botarse á auga e sacar aquel tolo; outros pensan que é perigoso, que mellor esperar. Pero hai outros que intúen o deleite e que comenzan a subir río arriba, mentres o profesor, feliz, baixa na auga deixándose levar por ela. Vai feliz, ingrávido e feliz, coma unha táboa teso, deixándose levar. E aturuxa, aturuxa forte no medio do Durance, no medio da Provenza, e aquel berro que ninguén coñece soa a triunfo e a reto e a ledicia recobrada; e a xente disténdese, e cando o profesor chega ó relanzo que hai no bandullo do primeiro meandro, hai mozas que aplauden e rapaces que o felicitan e el feliz, exultante, sen saír do río, explícalles que aquilo non é nada, que de neno, no seu país, que ten ríos fermosos e cheos de auga, xogaban a vida baixando polo Pai Miño, o pai dos ríos de Galicia que baixa grave e maxestoso dende hai séculos, o mesmo que hai séculos, ata que chega ós cachóns e troa coma un petrucio, enoxado e colérico, que se torna perigoso sen chegar a perde-la compostura.

E velaí veñen xa os rapaces que o seguen na pequena aventura do Durance, mentres que outros non se atreven. "Se viséde-lo Miño", non se resiste a repeti-lo escritor ós seus alumnos. E volve subir río arriba, seguido dos rapaces ós que lles explica os segredos para unha baixada segura, para escudi-los remuíños, para gozar que, ó fin e ó cabo, é do que se trata.

Lucille observa dende a ribeira, avisada que foi por unha alemana de Aquisgrán que é traductora e ten o pelo curtiño, rapado, das feministas emboscadas. Cando remata a segunda viaxe, achégase á orella e dille toda acontecida:

– Vostede está tolo, ou é un inconsciente.

O escritor sen nada que contar sorrí feliz.

From There Goes the Griffin on the Wind, *1984*

The Durance brings water from the Verdon, perhaps from the Lac de Sainte Croix; it is certainly blue, at least at this time of evening when a flock of cars and accents invade its banks, and new strange bodies meet once more in the presence of the miracle of water.

The students don't very well know why they are there. The sea is very near, the beaches, even the swimming pools in Aix; nevertheless they are here, in this bank full of stones and trees that are scarcely sweet. There is an old abandoned mansion half in ruins, into which the boys enter ill-timedly going through it all, in all its antiquity.

The best-preserved part are the former stables in which old stone arches hold up some domes which time and disasters couldn't destroy. It's a strange mansion with four cylindrical towers still standing, that could have been an inn or a monastery, a fort or a frontier mission: it's beside the river and that doesn't look like fertile land; although perhaps it was at one time.

Lucille, the person directly responsible for the class and the journey to that cel-ebrated and unwelcoming spot, gets the gas cooker ready, helped by her acolytes, pots and tasteless sausages made of white meat, fat sausages with their only merit being that they are spicy and you drink more wine which, warm like it should be and with the heat, is instead self-defeating. It's, as far as you can see, a university picnic. The students are having a swim.

The river is full of stones and it even has rapids from which the water gathers speed, very little, but it makes the students unwilling to get in and be taken off with the currents. The visiting teacher is reminded then of the rapids of Father Miño; those May mornings when there were no classes, in which they started off on a walk upriver, eight, ten, twelve kilometres, until the sun said that it was time to go back, to the Oira which Don Vicente loved, and then they went into the river and left themselves be carried off by it, happy in their thoughtlessness, light as feathers. The river flowed swiftly and, getting to the rapids, one had to go to the appropriate place, through the channels that went to the mill, beside them, always where the water wasn't broken by rocks. If you didn't find the appropriate way through, death or resurrection would be your destiny, in the middle of so much foam, with your body numb from being hit and from strong emotions. But if you went the correct way a dizzy, crazy speediness took you down river like a bolt of lightning, perhaps like a fairy, that Old Eduardo caught a glimpse of before nightfall, with his body stretched to all its length. You went down that way, full of excitement and fear, always afraid of hitting your knees on the stones because the water was low after the rapids and you saw it going by under you, as if it were the stones that moved and you felt inside you only that material lightness that water gives you.

The visitor, the oldest of all the visiting teachers, the least sociable of all, can't resist the temptation and he goes away, little by little, quickly upriver, against the current, until he gets to within a hundred metres of the dam, where the water begins to gather strength. There were those who saw that difficult and slow approach over the stones on the bank, ridiculously maintaining his balance, and enjoying the turns that the old writer had to take; taking pleasure in the odd postures that he adopted, that he had to go on all fours more than once; and that now observe, amazed, how that madman gets into the river and swims, one would almost say majestically, towards where the water gathers strength. And he makes signs. The most daring of the boys tauten their bodies and show that they are ready to jump into the water to get that madman out; others think that it is dangerous, that it's better to wait. But there are others that sense the pleasure and that start going upriver, while the happy teacher lets the water take him on. He's happy, weightless and happy, tense like a bow, letting himself be taken on. And he whoops with joy, he whoops loudly in the middle of the Durance, in the middle of Provence, and that shout that nobody knew before gives an impression of triumph, and challenge and recovered joy. And the people are relieved, and when the teacher gets to the bend in the stomach of the first curve, there are girls that applaud and boys that congratulate him, and he's happy, exultant, without leaving the river he explains to them that that's nothing, that as a boy, in his country, that has beautiful rivers full of water, they risked their lives going down Father Miño, the father of all Galician rivers, that has flowed gravely and majestically for centuries, the same for centuries, until it gets to the rapids and it thunders like a patriarch, angry and irate, it becomes dangerous without even losing its composure.

And there come the boys who follow him in the little adventure at the Durance, while others don't dare. "If you had seen the Miño", the writer couldn't help repeating to his students. And he went upriver again, followed by the boys to whom he explains the secrets of making a safe swim downstream, how to avoid the eddys, how to enjoy oneself as, in the long run, that's what it's all about.

Lucille observes everything from the shore, after being called by a German girl from Aquisgrán who is a translator and has short hair, cropped, a camouflaged feminist. When the second journey ends, she whispers in his ear sadly:

– You're mad or thoughtless.

The writer, who had nothing to say, smiled happily.

Marilar Aleixandre (1947–)

From Lobos nas illas, *1996*

Disque na illa hai un lobo, conta dona Lucinda unha noite, os ollos enterrados na calceta, nas agullas que brillan como coitelos ó resplandor do quinqué. A luz falta moitas noites, hai que ir protestar ó Xallas. ¿Quen o viu?, pregunta Amalia mirando os ollos abertos de Miguel. Non o viu ninguén, rouboulle un pedazo do cabrito que tiñan para asar os fillos de Paco o domingo pasado. Rita e Amalia nunca ían á illa os domingos. Nós, di Amalia, non vimos lobo ningún ¿como vai haber lobos na illa? Pode haber, di dona Lucinda, ou debeu haber en tempos, de aí o nome. O pai non dá creto a esas etimoloxías da silveira, os nomes veñen de ser propiedade duns López, tantos como hai na parroquia, ou noutras parroquias da ría, despois a xente non distingue entre o pe e o be, ou calquera sabe ¡lobos na illa, que insensatez!

Non me gusta que vaiades á illa, repite dona Lucinda. Iremos a Sardiñeiro, di Rita lanzando unha ollada rápida cara a Amalia, unha ollada que nega as súas palabras, non te preocupes que non nos han comer os lobos.

En Lobeira hai nais que non asustan ós fillos falando do cocón, ou ameazándoos co lobo, senón con Foucellas. Non todas, tamén hai outras que foron anarquistas cando a guerra, e para elas Foucellas non é un bandido, senón un heroe, aínda que destas cousas só é dado falar baixiño. Foucellas non pode xa meter medo a ninguén, non sendo ós que temen ás pantasmas, porque o vinteseis de xullo fixo catro anos que lle deron garrote vil. Tamén mataron a Pancho, hai un ano, pero quedan no monte outros fuxidos, como aquel que lle din o Piloto e algúns máis, disputando as presas ós lobos. Indo para Coruña, pasado Lobelos, vive unha moza que ten máis que chorar por Foucellas que as outras; polo menos así conta Flora.

Desde que os fillos de Paco miraron lobos, hai que ir á illa ás escondidas. Antes era un paseo, e agora é unha aventura; se o sabe dona Lucinda mandará encerrar a buceta baixo chave. Mellor non fales nada, dille Rita a Amalia, ti non sabes mentir. Coa excitación da aventura Amalia non durme, só dá voltas na area, desacougada, esperando algo. Vai calmizo, hai nubes baixas, como se tecesen unha tormenta, e Amalia levántase chamando por Rita, pon as sandalias, e penetra na illa buscando a Rita. Buscando a Rita percorre os canavais, o mato, con cuidado de non espiñarse cos toxos; segue o camiño que leva ó faro, á torre arruinada. Caen as primeiras gotas, e cruza a porta, sen saber por que, dentro non queda teito que ampare da tormenta. Sobre unha manta vella hai dous corpos enlazados, o peito de Rita é dun branco de area onde sempre o cubriu o bañador, o home ten cabelo e barba hirsutos, como deben ter os lobos. Ó contrario do que sempre imaxinou Amalia, ela está encima, e el debaixo. Dá media volta e corre, corre baixo a chuvia cara á praia, pon o vestido, e envolta nunha toalla, apertando xunto ó corpo o vestido de Rita para que non se molle, agarda por ela un tempo interminable.

Cando chega xa pasaron as bategadas, a chuvia é un orballo fino que adhire as roupas á pel. Amalia mira o corpo de Rita, procurando os signos do que viu, un brillo na pel, un tremor nos peitos, certa languidez como exhiben as amantes no cine ou nos cadros; unha non pode medir o seu corpo, enguedellar o seu cabelo co de homes que parecen lobos e despois ficar a mesma, ter a mesma cara de rapaza de dezasete anos que murmura, é a última vez que vimos a illa, e por iso..., cos ollos mollados, non se sabe se por causa da chuvia.

Gracias a Flora que vai rosmando traer roupa seca, poden cambiarse na cociña, sen que ninguén máis saiba o estado en que chegaran a casa. Durante unha semana non foron moito á praia; tampouco o tempo era apropiado. O luns seguinte, despois da cea, dona Lucinda conta que o domingo houbera unha batida na illa á procura do lobo. ¿Encontráreno?, pregunta Amalia. Nin rastro, di dona Lucinda, e non deixaron pedra sobre pedra, ata plantaron lume á toxeira por se estaba agochado nela, engade brandindo as agullas entre a lá vermella, da cor que lle din sangue de touro, e que podía ser sangue de calquera outro animal, á fin todo o sangue é vermello. E o pai apunta se sería o propio can dos fillos de Paco quen roubara o cabrito, xa dixen eu que na illa non pode haber lobos, que idea tan absurda. Por unha noite a illa volveu emitir luz, como se houbese outra vez un faro, como se os faros mortos enxendrasen pantasmas que iluminan ós mareantes por unha noite.

From Wolves on the Islands, *1996*

They say there's a wolf on the island, Dona Lucinda tells them one night, her eyes buried in her knitting, in the needles that shine like knives in the glow of the oil lamp. The electricity's often cut off at night, we must go to the River Xallas power station and complain. Who's seen it? – asks Amalia looking at Miguel's wide-open eyes. Nobody's seen it, it stole a piece of goat-meat that Paco's children were going to cook there last Sunday. Rita and Amalia never went to the island on Sundays. We, says Amalia, have never seen any wolves; how could there be any wolves on the island? There might be, says Dona Lucinda, or there must have been once, hence the name. Their father doesn't believe in these folk etymologies, names like Lobeira come from being the property of people called López, with so many of them in the place, or in other places around the ria, and then people don't distinguish between the 'p' of López and the 'b' of lobo, who knows; wolves on the island, how silly!

I don't like you going to the island, Dona Lucinda repeats. We'll go to Sardiñeiro instead, says Rita, throwing a glance towards Amalia, a glance that belies her words: don't you worry, the wolves won't eat us.

In Lobeira there are mothers who don't frighten their children by talking about the bogeyman, or threatening them with the wolf, but with Foucellas. Not all of them, there are others who were anarchists during the war, and for them Foucellas isn't a bandit but a hero, although one can only speak about these things in hushed tones. Foucellas can't frighten anyone anymore, except those who fear ghosts, because on the twenty-sixth of July four years ago they garrotted him. They killed Pancho, too, a year ago, but there are other fugitives in the wilds, like that one they call the Pilot and a few others, competing with wolves for prey. On the way to Corunna, just past Lobelos, lives a girl who has more reason to mourn for Foucellas than the others; at least that's what Flora says.

Ever since Paco's children saw wolves there, the island has to be visited in secret. Previously it was a little trip, now it is an adventure; if Dona Lucinda finds out she will have the skiff locked up. You'd better not say anything, says Rita to Amalia, you're no good at lying. Excited by the adventure, Amalia doesn't sleep, she just turns over in the sand, uneasy, waiting for something to happen. It's muggy, there are low clouds, as if a storm was brewing, and Amalia stands up calling for Rita, puts her sandals on, and heads inland looking for Rita. She searches for Rita in the reed-beds, in the scrub, taking care not to scratch herself on the gorse; she follows the path that leads to the lighthouse, to the ruined tower. The first drops of rain are falling, and she goes through the door, not knowing why, there isn't any roof in there to protect her from the storm. On an old blanket there are two intertwined bodies, Rita's breast is a sandy white where her bathing costume has always covered it, the man's beard and hair are thick, just like wolves' hair must be. The opposite of what Amalia had always imagined, she is on top and he is underneath. She turns and runs, runs in the rain back to the beach, puts on her dress and, wrapped in a towel, pressing Rita's dress to her body so that it does not get wet, waits an interminable time for her.

When she arrives the squalls are over, the rain is a fine drizzle that makes clothes stick to the skin. Amalia looks at Rita's body, searching for signs of what she has seen, a sheen on her skin, a quivering in her breasts, a certain languor like that shown by lovers in films or in paintings; one cannot lie with, entangle one's hair with men who look like wolves, and then stay the same, have the same face of a seventeen-year-old girl who murmurs, it's the last time we're coming to the island, and that's why we..., with wet eyes, perhaps because of the rain.

Xavier Alcalá (1947–)

From A nosa cinza, *1980*

Naufragando recomecei o curso. Os profesores lanzábanse a cubrir o segundo trimestre cun ritmo forzado, en canto eu ía deixando o estudio retrasado ata os fins de semana, cando o debía facer por forza – por medo ó que non quería aceptar de ningún modo: o suspenso. Aínda me quedaba orgullo:

Isto reflexioneino unha noite cando xa os ollos me laiaban e o sangue me batía nas tempas. Estaba a ler a crónica dun Cieza de León sinistro que fora conquistador do Perú. Parei en certo parágrafo, con remordementos, a conciencia a acusarme: non durmía, non descansaba ben, non rendía á mañá seguinte. Así un día e outro, co vicio de ler para despois pensar e discutir de socioloxía, de historia, de cousas despersonalizadas, ben lonxe do que me afectaba, me preocupaba, me proía... Tiven un calafrío interno, sen tremor; e medo. Voltei ó relato de Cieza (só uns minutos máis, díxenme) e o conquistador emocionábase describindo a chegada dos castellanos a un templo onde había duascentas virxes adoratrices do sol.

Así foi como me decatei de que algo estrañísimo me estaba acontecendo. Non comprendía o texto; pensei que fose a dificultade do castellano do Renacemento. Relín; nada entendía; só as palabras tiñan algún significado sen relación dentro da frase. Pero as palabras mesmas logo se convertían en sílabas inconexas e, por fin, as sílabas eran grupiños de letras sen sentido... Sorprendinme a ler en alta voz, silabeando, repasando as letras á luz intensa do flexo.

¿Que era aquilo?, ¿que era?, ¿que me pasaba? Seguindo algún instinto, deiteime, e axiña me desconectaba da realidade. Durmín pesadamente, tanto que non sentiría o despertador ás poucas horas. Tívome que chamar a Felisa e perdín dúas clases da mañá.

A terceira clase era de literatura. O profesor falaba de rima e ritmo, e puña por exemplo algunhas estrofas de Rubén Darío:

"Esto ocurrió en el reinado de Hugo,
emperador de la barba florida..."

Como por costume, dirixíuseme cunha pregunta acerca do autor. Para a miña desesperación, non fun capaz de lembrar nada relacionado con el. Daquela o profesor foime facendo preguntas cada vez máis elementais ata chegar ó significado dos arquicoñecidos "cachorros de león hispánico." Pero nin iso souben comentar. Ó fin da clase, corrín á clínica do vello.

Meu pai deume un enderezo e alá fun. O rótulo á porta do seu colega e amigo asustoume: "Psiquiatra." Entrei no despacho vencendo unha repugnancia como nunca sentira; porque estar tolo era unha vergoña, era a destrucción. O Avelino repetíao: que a mitoloxía clásica o deixaba ben claro: cando os deuses querían acabar cun humano, primeiro tirábanlle o siso...

O psiquiatra escoitoume e deu un rápido diagnóstico:

– Fatiga cerebral. Andas a cocer demasiadas cousas na pota, rapaz... Así que agora un descanso, cama e ácido glutámico. E prohibidos os libros, ¿eh?

Obedecín ó médico. Pasaba horas sen conto deitado na penumbra familiar do cuarto, coa radio prendida a baixo volume. Durmía, durmiñaba embalado pola música, distraíame a remoer as conversas dos que me viñan visitar: a Rosiña contoume como as monxas a castigaran a principio do curso por apañar castañas no patio do convento: o producto dos castiñeiros daba para a sobremesa das pupilas; as esposas de Cristo (gocei cos termos utilizados polo Lourenzo) eran cruelmente aforrativas... O Sindo tróuxome da aldea a colección de selos do avó, "Selos da Diáspora", e relatoume o caso dun rapaz veciño da parroquia que era "moi listismo de Dios" e o trouxeran do seminario a morrer na casa "dunha cousa que se lle agarrara na cabeza de ler tanto en latín."

From Our Ashes, *1980*

By drowning I was able to take up my studies again. The teachers were in a hurry to give the second semester at a quick pace, while I was leaving my work until the weekends, as I had no choice but to do it – for fear of what I didn't want to accept by any manner of means: failure. I was still proud.

I thought about this one night when my eyes were tired and my temples throbbed. I was reading the account of one sinister Cieza de León who had been a conquistador in Peru. I stopped at a certain paragraph, guiltily, my conscience accusing me: I couldn't sleep, I didn't have a good rest, I was not in top form the next day. In this way the days passed, with me acquiring the habit of reading to think afterwards and argue about sociology, history, about impersonal things, very far from what affected me, from what worried me, from what obsessed me… I had internal shivers without shaking; and I was afraid. I went back to the story of Cieza (only some minutes more, I told myself) and the conquistador became excited when describing the arrival of the Spanish to a temple where there had been two hundred virgins adoring the sun.

This was how I realised that something very strange was happening to me. I didn't understand the text; I thought that this was due to the difficulty of Renaissance Spanish. I read it again; I didn't understand anything; the words only had meaning without any relationship within the sentences. But those same words immediately became unconnected syllables and, at last, the syllables were little groups of letters without meaning… I surprised myself reading aloud, syllable by syllable, going over the letters in the bright light of the reading lamp.

What was that? What was it? What was happening to me? Following some instinct, I went to bed and immediately I lost touch with reality. I slept heavily, so much so that I didn't hear the alarm clock a few hours later. Old Felisa had to call me and I missed two morning classes.

The third class was literature. The teacher spoke about rhyme and rhythm and gave as an example some verses from Rubén Darío:

"This happened in Hugo's reign,

Emperor with the florid beard…"

As usual, he asked me a question about the author. To my desperation, I wasn't able to remember anything about him. Then the teacher began to ask me questions which were more and more elementary until getting to the meaning of the very well-known "cubs of the Hispanic lion". But I wasn't even able to comment on that. At the end of the class I ran to my old man's clinic.

My father gave me an address and I went there. The sign on his colleague and friend's door frightened me: "Psychiatrist". I went into the office, overcoming a repugnance like I had never felt before; because to be mad was shameful, it was destruction. Old Avelino repeated it: that classical mythology left no room for doubt: when the gods wanted to finish off a human being first they took away his mind…

The psychiatrist listened to me and gave a quick diagnosis:

– Brain fatigue. You'r cooking too many things in the same pot, young fellow… So that now you must rest, bed and glutamic acid. And no books, ok?

I obeyed the doctor. I spent innumerable hours lying in the darkness of my bedroom with the radio on low. I slept, I dozed, lulled by the music, I passed the time thinking over the conversations of those who came to visit me: Old Rosiña told me how the nuns had punished her at the beginning of the year for collecting chestnuts in the convent courtyard: the chestnuts were for the pupils' dessert; Christ's brides (I liked the term used by old Lourenzo) were cruelly parsimonious… Old Sindo brought me his grandfather's collection of stamps from his hometown, "Stamps from the diaspora", and told me the case of a boy from the parish who was "as clever as they come" and they had taken him out of the seminary to die at home "of a thing that had got into his head from reading so much in Latin".

Carlos Reigosa (1948–)

From Crime en Compostela, *1984*

– Aló polo ano 1962 – continuou Carlos –, estes dous homes, Aurelio Xieiro e Terencio Rancaño, aparecen como socios nunha contrata de obras e, tres anos despois, forman unha sociedade constructora con outros dous socios. Fixeron varios edificios grandes entre 1965 e 1970, e en 1971 separáronse e cada un tirou polo seu lado. Ámbolos dous eran xa ricos daquela.

– ¿Tan rápido?

– Si, aqueles foron anos moi bos, anos dun crecemento tresloucado, e os que máis gañaban eran os que máis arriscaban. Aurelio e Terencio xogaron forte, todo o forte que puideron, sempre ó límite do seu crédito e empeñándoo todo cando facía falla. Pero as cousas saíronlles ben, o diñeiro inzou e multiplicouse nas súas mans e gañaron moitos millóns. Especularon todo o que había para especular, neses anos en que a especulación, e sobre todo a especulación do chan, era o mellor negocio. Mercaron terreos e, en menos dun mes, chegaron a vendelos polo dobre. Non é doado de entender, pero foi así. Eu teño copias dos documentos privados dalgunhas das operacións, nas que, por certo, figuran cantidades que non teñen nada que ver coas das escrituras oficiais diante do notario, e podo mostrarche como un terreo comprado en pouco máis de dous millóns foi vendido ós once meses en máis de oito millóns. ¿Como foi posible? ¿Como eran posibles estas cousas? Pois como foron posibles sempre: Xuntando unha boa información, conseguida mediante xenerosas propinas, dádivas e regalos a secretarias e funcionarios, e unha axeitada intervención nos niveis de decisión, con extraordinarias atencións para os peixes gordos que, desde a sombra, toman os acordos máis proveitosos para os seus intereses… Máis ou menos, como se fixo en todas partes.

Carlos Conde calou de novo e permaneceu abstraído, coa ollada perdida sobre o asfalto que se estendía diante deles. Nivardo, despois dunha pausa breve, comentou:

– Sospeito que me queda aínda moito por saber.

– Abondo, si. Pero agora chegou o momento de incluír outro personaxe clave nesta leria: a muller de Terencio Rancaño. Porque Terencio, en 1966, cando os negocios lle ían vento en popa e el se convertera nun home rico, regresou a Noia e pretendeu en matrimonio a unha rapaza de boa casa, pero vida a menos. Gabouse e xactouse de toda a súa fortuna económica para seducir e engadelar á familia e, ó pouco tempo, conseguiu casar coa Teresa, unha moza bemposta que sempre vivira recluída cos seus pais e que acababa de face-los vintedous anos. Terencio tiña daquela 39, cinco máis có seu socio Aurelio Xieiro. Casaron e viñeron vivir a Santiago. E os anos foron pasando sen problemas, mentres as súas contas bancarias medraban e medraban sen parar. Pero en 1973, Teresa e Aurelio, sen que Terencio sospeitase nada, convertéronse en amantes. Ó parecer, Terencio volvérase enteiramente para os negocios e descoidara a casa...

– Esta é a pista que ti tes e non ten a policía. Eles non saben que Teresa e Aurelio foron amantes.

From Crime in Compostela, *1984*

– Around 1962 – Carlos continued –, these two men, Aurelio Xieiro and Terencio Rancaño, appear as partners in a building contract and, three years later, they form a construction company with two others. They built several big buildings between 1965 and 1970, and in 1971 they separated and each went his own way. By then, both were very rich.

– So quickly?

– Yes, those were very good years, years of uncontrolled growth, and those who earned most were those who risked most. Aurelio and Terencio played hard, the hardest they could, always at the limit of their credit and pawning everything when it was necessary. But things went well for them, money grew and multiplied in their hands and they earned millions. They speculated all that they could, in those years when speculation, and most of all speculation in land, was the best business. They bought sites and, in less than a month, they sold them for double the price. It's not easy to understand, but that's the way it was. I have copies of the private documents of some transactions in which, by the way, there are sums which have nothing to do with those in the official deeds, and I can show you how a site bought for little more than two million was sold eleven months later for more than eight. How was it possible? How were these things possible? Well, how they were possible always: getting together valuable information, got through generous tips, gifts and presents to secretaries and civil servants, and an adequate control over the powers that be, with extraordinary attention to the bigwigs that, from the shadows, take the decisions most advantageous to their interests... More or less how things were done everywhere.

Carlos Conde went quiet again and was meditative, with his look lost on the asphalt which extended in front of them. Nivardo, after a brief pause, commented:

– I suspect that I still have a lot to learn.

– A lot, yes. But now the moment came to include another key person in this muddle: Terencio Rancaño's wife. Because Terencio, in 1966, when his business was thriving and he had become a rich man, went back to Noia, hoping to marry a girl from a good family, fallen on hard times. He boasted of and bragged about all his fortune to captivate and soft-soap the family and, a short time after, he succeeded in marrying Teresa, an attractive girl who had always lived shut away with her parents and who had just turned twenty-one. Terencio was then thirty-nine, five more than his partner Aurelio Xieiro. They got married and came to live in Santiago. And the years went by without problems, while their bank accounts grew and grew. But in 1973, Teresa and Aurelio became lovers, without Terencio suspecting anything. It seems, Terencio had given himself over completely to his business and paid no attention to his family…

– This is the clue that you have and the police don't. They don't know that Teresa and Aurelio were lovers.

Afonso Pexegueiro (1948–)

From Seraogna, *1976*

A muller de Seraogna

Renxe o mastro da noite no tempo
e na ribeira do silencio dorme afanosa
a muller de Seraogna. Espiga de luz,
muller de tiza, introdúcese núa
na terra que traballa, abertos os seus seos e o seu sexo.

Cheira a silva e confúndese co gran
a muller de Seraogna. Saben a vaca os seus dedos
e a leite os seus beizos que o sol mata no centro da eira.

Sabe a tempo, a vida, a río e a soño
a muller que non sabe de contas,
que se perde na praza regateando dúas pesetas e o peso.

Sabe a sol, a uva, a resina recenden
os seus peitos cando anceiosa e cansa me ofrece o seu corpo.
Salvaxe, hierática, muller de herbaluísa,
de fiúncho e de fresa. Qué ben me sabes
cando te bico confundido coa túa carne, no chan, no leito.

Humedécente os sabios e os reis ao mollaren
na súa saliva a túa esperanza – icovardes! –.
E só o home que te bebe coñece a túa tristura.
Só el sabe a color das túas pernas
e o cheiro a terra que delas se desprende, muller
de saudade
que con zocas e sen lúa pretendes cruzar a noite.

The woman of Seraogna

The mast of the night creaks in the midst of time
and on the banks of silence she sleeps avidly,
the woman of Seraogna. Corn-ear of light,
woman of chalk, she goes naked
to the land she works, her bosom and her pudenda open.

She smells of brambles and she fuses with the grain,
this woman of Seraogna. Her fingers taste of cow,
and of milk her lips that the sun destroys in the middle of the
                                        threshing-floor.

She tastes of time, of life, of river and of sleep,
this woman who does not understand accounts
and who gets lost in the market-square haggling over two pesetas
                                        and weight.

She tastes of sun, of grapes, a perfume of resin exudes
from her breasts when avid and weary she offers me her body.
Wild, hieratic, woman of lemon verbena,
of fennel and strawberry. How good you taste
when I kiss you fused with your flesh on the ground, in bed.

Wise men and kings wet you when they soak
your hope in their saliva – the cowards!
And only the man who drinks you knows your sadness.
Only he knows the colour of your legs
and the smell of earth issuing from them, woman
of sadlonging
who in clogs and moonless tries to cross the night.

Vítor Vaqueiro (1948–)

From A cámara de néboa (The Chamber of Mist), *1989*

E soñamos daquela coas viaxes...

E soñamos daquela coas viaxes
indescriptíbeis. Coas viaxes na noite
furando aqueles túneis como tobos
e nós, os rilladores, procurando
a chegada da luz. E coas lanternas
afincándonos afincadamente
en cada treito escuro, alavancando,
ao avantarmos, cun nocturno, un nocturno.

E iamos marchando, ou navegando,
ou borrifando ao rente dos esgotos,
nos zudres estilados por paredes
sen nome, ou valadares lenturentos
que atuían os ollos, que atuían
o berro, que atuían a xordeira.
E era todo un silencio. Unha embaixada
de noite desde o zénite do tempo.

And we dreamt then of journeys...

And we dreamt then of journeys
indescribable. Of journeys in the night
digging those tunnels like burrows
and we, the gnawers, seeking
the arrival of light. And with our torches
kneeling resolutely
in each dark stretch, levering,
as we pressed on, with a nocturne, a nocturne.

And on we went, or sailed,
or sprayed alongside the gutters,
in the sludge seeping down nameless
walls, or damp palisades
that choked eyes, that choked
the yell, that choked deafness.

And all was one silence. An embassy
of night from the zenith of time.

Xesús Rábade Paredes (1949–)

From Branca de Loboso, *1991*

Tiña dezaseis anos recén feitos cando coñecín aquel por quen me paga a pena ter
nacido. Acórdaseme ben, que era o día de San Roque. E cada vez que acode á miña
mente o baile daquel día no adro da Capela, arreguízaseme o sangue e sinto que me
toma todo o corpo un aire ou cousa leve que me deixa por dentro moito gozo e
tamén moita tristeza.

Vai para catro anos que me puxeron a existencia mesmo ás beiras da morte, e hai
xa tres que me meteron a servir neste convento de Belvís, non sei por qué motivo.
Hei facer confesión – anque odio esta palabra, que me trouxo tantos males – de que
fun denunciada, procesada por meiga, torturada, posta nos sotos humedentos dun
presidio que me entumeceu o corpo e finalmente absolta polo mesmo tribunal do
Santo Oficio de Santiago que neste mesmo escrito direi logo. Por recomendación
do cal e mediación comenenciuda do arcipreste de Saavedra, que din Servando
Fontes, fun traída a esta casa de monxas onde á sazón me atopo, din que para purgar
enteiramente a alma de pecado e facer así mesmo humildosa renuncia e contrición
da vida pervertida en que ó parecer me puxo un verdadeiro enviado do maligno, o
meu aínda moi amado Antonio Aldán, a quen quixen e quero por sobre todas as
cousas deste mundo.

Aquí fago o oficio de criada e mandadeira. E destas vintecatro mulleres coas que
vivo nada malo hei de dicir, pois son de moita paz e trátanme con moito mira-
mento. Algunha vez fago tamén recados que me piden de fóra do convento. Estas
benditas, sei que para animarme, pídenme que borre da cabeza o meu pasado
negro, dicíndome a cadora que o peor do meu caso está pasado. Eu contesto que
ben, que pode ser, para non contradicilas, pero síntome moi triste nos adentros e
moi soa sen o Toño. Cada ano visito de ofrecida os Milagres de Saavedra, só
cumprindo os desexos do pai, meu infeliz, e non lle faltarei nesta súa vontade mentres me quede vida. Disque o ano que vén quere levarme ó Santo André e á Virxe
dos Remedios. Sei que o meu pai argalla todo isto por me ter cabo de si uns días e
de paso por sacarme deste lugar pechado, pois sempre el opinou que esta non era
solución ningunha para unha filla no mellor da mocidade. E sei que el coñecía o
meu con Toño. E sei que sofre porque entende o que neste punto eu sufro...

Toño viña pasar case todos os agostos e setembros a cabo duns parentes de seu
no lugar que lle din de Cal da Loba, e xa non faltou nunca desque nos coñecemos e
me pediu palabra no baile de San Roque. ¡Que espigadiño era! En fin, segundo
miña nai, eu andaba daquela bolonia e soñadora. Non tardou moito, ben seguro, en
llo comunicar a don Servando, que xa por entón lle quentaría a cama. Dicíame

tamén que por mor diso, de andar dada ós paxaros, me visitaba o demo na figura dese estudiante alleo, un real mozo de presencia baril e gasalleira, que aparecía e desaparecía xusto cada verán, sempre vestido cun traxe a raias negro, para me levar á tentación e me perder na golosume da carne e na concupiscencia.

Endexamais eu crin en tales cousas. Pero de tanto repetirmo el, o arcipreste de Saavedra, por boca da miña propia nai, unha empezou sen querer a figurarse na imaxinación como sería o demo e qué de marabillas non obrarían as súas artes cando se vía precisamente escarnecido por xente de sotana e auga bendita, sempre amargada, reprendedora e mouca ante as alegres mostras de vivir da xente nova. A verdade é que eu tiña o vezo dentro do meiguísimo del, de Toño Aldán, e que a súa aparición case me toleaba e me perdía. E así pasou que a por de mo pintaren cos propios atributos e engados do maligno, cheguei mesmo a soñar, non sei se a convencerme, de que o de Aldán podía moi ben ser demo, demoro ou preso da meiguice. Nada se me daría que o fose, senón todo o contrario. Mesmo se penso agora nel, no punto en que isto escribo, como enviado misterioso que vén do máis alá para facerme as beiras e tentarme só do modo que el sabe, sinto por todo o corpo a comezón e o sangue en arreguizo por ser eu precisamente a muller escollida entre tantas e tantas para gozar da regalía de home tan cobizado e tan bo mozo, que ningunha cousa mala pode haber en que unha fachendee e queira para sempre e para si o que resulta de inclinación universal e de natura. ¡Tiña os ollos azuis do mar de Aldán! ¡Meu meigo, oxalá resucitase!

E aínda digo que o demo me é simpático. E estou segura, pero non pola experiencia torcida que o Tribunal me apuxo, de que se trata dun ser ben paciente e divertido. Porque é preciso ter verdadeiros dotes de renarte e un sentido do humor moi aguzado para saír triunfante de tantas armadillas, tanto divino marteleo, persecución, maldición gratuíta e asañamento.

From Branca de Loboso, *1991*

I was just sixteen when I met the one person it was worth being born for. I remember it very well. It was San Roque day. And every time I recall the dance held that day in the chapel yard it makes me shiver, and a mixture of joy and deep sadness runs through my whole body. "It is almost four years ago now that my very life was taken to the verge of death, and then, three years ago, for what reason I know not, I was sent to serve in this convent in Belvis. I must make a "confession", although I hate that word – which has brought me such suffering. I was betrayed, judged as a witch, tortured, thrown into a damp prison cell where my body became as stiff as a board, and finally released by the same Inquisition court in Santiago that I shall talk of later. By recommendation of the said court and with the mediation of the Archbishop of Saavedra, by name of Servando Fontes, I was brought to this nuns' convent where I now dwell, it was said, "in order to wholly purge my soul of sin" and humbly renounce and make penance for the perverse life I was apparently led on to by one who was a true messenger of evil, my beloved Antonio Aldán, whom I still love above all else in this world.

Here I do the job of a servant and run errands. I cannot say a word against the twenty-four women I live with; they are gentle and treat me kindly. Sometimes, I also do the odd jobs they ask me to outside the convent. These blessed creatures, in order to cheer me up, ask me to blot out my dark past from my mind, telling me that the worst is now past. I reply that such may well be the case, so as not to contradict them, but deep down inside I feel so lonely without my young man, Toño.

Each year I pay a visit as a pilgrim, to fulfil the wishes of my father, that unfortunate man, who I will not let down until the day I die. It is said he wants to take me to Santo Tomé and Our Lady of the Remedies next year. I know he arranges all this so as to have me around for a few days, as well as to release me from this shut-in place, which, even so, he always said was the best way out for a daughter in the prime of her youth. And I know he was aware of my affair with Toño. And I know he suffers because he understands how much I too am suffering now.

Toño came to spend almost every August and September in the house of some relatives of his in a place called Cal da Loba. He has never once failed to come since the day we met at the San Roque dance when he asked me to become engaged to him at the San Roque dance. What a tall, gangling young man he was! Anyway, according to my mother, I was a foolish dreamer. It certainly didn't take her long to report the matter to Don Servando, who, by then, was sharing his bed with her. He also used to say that because I was so fond of birds, the devil used to visit me in the guise of a handsome, manly student from far away, who appeared and then vanished each summer like a migratory bird, always dressed in a black pin-striped suit, to tempt me into the sins of lasciviousness and lechery.

I never believed in those things myself. But because the Archbishop of Saavedra repeated it to me so often, by word of my mother, I unwillingly began to imagine what the devil was like and turned over in my mind the miracles he would perform when he found himself ridiculed by those people in black surplices and with holy water, always nagging and scolding, bitter at the way young people had so much fun. The truth is that I had really fallen for Toño Aldán, which made me lose my head – and myself – in the process. And so it happened that, because they made him out to have the features and the tricks of the devil himself, I ended up daydreaming, and convincing myself that Aldán might really be the devil, or a demon or the slave of some heavenly enchantment. It would make no difference what he was. Quite the opposite. Even now when I imagine him, at this point in my writing, as a mysterious go-between who comes from the beyond to seduce me and tempt me in the way only he knows how, I feel my flesh creep. My blood freezes, imagining I am the woman chosen, among so many, to enjoy, freely such a handsome, desirable young man, without one stain on his character. It cannot be a sin for a girl to boast about having a man like him, and wanting to have him for herself. It's only natural, and happens to girls all over the world. He had eyes as blue as the Aldán Sea. My bewitcher, would that you could come back to life!

I still find this devil amusing – and I am equally certain that unlike the court's crookedly unjust sentence proclaimed, he is a patient and entertaining creature. Why? Because you need to be really cunning and to have a razor-sharp sense of humour to emerge victorious from so many skirmishes, from all that persecution, needless evil and cruelty.

Millán Picouto (1949–)

From O poema dos lustros (The Poem of the Lustra), *1984*

Ao Miño en marzo

Xa a invernía se vai das túas veigas,
    Miño, eixo da patria,
e dun soño de ouveos e de chuvias
    saes de aceiro lucente
e feroz, pero os días han cubrirte,
    han cubrirte de calma.
Lugo segue ao teu lado, a poderosa,
    segue Ourense, a sorrinte,
como deusas que veñen coroarte
    con grinaldas de homes,
e ti segues, anciao reverdecido,
    cara ao Tegra e a Guarda.
Así sempre has florir dun ano pra outro,
    e os meus versos contigo,
e por riba dos dous ese arco-iris
    con beleza impalpábel
selará celestial a grande alianza
    entre ti e o meu pobo.

To the river Miño in March

Harsh winter is leaving your water-meadows,
    Miño, axis of the fatherland,
and from a dream of howls and rains
    you emerge made of steel, shining
and fierce, but the days will cover you,
    will cover you with calm.
Lugo the powerful still stands by your side
    as does Ourense the smiling,

like goddesses coming to crown you
>with garlands of men,
and still you move on, rejuvenated ancient,
>towards Mount Tegra and A Guarda.
And so you will always flower, year after year,
>and my verses with you,
and over us that rainbow
>with impalpable beauty
will celestially seal the great alliance
>between you and my people.

Xavier Rodríguez Baixeras (1950–)

From Fentos no mar (Ferns in the Sea), *1981*

Como un río

El non nos ve. Con este vento frío,
case outonal, despido xa de aromas,
chegan as horas, o vacío.
El non nos ve.

E, súbito, ti agromas,
acordas no seu sono; alí te asomas
grande e dispersa, lume e desvarío,
fondo alento dun medo onde nos tomas.
El non nos ve. O sono é como un río.

Como un río de tempo sen idades,
un lento decorrer de soidades,
un ceo andando para calquera día.

Como un neno tal vez. Mais estas horas
soben rotas das augas, e ti choras.
El non nos ve. O rostro se esvaía.

Like a river

He does not see us. With this cold wind,
almost autumnal, stripped now of aromas,
the hours arrive, the emptiness.
He does not see us.

And, suddenly, you sprout up,
you awake in his sleep; there you appear
great and dispersed, fire and delirium,
deep breathing of a fear where you capture us.
He does not see us. Sleep is like a river.

Like a river of time without ages,
a slow slipping along of sadlongings,
a sky moving towards any day.

Like a child perhaps. But these hours
rise broken from the waters, and you weep.
He does not see us. The face was fading away.

From Visitantes (Visitors), *1991*

Sós

Estamos aquí sós, no corazón do frío,
tentamos os aromas que a neve nos sepulta,
dos nosos corpos nus despréndense regatos
de sol e bolboretas que se abrasan, nocturnas,
e ventos que nos levan por un mesmo camiño;
dicimos as palabras que milagrosamente
dun fondo me arrebatan o teu pasado escuro
e mesmo o que hai en min, apenas xa pasado
no que imprimir o musgo tecido nas caricias
doutras noites lonxanas que non han de voltar
ao corazón do frío, onde non teño casa,
nin leito, e me procuro nos teus ollos furtivos.

Alone

We are here alone, in the heart of cold,
we feel the aromas that the snow buries from us,
out of our naked bodies flow streams
of sun and moths that are burnt up,
and winds that carry us along one same path;
we speak the words that miraculously
tear from some deep place your dark past
and even what there is in me, hardly past at all
on which to lay the moss woven in the caresses
of other distant nights that will not return

to the heart of cold, where I have no house,
or bed, and I seek myself in your furtive eyes.

Vicente Araguas (1950–)

From O gato branco (The White Cat), *1995*

Cando ela dorme..

CANDO ELA DORME
é un sabor
de laranxa
brava.
E o fume
do cigarro
doce como
nata montada.
Cando ela dorme:
un biscoito
despenado
na alba.

When she sleeps...

WHEN SHE SLEEPS
she's a taste
of bitter
orange.
And the smoke
from the cigarette
as sweet as
whipped cream.
When she sleeps:
a cake
flung down
into the dawn.

From Paisaxe de Glasgow (Glasgow Landscape), 1978

Eu fun o amante de Lady Chatterley...

EU FUN O AMANTE DE LADY CHATTERLEY
ao rachar do serán a curvatura.
As nádegas da lúa apontaban en ningures
o novo rumbo dos equinoccios.
Flossie ouveaba choivas de azures,
xofre adolescente na derradeira batalla,
Flossie do solpor, alpendre, dafodilo,
velaí Constance que coñecía.
Non é bo asimilar esposos paralíticos,
tampouco secarse baixo a mesma volvoreta,
sentir que a bágoa caeu na mina de volframio,
nin sequera sei onde puxen as muletas.
Se eu fose gardaboscos envolveríate, Constance,
cun vagalumes roubado dun Bentley vello estilo,
mais hoxe, calquera necesita un pai
e un rumor de sabas para se cubrir alleo.

I was Lady Chatterley's Lover...

I WAS LADY CHATTERLEY'S LOVER
while the nightfall was fracturing the curvature.
The moon's backsides were directed at nought,
the newborn track of the equinox.
Flossie barked torrents of blues,
adolescent sulphurs at the final affray,
Flossie at sunset, the hut, the daffodil,
that was all that Constance knew.
It doesn't do to take on crippled consorts
or to dry ourself under the same butterfly,
to feel the tear dropt into the tungsten pit
I don't even know where I left the crutches.
If I were a gamekeeper I'd cloak you, Constance,
in a glow worm pinched from a vintage Bentley,
but today, everybody needs a father
and a distant noise of sheets to cover us, strange.

Xosé María Álvarez Cáccamo (1950–)

From Cimo das idades tristes (Summit of the Sad Ages), *1988*

Coitelos

A vida prepara con dedicación artesanal
os seus coitelos máis finos e máis tristes
para que algun día unha folla azarosa toque con feitizos
a parte da pel en que máis confiamos. E trae
as navallas precisas, armas
que apenas mostran a ferida aberta, o río de excesivo
desprendimento e pranto.
Parecen os coitelos, que son palabras amistosas
e ás veces son caricias,
instrumentos fermosos para acompañar a solemne
festividade da mesa. Ninguén pensa
que logo da alegría e dos felices
pratos que nos foron servidos e tamén
daquel fluír de rostos que se falan
con moito amor despois do viño
os coitelos puidesen abrir follas dentadas,
florir rosas de óxido, brillar
con violenta intención. Pero hai un día
en que todas as navallas e coitelos que foran simplemente avisos
para a prudencia
medran ata facerse ferros dun terror que sabe matar.
A vida leva moitos anos preparando armas delicadas
e todas as feridas milimétricas,
os cortes paralelos de lenta miniatura,
non foron máis que agoiros dunha crecida de sangue
que nos fará homes mui tristes e mui pacíficos para sempre.

Knives

Life prepares with the dedication of an artisan
its finest and saddest knives
so that one day a chance blade can touch with spells
the part of our skin in which we most trust. And it brings
the knives it needs, arms
that hardly show the open wound, the river of excessive
emission and weeping.

Knives, which are friendly words
and are sometimes caresses,
seem to be beautiful instruments for accompanying the solemn
festivity of the table. Nobody thinks
that after the happiness and the cheerful
dishes we were served and also
that flow of faces talking to each other
with great love after the wine
the knives could open serrated blades,
flower roses of rust, gleam
with violent intent. But there is a day
when all the knives that had been simply alerts
to prudence
grow until they become the tools of a terror that can kill.
Life has for many years been preparing delicate arms,
and all the millimetric wounds,
the parallel cuts in slow miniature,
were only omens of a flood of blood
that will make us very sad and very peaceful men for ever.

From Calendario perpetuo, *1997*

É Domingo na casa dos avós. Nace o Domingo do perfil da herba, como fonte de seda. Baixa a cor do Domingo pola rúa grande, vén dos parques, percorre o canellón e dá primeira man de minio nas cancelas. Entra un vento amoroso nas tabernas e as xentes da parroquia camiñan con prudente paso de zapatos brancos.

Coñécese o Domingo na casa dos avós porque proclama o ritmo dos costumes lenes. Retarda o noso avó diante do espello o ritual dos dedos para compor o nó da gravata. A avoa na despensa clasifica as especias e as cores do betume e as etiquetas para confituras.

O nenos cremos que hai un home louco nunha alcoba que chaman Cuarto Escuro, o das baldosas negras.

From Perpetual Calendar, *1997*

It is Sunday in our grandparents' home. Sunday is just being born from the blades of grass, like a silken fountain. The colour of Sunday comes down the High Street, coming out of the parks, running down the gutter, spreading the first coat of primer on the garden gates. A soft breeze in the pubs; the people of the parish walking cautiously in their white shoes.

Sunday is famous in our grandparents' house, its arrival heralding the gentle rhythm of soothing habits. Our grandfather slowly and deliberately fingers the knot of his tie in front of a mirror. Grandma, in the pantry, brings order to the spices, tins of shoe polish and jam-jar labels.

We children believe a madman is on the loose in the room they call the dark-room, the one with black floor tiles.

Cesáreo Sánchez Iglesias (1951–)

From O rostro da terra (The Face of the Earth), *1996*

A neve cae...

A neve cae
na imensidade vacía.
Cae o rumor do branco silencio.

Muda claridade
na pel do tempo:
pequenas flores húmidas.

Escóitote
cando xa teño soñado
a túa luz vexetal.

A paisaxe é un ser
a se encarnar.

Dentro do silencio
o presente non existe.

Unha ave busca o seu niño
nas árbores cargadas
de soidade.

A neve borra
as túas pegadas
sobre a neve.

The snow falls...

The snow falls
in the empty immenseness.
The murmur of the white silence falls.

Mute clarity
on the skin of time;
small damp flowers.

I listen to you
when I have already dreamt
your vegetal light.

The landscape is a creature
being embodied.

Within this silence
the present does not exist.

A bird seeks its nest
in trees laden
with sadlonging.

The snow effaces
your footsteps
in the snow.

Víctor Freixanes (1951–)

From O triángulo inscrito na circunferencia, *1982*

Santo Alberte Magno, doutor da Santa Igrexa, mestre da Universidade de París, sabio entre tódolos sabios do seu tempo, construíu un día, logo de moitos estudios e traballos, unha enorme cabeza que falaba: o androide. E non só falaba, senón que podía adiviñar o futuro, curar as doenzas do corpo, descubrir tesouros escondidos e revelar os segredos máis profundos do tempo pasado. Era unha cabeza de ferro e madeira que o santo varón eclesiástico tiña gardada nas súas cámaras privadas e non amostraba a ninguén, sabedor que era de que moitos non o entenderían. Un día – un día verdadeiramente parvo – amosou o segredo a un seu discípulo moi querido, aquel que máis salientaba nos estudios da lóxica, a matemática e a teoloxía, e que se chamaba Tomás: Tomás de Aquino. Tomás viu cos seus ollos e escoitou cos

seus ouvidos o milagre da Cabeza parlante, milagre da Razón, da intelixencia constructora do seu mestre. Preguntoulle ó mecanismo aquel todo o que quería saber.
Empezou primeiro polas cuestións máis pequenas e sinxelas, coma quen enreda
cun brinquedo gracioso, pero foi pasando despois ás máis complexas, segundo descubría as posibilidades da máquina; quixo saber, sentiuse aguilloado pola curiosidade, avanzou polos camiños da Fe, os Grandes Misterios, as Verdades Absolutas,
os camiños prohibidos do Dogma e os Altos Destinos. A Cabeza contestábao todo.
Nada deixaba sen responder.

– ¿Onde está o segredo primeiro do Mundo, o Motor único e principal de todo
canto vemos, sentimos e enxergamos ó noso arredor? – preguntou Tomás.

– O segredo está no Triángulo – díxolle a Cabeza.

– O Triángulo... O indescifrable misterio da Santísima Trindade, o máis profundo dos misterios divinos – comentou admirado o de Aquino –. ¿Que fe
relixiosa, que teoloxía podería facérnolo comprender na súa perfecta plenitude?

– Eu non falo de relixión, nin de fe, nin de teoloxía respondeu a Máquina –. Eu
falo da ciencia antiga do número e da equidistancia, o equilibrio harmónico da
suprema xeometría, que tracexou as liñas directrices do Universo hai miles de
millóns de anos. O segredo está no Triángulo.

– ¿Pero non é a teoloxía a ciencia suprema do coñecemento de Deus, filosofía de
tódalas filosofías?

– Deus está na Razón. E a Razón está no Triángulo – volveu respostar a Cabeza
mecánica.

Tomás pillou medo. Entroulle un medo terrible, medo dediante do misterio que
non entendía, medo de saber, medo da nova Revelación, pois diso se trataba. Era
feble, fraco de espírito – anque as historias nolo apresenten doutra maneira – e non
foi quen de se arriscar a alancar por aquel camiño que dediante de si se lle abría.
Tivo a súa oportunidade e non a aproveitou. Pasa sempre. Perante o que non coñecemos, perante aquilo que esperta en nós a inseguridade dun mundo distinto do
que decote habitamos, perante o que non sabemos aínda explicar, pero existe, reac-
cionamos coa violencia e o anatema, a excomuñón e o dogma, a rabia que nace da
nosa propia impotencia. Todo coñecemento ten o seu risco. O acto de coñecer é, de
seu, un acto revolucionario, pois leva dentro de si a esencia da mutación. Cada verdade nova que aparece dediante de nós cuestiona e critica irremediablemente todo
o aparello tecido polas verdades anteriores. O edificio da realidade cambalea. Iso foi
o que asustou a Tomás: a certeza do derrubamento das vellas teorías (vellas e
sacrosantas), o abismo que de súpeto podía abrirse baixo de si. Puido deixarse levar,
mergullarse naquel mundo novo e marabilloso, como fixeron outros (coma
mesmo fixo o seu mestre), pero botou man dun martelo de ferro que había a carón
del e, sen que o outro tivese tempo de o parar, bateu na cabeza aquela con tódalas
súas forzas, machacouna ata que non foi máis ca un cangallo de ferros retortos e
escachifados. "Era cousa do Diabo", dixo. "Era a máquina do Inferno, unha andró-
mena para nos confundir e condenar."

Non se sabe o que lle respondeu daquela San Alberte Magno, se rifaron entre eles, se chegaron ás mans sen que ninguén os vira ou se o mestre, abafado pola acción do discípulo, recoñeceu o seu erro e pediu a penitencia. Tanto ten. O conto é que alí acabou a historia do androide, a Cabeza parlante. E nunca tanto medo se viu na cara dun home coma nos ollos arrepiados de Tomás de Aquino.

A historia, tal coma aquí se conta, cáseque coas mesmas palabras, vén no segundo dos Cartapacios Verdes de don Xoán Manuel, aquel onde o navegador presenta e desenvolve a súa teoría do Triángulo inscrito na Circunferencia, que logo Quinteiro estudiou nos manuscritos da biblioteca. Así empeza a teoría do Triángulo: con esta historia. Alberte Magno, doutor universalis, aínda sendo cristián, lera nos textos prohibidos a Ciencia da Razón, ciencia maldita que moitos pagaron coa fogueira, ciencia das verdades profundas e dos secretos mecanismos do Universo que os homes, certamente, coñeceron unha vez, pero logo esqueceron. Esta era a base principal do traballo de don Xoán Manuel filósofo e precursor. Abofé que outros moitos falaron disto, e aínda máis nestes séculos laicos de anticlericalismo e rebelión contra das teoloxías, as teocracias e os poderes absolutos. ¡Louvor á antiga ciencia da Razón e a luz ordenadora que tira dos ollos dos homes as tebras ruíns da ignorancia e do medo; ciencia da harmonía total que chegará ordenar, andando os anos, o mecanismo marabilloso do Universo todo! ¡Luz da Intelixencia, que pon no corazón dos homes certezas e verdades que transformarán o mundo! Así pensaba xa don Xoán Manuel moito antes de que outros que agora pasan por precursores naceran. E aínda foi mais alá, que disto falaba Quinteiro co inglés cando fixeron xuntos a viaxe a Compostela. A Razón de don Xoán Manuel non é o racionalismo estreito dominante, non é tampouco o positivismo nin o culto devoto e cego ás ciencias empíricas (anque moito teñamos que deprender delas), non. O sabio navegador sabía que a Razón é a outra porta do Universo, a vía secreta e secularmente prohibida que ha levar ó home ós Paraísos Perdidos, á Primeira Idade, ás orixes, tal como pensou tamén no seu tempo Alberte Magno, e outros moitos que non o dixeron ou que calaron na fogueira dos poderes absolutos...

From The Triangle Within the Circumference, *1982*

Saint Albert the Great, a Church doctor, a Master in the University of Paris, the wisest of all the wise men of his time, one day built an enormous talking head, after a lot of work and study: the android. And it didn't only talk, but it could also tell the future, cure corporal illnesses, discover hidden treasures, and reveal the most profound secrets of the past. It was a head made of iron and wood that the holy, ecclesiastical man kept in his private chambers and didn't show to anyone, conscious that many would not understand it. One day – one stupid day – he showed the secret to a very much-loved disciple of his, the one who was most outstanding in Logic, Mathematics and Theology, and who was called Thomas: Thomas Aquinas. Thomas saw with his own eyes and heard with his own ears the miracle of the Talking Head, the miracle of Reason, of the creative intelligence of his master. He asked that machine all that he wanted to know. First he started with the smallest, simplest questions, like someone who was enjoying himself with an entertaining pastime, but then he proceeded to more complex questions, as he discovered the machine's potential; he wanted to know, he was driven by his curiosity, he advanced through the paths of Faith, the great Mysteries, the Absolute Truths, the forbidden paths of Dogma and High Destinies. The Head answered everything. He left nothing without an answer.

– Where is the first secret of the World, the only and the First Mover behind everything that we see, feel and descry around us? – Thomas asked.

– The secret is in the Triangle – the Head told him.

– The Triangle… The indecipherable mystery of the Holy Trinity, the deepest of the divine mysteries – Aquinas commented admiringly –. What religious faith, what theology can make us understand it in all its complexity?

– I'm not talking about religion, or faith or theology – the Machine answered –. I'm speaking about the ancient science of numbers and of equidistance, of the harmonious equilibrium of supreme geometry that drew the guidelines of the Universe, a billion years ago. The secret is in the Triangle.

– But is Theology not the supreme science of all divine knowledge, philosophy of all philosophies?

– God is in Reason. And Reason is in the Triangle – the mechanical Head answered once more.

Thomas became afraid. A terrible fear took hold of him, fear of the mystery that he didn't understand, fear of knowing, fear of the new Revelation, because that's what it was about. He was weak, weak-spirited – although history tells us a different story – and he wasn't able to risk taking that road which opened up before him. He had his opportunity and he didn't take advantage of it. It always happens. Faced with what we don't know, faced with that which awakens in us the insecurity of a world different to that which we usually inhabit, faced with that which we don't yet know how to explain, but that exists, we react with violence and anathema, excommunion and dogma, the rage that comes from our own impotence. All knowledge is risky. The act of knowledge is, in itself, a revolutionary act, because it has within it the essence of change. Each new truth which appears before us questions and criticises irremediably the properties woven by anterior truths. The construction of reality shakes. That's what frightened Thomas: the certainty of the dismantling of old theories (old and sacrosanct), the abysm that could suddenly open up under one. He could have gone with the tide, submerged himself in that new, wonderful world (even as his master had done), but he took an iron hammer that was beside him and, without the other being able to stop him, he hit that head with all his might, he destroyed it until it was no more than a jumble of twisted, squashed iron. "It was the Devil", he said. "It was a machine from Hell, a fantasy to confuse us and damn us".

Nobody knows what Saint Albert the Great answered then, if they argued amongst themselves, if they hit each other without anyone seeing them, or if the master, ashamed by his student's acts, recognized his mistake and asked for penance. It doesn't matter. The fact is that there the story of the android ended, the Talking Head. And so much fear was never seen in a man's face as in Thomas Aquinas's terrified eyes.

The story, just as it is told here, almost with the same words, is found in the second of Xoán Manuel's Green Folders, where the navigator presents and develops his theory of the Triangle within the Circumference, that afterwards Quinteiro studied in the manuscripts in the library. That's how the theory of the Triangle begins: with this story. Albert the Great, doctor universalis, in spite of being a Christian, had read about the Science of Reason in the forbidden texts, an accursed science which many paid for at the stake, a science of deep truths and of the secret mechanisms of the Universe that men certainly once knew but soon forgot. This was the chief basis of philosopher and pioneer Xoán Manuel's work. It's true that many others spoke of this, and even more in these lay centuries of anticlericalism and rebellion against theology, theocracy and absolute power. Praise be the ancient science of Reason and the ordering light that eliminates the contemptible darkness of ignorance and of fear from the eyes of men; a science of total harmony that will eventually order the marvellous mechanism of the whole Universe as time goes by! Light of Intelligence, that puts into men's hearts certainties and truths that will transform the world! That's how Xoán Manuel thought a long time before others, who pretend to be pioneers, were born. And he went even further because Quinteiro spoke with the Englishman of this when they made the journey to Compostela. Xoán Manuel's Reason is not a narrow and dominating rationalism, nor is it positivism either nor the devout, blind devotion to empirical science (although we have a lot to learn from it), no. The wise navigator knew that Reason is the other door of the Universe, the secret way, forbidden for centuries, which will take man to Forbidden Paradises, the Golden Age, to his origins, as Albert the Great thought in his time, and many others who didn't say it or were silenced at the stake of absolute power…

Margarita Ledo Andión (1951–)   •

From Mamá Fe (Mother Faith), *1983*

Ironpark crime

A aureana respondía por este nome coa súa orixe en Merza, en ríos pequechos onde peneiraba areas e verdello para escolma-lo prodixio, as pebidas de ouro que o Miño, baixando raiano Cortegada, non producía.

As marxas que ascenden na bocarribeira, o paso diario con wolfram chegado de Verín, o cornello en papel de estraza e as bolas, culminaban as especias contrabandeadas cara ó sur, igual que os fíos, as medias, o aceite sen refino entraba sen apuros.

Dez anos afastaran aqueles meses, o ferro, a ponte, os campos convertidos nun parque de ferro. Aureana termou sempre do prodixio que había producirse sen querer zafar, tampouco, un aquel triste, acochada no canaval, cando sentiu para-lo camión.

A cuadrilla sae da cabina a cara descuberta, sen apaga-lo motor diésel, cos faros acesos e renxe, seco, o aceiro cando o chofer mete o freo de man.

Tres sombras axustan as carabinas e as machadas ó cinto, sombras que aureana non quixera turbar nin co alento, inmóbil, na súa covacha de hedras e que, nos anos que ían pasando, nunca máis utilizará para o seu salto de contrabandista solitaria.

O vento estaba sur, mesto, pesado no seu devalo escuro apampándose nos faros acesos que sinalaban un final de xornada a escasas horas do mencer.

Da caixa do diésel renxen, agora, as bisagras e caen como fardos, apilados, respirando o gas carbónico do escape. Móvense arredor dúas sombras, as mesmas que foran facendo a descarga e chéganlle as frases nas que só distingue certos sons como cando os chaláns cruzan os caiados e pechan o tira e afrouxa dunha operación que levou toda a feira.

Aureana sabe permanecer horas e horas cabeceando, dando espreitadelas, collendo o sono embaixo do manto de merino que lle dá boa sorte, permanecer aniñada como se peneirara nas augas o prodixio das pebidas de ouro.

O bafo das dúas sombras alampea entre os grilos e xa collen cada brazado, a dous, que ascende a ponte e faise vango ata un bruído grave que esnaquiza a corrente parsimoniosa do Miño.

Sen atafegos, con tempo de prende-los cigarros, as sombras reenganchan o seu traxecto curto que se repite cinco veces, cando aureana descobre que aquel quinto vulto estira os brazos e sente a mordedela nos dedos agarrando o petril mentres as sombras aguilloan o espacio escurísimo cun alarido e méxense veloces, cara á ponte, e as culatas chocan coa pedra, chocan cos dedos, os dedos non soltan o petril, a culata mete o seu óvalo nas unllas que ataniscan o muro.

Aureana ve, entón, a terceira sombra que xa tiña esquecida, vea saca-la machada, o relustro ó pasa-los faros, a terceira sombra, de vagar, que esmaga o seu cigarro e vai reunirse cos culatazos que paran en seco no tempo de erguerse a machada, que vai corta-los dedos no petril para ouvirse o vulto, o corpo entrar nas augas.

Saen as tres sombras para a cabina. O motor mete un tropel que as rodeiras deixan marcado no camiño e vaise o diésel, choqueleando, coa cancela da caixa pendurada nas traseiras, co vento sur arrequecido de súpeto e aureana dórmese sen sabelo.

Pasan os anos dos paseadores, volta a rutina raiana, Cortegada esvae unha memoria que campea nalgúns axustes de contas por Coles, por Taragoña, en Foz, recupera a ruta do sur e a tan agardada tranquilidade noitébrega. Ós dez anos calquera cronista faríanos dunha vila ben organizada, disposta ó intercambio, cos estraperlistas vencellados como en calquera lugar á comisaría de abastos da súa capital de provincia.

No bar da estación, outravolta, péchase tarde e despois do último relevo entra a parella de fronteiras porque sempre quedan mesas con partidas en aberto.

Adoitan verse pola vila visitantes do sur. Distínguense por ter pouca présa e dar un aspecto de adicar certo tempo ó coidado persoal. Traen os zapatos recén limpos, chambras de feltro remarcadas con colares de raposo loiro. Adoitan vir artellar algunha encomenda forte, controla-los seus mellores puntos, exercer sen demoras o suborno de fronteiras, asegurarse dos camións cargados de ovos, si, ou de mineral. É unha caste de visitante ben acollida, con trato suavizado, sempre co mesmo cuarto na pousada, e que regresan ó sur sen botar máis de dous ou tres días ou collen o comboio para Ourense. O día que fan noite en Cortegada habitúanse a frecuenta-las partidas ou fano cando están á espera de coller un tren.

A mesa próxima ó mostrador goza do privilexio da reserva sen outra razón que a de ser ocupada, dende cedo, pola mesma peña e tamén para poderse servir, eles mesmos, na barra cando sae unha man de cartas litixiosa e cómpre medir ben as forzas.

Os visitantes fíxanse naquela mesa. Achéganse para asexar, silenciosos, as últimas operacións dos xogadores. Os xogadores míranse, acóllense a uns segundos de respiro para cavilar na combinación precisa, segundos que ninguén interrompe e nos que, polo común, as facianas adoptan un aire de certa rixeza.

Os visitantes coñecen a norma, o prezo deses segundos. Teñen as mans nos petos. O do centro, xa máis preto, vaise permitir, ousado, fende-la norma, fende-la gravidade do momento con algo tan banal como dirixirse a un dos actores familiarmente cun ¿nón me coñeces, ti?, que o interrogado despacha, distante, cun pois non, que o visitante acompaña nun movemento de brazos tensos que desenfunda da chambra e que sitúa, xusto, no feltro verde.

As sillas dos xogadores van recuar lenes. Os xogadores que se retiran. Non se escoita outra palabra no bar da estación. E o patrón desaparece pola trampilla da bodega.

Só el queda chantado diante do visitante. Que garda, sen présa, as mans no peto cando os seus dous amigos, como liscas, baleiran ó unísono un par de cargadores no mellor xogador de Cortegada.

Ironpark Crime

The golddigger answered to this name with her origin in Merza, in small rivers where she sifted sand and mud to select the prodigy, the gold nuggets that the Miño, going past Cortegada, didn't produce.

The stains all along the shore, the daily walk with wolfram that comes from Verín, with bread wrapped up in paper and rolls, were the height of the smuggled merchandise to be taken to the South, the same as thread, stockings and unrefined oil got in without problems.

Ten years had passed since those months, since the iron, the bridge, the fields that had turned into iron parks. The golddigger always held the prodigy that had to be produced without trying to avoid giving a sad impression either, hidden in the reedbed, when she heard the truck stop.

The gang left the cabin with their faces uncovered, without switching off the diesel engine, with the headlamps on, and when the driver put on the handbrake the steel screeched drily.

Three shadows fix their rifles and knives in their belts. Shadows that the golddigger didn't want to bother even with her breath, without moving in her ivy-covered hovel and that, in the years that would pass, she would never use again for her solitary smuggling.

The wind came from the South, dense, heavy in its dark descent against the lighted lamps that showed the end of the day a few hours from dawn.

The hinges of the diesel truck screech now and like sacks, one on top of the other, breathing the fumes from the exhaust pipes, they fall. Two shadows move around, the same that were unloading, and she hears sentences in which she only makes out some sounds as when dealers spit on their hands and close the haggling of a deal that lasted the whole fair.

The golddigger knows how to doze for hours and hours, taking a peek from time to time, getting to sleep under the sheep's wool blanket that brings her luck; she knows how to stay nestled up as if she were sifting the prodigy of gold nuggets.

The steam of the two shadows advances among the crickets and they pick up an armful between the two of them, which goes up the bridge and it becomes weightless until there is a low sound that breaks the parsimonious current of the Miño.

Without hurrying, with time to light some cigarettes, the shadows start their short route again repeating it five times when the golddigger discovers that that fifth bundle stretches its arms and she feels the bite in his fingers clutching the railing, while the shadows stab the dark space with a shout and they move quickly towards the bridge, and the butts hit the stone, they hit his fingers, his fingers don't let go of the railing, the butts with their wide end stick in his nails grasping the wall.

The golddigger sees, then, the third shadow that she had forgotten about, she sees it taking out a hatchet, and it shines under the lamps; the third shadow slowly stamps on its cigarette and goes to join the butters that stop suddenly as he raises the hatchet, he's going to cut the fingers on the railing so as to hear the bundle, the body, falling into the water.

The three shadows go towards the truck. The engine acclerates so that the wheels leave marks on the road and the diesel lorry goes away, rattling, with its back door hanging off, with the South wind rising suddenly, and the golddigger sleeps without knowing it.

The time of the walkers is past , the border routine comes back, Cortegada banishes a memory that shows itself in some settlings of scores around Coles, around Taragoña, in Foz; it recovers the route to the South and the so longed-for tranquility at night. Ten years afterwards historians would describe it as a well-organized town, prepared for interchanges, with the blackmarketeers taking charge of the supply of its provincial capital, as in any other place.

Once more the station bar closes late and after the last shift a pair of frontier guards come in, because there are always tables with a card game going on.

One can see visitors from the South around town. They are identifiable because they are never in a hurry and because they give the impression of spending time on their personal appearance. Their shoes are always clean and they wear felt smocks with red fox collars. They usually come to get a good payment, to supervise their best places, to ask for the border bribe without delay, to make sure there are trucks full of eggs, yes, or of minerals. They are visitors who are very welcome, with the most favourable reception, always with the same room in the inn, and who go back to the South after two or three days or they take the train to Ourense. The day that they sleep in Cortegada they usually play cards, or else they do it when they are waiting for the train.

The table closest to the counter is special in that it is reserved without any other reason than that it has been occupied early by the same circle, and also so that they can get themselves drinks from the bar, when they argue over a game and it's necessary to be careful about what they say and do.

The visitors notice that table. They go up to watch silently the movements of the players. The players look at each other, they take a break for a few seconds to think about their next move, seconds that nobody interrupts and during which, usually, the faces adopt a serious air.

The visitors know the rule, the price of those seconds. Their hands are in their pockets. The one in the middle, comes closer, he's going to allow himself to dare to break the rule, break the gravity of the moment with something as banal as addressing himself to one of the players with familiarity, with a "don't you know me?", which the interrogatee attends to distantly with a "well no", that the visitor accompanies with a movement of his tense arms, taking them out of his pockets and situating them just over the card table.

The players' chairs are pushed back slightly. The players go away. Another word isn't heard in the station bar. And the owner disappears by the trap door to the wine cellar.

Only he remains standing in front of the visitor, who waits, without being in a hurry, his hands in his pockets when his two friends, in a flash, empty in unison a couple of chambers of bullets into the best player in Cortegada.

Ánxel A. Rei Ballesteros (1952–)

From Dos anxos e dos mortos, 1977

"O coche", balbuciou.

O corazón choutáballe agora no peito ata lle facer sentir dor.

Espreitábao. Podía dar tres pasos, entrar nel, e poñer o motor en marcha. Pero non o facía. Non se moveu. Non era capaz. E, cun suspiro, soltou o bulso e deixou caer os brazos nun súpeto abandono de si mesma ó longo do seu corpo. Sentía unha canseira inmensa, coma se as súas forzas lle fallasen. A súa boca sorriu na soidade. E, xa sabías que che ía pasar esto, pensou. Pero notou que xa que as bágoas debruzaban nos seus ollos e que, dun momento a outro, ía sentir degaros de chorar. Mais, nun último intento, tratou de evocar a imaxe salvadora de Vicente, con calor. Pero esta vez, no lugar da imaxe garimosa á que ela estaba acostumada, na súa fantasía abriuse paso a dun home case descoñecido, a dun avogado, que a ollaba frío e indiferente, avés cun sorriso orgulloso de ironía, na porta da súa casa. E ante este novo cariz que adquiría o ser que amaba, ante aquela imaxe arrepiante, inesperada, sentiu medo, e notou que se lle as pernas debilitaban e era como se algo frío, unha cousa fría, de xeo, se lle puxera no estómago. Entón deixouse caer contra a parede, co seu corpo todo inerte, e pechou os ollos. E sacudía a cabeza entre xemidos, sentindo xa na súa cara a caricia morna e suave das bágoas. Chorou un anaco na soidade do garaxe, encostada no húmido cemento da parede. Choraba: O naufraxio dos soños que morrían cun pranto profundo e ferido de tristeza. Cando se tivo sosegado outra vez, limpou as bágoas, compúxose un pouco a súa roupa, retocouse o cabelo brevemente, e dirixiuse de novo cara á porta para saír. Pero antes, cando xa se dispuña ao facer, deñou coa súa vista no coche, unha vez máis, e parouse uns minutos, inmóbil, diante del. Espreitábao no silencio. Dirixiulle unha última mirada longa e triste, e cunha dozura infinda e inexpresable. Logo, deu media volta e abandonou o garaxe.

From About Angels and About the Dead, *1977*

"The car", she stuttered.

Now her heart jumped in her chest so much that it caused her pain.

She watched it. She could take three steps, get into it, and start the engine. But she didn't do it. She didn't move. She wasn't able to. And, with a sigh, she dropped her bag and let her arms fall down by her sides in a sudden abandoning of herself. She felt an enormous fatigue, as if her strength failed her. There was a smile on her mouth in the solitude. And she thought: you knew that this was going to happen to you. But she noticed that tears were already forming in her eyes and that, in a moment or two, she was going to feel like crying. However, in a last effort, she tried heatedly to remember the life-saving image of Vicente. But this time, instead of the affectionate image that she was used to in her fantasy, an almost unknown man appeared on her doorstep, a lawyer who looked at her coldly and indifferently, with scarcely an ironic smile. And faced with this new aspect which the person she loved had, faced with this terrible, unexpected image, she felt afraid, and she noticed that her legs became weak, and it was as if something cold, a cold icy thing, was in her stomach. Then she leaned against the wall, with her body completely inert, and she closed her eyes. And she shook her head while she moaned, feeling the tepid, gentle caress of tears on her face. She cried a while in the solitude of the garage, leaning against the damp cement of the wall. She cried: dreams drowning in the profound, injured weeping of sadness. When she became calm again, she wiped her tears, she fixed her clothes a little, she touched her hair quickly, and went to the door to leave. But before she started to go, she looked at the car once more, and stopped a few minutes, motionless, in front of it. She watched it silently. She gave it a last, long, sad look, with immense, inexpressible sweetness. Then, she turned around and left the garage.

Luís González Tosar (1952–)

From A caneiro cheo (Full Channel), *1986*

Auga de amor sen nome

Cumpríame ás veces estar cos puños pechos
e cavilar un pouco coas mans preto do lume,
poder afalarlle desde min mesmo á túa sombra
e ir compondo de vagar unha figura nova,
que é como sentila vir ardendo na forma
e ímpeto dun lentísimo boi rubio, inmenso.
Cando acudo á frescura deses ríos
ou bebo das entrañas afumadas do licor,
estou entrando no ferro dóçe do teu corpo,
subindo un mar que principia polas pernas,
que fai abalear as cousas e os bruídos familiares
anunciando un canto de malvises imposibles
no remol dunha ínsua lonxíncua e coñecida.
Nesta luz incerta que separa os nosos corpos,
ben me decato de ser un barco triste
con ansia de sombra nun porto pola tarde.
Sigo topeñando nas rochas e raíces máis estrañas,
escorándome de vez no acedo da soidade,
oíndo de hora en hora a chamada das buguinas,
esas que fan erguer as ondas sobre a proa.
É a máxica visión que a modo vai queimando
toda a ardentía e cor que colle nas palabras.

Water of nameless love

I need at times to sit with clenched fists
and muse a little with my hands close to the flame,
be able, from within my self, to urge your shadow into action
and gradually compose a new figure,
which is like feeling it come burning in the form
and with the impetus of a slow, vast brown ox.
When I go to the freshness of those rivers
or drink from the smoky heart of that liqueur,
I am entering the sweet iron of your body,
rising through a sea that begins at your legs,
that makes things and familiar noises sway

announcing a song of impossible redwings
on the embers of a remote and well-known island.
In this uncertain light that separates our bodies,
I can well see that I am a sad boat
yearning for shade in a port in the afternoon.
I still collide with the rocks and the strangest roots,
sometimes shored up on the acid of solitude,
hearing every so often the call of the sirens,
the ones that make waves rise over the prow.
This is the magical vision that is slowly burning
all the ardour and colour that words can contain.

From Seis cantos labrados co recordo de seis cidades mouras (Six Cantos Fashioned from the Memory of Six Moorish Towns), *1986*

Azrou, amiga triste

Cando nace a lúa branca das vendimas
aló no meu país de lumes no Fisterra,
chego eu a Azrou, triste amiga montañesa
chantada no val fondo, ferida pola luz.

Coa noite van entrando ringleiras de homes.
Veñen do sur amargo e avantan lentamente,
están marcados todos coa negra cor da fame.
¿Quen labrou eses rostros?
¿Por que me acenan as súas mans de medo?

Azrou, pequena amiga, non volvas a ensinarmos,
dáme a beber o sangue do corazón dun cedro,
abre os nimbos que pesan no alto deses montes
e que o poema recolla os labios dos amigos.

Azrou, sad friend

When the white moon of the grape-harvests is born
away in my country of fires in Finisterre,
I reach Azrou, my sad mountain friend
set in the deep valley, wounded by the light.

As night falls rows of men come filing in.
They are from the bitter south and advance slowly,

all are marked by the black colour of hunger.
Who fashioned those faces?
Why do their hands of fear gesture to me?

Azrou, little friend, don't show me them again,
give me the blood of the heart of a cedar to drink,
open the halos that weigh on the peaks of those mountains
and may the poem gather up the lips of friends.

César Antonio Molina (1952–)

From **Eume,** *2007*

Leteos

Que río podes desexar despois de terme visto?
di o Neva.

Que río podes desexar despois de terme visto?
di o Hudson.

Que río podes desexar despois de terme visto?
di o Tíber.

Que río podes desexar despois de terme visto?
di o Rin.

Que río podes desexar despois de terme visto?
di o Sena.

Que río podes desexar despois de terme visto?
di o Danubio.

Que río podes desexar despois de terme visto?
di o Texo.

Leteoneva Leteohudson Leoteotíber Leteorín Leteosena
Leteodanubio Leteotexo

Eu só son a túa epifanía!
di o Eume.

Lethe

What river can you want after seeing me?
says the Neva.

What river can you want after seeing me?
says the Hudson.

What river can you want after seeing me?
says the Tiber.

What river can you want after seeing me?
says the Rhine.

What river can you want after seeing me?
says the Seine.

What river can you want after seeing me?
says the Danube.

What river can you want after seeing me?
says the Tagus.

Letheneva Lethehudson Lethetiber Letherhine Letheseine
Lethedanube Lethetagus

I alone am your epiphany!
says the Eume.

Darío Xohán Cabana (1952–)

From Canta de cerca a morte (Death Sings Nearby), *1994*

Aquelas noites mornas e sombrías

Aquelas noites mornas e sombrías,
eu no valtrón velando e tu no río
coa rede e mais coa luz, e o marmurío
das populosas augas que esfendías,

meu pai, comigo van, nas lucidías
augas do corazón que de cotío

te lembra así, señor, señor do estío,
dono das troitas, amo das anguías.

E a vez que vin aquela cousa rara
coma un lostrego escuro, e tu berrando
¡esa escopeta, que é unha lontra, home!,

e eu non tirei, e espaventei ollando
unha palabra que de ti escoitara
nadar fuxindo e merecendo o nome.

Those mild, dark nights

Those mild, dark nights,
I on the bank on watch and you in the river
with the net and the light, and the murmur
of the teeming waters you were ploughing,

father, are with me always, in the splendent
waters of the heart that every day
remembers you thus, sir, sire of the summer,
lord of the trout, master of the eels.

And the time I saw that strange thing
like a dark lightning flash, and you yelling
'the shotgun – it's an otter, look!'

and I did not shoot, and I was scared watching
a word that I had heard from you
fleeing through the water and deserving the name.

From Vidas senlleiras (Great Lives), *1992*

O Vello da Montaña

En xaneiro de 1809, ía o bestilleiro de Retizós para a Feira do Oito de Escairón cando lle saíu ó camiño un escuadrón de remonta do exército francés que entrara en Galicia ás ordes do Mariscal Soult. O bestilleiro, Salustiano Yanes chamado, aínda quixo discutir, pero de nada lle serviu, pois aqueles homes falaban pouco, seco e estraño. En vista de como se poñían as cousas, tivo que resignarse a deixar ir con eles catro cabalos e un macho moi bo que levaba. Era unha mañá fría e desapracible.

O señor Salustiano, que tal tratamento merecía xa a pesar de non ter máis de corenta anos, volveu andando para Retizós, a onde chegou con noite, os pés en carne viva e medio derreado pola falta de costume. Entrou na casa coma se nada pasara, mandou que lle quentasen unha baldeta de auga para desapegar os piúcos, preguntou polas bestas que deixara na corte, pediu algo de cear, e foise deitar coa muller.

Ó día seguinte pola mañá afiou a bisarma, cargou escopeta e pistolas, aparellou dous cabalos, colleu consigo o seu primoxénito, que xa andaba polos dezaseis anos, e deixándolle á muller o cargo da casa e dos outros seis fillos que tiñan, todos varóns, uniuse á guerrilla en defensa da patria.

A prudencia e o valor do señor Salustiano convertérono pronto en capitán elixido dunha partida, na que non permitiu crego con pendón por certas opinións secretas que tiña. Primeiro combateu seguindo, ou facendo que seguía, as consignas da Xunta Suprema do Reino, pero axiña se uniu ás forzas do coronel García. Este coronel sempre andaba con grandes barbas e moi embozado, quizais para que non lle visen a cara, e ás veces oíuselle falar francés, pero case non sabía o castelán. O galego, sen embargo, falábao de corrido, coma se lle fose natural, senón que mesturado de palabras moi raras. Andaba tamén o falacio de que en realidade viñera coas tropas de Napoleón, e que terminara levantándose contra el e pronunciándose pola república. Fracasado o ideal, desaparecido o seu coronel e os franceses xa ben lonxe de terras galegas, o señor Salustiano non quixo saber máis da guerra e volveu á súa casa e ás súas ocupacións, non sen algunhas riquezas adquiridas lexitimamente en combate.

Á parte do trato das bestas, que era o que máis lle daba, os Mercadores – así lles chamaban de sempre na parroquia – labraban algunhas terras, polas que pagaban foro ó mosteiro de Meira. Polo San Miguel do ano que volveu para a casa, o señor Salustiano tivo unha forte discusión cos frades, ó lor duns máis e duns menos nas medidas, e dunha cousa na outra acabouse reñendo pola mor da política. Saíron a relucir os vellos agravios do guerrilleiro contra a santa relixión católica en persoa dos seus ministros, e un frade colérico anuncioulle que cando voltase o desexado rei Fernando Sétimo habíano traer ó rego, a el e mais a outros coma el.

O bestilleiro volveu pensativo co seu carro baleiro e falou coa muller. Despois de lle daren moitas voltas ó asunto, pareceulles que o mellor sería mudárense de aires polo que puidera pasar. Aquel ano xa non outonaron, e o Salustiano e os fillos, coa axuda alugada dunha cuadrilla de canteiros de Román, construíron unha casa bastante grande no alto da serra, aproveitando pedra que parecía dunha torre derrocada. O sitio que escolleron era moi rico de fontes, visitado de lobos, ben desviado de casas e labradíos, e non lonxe do soar nacía un regato de augas cristalinas. Aquel mesmo inverno, os Mercadores deixaron a súa parroquia cunha recua moi lucida cargada con cantas mantenzas e mobles había na casa vella que, falta de poboadores, pouco tardou en cubrirse de hedra e herbas cativas.

A casa nova era de baixo e sobrado, arriba con fiestras grandes e abaixo con regandixas que a penas deixaban pasar un pouco de luz. As cortes estaban ó carón da cociña, para aproveitar toda a calor dos animais e do lume na calefacción do cuarto, pois aquelas terras son de invernos moi fríos. Orientábase ó mediodía, para coller ben o sol, e pola parte de atrás erguíase súpeto un píncaro que a defendía contra os aires do norte. O curral, que abranguía toda a fachada, estaba cercado de pedra a máis altura ca dun home, e un manantío moi oportuno enchía un enorme pío de cantería que se derramaba costa abaixo por un burato que deixaran ó carón da portada.

Gobernados por súa mai, os fillos máis novos escorrentaron o frío cavando o monte cerca da casa. Chegado o tempo, puxeron un anaco a horta e a castañas mariñas, que algúns chamaban patacas. As bestas pacían polas valigotas, veladas polo señor Salustiano e os fillos máis vellos. As feiras principais das sete provincias vían chegar o bestilleiro montado no seu cabalo, coa escopeta ó lombo e a bisarma ó traveso, diante da reata que algún fillo, armado tan ben coma o pai, lle axudaba a guiar. A onde non ían nunca era á cercana feira de Meira, famosa de mular para os señores frades bernaldos.

A eguada foi aumentando. O señor Salustiano mercaba e vendía os cabalos sen dó ningún, pero as eguas de mellor ventre deixábaas na casa. A pór de cavaren, chegaron a coller algo de centeo, pero o monte non pagaba moito o traballo. Unha rabañada de ovellas e cabras daba carne e leite, e la para xergóns e para fiar, e os montes e os ríos tamén eran xenerosos coas escopetas e as redes. Entre o que se collía e o que se mercaba, de comer a xente non tiña falta; os fillos pequenos medraban robustos, e os grandes refacíanse. Desque casaran, a Mercadora fora dando un por ano, con menos dun mes de diferencia, pero unha vez parido o sétimo, o seu ventre declarouse en folga e non daba agarrado, anque seguía facendo os labores de costume. E mais non deixaban de ter gana dunha pequena, despois de tanto varón.

Nestes medios, os franceses terminaron marchando de España, e na primavera de 1814 volveu o indesexable Fernando. O señor Salustiano non se preocupou gran cousa de primeiras. Sen embargo, a execución de Sinforiano López, un mestre seleiro da Coruña coñecido seu, que fora dos primeiros en levantarse contra o francés, deixouno arrepiado. Pouco despois, don Xoán Díaz Porlier alzouse contra o absolutismo e formou a nova Xunta de Galicia; ó señor Salustiano volveulle parecer que xa non había de que ter medo. Pero o xeneral Porlier foi preso polos seus propios sarxentos, mercados polo arcebispo de Compostela. O bestilleiro soubo do seu aforcamento na feira de Dompiñor, seis días despois do crime, pola conversa duns cregos que facían moita farra coas contas que pensaban arranxar, agora que a Católica Maxestade de Fernando mandaba como lle daba a real gana. De volta para a casa, veu todo o camiño pensativo, e ó chegar ó Vertedoiro, non querendo pasar por Meira, meteuse por travesíos e foi saír a Rixoán pasando por Vilar de Mouros.

Pero por moito que eles non buscasen a ninguén, alguén podía buscalos a eles. Había que facer fronte ás cousas, e así o falaron na casa aquela mesma noite.

O quince do seguinte mes, Salustiano Yanes entrou na vila de Meira montado nun cabalo branco, a bisarma terciada no arzón, a escopeta Cruzada ó lombo, a chaqueta aberta deixando ver dúas pistolas remetidas na faixa. Tras del cabalgaban os seus sete fillos, o máis novo querendo xa ser mociño, todos os sete con semellante armamento. A feira abriuse para velos pasar, e as fiestras do convento enchéronse de miradas.

O señor Salustiano desmontou e deixoulle o cabalo ó fillo máis novo. Deu lentamente unha volta por entre o gando, preguntando como habían mandar por algunhas bestas que lle enchían o ollo. Trataba humilde pero serio, falando con cortesía e sen apuro, deixando os tempos debidos ó pensar e ó trasacordar. Acabou mercando tres eguas leonesas, dúas delas preñadas, e mais unha burra para o servicio da casa.

A media mañá, deu a súa feira por rematada e montou a cabalo. Seguido polos seus fillos, chegouse lentamente ó convento dos bernaldos, que cerra o campo da feira por unha banda, e petou na porta sen descabalgar. O frade porteiro estaba á espreita e abriu de contado. O bestilleiro falou.

– Fágame a mercé de lle dicir ó señor abade que está aquí o seu servidor Salustiano Yanes, que foi de Retizós, e que lle quere falar se non lle for molestia.

Tamén o abade debía estar agardando, porque de contado fixo saír á porta a súa venerable redondeza rodeada doutros catro monxes.

– ¿E logo que quere o noso amigo e foreiro?

– Amigo lle quero ser, señor abade, que foreiro fun e non son, e nunca máis pra señores botarei pan. Mais como é propio de amigos falar as verdades, veño dicirlle a miña á súa reverencia, se ma quere escoitar. Teño unha casa na serra, e cincuenta cabalos pacendo polas terras de Deus. Teño sete fillos comigo, todos eles máis grandes ca min. Nin eles nin eu nos metemos coa xente, e nin eu nin eles deixamos que a xente se meta con nós. Se alguén se equivoca e nos vén molestar, ten a miña bisarma o gadañete á medida da gorxa máis grosa. E agora, se me dá licencia, volvo prá miña montaña, onde teño ben que facer. Pense a súa reverencia e mande en qué o sirva, que en podendo e querendo non lle hei de faltar.

Labregos e feirantes fóranse achegando en silencio, e formaban un semicírculo a respectuosa distancia dos oito homes. O señor Salustiano fixo virar o seu cabalo, e a multitude abriuse para deixalos pasar.

Pasaba o tempo, e os montañeses prosperaban tranquilos na cría e nos tratos de cabalar. As vereas e as corredoiras víanos pasar camiño das feiras, case sempre catro xuntos, pois os outros quedaban gardando na casa; e a súa palabra valía unha escritura desde a Fonsagrada ó Padrón e desde Moeche a Monterrei. O petrucio deixara medrar a barba, que xa lle empezaba a branquear. A xente seguíalle chamando señor Salustiano, cada vez con máis respecto, pero o alcume de Mercador fora deixando paso a outro que se ía estendendo pouco a pouco polas terras que andaba, coma unha lenda. O Vello da Montaña sorría e agarimaba na súa barba florida.

As vicisitudes políticas non os favorecían nin os prexudicaban: mandasen uns ou mandasen outros, todos eran uns en deixalos en paz, xa que non se metían con ninguén e andaban tan ben armados. Parece ser que algunha vez o gobernador militar de Lugo pensara en facer algo, premido polo clero e a fidalguía, que se laiaban do mal exemplo que daban; pero decidiu non gastar esforzos e xente nunha limpeza que agoiraba bastante máis cara do que en realidade valía. O mesmo don Nazario Eguía, que cando viñera de capitán xeneral espertara moitas esperanzas no señorío pola súa brutalidade, preferiu ignorar as queixas que lle chegaron. Ademais, entre a xente andaba o falacio, quizais ben fundado, de que era imposible acabar con todos dun golpe, porque o monte de tras da súa casa estaba furado de galerías polas que podían escapar facilmente dun ataque masivo. Dicíase tamén que tiñan feito un xuramento terrible: que se algún deles morría de morte militar, os que quedasen habían de matar polo menos o abade de Meira, o gobernador de Lugo, o arcebispo de Santiago e o propio capitán xeneral de Galicia, anque lles custase tamén a eles a vida. E eran ben capaces de facelo, e mesmo de contar con axuda, pois se o Vello da Montaña tiña inimigos, tampouco non lle faltaban amigos.

De inverno, as noites facíanse algo longas na casa da serra. Entón, os mozos montaban a cabalo e ían de rúa ás casas de Fonteo e da Braña, de Caraño e de Librán, ou mesmo á nativa parroquia de Retizós. O vello deixábaos marchar cun sorriso, de dous e tres xuntos. Pero cando se trataba de ir a algunha foliada de xente, o señor Salustiano aparellaba tamén a súa besta, montaba a muller na garupa, e acompañaba os fillos á diversión. Chegados ó turreiro, o pai recibía de cada un escopeta e pistolas, e quedáballelas gardando á beira do baile. Só lles deixaba as zochudas caxadas, por se acaso había paos. Pero rara vez os había: os mozos eran pacíficos de seu, e temidos de todos.

A eguada multiplicábase case salvaxe, mais non por iso había perdas nin interquinencias. Os bestilleiros botaban o máis do día polos montes, tornando as bestas para que non fixesen danos nas chousas dos vales; e cando os facían, daban satisfacción antes de ser requiridos. Como nas cortes da casa xa non cabía tanta habenza, nin era cousa tampouco de facela andar tanto, foron construíndo alboios aquí e acolá para que os animais se defendesen de xeadas e nevaradas. As súas escopetas libraban o país de lobos, e eran moi estimados dos labradores polo servicio.

Para o día da rapa, que facían sempre o primeiro domingo do verán, asábanse ó espeto dous carneiros ou tres, chamábanse gaiteiros e eran convidados os veciños de máis cerca, que andaban con gusto unha legua por gozar da boa comida e do espléndido viño. As mozas sobre de todo acudían coma as moscas ó mel. Os sete bestilleiros saíran cortados polo patrón do seu pai, senón que eran aínda máis altos de corpo, e alegres e considerados coma ningún.

Cada vez que casaba un fillo, o señor Salustiano mandaba chamar os canteiros de Román e poñía toda a familia a traballar. Ó redor da casa petrucial fóronse erguendo as novas moradas, escudadas unhas nas outras, e desfíxose a cerca do curral vello para erguer un muro que as cinguira todas. Unha recovaxada de pícaros empezou a alegrar o rueiro do casarío. Unha das noras, que era filla de cura e fora para escolante antes de namorar, poñíalles algo de escola cando chegaba o seu tempo.

A vida transcorría sosegada e case monótona naqueles deitados píncaros, patriarcal e antiga. Mais a sede popular de marabillas é inesgotable, e a fantasía dos vales non paraba de ornar con volutas alexandrinas as lacónicas fazañas dos montañeses, que do que máis se prezaban era de coñeceren camiños e corredoiras e de trataren con astuta honradez. Co tempo, a controversia verbal cos bernaldos de Meira fora adquirindo proporcións de homérica batalla, e as respostas ásperas ou enxeñosas que sempre se producen no vai e vén dos tratos feirais asumían calidades heroicas ou epigramáticas cando a xente as contaba. As vellas accións guerrilleiras do señor Salustiano, xa case diluídas no tempo, eran inventadas de novo con épicas dimensións, e florecían en púrpuras claros nas noites invernais do Val de Baleira, tal como nos días vernais os seus queiroguentos montes.

O señor Salustiano sorría, e non parecía despracerlle o eco de tanta invención; mais non por iso deixaba que a fama volvese soberbios os seus, e impoñía un modo de comportarse suave e cortés, orgullosamente humilde, que non provocase nin refugase a confrontación. Parecían torres os bestilleiros; pero gardaban a súa dereita en todo camiño, e eran raros os tropezos, a non ser que batesen con xentes desalutas e destemperadas. Cando isto lles sucedía, as palabras eran poucas e firmes, e as máis das veces abondaba con elas e a sona.

Era, pois, a mesura norma dos montañeses. As súas serras retumbaban soamente cos rinchos dos garañóns, cos tiros dos cazadores e coas gaitas da festa da rapa. Só unha vez, cando o petrucio andaba xa cerca dos setenta anos, se formou distinto arruído. O señor Salustiano fixo vir catro mulas cargadas de foguetes variados e mandou encurralar todas as bestas ceibas. Un día, os poderosos estoupidos abalaron os montes desde a mañá deica a noite. O cheiro da pólvora embriagaba os cabalos, e ás eguas madriñas custoulles traballo sosegalos nos seus coutados. Foi o mesmo día que os frades bernaldos saían exclaustrados do mosteiro de Meira; pero o Vello da Montaña nunca quixo dicir se era por eles a festa.

Chegado o tempo, os netos máis vellos empezaron a subir as súas mulleres, e o casarío aumentaba. Algunha neta tamén tirou polo home para arriba, pero as máis delas baixaban de abastadas labradoras para os vales, levando un dote de bestas que a penas se notaba de falta nas grandes eguadas.

Pouco a pouco, o señor Salustiano foi deixando de ir ás feiras, e tampouco non saía moito ó monte. Botaba o máis do tempo coa muller, conversando os dous moi alegres e facéndose bromas, e contáballes contos ós bisnetos, que lle enguetaban os dediños nas longas barbas liñais. Vinte homes varudos, na flor da mocidade e na forza da madurez, velaban as eguadas polas serras impervias, e cansaban os camiños de tres reinos indo e vindo das feiras, sempre armados e sempre respectados, sempre a longa sombra do petrucio garantindo os seus tratos.

A súa sombra acompañábaos por fóra, e a súa palabra gobernábaos na Montaña. Ninguén era ousado de desobedecela; os seus xuízos eran a lei da tribo, e os seus consellos desfacían coma néboa as liortas de irmáns. E despois de acougalos, escoitaba as noticias recollidas nas feiras que xa non o vían entrar, pasmadas do seu aspecto real.

O primeiro domingo de cada verán, o vello sentábase diante da casa e recibía a homenaxe da familia afastada e dos veciños de abaixo, agarimando as cabezas dos fillos das súas netas, que se apuxaban uns a outros por achegarse ó grande avó das barbas de liño. E chegada a hora do xantar, posta a mesa no eirado, o señor Salustiano sentábase á cabeceira coa súa muller e contemplaba o seu reino.

Pero os anos corrían coma ríos, e o Vello da Montaña revía do seu corpo, por máis que o magnánimo espírito se arrepuxese contra o transcurso do tempo. A mediados do inverno de 1846 mandou vir toda a súa descendencia, a da montaña e mais a dos vales. A penas cabían na sala do sobrado. O patriarca, sentado na súa cadeira, dictou testamento de viva voz. Despois ergueuse traballosamente, apoiado na muller e no fillo máis vello, entrou no seu cuarto e deitouse a morrer. A velliña seguiuno antes da primavera.

A aldea da serra durou aínda uns anos, amparada pola lembranza da súa autoridade. Mais a memoria das cousas vaise esvaendo: a tribo foi perdendo o seu vínculo férreo, dividida en familias por xenreiras e cuestións de reparto, e os seus tratos xa non eran comúns. Os ricos bestilleiros acabaron collendo cadaquén a súa parte e buscando acomodo en lugares máis mansos dos vales e as chairas, uns lonxe dos outros. Hoxe aló arriba só quedan pedras caídas, e medran queirogas e herbas rastreiras onde noutrora se ergueu tanto orgullo.

The Old Man of the Mountain

In January 1809, the horse-breeder was going to the Oito de Escairón fair when he bumped into a mounted division of the French army who had entered Galicia under the orders of Marshall Soult. The horse-breeder, whose name was Salustiano Yanes, tried to hold a conversation with them, but without success, as they were taciturn, blunt and spoke strangely. Seeing how things were turning out, he had to give up four horses and a very good mule he had with him. It was a nasty, cold morning.

"Don" Salustiano, who deserved this title, in spite of being no more than forty years old, walked back to Retizós, his feet raw and bleeding as he was unused to walking, where he arrived at nightfall. He entered his house as if nothing had happened, requested a bucket of warm water to get rid of the thorns, asked after the animals he had left in the stables, ordered some dinner and then went to bed with his wife.

The following morning he sharpened his knife, loaded his rifle and pistols, saddled two horses, took his eldest son, who was about sixteen, and leaving his wife in charge of the house, together with the other six children, all boys, joined the people's militia to defend his country.

His sound judgment and bravery soon enabled him to be promoted to the rank of captain of a group of militiamen, from which he excluded clergy because of certain secret beliefs he held. At first he fought, following, or pretending to follow, the Supreme Rules of the Kingdom, but soon joined up with the forces of Colonel García. The latter had a large beard and was well muffled up, perhaps so that his face could not be seen; he was sometimes heard to speak French, but could hardly speak a word of Castilian Spanish. He did, however, speak fluent Galician, as if it came naturally to him, but with several alien-sounding words mixed in with it. He also tried to give the impression that he had actually come with Napoleon's troops, and that he had ended up changing sides and supporting the Republic. When his ideals were finally shattered, his colonel had finally vanished, and with the French far away, Don Salustiano returned home to get on with life as before, not without some wealth legitimately gained in combat.

Apart from the buying and selling of horses, which was his stock in trade, the Merchants – as they were called by the villagers – also ploughed a little land, for which they paid rent to the Monastery of Meira. Around Michelmas Day, the same year Don Salustiano returned home, he had a bitter argument with the monks over a question of weights and measures; one thing led to another, and it turned into an argument about politics. Ancient grievances arose in the heart of the old guerilla, against the Holy Catholic Church in the figure of its ministers, and one irate monk told him in no uncertain terms that when the longed-for King Ferdinand VII came back, Salustiano would be forced back to the strait and narrow, and others too who thought like him.

The horse-breeder returned home thoughtfully together with his empty cart, and spoke to his wife. After thinking it over, they decided it would be better to move to somewhere else just in case. They did not wait for autumn, but Salustiano and his sons, with the help of the piece-work done for him by the stone-masons of San Román, built a fairly big house higher up in the hills using the stone that appeared to be from the remains of a tower. The place chosen was very rich in springs of fresh water where the wolves refreshed themselves, well away from houses and farmland, and not far from a brook of crystal-clear water. That very winter the Merchants left their village with all their belongings and furniture from the old house, which, as no one now lived there, was soon covered in ivy and weeds.

The new house consisted of a ground floor and a first floor, the latter with larger windows and the former with smaller ones that hardly let in any light at all. The stables were next to the kitchen, to make the most of the heat from the animals' bodies and the fire in the hearth, as winters there were freezing cold. The house faced south, to take advantage of the sun's heat, and the back was made up of a huge natural rock that sheltered it from the north wind. The chicken coop, which took up the whole of the front of the house, was surrounded by a stone wall the height of a man, and a very handy stream filled a huge stone hollow, and then flowed out through a hole next to the front door.

Led by their mother, the younger sons escaped from the cold by digging in the hill nearby. In due course, they had cleared part of the orchard and planted some "sea-chestnuts" that some called potatoes. The cattle grazed in the little valley watched over by Salustiano and the older sons. The main fairs of the seven provinces would see the horse-breeder come, riding on his horse, with his gun at his back and his ammunition belt across his chest, in front of the wagon which one of his sons, armed just like his father, was helping to guide. The place they never went to was the nearby fair in Meira, well-known for its mules, which was often frequented by the monks.

The group of mares got bigger and bigger. Salustiano bought and sold with great zeal, but the best-looking horses were left at home. By digging, they managed to harvest some barley, but it was hardly worthwhile. A flock of sheep and goats provided them with meat and milk and wool for the mattresses and for making thread, and the hills and rivers were generous as well, for their guns and fishing nets. Between what they gathered and what they bought, they needed little else; the young boys grew strong and the older ones reproduced: since they got married his wife gave birth once a year with less than a month's difference between them, but once she had had her seventh baby, her womb went on strike and no longer swelled, although they went on trying. Besides, they always wanted a girl, after having so many male children.

In the middle of all this, the French finally left Spain, and in the spring of 1814 the un-longed-for Fernando the Seventh returned. Salustiano did not worry much at first, although the execution of Sinforiano López, a master engraver, an acquaintance of his, who was one of the first to rise up against the French, made his hair stand on end. Shortly afterwards, Xoán Díaz Porlier rose up against absolutism and set up a new Junta in Galicia; Salustiano once again believed there was nothing to be afraid of, but General Porlier was arrested by his own sergeants, who had been bribed by the Archbishop of Santiago. Salustiano found out about his execution at the Dompiñor fair, six days after it took place, when he overheard a conversation between some priests, who were boasting of the revenge they were going to take now his Catholic Majesty Fernando reigned as he pleased. He returned home pensively, and when he got to the Vertedoiro, as he was loathe to go through Meira, he went along side-roads and arrived in Rixoan going by way of Vilar de Mouros.

But no matter if they were not looking for any trouble, trouble might be looking for them. They had to face facts, and so they talked about it at home that very evening. On the fifteenth of the following month Salustiano Yáñez arrived in Meira riding a white horse, his ammunition belt over his shoulder and his shotgun across his back, the jacket unbuttoned, allowing two pistols to be seen sticking out of the belt. His seven sons rode behind him, the youngest pretending to be grown-up, and all of them equally well-armed. The fair opened up to watch them pass, and the windows of the monastery were crowded with eyes.

Salustiano got off his horse and left it to his youngest son. He strode unhurriedly among the horses enquiring about how to transport some he was keen on. He traded in a humble, serious way, talking courteously and nonchalantly, leaving due time to think things over. He ended up purchasing three mares from the province of León, two of them pregnant, and a donkey for the minor chores around the house.

Half-way through the morning, he put an end to his business at the fair and got on his horse, followed by his sons. He slowly reached the monastery, which lies to one side of the field where the fair is held, and knocked on the door without getting off his horse. The monk at the gate seemed to be half expecting him, and opened up straight away. The horse-breeder spoke: "Would you be so kind as to tell the Abbot that his servant, Salustiano Yáñez, from Retizós, is here, and wishes to talk to him if he pleases?"

The Abbot must have also been expecting him, for his venerable, portly figure immediately appeared, surrounded by another four monks. "Well, what does our worthy friend want from us?" "A friend is what I would like to be, Abbot, as I was on the other side, but now I am no longer, and will never again sell myself to any-one. But as true friends tell each other the truth, I have come to tell Your Reverence my truth, if you will kindly listen to it. I have a house in the hills, and fifty horses grazing on God's land. I have seven sons with me, all of them taller than me. Neither they nor I pose a threat to anyone, and we do not allow anyone else to threaten us either. If someone should come along by mistake and bother us, they find my scabbard and my ammunition belt are as broad as the widest throat. And now, if you will allow me, I will be getting along to my farm, where there is plenty of work to be done. Think, my lord, how I can best serve you, because where there's a will there's a way, and I have the will."

Farmers and traders at the fair were approaching in silence, forming a semi-cir-cle, keeping a respectful distance from the eight men. Salustiano turned his horse around, and the crowd opened up to let them pass.

Time went by, and the family prospered peacefully breeding and trading horses. They were seen to go to the fairs, nearly always four of the family together, while the other four remained at home taking care of the house; they were known to be true to their word just as if it had been written in letters of gold, from Fonsagrada to Padrón and from Moeche to Monterrei. The head of the family let his whiten-ing beard grow long. People continued to call him Don Salustiano, with more and more respect as time went on, but the nickname of the cattle-drover was forgotten, and another took over little by little in the lands he was seen in, as if he were a leg-end. "The Old Man of the Mountain" smiled into his bushy beard.

The political events neither helped nor hindered them; no matter who was in power, everyone left them in peace, as they did not bother anyone and were very well armed. It seems that on some occasions the military governor of Lugo had a mind to do something about him, goaded by the clergy and the squires, who were obsessed by the bad example the family set, but he decided not to waste time and effort on rooting out a problem that promised to be more trouble than it was really worth.

Even Don Nazario Eguía himself, whose reputation for brutality gave great hope to the squires, ignored all the complaints he heard when he became Captain General. Besides, among the people it was rumoured that it was impossible to fin-ish them all off at once, because the hill that the back yard gave on to was full of caves and tunnels, through which they could all make off. It was also said that they had made a terrible oath: that if any of them were killed by the army, those who remained alive were to kill at least the Abbot of Meira, the Governor of Lugo, the Archbishop of Santiago and even the Captain General of Galicia, before they paid for it with their lives. And they were quite capable of doing so, as they could count on help: although "The Old Man of the Mountain" had enemies, he did not lack friends either.

In winter, the nights became rather long and tedious in the house on the mountain. Then the sons rode their horses into Fonteo and Braña, Araño and Librán, or even to their birthplace, the village of Retizós. The Old Man let them go three by three, with a smile. But when there was a gathering for singing and dancing, the Old Man got his own horse ready, and with his wife mounted behind him, he accompanied his sons to the event. Once they got to the dance, the father took the guns from each one, and kept them by his side, just beside the dance-floor. He let them carry only a rounded wooden stick, just in case. But there was hardly ever any violence; the young men were of a peaceful nature and were feared by all.

The herd of mares grew in number, almost wild, but even so he did not lose money or have any trouble. The horse-breeders spent most of their time on the hills, guiding their animals properly so that they should not harm other people's property in the valleys. And when they did so, they compensated the owners before they were asked to. As the yard was not big enough for the sheep they had, and they did not want them to walk so far back home, they built shelters here and there for them to take refuge from the ice and snow. Their shotguns freed the countryside of wolves, and this was much appreciated by the locals.

The day of the trimming of the horses' manes, which always took place on the first Sunday in summer, they roasted two or three lambs, the bagpipes played, and they invited all the people from nearby, who did not need to think twice before they came to taste the fine meat and wine on offer. Girls, above all, appeared like flies round honey. The seven sons were a chip off the old block, but were even taller, and were good-tempered and better respected than anyone else around there.

Every time one of his sons got married, Don Salustiano sent for a stone-mason from Román and put the whole family to work. Surrounding the family house were the new family homes, each one shielded by the others, and he removed the fence from the chicken-coop and built a wall which circled them all. A group of children began to brighten up the yard of the farmhouse. One of the daughters-in-law, the daughter of a priest, had been a student before falling in love; she gave them a taste of education when the time was due.

Life passed quietly and almost monotonously in those craggy patriarchal heights. But people's thirst for miracles and heroic deeds is insatiable, and the legends in those valleys continued to ring with the praise of the family of the Man of the Mountain. What they were proudest of was their knowledge of the local highways and byways, and their honesty in business. In time, the quarrels with the clergy in Meira reached Homeric heights, and the rough answers that are always produced in the heat of haggling in the fairs acquired heroic proportions when retold. The nearly-forgotten actions of the ex-guerrilla, lost in the mists of time, were again retold and exaggerated, flourishing in the forest clearings during the winter nights in the Baleira Valley, just as the oak-covered mountains bloomed in the summer.

Don Salustiano smiled and seemed not to be displeased by the popularity of these made-up stories; but did not allow them to make his family arrogant, and he made sure they behaved in a proud but courteous way, thus avoiding confrontations. They looked like towers, but always kept to the right side of the road when they drove, and seldom had altercations with anyone, unless they bumped into people who were looking for trouble. Whenever this happened, their words were few and firm: this was nearly always quite enough.

Moderation, then, was the rule of the people from the mountain. From their lands one could only hear the neighing of stallions, hunters' shots ringing out, and the music of the bagpipes celebrating the day when the horses' manes were to be trimmed. Only once, when the patriarch of the family was in his seventies, was a different sound to be heard. Salustiano brought four mules loaded with fireworks of different types, and ordered all the free-grazing animals to be kept safely in the stables. One day the powerful explosions made the hills shudder from dawn till dusk. The smell of gunpowder made the horses nauseous, and the older mares struggled to keep them calm in the stables. It was that same day when the monks left the monastery of Meira, but the Old Man of the Mountain never let on that the celebrations were in their honour.

In due time, the eldest grandchildren began to come up to live with their wives, and that enormous house got even bigger. Some grand-daughters also persuaded their husbands to move up there, but most of them went down to the valleys to work as farmhands, taking with them a dowry of horses, but their loss was hardly noticed because of the huge number of mares that were left.

Little by little, Salustiano stopped going to the fairs and even to the hills. He spent most of the time with his wife, chatting and talking wittily, making jokes and telling his great-grandchildren stories, the tiniest ones running their fingers through the long hairs of his beard. Twenty robust men, in the prime of their lives, looked after the mares on the unyielding hills and ranged through the highways and byways far and wide, going to the fairs, armed to the teeth and highly regarded, with the long shadow of the patriarch a guarantee of fair treatment.

His long shadow went with them wherever they went, and his word was law the length and breadth of those hills. No one would dare to disobey; his judgment was the law, and his advice banished the arguments among the brothers. After they were soothed, he listened to the news that had been gathered from the fairs, where he was no longer seen.

Every first Sunday of the summer, the old man sat outside his house and received homage from those of his family that lived far away, and neighbours from further down in the valley, patting the heads of his granddaughters' children, who jostled each other for the chance to reach the grandfather, whose beard was like threads of linen. At dinnertime, when the table was laid outdoors, Salustiano sat next to his wife at the head of the table to contemplate his kingdom.

But the years passed like the water of the rivers, and the body of the Old Man of the Mountain shriveled up, much as his spirit fought against the course of time.

Half-way through the winter of 1846 he called in his descendants from the mountains and from the valleys. They could hardly fit into the upstairs room. The patriarch, sitting in his chair, dictated his last will and testament aloud. After getting to his feet with great difficulty, holding on to his wife and his eldest son, the Old Man entered his bedroom and lay down to die. His wife followed before the next spring.

That village in the hills lasted for several years, sustained by the memory of his authority. But the memory of things fades away: the tribe began to lose its strong cohesion, because of matters relating to in-laws and the share-out of belongings, and reunions became rarer and rarer. The wealthy horse-dealers ended up taking what was theirs and going away to look for comfort in milder valleys and plains, far away from each other. Nowadays, there are only broken stones left up there, and gorse and grass grow where once such pride held sway.

Xulio López Valcárcel (1953–)

From Alba de auga sonámbula (Dawn of Sleepwalking Water), 1983

Habitas rúas de medo

Habitas rúas de medo e buscas
en cada neno que cruzas aquel neno que fuches.

Nunha luz oblicua da memoria onde se perden
as horas en labirintos escuros,
invernos longuísimos, cinza da túa historia,
chegan a ti campás melancólicas, días sen paxaros,
misais, rosarios, remol de leitos onde se amou.

Por anchos corredores cruzan sombras que te precederon,
bouga de pregos esluídos nunha luz neboenta
que che trae ecos silenciosos.

Esculcas cadros
que te miran desde aló, obxectos
que outras mans tocaron,
frías caricias no muro da derrota.

Se voltas e te achegas respiras o ar que outros deixaron
en mestas atmosferas de desarraigo.
Flores artificiais, caixas de música,

funerarias monecas, universo en sombra
no clarescuro desfarrapado da lembranza.

Sairás á rúa.

E recoñeceraste nese neno que xoga,
neses ollos inmensos que miran asustados.

You live in streets of fear

You live in streets of fear and seek
in every child you meet the child you were.

In an oblique light of memory where the hours
are lost in dark labyrinths,
long, long winters, the ash of your history,
melancholy bells reach you, days without birds,
missals, rosaries, embers of beds where love was made.

Along wide corridors pass shadows that went before you,
the rustle of papers that are dissipated in a hazy light
that brings you silent echoes.

You examine pictures
that look at you from over there, objects
that other hands have touched,
cold caresses on the wall of defeat.

If you return and come close you breathe the air that others have left
in dense atmospheres of rootlessness.
Artificial flowers, music boxes,
funerary dolls, a universe in shadow
in the ragged chiaroscuro of memory.

You will go out into the street.

And you will recognize yourself in that child playing,
in those immense eyes that gaze in fear.

From Memoria de Agosto (Memory of August), *1993*

Outro poema dos dons

Gracias quero dar
pola noite e a chuvia
que nos devolven a memoria da nai.
E pola muller
que dá forma á beleza.
Polo sexo
que une nunha soa carne
dúas soidades
e polo soño que nos permite
a viaxe á morte
e o regreso.
Polo vento
que nos fai estraños de nós mesmos
e pola pedra
que aspira a soñar a eternidade.

Gracias quero dar polos nenos
que non coñecen nin a culpa nin a morte.
E pola música,
leve espírito do vento.
Pola luz
que nos devolve o mar nos ollos da amada
e polo aire, vivificante e saudábel.
Pola beleza,
que nos enche e acovarda,
e polo mencer
que nos ofrece a ilusión
da primeira vez.

Gracias
pola xuventude e polos sentidos.
Polo loureiro e o trigo,
pola herba, máis tenaz que o tempo,
e pola arte,
que nos transcende e sobrevive.

Gracias quero dar
polos días que compartes comigo,
pola caricia e polo beixo.

Gracias polo mar, absoluto e poderoso.

Gracias polo silencio e polo verso.

Another poem about gifts

Thanks I wish to give
for night and rain,
which bring back to us the memory of mother.
And for woman,
who gives form to beauty.
For sex,
which unites in one flesh
two solitudes,
and for dreams, which allow us
the journey to death
and the return.
For the wind,
which makes us strangers to ourselves
and for the stone,
which aspires to dream eternity.

Thanks I wish to give for children,
who do not know blame or death.
And for music,
the gentle spirit of the wind.
For light,
which gives us back the sea in the eyes of the beloved
and for air, invigorating and healthy.
For beauty,
which gratifies and intimidates us,
and for the dawn,
which offers us the same thrill of hope
as the very first time.

Thanks
for youth and for the senses.
For the laurel and for wheat,
for grass, tougher than time,
and for art,
which transcends and survives us.

Thanks I wish to give

for the days you share with me,
for the caress and for the kiss.

Thanks for the sea, absolute and powerful.

Thanks for silence and for verse.

Xavier Seoane (1954–)

From Iniciación e regreso (Initiation and Return), *1985*

Cando a miña alma se erga e voe sobre o mar...

Cando a miña alma se erga e voe sobre o mar
hei de voltar para contarche a fortuna do retorno dos paxaros
e a choiva de primavera sobre os campos

que nada é tan fermoso nesta vida
nin tampouco tan cruel quizais
como volver ao país amado e reencontrarte
a enfiar o nobelo dunha nosa mocedade que non morreu xamais

cando sobre esas illas se sinta o ar traspasado
dun espírito que foi meu e que se esvae
haberá un estremecimento nas vellas cousas que nos ataron
un silencio que matina no retorno dunha voz que en min cantaba

sé xenerosa
e cando a miña alma erga e voe alén do mar
érguete e canta
sobre a terra que amamos

When my soul rises and flies over the sea...

When my soul rises and flies over the sea
I shall come back to tell you of the fortune of the return of birds
and the rain of spring over the fields

for nothing is as beautiful in this life
or as cruel perhaps
as coming back to your beloved country and finding
that you are yet again spinning the yarn of a youth of ours that never died

when over those isles is felt the transported air
of a spirit that was mine and that is vanishing
there will be a trembling in the old things that bound us together
a silence that ponders on the return of a voice that sang inside me

be generous
and when my soul rises and flies beyond the sea
rise too and sing
on the land we love

From Eu tamén oín as voces do orballo (I, Too, Heard the Voices of the Rain), *1994*

A ave

A Manuel Vilariño

Atravesei o umbral, e vin a ave.
Atravesei o sangue.

Mireime nos seus ollos,
que soñaban paraísos desolados
e primaveras amargas.
Mireime na súa alma espida e namorada.

Sentín o día caer, sobre os meus ollos, canso.
Sentín pasar neboeiros
nunha brisa que a ningures levaba.
Sentín que o espacio aberto era soñado.
Que un deus enamorado
me conducía das tristezas da alma
ao insomnio da carne.

Deixeime ir aonde a sombra,
máis amábel que a luz,
por destruírme me amaba.

Contempleime palabra suspensa no vacío.
Deixeime ser ferida e fonte amarga.

Atravesei o umbral.
Atravesei o umbral, e vin a nada.

The great bird

For Manuel Vilariño

I crossed the threshold, and I saw the bird.
I crossed the blood.

I looked at myself in its eyes,
which were dreaming of desolate paradises
and bitter springtimes.
I looked at myself in its naked, enamoured soul.

Weary I felt the day falling on to my eyes.
I felt mists passing by
on a breeze that was taking them nowhere.
I felt that open space was a dream.
That an enamoured god
was bearing me from the sorrows of the soul
to the insomnia of the flesh.

I let myself be carried to where shadow,
more amiable than light,
was loving me to destroy me.

I contemplated myself a word suspended in the void.
I let myself be a wound and a bitter fountain.

I crossed the threshold.
I crossed the threshold, and I saw nothingness.

Chus Pato (1955–)

From Heloísa (Héloïse), *1994*

Dígovos que a muller que danza..

Dígovos que a muller que danza no meio das leiras de centeo
bate cos seus pés a planura da morte.

Que non existindo árbores ao redor da meta
en que doce veces dá voltas a carreira de cabalos,
remontei o camiño que conduz cara o cervo de cornamenta áurea.

Como, conceber entón o país dos Hiperbóreos?
Que atoparía no interior do alpendre un carro completamente
inzado por bolboretas, erva
e unha parede, broncínea, onde aniñan os pardais
que podería contemplar a torre
que no lugar central da torre medraría unha árbore
e na árbore a serpe branca das cen cabezas brancas
a serpe dos mil e un silvos violeta.

A muller danza sobre o bronce
enguirlanda a súa voz.
Exánime
exhausta.

I tell you all that the woman who dances...

I tell you all that the woman who dances in the middle of the rye fields
is beating her feet on the plain of death.

That, there being no trees around the winning post
where the horse-race lasts twelve laps,
I returned along the road that leads towards the stag with golden
                                        horns.
How, then, to conceive of the land of the Hyperboreans?
I would find inside the barn a cart swarming with butterflies, grass
and a wall of bronze where sparrows nest,
I would be able to contemplate the tower,
in the central part of the tower a tree would grow
and in the tree the white serpent with a hundred white heads,
the serpent with a thousand-and-one violet hisses.

The woman dances on the bronze,
she garlands her voice.
Exhausted,
spent.

Xesús Manuel Valcárcel (1955–)

From Rosa clandestina (Clandestine Rose), *1989*

Nas remotas rexións

Nas remotas rexións
que con hostilidade e tenrura deixo amado,
á sombra dun carballo ou na alta noite,
dispoño que bebades con orgullo e con calma
por min, e que os acios se vos medren de alegría
e que as cuncas se agranden como océanos
se agora mesmo arredades os traballos
e ides amar ós bosques que eu vos digo.

Aquel que despreciase beber ou a verdade
sexa traficante de ofidios sen fortuna
e non teña acomodo nin acougo
nin campa nos outeiros. Pero vós, que viñestes
comigo polas bandeiras da aventura
e que queimastes comigo as naves nun ocaso
amaredes de vagar e sen miseria
e se cantades canción de rebeldía
que atopedes en taberna ou en pousada
no primeiro esbicar o mundo todo.

Deixo encomenda de festa interminable
por min, e algúns gromos, cativiños, de tristura
e que se toque tamén unha muiñeira
e se coma e se beba e se baile nun pé.

Quen así non fixese sexa trasno
e non suba de mil amores ós bacelos
nin veña despedirse co poeta
no galano dos eternos amadores,
e non abra as trapelas do mar tan misteriosas
no alleo bater, nin os ollos do lobo noutra selva
nin comprenda este recado que aquí escribo.
E que máis cedo ou máis tarde atope axiña
polas remotas rexións que deixo amado,
á sombra dun carballo ou na alta noite,
a miña semblanza de antigo asasino.

E que en portos solitarios de amargura
mariñeiros con luces de verbena
relaten historias da cobra dos mil ollos
debullando os medos da augardente.

In the remote regions

In the remote regions
that with hostility and tenderness I am leaving, loved by all,
I hereby stipulate that, in the shade of an oak or in the small hours,
you drink with pride and with calm
to me, and that the grape-bunches swell with joy
and that the wine-cups grow like oceans
so long as you immediately put aside your work
and go to love in the woods that I specify.

May he who scorns drinking or the truth
be a luckless trafficker in ophidians
and may he have neither repose nor serenity
nor a gravestone in the hills. But you who came
with me for the flags of adventure
and who with me burnt our boats in a sunset
will love unhurriedly and unstintingly
and if you sing a song of rebellion
may you find in tavern or in hostelry
the whole world in the first sip.

I leave provision for an interminable party
for me, and a few swigs, small ones, of sadness,
and let a lively muiñeira be piped, too,
and let people eat and drink and dance most merrily.

Let whoever fails to do so be a goblin
and may he not climb with a will to the vines
or come to say farewell with the poet
in the gift of the eternal lovers,
or open the trapdoors of the sea, so mysterious
in their alien beating, or the eyes of the wolf in another jungle,
or understand this message that I am writing here.
And may he sooner or later quickly find
in the remote regions that I am leaving, loved by all,
in the shade of an oak or in the small hours
a brief account of my former life as a murderer.

And in solitary ports of bitterness
may sailors under night-festa lights
tell stories about the snake of one thousand eyes
as they peel away the fears of firewater.

Xosé Miranda (1955–)

From Morning Star, 1998

A miña infancia na Taberna da Disputa

A Disputa era o nome da taberna do meu pai, situada nas proximidades da cidade de Pontevedra, no vello camiño que leva a ela desde Santiago de Compostela. Desde a taberna nin sequera se albiscaban as últimas casas rurais, xa cercanas ó Burgo, esparexidas pola estrada, e en realidade só se entrevía algunha das pequenas aldeas máis achegadas á cidade, pero adiviñábase a presencia desta polo frecuente paso de coches, dilixencias con pasaxeiros e carros con mercadorías, ademais dos correos reais a cabalo e dos variados viaxeiros que acostumaban parar na nosa casa a tomar un grolo ou un descanso. Pontevedra non distaría media hora co cabalo ó paso, e nos días en que sopraba o vento desde o sur podíanse oír sen moito esforzo as campás da Peregrina e de Santa María chamando a misa ou tocando a morto desde a outra beira do Lérez.

A Disputa, un caserón vello e escanastrado, de grandes cachotes de granito e planta rectangular, coa maior parte dos cuartos baleiros e estragados, erguíase sobre un pequeno outeiro desde o que se divisaban os bosques tupidos que se estendían terra a dentro, os escarpados picos do Castrove e do Acival, algúns anacos da estrada nas chairas e, forzando a vista, as rompentes brancas contra a afastada costa nos días máis claros do ano. O aire da ría penetraba ata nós, enferruxaba gonzos, armelas e picaportes, humedecía as sabas e os vestidos, botaba a perder os chourizos e os xamóns e relaba portas e fiestras, obrigándonos a pintalas todos os anos e a lucir e calear moitas veces as paredes. Maldicía meu pai, nas agres tardes de inverno nas que a penas entraban clientes, o xudeu que lla vendera e a mala hora na que se lle ocorrera meterse naquel oficio. Sentaba entón nunha das mesas, cunha botella de augardente e unha cunca, e de nada servían as miñas lágrimas e a desesperación da miña nai. Grolo vai grolo vén, despachaba a chisca, poñéndose cada vez de peor humor, ata que remataba a botella ó mesmo tempo que o día e marchaba vencido a se estombaillar no leito.

Meu pai era un home violento e de man lixeira, que me zorregaba cada vez que eu facía algunha trasnada ou algo que a el llo parecía, ou sinxelamente cando tiña algún tropezo ou algunha cousa non lle saía ó seu gusto. Só me valían nesas ocasións os auxilios da miña mai, que corría a interpoñerse entre nós e lle recriminaba o seu comportamento. Unha soa palabra dela bastaba para calmalo. Tornábase daquela melancólico, escurecíanselle os ollos e rosmaba para si, apartándose de todos, tal vez arrepentido de terme levantado a man. Polo demais, non podo dicir que non me quixese. Era descoidado nos seus afectos e case non me prestaba atención, pero preocupábase pola miña roupa e a miña comida, tratábame case como a un igual e unha certa camaradería foi afirmándose entre nós co paso dos anos. Desde pequeno acostumoume a ir cazar con el nos montes próximos e a vagar polos arredores, deixando a miña mai ó coidado da cantina. A cambio, tiven que me facer home desde moi novo e axudar nas ocupacións da taberna, que tamén servía de pousada cando alguén o requiría, e así habitueime a servir xerras de viño e perdices estufadas, liscas de touciño fritidas, pratos de caldo e botellas de augardente, a limpar as mesas, a usar a vasoira, a catar o viño que nos ofrecían os arrieiros, a muxir a vaca, a metela e sacala das cortes, a alindala nuns prados próximos, a rozar os toxos e botarlle o estrume, a limpar as cortes, a cebar os porcos e a gardalos nun soutiño que posuiamos, case a carón da Disputa, a axudar na matanza, e, nos últimos tempos, coa miña mai enferma e o meu pai completamente vencido, a aviar os cuartos, a fregar, coser a roupa e facer a comida. Tamén aprendín a relear e a tratar cos clientes difíciles. O que non aprendín foi a ler e a escribir, aínda que se comentaba, e despois souben que era certo, que meu pai era de xente fidalga e fillo dun escribán, e no seu dormitorio gardaba unha Biblia e dous libros de Medicina, que pretendía seren un recordo da súa época de estudiante na Universidade. Pero non se molestou en aprenderme tan insignificante habelencia nin permitiu tampouco que a miña mai me mandase a unha escola, seguramente porque carecía de medios para lle pagar a un mestre e porque ademais non quería desprazarse ata Pontevedra cada día. Se podo agora escribir estas memorias, a petición dos meus parentes e dos meus amigos, é porque a sorte me axudou e porque un anxo se preocupou de me dar a coñecer as letras.

Malia vivirmos tan preto, eu a penas coñecía esa cidade. O meu pai non adoitaba achegarse alí máis ca por unha necesidade, para realizar unha compra ou para chamar un médico. Case todas as compras, ademais, faciámosllelas a arrieiros ou labregos da veciñanza, ou utilizando terceiros. Houbo moitas murmuracións entre os fregueses sobre os verdadeiros motivos do meu pai para evitar esas visitas. A máis insistente – que eu non puiden deixar de oír – pretendía que o meu pai era un fuxido da xustiza, que vivía cun nome falso e que non quería ser recoñecido se frecuentaba segundo que lugares. Iso cadraba ben con vivirmos na soidade, con que eu non soubese nada dos meus parentes, con que o meu pai deixase deteriorarse pouco a pouco o caserón e se desinteresase do negocio e ata cos seus súbitos accesos de tristura. Sexa como for, íaseme facendo claro que o meu pai gardaba un segredo, que tivera outra vida ou outro oficio na súa mocidade, se cadra nómade ou aventureira, e que botaba de menos a liberdade perdida ou unha vida máis fácil e regalada.

Non pasaron de vinte as veces que atravesei a vella ponte, traspasei a porta arruinada da muralla e me acheguei ata máis alá do Burgo, por visitar unha curmá da miña mai, única parente que recordo, que nos recibía sempre con moito alborozo, a pesar de que poderiamos pasar doadamente por desagradecidos, tan pouco era o noso interese – o interese do meu pai, en realidade, pois ben sabía eu que a miña mai iría alí moitas outras veces de boa gana – en cumprimentala. Nesas vinte veces teño que incluír as que, ás escondidas do meu pai, que andaba de caza, aproveitamos para pechar a taberna e fuxirmos ata a cidade. Ela, pola súa parte, non se achegou nunca ata A Disputa, se cadra porque consideraba que a clientela deixaba moito que desexar. Chamábase Ánxela, mais como se trataba dunha señora moi maior, todos lle chamabamos Mai Ánxela. Tiña a súa casa nunha canella minúscula e de triste aspecto, o Canellón do Carboeiro, que outros chamaban Rúa Cega, sen saída, de edificios case en ruínas e na que abundaban os gatos. As lastras estaban todas levantadas e un rego de inmundicia salfería as beirarrúas cando pasabamos no carro. Máis ca casa, o seu era unha bufarda estreita e escura, chea de lembranzas do seu home, que fora capitán carlista, e dos seus fillos. Mai Ánxela quería moito á miña mamá e tamén a min, pero non soportaba a meu pai. Sempre me agasallaba co que podía ás súas costas. Aínda lembro unhas roscas de anís, tal vez degustadas nunhas festas patronais, porque vagamente asocio o seu sabor coas multitudes e coa ausencia do meu pai.

Con esa señora vivía un rapaz dunha idade similar á miña, non sei se un ano ou dous maior, o seu neto Carlos, ó que eu trataba de primo e co que simpatizaba moito. Creo que lle puxeran ese nome en honor do seu pretendido rei. Pero Carlos só pensaba en xogar cos outros rillotes e, nos días en que non estaba o meu pai, levoume a visitar os barrios dos arredores, as Moureiras e o Porto. Despois, cando volviamos á taberna, ía eu malhumorado, pensando que pasarían se cadra seis ou oito meses antes de que puidese ver de novo o que era o meu único amigo.

Vivín naquel lugar salvaxe e xabreiro, case coma un recluso, sen saber nada do mundo nin da vida, ata o día nefasto no que se presentou na taberna un descoñecido de mediana idade, moreno coa mesma cor do polbo cocido, alto de máis de dez cuartas, desamañado e case calvo.

Agora que rememoro a súa figura véxome, de obra de trece anos, gardando o verroallo no souto a carón da estrada, mentres el se aproximaba cabaleiro nun mulo pintado, con grandes alforxas, un traxe moi usado que non me pareceu do país e unha zamarra de coiro a medio abrochar. Levaba barba de varios días e todo no seu aspecto impoñía. Achegouse a min e levantou levemente o chapeo, como para mirarme mellor. Levantouno coa man esquerda e tamén coa man esquerda acariñou despois a caluga do mulo. Entón decateime de que a man dereita parecía seca, cos dedos ríxidos e encrequenados, aínda que a mantiña medio oculta baixo a manga. Despois tiven ocasión de ver un costurón que atravesaba a man e continuaba brazo arriba. Tomou o seu tempo e preguntou:

– ¿Esta é a taberna de Lourenzo Tasende?

– Non, señor – contesteille eu –. Esta é de Lourenzo Gómez, meu pai.

– ¿Gómez? – rosmou entre dentes –. Vós sodes tan Gómez como eu frade. ¿Está o teu pai na casa?

– Está, si, pero o meu pai é Lourenzo Gómez – repetinlle.

Sorriu sen contestarme e foi asubiando ata a porta do caserón, baixou do mulo e atouno nunha das armelas. Quixo a casualidade que nese momento saíse a miña mai cunha grande cesta de roupa que levaba para poñer ó clareo. Ó velo detívose, lanzou un berro e levou as mans á boca, deixando caer o cesto e esparexendo a roupa polo chan. Sen dicir nada entrou outra vez na casa e correu escaleiras enriba. O descoñecido soltou a gargallada, unha das súas gargalladas altas, sonoras e desprezativas, que tantas veces oín despois e que tanto temín e tanto odiei, e sen preocuparse pasou entre a roupa estrada polo chan e introduciuse na taberna.

Deixei o porco ceibo e corrín detrás da miña mai. Na taberna había un só freguês, un vello pastor de ovellas e caseteiro ocasional, que vivía non moi lonxe. Non tiña nin para pagar o que bebía, pero meu pai, se cadra por compaixón, aturábao e íalle servindo algunha cunca de augardente. O vello sentaba nunha mesa nun cornello e pasaba as tardes en silencio, coa ollada perdida. Pero naquel momento ollaba ó home que tan inesperadamente irrompera nas nosas vidas, e ollábao estupefacto: o home inclinábase sobre o mostrador, collía do estante unha das garrafas e bebía a grandes grolos, mentres meu pai, que tiña xusta sona de colérico, paseaba ansioso sen ocultar a sorpresa, pero sorrindo entre dentes e sen a menor preocupación. Por fin advertiu o meu abraio e fíxome coa man xestos de que me retirase. Con isto o mangallón volveuse cara a min, tirou a garrafa da boca, eructou ruidosamente, limpou os beizos coa manga da zamarra e dixo:

– ¡Así que tes un fillo, gandulo! A Rosiña agarroute ben agarrado.

A Rosiña era a miña mai. Aínda que escuramente, non deixaba eu de captar o sentido daquelas palabras, que me pareceron inxuriosas. Sorprendín un brillo malévolo nos ollos daquel home, dun azul tan claro que había que esforzarse para percibilo tanto como para percibir o das ondas do mar desde o alto da cuíña.

– Si. É o meu fillo Lourenzo – contestoulle meu pai, pero non dixo nada máis nin me presentou ó descoñecido e repetiu o xesto coa man.

Subín rapidamente as escaleiras, alancando os banzos de dous en dous e polo corredor escoitei os saloucos apagados da miña mai. Entrei na súa alcoba. Ela estaba sobre o leito, chorando. Apertoume convulsivamente.

– ¿Que pasa? – preguntei –. ¿Quen é ese home?

– É a Desgracia – díxome, con palabras entrecortadas –. A Desgracia: Lázaro Rivadulla.

My Childhood in the Disputes Tavern

The Disputes was the name of my father's tavern, which lay on the outskirts of the city of Pontevedra, on the old road that leads to Santiago de Compostela. From where this tavern was you couldn't even make out the last of the cottages scattered along the road near O Burgo, and in fact one could only discern some of the little hamlets nearest to the city, but one could guess the city's presence because of the frequency of the cabs, coaches with their passengers and carts with goods piled on top of them, the horse-drawn mail-coaches and the different sorts of travellers, who all used to stop at our place to have a drink or a rest. Pontevedra was not more than an hour away on horseback, and on the days when there was a southerly wind, you could hear the Peregrina and Santa María bells, calling the faithful to Mass or to a funeral from the other side of the River Lérez.

The Disputes, an old detached big house half in ruins, constructed from thick granite slabs and with a rectangular base, with most of its rooms empty and neglected, stood on a small piece of high ground. From here, on the clearest days of the year the dense woods were just visible spreading inland, the craggy peaks of Castrove and Acibal, a few stretches of road in the valleys and wide jutting cliffs, could be seen with the background of the distant coast. The wind from the *ría* reached us, rusted the hinges, handles and door-knobs, made the sheets and dresses damp, ruined the chorizos and hams, and stripped the paint from the doors and windows, so that we had to repaint them every year, and also paint the walls white with lime very often. My father would frequently curse both the Jew who had sold him the place and the day it had occurred to him to run a business like that, during the long, bitter winter evenings when we had hardly any customers. He then used to sit at one of the tables with a bottle of liquor and a glass, and he cared about neither my mother's despair nor my tears. Gulp after gulp, he drank from the bottle, becoming more and more bad tempered, until he emptied it at the evening's end and stumbled off to bed exhausted.

My father was a violent man, with a long arm to hit me each time I did something silly, or he thought it was, or simply when he himself made a mess of something, or something didn't turn out as he expected. Only my mother's help was any good on those occasions, as she ran between my father and me and told him off for his behavior. Just one word from her was enough to calm him down. Then he became melancholic, his eyes grew dark, and he started murmuring to himself, going away on his own, perhaps regretting lifting his hand to hit me. Apart from that, I daresay he loved me. He was careless in his affections, not paying much attention to me, but he cared about my clothes and food, and treated me almost as an equal, a certain comradeship setting in between us as the years went by. Ever since I was a child, he used to take me hunting with him in the surrounding hills, and we wandered around near the house, leaving my mother in charge of the tavern. In exchange, I had to become a grown-up from a very early age and help with the chores in the tavern, which in time became a hostel, when somebody needed lodgings, so I got used to serving jugs of wine, stewed partridges, pork crackling, broth and bottles of liquor, cleaning tables, using the broom, tasting the wine offered by wine traders, milking the cows, taking them out to the meadows and back to the stables, putting them out to graze in the nearby meadows, cutting the gorse and laying it on the stable floor, cleaning the stables, feeding the pigs and confining them in a copse we owned just around the corner from our house, helping in the slaughter of the pigs, and, in time, when my mother was ill and my father completely disheartened, tidying the rooms, washing up, sewing the clothes and cooking. I also learnt to haggle and deal with even the most difficult of customers. What I never learnt was to read and write, even though it was often said, and I established that it was true, that my father belonged to a family of local gentry, was the son of a public notary, and that in his bedroom there was a Bible and two books on medicine, which were intended to be a reminder of his period at university. But he couldn't be bothered to teach me anything as pointless as reading and writing, nor did he allow my mother to send me to school, perhaps because they could not afford to pay the teacher, and besides he didn't want to go all the way to the school in Pontevedra every day.

It is only now that I can write my memoirs at the request of my relatives and friends it is because I have been lucky enough and because an "angel" committed himself to teach me. Despite living so near to the town, I was hardly acquainted with it; my father wouldn't go near the place unless it was absolutely unavoidable in order to do the shopping or see the doctor. Besides, we obtained nearly all the shopping from the traders who passed by, or from the neighbouring farmers or middle men. There was a lot of gossip among the parishioners about the real reasons why my father avoided those visits. The most common one, which I heard again and again, was that my father was on the run, living under a false name, and did not want to be recognized when he visited certain places. That fitted well with the fact that we lived so far off the beaten track, with the fact that I knew hardly anything about my relatives, and with my father letting the whole house fall more and more into neglect and his lack of interest in how the business went, and would also account for his sudden fits of melancholy. Whatever it might have been, it was becoming clear that my father had a secret, that he had a previous life, or another profession in his youth, either as a wanderer or adventurer, and that he missed his lost freedom, or perhaps the comfortable life he had enjoyed.

I did not cross the old bridge more than twenty times in all, going through the broken-down wall and walking as far as O Burgo to visit one of my mother's cousins, the only relative I can remember, who always welcomed us with open affection, although we could easily have seemed ungrateful we went so seldom, because we hardly showed any interest to pay a courtesy call to her, which was really my father's lack of interest. As far as I know, my mother would have liked to go more often. Within those twenty times, I must include those when, behind my father's back (he was hunting), we took advantage of his absence and closed the tavern to escape to town. On her part, this cousin never got to the Disputes, maybe because our customers were not to her liking. Her name was Angela, but as she was quite an old lady, we used to call her Mother Angela. Her house was located in a tiny, gloomy alleyway named Canellón do Carboeiro, which others called the Dead-End Street, where nearly all the buildings were in ruins, and where many cats had ended up literally scratching a living. The stones on the streets were nearly all uneven and we splashed water from the stream of filth onto the pavement as we passed by in our cart. Rather than a house, it was really just a garret, narrow and dark, full of memories of her husband (who had been a captain in the uncrowned King Charles's "Carlista" army) and her sons. Mother Angela loved both my mother and me very much but she could not bear my father. She always presented me with whatever she could afford. I still remember some aniseed biscuits, perhaps from some village festival, because I slightly associate its taste with crowds and with my father not being home.

There was a child of about the same age as mine living with her. He might have been a year or two older than me. He was her grandson, Carlos. I considered him as my cousin and used to get on well with him. I think the boy was given the name on account of the Pretender to the throne. But Carlos only thought about playing with the other naughty boys, and those days when my father wasn't there he took me round to call on the surrounding areas such as Moreiras and Porto. Later on, when we came back to the tavern, I was always in a bad mood, thinking that perhaps it would not be less than six or eight months before we met Carlos again, my only friend.

I lived in that wild and windy place, almost like a prisoner, without knowing anything about the world or life, until that ill-fated day when a middle-aged stranger appeared in the tavern; he had a dark complexion, the colour of a boiled octopus, and was over two metres tall, shabbily dressed and almost bald.

Now that I recall his figure, I can see myself at thirteen years of age, tending the pig on the hills near the road, watching him come along on a piebald mule, with big saddle-bags, a worn-out foreign-looking suit, and a leather jacket, half buttoned up. He was wearing a beard several days old and his appearance would have impressed anyone. He approached me and lifted his hat slightly as if he wanted to see me better. He raised it with his left hand and with the same hand he patted the mule's neck. Then I noticed his right hand looked withered, the fingers stiff and crooked, although it was half hidden under his sleeve. After that, I could see the scar that ran up his hand and further up his arm. He took his time, asking: "Is this Lorenzo Tasende's tavern?"

"No, sir", I answered, "this is Lourenzo Gómez's, my father's tavern." "Gómez," he grunted. "You are as much a Gómez as I am a monk. Is your father home?" "Yes, but my father is Lourenzo Gómez."

He did not answer but smiled, and continued, whistling as he went, towards the gate of the big house. He got off the mule and tied it to one of the chains of the fence. My mother happened to come out at that very moment with a big basket full of clothes, to lay them on the grass in the sun. On seeing him, she stopped, screamed, and put her hands up to her mouth, dropping the basket and scattering the clothes all over the ground. Without a word she re-entered the house and ran upstairs. The stranger laughed a loud laugh, one of those disdainful, scornful, loud laughs I would hear again and again later on and would grow to loathe and fear. And carelessly, treading on the clothes on the ground, he entered the tavern.

I left the pig alone, and ran after my mother. Inside the tavern there was only one customer, an old shepherd and occasional day-labourer who lived not far away. He never had enough to pay for the drinks, but my father, perhaps out of sympathy, used to serve him one free. The old man sat at a table in the corner and spent the afternoons in silence, staring into nothingness. But at that moment he stared at the man, who had broken so unexpectedly into our lives. And his stare was a shocked one: the stranger leaned on the counter, took one of the bottles from a shelf, and gulped down its contents, while my father, who was rightly considered a bad-tempered man, paced up and down anxiously without hiding his surprise, but grinning and not showing the least concern.

Finally, he noticed my amazement and gestured with his hand for me to leave. At this, the tall stranger turned towards me, moved away the bottle from his lips, burped loudly, wiped his lips with the jacket sleeve, and said: "So, you've got a son, you bastard. So, little Rosa got you into her grip."

"Little Rosa" was my mother. Although incompletely, I could understand what his words meant, and they seemed to me to be insulting. I noticed an evil gleam in his eyes, which were such a light blue that you needed as much of an effort to see the colour as you did to make out the waves on the sea from the top of a tall cliff.

"Yes, he's my son Lourenzo," my father answered, but said nothing more, nor did he introduce me to the stranger, and he made the gesture with his hand once again.

I went upstairs quickly, climbing the steps two by two, and from along the corridor I could hear my mother weeping bitterly. I entered her room. She was lying on the bed, sobbing. She squeezed tightly and held me to her.

"What's wrong?" I asked. "Who's that man?"

"He is Misfortune," she told me with broken speech. "Misfortune: Lázaro Rivadulla."

Claudio Rodríguez Fer (1956–)

From Historia da lúa (History of the Moon), *1984*

A brétema

A brétema que vén da mar batida
afinca en Mondoñedo néboa macia.
Vila de pedra antiga marco recio
onde repousa a voz e falar sabe
a vellas augardentes e viños escuros.
Poetas pantasmais vagan nas rúas
enchidas de lembranzas nas engrelas do tempo.

Conversar nesta tarde é lene talla
de centenario arte.

Fog

The fog that comes in from the heaving sea
settles in Mondoñedo as pale mist.
A town of ancient stone, a sturdy frame
in which voices repose and know the way
to speak to vintage spirits and dark wines.
Phantom-like poets wander through the streets
replete with memories in the leaf-buds of time.

To talk this afternoon is a soft carving
of an ages-old art.

Suso de Toro (1956–)

A Paixón segundo San Mateo, *1988*

En sentindo a música ficou inmóbil sen sentir a auga quente que saía da billa e caía na man que suxeitaba o prato enxaboado. "A Paixón segundo San Mateo". Volvíao invadir aquel malestar xa case esquecido, aquela mestura de medo e desacougo que o abandonara había catro anos. Volvera. Era ela. Sacou a man de debaixo da auga quente, notouna algo dorida. Na sala estaba a nena, soa. Cerrou a billa despacio, secou as mans no mandil, outra vez ela, e camiñou despacio á sala mentres lle ía subindo do fondo da memoria aquela sensación de maldade tan familiar.

O día en que o psiquiatra lle dixera que podía suspender toda medicación, que estaba curado, sentiu un oco dentro de si. Un oco, iso era o único que notaba.

Aceptara o tratamento porque teimara a súa nai e tamén, en parte, porque prefería pensar que realmente tiña unha obsesión paranoide a aceptar que ela se estaba a vingar del. E ademais onde máis lle doía, na nena, o que máis quería.

A culpa non fora del, el non a obrigou a nada. Se tivo a filla foi porque ela quixo. Ela non quería ter fillos e el si, pero el nunca lle insistiu. Con Rita o peor era teimar nalgunha cousa, era a mellor maneira de facerlle levar a contraria. O da viaxe a Berlín por exemplo, bastou que el dixera que lle apetecía de verdade ir a Berlín para que ela lle collese teima a Berlín, nunca iría a Berlín, os alemáns eran todos uns nazis noxentos, non pisaría Alemania na súa vida. Sempre era así e el prefería non levarlle a contraria. Cando empreñou era culpa del. ¿E por que era culpa del? Home claro, o que a empreñou foi el. Pero, se imos ao caso, tamén foi porque ela quixo. O caso é que empreñara, ían ter un neno, ou unha nena. El quería ter o neno. Se ela quería, claro. Ela non quería ter o neno, pero como a el lle apetecía, pois teríao. Pero non, el así non quería, el non dixera iso, el quería o neno só se os dous o querían. Non houbo maneira, ían ter o neno.

Os meses de embarazo foron terribles, cheos de complicacións. Ela case non comía, adelgazou moito e estaba moi feble. O médico fíxolle unha dieta cos alimentos e as cantidades que obrigadamente debía tomar se non quería danarse a si mesma e ao feto, prohibiulle o tabaco e o alcohol. Como se nada. Perdera o apetito disque, e non podía deixar de fumar porque estaba nerviosa. Gorentáballe ver como sufría el cada vez que prendía un cigarrillo, é que estou nerviosa. Como se non soubese que o monóxido e a nicotina afectaban ao feto, claro que o sabía. Rita estaba máis cruel e insoportable que nunca. Nove meses cheos de reproches, ela estaba así por causa del, non quería saber nada del, maníaco sexual, que non a tocara, era unha besta que a forzara, dáballe noxo, oxalá o neno nacera mal. Que o neno nacera mal. ¿Como podía dicir aquilo? Ela, que era a nai. El sempre a quixera, e seguíaa querendo, pero non aturaba aquelas olladas cheas de odio que lle botaba. Si, si, que non o negara, estábao mirando con odio. E o que o desesperaba eran aquelas risiñas histéricas cheas de maldade que botaba ás veces sen vir a conto. Ao remate do embarazo eran como dous estraños. Ou como dous inimigos que se axexaran mutuamente. Foron nove meses moi duros.

E a morte de Rita. Un parto difícil, ela morrera, aí estaba a nena. Xa nin se lembraba do que sentira pola súa morte. Doeríalle, o máis seguro, el queríaa moito, estaba afeito a vivir con ela, seis anos sempre xuntos. Eran moitos anos. Debeulle doer moito. Pero xa non lle quedaba nin o recordo de ter experimentado eses sentimentos, quedaba tan atrás todo o anterior ao nacemento da nena. De aí en diante todo foi a nena. Axudáralle a súa nai, pero el fixo as veces de pai e nai, cambiou cueiros, preparou biberóns, velou catarros. Nunca pensou que puidese querer tanto a ninguén.

E foi no cuarto mes cando ela volveu. Ou, se cadra, nunca marchara e sempre estivera alí mirándoo pasar traballos e facerlle aloumiños á nena. Pero foi un día do cuarto mes cando a nena empezou a chorar daquela maneira mentres el puña a lavadora. Nunca a sentira chorar asi, con aquel pranto histérico. Foi correndo á habitación. A nena estaba destapada e estremecíase nun pranto intermitente e agudo. Notou unha presencia maligna e insoportablemente hostil alí dentro. Instintivamente colleu a nena en brazos e sacouna correndo da habitación. Pouco a pouco a nena foi acougando. Tardou un bo anaco en entrar outra vez na habitación. Para aquela, pareceulle que todo estaba normal, todo tiña a atmosfera familiar de sempre. Deixo que fora cedendo o desconcerto e acabou atopando unha explicación lóxica, a nena asustouse de algo un hipo cecais, e rompeu a chorar destapándose toda. Cousas de nenos, díxose. Pero non eran cousas de nenos.

De alí a uns días estábase duchando mentres durmía a nena, cando oíu a música. ¿Quen puxera a música? Era a "Paixón segundo San Mateo", o disco favorito de Rita. Berros da nena. Saíu espido e mollado da ducha, pasou por diante da sala de onde saía a música e entrou na habitación. A nena chiaba a morrer enriba da cama, espida e vermella coma un tomate. Colleuna contra si envolvendo co seu corpo aquel feixiño de chíos que se lle cravaban moi dentro, moi dentro. Entrou na sala coa nena no colo e apagou aquel puto disco, que foi parando de dar voltas, parando de dar voltas, ata que quedou inmóbil. E quedou así de pé coa nena chorando contra el, mirando o disco parado. Sentou no butacón e rompeu a saloucar coa nena moi apretada contra si.

Rompeu o disco e tirouno, pero foi o mesmo. Os ataques á nena continuaron. Sempre era igual, cando el estaba noutra habitación molestaba á nena, que sempre choraba aterrorizada e aparecía destapada ou fóra do berce, enriba da cama ou no chan. Cando xa sucedera cinco ou seis veces comentouno coa súa nai. Ela díxolle que non dixera tal cousa, mentres se persignaba e apretaba a nena contra ela, que era unha teima del. El sabía que non era certo, pero aceptou ir a un psiquiatra. Mais sen comentalo coa nai, acordou mudarse axiña de piso. Tiña que sacar à nena dos seus dorninios. Aquela mesma noite, mentres picaba as patacas para unha tortilla, sentiu os chíos desesperados entrecortados da nena. Entrou coma un tolo na habitación. Notou un frío que lle arreguizou os pelos. A súa filla botaba coma unha pelota enriba da cama co pranto entrecortado polos botes. Como se algo a erguese a unha altura de vinte centímetros e logo a sacudise contra a cama, a volvese erguer e a volvese sacudir. A nena parecía un pedazo de carne tenro e encarnado, do nariz saíanlle uns carreiriños de sangue que caían pola fazula. Botouse á cama enriba dela e cubriuna co seu corpo, notou como o corpiño dela seguía sacudíndose debaixo do seu peso. Agarrouna e sacouna a rastras da cama, pesaba coma unha adulta. Saíu correndo do piso coa nena en brazos e, nun taxi, levouna ao hospital. Diagnosticáronlle un shock, fixéronlle análises e placas e non viron nada anormal, déronlle uns tranquilizantes para a nena e outros para el e dixéronlle que a levase o día despois a Pediatría. Aquela noite quedou a durmir coa nena na casa da súa nai. Dedicou os días seguintes a buscar piso, de alí a quince días mudárase ao novo.

O novo piso non tiña a luz do anterior nin era tan céntrico. Aínda que estaba máis preto da casa da nai, o cal non lle viña nada mal para deixar a nena. Pero aínda que o piso non fora tan bonito tanto lle tiña, sentíase tan ledo que non lle importou acudir regularmente, unha vez cada semana o primeiro mes e unha vez ao mes logo, durante seis meses ao psiquiatra. Non lle importou aceptar que sufría unha obsesión paranoide nin tomar medicinas. Sentíase tan ledo e a nena volvía estar tan ben. Recuperara o sono tranquilo e o apetito regular, a cousa marchaba outra vez. E aínda que sempre deixou acesa unha luciña de alerta no fondo de si, volveu vivir.

Un ano e medio máis tarde coñeceu a Clara. Era tan diferente de Rita. Non estaba afeito a que alguén se puidese entusiasmar con el, ¿que podía ver Clara nel de interesante? Ás veces, cando Clara o miraba atenta con expresión de afecto, el paraba de falar e esculcaba naquel rostro. Pero non, non finxía. ¿Que lle pasaba que a miraba así? Non, nada. Non pasaba nada. Estaba tan contento que prefería non falar de Rita nin do pasado con Clara. Ata volveu mercar "A Paixón segundo San Mateo" e cando a volveu oír reconciliouse con aquela música de sentimentos nobles. Acordaron vivir xuntos, Clara trasladouse ao piso.

Deixáronse de alí a un ano. A nena nunca pareceu aceptar a Clara. Nin o máis pequeno xesto de confíanza. Como se fose unha descoñecida, cando xa levaba vivindo na casa seis meses. A Clara fóiselle facendo insoportable, que a nena a rexeitaba. Como a ía rexeitar, se era unha nena de dous anos e medio. Tería algo de ciumes dela, pero xa lle pasarían. Pero non, foi como unha cuña entre eles dous que foi fendendo, fendendo. Cando Clara dixo que marchaba el non dixo nada, serviuse outro café e suspirou.

Ritiña seguiu medrando. Recordaba moito á nai, aínda que el se abstivo sempre de dicirllo ou de ensinarlle fotos. Era moi lista, parecía ter o entendemento dunha persoa maior, e tamén moi caprichosa. Os anos de coidados do pai facían que a nena dependese moito da súa presencia. Iso obrigábao a renunciar a case toda a vida social. Pasaba case todo o tempo libre coa nena. Pero non lle importaba estar atado aos seus antollos, ela era a súa vida.

Cando entrou na sala viu a nena coa carpeta do disco na man, mirou para el e riu con aquela risiña histérica tan coñecida del. Volvera para ficar e quitarlle a nena.

El adiantou os brazos e camiñou cara a ela, a súa meniña, que o estaba a mirar con aquela ollada de odio e ría histérica ollándoo vir.

Santiago de Compostela, 23 de agosto de 1988.

The Passion of St Matthew, *1988*

When he heard the music he remained still, without noticing the water running from the tap and falling on the hand that held the soap-dish. "The St Matthew Passion". He felt uneasy and experienced again that sensation he had almost forgotten, that mixture of fear and emptiness which he had not felt for the last four years. It had come back. It was her. He took his hand away from under the hot water; it hurt a bit. In the sitting room was the girl, alone. He turned off the tap slowly, dried his hands with his apron, it was her again, again, and he walked slowly towards the sitting room while the familiar sensation of evil arose from the depths of his memory.

The day when the psychiatrist told him he could stop taking all the medication, that he was cured, he felt a sinking feeling inside him. A hole inside was the only thing he could feel. He had accepted having the treatment because of his mother, and also, partly, because he would rather think he really had a paranoid obsession and accept that she wanted to take revenge on him. Besides, what hurt him most, the baby, was also what he loved most.

It hadn't been his fault; he hadn't made her do it. If she had had the baby it was because she had made up her mind to. She hadn't wanted to have children although he had wanted them, but he had never insisted on it. The worst thing you could do with Rita was insist on something, because then she was sure to do the opposite. For instance, the trip to Berlin: he only had to tell her that he really wanted to go, and she got the chills about Berlin, and refused point blank to go; the Germans were all dirty Nazis, she would never set foot there for the rest of her life. It was always the same with her and he preferred not to gainsay her. When she fell pregnant, she said it was his fault. Why was it his fault? Obviously, because it was he who had made her pregnant. But, if we only consider it carefully, it was because she had wanted it. The thing was that she was pregnant, they would have a boy or a girl. He wanted a baby boy, but only if she agreed. She didn't want to have the baby, but as he wanted it, she would have it. But he didn't want it to be that way, he didn't say so, he wanted a baby provided they both agreed. But there was no way out now: they would have the baby.

The months of her pregnancy were awful, full of complications. She hardly ate, lost a lot of weight and was very weak. The doctor made a list of foods and the amounts she had to eat if she didn't want to damage her own health and that of the fetus, and he also forbade her to smoke or drink alcohol: all in vain. Apparently, she lost her appetite and couldn't stop smoking because she was nervous. She grinned with glee when she saw him suffer every time she lit up a cigarette: "I'm nervous, you know". She knew very well how monoxide and nicotine affected the fetus, of course she did. Rita became crueler and more unbearable than ever.

Nine months of reproach: she was like that because of him, she didn't want to have anything to do with him, she didn't want him to touch her, he was a wild animal who had violated her, and he disgusted her. She hoped the baby would be born sick. Hoped the baby would be born sick? How could she say that? She, who was the creature's own mother. He had always loved her and still loved her, but he couldn't deal with those looks, filled with hatred, that she darted at him. Oh yes, she never denied it, she looked at him with hatred. And what he hated most about her was that evil, hysterical, cackling laughter without any cause. By the end of her pregnancy they were like two strangers. Or rather, like two foes spying on each other. They were nine very hard months.

Then, there was Rita's death. A difficult delivery; she died after it, and then there was the baby girl. He hardly remembered what he had felt on her death. It must surely have hurt him, as he was deeply in love with her. He was used to living with her; they had been inseparable for six years. It must have hurt him a lot. But he didn't recall having had those feelings, which dated back so long before the girl's birth. From then on, there was nothing but the girl. His own mother helped him, but he acted as both father and mother, changed her nappies, prepared her bottles of milk, watched out for colds. He never thought he could love anybody so much.

And it was after four months when she came back. Or maybe she had never gone away, and had always been around to see him working and hugging the baby girl. It was one day during the fourth month when the girl began to scream like that while he was busy with the washing. He had never heard her cry like that, hysterically. He rushed to her room. The girl had thrown off her bedclothes and was squealing in a high-pitched voice, on and off. He noticed an unbearable, hostile, evil presence in there. Right away, he took the girl into his arms and ran with her out of the room. Little by little the girl began to calm down. It was a long while before he ventured back into the room. By then the room seemed to be back to normal, everything had the same familiar atmosphere as usual. He refused to believe his own suspicions and finally found a logical explanation for it all: the girl was scared for some reason, and had burst into tears, throwing off the bedclothes.

Things like that often happen to babies. But of course it wasn't so.

A few days later he was taking a shower while the baby slept, when he heard the music. But who had put the music on? It was the Passion of Saint Matthew, Rita's favourite record. The girl screamed. He rushed, naked and wet, out of the shower, walked past the sitting room where the music came from, and entered the bedroom. The girl was shrieking like a mad thing on top of the bed, naked and red as a tomato. He hugged her against his chest, sheltering that bundle of screams which stabbed him deep inside. He entered the sitting room with the girl in his arms and turned off that damned record, which went round slower and slower, until it stopped. And he stayed there on his feet, pressing her tightly to his chest, the girl crying, while he stared at the record. He sat down in the armchair, with the baby held tightly in his arms.

His broke the record into pieces and threw it away, but it made no difference. The attacks on the girl went on. It was always the same: when he was in another room she scared the girl, who always wept inconsolably and appeared uncovered or out of the cot or in his bed, or on the floor. When this had happened five or six times, he talked about it with his mother. She told him to keep quiet, while she herself made the sign of the cross and hugged the girl tightly, saying it was just something feeding on his mind. He knew it wasn't so, but agreed to see the psychiatrist. But without telling his mother, he made up his mind to move soon to another flat. He had to take his daughter away from her domains. That same night, while he was cutting up the potatoes to make an omelet, he heard the girl scream intermittently. He rushed into the room like a madman. He noticed she was so cold that her hair stood on end. His daughter was bouncing up and down on the bed like a ball, crying on and off. It seemed as if someone was lifting her up about six inches, and was throwing her down against the bed, again and again. The girl looked like a piece of tender red meat. Two threads of blood flowed from her nostrils and down across her rosy cheeks. He jumped on top of the bed and covered her body with his, but still her little body kept shaking under him. He dragged her out of the room; she weighed like an adult. He ran out of the apartment with the girl in his arms, and took her to hospital in a taxi. They diagnosed shock, made blood tests and X-rays, and found nothing amiss. So they gave her some tranquilizers and told him to take her to the children's doctor the following day. That night he slept in this mother's place together with his daughter. He spent the following two days flat-hunting and in a fortnight he was settled in a new apartment.

The new flat was not as well-lit or near the town centre as the old one, though it was near his mother's, which was very convenient when he had to leave the girl with her. But even though this flat was not as good as the other one, he didn't care. He felt so happy that he didn't mind going to the psychiatrist, first once a week, then once a month, for the next six months. He didn't mind admitting he had a paranoid obsession or the fact that he had to take medication. He felt so happy and the girl got so much better. He recovered his normal sleep routine and began to eat properly; things began to go smoothly. And although a little alarm-light on deep down was still on, he began to live again.

A year and a half later he met Clara. She was so different from Rita. He was not used to someone who could be so interested in him. What could Clara see in him? At times, when Clara stared tenderly at him, he stopped talking and scanned her face. But no, she was not pretending. Why was he looking at her like that? No, nothing. Nothing was wrong. He was so glad that he preferred not to talk of his past or of Rita with her. He even bought The Passion of Saint Matthew again, and when he heard it again he made his peace with the music. They decided to live together, and Clara moved in.

A year later they split up. The girl never seemed to accept Clara. There was never the slightest sign of trust. It was just as if she were a stranger, even when she had been living in the same house for six months. It was unbearable for Clara to be rejected by the girl. How could a two and a half-year-old girl reject her? She was probably jealous of her, and that would pass. But it didn't. It was like a solid block between them that pushed them further and further apart. When Clara said she was leaving, he said nothing. He helped himself to another cup of tea and sighed.

Little Rita kept growing. She reminded him a lot of her mother, although he had always avoided telling her that or showing her photos. She was very clever, seeming to have the intelligence of a grown-up, and was also very spoilt. All those years of being looked after by her father made her depend a lot on his presence. That fact made her father give up nearly all his social life. He spent nearly all his spare time with the girl. But he didn't mind devoting his life to her whims and fancies, as she was all his life.

When he entered the sitting room one day, he noticed the girl had a record-cover in her hand; she looked at him and laughed that hysterical laugh he knew so well. Rita was back to stay and take the girl away from him.

He reached forward for her and stepped towards her, his precious little girl, who was looking at him with hatred in her eyes and cackling with laughter.

Santiago de Compostela, 23 August 1988

From Tic-tac, *1993*

A dolor é coma o resto das cousas, unha cousa que está aí. O caso é quen controla. Quen controla a quen, a dolor a ti ou ti a dolor. Velaí o choio. Positivamente. Ademais que gusta ser un quen a controlar a dolor. E hai casos nos que mesmo dá gusto. Mira, vou poñer un exemplo. Esto é un exemplo. Fagamos unha comprobación. Collamos agora unha xerra con medio litro de viño. Ou mellor, con cervexa, que dá máis ganas de mexar. A cervexa tamén se chama diurética, que disque quere dicir "que dá gana de orinar." Pero ti non vaias pedir a ningún bar que che poñan "unha diurética", porque non te entenden. A xente ten escaso nivel de información. Pero collamos a xerra con medio litro de cervexa. Agora bebémola, ras. Agardamos a que vaian vindo as ganas. Agardamos a xuntar ben ganas. E cando teñamos ganas, pero ganas a base de ben, é cando hai que empezar. Trátase de aguantar, hai que aguantar. Hai que aguantar canto máis mellor. Pensar noutra cousa, asubiar, falar o que sexa, pero aguantar. Ata que non poidas máis, ata que vas rebentar. Entón, xa cando che vai rebentar a vexiga colles a xerra de medio litro da que bebiches e mexas nela. Verás que gusto dá. Ese si que é un gusto. Un pracer. Canto máis aguantas e canto máis mal o pasas antes máis gusto che dá despois de orinar. E mesmo cando orinas, ou sexa cando mexas, non sabes se dá gusto ou doe, ti mira como é. É dicir que para que che dea gusto hai que pasalo mal primeiro. Ou sexa, digo eu para min, que non hai gusto sen traballo nin pracer sen dor. Positivamente. Esta é unha comprobación bastante científica que pode estar ao alcance de calquera individuo humano. Digo eu. Eu como teño pouco trato con mulleres, bastante pouco, a verdade. Aínda que é raro o ano que non boto un foguete. Pero como me dou pouco gusto con mulleres pois de cando en vez fágome unha cousa destas para darlle unha malleira ao corpo e mais para ter sensacións, que se di. O caso é que, como poderá observar quen practique esta comprobación sobre os líquidos, nunca se mexa o mesmo que se bebeu. Nunca. Sempre che queda unha parte dentro. Por moito que mexes sempre queda unha parte dentro. Sempre hai un desgaste. Sempre. Como se dixeramos, nada é inmune. Non hai cousa que sexa de gratis, sempre hai que pagar un prezo. Por exemplo, bebes medio litro, pero saír, sae menos. Hai unha parte que queda para a empresa. A min gustaríame escribir un libro de tipo técnico con todos os meus inventos e comprobacións. Para min que lle había axudar moito á xente a vivir. Non digo a ser feliz, porque non, por que habemos enganar a ninguén se non gañamos nada. Gañando algo compréndese, pero sen gañar nada xa me diredes. A vida non dá para moita felicidade e tampouco sabe un moito que é mellor facer. Un nunca sabe que cousa ten máis mérito, se estarse quieto e aturar tanto ataque e tanta cousa que che tiran, ou se saír á vida botándolle peito ao asunto e afrontar unha chea de calamidades e vencelas. Velaí o choio. Esa é a cuestión, como se dixeramos, ou se é ou non se é. E eso é o que me pasa a min, que nunca me souben decidir por unha cousa ou pola outra. E cando te pos a dar voltas a unha cousa, malo. Porque se na vez de decidirte a seres poste a cavilar e darlle voltas á cousa, que se é mellor ser ou non ser, pois o que pasa é que ao final non es. Eso é o que pasa. Que foi o que me pasou a min, que non me decidín a nada e agora non son. Home, como ser, ser, claro que son. Son eu dentro do que cabe. Digo eu. Pero quero dicir que puiden ser moitas cousas, e mesmo moitas persoas, pero funme deixando estar, funme deixando estar, e cando te dás de conta xa tocou a campá. Xa pasou o tempo, fóra de combate. Que foi o que me pasou a min. Por eso, que a vida éche un soño e cando te dás conta xa toca o reloxo espertador, acaba o soño e ala, para a pataqueira. A criar patacas. Positivamente. Todos os que somos de carne non che somos máis ca herba, e todo canto mérito temos éche como as flores da herba. E a herba vai e seca e a flor, pois murcha. Así mesmiño é.

From Tick-tock, *1993*

Pain is like everything else. It's something which is there. The thing is, who is in charge? Who controls what? You control pain or pain controls you. That's the point. It really is. Besides, one likes to be somebody who controls pain. And there are times when it's really great. Look, let me give you an example. This is it. Let's just check on this. Take a jug with half a litre of wine in it. Even better, beer, which makes you pass water. Beer is also called a "diuretic", which means "it makes you pass water." But you wouldn't go to a pub and order a diuretic, because they wouldn't understand you. People are so badly informed. But let's get back to that jug with half a litre of beer in it. Now, drink it. Then, wait until you begin to feel you need to pass water. Wait until you really need to go. And when you really do, then this is when you have to start; the question is to control your instincts. The longer you can wait the better. Think of something else, whistle, talk about something, or whatever you like, until you just can't wait any longer, until you think you're going to burst. Then, when your bladder is going to burst, you take the jug you drank the half-litre from and pass water there. You'll see what a relief it is. It's really a fantastic feeling. What a pleasure. The longer you waited and the worse you felt before, the more pleasure you'll have after you've passed water. And while you're doing it, that is passing water, you don't really know if it hurts or gives you pleasure, you know. Which means that in order to feel pleasure you have to go through pain first. I mean, as I tell myself, there's no rest without work and no pleasure without pain. Really. It has been scientifically proved, so any human being can check it out. That's what I say. I do not have much contact with women, not much at all, and that's the truth of it. Although rarely a year goes by without my having a screw at some time. But as I don't get much pleasure from women, from time to time I do one of these things to punish my body, and also to feel more sensations, or whatever they call them. The thing is, as those who carry out this test on liquids may find out, you never piss the same amount you've drunk. Never. There is always a small amount left inside. However much you piss, there's always some left inside. There is always some wasted. Always. As we said before, nothing comes without a cost. There is absolutely nothing free, there is always a price to pay. For instance, you drink half a litre, but it's always less that comes out. There is always part that's left for business. I would like to write a technical manual myself, with all my inventions and the conclusions I've come to. I am under the impression that such a manual would be a great help for people to get by. I don't mean it would make them any happier, because it wouldn't. Why should we take people in if we get nothing out of it? If you gain something out of it, all right, but if you don't, why do it? Life's not a bowl of cherries and often one doesn't know what's best to do. One never knows whether it's more sensible to keep quiet and withstand the slings and arrows of outrageous fortune, or go out, face up to life and fight back, take arms against a sea of troubles and, by opposing, end them. Aye, there's the rub. That is the question, as we could say, to be or not to be. And that is my case. I could never make up my mind one way or the other. And when you go round and round in circles about something, you never get anywhere. Because if one day you decide to be, you end up hesitating and turning things over in your head, whether it's better to be or not to be, and in the end, you end up not being. That's what's happened to me: I didn't commit myself to being anything, and now "I am not". Well, when I say "to be" of course "I am". I am myself up to a point. But what I mean is that I might have been much more and even could have been many people, but I let myself stand still, and when I realized it, the bell had already tolled. Time is up, game over. That's what happened to me. That's why, life is a dream, and when you realize it, the alarm clock's rung, the dream is over, you're gone to push up daisies. Absolutely. All those of us that are flesh and blood are just grass, and all the glory we achieve is like the flowers of the field. The grass dries up, the flowers fade away, and that's all, folks.

From A sombra cazadora, *1994*

Eu queríalle moito ao meu pai, aínda non dando el oportunidade de dar ou recibir cariño, e el sabía que eu lle quería como eu sabía que me quería el. Pero o seu amor era triste e non me daba axuda nin calor, achegándose cada vez máis, conforme pasaban os anos e medraba eu, á lástima que se sente por alguén doente sen cura. A súa era unha doenza egoista na que só había lugar para a autocompaixón e para asumir uns "deberes" cos seus fillos.

Só recibín atención verdadeira da miña nai e unha nena comprende cando recibe amor que esa é a verdade, que non hai outra cousa verdadeira nin importante. Poderíase dicir que todo está ben cando te queren e que ningunha cousa está no seu sitio cando ninguén te quere. Iso apréndese nun instantiño a penas, basta que a mamai se anoxase e mirase para ti con fastío e unha miga de resentimento para que o terror asomase, abrise un precipicio no chan e un terremoto esfarelase o mundo. Cando se lle pasaba, de contado, e volvía abrollar nos seus ollos o amor por min comprendía que todo estaba ben así, que así había ser o mundo sempre. "Miña nai, miña naiciña, como miña nai ningunha, que me quentou a cariña coa calorciña da súa", ensináreme a cantar ela mesma.

Eu sabía que desde que morrera miña nai a nosa vida non estaba ben, estaba "fóra de madré", saída do seu centro. E por máis que eu miraba de que a vida diaria tivese xeito e senso para que a meu irmán non lle faltase de nada eu sabía que era un engano, unha caricatura da vida verdadeira. Escoitaba con atención e corrixía o falar do meu irmán por ver se curaba o seu gagueo, se volvese falar ben sería un signo de normalidade, de que as cousas volvían ao seu, pero meu irmán seguía a tatexar. E así non había ningún signo na miña vida que me axudase a ter ilusión ou esperanza de que cambiaría para mellor.

Aínda que eu vivía na aceptación da miña sorte, recordo que cando cumprín os catorce anos empezou a nacer dentro de min cada vez máis viva a curiosidade primeiro e o degoxo despois polo mundo exterior.

Sempre aceptara como "natural" o vivir arredados dun mundo que o meu pai calificaba de "perverso" e "infernal". O mundo verdadeiro era o noso, aquel que habitabamos nós os tres dentro dos valos que arrodeaban a finca. Todo o que nós sabiamos do mundo exterior era o que el nos quería contar, e el non quería falar do asunto.

Eu lembraba algo de cando era moi pequena, debeu ser nos primeiros anos do encerro da miña familia e por entón o meu pai aínda permitía que eu saíse de cando en vez, acompañándoos a el e a mamai nas viaxes ao hipermercado. Aínda teño as imaxes infantís de viaxar subida nun carriño metálico por corredores cheos de latas de cores e moitas persoas falando e puxando carriños cargados de cousas ao meu redor. Lembro perfectamente unha rapaza sentada diante da máquina rexistradora a quen meu pai entregaba unha tarxeta e recordo como me ofreceu ela uns caramelos. Tamén lembro como meu pai mos quitou e como só ante os meus choros e as súplicas da miña nai consentiu en darme un. Durante moitos anos gardei na memoria o sabor, de limón do caramelo, soñando en que o había volver sentir na miña boca. Padre só traía de fóra as cousas "imprescindibles", e os caramelos non eran imprescindibles. Por iso debezo polos caramelos de limón, anque sei que fan mal aos dentes.

Paréceme ter tamén vagas lembranzas da paisaxe de edificios, coches, estradas, ...vistos desde dentro do noso automóbil. O mesmo auto que tiñamos e que, a pesar dos poucos coidados do chambón do meu pai, seguíalle permitindo a el ir unha vez cada dous meses a buscar provisións e algún outro recado cada dous meses a buscar provisións e algún outro recado que só el sabería. E algo creo recordar da estancia no hospital cando me levaron a que me trataran da poliomelite, lembro unha habitación branca e ao papá e á mamá sentados a carón da cama.

Pero case todo o que sabía sobre o mundo de fóra era por miña nai. Ás veces estabamos as dúas na horta ou traballando na casa e, mentres, cantabamos cancións que ela me ensinaba, incluso sabía unha mesma canción en varios idiomas, o cal era unha maneira de tolearme ben a min a cabeza que a quería cantar en galego e cantábaa ela en francés ou viceversa. A miña nai tiña as veces o costume de me facer rabear, levábame mesmo ata a beiriña do pranto e entón viraba e dábame un beixo para consolarme. Era forte e cariñosa, mais non deixo de ver tamén que facía pequenas maldades, polo menos comigo. Debía ser o seu xeito de poñer algo de sal naquela vida.

Recordo unha vez na que padre estaba apañando herba coa segadora e cando mamai empezou a tocar co seu violoncello o petardeo do motor calou de inmediáto. Supoño que ficaría calado ao sol, suoroso, escoitando no medio do prado. É difícil imaxinar o ben que soaban na nosa solitaria casa as cordas do seu instrumento. Pena que a min non se me dese tan ben. Eu creo que na desmedida afección da miña nai por ler novelas e en cantar era onde ela libraba as tensións e padecementos que aquela vida lle supuña. Nunca acabei de entender como a miña nai aceptou aquela vida e nunca o acabarei de entender. Dígome que por amor ao meu pai, pero debeu haber tamén debilidade pola súa parte, penso eu. E dóeme pensalo.

Pero ela a toda hora cantaba e tiña un cantar para cada hora. E cando non lía nin cantaba prendía a falar e aí víase que tiña soidades da súa vida anterior, porque sempre lle asomaba na punta da lingua un "antes". Eu dáballe polo pao por ver se deixaba os asuntos diarios e contaba algo da súa xuventude e da súa vida. Ela facía como que non quería, e era certo que por non enfadar ao meu pai non quería, pero logo, se non estaba el diante, empezaba a falar moi despacio. Aqueles momentos nos que mamai vencía os reparos e comezaba a contar algo, pouco e pouco, eran momentos máxicos nos que o medo porque rompesen, e se volvese refuxiar nunha canción ou nos asuntos cotiáns, se xuntaban co pasmo por vela revivir.

Moitas veces teño collido do aparador da miña habitación a foto enmarcada de mamá, apertábaa e cantaba algunha canción que me ensinara mentres lembraba os recordos da súa vida que ela me contara. Eu dáballe voltas e imaxinaba novas situacións nas que a miña nai tiña a miña cara e viaxaba a Londres en avión, a París en ferrocarril... Un mozo que viaxaba no meu compartimento do tren lía o xornal, eu ollaba a paisaxe. Logo ese mozo encartaba o xornal e ollábame.

From The Hunting Shadow, *1994*

I really loved my father, even though he never showed his love or gave me the chance to show him that I loved him. But he knew that I loved him, just as I knew that he loved me.

But his was a sad love, and it didn't help me or give me any warmth, and as the years went by and I grew, so did the feeling of pity, the type of pity you feel for someone who has an incurable disease. His was a selfish illness which only left room for self-pity and carrying out his "duty" to his children.

The only person who ever paid any attention to me was my mother, and a young girl understands when the love she receives is real – then its the only thing that matters.

You could even say that everything is great when you're loved, and that nothing is right when nobody loves you. This is something you learn in no time at all. All your mother has to do is to get cross and give you a stern look, and a huge gaping hole appears before you and an earthquake seems to destroy your world. When she stopped being cross, and I could once again see all her love for me in her eyes, I knew that everything was going to be all right, and that things should always be that way.

I knew that since my mother's death our lives weren't as they should be. A world without Mum seemed all lopsided. Even though I tried to put some order and reason into our day-to-day life so that my brother wouldn't have to do without anything, I knew that this was all false, a sort of caricature of real life. I listened carefully to my brother and corrected him when he talked, to try to get him to stop stuttering. If he started speaking correctly again it would be a sign that everything was back to normal. It didn't work though, and he kept on stuttering, so I didn't have anything to help me to look forward to the future, or to feel hopeful about how things were going to turn out.

I accepted my lot, but even so, I remember that when I reached the age of fourteen I started to feel curiosity to know more about the world outside, and this curiosity soon turned into a real longing. It always seemed perfectly natural for me to live shut off from a world which, according to my father, was "evil" and "hellish". The real world was the one in which the three of us lived, inside the fence that surrounded the farm. All we knew about the outside world was what our father told us, and he didn't like to talk about it.

I can remember something happening once when I was very young, it must have been quite soon after we'd shut ourselves off, and my father still let me go out every now and then, to the hypermarket with my mummy and him. I still remember vaguely riding up and down the aisles in a metal trolley, seeing the stacks of coloured tins and hearing people all around me, chatting away and pushing their trolleys. I remember a girl sitting at a till, and my father handing over a card, and I remember she gave me some sweets. I also remember how my father took them from me, and how he only agreed to give me one after I burst into tears and my mother pleaded with him. For years after I could still remember the lemon flavour of the sweet, and I dreamt that one day I'd be able to taste it again. Father only brought "essentials" from the outside, and sweets were not essential. That's why I have a weakness for lemon sweets, even though I know that they're bad for your teeth.

I also seem to remember vaguely the buildings, cars, the roads, …all seen from inside our car. It was the same car we had always had, and which, thanks to my father tinkering with it every once in a while, could still be used once every two months to go and pick up supplies or whatever other things my father might have to do.

I also think I can remember something about when I was taken to hospital to get treatment for my polio; I remember a white room, and Mummy and Daddy sitting beside the bed.

Nearly everything I knew about the outside world I had learned from my mother. Sometimes we would both be peeling potatoes or cleaning the house, and we would sing the songs she used to teach me. She even knew the same songs in several languages, and that used to drive me crazy. My mother would laugh at me sometimes, I would be just about to break down in tears when she'd change all of a sudden and give me a kiss. She was strong and loving, but that didn't stop her from being naughty every now and then, like a spoilt child. It must have been her way of putting a bit of fun into her life.

I remember once that my father was mowing the grass, and when my mother started to play her cello the spluttering of the motor stopped. It's hard to imagine how lovely the strings of her instrument sounded in that lonely house. It's a pity I could never play as well. I think my mother's excessive fondness for reading novels and singing was a way of getting rid of her tensions and all the sufferings that stemmed from our way of life. I never could, and never will, be able to understand why my mother accepted that lifestyle. I suppose it was the love she felt for my father, but I reckon there must have been a certain amount of weakness on her part as well. It hurts me to think that.

But she sang all the time, and she had a different song for each moment. When she wasn't reading or singing she would chat, and you could see she was nostalgic about the past, because the words "in those days" were always on the tip of her tongue.

I tried to get her to stop doing the housework and tell me things about her life when she was young. She used to pretend that she didn't want to, and to some extent this was true because she didn't want to make my father angry, but if he wasn't around, she would gradually start talking. Those times when Mummy left her reservations aside and slowly started to tell me a story were magical moments, and I would feel a mixture of fear that she would stop and go back to her routine, and surprise at seeing her come alive again.

I've often taken the framed photo of my mother off the sideboard in my room and hugged it against me, singing a song I'd been taught by her while I remember all the details of her past life that she had told me about so often. I imagined new situations where I was Mum, and I travelled to London by plane and Paris by train... A young man in my compartment was reading a newspaper and I was watching the scenery, a closed book resting on my crossed legs. Then the young man folded his paper and looked at me.

Manuel Rivas (1957–)

From ¿Que me queres, amor? (What Do You Want of Me, O Love?), *1995*

O inmenso camposanto da Habana

Eu tamén tiven un tío en América. E agardo telo aínda, a regar rosanovas no Panteón Gallego co seu cubo de cinc.

O meu tío chamábase Amaro e morrera polo menos oito veces antes de morrer. Era un especialista en morrer e sempre o facía con moita dignidade. Da morte volvía perfumado con xabóns La Toja, peiteado á maneira do acordeonista da Orquestra Mallo, cun traxe novo Príncipe de Gales e cunha historia sorprendente. Unha vez fixo unha descrición moi detallada do menú do Banquete Celestial, no que, segundo el, abundaba o lacón con grelos.

¿E había cachola?, preguntou o meu pai con retranca.

¡Home, claro! Unha cabeza de porco en cada mesa, con dúas poliñas de pirixel nas ventas e un colar de margaridas.

¿Que tal tempo ía?

Soleado, pero algo frío. No purgatorio, non. No purgatorio ía un nordés arrepiante. Aquilo é unha uceira desarborada.

Esa capacidade de morrer sen morrer de todo atribuíaa a unha estraña natureza de neno vaqueiro de sangue azul, extremo este que Amaro demostraba en festas partindo o seu nariz, a igual que cristal de xeada, con só facer pinza cos dedos. Esvaraban entón dous azulísimos fíos que sorbía como anís de menta.

Coido, non obstante, que aprendera a morrer no inmenso camposanto da Habana.

Aínda se movía o océano baixo os meus pés cando alguén puxo unha vasoira e un cubo de cinc nas miñas mans. Así contaba el aquela súa primeira viaxe, da aldea de Néboa ao Caribe. Era tan mozo que non coñecía a navalla barbeira. Seguín os pasos de Mingos O' Pego, o paisano ao que me encomendaron meus pais, e con vasoira de palmitos e aquel balde luminoso entrei na intendencia do Cristóbal Colón, o máis principal cemiterio de América. E non saín durante un mes, créalo ou non. O' Pego era un devoto do ron. Tiña toda unha adega oculta nun dos nichos do Panteón Gallego. Mira este defunto, díxome, he, he. E avisoume ben avisado: ¡Ti, nin tocalo, eh rapaz! Corría da súa conta buscarme un cuarto na parroquia dos vivos, pero mentres tanto traballaba alí todo o día e alí durmía, nun cabanote do camposanto, entre coroas de flores e cruces de mármore. Alí aprendín a oír voces e músicas que os demais non escoitaban.

Acurrunchábame no colo de Amaro e o meu medo parecía animalo.

¡Que noites no camposanto da Habana! ¡Indios, negros, galegos! ¡Tambores e gaitas! ¡Todos danzando na noite cálida, mentres O' Pego roncaba sobre almofada de rosanovas e coroas de caraveis! Tiñamos un gato que se facía moi grande pola noite, ocelote ou xaguar, e papaba ratas grandes coma lebres, he, he. ¡La Habana, habanita mía, que bonito é todo na Habana! ¡Ata ser enterrador na Habana era bonito!

Os meus pais rexentaban unha tasca na rúa coruñesa do Orzán, tan mariña a rúa que o océano subía ás veces polo ollo do retrete. E a clientela era fixa, tan fixa que tiña as tazas numeradas. A de Amaro era a 36. Ao contrario que o común, o meu tío bebía en pequenos grolos, delicadamente, achegando con solemnidade a porcelana branca. Logo, miraba con ollos húmidos o pouso do viño ribeiro, como quen mira un dramático bordado. ¡O mundo! ¡Se souberas que pequeno é o mundo, criatura!

¡A ver, paspán, dime! ¿Que é máis vella, a Torre de Hércules ou a catedral de Santiago?, preguntaba na barra a taza número 7.

¡A min. todo, tooodo, impórtame un carallo!, proclamaba a taza 9.

Están as nubes chorando
por un amor que morreu.
Están as rúas molladas
de tanto como choveu.

Quen cantaba era un mariñeiro que non tiña taza numerada e chegara arrastrando unha tormenta que deixou no couzón da porta, ouveando como un can abandonado.

¡Cala a boca, animal!, dixo a taza número 3, que era un deses solitarios mimetizado coa mesa de piñeiro vello e con arañeiras colgando dos ollos.

¿Vai iso por min?, preguntou desafiante o mariñeiro, sacando peito de lobo.

Oia, cabaleiro, mediou oportunamente o meu tío Amaro, ¿coñece vostede A Habana?

¿A Habana? ¡De morro a rabo!, berrou desde a barra. Achegouse logo, picado pola curiosidade. ¡A Habana, ceo santo, que fermosa é A Habana! ¡Bríncame o corazón só con dicila!

E a min dóeme, dixo o tío Amaro nun suspiro. ¿E o cemiterio Cristóbal Colón? ¿Coñece o inmenso camposanto da Habana?

Pois non. ¡Outra rota levaba!

Lástima. Alí fun eu oficial xardineiro maior, explicaba con sentido orgullo o meu señor tío.

Os crisantemos son bos para os mortos, dixo a taza 5.

¡Prefiro as dalias!, proclamou a seguinte.

¡Borrachos!, berrou un solitario que non se tiña, despois dun longo grolo.

¿Hai moito que se veu?, interesábase o mariñeiro.

Foi cando Aquilo. Eu era pobre, pero tiña un dente de ouro, e alguén chegou berrando que a Revolución me sacaría o meu dente de ouro. Aínda o conservo. E abriu a boca para mostrar a prótese dourada ao mariñeiro, quen inclinou a cabeza con moito interese. Cando me dei conta, perdera A Habana, dixo o meu tío despois de rebrillar o dente coa gamuza da lingua.

Nestes casos, comentou o mariñeiro con voz sentenciosa, sempre vai un detrás dos outros e ás veces mete o zoco.

¿A canto sae agora calzarse un dente de ouro?, inquiriu a taza número 12.

¡Non chega coa paga de Nadal!, dixo a 7.

¿E como quedaba A Habana?, preguntou o meu tío con ton ferido.

Despintada... e bonita.

Así a deixei eu. E logo alegraba a voz: ¡Desfollemos a rosa do ribeiro na súa memoria!

Maldita gracia que facían a papá aquelas rondas impagadas. Amaro non tiña un peso e sempre acababa morrendo despois de brindar pola Habana. E así foi. Fartos do seu traxín dun mundo a outro, esta vez os meus pais non lle prepararon velorio, nin houbo perfume, nin peiteado, nin traxe.

Estate aí, ordenou o meu pai, e avísanos cando volva.

Fiquei durmido ao seu carón, pero ao espertar estaba frío e con aspecto de non volver nunca desa viaxe. Tiña un sorriso dolorido e, na boca entreaberta, botábase de menos o seu dente de ouro. Non regresou, por agora, da travesía. Meter metérono nun nicho na aldea de Néboa, pero eu imaxínoo nalgunha alfándega, intentando pagar o billete co seu dente na palma da man como precioso grao de maínzo, e facendo xestións para volver ao inmenso camposanto da Habana.

The Huge Cemetery in Havana

I had an uncle in America, too. And I hope he's still there, watering the roses in the Galician Mausoleum with his zinc bucket.

My uncle's name was Amaro, and he died at least eight times before he actually did so. He was an expert on dying, and always used to do so with a great deal of dignity. From death he returned with the scent of La Toja soap, his hair combed the way the accordionist in the Mallo band used to comb his, with his grey checked jacket on and with some amazing new story. One day he gave an exact description of the menu in the Heavenly Banquet, in which, according to him, there was an abundance of ham and turnip tops.

"And was there pig's head?" my father asked sarcastically.

"Of course! There was a pig's head on every table, with two sprigs of parsley coming out of the nostrils and a necklace of daisies."

"And what was the weather like?"

"Sunny, but a bit chilly. But not in purgatory. There, a north-east wind blew. There, it's treeless heathland."

He put his ability to die, without actually dying, down to a strange kind of blue-blooded cowboy, a fact which he always proved to be true in the fairs, breaking his nose as if it was made of thin frost-like glass, just by pinching his nose. Then two thin threads of blue blood ran down his nose, which he swallowed as if it was a peppermint drink.

Nevertheless, I gather he had learnt to die in the huge cemetery in Havana.

"The ocean was still heaving under my feet, when someone put a zinc bucket and a broom in my hands." That's how he used to talk about his voyage from the village of Néboa to the Caribbean. He was so young he had never used a razor-blade. "I followed in the footsteps of Mingos O'Pego, the compatriot to whom he was commended by his parents, and with the broom made from palm leaves and the shiny bucket I got a job in the Cristóbal Colón Cemetery, the largest in America. And I didn't leave until a month had passed, believe it or not. O'Pego was so given to drinking rum that he had a cellar full of spirits hidden under one of the tombs in the Galician mausoleum. "Look at this dead man," he used to say, and he threatened me: "Don't you dare touch this, my boy." It was his responsibility to provide me with a room in the land of the living, but the rest of the time day I worked there from dawn till dusk, and afterwards I slept in a shack in the cemetery, among floral tributes and marble crosses. There, I learnt to listen to voices and music others could not even hear.

I curled up on Amaro's lap and my fears seemed to lift his spirits.

What nights we spent in the Havana cemetery! Indians, blacks, Galicians! Drums and bagpipes! All of them dancing away the warm nights while O'Pego was snoring on a new rose and carnation pillow. We had a cat which became bigger by night, became a cheetah or a jaguar, and ate rats as big as hares, hee, hee! My own Havana, my own little Havana, how pretty all Havana is! Even being a gravedigger in Havana was great.

My parents ran a bar in a street in La Coruña called Orzan, a street so near the sea that the seawater sometimes surged up through the hole in the floor that was the toilet. And the regular customers were so regular they had their number on the wine-cups. Amaro's was number 36. Unlike what most people did, my uncle sipped wine gently, lifting the white china to his lips. Then he looked with tear-filled eyes at the dregs of Ribeiro wine as if he was looking at a dramatic tapestry design. Oh world! If only you knew how small the world is, my boy!

"Come on, you silly ass, tell me! Which is older, the Tower of Hercules or Santiago Cathedral?" asked cup number 7, who was at the bar.

"As far as I'm concerned, I don't care a fig!" said cup number 9.

The clouds are weeping for a love that is dead.

It's rained so much that the streets are all wet.

The singer of this song was a sailor, whose cup was unnumbered, who had come in dragging in a storm, which he left by the door, howling like a stray dog.

"Shut your trap, you beast!" said cup number 3, who was one of those lonely ones camouflaged by the old pinewood table he sat behind, with sleepy-men in his eyes.

"Is it me you're talking to?" asked the sailor defiantly, puffing out his chest.

"Listen, my man," said my uncle Amaro just in time, "Are you acquainted with Havana?" "Havana? From one end to the other!" he cried from the bar. Then he approached, spurred on by curiosity. "Havana, my God, how beautiful Havana is! My heart skips a beat when I hear the name."

"And it hurts me," said my uncle with a sigh. "And the Cristóbal Colón cemetery? Have you ever been to the huge cemetery of Havana?"

"Well, no, I haven't. I took a different route."

"A pity. I was deputy head gardener," my uncle exclaimed with a certain pride.

"Chrysanthemums are good for the dead," said cup number 5.

"I prefer dahlias," replied the man beside him.

"You load of drunks!" cried out a lonely man who could hardly stand up, after gulping down some more wine.

"Have you been back long?" enquired the sailor.

"It was a long time ago. I was poor, but I had a gold tooth, and someone came along, shouting that the Revolutionaries would remove my gold tooth. I've still got it." And he opened his mouth to show the gold implant to the sailor, who leaned over with great interest. "Then, when I turned back round, I had lost Havana," said my uncle after wiping his tooth with his tongue as a cloth, so as to make it shine.

"In these cases," asserted the sailor, "we follow in each others' footsteps, and sometimes we make crass errors."

"And how much does it cost to fix a gold tooth?" enquired cup number 12.

"Your Christmas bonus wouldn't be enough," said number 7.

"And how was Havana the last time you saw it?" my uncle asked, in a hurt kind of way.

"With the paint chipped off, but pretty all the same."

"The same as how I left it, then." And then his voice cheered up. "Let's drink a toast to her name in Ribeiro wine."

All those unpaid-for drinks didn't amuse my father at all. Uncle Amaro was always broke, and always ended up "dead" after toasting Havana. And so it was. Fed up with dragging him to and fro, from life to death and back, this time my parents did not prepare his laying out, nor his perfuming nor his combing, nor his laying-out suit.

"Stay there," ordered my father, "and let us know when he comes to."

I remained there asleep by his side, but when I woke up he was cold, and looked as if he would never come back from that journey this time. He had a pained smile on his lips, his mouth was half-open, and through the gap you could see his gold tooth was missing. He hasn't returned, as yet, from that voyage. He was taken and put in a niche in the cemetery of the village of Néboa, but I can picture him at some frontier, trying to pay his fare, with his gold tooth in his hand, as if it was an ear of corn, making all the arrangements to go back to the huge cemetery of Havana.

From O lapis do carpinteiro, 1997

A campaña internacional, por esta vez, produciu efecto. No último momento. A petición do goberno de Cuba, ao doutor Da Barca conmutáronlle a pena de morte por unha de cadea perpetua.

El, con aquela maneira de ser que tiña, fixérase como quen di socorro da prisión, contoulle Herbal a María da Visitação. Era coma un menciñeiro deses que curan as espullas a distancia só cunha copla. Mesmo cando estivo cun pé aquí e outro alá, á espera da execución, andara a dar azos a todo o mundo.

Os presos políticos funcionaban coma unha especie de comuna. Xentes que non se falaban na rúa, que se tiñan verdadeira xenreira, como os anarquistas e os comunistas, axudábanse dentro do cárcere. Chegaron a editar xuntos unha folla clandestina que se chamaba *Bungalow*.

Os vellos republicanos, algúns veteranos galeguistas da Cova Céltica e das Irmandades da Fala, co seu aire de antigos cabaleiros da Táboa Redonda, que mesmo comungaban na misa, facían as veces de consello de anciáns para resolveren conflictos e querelas entre os internos. Rematara o tempo das sacas sen xuízo. Os paseadores seguían a facer fóra o traballo sucio, pero os militares decidiran que tamén nas caldeiras do inferno debía imperar unha certa disciplina. Os fusilamentos continuaron previo trámite de consello de guerra sumarísimo.

Con aquela administración paralela, os presos foron mellorando no posible a vida no cárcere. Tomaron pola súa conta medidas de hixiene e de reparto alimentario. Superposto ao horario oficial había un calendario non escrito que era o que de verdade rexía as rutinas diarias. Distribuíronse tarefas con tal organización e eficiencia que moitos presos comúns acudían a eles en petición de axuda. Tralas reixas, había un goberno na sombra, nunca mellor dito, un parlamento asembleario, e uns xuíces de paz. E tamén unha escola de humanidades, un estanco de tabaco, un fondo común que facía de mutua, e un hospital.

O hospital dos presos era o doutor Da Barca.

Había algún persoal máis na enfermería, contoulle Herbal a Maria da Visitacão, pero era el quen levaba o peso de todo. Ata o médico oficial, o doutor Soláns, cando viña de visita, atendía as súas instruccións, coma se dun auxiliar accidental se tratase. Este Soláns a penas abría a boca. Todos sabiamos que se picaba con algunha droga. Víase que lle daba noxo o cárcere, aínda que el estaba por fóra. Parecía sempre ido, abraiado polo lugar no mundo en que lle tocara caer cunha bata branca. Pero o doutor Da Barca trataba a todos os presos polo nome e sabíalles a historia, fosen políticos ou comúns, sen necesidade de ficheiros. Non sei cómo facía. Corríalle máis a cabeza có almanaque.

Un día apareceu na enfermería un enviado da inspección médica militar. Mandou pasar consulta na súa presencia. O doutor Soláns estaba nervioso, coma se se sentise vixiado. E o doutor Da Barca colocouse adrede nun segundo plano, pedíndolle consello, dándolle a iniciativa. De repente, ao inclinarse para sentar, o inspector fixo un estraño e caeulle unha pistola da funda do sobrazo. Nós estabamos alí para ter conta dun preso considerado perigoso, o Gengis Khan, un que fora boxeador e loitador e que andaba algo tocado da cabeza e dábanlle arroutadas. Metérano preso porque matara un home sen querer, só por darlle un susto. Fora nunha exhibición de loita libre. Desque comezara o combate entre o Gengis Khan e un que chamaban o Touro de Lalín, o homiño aquel, sentado na primeira bancada, pasou o tempo berrando que había tongo. ¡Tongo, tongo! Gengis Khan botaba sangue polas ventas, tiña esa habilidade, pero aínda así o repugnante aquel non se deu por satisfeito, coma se o aparatoso da ferida confirmase as súas sospeitas de combate amañado. E entón Gengis Khan tivo unha das súas arroutadas. Colleu ao Touro de Lalín a pulso, un saco de home de cento trinta quilos, e chimpouno con toda a forza enriba do homiño que berraba tongo e que xa nunca máis se sentiu estafado.

A cousa é que, na enfermería, todos miramos para aquela pistola coma se fose unha ra morta. E o doutor Da Barca dixo todo pousón: Caeulle o corazón ao chan, colega. Ata o grandón aquel que levaramos esposado, o Gengis Khan, ficou abraiado; logo ceibou unha gargallada e dixo: Si, señor, un tipo con tres collóns! E dende aquela tívolle tal lei ao doutor Da Barca que andaba sempre a canda del nas horas de patio como se lle gardara as costas e acompañábao ás clases de latín que daba o vello Carré, o das Irmandades da Fala. Gengis Khan empezou a utilizar expresións moi paveras. Dicía de calquera asunto que non era *pataca minuta* e tamén, cando as cousas se torcían, *imos de caspa caída*. Dende entón, Gengis Khan foi coñecido como Pataca Minuta. Medía dous metros, aínda que era algo carrancas, e levaba botas abertas pola biqueira, por onde lle asomaban as dedas como raíces de carballo.

E no cárcere os presos organizaron tamén unha orquestra. Había entre eles varios músicos, bos músicos, o mellor das Mariñas, que fora na República zona de moitos bailes. Os máis deles eran anarquistas e gustaban dos boleros románticos, coa melancolía do lóstrego luminoso. Non había instrumentos pero tocaban co vento e coas mans. O trombón, o saxo, a trompeta. Cadaquén reconstruía no aire o seu instrumento. Percusión había auténtica. Aquel a quen chamaban Barbarito era quen de facer jazz cun penico. Discutiran se chamarlle Orquestra Ritz ou Orquestra Palace, pero ao final impúxose o nome de Cinco Estrelas. Cantaba Pepe Sánchez. Detivérano, con outras ducias de fuxidos, nas adegas dun pesqueiro, a piques de saír rumbo a Francia. Sánchez tiña o don da voz e, cando cantaba no patio, os presos miraban cara á liña sobranceira da cidade, porque a cadea estaba nun devalo entre o faro e a urbe, como dicindo non sabedes o que perdedes. Nese momento, calquera deles pagaría por estar alí. Na garita, Herbal pousaba o fusil, debruzábase na almofada de pedra e pechaba os ollos como o bedel dun teatro da ópera.

From The Carpenter's Pencil, *1997*

The international campaign had its desired effect this time. At the last moment the Cuban government's plea on behalf of Doctor Da Barca meant his death penalty was commuted to that of life imprisonment.

With that character of his, he acted as a kind of helper in the prison, Herbal told Maria da Visitaçao. He was like a witch-doctor, one of those who cures sores from a distance, just with a song. Even when he was on the verge of losing his life, waiting for his execution, he used to give hope to everyone.

The political prisoners worked together as a mutual assistance group. People who did not communicate when they met in the streets, who really hated each other, like the communists and anarchists, helped each other within the prison walls. They even edited a clandestine newsletter called *Bungalow*.

The old Republicans, some of them veteran Galician Nationalists from the Cova Céltiga and the Galician Language Brotherhoods looked very much like those Knights of the Round Table, who could either go to Mass to take communion or become a Council of Elders, resolving conflicts and disputes among inmates. The time of the executions without trial was over. They went on doing the dirty work of taking people "for a walk" and shooting them, but the army people had decided that even in the cauldrons of hell there should be some kind of order. The shootings went on after instant courts marshal.

With that parallel administration existing, the prisoners' living conditions began to improve. They took steps to improve their own hygiene and food supplies. Overlapping with the official schedule, there was another unwritten calendar, which was the one that regulated the daily routines. The chores were assigned with such efficiency that many common prisoners came to them to ask for assistance. Behind bars, there was a "shadow cabinet", a parliamentary assembly, and some justices of the peace. There was also a grammar school, a cigarette shop, a prisoners' co-op that worked like an insurance company, and a hospital.

The inmates' hospital was Doctor Da Barca.

There were some other nursing staff in the infirmary, Herbal told Maria da Visitaçao, it was the doctor who was in charge of everything. Even the official doctor, Doctor Solans, when he came to visit the inmates, followed his instructions, as if he were the doctor's assistant who had come to lend a hand as if by chance. This Doctor Solans hardly said a word. We all knew he took drugs. One could see he couldn't stand the prison, even though he only visited. He always looked absent-minded, overwhelmed by the kind of world he happened to work in, in his white uniform. But Doctor Barca called all the inmates by their first name and knew all their medical records, no matter whether they were political or common prisoners, and he never needed written records. I don't know how he did it. His head was more up to date than a calendar.

One day a representative from the army clinical inspectors arrived. He ordered the doctor to see the patients in his presence. Doctor Solans was very nervous, as if he was being spied on. Doctor Barca deliberately avoided being the centre of attention, asking him for advice and letting him take the initiative. Suddenly, when the inspector was bending down to take his seat, he made a strange movement and a gun dropped from the holster under his arm. The reason why we were there was to watch a very dangerous inmate, "Genghis Khan", who had been a boxer and prize-fighter, who was a bit unpredictable and was prone to occasional fits of anger. He was in prison because he had killed a man, just for giving him a bit of a shock. It was in a wrestling exhibition bout. Since the combat began between Genghis Khan and a man they called the Bull of Lalín, this man, who was sitting in the front row, was calling out constantly that the fight had been rigged. It's a fix! It's a fix! Genghis Khan's nose was bleeding, he was skilled at that, but even so, that fool was not satisfied, as if the extent of his wounds confirmed his suspicions of fraud. And then Genghis Khan had one of his fits. He lifted up the Bull of Lalín as if he was a sack weighing one hundred and thirty kilos, and hurled him against the man who had been protesting with all his might, so he would never again feel he had been cheated.

The thing is that, in the infirmary, we all looked at the gun as if it had been a dead frog. And Doctor Barca said calmly: My friend, your heart has fallen on the floor. Even the huge man who had been taken their in handcuffs, remained motionless, amazed; and then he blurted out: Yes, sir, a man with spunk if ever there was one! And from then on, he became so loyal to Doctor Barca that he used to follow him when he went out to the patio, as if he was his personal bodyguard and accompanied him to old Professor Carré's Latin lessons, the one from the Galician Language Brotherhoods. Genghis Khan began to use very funny expressions. He used to say something was just a "venereal sin" instead of a "venial sin", and when things went wrong, that they were in "flea fall", instead of "free fall". From then on, Genghis Khan was known as "venereal sin." He was six feet tall, even though he was a bit bow-legged, and his boots torn open at the front, where you could see his toes sticking out as if they were the roots of an oak.

In prison, the inmates also got together an orchestra. There were some musicians there, good ones too, the best in the Mariñas area, where a lot of dances had been held in the days of the Republic. Most of them were anarchists, and liked romantic boleros, with all the melancholy of a streak of lightning. There were no instruments, but they played with their breath and their own hands. The trombone, the saxophone and the trumpet. Each one of them played his make-believe instrument in mid-air. Here there was a real percussion section. The one they called Barbarito played jazz with a bed pan. They argued about whether to call it The Ritz Orchestra or the Palace Orchestra, and ended up calling it The Five Stars. The lead singer was Pepe Sánchez. They arrested him, along with another dozen people, in the hold of a fishing boat, when it was about to sail for France. Sánchez had the gift of a fine voice, and when he sang in the prison yard the inmates looked towards the city skyline, because the prison was on a slope between the lighthouse and the town centre, as if saying: You don't know what you're missing. At that moment, anyone in town would have paid to be there. In the sentry-box Herbal put his gun down, settled his head on the stone pillow and closed his eyes as if he was an usher in an opera-house.

From Ningún cisne (No Swan), 1989

Conto

Eu lía o xornal e o neno rebulía.
Decidín adormecelo co conto dun cabalo.
Repetinllo dúas veces.
Outra vez, dixo o neno. Só outra vez.
O conto do cabalo.
E mireino marchar,
sen poder facer nada,
no seu cabalo,
polas chairas inmensas.

Story

I was reading the paper and the child was tossing and turning.
I decided to send him to sleep with the story about a horse.
I told him it twice.
Once more, said the child. Just once more.
The story about the horse.
And, unable to intervene,
I watched him ride away,
on his horse,
across the immense plains.

From Costa da Morte blues, *1995*

Red rose, proud rose, sad rose

Coñecín algúns homes que levaron a bandeira vermella
cando era pecado e fermosa
como baga do acevro.
Eu mesmo tiven unha nas mans, unha bandeira vermella,
cando era pecado e fermosa
coma o bico dunha cegoña.
Oín dicir que hai homes en Calcuta e Soweto
que aínda levan bandeiras vermellas,
fermosas coma camelias nos dentes.
Pero eu hoxe non quería falarvos
da orgullosa, vermella e triste bandeira
que quenceu as mans dos que estaban debaixo,
pecado e fermosa coma a lapa do carbón.
Só quería falar
da baga do acevro,
do bico da cegoña,
da camelia entre os dentes,
da lapa do carbón,
e da orgullosa, vermella, triste rosa de Yeats.

Red rose, proud rose, sad rose

Once I met some men who bore the red flag
when it was sinful and as beautiful
as a holly berry.
I myself once held one, a red flag,
when it was sinful and as beautiful
as a stork's beak.
I have heard that there are men in Calcutta and Soweto
who still bear red flags,
as beautiful as camellias held between the teeth.
But today I didn't want to talk to you
about the proud, red, sad flag
that warmed the hands of the underdogs,
sinful and as beautiful as a coal flame.
I just wanted to talk
about the holly berry,
about the stork's beak,
the camellia held between the teeth,

the coal flame,
and the proud, red, sad rose of Yeats.

Xavier Queipo (1957–)

From Ártico e outros mares, *1990*

Château Saignant (fragmento)

Estás soa na mesa do apartamento parisiense 40, rue Dufour, *rive gauche*, por máis datos. Sei que es infeliz. Estou so na mesa 12 do comedor do cruceiro Sagres. Saberás que soño contigo. Os vaivéns divírtenme. O balance non é igual todos os días malia a presenza de estabilizadores. Admírome descubrindo a súa cadencia, o seu ritmo, a súa amplitude variábel e mesmo regular. O desexo. Volta o desexo. O camareiro nórdico e pesado retírase. Dous mascatos voan no aire. Non lle pidas un *chateâu saignant*. Non. Agora non. O camareiro solícito traeracho e terás que lle sorrir mentres el – profesional – agarda a túa compracencia en perfecto mutismo. Non o pidas.

A estas horas un home de mundo pide un vodka, ou quizais un ron torrado ou máis sensatamente unha copa de *Perrier*, ou nada, ou compaña, ou cama. Pero non un castelo sanguento, que é unha petición absurda.

Achégome á varanda. A néboa vai esvaecendo. Pódese sentir a proa afundíndose no mar e deixando ronseis de escumas ó seu tránsito. A praia. A auga transparente é verde de alga e mar. Os negros. Miles de negros na praia. O mar inzado de algas e de negros. O mar verde cheo de negros que non nadan, só choutan entre as ondas e as algas. A praia xaspeada de algas e de negros. A auga salferíndome a faciana adormecida. A noite. A lúa – branca – ilumínao todo. Reflexa nun mar de negros e de algas. Tremelocen as algas e os negros coas costas rebozadas en area e *noctilucas*. Soño. Tal vez mañá na praia. Soño que ficarás en París. *Wild thing. My little wild thing.* Yen yeré cumbé. Imposíbel regresar. Xa todo serán illas e negros e noites cando remate este cruceiro en Durban. *Wild thing. My little wild thing. Yen yeré cumbé.*

Voume deitar. O camarote é estreito e cheira a gasóleo e ós fumes da cociña. Tentarei durmir. Xa soñei abondo esperto. Sei que un día acordarei tras unha porta e non saberei qué a pechou nin qué é o que, agora a modiño, a abre e se apoia no marco esperando non sei que, ou sinxelamente deixando pasar o aire. Estarei cego, ou morto, ou soñando, e xa tanto me terá quen entre ou saia da miña vida. Pero agora non, agora é tempo de relaxar o meu corpo consumido pola ansia. *È così bella*, dicíasme cando nos amabamos sen freo naquel hotel do que non saïamos porque chovía, ou ía calor, ou simplemente se estaba tan ben así xuntos, amándonos ás ondadas, como cando os cheyennes atacan tomahawk en man, po e cabalos pintados montados a pelo, unha caravana de mulleres camiño do ansiado Oeste, ateigado de aventureiros de lenda, de lendas, de aventureiros e de búfalos.

Nesta hora anguriante, cando as sombras se fan vagas e me enfronto so coas cascudas que saen da cociña sometidas ó furor Cucal do cociñeiro axudante, véxote facendo e refacendo unha carta no teu italiano orixinal, que logo traducirás ó noso común francés cheo de expresións inacadémicas. Tal vez non nunca sexas quen de ma mandar. Eu debería facer o mesmo. Escribirche. Escribirche e non repetir, nunha versión permanente da Odisea, *that my name is no one, no one, anyhow*. *La brume du matain* sobre a cuberta. O espazo baleiro das hamacas recollidas. É moi cedo. Aínda non foi servido o almorzo. Serás o único, e a esas horas un home de mundo pediría un zume de tomate con salsa Perrins e un ovo. Pero ti es do mundo de teu e malia a resaca – só bebedes os perdedores – pedirás un zume de laranxa e o camareiro, nórdico e andróxino, traerache néctar de laranxa e non lle poderás dicir que non, nunca saberá se porque é nórdico ou porque é andróxino. Beberás daquel bebedizo inmundo mentres as primeiras lurpias xa se achegan ás súas mesas, o vello de traxe de liño branco retoma o exemplar do *Financial Times*, e dúas virxes de Brabante (unha sen dúbida chamarase Geneviève e outra Caroline, ou Martha, ou Catherine, pero a outra, seguro que si, que Xenoveva).

Esvaecerá a néboa? Poñeranse as brabantinas coma tizóns? Conseguirá o home do *Financial Times* os favores sexuais do camareiro andróxino? Chegarán os loros a Durban a tempo para o mercado de escravos? Volverei verte, tocarte, esvarar a miña lingua pola praia do teu peito? Si. A néboa non pode durar, nin nas proximidades de Cabo Verde, nin no corazón do nórdico, nin na miña propia ollada.

Château Saignant (extract)

You are alone at the table in your Paris flat, 40 rue Dufour, rive gauche, what is more. I know that you are unhappy. I am alone at table 12 in the dining-room of the liner Sagres. You must know that I dream about you. The pitching and rolling amuses me. The movement is not the same every day despite the stabilizers. I am amazed as I discover its cadence, its rhythm, its variable yet regular amplitude. Desire. Desire returns. The sluggish Nordic steward goes away. Two gannets fly by. Do not ask for a *château saignant*. No. Not now. Do not ask him for it. The solicitous steward will bring it and you will have to smile at him while he – ever the profes-sional – awaits your satisfaction in perfect silence. Do not ask for it.

At this time of day a man of the world asks for a vodka, or perhaps a dark rum or more prudently a glass of *Perrier*, or nothing, or some company, or a bed. But not a Bloody Castle, an absurd thing to ask for.

I walk over to the guard rail. The mist is clearing. The bow can be heard plung-ing into the sea and leaving wakes of foam behind. The beach. The transparent water is green with weed and sea. The blacks. Thousands of blacks on the beach. The sea teeming with weed and blacks. The green sea full of blacks who do not swim, they only leap among the waves and weed. The beach speckled with weed and blacks. The water splashing my sleepy face. The night. The moon – white-illuminates everything. It is reflected in a sea of blacks and weed. The weed and the blacks glint, their backs coated in sand and *noctilucas*. I dream. Perhaps tomorrow on the beach. I dream that you will stay in Paris. *Wild thing. My little wild thing. Yen yeré cumbé*. Impossible to return. Everything will be islands and blacks and nights by the time this cruise finishes in Durban. Wild thing. *My little wild thing. Yen yeré cumbé.*

Off to bed. The cabin is small and smells of diesel oil and kitchen fumes. I shall try to sleep. I have daydreamed enough. I know that one day I shall wake up behind a door, not knowing what shut it nor what it is that, slowly now, opens it and leans against the frame awaiting I know not what, or simply letting the air in. I shall be blind, or dead, or dreaming, and by then it will not matter to me who enters or leaves my life. But not now; now it is time to relax my anxiety-consumed body. *È così bella*, you would say to me when we were making boundless love in that hotel that we never left because it was raining, or it was hot, or simply because it was so good to be together like that, making love in great waves as when the Cheyennes, grasping their tomahawks – dust and painted horses ridden bareback – attack a caravan of women on their way to the longed-for West, packed with legendary adventurers, with legends, with adventurers and with buffaloes.

At this hour of anguish, when the shadows become indistinct and I confront alone the cockroaches that emerge from the kitchen fleeing from the kitchen assistant's Rentokil fury, I see you, writing and rewriting in your native Italian a letter that you will later translate into our shared French, full of unacademic expressions. Perhaps you will never be able to send it to me. I should do the same. Write to you. Write to you and not repeat in a permanent vision of the Odyssey, *that my name is no one, no one, anyhow. La brume du matin* on the deck. The empty spaces left by the cleared-away deckchairs. It is very early. Breakfast has not yet been served. You will be the only one, at that time of day a man of the world asks for a tomato juice with Perrins sauce and an egg. But you are a man of your own world and despite your hangover – only you losers drink – you will ask for an orange juice, and the steward, Nordic and androgynous, will bring you the sickly-sweet sort and you will be incapable of saying no, he will never know whether it is because he is Nordic or because he is androgynous. You will drink that foul concoction while the first witches approach their tables, as does the old man in the white linen suit who picks up the copy of the *Financial Times* again, and two virgins from Brabant (one will doubtless be called Geneviève and the other Caroline, or Martha, or Catherine, but the first will definitely be Geneviève).

Will the mist clear? Will the little women from Brabant go as brown as berries? Will the man with the *Financial Times* gain the sexual favours of the androgynous steward? Will the parrots reach Durban in time for the slave market? Will I see you again, touch you, run my tongue over the beach of your breast? Yes. The mist cannot last, not in the environs of Cape Verde, nor in the heart of the Nordic man, nor in the way I see things.

Antón R. Reixa (1957–)

From Historias do rock-and-roll (Stories of Rock-and-Roll), 1985

murrai anda a matinar...

murrai anda a matinar nun estudio profundo sobre
a ignorancia mais non quere adicarse a escribilo
ata non adquirir maior descoñecemento das cousas
si si as toallitas para
despois de

murrai is pondering...

murrai is pondering a profound study on
ignorance but does not want to devote himself to writing it
until he acquires greater general unknowledge
yes yes the paper towels for
after

madagascar lalín...

madagascar lalín namibia ortigueira chad mondoñedo guiné bissau
cambados costa de marfil monforte senegal corcubión burundi
mondaríz zambia camariñas malí guitiriz camerún a estrada gabón
cerdedo etiopía ribadavia níxer negreira mauritania boimorto serra
leoa tomiño lesoto becerreá libia a fonsagrada somalia trasmiras
kenia arzúa congo xinzo sudán rianxo liberia soutomaior togo
forcarei ghana laza zaire melide tanzania mos uganda santa
comba angola vilardevós
alto volta
a lúa ponse saharaui en vigo
hostia en dios cristo en biafra

madagascar lalín...

madagascar lalín namibia ortigueira chad mondoñedo guinea-bissau
cambados ivory coast monforte senegal corcubión burundi
mondariz zambia camariñas mali guitiriz cameroon a estrada gabon
cerdedo ethiopia ribadavia niger negreira mauritania boimorto sierra
leone tomiño lesotho becerreá libya a fonsagrada somalia trasmiras

kenya arzúa congo xinzo sudan rianxo liberia soutomaior togo
forcarei ghana laza zaire melide tanzania mos uganda santa comba
angola vilardevós
upper volta
the moon sets saharan in vigo
holy shit in biafra christ

Ramiro Fonte (1957–2008)

From Pasa un segredo (A Secret Passes), *1988*

Antes que ti foses viaxeiro

Cando veñas ó norte, non preguntes
Por unha casa vella;
Pola sombra de seu, nas calexas deitada
Como se deita o inverno
Con derrotados meses sobre o mundo e as choivas.

Cando veñas ó norte, vello amigo,
Non preguntes ás brétemas que furtan
Os segredos das cousas;
Non interrogues fondas baixamares
– E menos nun agosto de altas lúas –,
Nin os bosques de antano,
Onde soñan as faias e as carballeiras nobres.

Hai unha casa branca. Agardareite
Aireando os seus cuartos,
Abrindo as contras, para que a luz reciba
Aquilo que foi meu;
Ordenando papeis dos meus esquezos,
Libros daquela, versos
Por rematar aínda,
Escuros calendarios que escribiron
Anos mozos e nomes de rapazas.

E esta canción que é túa, e escribín para ti,
Antes que ti foses viaxeiro,
Moito antes quizais
De que tiveses sede, e decidises

Partir, soñar, ama-lo corazón
Destas palabras poucas.

Cando chegues ó norte, non preguntes.
Dirache o teu desexo que eu estaba agardando.

Before you were a traveller

When you come to the north, do not ask
for an old house;
for its shadow, cast in the alleys
as winter is cast
with defeated months over the world and the rains.

When you come to the north, old friend,
do not ask the mists that steal
the secrets of things;
do not question deep low tides
– and even less in an August of high moons –
or the forests of yesteryear,
where the beeches and the noble oak-glades dream.

There is a white house. I shall be awaiting you,
airing its rooms,
opening the shutters, so that the light can receive
what was once mine;
ordering papers fallen into oblivion,
books of those times, verses
yet to be completed,
obscure calendars inscribed
by years of youth and names of girls.

And this song that is yours, that I wrote for you,
before you became a traveller,
perhaps long before
you felt thirsty, and decided
to leave, to dream, to love the heart
of these few words.

When you reach the north, do not ask.
Your desire will tell you I was waiting.

From Luz do mediodía (Midday Light), *1995*

Luces de mediodía

O mediodía escribe
as mellores palabras sobre a noite;

no seu xardín a flor
amígase coa estrela insubornable.

Nas copas en que xuntos afogamos
as augas moribundas doutras lúas,
xa estaba a luz
serena para sempre, presentida.

Aqueles ollos meus
que nunca se cansaron de mirarte.

Midday lights

Midday writes
the best words about night;

the flower in its garden
is reconciled with the incorruptible star.

In the wineglasses where together we drowned
the dying waters of other moons,
the light was now
serene forever, presaged.

Those eyes of mine
that never tired of gazing at you.

Pilar Pallarés (1957–)

From Livro das devoracións (Book of Devorations), *1996*

renazo nos límites acuosos...

renazo nos límites acuosos
entre a palabra sombra
e o terror do abandono

soérgome da nai que aínda me nutre
deste silencio escuro que me bebe
e evádome nun fío sensitivo
nun regueiro de lava acre e salobre

e grítome e suplícome
nocturna flor crescida do desexo
pouta de tigre que a hora despreguiza
e tanxe nos meus nervos

renázome e reiníciome
e unha maré sen tregua en min reinvento
e refágome en lama
nunha estrela de sangue acedo e quente
neste medo nupcial en tanto visgo

regrésome e suplíciome
e digo-me que son
que teño un nome
unha inicial de lume
unha letra escarlate que me sinala a frente para os deuses

retorno aos meus cartílagos
a esta esfera solar que o inverno esfuma
a un ídolo de bronce balorento
a unha espiral larvada
á miña fame

i am reborn on the watery boundaries...

i am reborn on the watery boundaries
between the word shadow
and the terror of abandonment

i raise myself a little above the mother who still nurtures me
above this dark silence that drinks me
and i evade myself on a sensitive thread
on a stream of acrid salty lava

and i shout at myself and i beg myself
nocturnal flower grown from desire
tiger's claw that the hour rouses
and plays on my nerves

i revive myself and reinitiate myself
and i reinvent a relentless tide in myself
and i remake myself in mud
in a star of blood bitter and warm
in this nuptial fear in so much birdlime

i return myself and torment myself
and tell myself that i am
that i have a name
an initial of fire
a scarlet letter that marks my brow for the gods

i return to my cartilages
to this solar sphere that winter darkens
to an idol of ancient bronze
to an insidious spiral
to my hunger

No resplandor das horas...

No resplandor das horas
son o escriva sentado
e agardo a que o día esqueza
na miña tabuleta
un risco diagonal, o rosto dun efebo,
algo de sangue e especias,
o aroma da artemisa,
as coxas imantadas dunha muller que danza.

Inhábil para a vida,
transcribo o que me excede,
fixo en trazos esguíos o amor e os seus detritus,
a contracción das bocas no leito e na batalla,
as pupilas dos gatos.

Que os deuses me perdoen a renuncia
ao caudal da existencia:
deixo escoar as augas entre os dedos
e a miña xuventude,
e en tanto dilapido os meus minutos
reteño outras historias,
acaparo outros corpos
e aos seus membros precarios dou a forma do eterno.

Quizais un día futuro,
cando as fauces do tempo
tiveren devorado a miña carne
e a dos vermes da miña carne
e a xeración seguinte,
alguén descorra o po da tabuleta
e no fulgor extinto dos seus signos
me descifre,
para saber que eu fun o efebo e a doncela,
o elmo do guerreiro,
a raíz da artemisa,
a sede do felino,
o crisantemo.

In the splendour of the hours...

In the splendour of the hours
I am the seated scribe
and I wait for the day to forget
on my signboard
a diagonal line, the face of an ephebe,
traces of blood and spices,
the aroma of wormwood,
the magnetized thighs of a woman dancing.

Useless for life,
I transcribe what goes beyond me,
I fix in slender strokes love and its detritus,

the contraction of mouths in bed and in battle,
the pupils of cats.
May the gods forgive me for my renunciation
of the rivers of existence:
I let the waters slip through my fingers,
as well as my youth;
and while I waste my minutes
I retain other stories,
I hoard other bodies
and to their precarious members I give the form of the eternal.

Perhaps one future day,
when the jaws of time
have devoured my flesh
and the flesh of the worms of my flesh
and the following generation,
someone will brush the dust off my signboard,
and in the extinct glow of its signs
will decipher me,
to discover that I was the ephebe and the girl,
the helmet of the warrior,
the root of the wormwood,
the thirst of the cat,
the chrysanthemum.

Gonzalo Navaza (1957–)

From Erros e Tánatos (Errors and Thanatos), *1996*

Bull & Mignonne

Este tipo que ves aquí – dicía Moreiras estendendo sobre a mesa un recorte de xornal en alemán – é Emiliano Zingarelli, un italiano que coñecín en Suíza, atravesando os Alpes.

Era unha tira estreita e longa, xa medio desgastada polas pregaduras. Na marxe dereita, escritos en tinta vermella coa descoidada caligrafía do propio Moreiras, podíanse ler con dificultade a data e mailo nome do xornal, *Die Zeitung*, de Zurich. Nunha foto grande víase unha aristocrática mansión con porche de columnas brancas. Noutra máis pequena, o retrato dun home de trinta e poucos anos.

– Coñecino a primeiros de decembro do oitenta e oito – continuou dicindo –. Unha boa época para min aquela. A miña irmá Lucía andaba medio enleada con Rafael Vaz, cando Rafael Vaz aínda pintaba moito na Televisión Galega, e de cando en cando caíame algún encargo como axudante de producción en gravacións de campo. Nesa ocasión estiveramos no Ticino suízo, preto de Lugano, filmando unha reportaxe sobre certa pinacoteca privada da que se dicía, daquela era aínda un rumor, que ía ser vendida, ou arrendada, ou cedida ó Estado español. Despachámo-lo traballo en dúas intensas xornadas, moito antes do previsto, e cando os outros colleron o avión de volta eu resolvín quedar un días por alá e facer algo de turismo.

A primeira tarde boteina enteira no meu cuarto, entregado á nugalla. Á mañá seguinte, antes de raia-lo día, abandonei o hotel sen proxectos definidos, co meu cartón da SBB para viaxar en tren durante unha semana, a tarxeta de crédito na carteira e por toda equipaxe un pequeno bolso e o paraugas. Na estación non parei demasiado: o que me levou entrar no posto das revistas e mercar *Il Corriere del Ticino* e unha guía dos camiños de ferro suízos. Saín ás plataformas, bebín a correr un potente café negro en vaso de plástico, ripei dos expositores algúns folletos turísticos e saltei literalmente ó primeiro tren que saía: un expreso en dirección a Interlaken. Non era mal destino, a xulgar polo que dicían os folletos, que prometían con lambida prosa publicitaria o íntimo pracer de sentirse no teito de Europa. Podería hospedarme nun hoteliño e descansar un par de días, e se acaso facer algúns dos paseos que recomendaban "por carreiros serpeantes ó pé das neves milenarias, a través de praderías virxes onde florece o edelweiss." O traxe oficial de paseante alpino (sombreiro tirolés, pantalón curto con tirantes, medias de la ata o xeonllo, caxato de pegureiro, zapatóns...) podíase alugar en calquera oficina de turismo ou nos servicios de información da SBB.

Cando cheguei a Interlaken, sen embargo, tiven que cambiar de idea. Había unha néboa mestísima que non só ocultaba os famosos cumes, senón que mesmo difuminaba os perfís dos magníficos hoteis. Aínda por riba non levaba a roupa axeitada e ía unha viruxe que tradeaba os ósos, de maneira que botei na cidade unha hora escasa. O xusto para xantar de pé unha especie de longaínza nun barciño, percorrer de présa algunhas rúas morto de frío e tomar unha infusión con ron na cafetería dun requintado hotel onde certo célebre músico romántico vivira os seus últimos anos.

Pouco despois estaba outra vez na estación, tratando de escoller un destino diante dos paneis electrónicos. Agora inclinábame máis ben pola parte francesa, onde imaxinaba que atoparía mellor clima, ademais da vantaxe do idioma. Mentres consideraba as ringleiras de luces vermellas que se acendían e apagaban no mapa conforme calcaba un ou outro botón no taboleiro, achegóuseme por detrás este mesmo individuo que aparece na foto e comezou a falarme en italiano:

"Vexo que quere ir a Montreux, amigo... Non lle aconsello agardar polo Panoramic-Express, porque nesta época do ano xa é noite dentro de hora e media. No das 15.17 terá igualmente unhas vistas magníficas e chegará moito antes."

Estendeume a man e presentouse como Emiliano Zingarelli, veneciano de Marghera e veciño de Lausanne, fotógrafo de prensa. Ía para Montreux. Eu tatexei o meu nome dándolle a man. Como non se me ocorría unha idea mellor, díxenlle que ía para Montreux tamén, e el, satisfeito de ter adiviñado o meu propósito, empezoume a tratar con total confianza.

Tomárame por italiano polo xornal que levaba, pero axiña notou a miña torpeza na súa lingua. Era un tipo simpático e locuaz, con media melena crecha, sorriso fácil e enormes ollos claros, aínda que na foto non se aprecia ben. Falaba arqueando alternativamente as cellas e subliñaba cada saída con carantoñas de pallaso. Despois de lle explicar eu de ónde viña e a qué me dedicaba, xa cunhas cervexas na man mentres agardabamos no bar da estación a hora do noso tren, chegou a pronunciar entre risas algunhas frases procaces en galego, aprendidas, segundo dixo, dunha moza que tivera, galega de Portonovo. Polas olladas predatorias que botaba a cada muller que entraba ou saía decateime de que era un auténtico obseso, pero tamén entendín, polas correspondentes chiscadelas de ollo con que buscaba a miña complicidade, que me tomara a min por outro. "As centroeuropeas tolean polos latinos...", díxome, e apelou á autoridade, cómo non, do seu famoso paisano Giacomo Casanova. Eu contestei en van dicindo que as miñas faccións e a cor da pel me aproximaban máis á Suabia ca ó Mare Nostrum, pero el ignoraba as miñas réplicas e fiou un curioso razoamento que emparentaba a cultura mediterránea e o catolicismo coas capacidades amatorias. Facíao con tanta gracia e vehemencia que non me quedou máis remedio ca asentir.

Media hora máis tarde, estando xa os dous confortablemente instalados nun vagón para fumadores e o tren a punto de arrancar, vimos a través da ventá chegar á plataforma unha muller alta, loura, fermosa, camiñando envolta nun abrigo de peles de cor branca. Tras ela, un chofer fardado de almirante, teso coma un fuso, turraba dunha voluminosa maleta e un equipo de esquí. O Emiliano sinaloumos cun aceno de cine mudo e volveume chisca-lo ollo.

Abriuse a porta do noso vagón e subiu a muller. Tamén entrou con ela o chofer, que a axudou a desprenderse do abrigo antes de arromba-la maleta e os esquís sobre a rede e retirarse respectuosamente. O meu compañeiro comezou entón a facer caretas para min pondo os ollos en branco e cousas polo estilo así que viu a suxestiva figura da loura a corpo xentil.

Viña tan perfumada que esparexía por todo o vagón un recendo de madeira preciosa. Mentres se acomodaba no asento, xusto á miña altura pero da outra banda do estreito corredor (o Emiliano viña ó meu lado, contra a ventá), dirixiume unha ollada fugaz que non souben cómo interpretar.

O tren iniciou a marcha axiña, coa proverbial puntualidade dos trens suízos. A nosa veciña abatera o encosto do asento e puxérase a follear unha revista de modas, e ó cabo duns minutos empezoume a parecer que de cando en vez miraba para min de esguello, tusindo lixeiramente. Ó primeiro pensei que eran figuracións miñas, pero pouco a pouco fun convencéndome do contrario. Tamén se deu de conta o Emiliano, que me deitou no oído con voz de experto:

"Douche un cuarto de hora. Pasado ese prazo, se non fixeches nada cámbiasme de sitio e déixasme a min."

Eu mireino con ollos atónitos. Reparou na miña confusión e achegóuseme outra vez á orella para enumerarme co polgar e o índice o seu par de verdades indubidables: aquela beleza botárame o ollo e o meu deber era actuar. Eu escachei a rir: "¿O meu deber de qué..., de católico, de latino?" Aquilo xa me estaba empezando a pór nervioso. "O teu deber de home", dixo el todo serio, sen vacilar.

"Se cadra encontroume parecido con alguén", argumentei. O Emiliano burlouse da miña inxenuidade. As olladas da outra eran cada vez máis descaradas e elocuentes, e conforme aumentaba a súa insistencia maior era a miña turbación. Nun momento sostívenlle a mirada e aí si que quedei entalado, porque era unha muller de beleza inquietante. Tiven que disimular, baixa-la cabeza e pecha-los ollos, coma se quixese durmir. A ela non lle debeu de facer moita gracia o meu comportamento evasivo. Diríase que xa se ía contaxiando do meu nerviosismo, porque se movía intranquila e pasaba con precipitación as follas da revista. De alí a un pouco ergueuse do asento e atravesou lentamente o corredor en dirección ós servicios. Emiliano seguiuna coa mirada, arregalando os ollos, ata que se perdeu ó fondo do vagón. Logo virouse para min e mostroume o reloxo:

"Quédanche once minutos."

Debían de quedar unicamente tres ou catro cando regresou ela de novo polo corredor adiante, agora coa melena recollida, envolta na súa nube de perfume. Ó pasar ó meu lado creo que me rozou levemente a mantenta, e así que se acomodou outra vez no seu sitio atrevinme a dirixirlle un sorriso.

Nesas fixo o tren a súa primeira parada. Mentres a loura andaba a buscar algunha cousa no interior do bolso de man, tal vez un cigarro, atraeron a miña atención unhas voces que proviñan da plataforma, falando algo que semellaba galego. Cando se abriu a porta decateime de que o que falaban era portugués. Un mozo robusto, moreno, o pelo recollido en cola na caluga, enfundado nunha gabardina longa, ó brazo unha especie de macuto militar, despedíase da parella que ficaba na plataforma. O mozo entrou no vagón a grandes pasos, facendo soa-las botas de tacón alto, e xa ía colocarse tres ou catro asentos máis alá da fila que ocupabamos nós cando de súpeto viu que a nosa veciña estaba ollando para el cun cigarro sen prender na boca. Reaccionou de contado e acudiu solícito cun acendedor electrónico de chama azul.

"¿Vai para Gstaad, a esquiar?", preguntou mentres a outra prendía lentamente o cigarro rodeando coas dúas mans a man que lle ofrecía lume. "Eu son un fanático do esquí."

Falaba un perfecto francés con voz aveludada de galán de cine. Emiliano deume un golpe co cóbado e botoume unha ollada fulminante cando o portugués comezou a dicir:

"¿Non lle importa se sento ó seu lado, señorita?, non hai cousa máis bonita que viaxar con bonita compañía."

Mentres facían a presentación (Charlie Fernandés, ou algo así, tanto gusto, Dénise Le Dantec, o mesmo digo), Emiliano miraba para min contendo a risa e eu enxerguei nos seus ollos un aquel de desprezo. Baixei a cabeza, engruñeime no asento e, con máis sorpresa que rabia, dediqueime a pór oídos á conversa da nova parella.

O portugués levou a iniciativa nos primeiros momentos, pero ó pouco xa era a loura a dona da situación e el limitábase a articular breves comentarios ou respostas monosilábicas. Ela falaba dun xeito acelerado, saltaricante, compulsivo, e en tan alta voz que case se podería segui-lo parrafeo desde o outro extremo do vagón. Referiu atropeladamente que viña de pasar un tempo nun hospital en St. Gallen e que andaba co proxecto de escribir un libro sobre o poder curativo das pirámides. Tamén falou de que tiña problemas familiares porque estivera perdidamente namorada do seu padrasto, e da súa nai dixo que era unha puta odiosa e noxenta. Cando explicou que fora a Sant Gallen para esquece-la morte dun pianista ase-xuado que a pretendía e que acabara suicidándose por amor a ela, eu mirei para o Emiliano refungando, dando a entender que o portugués nos librara dunha boa.

Resultaba divertido oíla, laretando sen parar, saltando dun tema a outro seguido, enfiando as frases e os desatinos. "Agora os médicos recoméndanme descanso e moitas festas e diversións", repetiu un par de veces entre gargalladas. Pareceume, aínda que non me atrevía a mirar directamente, que a esas alturas xa estaba acariñando o brazo do portugués.

"¿Dixeches que ías a Montreux?", preguntoulle.

Respondeu que ía a Chateau d'Oex, onde traballaba de recepcionista nun hotel.

"Eu vou a Chamby. Unha casa preciosa. Ata o martes vou estar soa. ¿Que pasa se non vas ó teu hotel e vés comigo a Chamby?"

El tardou en contestar que non podía faltar ó traballo, porque non só lle descon-taban o soldo correspondente a cada día de ausencia senón que penalizaban as fal-tas cunha especie de multa. Entón ela sacou do bolso un talonario de cheques e pasoullo polo nariz ó tempo que lle ofrecía por cada día que a acompañase o salario semanal dun recepcionista de hotel de categoría.

"E de propina outras sorpresas relacionadas coa paixón", engadiu.

Con aquela oferta o portugués xa perdeu toda reserva e creo que comezou a aloumiñar tamén os xeonllos e as coxas da muller. Pero entón ela apartoulle o brazo suavemente, ergueuse, "desculpa un momento, vou á toilette", e saíu ó corredor lucindo a súa linda figura.

Aínda non se perdera na porta do fondo cando Emiliano me fixo ademán para que lle cambiase o sitio. Para a miña sorpresa, comezou a falarlle ó portugués:

"Señor – espetoulle con absoluta naturalidade –, permítame que me presente. Son Emiliano Zingarelli, psiquiatra. Este – dixo sinalando para min – é o meu colega o doutor Hergé. Vimos acompañando a demoiselle Le Dantec. Xa advertiría vostede que non anda ben dos nervios. Quero felicitalo porque está sabendo seguirlle a conversa moi ben, e prevílo de que en determinadas circunstancias adoita ter comportamentos agresivos e perigosos. Aquí o doutor Hergé pode con-firma-lo que lle digo."

Eu atrevinme a asoma-la cabeza para asentir. Emiliano continuou:

"Hai dous anos, en Zurich, chantoulle un bolígrafo na barriga a un mozo que acababa de coñecer nunha discoteca. O mozo morreu desangrado e ós avogados non lles foi difícil cambia-lo cárcere polo hospital psiquiátrico de St. Gallen, ó que pertencémo-lo doutor Hergé e mais eu. Durante ano e medio foi unha interna perigosísima, pero nos últimos meses comezou a mellorar e iniciáronse os trámites para un réxime aberto. Onte deixou o hospital por primeira vez despois de todo este tempo, e esta mañá xa provocou un pequeno incidente. Levámola sedada, con quince miligramos de valium en vea, pero dúranlle pouco os efectos. De tódolos xeitos, se segue vostede como ata aquí, procurando non contradicila, non haberá problemas."

Ó portugués aquela información deixouno algo contrariado. Calaba coma un peto e escoitaba con atención. Emiliano faláballe de vagar, modulando a voz, moi posto no seu papel de psiquiatra:

"Por último – engadiu con extrema cortesía –, quero pedirlle un favor. Cando cheguemos á súa estación, procure que non se note con antelación que vai descender. Agarde ata que o tren pare por completo e entón recolla rapidamente a súa equipaxe e baixe axiña. Se Dénise reacciona mal, xa nos ocupamos nós dela."

Cando Dénise regresou polo corredor, o portugués mirou alternativamente para ela e para nós con ar de desconfianza e no seu rostro acendeuse o rubor. Ela ocupou o asento con despreocupación e retomou a latricada interrompida, falando agora da súa devoción pola música de Mendelssohn e do emocionada que se sentía por volver á casa de Chamby, onde a agardaban Bull e Mignonne, dous dobermann que criara desde cadeliños.

"Coma se fosen fillos meus. O que máis quero no mundo."

O portugués foi reducindo a súa participación na conversa ata deixala en esporádicos acenos de significado impreciso. Creo que entón foi ela quen pasou ó ataque, pois pareceume ver que se puña a acariciarlle a entreperna con lascivas maneiras.

Aquilo foi seguramente demasiado forte para o coitado recepcionista, que se levantou dirixíndonos unha mirada queixosa e saíu entre desculpas en dirección ó servicio. Eu a duras penas puiden reprimi-las gargalladas e Emiliano aproveitou para intercambiar un par de sorrisos e mesmo algunhas frases coa muller.

O portugués decidira encastelarse no reducido compartimento da toilette e só asomou o fociño inesperadamente un tempo despois, nunha parada, agarrando dun golpe o seu macuto e desaparecendo en catro alancadas pola porta para fóra. A loura ergueuse no asento sen dar creto ós seus ollos, e dirixíndose a Emiliano laiouse anoxada e estupefacta:

"¡Non hai nin dez minutos estaba disposto a pasar uns días comigo en Chamby!"

"Non tódolos recepcionistas de hotel saben estar á altura das circunstancias cando se encontran cunha muller fermosa", pronunciou melosamente Emiliano, erguéndose e estendendo a man dereita: "Emiliano Zingarelli, dramaturgo; Emiliano, para servila."

Cando ela tamén lle tendeu a man dicindo o seu nome, el colleulla con delicadeza e bicoulla. Logo, sen soltarlle a man, convidouna a tomar algo no vagón restaurante.

Regresaron ó cabo dunha boa miga, collidiños da man, tal como foran, cando o tren entraba na estación de Chamby. Mentres recollían as equipaxes, Emiliano presentouma como o amor da súa vida e a min presentoume como director de orquestra.

"Do Finisterrae de Galicia, a verdadeira patria de Colón", díxolle.

Desde a porta do vagón, coa maleta e os esquís da loura ó lombo, despediuse de min berrándome un *ciao* renarte e erguendo o polgar co puño pechado. Supuxen que non o volvería ver nunca máis e estaba no certo.

Cinco días despois, no avión que me traía de Zurich a Santiago, folleando distraído os xornais que repartían a bordo, abrín *Die Zeitung* e dei con esta cara que me resultou familiar. Ó principio non o recoñecín, tan circunspecto e con gravata, pero axiña caín da burra cando vin que os titulares facían referencia a un fotógrafo italiano. Non había dúbida: Emiliano cuspido. Lin e relín o texto alemán por ver se daba entendido algo e atopei o nome: Emiliano Zingarelli. O mesmo. A casualidade quería permitir dese xeito que eu puidese conservar unha foto súa, aínda que fose collida da prensa, para ilustra-la lembranza daquela viaxe en tren.

Arrinquei a folla, dobreina e gardeina na carteira. Aínda me veu a risa ben de veces durante o resto da viaxe lembrando o meu encontro con aquel curioso tipo, os detalles da historia da loura perfumada e as artes con que escorrentara ó portugués.

Esa mesma noite, en Santiago, tomando unhas copas co meu amigo Lema, conteille isto mesmo que che estou contando. Eu xa nin recordaba que Lema sabe alemán, pero cando saquei a folla da carteira para mostrarlle a foto, colleuma con ollos abraiados e comezou a traducir: "Fotógrafo italiano devorado por dous dobermann no xardín dunha mansión en Chamby..."

Bull & Mignonne

"This man you can see here," said Moreira, laying out a German newspaper on the table, "is Emiliano Zingarelli, an Italian I met in Switzerland while crossing the Alps."

It was a long narrow article, torn at the folds. In the right hand margin, written in red ink, in Moreira's own careless handwriting, you could barely read the name and date of the newspaper, *Die Zeitung*, Zurich. In a large photograph you could see an aristocratic mansion with a porch and two white columns. In another smaller one there was the face of a man in his early thirties.

"I met him at the beginning of December of '88," he continued. "That was a good time for me. My sister Lucía was sort of half engaged to Rafael Vaz, when he was still someone important in Galician Television. And from time to time I could get a job as assistant producer filming on location. On that occasion we were in the Swiss part of Tiziano, near Lugano, filming a documentary about a private museum which, it was said, was going to be sold (at that time it was still just a rumour) to the Spanish government. We finished the job in two busy days, much sooner than we had planned, and when our colleagues took the plane back I decided to stay on for a few days to travel around.

"The first afternoon I stayed in my hotel room lazing about. The following morning, before sunrise, I left the hotel without any real plan in mind, with my SBB rail pass for a week's travel, my credit card in my wallet and my luggage: a small suitcase and an umbrella. I didn't have to wait long at the station, but I popped into a magazine store just long enough to buy *Il Corriere del Ticino* and a Swiss rail map. I went out onto the platform and drank a strong coffee from a plastic cup, took a few brochures from the racks and literally leapt onto the first train leaving: an express bound for Interlaken. It wasn't a bad route, at least according to the brochures, which spoke in glowing terms of the profound pleasure of finding oneself on 'the roof of Europe'. I could stay at a small hotel and rest there for a couple of days, and perhaps take one of those walks recommended along those 'winding paths at the foot of the eternal snows, through virgin meadows where the Edelweiss blooms.' The typical dress of the Alpine walker, (Tyrolean hat, shorts with braces, woollen knee-length stockings, walking stick and walking boots) could be hired in a tourist office, or at the SBB's own information offices.

"When I reached Interlaken, however, I was forced to change my plans. There was a thick fog, which not only hid the famous summits, but also blurred the outline of the magnificent hotels. To make matters worse, I was ill-dressed, and a cold wind chilled me to the bone, so as a result I spent less than an hour in that town, just long enough to eat a kind of long thin sausage in a small bar, standing up, hurry through some of its streets, freezing cold as I was, and have a herbal tea with rum in a cafeteria that was part of a posh hotel where some famous Romantic musician had spent his last years.

"Not long after I was back at the station, in front of the electronic display boards trying to choose a destination. Now I was more inclined to go to the French part, where I hoped to find better weather, apart from the fact that I knew the language better. While I was watching the lines of red lights that winked on and off on the rail map as I pressed one or another of the buttons on the board, somebody approached me from behind. It was the man in the photo, and he began to speak to me in Italian. 'I imagine you want to go to Montreux,' he said. 'I wouldn't recommend you wait for the panoramic express because at this time of year it gets dark within an hour and a half. On the 15.17 you'll see magnificent views just the same and you'll arrive much earlier.'

"He stretched out his hand and introduced himself as Emiliano Zingarelli, a Venetian from Marghera, a citizen of Lausanne, and a press photographer by trade. He was on his way to Montreux. I stammered out my name while we shook hands. As I had nothing better to do I told him I was going to Montreux as well, and the man, well-pleased at having guessed my intention, began to treat me as if we were close friends.

"He had taken me for an Italian because of the newspaper I was carrying, but he soon noticed how I stumbled over the words. He was a witty and talkative fellow-traveller, with longish curly hair, an easy smile and huge pale eyes, though one doesn't get this impression from the photograph. He talked and talked, arching his eyebrows alternately and exaggerated every gesture in a clownish way. After explaining where I was from and what I did for a living (we had glasses of beer in our hands while we waited for the train at the station bar) he managed to pronounce some sentences in Galician, chuckling as he did so, which he had learnt, he said, from a Galician girlfriend of his from Portonovo.

"From the way he looked at all the women coming in and out of the bar, I realized he was a real womanizer, and I also understood, by the way he winked at me with an air of complicity, that he thought I was another. 'Central European women go mad about Latin men', he told me, and cited his fellow-countryman Giacomo Casanova as an example. I answered in vain that my features and complexion were more those of a Swede than of someone from the Mare Nostrum, but he ignored my reasons and resorted to a saying that related Mediterranean culture, Catholicism and the ability to seduce. He did it so wittily and convincingly that I had no alternative but to agree.

"Half an hour later, and with both of us seated in a smokers' compartment, and the train on the point of leaving, we observed, through the window, a beautiful, tall, blonde lady walking along the platform wrapped in a fur coat. Behind her was a chauffeur in an admiral's uniform, as stiff as a board, pulling behind him a cumbersome, weighty suitcase together with a complete skiing kit. Emiliano pointed at her, with the gesture of an actor in a silent film.

"Our carriage door opened and the woman got in, the chauffeur with her, helping her to take her coat off and placing the case and the skiing kit up on the luggage rack. Then he vanished respectfully. My fellow passenger began to grimace towards me, showing the whites of his eyes, as soon as he saw the seductive figure of the blonde, with the body of a model.

"She had so much perfume on that a scent of some exotic wood spread throughout the carriage. While she was settling down in her seat, opposite mine but on the other side of the central aisle, she glanced briefly in my direction (Emiliano was beside me next to the window), giving me a look I didn't quite know how to interpret.

"The train set off straight away, with proverbial Swiss punctuality. By then our lady friend had reclined the back rest and begun to leaf through the pages of a fashion magazine; after a few minutes I got the impression that she was looking at me out of the corner of her eye with a slight cough. At first I thought it was my imagination, but gradually I began to believe otherwise. Emiliano also noticed it, and whispered in my ear with the voice of an expert: 'I'll give you a quarter of an hour. After that, if you have made no progress, we'll swap seats and you'll leave her to me.'

"I looked at him in astonishment. He took note of my confusion and approached my ear again to tell me a couple of home truths in no uncertain fashion with the help of his thumb and index finger. That beauty had set her eyes on me and it was my duty to act. I burst out laughing: 'My duty as what? As a Catholic, as a Latin lover?'

"That situation was beginning to put me on edge. 'Your duty as a man,' he answered seriously, without hesitating. 'She must have found a likeness between me and someone she knew', I argued. Emiliano mocked my naivety. The looks she gave me were more and more evident and spoke louder than words, and the more insistently she looked at me, the greater my embarrassment.

"For a moment I held her look, and it was then that I was captivated, as she was truly a woman of astonishing beauty. I had to hide my feelings, put my head down and close my eyes, pretending I wanted to go to sleep. My evasive attitude cannot have pleased her. I daresay I was passing on to her my own nervousness, because she also became restless and turned over the pages of the magazine with great haste. After a while she rose from her seat and slowly walked the length of the aisle towards the toilets. Emiliano followed her with his gaze until she vanished at the end of the carriage. The he looked at me and pointed at his watch. 'You have eleven minutes left.'

"It must have been down to about three or four minutes by the time she came back along the aisle. This time her hair was tied at the back, and she was as if wrapped in a cloud of perfume. As she walked past me I had the feeling that she touched me slightly on purpose, and when she was back in her seat I plucked up enough courage to smile at her.

"It was then that the train made its first stop. The blonde lady, in the meantime, was searching for something in her handbag, perhaps a cigarette, and then something drew my attention. It was the sound of some voices coming from the platform, talking in a language that could have been Galician (my mother tongue). When the door opened I realized they were speaking Portuguese. A burly brown-haired young man appeared, with his hair tied back in a pony-tail, wearing a long raincoat, holding a kind of large army satchel and waving good bye to a couple on the platform. The young man strode into the carriage, his high-heeled boots making a loud noise on the floor as he did so. He was going to sit about three or four rows away from ours when I suddenly noticed our new lady friend was looking at him, with the cigarette dangling out of her mouth, still waiting to be lit. He reacted at once and rushed attentively holding out an electric lighter with a blue flame.

'Are you going skiing in Gstaad?' he asked, while the blonde was slowly lighting her cigarette, placing her hands round his. 'I myself am a great fan of skiing.'

"He spoke perfect French, with the soft voice of a film star. Emiliano elbowed me sharply and if looks could kill, I would have dropped dead on the spot. The Portuguese began to say: 'Would you mind me sitting next to you, young lady? There's nothing makes a journey more pleasant than travelling in pleasant company.'

"While they were still introducing themselves ('Charlie Fernandes', or something like that, 'at your service,' 'Dénise Le Dantec, the pleasure is mine'), Emiliano was looking at me attempting to hold back his laughter, and I noticed in his eyes a look of scorn. I lowered my head, settled down in my seat, and, surprised rather than angry, started to listen to the couple's conversation.

"The Portuguese took the initiative to start with, but gradually the blonde took control and he just answered 'yes' or 'no' or commented briefly on something. She spoke hurriedly, compulsively, in a staccato fashion, and so loudly that anybody could hear her right at the end of the carriage. She told him, stumbling over her words, about the time she had just spent in the St Gallen hospital, and about her plans to write a book regarding the healing powers of the pyramids. She also talked about her family problems that arose when she had fallen desperately in love with her stepfather, and, talking about her mother, she said she was a hateful, dirty old whore. When she explained that she had gone to St Gallen in order to forget about the death of a pianist of uncertain sexual tendencies, who had made advances towards her and had committed suicide when she rejected him, I looked towards Emiliano meaningfully. We had been saved by the Portuguese from a real disaster. It was fun to listen to her, chatting away non-stop, jumping from one subject to another, linking together phrases and pieces of nonsense: 'Now the doctors have prescribed me lots of parties and fun.' She repeated this a couple of times, giggling as she did so. I had the impression, although I did not dare look directly at her, that at that point in the conversation she was stroking the arm of the Portuguese.

'You said you were going to Montreux?' she asked. He replied that he was going to Chateau d'Oex, where he worked as receptionist at a hotel. 'I'm on my way to Chamby. A lovely house. I shall be there alone until Tuesday. What about coming to Chamby instead of going to your hotel?'

"It took some time for him to answer that he couldn't absent himself from work, as not only would they deduct the lost time from his salary but would fine him. On hearing this, the lady took out her cheque book from her handbag and waved it in front of his nose, while she offered him a receptionist's weekly wages in a top-class hotel for every day he spent with her. 'And as a tip, other surprises that have to do with passion!' she added.

"With all that on offer, the Portuguese had already lost all his inhibitions, and began to stroke her knees and thighs. But then she gently moved his arm away, stood up. 'Excuse me for a moment. I'm going to the ladies' room.' And she left, stepping into the corridor, showing off her slim, elegant figure.

"She could still be seen from where we were, but Emiliano gestured to me to change seats. To my surprise he began to talk to the Portuguese. 'Sir', he began, with absolute normality. 'Let me introduce myself. I am Emiliano Zingarelli, a psychiatrist. This man here, he said, pointing at me, is my colleague, Doctor Hergé. We are traveling with Mademoiselle Le Dantec. You must have realized that she is mentally unbalanced. I wish to congratulate you, because you have been able to hold a conversation with her in a very natural way, and I also wish to warn you that in some circumstances her behaviour can become aggressive and dangerous. Doctor Hergé here can confirm what I am saying.'

"I dared to stick my head out enough to nod as if in agreement. 'Two years ago, in Zurich, she stabbed a boy she had met in a discotheque in the stomach with a ball-pen. The young man died after losing a lot of blood, and the lawyers did not find it difficult to change imprisonment for the psychiatric hospital of St Gallen, which is where Dr Hervé and I work. For eighteen months she has been a very dangerous inmate, but for the last few months her mental state has been improving and she is now in the process of applying to become an outpatient. Yesterday she left the hospital for the first time after so long, and this morning she has already provoked a small incident. She is under sedation, an injection of fifteen milligrams of Valium, but that soon loses its effect. Anyhow, if you carry on like you have so far, trying not to contradict her, there won't be any problem.'

"The Portuguese looked rather upset by that news. As quiet as the dew, he listened attentively. Emiliano spoke unhurriedly, with a gentle voice, taking his role as a psychiatrist very seriously. 'Lastly,' he added, with extreme courtesy, 'I want to ask you for a favour. When we arrive at the station, do not let her notice in advance that you are getting off; wait until the train has come to a complete stop, and then very quickly, pick up your bags and get off as fast as you can. If Dénise reacts violently, we'll take care of her.'

"When Dénise came back down the corridor, the Portuguese looked backwards and forwards between her and us with distrust, and then blushed with shame. She sat down in an unconcerned way and carried on with her non-stop talking, now talking about her devotion for Mendelssohn's music, now about how moved she felt on coming back to her house in Chamby, where Bull and Mignonne, the two Doberman dogs she had looked after since they were puppies, would be waiting for her. 'As if they were my own children. What I love most in the world.'

"The Portuguese was gradually taking a less and less active role in the conversation, until his answers were just meaningless grunts. I believe it was then when she started to go on the offensive, as I thought I saw her stroking the inside of his thighs lasciviously.

"That was probably too much for the quiet receptionist, who stood up, looked at us accusingly and left for the toilets, apologizing all the time. I could hardly suppress a guffaw, and Emiliano took advantage of the situation to smile at the lady and exchange a few words with her.

"The Portuguese had decided to take refuge in the tiny toilet compartment and only stuck his nose out, unexpectedly, just after the train had stopped, grabbing his rucksack from the rack and hurrying out of the door. The blonde sat up, unable to believe what she saw, and addressing Emiliano cried in anger and astonishment: 'Not ten minutes ago he was prepared to spend a few days with me at Chamby!' 'Not all hotel receptionists come up to expectations when they are faced with a beautiful lady,' Emiliano replied sweetly, standing up, stretching out his right hand: 'Emiliano Zingarelli, playwright, Emiliano to you, at your service.'

"When she also stretched out her hand towards him, saying her name, he took it courteously, with great care, and kissed it. Then, without releasing it, he invited her to have something in the restaurant car.

"They came back after a long while, holding hands, just as when they had left, when the train was just drawing in to Chamby station. While they were picking up their luggage, Emiliano introduced her to me as if she were the love of his life, and I was introduced as an orchestral conductor. 'From Finisterrae, from Galicia, the real home of Christopher Columbus,' he told her.

"From the carriage door, carrying the blonde's case and skis on his back, he said goodbye to me, shouting 'Ciao' and giving me a thumbs up sign. I presumed I would never see him again, and I was right.

"Five days later, on the plane back from Zurich to Santiago, turning over the pages of the newspaper they give you free on the plane, I opened *Die Zeitung* and came across a familiar face. At the beginning, I couldn't recognize him, so serious and wearing a tie, but at once I realized, when I saw the headlines, referring to an Italian photographer. There was no doubt: Emiliano, it was his spitting image. I read the article over and over again in German to see if I could gather anything and found the name, Emiliano Zingarelli himself! This coincidence allowed me to keep a photograph of him, and even though it was a newspaper photograph it was good enough to illustrate the memory of that train journey.

"I tore out the page, folded it and kept it in my wallet. I chuckled to myself many times during the rest of the flight, about my encounter with that odd character, the details of the story of the perfumed blonde and the crafty way he stole her from the Portuguese.

"That same night in Santiago, having some drinks with my friend Lema, I told him the story. I didn't remember that Lema speaks German, and when I took the photo out of my wallet to show it to him, he took it from me with wide-open eyes, and began to translate: 'Italian photographer mauled to death by two Doberman dogs in the garden of a mansion in Chamby.'"

From Fábrica íntima (Intimate Construction), *1991*

Fábrica íntima

Tece soa a súa tea a lenta tarántula.
Escura nun recanto da confusión do asedio
recolle entre as ruínas da desfeita
os trofeos da morte. Receosa
do fado quebradizo coma de un tesouro
acaricia na sombra as súas propias feridas
e vive de convicción de que a vida prosegue
mentres no peito aínda un corazón latexe.
Sabe que todo está perdido, sabe
que nada será igual, e non obstante,
soa e inerme no medio da noite
prende un cativo lume que escintila
pola gándara erma do silencio
coma se fose unha voz. Humildemente
tece soa a súa tea a lenta tarántula
e mide na dor a estatura da vida.

Intimate construction

The slow tarantula weaves its web alone.
Dark in a corner of the confusion of the siege
it collects among the ruins of the catastrophe
the trophies of death. Suspicious
of brittle fate as of a treasure
it caresses in the shadow its own wounds
and lives in the conviction that life continues
so long as a heart still beats in the breast.
It knows that all is lost, it knows
that nothing will be the same, and nonetheless,
alone and defenceless in the night,
it lights a small flame that shines out
in the wastelands of silence
as if it were a voice. Humbly
the slow tarantula weaves its web alone
and measures in grief the stature of life.

From A torre da derrotA (The Tower of DefeaT), *1992*

A rosa ve...

A rosa ve, evasorA,
A torre da derrotA.

A lúa é aulA,
Adival a vidA.

The rose sees...

The rose sees, evasively,
the tower of defeat.

The moon is a classroom,
life a rope.

Luísa Villalta (1957–2004)

From **Música reservada (Reserved Music),** *1991*

En soneto de sons que soan sendo...

En soneto de sons que soan sendo
a melodía do que eu son na esencia
inconsciente de ser, unha presencia
sen máis sentido que soar sabendo,

a monodia do viver entendo,
fluíndo como o son, en transcendencia,
improvisado ritual, ausencia
no eco que a memoria vai perdendo.

Número e canto, necesaria vía
por que ascendo as escadas, se afastasen
a razón da intuición que o ritmo cría,

e transgrido a palabra, se soasen

outras voces que o sentido ouviría
cando os sons da súa música calasen.

In a sonnet of sounds that sound out and are...

In a sonnet of sounds that sound out and are
the melody of what I am in the unconscious
essence of being, a presence
with no more sense than sounding out and knowing,

I understand the monody of living,
flowing like sound, in transcendence,
improvised ritual, absence
in the echo that memory is slowly losing.

Number and song, the necessary way
in which I would climb the stairs, if reason
were separated from the intuition that rhythm rears,
and I would transgress the word, if there sounded out

other voices that the senses heard
when the sounds of their own music fell silent.

From Ruído (Noise), *1995*

AMOR, asfalto...

AMOR, asfalto, veloz, terraza, servir, reveso, como!, salubre, cansazo, saltando, sublime por que?, agora, invento, tardarei, NON!, anterior, serán, rotas, ritos, ritmos, rictus, cantos, cantas palabras desde o primeiro día, e o sonido, en que cada lingua se solta, ameaza, expande, ferve, constrinxe, alimenta, camiña pola beira dos ares até o ponto máis alto ou máis afastado, chantando pequenos estandartes, infalíbeis substáncias, cumprindo as escadas que sempre retornan ao início da ignorancia e ao final como intento, sen atinxir a ver o proxecto, as estradas por onde se perde o eco de todo sentido, aínda que sempre fica un repouso como o daquel que morre comprendendo que o fin da metáfora é deixar de selo.

LOVE, asphalt...

LOVE, asphalt, speedy, terrace, serve, reverse, how!, salubrious, weariness, jumping, sublime why?, now, invention, I shall be late, NO!, earlier, afternoon, broken, rites, rhythms, rictus, songs, how many words from the first day on, and the sound, in which each tongue loosens itself, menaces, expands, boils, constricts, feeds, walks at the edge of the breezes to the highest or furthest point, setting up small flags, infallible substances, completing the stairs that always return to the beginning of ignorance and the end as an attempt, without managing to see the project, the roads in which the echo of all sense is lost, although there always remains a respite such as that of the one who dies understanding that the purpose of the metaphor is to cease to be one.

Miguel Anxo Fernán-Vello (1958–)

From Memorial de brancura (Memorial of Whiteness), *1985*

Mulleres do verao

Cando as mulleres do verao pasan en ámbar luz
na tarde que se detén nos seus pasos que van
con grácil ventura nos meus ollos que levan

cando os ombros delas son a frescura do ar
que eu sinto nos labios como unha nudez pura

ou subtil redondeza no milagre interior
dun equilibrio que soñarían aves delicadas

cando pasan os seus corpos que son como séculos
que a beleza destinara ao amor que non morre

cando pasan na súa marabilla clarísima
e eu sinto un perfume de ceo na súa pel
transpasada de sol como unha flor moi íntima

cando pasan así esas mulleres do verao tan fermosas
un desexo desangra a miña vida e morro
en instantes crueis que me iluminan toda a carne
e morro nese asombro constante da beleza.

Women of the summer

When the women of the summer pass by in amber light
in the afternoon that comes to a halt in their steps that go
with graceful happiness in my eyes that they carry away

when their shoulders are the freshness of the air
that I feel on my lips like pure nudity
or subtle roundness in the inner miracle
of a balance that delicate birds would dream

when their bodies pass by that are like centuries
that beauty had destined for love that does not die

when they pass by in their clear marvel
and I sense a perfume of heaven on their skin
transfixed by sun like an intimate flower

when those lovely women of summer pass by
a desire bleeds my life and I die
in cruel instants that illuminate all my flesh
and I die in that constant amazement before beauty.

From Poemas da lenta nudez (Poems of Slow Nudity), *1994*

A viaxe

A Jordi Virallonga

Desexo neste poema que a flor da lonxanía
veña azul sobre min, agora que parto e deixo o mar
e unha terra escura descobre no meu sangue
o vello camiño da tristeza.

Vou ao Sul. Procuro a suave dirección doutros días,
a luz branca doutros corpos.
Abandono a cinza e a miseria deste tempo
atado aos homes e ás mulleres dunha cidade estraña
como o vento que cruza desolado as súas rúas.
Vivo entre bárbaros e todo horizonte é un alivio.
Por iso me despido da última árbore
e conservo nos meus ollos como un gume de asombro
o beixo da chuvia e os crepúsculos.

Porque é preciso inaugurar unha nova saúde
que ilumine nos meses a patria do desexo
e deixar que as raíces medren coa sede dunha estrela.

Sei que todo é unha rara alianza
entre o vacío, a nada e un segredo que brilla
no corazón.

E a esa luz me entrego, nudez e queimadura,
fervor de alba, perfil de ceo que treme
neste verso que foxe, como un soño,
do tempo e da morte.

The journey

To Jordi Virallonga

In this poem I desire the flower of remoteness
to come upon me blue, now that I depart and leave the sea
and a dark land is discovered in my blood
by the old road of sadness.

I am going to the South. I seek the smooth direction of other days,
the white light of other bodies.
I abandon the ash and the wretchedness of these times
bound to the men and women of a strange city
like the wind that blows desolate through its streets.
I live among barbarians and every horizon is a relief.
This is why I say goodbye to the last tree
and retain in my eyes like a knife-blade of astonishment
the kiss of the rain and the dusks.

Because it is necessary to inaugurate a new health
that will illuminate in the months the fatherland of desire
and to let the roots grow with the thirst of a star.

I know that everything is a strange alliance
between emptiness, nothingness and a secret that shines
in the heart.

And to that light I give myself, nakedness and burn,
fervour of dawn, profile of a sky that quivers
in these verses that flee, like a dream,
from time and death.

Manuel Forcadela (1958–)

From O regreso das ninfas (The Return of the Nymphs), *1985*

Odisea

Do antigo mar que sulcan as palabras
en naves cheas de ánforas e hexámetros
só lembro o vello aroma do crepúsculo
e esa vaga circular efixie que na noite
despois das chuvas fértiles do Abril,
emerxe desde o fundo,
atravesando espazos co seu corpo
e abrindo a leve xanela do verán
con un fulgor lunático.
Do resto gardo un eco fráxil,
esvaído como a pomba da mañá
sobre un muro de cal,
e só, ás veces,

cando o ingreso do outono é violento
e embalsamo o desexo con flores antigas,
lembro a lúa a caír,
vertixinosa, acesa,
sobre o doce perfil e a sombra do teu corpo,
Nausícaa.

Odyssey

Of the ancient sea ploughed by words
in ships full of amphorae and hexameters
I only recall the old aroma of dusk
and that vague circular effigy that in the night
after the fertile rains of April
emerges from the depths
crossing spaces with its body
and opening the slight window of summer
with a lunatic fervour.
Of the rest I retain a fragile echo,
faded like the dove of morning
upon a whitewashed wall,
and I only, at times,
when autumn's entry is violent
and I embalm desire with ancient flowers,
recall the moon falling,
vertiginous, alight,
upon the sweet profile and the shadow of your body,
Nausicaa.

From Profecía (Prophecy), *1992*

Eu, que sempre quixen ...

Eu, que sempre quixen ter morada no Parnaso
e asistir aos concertos vocais dos poetas antigos
para ollar como limpaban as feridas das súas linguas
e arrincaban o voo dunha flor ás súas chagas de anos,
senteime a descansar no medio do camiño
e só ollei os outeiros ao lonxe.
Preferín ficar ollando os camiñantes,
o val verde,
os cabaleiros,
as padiolas de cinsa que vía pasar

dando conta do naufraxio.
E ollei a xente que agardaba na antesala dos quirófanos,
perdida no interior da súa debacle,
apalpándose os sinais de ignoradas doenzas,
como escravos que soñasen coa chegada dalgún barco
entre gritos de mulleres e ambulancias. Viñan sempre dalgún río
coas familias ensumidas nos seus panos de quebranto
preguntándose por que
e, despois de coñecer que aquel fluído se detiña,
desfacían os seus rostros co trazado dunha bágoa,
antepuñan á poesía as pregarias do olvido
e, virándose na néboa, entre o arrecendo de lexivia,
espreitaban os cadáveres,
fragmentos do seu tempo que se foran derrubando
para abrirlles un crepúsculo nas bocas
que xa nunca calaban. Debo ser dos que descían para ollalos chorar
cada tarde entre os sonidos do inverno
coa carreta das mortallas a través do corredor.

I, who always wanted...

I, who always wanted to own a dwelling on Parnassus
and attend the vocal concerts of the ancient poets
to watch how they cleansed the wounds on their tongues
and plucked the flight of a flower from their sores of years,
sat down to rest in the middle of the road
and only watched the hills in the distance.
I preferred to stay watching the passers-by,
the green valley,
the gentlemen,
the stretchers of ash I saw passing by
informing of the shipwreck.
And I looked at the people waiting in the ante-rooms of the
                                            operating theatres,
lost inside their debacles,
feeling for the signs of unknown ailments,
like slaves dreaming of the arrival of some boat
amidst screams of women and ambulances. They always came from
                                            some river
with their families consumed in their cloths of grief
wondering why
and, after learning that the fluid was obstructed,
broke their faces with the course of a tear,

preferred prayers for oblivion to poetry
and, turning in the mist, amidst the perfume of bleach,
watched over the corpses,
fragments of their time that had been slowly collapsing
to open a twilight in their mouths
that never now were silent. I must have been one of those that went
down to watch them weep
each evening amidst the sounds of winter
with the cart of shrouds across the corridor.

Lois Pereiro (1958–1996)

From Poemas 1981–1991 (Poems 1981–1991), *1992*

Car crash (Da morte en negativo)

Á sombra deste horror metalizado
escribirás os diálogos da morte
da cóxega homicida da memoria
no centro xeométrico do choque
deixando a porta aberta a outras escenas
na emulsión dos meus ollos que impresionan
imaxes de accidentes e feridas.

Car crash (of death in a negative)

In the shade of this metallized horror
you will write the dialogues of death
of the murderous tickling of memory
in the geometrical centre of the crash
leaving the door open to other scenes
on the emulsion of my eyes exposed to
images of accidents and wounds.

Dandy

O espello da elegancia dediante dos meus ollos
e as pálpebras dormen un soño nervudo
en liñas líquidas dos xestos debuxados
nun rostro de crueldade aproximada á miña

Convírtome no medo no asasino
e mentres pasa un anxo un ange passe
todos quixeran ver despois da orxía
se o que levo gardado é un pensamento
enfiado en agullas de ironía.

Dandy

The mirror of elegance before my eyes
and my eyelids sleep a sinewy sleep
in liquid lines of the expressions etched
on a face of cruelty close to mine.

I become fear the murderer
and while an angel passes un ange passe
all would like to see after the orgy
if what I have kept back is a thought
threaded through needles of irony.

Xosé Cid Cabido (1959–)

From Grupo abeliano, *1999*

Non levabamos nin media hora viaxando pola autopista sen case pronunciarmos palabra, de tan a gusto que iamos, cando apareceu o sinal dunha estación de servicio con restaurante. O que guiaba non preguntou, pero foi como se nos adiviñara o pensamento porque ninguén se opuxo á idea de facer unha paradiña. Unha vez na gasolineira, o que guiaba quedou a cargar un chisco o depósito mentres os demais nos fomos achegando á cafetería-restaurante, moi semellante a unha cafetería de aeroporto nalgúns aspectos, con certas pretensións de aire internacional e cosmopolita; non debín ser o único en decatarse de que máis dun empregado se comportaba como se fose un emigrante que traballa na hostalería nalgún país de centro Europa, e niso tiñan non pouco que ver os seus esforzos por simular un acento que se recoñecía como falso mesmo na pronunciación das curtas frases necesarias para atender ós clientes. En realidade, creo eu, a ninguén lle sorprendería que moitos daqueles empregados fosen naturais das aldeas próximas á estación de servicio.

Cando chegou o que guiaba, xa nos instalaramos nunha mesa ben grande, na que collerían de sobra dez comensais. Tiñamos as cartas plastificadas na mesa, e unha muller cun pano á cabeza – as cores do seu uniforme, listas verdes e brancas, tamén estaban presentes nalgúns elementos decorativos do local – agardaba disposta para tomar nota dos pratos. A comida non ofreceu problema, cada un pediu o que lle pareceu máis apetecible e todos felices. Pero na bebida resultou que cada un quería unha marca distinta de viño, e ninguén se conformou con pedir só media botella, así foi como acumulamos seis ou sete botellas enteiras, das de tres cuartos, cada unha de seu pai e a cal máis cara, pero igualmente todos felices.

Decateime, e creo que non fun o único, de que unha muller co uniforme de Autopistas alancaba cara a nós moi ocupada en administrar un xeneroso excedente de cólera.

Chantouse diante do noso que mellor conduce, e díxolle, vostede marchou sen pagar a gasolina, ó que o noso respondeu moi calmado, efectivamente, enchín o depósito hai uns minutos.

Que o encheu seino eu moi ben, pero ten que aboarme tres mil setecentas corenta e sete pesetas, digo eu, non pensará que lle vou regalar a gasolina.

Como vai regalarma, señorita, se non é súa.

¡¿Ai non é miña?!

Pois miña non será pero súa tampouco.

Se se trata dunha confusión, por min non hai problema, pero...

Pois se non hai problema, todos contentos, aproveitou o noso.

¡Pero como contentos! ¡Ten que me pagar!

Sentímolo moito pero non dispoñemos de fondos para gasolina, dixo un de nós, por aquela cousa de botarlle unha man ó que mellor conduce, que tampouco é manco, pola parte da lingua escaqueativa.

¡Están de broma! Supoño que estarán de broma, vamos.

Ollámonos cunha miga de cinismo mal disimulado e varios de nós negamos coa cabeza en dirección á cobradora.

Entón ela deu a volta, máis encabuxada do que viñera, e marchou, imaxinamos nós, a pedir reforzos ou apoio moral, ou quizais un combinado forte das dúas cousas.

Trouxéronnos o xantar e iso centrou a nosa atención bastante lonxe dos pequenos inconvenientes. Alí despachamos boas carnes e bos peixes, a cociña non era de clase superior pero aínda merecía un aprobado para todos, quizais coa excepción daquel de nós que proviña de boas familias e tiña o padal máis enviciado nos manxares exquisitos do que o tiñamos o resto. Así e todo, a comida, máis ben comida merenda, transcorreu gratamente. Só que o tempo, por ese motivo, tamén se nos foi sen sentir, entre o xantar e a sobremesa, os cafés, as copiñas e mesmo algún puro que un de nós pedira con moita intención.

Nunha mesa moi próxima medio recordo un home groso e barbudo, de voz grave, e unha muller de cara batida e xesto nervioso, que falaban un galego inusitadamente fiel á normativa estándar. Pronunciaban con escrúpulo profesional palabras como olfacto, vestiario, collesemos, afección e outras rarezas polo estilo. Poñendo a orella sen querer, cheguei á conclusión de que os dous eran dobradores, é dicir, actores de dobraxe, vivían nalgunha das cidades do norte e intercambiaban información – ó parecer valiosísima para eles aforrar tempo nas súas viaxes de traballo – sobre a ruta de penetración máis adecuada para chegar ó barrio da grande urbe costeira do sur, onde tiña as súas instalacións a empresa de dobraxe que habitualmente os convocaba. Nun ínterim que situaría entre o segundo prato e os postres sen medo a equivocarme, pensei que o seu relato contrastado sobre as rutas máis aconsellables para entrar e saír naquela cidade caótica mesmo dependendo das horas xa rematara, pero non, logo duns minutos en silencio, os dous coa ollada un chisco perdida nas augas do interior da ría, reanudaron a conversa sobre a mesma cuestión, xuraría eu que non pouco satisfeitos por estar de acordo na solución variable dun problema para eles tan crucial.

Nalgún preciso momento creo eu que lembramos todos a cita coa empregada da lavandería e decidimos dar por terminada a grata sobremesa. Xa que estabamos obrigados a pagar a peaxe abusiva da autopista para non prexudicar ó dono do coche, todos deducimos, sen comentalo sequera, que a comida podía considerarse incluída nese prezo; é dicir, nós intuiamos que aquel non era o trato por parte da cafetería-restaurante da autopista, pero non por iso deixaba de ser para nós un trato razoable, e así'llo expresou o de nós que mellor manexa a palabra en momentos de conflicto e confusión, primeiro á moza que nos servira o xantar, e logo, como iso non parecía ser suficiente, ó encargado, que, por certo, acabou poñéndose algo nervioso (ou tenso, quizais a palabra sexa tenso). O que mellor fala nestes casos explicoulle que a autopista era un pouco cara de máis e que o firme estaba moi descoidado, e que mesmo o trazado non era un trazado realmente propio dunha autopista, e nomeoulle tamén outros defectos que todos coñeciamos (tramos de alta sinistralidade, etc.) e cando digo todos refírome non só a nólos seis ou sete senón a todos os clientes que se atopaban naquel momento na cafetería-restaurante, que, por certo, tiveron o detalle de non inmiscirse para nada na discusión, que nós non desexabamos, sobre o pago da comida e o prezo da autopista en relación coa súa calidade.

Un dos clientes aproveitou a ocasión para relatar o que lle sucedera a el había pouco. Como estaban en obras, o tráfico fora desviado a un carril provisional durante días. Pero de alí a pouco, aínda co asfalto demasiado fresco, volvéranos reconducir ó trazado orixinal. Ó chegar á casa decatouse de que os fondos e boa parte do lateral dereito do coche estaban salpicados de piche (*celpicados*, dixo el).

Fun pró outro día falar cos das oficinas e déronme un folleto para que o recubrise cos meus datos e contara o problema que tiña por escrito. O folleto chamábase *Opino que…*, non falaba para nada de reclamacións. Pasando un mes, chegoume unha carta na que Autopistas me facilitaba o nome, o enderezo e o teléfono da empresa que realizara as obras de reforma naquel tramo, para que lles fose reclamar a eles. É dicir, Autopistas non se fai responsable dos danos que ocasionan as empresas que mete a traballar dentro do seu recinto.

Por suposto, este relato foi interrompido varias veces polo encargado, a quen nós tamén varias veces lle pregamos que mantivese a calma e deixase falar á xente.

Sobra dicir que o caso do home do coche lixado de piche foi utilizado convenientemente polo noso que defendía a postura do grupo naquel momento.

O que lle pasou a este señor, quería rebater así o encargado, hai dous ou tres meses, ou o que lle pase mañá con outra obra da autopista, iso agora non vén a conto. Nós estamos falando de que vostedes veñen aquí a comer e séntanse e piden de comer. E nós atendémolos como é debido. ¿Comeron mal?

Non, ho, dixemos, comeuse bastante ben. Se iso non é o que se discute.

Pois, daquela, non se fale máis. Aquí teñen a conta e punto.

Non, e punto nada diso.

Como que nada diso, alporizábase e púñase rubio de coraxe o encargado. Eu son un traballador.

Vostede será o encargado.

¡Eh! Son o encargado pero son un traballador. ¡Quen me vai pagar a min todo isto! Autopistas non mo paga.

Pero como que non llo paga se o restaurante pertence á empresa de Autopistas.

Non se fale máis, morreu o conto. ¿Vanme pagar?

Nós, non, dende logo.

Ó escoitar semellante resposta, o encargado púxose tan nervioso e tan violento que comezou a bracexar, levando as mans por enriba da cabeza como se quixese poñerse a bailar a muiñeira e mesmo ameazou con chamar á policía, ó cal o noso respondeu que non tiñamos ningún inconveniente, se el cría que con iso adiantaría algo. Igualmente debía el comprender que naquel mesmo instante abandonaramos o local, posto que tiñamos unha cita, e xa chegabamos tarde. O encargado non soubo qué responder e, coa cara violeta de excitación, alí quedou explicándose por teléfono coa policía mentres nós montabamos no coche. Algunha xente non sabe controlar o nerviosismo interior.

Sobra dicir que cando a cobradora da gasolina regresou, en compaña dun mozo algo extenso, nós xa estabamos en plena zambra co encargado; ela quixo meter baza e incluso aquel mozote fixo intención de impoñer un par de criterios, pero non houbo caso porque alguén de nós lle centrou as ideas ó instante con pouco máis ca unha mirada tesa e aquel detalle de respirar polo nariz moi repousado, recursos sempre eficaces para casos de agresividade embrionaria.

From Grupo abeliano, *1999*

We had hardly been driving for half an hour along the motorway, with scarcely a word spoken between us, so happy were we in each others' company, when the sign for a service station with a restaurant appeared. The driver didn't ask, but it was as though he could read our minds, for nobody complained when he drew in. Once there, the driver said he would tell them to top up the tank while the rest of us went in the restaurant, which looked in some ways very much like those cafeterias you find in airports, those that have a kind of pretentious international, cosmopolitan air about them.

Apparently, I was not the only one to realize that several of the workers were there behaving like immigrants who had been working in the service sector of some central European country, and this had a lot to do with the fact that they made a great effort to pretend to have a certain accent which I found a bit artificial, like for instance, the pronunciation of certain short sentences used when serving the customers. To tell the truth, as far as I am concerned, nobody would have been surprised to find, from the accents, that those employees were people from villages near the service station.

When the driver arrived, we were already seated round a big table where ten customers would have fitted easily. We had plastic-covered menus on the table, and a woman with a scarf on her head – the same colours as her uniform (green and white stripes) were also present in some of the decorative elements round the premises – stood ready to take down our orders. The food was all right and each of us ordered what seemed nicest, so everything was going fine. But as for the drinks, it so happened that everyone wanted a different sort of wine, and none of us seemed to be happy with just half a bottle. That way, we managed to collect six or seven whole bottles, three quarters of a litre size, each one more expensive than the last. But then again, everyone was content with their lot.

I then realized (and I was apparently not the only one who did), that a woman in the motorway uniform was charging towards us, seemingly ready to vent all her rage on us. There she stood in front of our good driver and accused him of having left without paying for the petrol, to which our man replied calmly:

Yes, indeed, I filled up just a few minutes ago.

I know that for a fact, but you still owe me three thousand seven hundred and forty seven pesetas, unless you think I'm giving it away.

You can scarcely do that, young lady, as it is not yours to give away.

So it's not mine, then?

Well it might not be mine, but it's not yours either.

If there's been a muddle, there's no problem as far as I'm concerned, but ...

Well, if there's no problem, we're all happy as larks then, said our man.

What do you mean we're all happy? You have to pay up.

We're very sorry but we don't have enough money for petrol, replied one of us, trying to help out our good driver, who wasn't bad at talking his way out a scrape either.

You're joking, of course! At least I hope you are.

We all watched with badly concealed irony and several of us shook our heads in the direction of the petrol pump attendant. Then she turned round, even more irate than when she had come, and stomped off, we imagined, to get help or moral support or a good dose of both.

Lunch was brought, and that took our minds off the troubling little incident. We shovelled down good meat and good fish. Although the cooking was not haute cuisine it was awarded a good pass mark from all of us, except for one, who came from a wealthy family and had a more delicate palate, having been spoilt when he was brought up. Altogether, lunch, or rather high tea, went on smoothly, and perhaps because of that, time flew without us noticing it, what with lunch, chatting together, coffee, drinks and even the odd cigar that some of us had ordered (in bad faith).

At the next table I remember there was a fat man with a beard and a deep voice, talking with a woman, sad-faced and nervously gesturing; they were talking in the local language, using the most academic standard forms. They pronounced words with a well-chosen professional sound, such as "fragrance", "armoire", "should we secure…", "indisposition", and other similarly quaint expressions. Overhearing them (though without meaning to), I reached the conclusion that they were actors who did dubbing, that they lived in one of those northern towns, and that they were exchanging information – seemingly very important information, so that they could save time in their travels in the course of their work – about the best route to get to some area within a large town on the south coast where the dubbing company which normally contracted them had its offices. During the time between the main course and the dessert, I can say without a doubt that I thought the conversation about the best routes in and out that chaotic city (depending on the time of day) was over, but not so; after a few minutes' pause, both of them, with rather a lost expression on their faces, looking towards the waters of the nearby inlet, renewed their conversation on the same theme; I could swear they were eventually very glad to have agreed on the solution to such a crucial matter.

At some time I believe we all remembered our appointment with the laundry worker, and we decided to put an end to that nice little chat. As we were obliged to pay the unreasonably high motorway toll, which we had decided to do between all of us, so as not to charge the coach-driver, we all came to the conclusion that lunch should be included in the toll; we agreed upon that without a word being said; that is to say, we shared the opinion that this was not the right way to be treated by the restaurant, though we could not in fact deny that it was reasonable treatment. Indeed one of us, who chose the right words at times of conflict or confusion, said as much. First we addressed the woman who served us lunch, and then as we didn't seem to be getting across well enough, the manager, who, by the way, ended up becoming rather nervous (perhaps a better word is "tense"). The one of us who best expressed himself explained to him that the toll was rather too high, the road surface had been very much neglected and the motorway route itself had been wrongly designed, and he listed other deficiencies besides, those all of us know, such as accident black spots. When I say "all of us" I mean not only the six or seven of us but all the other customers who were there at that moment in the restaurant, the customers who, by the way, had the gentility not to interfere in the row at all (as we did not wish them to), about the price of lunch and the motorway toll in relation to the poor quality of the road.

One of the customers took advantage of the situation to tell us what had happened to him not long before. As there was work in progress on the motorway, the traffic had been diverted along one of the carriageways for some days. But not far from there, and as the asphalt was still fresh, they were send back along the original route. When he got home he realized that the bottom of the right hand side of his car had been "splotched" with asphalt.

Soon, I went to the office to make a complaint, and they gave me a form to fill in

with my personal data, and the complaint I had. The form was headed In my opinion… and was not really a claim form at all. After a month, I got a letter from the
motorway company in which they gave me the name, address and telephone number of a company that was performing the road works in that particular area and so
I could claim from them. That means the motorway will not take responsibility for
the damage caused by the company that works on their property.

Of course, this story was interrupted several times by the manager, whom we
asked to keep calm and let people have their say.

Needless to say, we used the case of the man whose car was "splotched" with
asphalt (very conveniently) to defend our own cause.

What happened to that man three or four months ago, the manager claimed, or
whatever might happen tomorrow in some other stretch of the motorway, had
nothing to do with the issue now. We were, he said, talking about the issue of our
coming here today and ordering lunch:

And we served you properly – he said – or did you not eat well?

Well, we ate reasonably well, but that is not the issue.

So let's not talk any more about it. Here's the bill, and that's that.

No, that's not that at all.

What do you mean?

The manager went red with rage.

I'm only a worker here.

You're the man in charge.

Well, I'm in charge but I am a worker. Who's going to pay me for all this? The
motorway company won't.

What do you mean they won't; the restaurant belongs to the motorway company.

That's enough of this nonsense. Are you going to pay or not?

What, us? No, of course not.

On hearing this, the manager became so nervous and violent that he began to
gesticulate, lifting his arms above his head as if he was going to dance the local
dance, the muiñeira, and threatened to call the police, at which our driver answered
that he didn't mind, that calling them would do him no good at all. At the same
time, he should understand that we were going to leave the restaurant at that very
moment as we were already late for our appointment. The manager did not know
what to say, and with a face flushed with rage, stayed put, explaining the matter to
the police on the phone, while we were getting into the coach.

Some people don't know how to control themselves, we said.

Needless to say, when the petrol attendant came back, accompanied by a burly
young man, we were in the middle of a row with the manager. She wanted to interfere, and even the thickset young man made an attempt to make his opinion
known, but no way. One of us made him change his mind right there and then
with a meaningful look and by breathing very hard, one of those things you can
resort to in the event of primitive aggression.

Román Raña (1960–)

From Extramuros da noite (Outside the Walls of Night), *1985*

Nunca direi desexo

É inútil o nocturno viño, o apego
ás formas e ao que morre, son inúteis
os muros solitários, o xemido da espiña
nos adentros, o prodixio
obscuro das adelfas ou as tardes
que embriagan con sois a flor submisa.
Falarei novamente de ti ou nunca
direi desexo, labios abismados,
illas de alcool, setembro adolescente,
amor, delta de todos os silencios.

Never will I say desire

No purpose is served by nocturnal wine, adherence
to forms and to what is dying, no purpose is served
by solitary walls, the groan of the thorn
inside one, the dark
prodigy of oleanders or evenings
that intoxicate the meek flower with suns.
I will speak again of you or never
will I say desire, engrossed lips,
islands of alcohol, adolescent September,
love, delta of all silences.

From Ningún camiño (No Road), *1997*

Terra pretérita

Veronza, escurécesme.
Non son aquel que fun, mais cheo de ecos digo
lúcidas ondas do río bañan o teu curso
e sei entrar en ti ben fría e de ribeira herbosa.
Ás veces alóxanse no peito
os ledos pasos de outrora
cando habitabas de amor as alamedas
e enviabas noites de libélulas amigas no teu dorso

florecéndoche lirios, farna
colmándome de lumes sinuosos, bicos
que nos ramos xamais fixeron niño.
Agora comprendes por que nos meus versos
fuxo do teu curso, aínda que cando máis lonxe estou
máis me desfago e me consumo,
porque non te sei esquecer
e levas na túa tona a miña infancia.

Land of the past

Veronza, you darken me.
I'm not the man that once I was, but full of echoes I say
lucid waves of the river bathe your course
and I know how to enter you cold as you are and with overgrown banks.
Sometimes my breast houses
the happy steps of yesteryear
when you peopled avenues with love
and sent nights of friendly dragonflies on your back
as lilies flowered on you, pollen
filling me with sinuous flames, billing and cooing
that never produced nests in branches.
Now you understand why in my verses
I flee from your course, although the further away I am
the more broken and consumed I am,
for I cannot forget you
and on your filmy surface you carry my childhood.

Paulino Vázquez (1962–)

From Un áspero tempo de caliza (A Harsh Time of Limestone), *1994*

Consideración última

A Xosé Luís Méndez Ferrín

A indiferencia ante todo aquilo que non provoque
        unha profunda emoción
as xentes e os humildes de vilanova dos infantes
no verao (un alento inerte parecían os anos
        por vir, un van alento os anos deixados atrás)

os restos dispersos do tempo
e as cinzas de Blackburne, Lancashire
as celadas que o amor nos depara, un sono
semellante á morte, os ocres fragmentos de arxila
    derramados como un tempo detido en arañeiras
– o oscuro rumor do mar
con os seus ecos, e as pertenzas dos estranxeiros mortos.

As teselas dos mosaicos en Ravena
(O ANTIGO ESPLENDOR DOS FERMOSOS OLLOS
                                  XÓNICOS)
as páxinas amarelentas dun libro
    que o mundo esquencerá
(a desgastada voz
dun amigo morto antes de tempo, inevitabelmente entre nós)
as landas orballadas próximas a Doncaster
as areas do deserto onde uns ósos xacen calcinados
    para expiación do olvido
– todo o que foi perdido
e nunca máis será; o que foi e o que puido ter sido
o que prevalece á morte e o que dura como un soño
o beneficio e a perdida, as palabras que non foron escritas
                             no poema

O Tempo que nos arrastra
    cara a destrucción deixándonos a inminencia
    dunha revelación que nos reserva para despois da Morte.

Final consideration

To Xosé Luís Méndez Ferrín

Indifference in the face of all that which does not provoke
    a deep emotion
the people and the humble of vilanova dos infantes
in the summer (the years to come seemed like
    an inert breath, the years left behind a vain breath)
the scattered remains of time
and the ashes of Blackburn, Lancashire
the ambushes that love prepares for us, a sleep
similar to death, the ochre fragments of clay
    spilt like a time held in spiders' webs
– the dark murmur of the sea
with its echoes, and the belongings of dead foreigners.

The tesserae of the mosaics at Ravena
(THE ANCIENT SPLENDOUR OF THE BEAUTIFUL IONIC
EYES)
the yellowing pages of a book
    that the world will forget
(the worn voice
of a friend who died too soon, inevitably among us)
the dewy moors close to Doncaster
the sands of the desert where sun-bleached bones lie
    for expiation of oblivion
– all that which has been lost
and never again will be; which has been and which could have been
which prevails over death and which lasts like a dream
the gain and the loss, the words that were not written in the poem

Time that drags us along
    towards destruction leaving us the imminence
    of a revelation that it reserves for us after Death.

Eusebio Lorenzo Baleirón (1962–1985)

From O corpo e as sombras (The Body and the Shadows), *1985*

Dous cisnes

Tal vez non coñeceron esa tarde
o canto epigonal da súa estirpe
nin o sol a beixar as superficies
míticas da onda.
Tal vez non chegaron a tempo
aquela vez; non puderon ser
a barca que urdía o canavial
cando amañece,
o centro no convite dos domingos
entre os cantos e o pan que achegan nenos.
Así dispuxo a Morte o seu banquete,
o cruel sinal distinto da elegancia,
así a sombra cruel que tece a Morte.
Roxa será esta alba
de sórdidos agoiros
xa que tal vez convosco morre o que Yeats amara.
Swanehals, recordarás por sempre a túa sorte

porque eles, sobre a morte do corpo
e sobre a ausencia, duran.

Two swans

Perhaps they did not know that afternoon
the epigonal song of their breed
or the sun kissing the mythical
surfaces of the wave.
Perhaps they did not arrive in time
on that occasion; they could not be
the boat that the reed-bed was weaving
as day breaks,
the centre-piece of the parties held on Sundays
amidst the songs and the bread brought by children.
Thus Death prepared its banquet,
the cruel distinct sign of elegance,
thus the cruel shadow that Death spins.
It will be red, this dawn
of sordid omens
since perhaps with you what Yeats loved will die.
Swanehals, you will forever remember your fate
because they, beyond the death of the body
and beyond absence, endure.

From A morte presentida (Death Presaged), *1988*

Linguaxe

Palabras como días claros,
sen fronteiras
para nomear cervos e rosas e
algún comezo que se escapa ao Tempo,
pronunciar o teu nome
en todos os desertos,
recuperar un intre de espadas e de beixos
con que negar a morte.
En ti comparto os días e os silencios,
as mañás transparentes, as futuras.
Entrégome a este mar de luz e signos,
a unha branca extensión que se perfila
no interior secreto de min mesmo.
Busco o clamor dos corpos, das palabras
neste mar que convoco e non responde.

Language

Words like clear days,
without boundaries
to name deer and roses and
some beginning that escapes from Time,
to say your name
in all the deserts,
to regain a moment of swords and of kisses
with which to negate Death.
In you I share the days and the silences,
the transparent mornings, the future mornings.
I give myself up to this sea of light and signs,
to a white expanse that takes shape
in the secret interior of my self.
I seek the clamour of bodies, of words
in this sea to which I call and which does not reply.

Ana Romaní (1962–)

From Das últimas mareas (From the Latest Tides), *1994*

Ennobelar pensamentos nos aneis...

Ennobelar pensamentos nos aneis,
perder os ollos nas montañas,
aniñar no silencio tan temido
e tecer esperanzas no zaguán.
Ese foi o único erro
que esqueceu Penélope.

Winding thoughts over rings...

Winding thoughts over rings,
losing her eyes in the mountains,
nesting in the much-feared silence,
and weaving hopes in the vestibule.
This was the only mistake
that Penelope forgot.

From Arden (They're Burning), *1998*

Xunto á tarde...

Xunto á tarde hai algo que salta
unha memoria breve
    quizais auga
as gamelas en domingo desasidas

Hai algo que reclama
a extensión do plancto
os pés de chapapote

Como se fose

Como se algo tivera sido

Near the afternoon...

Near the afternoon there is something bobbing
a brief memory
    maybe water
the little boats unmoored on Sundays

There is something claiming
the expanse of plankton
the feet of tar

As if it were

As if it had been something

Xelís de Toro (1962–)

From Antoloxía do conto de medo (Anthology of Horror Stories), *1995*

Insomnio (fragmento)

Vaguei polas rúas un tempo que non fun quen de contar, só sei que pasei por moitas rúas con cans que ladraban, moitas rúas con farolas ás que lles faltaba un cristal, moitas rúas con coches aparcados riba das beirarrúas cos cristais rotos a través dos que se lle vían cables arrincados, como se lles sacasen os nervos e veas a unha máquina, moitas rúas que non tiñan nada que contar, máis que casas amontoadas e pegadas de si, cos ollos escuros e as pálpebras caídas en enrugas. Odiaba o meu insomnio con toda a brutalidade con que un home pode odiar; recordábame ao pecado orixinal, ao castigo que se paga pola vida, ao inferno, ao mundo escuro e sen cobixo que nos espera tras da morte. Só os que o padecen saben do que estou a falar. O insomnio é estar tan cerca da sombra que se lle coñece o bafo, que se sente unha aperta pegañenta e visgosa como se os vapores das ánimas che estivesen tomando as medidas.

E foi sen embargo no insomnio onde o meu cerebro atopou lugares descoñecidos, viviu afastado do meu corpo, pensou sen os meus medos, e sentiuse ceibe dos sórdidos problemas co que o atormentaba no meu vivir. Foi por iso que primeiro o respectei e lle gardei lei, alieime e xoguei con el; pero sen tino despois provoqueino, desafieino e definitivamente perdín.

Lémbrome ben da primeira vez, non fora na súa busca, como moitas veces acontece cos máis ricos achádegos; unha man oportuna, e por un módico precio, estendeu un puñado das agora fóra de circulación Dixidrinas. Foi así que dei con este outro vivir. Ao principio a experiencia da anfetamina e a do insomnio veu mesturada e non era quen de sinalar os seus límites. Nin tan sequera era quen de saber a que era que me estaba afeccionando. Estiven coas Dixidrinas por un tempo, unha gang de nós acostumabamonos a xuntar á porta das farmacias de garda a coar as nosas receitas falsificadas. Cando as autoridades se puxeron duras coas Dixidrinas fomos polas anfetaminas portuguesas. Abríraseme unha porta que xa nunca quería pechar, ou polo menos iso pensei daquela.

Pouco a pouco a medida que fun entrando no coñecemento do meu secreto compañeiro, o meu secreto lugar, o paraíso do desvelo, fun atopando as covas e pasadoiros para acceder sen necesidade das anfetaminas. O insomnio entrara en min para xa nunca marchar. Como todas as amizades ofrece os seus favores e complicidades, os seus xogos en común, e acaba ofrecendo tamén as súas escravitudes e maltratos. Pero disto último tardei en saber. Mentres o dominei, mentres o chamei e veu, mentres eu fun o guía, o gracioso, o capitán, o das ideas, o que chama polas aventuras e el me seguiu, foi dunha grande ledicia para min. Xoguei a ser o amante das sete camas, a sombra da noite, a chuvia miúda, o sereno do barrio, o poeta desangrado e lunático. Que me importaban os comentarios ao día seguinte da miña fasquía, o meu desarreglo xeral, as miñas olleiras perennes, os meus ollos tinxidos de sangue, as miñas guedellas sen peitear e graxentas. Eu sabía que vivía dúas veces, con eles, o mundo, e outra vez máis, cando eles dormían. Eu sabía que vivía doble, o que non sospeitaba é que tería que pagalo. Foron anos que vivín coma se dese cun tesouro, un talismán ao que poucos teñen acceso, un feitizo segredo. Ao seu amparo escribín incontables poemas, tracei ideas e xoguei con palabras. Fíxenme habitante da noite e dos seus misterios, escrutei na escuridade, escoitando os ruídos das sombras, sabendo dos seus amores agochados, do ecoar dos pasos, dos seus licores, das súas servidumes. Xa daquela sabía que a noite tiña outros habitantes, só de un fuxín: o terror, o medo. Non podo recordar a primeira vez que sentín terror, porque nin sequera me permitin sentilo plenamente, sabía que ocupaba un lugar na noite que eu non quería traspasar. Confiei que nos respectásemos, como me respectei cos gatos. Cando presentía que o medo podía estar cerca, sentía un arreguizo subíndome pola espiña, un cravo na alma, e botábame enriba de papeis, sempre escribindo, escribindo cara adiante.

Insomnia (extract)

I wandered through the streets for I couldn't tell how long, I only know I went down many streets with dogs barking, many streets with their lamps missing a pane of glass, many streets with cars parked on the pavement with broken windows through which dangling wires could be seen, as if the nerves and veins of a machine had been pulled out, many streets that had nothing to say but houses jumbled together and stuck to each other, with dark eyes and eyelids drooping in wrinkles. I hated my insomnia with all the brutality a man can hate with; it reminded me of original sin, the punishment received for living, hell, the dark and shelterless world that awaits us beyond death. Only those who suffer from it know what I'm talking about. Insomnia is being so close to the shadow that you recognise its breath, that you feel a sticky, slimy embrace as if the vapours of spirits were sizing you up.

And yet it was in insomnia that my brain discovered unknown places, lived far from my body, thought without my fears and felt free from the sordid problems with which I tormented it in my everyday existence. This was why at first I respected it and kept faith with it, joined forces and played with it; but later I foolishly provoked it, challenged it and suffered a definitive defeat.

I remember the first time well; I hadn't gone in search of it, as often happens with the best finds; a timely hand, for a reasonable price, held out a fistful of the now unobtainable Dixidrines. This was how I came across this other existence. At the beginning, the experience of the amphetamines and that of the insomnia came mixed together and I wasn't able to define their borders. I wasn't even able to work out what it was that I was beginning to enjoy. I took Dixidrine for a while, a gang of us used to gather outside the duty chemist's to pass off our forged prescriptions. When the authorities got tough on Dixidrine, we went for Portuguese amphetamines. A door had opened that I would never want to close, or at least this was what I thought then.

Little by little, as I made the acquaintance of my secret companion, my secret place, the paradise of wakefulness, I began to discover the tunnels and pathways that led me there without any need for amphetamines. Insomnia had taken hold of me, never again to let go. Like all friends it offers favours and complicity, shared games, and in the end it also offers servitude and ill-treatment. But it was some time before I found out about the latter. So long as I was dominant – so long as I called for it and it came, so long as I was the boss, the joker, the leader, the one with ideas, the one who seeks out adventures – and it followed me, it was all a great joy for me. I played at being the lover of the seven beds, the shadow of the night, the misty rain, the neighbourhood night-watch, the anaemic, lunatic poet. What did I care about the comments the next day on my appearance, my general scruffiness, my bloodshot eyes, the rings always under them, my uncombed greasy lank hair. I knew I was living two lives – with them, the world, and then again while they were sleeping. I knew I was living twice; what I didn't suspect was that I was going to have to pay for it. Those were years when I lived as if I'd come across a treasure, a talisman to which few have access, a secret spell. Under its protection I wrote innumerable poems, sketched out ideas and played with words. I became a denizen of the night and of its mysteries, I scrutinized the darkness listening to the sounds of the shadows, learning of their hidden loves, the echoing of their footsteps, their absinthes, their servitudes. Already then I knew the night had other denizens, but I fled only one of them: terror, fear. I can't remember the first time I felt terror, because I didn't even allow myself to feel it fully; I knew it occupied a place in the night into which I didn't want to venture. I trusted that we would respect each other, in the way that cats and I felt mutual respect. Whenever I sensed that fear might be close, I felt a shudder running up my spine, a nail in my soul, and I threw myself at papers, always writing, writing on and on.

Xurxo Borrazás (1963–)

From Contos malvados (Evil Stories), *1998*

Plusvalía (fragmento)

Senteime no sofá e el foi ao estante coller o libro. Aínda tiña o plástico.

– Ábreo.

– Non.

– Ábreo.

El ollaba o envoltorio con desesperación. Choraría en calquera instante. Eu soltei un botón máis da blusa e achegueime a el. Rachei o plástico e guindeino ao chan. A blusa transparentaba e eu soletreei Ludwig Wittgenstein interiormente para lle dar tempo a agarrarme as cachas.

– Enfría o café – dixo, recuando un paso. Pisou o plástico e sobresaltouse, monicreque. Co susto empurrou varios dicionarios ata o fondo do estante. Realiñounos milimetricamente e eu olleino en silencio.

– Teño que marchar.

– Non.

– De onde sacas pelas para todo isto? – mirou o teléfono, a cámara de fotos, os marcos de prata, os lentes de sol. Coma un policía.

– Mángoo – declarei. E paseille o *Tractatus*, facendo un abano co dedo gordo sobre o canto das follas. El colleuno e volveu pousalo no andel. Desde a súa altura víame perfectamente as tetas endurecidas dentro do sostén de encaixe.

– Mángalo?

– Todo. Menos o butano. As tendas son centros de humillación multinacional.

Nunha ocasión estiveron a piques de pillarme e corrinme toda. Agora sei o que senten os sublevados.

El non ousou preguntar polo servicio. A calefacción era excesiva e a súa carta de identidade caducaba hoxe. Na carteira levaba tres fotografías tamaño carné.

– Sei que detectores funcionan e cales non – proseguín –. Coñezo a letra dos convenios de seguridade, unhas condicións laborais indignantes. Desapego un prezo ou un código de barras en quince segundos e unha vez manguei un aparello para arrincar as pinzas magnéticas da roupa e o calzado. Desde entón sempre entro fresca nos grandes almacéns.

– Estás pirada.

– Ás veces mango cousas que non me serven para nada, por se acaso. Como os tubos de óleo, por exemplo. Ou lámpadas halóxenas. Gárdoo todo nos caixóns e logo ofrézollo ás visitas.

– Xa.

– Máis café?

– Non, grazas.

– Non me cres? As miñas medias valen máis cá túa chupa cando era nova. Queres saber canto? – leveille a man aos collóns e non sentín nada. Doce horas máis tarde souben que era homosexual.

Estes días foron duros. Antonte fun ao Alcampo mercar comida. Engadín dous kiwis na bolsa dos xa pesados, abrín uns bombóns e comín media ducia, e saín cunhas lascas de salmón afumado no lombo. Na cesta levaba unhas acelgas, panos de mesa e os kiwis. A caixeira era a morena do brazo queimado. Despois pasei polas galerías e liguei unha máquina de depilar, que estaba de oferta; pero ao chegar á casa fixen a cera, coma sempre. Comín o salmón e estudei os feitos.

O Estado aliábase máis ca nunca co grande capital e a plusvalía tiña que ser recobrada a dentadas, pola subversión, como ela o facía. Pero había babións que non o entendían e amoreaban carnés. Meteuse no baño e masturbouse submariña. Quixo cantar pero o eco asustouna. O apartamento cheiraba e limpou nel ata a medianoite; logo abriu as xanelas e apagou as luces.

Onte no Claudio mercou unha barra de pan e un cartón de zume de laranxa, e no bolso interior do anorak agachou unha bolsiña de cera para o parqué. Fóra das caixas había un garda, que en voz baixa lle pediu que o acompañase.

Isto é que me foderon, pensou. Parece incríbel. E o corazón estaloulle no peito antes de desfalecer. Cando a reanimaron ela non dixo ren. Abroncárona, ameazárona e cacheárona. E volveu desfalecer. Sempre se coidara de non levar consigo documentos que a identificasen, pero viña de encargar unha bombona de butano e no peto traía o recibo, co seu nome e enderezo. O garda chamou á policía e estes levárona ao ambulatorio.

Non esperedes tirarme unha confesión, falaba para si. Na dianteira do coche Z o policía acompañante ollábaa de cando en vez a través da reixa. Así viva cen anos e me torturedes sen pausa.

A cidade estaba fermosa e ela colleu folgos.

– Vai ficar ingresada – dixo alguén.

– Este é o seu enderezo.

Todo tiña a intensidade da verdadeira poesía.

Ao abriren a porta os policías olláronse e enrugaron as cellas. A luz entraba en torrente polas persianas abertas e todo estaba limpo e ordenado. Os fabricantes de cera poderían estar contentos.

Os productos roubados, pensaredes vós, non se distinguen dos demais; pero ese é un dos vosos erros. As cousas compradas non transmiten emoción ningunha, son elos de vulgaridade na cadea do aborrecemento. Pola contra, un mero pintauñllas roubado fai que me estremeza de gusto. Calquera que non sexa un necio sentiría o mesmo.

Pero os policías non notaron nada. Tiraron de panos e abriron portas. Os meus delictos lucían por todas partes diante dos seus ollos, pero os parvos deles só reaccionaron cando no dormitorio baleiro atoparon o corpo espido do rapaz, cuberto de prezos e códigos de barras. Saíron a respirar ao relanzo e un deles vomitoume no parqué.

Surplus Value (extract)

I sat down on the sofa and he went to the shelves to fetch the book. It was still wrapped in plastic.

"Open it."

"No."

"Open it."

"No. I won't…"

He was looking at the wrapping in desperation. He was going to cry at any moment. I undid one more button on my blouse and moved closer to him. I ripped the plastic off and threw it on the floor. The blouse was see-through and I spelt Ludwig Wittgenstein in my head to give him time to grab my bum.

"The coffee is getting cold," he said, taking a step backwards. He trod on the plastic and started, the dummy. In his consternation he pushed several dictionaries to the back of the shelf. He realigned them millimetrically and I watched him in silence.

"I must be going."

"No."

"Where do you get the dough for all this?" He looked at the phone, the camera, the silver frames, the sunglasses. Like a policeman.

"I nick it," I declared. And I handed him the *Tractatus*, flicking over the pages with my thumb. He took it and put it back on the shelf. From up there he had a perfect view of my tits, firm inside my lace bra.

"You nick it?"

"All of it. Except the butane cylinders. Shops are centres of multinational humiliation. Once they were about to catch me and I just came completely. Now I know what insurgents feel."

He didn't dare ask where the toilet was. The heating was on too high and his identity card expired today. In his wallet he had three passport-size photos.

"I know which detectors work and which don't," I continued. "I know all the print of the security agreements – humiliating working conditions. I peel off a price or a bar code in fifteen seconds and once I nicked a device for pulling the magnetic clips out of clothes and shoes. Since then I've always gone lightly dressed into department stores."

"You're nuts."

"Sometimes I nick things that are of no use to me at all, just in case they come in handy. Tubes of oil paint, for example. Or halogen lamps. I put it all away in my drawers and then I offer it to visitors."

"Right."

"More coffee?"

"No thanks."

"You don't believe me? My tights are worth more than your leather jacket when it was new. Do you want to know how much?" I put my hand on his balls and couldn't feel any reaction. Twelve hours later I found out he was homosexual.

These last few days have been hard. The day before yesterday I went to the Alcampo supermarket to buy food. I added two kiwis to the bag that had already been weighed, opened a box of chocolates and ate half a dozen, and left with some slices of smoked salmon down my back. In my basket I had some greens, table napkins and the kiwis. The checkout-girl was the dark one with the burns on her arm. And then I walked through the shopping centre and swiped a Ladyshave that was on offer; but on getting home I waxed, as usual. I ate the salmon and studied the facts.

The State was allying itself more than ever with big business and the surplus value had to be recovered bite by bite, through subversion, as she was doing. But there were morons who didn't understand that, and hoarded loyalty cards. She got into the bath and masturbated, sub-aquatic. She tried singing but the echoes scared her. The flat stank and she cleaned and cleaned until midnight; then she opened the windows and turned out the lights.

Yesterday in the Claudio supermarket she bought a baguette and a carton of orange juice, and in the inside pocket of her anorak she hid a bag of wax for the parquet. Beyond the tills there was a security guard, who asked her in a very low voice to accompany him.

This means I'm fucked, she thought. It seems incredible. And her heart burst in her chest before she fainted. When they brought her round she said nothing. They shouted at her, threatened her and searched her. And she fainted again. She had always been careful not to carry documents that would identify her, but she'd just ordered a butane cylinder and she had the receipt in her pocket, with her name and address. The security guard phoned the police and they took her to the clinic.

Don't expect to get a confession out of me, she was saying to herself. From the front of the police car the officer in the passenger seat looked at her now and again through the grille. Though I live a hundred years and you torture me non-stop.

The city looked beautiful and she gathered strength.

"She'll be an in-patient," someone said.

"This is where she lives."

It all had the intensity of true poetry.

As the policemen opened the door they exchanged glances and frowned. Light poured in through the open blinds and everything was clean and tidy. The wax manufacturers could be satisfied.

Stolen products, you people may think, cannot be distinguished from the rest; but that is one of your mistakes. Bought things do not convey any emotion whatsoever: they are links of vulgarity in the chain of boredom. On the other hand, mere nail polish, if stolen, makes me quiver with pleasure. Anyone who isn't a cretin would feel the same.

But the policemen didn't notice anything. They grabbed their handkerchiefs and opened doors. Everywhere my crimes shone before their eyes, but the fools only reacted when in the empty bedroom they found the lad's naked body, covered in price tags and bar codes. They went out on to the landing to breathe, and one of them vomited on my parquet.

Xosé Carlos Caneiro (1963–)

From Tal vez melancolía (Perhaps Melancholy), *1999*

Tren

Ana, a cantante, tamén morreu. Ela foi a terceira víctima que tivo relación coa miña vida. O acomodador e o marido de Mamá foron as primeiras. Sóubeno polo xornal. Hai cinco anos, despois do meu retiro. Cando regresei de perseguir, por amor, as súas cancións e os seus ollos de rula. Estiven días pechado no cuarto. Cando saín furguei na terra e o sábado, como sempre, fun á taberna.

Mira, Pirata. ¿Que? Apareceu morta a cantante de boleros. Pero Ana non foi a única víctima. Ao día seguinte o xornal anunciaba un novo óbito na mesma cidade, un individuo que practicaba o boxeo nas súas horas libres. Probablemente o mesmo que golpeara o meu rostro. Catro, xa eran catro. Pero Mamá non foi. Mamá nunca foi. Aínda que souben, polo Purísima, que ela estivera ausente un par de días, mentres eu agardaba un mellor estado psíquico pechado no meu cuarto. Ademais é moi difícil matar a dúas persoas. Pero Mamá, ademais de bebedora, traballou nunha farmacia. E gracias a iso podemos ir tirando. Non, Mamá non foi. Mamá é boa. Ás veces caio na tentación de pensar as cousas que pensaría calquera que coñecese o caso en profundidade. Pero non, Mamá non foi. Sempre coidou de min, e da avoa. Ata que morreu. Eu creo que a avoa morreu de pena. Óbito feraz, ruín. Óbito cínico. Un ano no que tardou catro meses en chover. Porque a avoa amaba a chuvia. E durante catro meses non puido saír comigo para alcanzar as gotas que eu recollía nun cazo de cor laranxa.

Train

Ana, the singer, died too. She was the third victim who had something to do with my own life. The usher and my mother's husband were the first. I found it out from the newspaper. Five years ago, after I retired. After I'd come back from hunting (out of love) her songs and her dove's eyes. I spent days locked away in my room. When I eventually came out I scratched away at the earth and on Saturday, as usual I went to the bar.

Look here, Pirate. What? The bolero singer has been found dead. But Ana was not the only victim. The next day the papers announced another death in the same town, that of a man who used to box in his free time. Most likely the same one who punched me in the face. Four down then, four down. But it wasn't mother. It never was. Although I found out, from the Most Pure Virgin, that she had been away for a couple of days, while I was waiting for my mood to improve so I could come out of my locked room. Besides, it is very hard to kill two people. But mother, apart from being a hard drinker, also worked at the chemist's. And thanks to that we are able to make ends meet. No, it wasn't mother. Mother is good. Sometimes I fall into the temptation of thinking things that anyone would think who knows the case in depth. But no, it wasn't mother. She always looked after me and grandma. Until grandma died. I believe she died of a broken heart. A cruel, a wicked death. A cynical death. That year, when it didn't rain for four months. For grandma loved the rain. For four months she couldn't go out with me to catch the drops I collected in an orange-coloured tin.

Senectude

Os budistas consideran o pensamento como un obstáculo decisivo para a iluminación. Cando a mente está centrada no pensamento, non pode experimentar a realidade.

Os budistas contan o mesmo que eu conto. Pero con outras palabras. Eu digo: pensar condúcenos ao infortunio. Eles din: o pensamento obstrúe a iluminación. Claro que os budistas e o Pirata parten de supostos completamente distintos. Eles cren na luz. Eu, sen embargo, só creo na escuridade.

De todos modos, igual que Denis e D'Alembert, podo facer un trato cos budistas para iniciar unha campaña en contra do pensamento e a favor da meditación. Meditar: centrar a atención nun determinado obxecto. Eu son un grandísimo meditador. Paso o día meditando na morte, no suicidio, no problema que me plantea Cirano coa súa presencia non presumida (En verdade, cando o Pirata e o Purísima falaban da voda de Mamá en primavera non pensaban que esa voda ía acontecer de modo efectivo e, moito menos, que o señor Cirano ía repousar cada noite, coa súa incontestable pero intencionalmente evitada senectude e o seu sobrio recitatio, no cuarto de Mamá. Eu, ao revés que Cirano, vivín sempre na senectude.

El non. É moito máis novo ca min. O home imposible, Pirata, eu, vive permanentemente na máis rotunda senilidade. Así é a vida).

Así é a vida.

Pura sorpresa variativa arredor da mesma fin.

Old Age

Buddhists believe that thought is a crucial obstacle to enlightenment. When the mind is focused on thought, it cannot experience reality.

The Buddhists say the same as I say. But in other words. I say: "Thought leads to misfortune." They say: "Thought obstructs enlightenment." Of course the Buddhists and the Pirate are departing from two completely different assumptions. They believe in light. I, on the other hand, only believe in darkness.

But anyway, just like Denis and D'Alembert, I could strike a deal with the Buddhists to start a campaign against thought and in favour of meditation. "Meditation: Focusing your attention on one particular object." I am a great meditator. I spend the whole day meditating on death, on suicide, on the problem Cyrano posed for me when he turned up unexpectedly. (The truth is, when the Pirate and the Most Pure Virgin talked about mother's wedding in spring they could never have imagined it would ever really take place, and even less that Cyrano would lie down every night with the old age he intentionally put off, and his sober conversation, in mother's room. I, unlike Cyrano, lived forever in old age. Not him. And then he was much younger than I was. The impossible man, me, the Pirate, I lived eternally in my old age. Life is like that.)

Life is like that.

Pure surprise arranged upon the same theme.

Xosé Manuel Millán Otero (1963–)

From As palabras no espello (The Words in the Mirror), *1995*

De palabra (II)

este o terror dos dedos calcinados
áspera agra aberta terra núa
esta a palabra inscrita marca e linde
e saber que foi árbore e morada

describo cauce a cauce o pleno día
e o sangue que abrollou onde houbo chaga
e o ollo a penas fóra do seu centro
disperso cáliz ou raíz efémera

vida adiada cando a noite insiste
en labios afiados que son sombra
en pasos que retornan que se apagan
apreixar o amencer en rodopío
plantar dentes de sal na madrugada
e forzar a ser canto non existe

Word of mouth (II)

this the terror of charred fingers
harsh open field naked earth
this the word inscribed limit and boundary
and knowing it has been tree and dwelling

I describe from river-bed to river-bed the full day
and the blood that spurted where there was a wound
and the eye a little out of centre
dispersed chalice or ephemeral root

life postponed when night insists
on sharpened lips that are a shadow
on footsteps that return that abate

to grasp the dawn in a whirl
to plant teeth of salt in the early morning
and to force into being all that does not exist

Perdida Carcasona a cidade os días os rostros que tiveches

nunca máis volverás a carcasona
di adeus á cidade encaramada nos outeiros
e á que repta e se adelgaza na planicie até o horizonte
e á que pendura do precipicio como agoiro

crerás que foi por desangrares as palabras
porque é bon inventar o mundo e rostros que o fecunden
necesario coma un viño tépedo e sal para a viaxe
aínda que en cada pulsación sexa a morte a que palpite
cando esixe o seu tributo en cicatrices

todo regresa con vagar para ser cerna
endurecido tal vez no adubo da nortada
onde o tacto é insensíbel e hai agullas

afiadas na mesma mola que a caricia
todo regresa ao seu centro e no seu límite

nunca máis procures carcasona
hai un bosque entre ti e o que xa fuches
milenario en húmus terra estéril
e anoitece con vagar entre os teus ollos.

Lost Carcasonne the city the days the faces you had

never again will you return to carcassonne
say goodbye to the city that perches in the hills
and that worms along and grows thinner on the plain as far as the
                                                                horizon
and that hangs from the precipice like an omen

you will think it was because you bled words
because it is good to invent the world and faces to enrich it
necessary like warm wine and salt for the journey
even though in each pulsation it be death that is palpating
when it demands your tribute in scars

everything returns unhurriedly to be heartwood
hardened perhaps in the tanning of the north wind
where touch is insensitive and there are needles
sharpened on the same whetstone as the caress
everything returns to its centre and within its limits

never again seek carcassonne
there is a forest between you and what you once were
that is millenary in humus sterile land
and night is slowly falling between your eyes.

Antón L. Dobao (1963–)

From **Caderno dos dereitos e das horas (Notebook of the Rights and the Hours),** *1993*

XVIII
Nesta noite tan fonda vaise todo ensumindo:
os cigarros, os fumes, os camiños de ferro

percorridos en lume; renxe o renxer da máquina,
alumea o silencio, unha nube debruza
o paseo ó outro cuarto onde agarda quen sabe.
Nesta noite tan fonda aparece a bufarda
ás veces de auga doce, outras veces de brétema
en que os cativos xogan a xogar xogos grandes;
chucha o tempo as auroras dos decenios inertes
e agavela os recantos das máis cálidas febres.
Nesta noite tan fonda hai amigos que cantan,
aparellos que á música non lle fan máis espacio;
hai luceiros que albiscan como o vento se move,
como mexe unha morna instantánea de lóstrego
as dores dunha vida que nos deixan en nada.
Sufro por esta noite o que sofre o que a canta,
ou máis, que a min me enxerga desde o teito das épocas,
que a min me busca louca como busco eu a rúa
do lugar do meu pobo nunha noite sen ollos.

XVIII

In this deep, deep night all is fading away:
the cigarettes, the smoke, the rails
traversed in fire; the creaking of the engine creaks,
the silence gives off light, a cloud casts down
the walk to the other room where the one who knows is waiting.
In this deep, deep night the skylight appears
sometimes of fresh water, sometimes of mist
in which children play at playing great games;
time sucks dry the dawns of the inert decades
and sheaves the corners of the hottest fevers.
In this deep, deep night there are friends who sing,
tackle that does not make room for the music;
there are stars that glimpse how the wind moves,
how a warm snapshot of lightning rocks
the griefs of a life that has been left in nothingness.
I suffer for this night as he who sings it suffers,
or more, for it espies me from the roofs of the epochs,
for it seeks me madly as I seek the street
of the village of my people in a night without eyes.

Manuel Outeiriño (1963–)

From Depósito de espantos (Warehouse of Horrors), *1994*

Hipopótamo (babilonio)

Ser un pousón. Ter mundo (subacuático).
Pousón do subacuático, animal de pel mol,
un animal con paxaros no lombo
(no pouquiño do corpo que levanta das augas).

Estar no río (a cousa heraclitana) a catro patas.
Te-las orellas a rentes das augas,
tirar por veces as ventas das augas.
Vivir na lama.

– Je suis l'hipopotame, le veuf, l'inconsolé,
le prince ad aquas, Taine a la tour abolie.

Hippopotamus (Babylonian)

To be a sluggard. To own a world (underwater).
Sluggard of the underwater, animal of soft skin,
an animal with birds on its back
(on the little bit of body it lifts from the waters).

To be in the river (the Heraclitian thing) on four legs.
To have ears at water level,
every so often to raise nostrils from the waters.
To live in mud.

– Je suis l'hipopotame, le veuf, l'inconsolé,
le prince ad aquas, Taine a la tour abolie.

From Letras vencidas (Defeated Letters), *1999*

Ardentía

Nun límite de sal e de solpor,
vivimos no salseiro e na semente,
nas trazas do remol e do ronsel,
na conversa continua,

na pausa que responde ós desmedidos,
na solercia que sabe como o raposo salta
pero non perde a pista, coma os cans, polo cheiro,

(no bruar dos piñeiros, na ardora
nos magníficos días da concordia
e nas pedras inscritas)

na cor e mais no con que non sabemos, no matiz,
tamén no trazo forte e veladura triste,
nunha irónica idea do pasado:
na cegueira que aprende ás apalpadelas
o natural fermoso, na xiria cálida
no bosque non témero,
no roxido da area nos arrastres
no reloxo de príncipes corsarios,
nos olorosos ferros oxidados:
celebrámo-lo mar.

Sea-glow

On a boundary of salt and sunset,
we live in the spray and in the seed,
in the traces of the ember and of the ship's wake,
in continuous conversation,
in the pause that replies to those who overstep the mark,
in the astuteness that knows how the fox jumps
but does not lose the trail, like dogs, because of the scent,

(in the roaring of the pines, in the glow of the sea
on the magnificent days of concord
and in the inscribed stones)

in colour and in the reef we do not know, in the nuance,
also in the strong line and the sad vigil,
in an ironical idea of the past:
in the blindness that learns by touch
about natural beauty, in warm courage,
in the forest that is not fearsome,
in the swishing of the sand under the trawl-nets,
in the clock of corsair princes,
in fragrant rusty iron:
we celebrate the sea.

Fran Alonso (1964–)

From Persianas, pedramol e outros nervios (Persian Blinds, Softstone and Other Nerves), *1992*

Escribireiche poemas de amor e morte...

Escribireiche poemas de amor e morte,
pura vinganza de días, de odios,
asasinados a cada intre en min
pola túa man pérfida, planificadora,
executadora das máis intrincadas xenreiras
que poida concibir o noso amor.
¿Coñeces acaso a dor da palabra escrita?
Será a miña vinganza, o meu odio,
a miña esperanza, o meu renacer.
Cóidate, loba, da miña palabra,
sucúmbeme antes da escrita,
derrótame nun imprevisto,
nun contrataque do inicio da batalla.
Despois, amor, todo estará perdido
para ti.

I shall write you poems of love and death...

I shall write you poems of love and death,
pure vengeance of days, of hates,
murdered each moment in me
by your perfidious, planning hand,
executioner of the most intricate grudges
that our love could possibly conceive.
Do you by any chance know the pain of the written word?
It will be my vengeance, my hatred,
my hope, my rebirth.
Beware, she-wolf, of my word,
overcome me before the word is written,
defeat me in a surprise move,
in a counterattack at the beginning of the battle.
Later, my love, all will be lost
for you.

Miro Villar (1965–)

From Ausencias pretéritas (Past Absences), *1994*

A quentura dos libros non conforta...

A quentura dos libros non conforta,
non enche a sequidade do vacío,
non outona nin dá fruto tardío,
non deixa de ser verso en folla morta.

A quentura dos libros nada aporta,
nada con que matar un arrepío,
nada con que escoitar un asubío,
nada con que vencer a unha comporta.

A quentura dos libros é vendaxe,
é gasa, sulfamida, esparadrapo.
É postema que axiña debilita.

A quentura dos libros é miudaxe,
é remendo cosido dun farrapo,
é dor de desamor que non se evita.

The warmth of books gives no comfort...

The warmth of books gives no comfort,
it doesn't fill the dryness of the void,
it does no autumn sowing or yield late fruits,
it's just verses on dead pages.

The warmth of books contributes nothing,
nothing to kill a shudder,
nothing to listen to a whistle,
nothing to defeat a lock-gate.

The warmth of books is a bandage,
it's gauze, sulphanilamide, sticking-plaster.
It's a boil that soon debilitates.

The warmth of books is triviality,
it's a patch sewn on to a rag,
it's the pain of inescapable lovelessness.

Miguel Anxo Murado (1965–)

From Ruído (Noise), *1995*

Grandes cambios no último minuto

– Con todo paga a pena – dixo M. –. A pesar de todo. Aínda que ás veces un se pregunta... Lémbrome dun caso. Tiñamos que levar combustible para facer funcionar a caldeira dun hospital. Durante días intentámolo en van. Os francotiradores non nos deixaban nin achegarnos coa carga. Pensabamos con tristeza que os enfermos se ían conxelar. Ata que ó cabo o logramos... Puidemos meter alí o combustible durante unha pequena tregua. E ó día seguinte un tiro de morteiro..., en fin, o combustible axudou a que todo aquilo ardera como unha pira. Varios morreron, moitos sufriron queimaduras horribles – tomou un minuto de tempo –. A pesar de todo paga a pena. ¿E sabes por que? Porque equivocarse é tamén unha forma de ser inocente.

En principio non estaba previsto atranco ningún. Tres controis, vintecinco quilómetros. E á ida todo foi ben. Os vehículos da Axencia da Solidariedade, brancos coma camións frigoríficos, cruzaron o primeiro control sen sequera deterse. A barreira – un tractor e un tronco de bidueiro – non estaba posta e os milicianos do HVO, lonxe da estrada, formaban un corro indolente. Xogaban cun coitelo de monte que o sol líquido de xaneiro facía escintilar como unha xoia valiosa. A partir de aquí o convoi comezou a lenta escalada polos camiños de montaña, arrastrándose penosamente cara ó norte. Ese era o lugar que escollera a agonía ultimamente na dolorosa xira por aqueles vales enfariñados polo inverno. Os eixes xemeron baixo o peso das toneladas. Os motores iguais, tusindo e restelando, arrolaron o sono de Anna.

Unha multitude de esquíos vermellos coma lapas atravesou a estrada e perdeuse entre a neve, e o sol, marelo e xeado coma un botón de uniforme, sobrevoou a cabeza de Anna cando sentiu unha presión no brazo e acordou. Armand zarandeábaa lixeiramente.

O cheiro da gasolina mal carburada – as sabidas restriccións na octanaxe ó longo da rota central – tróuxoa de volta á vixilia e cando abriu os ollos o convoi estaba parado e non viu os esquíos do seu soño senón unha pequena multitude indefensa sobre a neve, borrosos en medio do bafo do seu propio alentar.

– ¿Quen son? – preguntou Anna incorporándose e esfregando os ollos.

– Non o sabemos. Apareceron aí de golpe. Non apartan.

Os motores apagáronse e a enorme masa branca e pesada da neve absor beu o eco. Ese silencio que a neve provoca e que enche de soidade os bosques.

Anna e Armand, torpes coma astronautas dentro dos seus chalecos anti-balas azuis, saltaron do camión e aproximáronse acompañados polo intérprete. Este era un rapaz nado en Toronto, alimentado co esforzo dos seus pais durante dezaoito anos para vir acabar aquí, a falar o idioma dos seus avós en medio da ruína.

– *Tko ste vi? Kamo idete?*[1]

Respondeu un alboroto. As mulleres falaban desordenadamente e as nenas escoitaban cansas e nobeladas nos abrigos. A Anna pareceulle por un momento que ningunha tiña mans. E pensouno: "Non teñen mans, non teñen mans." Pero era o frío. Tiñan as mans gardadas dentro das mangas, como as chinesas.

– Veñen do outro lado da montaña. Os haveos[2] incendiáronlles a vila. Non hai combatentes. Só mulleres e as nenas. Camiñaron toda a noite.

– ¿Onde van?

– *Kamo idete?*... Non saben. Camiñaron toda a noite – repetiu o intérprete.

– Ben – dixo Anna, cun salaio de fatalismo –. Ímolos sacar de aquí. Se seguen nesta dirección, colleranos. Dilles que vimos controis, pero que cremos que os poderemos pasar.

– Pénsao ben – díxolle Armand –. Ó mellor non os damos pasado. Sabes que non é fácil.

Anna pensou un momento, logo dixo:

– Xa decidín. Pasarémolos. Eu asumo toda a responsabilidade.

Pero para facerlles sitio había que sacar a carga para fóra.

A carga: setenta caixas con roupa e medicinas empaquetadas en Dinamarca por mans brancas e secas, grampadas en caixóns por traballadores turcos do porto de Hamburgo.

En media hora as caixas foron depositadas sobre a neve diante da mirada indescifrable das nenas. Aínda que non era tan difícil. En realidade facían por adiviñar o que habería dentro. Armand e o intérprete achegáronse a Anna.

– Isto complícase, xefa. Ven ver isto.

Acovardados e avergoñados, as figuras grises de catro homes saíron do bosque e agora as mulleres e as nenas rodeábanos querendo ocultalos.

– Enganáronnos... Bojan – dixo Armand volvéndose ó intérprete –, dilles que non podemos levar combatentes.

Mentres Bojan daba as explicacións, Anna observou os ollos de mendigo daqueles catro homes tecnicamente mortos. De desertaren, estaban na estrada equivocada. As mulleres suplicáronlles que os sacasen de alí. Eles protexéranas. Non fixeran mal ningún, dicían.

– Nada de combatentes – recalcou Armand, algo nervioso –. Díllelo claramente.

– Ímolo intentar – dixo Anna –. Todo se pode negociar. Aquí non teñen posibilidade ningunha.

Empezaba a anoitecer cando subiron ós camións co agradecemento aparatoso dos desesperados. A escuridade apresurouse aínda máis ó pechar o ceo. Comezaron a caer folerpas, finas e xeadas, alborotando arredor dos cristais.

– Veremos se hai sorte – dixo Armand cando se aproximaban ó control.

[1] ¿Quen sodes? ¿Cara onde ides?

[2] Haveos, membros do HVO, Consello de Defensa Croata

Non a houbo. O tractor bloqueaba esta vez a estrada e os milicianos obrigaron ó convoi a deterse. Xa non estaban de bo humor. ¿Que cousa cambiara? Nada. A voda que beberan cambiárao todo, ou o aborrecemento. Ou o que fose. O facho cegador das lanternas invadiu o interior dos vehículos e fóra os milicianos arremuiñáronse arredor deles, dando ordes. Anna descendeu.

– Temos un salvoconducto asinado – dixo –. Autorizounos persoalmente o comandante de zona para que... – continuou Anna, superpoñendo a súa voz á da traducción. Sabía o importante que era non deixar de falar para manter a súa posición.

O oficial ó mando interrompeuna, ansioso, estirándose para mirar o contido dos camións por enriba do seu ombro.

– Recibimos ordes.

Anna comprendeu axiña. Fixouse ben nos milicianos. Leulles as miradas. Sabía algo acerca disto. Sabía o que significaba. Non moi lonxe escoitábanse raxadas de armas automáticas e de vez en cando un lóstrego iluminaba o contorno dunha montaña veciña.

Comezou daquela a negociación de verdade. Foi rápida, tensa, implacable. Anna sabía que non dispuña de moito tempo e a súa capacidade de manobra era moi limitada. Non era a primeira vez que negociaba e mentres o facía ía ela mesma sopesando todas as posibilidades. Intentaba salvalos a todos. Ata que o ton da conversa mudou. Entón entendeu que todo rematara.

– Levamos combatentes – dixo friamente –. Son vosos, pero deixádenos pasar.

Sacaron os combatentes dos camións a toda présa e colocáronos en rea na beiravía, coas mans na caluga. Todo se pode negociar. Anna subiu xunto ó conductor. Nin sequera se volveu para miralos. Decidira xa esquecer. Fixera o que crera que era o mellor. Fixera o posible por salvalos a todos, pero tiña que escoller. Desde había tempo sabía que non hai modo de ser inocente, que o crime nos busca e a culpabilidade nos espera.

Agradeceu a neve. Tivo o pensamento estraño e gratificante de que a neve arrastraría os cadáveres ata un lugar oculto.

Great Last Minute Changes

In spite of everything, it's worth it – said M–. In spite of everything, even though at times one does wonder. I remember one case. We had to transport fuel to make a hospital boiler work. Trying in vain for days. The snipers didn't even let up for a moment to let the cargo get near. We thought sadly that the hospital inmates were going to freeze to death, until after a time we succeeded: we were able to get the fuel there during a lull in the fighting. And then the following day, a mortar shot fell, well, the fuel helped, so everything went up in flames like a funeral pyre. Several people died, others suffered horrible burns; it only took a moment. In spite of everything it was worth it. And do you know why? Because making a blunder is also a form of innocence.

In the beginning, no incident was planned. Three controls, twenty five kilometres. On the way there, everything went fine. The vehicles from the Solidarity

Agency, as white as refrigeration lorries, went through the first control without stopping. The barrier – a tractor and a tree trunk – were not in place and the militia-men from the HVO, far from the road, made an unheeding circle. They played with their mountain knives, the January sunshine streaming down, making the blades shine like precious stones. From this point on, the convoy started its slow climb up the mountain roads, painfully northwards. This was a place fate had cho-sen for them in their painful journey through the winter-whitened valleys, the snow scattered around like flour. The lorry axis creaked from the weight, the engines the same, creaking, coughing and rattling, rocking Anna to sleep.

A crowd of destitute refugees, their skins flame-red, crossed the road and were lost in the middle of the snow, and the yellow sun, as freezing as a uniform button, was above Anna's head as she felt something pressing down on her arm and she remembered. Armand shook her gently.

The smell of the badly-burning petrol – the famous restrictions in octane levels all along the main road were to blame – jolted her back to the real world, and when she opened her eyes the convoy had stopped and she could no longer see the squir-rels in her dream, but a small defenceless crowd in the middle of the snow, blurred by the steam from their own breath.

– Who are they? Anna asked, sitting up and rubbing her eyes.

– We don't know. They just appeared out of the blue. They won't move aside.

The engines stopped and the huge heavy white mass of snow absorbed the echo: the silence produced by the snow and which fills the forests with loneliness.

Anna and Armand, clumsy as astronauts in their blue bulletproof jackets, jumped from the lorry and approached the crowd accompanied by their inter-preter. The latter was a young man born in Toronto, brought up, not without sac-rifice, by his parents for eighteen years, just so that he could end up here, speaking his grandparents' language here in the middle of the rubble.

– *Tko ste vi? Kamo idete?*[1]

He was answered by a roar from the crowd. The women answered back in no particular order while the girls listened wearily huddled up in their overcoats. It seemed to Anna for a while that none of them had hands, and she even thought to herself: "They have no hands, they have no hands." But it was the cold. They had their hands hidden under their coat-sleeves like the Chinese.

– They came from the other side of the mountain. The HVOs[2] burnt their vil-lage down. They are non-combatants. They have been walking all night.

– Where are they going?

– *Kamo idete?*... They have no idea. They have been walking all night, repeated the interpreter.

– All right, Anna said, with a fatalistic sigh. We're going to take them away from

---

[1] Who are you? Where are you going?

[2] HVOs. Members of the Croatian Defence Committee

here. If they keep on in this direction they'll be caught. Tell them we saw controls but that we think we can get them through.

– Think it over, said Armand. We may not succeed. You know it's not easy.

Anna thought it over for a moment and then said:

– I have already made up my mind. We'll take them through. I'll take all the responsibility on my shoulders.

But to make room we had to unload the lorry.

The load: seventy boxes full of clothes and medicine packed in Denmark with dry white hands, riveted in containers by Turkish workers in the port of Hamburg.

In half an hour, the boxes were unloaded onto the snow in front of the girls looking on in astonishment. Although it was evident what was inside, the girls were having trouble guessing. Armand and the interpreter approached Anna.

– This is going to get complicated, boss. Come and look at this.

In a cowardly and ashamed way, the grey figures of four men emerged from the woods and at once the women and girls surrounded them, trying to hide them from view.

– They have deceived us... Bojan – said Armand, turning to the interpreters –. Tell them we cannot take combatants.

While Bojan was giving explanations, Anna watched the eyes of those poor men, who were virtually dead. If they had deserted, they were on the wrong road. The women begged to be able to take them away from there. These men had protected them, and had done nothing wrong, they said.

– No combatants, said Armand firmly, getting a bit edgy. Tell them that clearly.

– We'll do what we can, said Anna. Everything is subject to negotiation. If they stay out there they'll have no chance at all.

It was getting dark when the four climbed into the lorries with the exaggerated gratitude reserved for the desperate. Darkness fell fast as the sky grew cloudy. Snowflakes began to fall, thin and ice-cold, noisily against the windscreen.

– We'll see if we're lucky, said our man, as we approached the police control.

We weren't. The tractor was blocking the way this time and the militiamen made the convoy stop. They weren't in such a good mood by now. What had made them change? Nothing. The vodka they had drunk, or perhaps boredom, whatever. The dazzling torchlight shone into the vehicles, and the militiamen gathered round outside giving orders. Anna got out.

– We have a signed safe-conduct – she said. We were given our permits personally by the area commander himself, so... – Anna continued, drowning out the interpreter's voice with her own. She knew how important it was to keep talking, to secure her position.

The officer in charge interrupted her, anxious, stretching his neck to look in at the lorry's load over her shoulder.

– We have our orders.

Anna understood right away. She observed the militiamen closely. She could read their looks. She knew a thing or two, she knew what they meant. Not far away, they could hear the sound of automatic weapons and from time to time a flare illuminated the shape of a nearby mountain.

Then the real negotiation began. It was fast, intense and implacable. Anna knew she did not have much time, and her margin for negotiation was very limited. It was not the first time she had had to negotiate and, meanwhile, she weighed up all the possibilities. She tried to save them all, until the tone of the conversation changed for the worse. Then she realized it was all over.

– We are carrying combatants, she said coldly. They are yours, but let us go through with them.

They took the combatants out of the lorries in haste and placed them in a line at the roadside, with their hands behind their necks. Everything is negotiable. Anna climbed up beside the driver. She didn't even look back to see them. She had already made up her mind to forget. She had done what she thought best. She had done her best to save them all but she had had to choose. Since some time ago, she had learned there is no way to be innocent. Crime searches us out and guilt awaits us.

She was grateful for the snow. It occurred to her, strangely, that the snow would drag the bodies away to some hidden place.

Marta Dacosta (1966–)

From Crear o mar en Compostela (Creating the Sea in Compostela), *1994*

Teño unha cidade agachada nos versos...

Teño unha cidade agachada nos versos,
unha cidade grande de pequenas ruelas,
de altos edificios, de casas estragadas,
de berros temperáns e fontes cantareiras.
Teño unha cidade agachada en cada verso,
unha cidade nova que medra no mencer,
espreguizando o corpo de cristais e de argazo,
estendendo as mans cheas de escuma e sal.

I have a city hidden in my verses...

I have a city hidden in my verses,
a great city with little lanes,
with tall buildings, with broken-down houses,
with early cries and singing fountains.
I have a city hidden in each line,

a new city that grows at dawn,
having a stretch, all glass and seaweed,
holding out its hands full of foam and salt.

From Pel de ameixa (Plum Skin), *1996*

E ti dirás quizais que non gustas dos versos...

E ti dirás quizais que non gustas dos versos
que constrúen ás veces os meus dedos cansados,
pois son versos vencidos, cal heroes de traxedia,
que nos abren os ollos a todos os fracasos.
E dirás que por que non falar da beleza,
do sol, da paz, do amor gozoso dos humanos.

E eu direi entón que os versos que me nacen
son fillos do presente e tamén do pasado,
reais coma a traxedia vivida cada día,
e perdedores sempre nas guerras que creamos.
E direi que por qué ocultar a verdade,
a dor, o pranto, o odio antergo dos humanos.

And you perhaps will say you do not like the verses...

And you perhaps will say you do not like the verses
that these my weary fingers occasionally build,
for they're defeated verses, like the heroes of tragedy,
that open up our eyes to all those wretched failures.
And you will say why don't you speak of beauty,
of the sun, of peace, of the joyful love of humans.

And I shall then say that the verses born from me
are children of the present and also of the past,
as real as the tragedy that is lived every day,
and always the losers in the wars we create.
And I shall say why should I hide the truth,
the suffering, the weeping, the ancient hate of humans.

Rafa Villar (1968–)

From Casa ou sombra (House or Shadow), *1997*

Levo...

levo
a casa
como un exilio
de sombras
desgastadas

ás costas
da miña pasaxe

a corazón
aberto

I bear...

I bear
my house
like an exile
of worn-out
shadows

on the back
of my passage

with open
heart

ningunha rosa...

ningunha rosa
do xardín
recoñece xa
os meus pasos
que regresan
sós

no rose...

no rose
in the garden
now recognizes
my steps
that return
alone

Martín Veiga (1970–)

From As últimas ruínas (The Last Ruins), *1994*

Hoxe a morte persiste obstinada nas pedras...

Hoxe a morte persiste obstinada nas pedras,
nos lenzos corrompidos das paredes,
sobre os xacintos do patio, nos estucos
mordidos polo tempo, destrozados;
hoxe vaga a morte nas últimas ruínas
abrazando os cipreses vellos, abrazando
os corpos como unha música antiga.
Retornan hoxe as máscaras da morte
a pousarse nos semblantes desolados,
a pousar a luz do abatemento
no invernadeiro con dalias, nas estancias
arrasadas como ceos de Turner, como templos
onde o silencio cerca a pedra derrubada.
Hoxe sentimos a morta baixamar do tempo
entre a enredadeira do xardín calado,
no sombrío claustro onde agardaba,
aquel soño amargo de amores e tapices,
aquel escuro soño de horizontes e navíos.
Hoxe vaga a morte nas últimas ruínas
ocultando o rostro negro nas columnas.
Hoxe atopamos pedras cando buscamos rosas,
procuramos cálidos ouros baixo os nardos,
atopamos no corazón a cinza.

Today death persists obstinately in the stones...

Today death persists obstinately in the stones,

in the decayed surfaces of the walls
on the hyacinths in the courtyard, in the stucco
gnawed by time, destroyed;
today death wanders among the last ruins
embracing the old cypresses, embracing
bodies like an ancient music.
Today they return, those masks of death,
to settle upon the desolate faces,
to settle the light of dejection
upon the greenhouse with dahlias, upon the rooms
razed like Turner skies, like temples
where silence besieges the demolished stone.
Today we hear the dead low-tide of time
through the creeper in the silent garden,
in the shadowy cloister where it was waiting
– that bitter dream of love and tapestries,
that dark dream of horizons and ships.
Today death wanders through the last ruins
hiding its black face among the columns.
Today we find stones when we look for roses,
we search for warm gold beneath the spikenards,
we find ash in our hearts.

Yolanda Castaño (1977–)

From Profundidade de campo (Depth of Field), 2007

Contos de fadas

ÉRASE unha vez
…e ao final do conto
a carapuchiña era unha loba,
a avoíña un leñador,
a devoradora unha asceta,
a libérrima un completo compendio de dependencias,
a mística unha frívola tinguida de temores,
o incomprendido un anxo,
a princesa un monstro,
a frívola unha mística tinguida de temores,
o monstro unha princesa,
o outro incomprendido un demo,
a suposta loba unha absoluta carapuchiña

e o camiño entre o bosque
un leñador.

Fairy tales

Once upon a time
...and at the end of the tale
little red riding hood was a she-wolf,
her granny a woodcutter,
the devourer an ascetic,
the liberated woman a complete compendium of dependences,
the mystic a frivolous girl tinged with fears,
the man no one understands an angel,
the princess a monster,
the frivolous girl a mystic tinged with fears,
the monster a princess,
the other man no one understands a devil,
the supposed she-wolf a total little red riding hood
and the path through the forest
a woodcutter.

Mª do Cebreiro Rábade Villar (1976–)

From Os Hemisferios (The Hemispheres), *2006*

Venus

O libro non ten sexo. O libro é unha árbore.

Ela era como o xeo da mañá.
El levaba un anel no dedo máis pequeno.

Non te quero fundir,
só quero ver a herba
debaixo do teu corpo.

E se temos ideas
é porque virá o xeo rescatalas.

Que feito parte en dous a nosa historia
se non temos historia,
só este verso?

Case non lembro a infancia.
Vou quedando durmido.
A cabeza pequena, sobre a mesa,
mentres os demais falan.

Era a lingua dos mortos,
a lingua dos teus mortos?

Non, e baixou a vista.

Era a lingua da escola,
era a lingua das máquinas.

Íntimo é unha palabra que se aplica
ao que está moi adentro.

Os poemas que gardo son os que non se pechan.

Ou os que non se abren?

Busco a lingua perdida,
a que me precedeu.

Se escribo ocupo o espacio.

Igual que os astronautas?

Case igual, case igual,
pero sen a bandeira.

Sen cravala no chan,
sen erguela do chan.

Nin a que leva un río
atravesado?

Nin a do fondo negro.

Ao ler trémelle a voz.
Ao escoitar verque o viño sobre a mesa.

(A vibración, o ritmo do desexo.)

Venus

The book is sexless. The book is a tree.

She was like the morning ice.
He wore a ring on his little finger.

I do not want to melt you,
I only want to see the grass
beneath your body.

And if we have ideas
it is because the ice will come to rescue them.

What fact divides our story in two
if we have no story,
only this verse?

I hardly remember my childhood.
I am falling asleep.
My little head, on the table,
while the others talk.

Was it the language of the dead,
the language of your dead?

No, and the gaze was lowered.

It was the language of the school,
it was the language of the machines.

Intimate is a word that is applied
to what is deep inside one.

The poems I keep are the ones that do not close.

Or the ones that do not open?

I am searching for the lost language,
the language that went before me.

If I write I take up space.

Like astronauts?

Almost, almost like them,
but without the flag.

Without ramming it into the ground,
without pulling it out of the ground.

Not even the one with a river
running across it?

Not even the one with a black background.

While reading, the voice shakes.
While listening, wine is spilt on the table.

(Vibration, the rhythm of desire.)

Select Bibliography

Álvarez Blázquez, X.M.: *Escolma de poesía galega II. A poesía dos séculos XIV ao XIX*, Vigo: Galaxia, 1959.

Arias Freixedo, X.B.: *Antoloxía da lírica galego-portuguesa*, Vigo: Xerais, 2003.

Beltrán, V.: *A cantiga de amor*, Vigo: Xerais, 1995.

Bernárdez et alii: *Literatura Galega Século XX*, Vigo: A Nosa Terra Edicións, 2001.

Brea, M. e Lorenzo Gradín, P.: *A cantiga de amigo*, Vigo: Xerais, 1998.

Carballo Calero, R.: *Estudos rosalianos. Aspectos da vida e da obra de Rosalía*, Vigo: Galaxia, 1979.

– *Historia da Literatura Galega Contemporánea*, Vigo: Galaxia, 3ª ed., 1981.

Davies, C.: *Rosalía de Castro no seu tempo*, Vigo: Galaxia, 1987.

Ferreiro, C.E.: *Curros Enríquez*, A Coruña: Moret, 1954.

Forcadela, M.: *A poesía de Eduardo Pondal*, Vigo: Do Cumio, 1993.

Gutiérrez Izquierdo, R.: *Lecturas de nós. Introdución á Literatura Galega*, Vigo: Xerais, 2000.

Hermida, M.: *Narrativa galega. Tempo do rexurdimento*, Vigo: Xerais, 1995.

Lanciani, G. e Tavani, G. (Coords.): *Dicionário da Literatura Medieval galega e portuguesa*, Lisboa: Caminho, 1993.

– *As cantigas de escarnio*, Vigo: Xerais, 1995.

López, A. e Pociña, A.: *Rosalía de Castro. Documentación biográfica e bibliografía crítica (1837-1990)*, 2 vols., A Coruña: Fundación Barrié, 1991 e 1993.

Mayoral, M.: *La poesía de Rosalía de Castro*, Madrid: Gredos, 1974.

Méndez Ferrín, X.L.: *De Pondal a Novoneyra*, Vigo: Xerais, 1984.

Murguía, M.: *Los precursores*, A Coruña: Latorre y Martínez, 1885.

Pena, X.R.: *Manuel Antonio e a vangarda*, Santiago de Compostela: Sotelo Blanco, 1996.

– *Historia da Literatura galego-portuguesa*, Santiago de Compostela: Sotelo Blanco, 2002.

Resende de Oliveira, A.: *Trobadores e xograres*, Vigo: Xerais, 1995.

Rodríguez, L.: *Poetas Galegos do Século XX*, A Coruña: Espiral Maior, 2004.

Rodrigues Lapa, M.: *Lições de Literatura Portuguesa*. Época Medieval, Lisboa: Coimbra, 9ª ed., 1977.

Tarrío Varela, A.: *Literatura Galega*. Aportacións a unha historia crítica, Vigo: Xerais, 1994.

Tarrío Varela, A. (Coord.): *Galicia Literaria. T. XXXII. O século XX. A literatura anterior á Guerra Civil*, A Coruña: Hércules de Ediciones, 2000.

– *Galicia Literaria. T. XXXIII. A literatura desde 1936 ata hoxe: poesía e teatro*, A Coruña: Hércules de Ediciones,2000.

Tavani, G.: *A poesía lírica galego-portuguesa*, Vigo: Galaxia, 1986.

Varela, J.L.: *Poesía y restauración cultural de Galicia en el siglo XIX*, Madrid: Gredos, 1958.

Vilavedra, D. (Coord.): *Dicionario da Literatura Galega*. T.I. Autores, Vigo: Galaxia, 1995.

– *Dicionario da Literatura Galega*. T.II. Publicacións periódicas, Vigo: Galaxia, 1997.

– *Dicionario da Literatura Galega*. T.III. Obras, Vigo: Xerais, 2000.

VV. AA.: *Historia da Literatura Galega*, 5 vols., Vigo: A Nosa Terra Edicións, 1996.

VV. AA.: *Lírica Profana Galego-Portuguesa*, Santiago de Compostela: Centro Ramón Piñeiro, Xunta de Galicia, 1996.

List of publishers and texts used in this anthology

Editorial Galaxia: Do ermo, O lobo da xente, O porco de pé, Retrincos, Cousas, Entre a vendima e a castiñeira, Arredor de sí, Os camiños da vida, Dos arquivos do trasno, Sombra do aire na herba, A esmorga, Xente ao lonxe, Os biosbardos, A medosa Blandina, Á lus do candil, Merlín e familia, Crónicas do Sochantre, Escola de menciñeiros, Xente de aquí e de acolá, Cantiga nova que se chama Ribeira, Dona do corpo delgado, Herba aquí ou acolá, Nimbos, Canle segredo, Nas faíscas do soño, Xente no rodicio, Cara a Times Square, Estacións ao mar, As torres no ar, Orella no buraco, Vento ferido, Ilustrísima, Os escuros soños de Clío, Querida amiga, A nosa cinza, Branca de Loboso, O triángulo inscrito na circunferencia, Dos anxos e dos mortos, Caneiro cheo, Eume, Canta de cerca a morte, Historia da lúa, Ningún camiño, Antoloxía do conto de medo, Que me queres, amor?, Ruído, Os hemisferios. *Edicións Xerais*: Cantares Gallegos, Follas Novas, A tecedeira de Bonaval, Aires da miña terra, O divino sainete, Na noite estrelecida, Estevo, Codeseira, De catro a catro, Fírgoas, Nao senlleira, O soño sulagado, Os eidos, Agosto do 36, Profecía do mar, Se o noso amor e os peixes, Entre o sí e o non, Con pólvora e magnolias, Poesía enteira de Heriberto Bens, Estirpe, Crónica de Nós, Arraianos, Mesteres, A chamada escura dos cavorcos, Xa vai o grifón no vento, Lobos nas illas, Crime en Compostela, Seraogna, Mamá Fe, Vidas senlleiras, Morning Star, A sombra cazadora, O lapis do carpinteiro, Costa da morte blues, Pasa un segredo, Erros e Tánatos, A torre da derrota, Grupo abeliano, Contos malvados, Persianas, pedramol e outros nervios, Casa ou sombra. *Sotelo Blanco*: Obras completas, Códice calixtino, De Courel a Compostela, Cantos caucanos, A cámara de néboa, Cimo das idades tristes, Ningún cisne, A morte presentida, Rosa clandestina. *Edicions do Castro*: Jacobusland, Lonxe, Futuro condicional, Memorias de un neno labrego, Fentos no mar, Música reservada, As palabra no espello. *Espiral Maior*: Orballa en tempo lento, Desmemoriado río o da memoria, A primavera de Venus, Tempo de ría, O gato Branco, Calendario perpetuo, Heloísa, Luces do mediodía, Livro das devoracións, Ruido, Memorial de blancura, Poemas da lenta nudez, Das últimas mareas, Arden, Talvez melancolía, Ausencias pretéritas, As última ruínas, Profundidade de campo. *Deputacion Provincial de A Coruña*: Pel de Ameixa, Luz de facer memoria, Un áspero tempo de caliza, Caderno dos dereitos e das horas, Memoria de agosto. *Edicións Positivas*: Ártico e outros mares, Poemas, Depósito de espantos. *La Voz de Galicia*: Fardel do exiliado, Cantares gallegos. *Pero Meogo*: O corpo e as sombras, O regreso das ninfas. *Akal*: Conto galego, No desterro, Non. *Bahía edicións*: Eu tamén oín as voces do orballo, O rostro da terra. *Nós*: O fin dun canto, Iniciación e regreso. *Ediciones B*: Tic-tac; *Promocións culturais galegas*: Era tempo de apandar. *Salnés*: Salterio de Fingió. *Via Láctea*: Fabulario Novo. *Autoedición*: O ar que nos leva. *Ediciones Galicia del Centro Gallego de Buenos Aires*: Advento. *Edicións do Cerne*: Tempo de Compostela. *Castrelos*: Paisaxe de Glasgow; *Sons Galiza Libros*: Profecía. *Diario 16 Galicia*: Extramuros da noite. *Noitarenga*: Letras vencidas. *El Correo Gallego*: Crear o mar en Compostela. *Edicións Celta*: Alba de auga sonánbula.